U.S. merchandise exports and imports by area
[Billions of dollars]

W9-BZC-624

Item	1982	1983	1984	1985	1986	1987	1988	1989	1990	1991 first 3 quarters at annual rate[1]
Exports................	211.2	201.8	219.9	215.9	223.4	250.3	320.3	361.5	389.6	412.9
Industrial countries....	127.3	128.4	141.0	140.5	150.3	165.6	207.3	233.8	254.1	260.0
Canada............	39.2	44.5	53.0	55.4	56.5	62.0	74.3	80.7	83.6	84.8
Japan.............	20.7	21.8	23.2	22.1	26.4	27.6	37.2	43.9	48.0	47.7
Western Europe.....	59.7	55.4	56.9	56.0	60.4	68.6	86.4	98.4	111.4	116.3
Australia, New Zealand and South Africa...	7.7	6.6	7.8	7.0	7.1	7.4	9.4	10.9	11.2	11.2
Australia..........	4.4	3.9	4.8	5.1	5.1	5.3	6.8	8.1	8.3	8.0
Other countries, except Eastern Europe......	80.1	70.4	74.6	72.0	71.0	82.4	109.1	121.9	130.6	147.9
OPEC[2].............	20.7	15.3	13.8	11.4	10.4	10.7	13.8	13.1	13.4	17.8
Other[3].............	59.5	55.2	60.8	60.6	60.6	71.7	95.3	108.9	117.2	130.2
Eastern Europe........	3.7	3.0	4.3	3.3	2.1	2.3	3.8	5.5	4.3	4.5
International organizations and unallocated.........	.1	.1	.0	.2	....	....	.1	.2	.6	.4
Imports................	247.6	268.9	332.4	338.1	368.4	409.8	447.3	477.4	497.7	485.3
Industrial countries....	144.1	159.9	205.5	219.1	245.4	259.7	283.4	292.5	299.3	291.8
Canada............	48.5	56.0	67.6	70.4	69.7	73.6	84.7	89.9	93.0	92.9
Japan.............	37.7	42.8	60.2	65.7	80.8	84.6	89.8	93.5	89.7	90.2
Western Europe.....	52.9	55.6	72.1	77.5	89.0	96.1	102.6	102.4	109.3	101.4
Australia, New Zealand and South Africa...	5.0	5.4	5.6	5.6	5.9	5.4	6.2	6.6	7.3	7.3
Australia..........	2.3	2.3	2.7	2.7	2.6	3.0	3.5	3.9	4.4	4.2
Other countries, except Eastern Europe......	102.4	107.6	124.7	117.1	121.1	148.2	161.8	182.8	196.1	191.7
OPEC[2].............	31.5	25.3	26.9	22.7	18.9	24.4	23.0	30.7	38.0	33.3
Other[3].............	70.9	82.3	97.8	94.5	102.2	123.8	138.8	152.1	158.1	158.4
Eastern Europe........	1.1	1.4	2.2	1.8	2.0	1.9	2.2	2.1	2.3	1.8
International organizations and unallocated.........	.0	.0	....	....	....	....	....	....	....	......
Balance (excess of exports +)............	−36.4	−67.1	−112.5	−122.1	−145.1	−159.5	−127.0	−115.9	−108.1	−72.4
Industrial countries....	−16.9	−31.5	−64.5	−78.6	−95.0	−94.0	−76.0	−58.7	−45.2	−31.8
Canada............	−9.3	−11.5	−14.6	−15.0	−13.2	−11.6	−10.4	−9.3	−9.5	−8.0
Japan.............	−17.0	−21.1	−37.0	−43.5	−54.4	−57.0	−52.6	−49.7	−41.7	−42.6
Western Europe.....	6.8	−.2	−15.2	−21.4	−28.6	−27.5	−16.2	−4.0	2.1	14.9
Australia, New Zealand and South Africa...	2.6	1.2	2.2	1.4	1.1	2.0	3.2	4.2	3.8	3.9
Australia..........	2.1	1.6	2.1	2.4	2.5	2.3	3.3	4.2	3.9	3.8
Other countries, except Eastern Europe......	−22.3	−37.2	−50.1	−45.2	−50.1	−65.8	−52.7	−60.9	−65.6	−43.7
OPEC[2].............	−10.9	−10.0	−13.1	−11.3	−8.5	−13.7	−9.3	−17.6	−24.6	−15.5
Other[3].............	−11.4	−27.1	−37.0	−33.9	−41.6	−52.1	−43.4	−43.2	−40.9	−28.2
Eastern Europe........	2.7	1.6	2.1	1.4	.1	.3	1.7	3.5	2.1	2.7
International organizations and unallocated.........	.0	.1	.0	.2	....	....	.1	.2	.6	.4

[1]Preliminary; seasonally adjusted.

[2]Organization of Petroleum Exporting Countries, consisting of Algeria, Ecuador, Gabon, Indonesia, Iran, Iraq, Kuwait, Libya, Nigeria, Qatar, Saudi Arabia, United Arab Emirates, and Venezuela.

[3]Latin America, other Western Hemisphere, and other countries in Asia and Africa, less members of OPEC.

Note.—Data are on an international transactions basis and exclude military.

Source: Department of Commerce, Bureau of Economic Analysis.

INTERNATIONAL ECONOMICS

INTERNATIONAL ECONOMICS

THIRD EDITION

James C. Ingram
University of North Carolina

Robert M. Dunn, Jr.
George Washington University

WILEY

JOHN WILEY & SONS, INC.

New York   Chichester   Brisbane   Toronto   Singapore

ACQUISITIONS EDITOR / Whitney Blake
MARKETING MANAGER / Carolyn Henderson
PRODUCTION SUPERVISOR / Elizabeth Austin
DESIGNER / Kevin Murphy
MANUFACTURING MANAGER / Lorraine Fumoso
COPY EDITING SUPERVISOR / Richard Blander
ILLUSTRATION / Jaime Perea

This book was set in Times Roman by Publication Services, Inc. and printed and
bound by Malloy Lithographing. The cover was printed by Lehigh.

Library of Congress Cataloging in Publication Data:
Ingram, James C.
    International economics. — 3rd ed. / James C. Ingram and Robert
  M. Dunn, Jr.
      p.   cm.
    Includes indexes.
    ISBN 0-471-61031-3
    1. International economic relations. I. Dunn, Robert M.
  II. Title.
HF1411.I392   1993
   337–dc20   92-19474
                                      CIP

Printed in the United States of America.
10 9 8 7 6 5 4 3 2

Printed and bound by Malloy Lithographing, Inc.

ABOUT THE AUTHORS

James C. Ingram, Professor of Economics Emeritus at the University of North Carolina at Chapel Hill, is a specialist in the field of international economics. He is the author of *Economic Change in Thailand* (2nd ed., 1971), *Regional Payments Mechanisms* (1962), *International Economic Problems* (3rd ed., 1978), and numerous articles on international trade and finance.

Professor Ingram has been a visiting scholar at the London School of Economics and at the Brookings Institution, and he was a visiting professor at Thammasat University (Bangkok) for two years. He was formerly president of the Southern Economic Association, managing editor of the *Southern Economic Journal,* and dean of the Graduate School at the University of North Carolina.

Robert M. Dunn, Jr., is a professor of economics at George Washington University. He did his undergraduate degree at Williams College, and his Ph.D. in economics at Stanford University. His primary area of teaching and research interest is international economics. He is the author of *Canada's Experience with Fixed and Flexible Exchange Rates* (1971), *The U.S.-Canada Capital Market* (1978), *The Many Disappointments of Flexible Exchange Rates* (1983), and numerous articles in the area of international trade and finance.

In addition to teaching at George Washington University, Professor Dunn lectures at the Foreign Service Institute of the U.S. Department of State. He has also been a consultant for the Brookings Institution, the Stanford Research Institute, and the Federal Reserve Board. From 1983 to 1989, Professor Dunn was the editor of *International Economic Perspectives: Portfolio,* which was published by the United States Information Agency.

PREFACE

This book is an introduction to international economics, intended for students who are taking their first course in the subject. The level of exposition requires, as a background, no more than a standard introductory course in the principles of economics. Those who have had both intermediate microeconomics and macroeconomics will find them helpful, but except for two or three of the optional sections (marked with an arrowhead ▶) the entire book is accessible to readers whose prior exposure to economics is limited to that introductory course.

The primary purpose of this book is to present a clear, straightforward account of the main topics in international economics. We have tried to keep the student's perspective constantly in mind and to make the explanations both intuitively appealing and logically convincing.

Reactions from users of the first two editions—both students and instructors—have been encouraging. However, the passage of time itself erodes the usefulness of a book in a field such as international economics, and we have therefore prepared this third edition.

This book covers the standard topics in international economics. Each of the two main parts, International Trade (Part I) and International Finance and Open Economy Macroeconomics (Part II), develops the theory first, and then applies it to particular policy issues and historical episodes. This approach reflects our belief that economic theory should be what Professor Hicks calls "a handmaiden to economic policy."

Wherever possible, we use economic theory to explain and interpret experience. That is why this book contains more discussion of actual historical episodes than most existing textbooks of international economics. The historical experience is used as the basis for showing how the analysis works. We have found that students generally appreciate this approach. However, some instructors may find that time does not permit a detailed discussion of some of these historical episodes. In that case, some extended discussions, as in Chapter 19, can be left for independent study, used as the basis for term papers, or simply omitted.

CHANGES IN THE THIRD EDITION: TRADE

The most important change in this edition is that the coverage of international trade has been moved to the first half of the book, followed by the presentation of international finance and open economy macroeconomics. This change was made because this appears to be the order in which the vast majority of instructors teach international economics. In Chapter 5 we have placed more emphasis on models of trade pattern determination other than Heckscher-Ohlin, with particular attention to cost advantages in imperfectly competitive markets created by economies of scale, resulting from large research and development expenses. There is more discussion of nontariff barriers to trade in Chapter 6 and of some of the newer arguments for protectionism, such as the industrial strategy approach, in Chapter 7.

We have now added a separate chapter (8) on regional trading blocs, a decision that was encouraged by the new U.S.-Canada free trade arrangement and by increased interest in the European Community as the 1992 program is negotiated and implemented. Chapter 9 covers the history of commercial policy, and it includes a discussion of the problems of the Uruguay Round and of issues such as intellectual property. The chapter in the previous edition on multinational corporations has been replaced by Chapter 11, which covers international factor mobility. Such factor movements are viewed as an arbitraging process, with the analogy to Heckscher-Ohlin trade emphasized. Coverage of labor migration in that chapter is followed by a discussion of capital flows, including those resulting from the operations of multinational firms.

CHANGES IN THE COVERAGE OF INTERNATIONAL FINANCE

The restructuring of the international finance half of the book is more extensive, because that area is more controversial and has undergone greater changes during the last few years. After discussion of balance of payments accounting and of exchange markets in Chapter 12 and 13, balance-of-payments determination and adjustment are first taught under the assumption of a fixed exchange rate in Chapters 15 and 16. We have adopted this approach for two reasons. First, the vast majority of the countries in the world retain fixed parities, and second and more important, we believe that students will find the subject easier to understand if it is presented in this manner.

An extensive discussion of changes in otherwise fixed parities and then of floating exchange rates follows in Chapters 17 and 18. The latter of these two chapters contains a discussion of open economy macroeconomics under alternative exchange rate regimes. The earlier chapter (15) on balance of payments determination puts considerable emphasis on the asset market approach, both in its monetarist and portfolio balance forms.

The standard IS/LM/BB graph is explained in Chapter 16 and is then used in Chapters 16, 17, and 18 to illustrate alternative routes to payment adjustment and the impacts of fiscal and monetary policies under fixed versus flexible exchange rates.

Chapters 19 and 20, which deal with early international monetary history, are largely unchanged, but the coverage of the period since 1973 in Chapter 21 has been rewritten to deal with events since 1985, with particular emphasis on the European Monetary System and the Latin American debt crisis.

INSTRUCTORS' ALTERNATIVES FOR THE USE OF THIS EDITION

Those instructors using this book for a full-year course can cover the entire volume and assign supplementary material such as a book of readings. Those who choose to use this book for a one-semester (or one-quarter) course will probably want to eliminate some chapters. The core chapters are Chapters 2 through 8 and 12 through 18. For a one-term course in international trade, Chapters 1 through 11 provide a compact, self-contained unit. For a one-term course emphasizing international finance or open economy macroeconomics, Chapter 1 and Chapters 12 through 21 are the appropriate choice.

In writing this book, we have accumulated a number of obligations: to our students and colleagues at the University of North Carolina and George Washington University and to international economists too numerous to mention whose work is drawn on in writing a textbook such as this. We also gratefully acknowledge the economics editors and outside reviewers at John Wiley and Sons—for the second edition, Maurice B. Ballabon, Baruch College, CUNY; Elias Dinopoulas, University of California, Davis; Geoffrey A. Jehle, Vassar College; Marc Lieberman, Vassar College; Don Schilling, University of Missouri; and Parth Sen, University of Illinois at Urbana/Champaign; for the third edition, Robert W. Gillespie, University of Illinois at Urbana/Champaign; Henry Goldstein, University of Oregon; Gerald M. Lage, Oklahoma State University; Robert Murphy, Boston College; William Phillips, University of South Carolina at Columbia; and Henry Thompson, Auburn University. Finally, we thank the users of the first two editions who have sent us their helpful comments and suggestions.

March, 1992

James C. Ingram
Chapel Hill, North Carolina

Robert M. Dunn, Jr.
Washington, D.C.

Contents

1

INTRODUCTION

A few decades ago international trade and finance were viewed in the United States as relatively minor areas within economics. Both macro- and microeconomics courses typically contained little or no reference to the role of international transactions, and relatively few students enrolled in international economics courses. The popular and financial press reflected a similar attitude; news stories concerning international business were seldom carried, and when they were they appeared at the end of the publication. The United States had a rather isolated economy, a fact that was reflected both in academic economics and in the world of business.

This situation has changed radically in the last few years. Enrollments in international economics courses (and in international affairs programs) in colleges and universities have risen sharply, and even domestic macro- and microeconomics courses make some reference to the role of international transactions. The business press carries many stories concerning international events and their impact on the U.S. economy. The United States is now a far more open or outward-oriented economy, and both academic and popular economics reflect that transformation.

A major reason for growing interest in international economics in the United States and in other industrialized countries can be found in Table 1-1. In three decades the share of foreign trade in the U.S. gross national product (GNP) rose by 127 percent. In all seven major industrialized countries, except Japan, there was a

TABLE 1-1 Exports Plus Imports of Goods and Services as a Share of GNP (percentage)

Country	1960	1970	1980	1990	1990 / 1960
United States	9.2	11.0	20.5	20.9	2.27
Canada	36.5	43.2	56.1	51.1	1.40
United Kingdom	41.5	43.2	52.0	51.6	1.24
Japan	20.7	20.4	28.3	19.9	0.96
Federal Republic of Germany	37.4	43.2	57.1	64.8	1.73
France	25.2	31.1	44.3	46.0	1.83
Italy	26.0	30.3	44.0	39.4	1.52
Unweighted average	28.1	31.8	43.2	42.0	1.49

Source: International Monetary Fund, *International Financial Statistics Yearbook*, 1991. Country tables. For France, gross domestic product (GDP) rather than GNP is used. Owing to a lack of data, the entry for Japan for 1960 is actually for 1965, and the 1990 entry is for 1989.

sizable increase in the share of foreign trade in GNP since 1960; for the group as a whole, the increase was from 28 to 42 percent of GNP.

Information on the extent to which international trade has grown faster than world output can be found in Figures 1-1 and 1-2. (Other current data on international trade flows can be found in the Appendix to this chapter). International trade is clearly a much larger part of both the U.S. and the world economy than was the case only three decades ago.

The growth in the role of international capital flows in U.S. financial markets has been even more striking than the growth of merchandise trade. In 1960–61 increases in U.S. assets abroad averaged only $4.8 billion per year, whereas increases in foreign investments in the United States averaged only $2.4 billion. By 1989–90, U.S. investments abroad were growing by $94.2 billion per year, whereas foreign assets in the United States increased by $151.1 billion. Total capital flows in and out of the United States increased by a factor of 172. U.S. capital markets are now closely tied to those of the other major industrial countries; thus U.S. interest rates and other financial variables are strongly affected by events abroad.

The linkages between the U.S. and foreign economies increased throughout the 1960s, but many Americans did not become aware of the United States' increased vulnerability to economic shocks from abroad until early 1974 when OPEC (Organization of Petroleum Exporting Countries) increased the price of oil from $3 to $8 per barrel. Later price increases which pushed the price of oil to a peak of $35 per barrel in the early 1980s increased U.S. awareness of its new dependence on foreign trade. The sharp increase in the vigor of competition felt by U.S. automobile and consumer electronics manufacturers throughout the 1970s and 1980s added to this sense of growing vulnerability. A wide range of U.S. markets for manufactured goods became far more competitive as the role of imports in U.S. consumption increased, and as a result U.S. profit rates in manufacturing declined during much of this era. U.S. firms faced very little competition from abroad for

(Average annual percentage change)

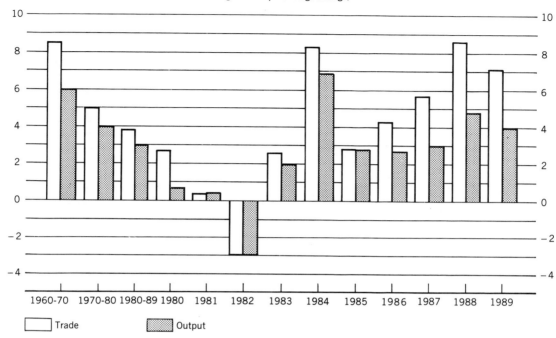

FIGURE 1-1 Volume of world merchandise trade and output, 1960–1989 (average annual percentage change). *Source: GATT, International Trade, 1989–1990, Vol. 2 (Geneva, 1990), p. 1.*

the first two decades after World War II and frequently behaved as though they virtually owned their markets. That situation changed dramatically in the following twenty-five years as imports became a threatening source of competition across a wide range of U.S. markets.

The U.S. macroeconomy has also become far more closely tied to events in the international sector. Changes in the exchange rate or shifts in the trade balance (export receipts minus import expenditures) meant relatively little to this economy a few decades ago, but the events of the early and mid-1980s make it clear that this viewpoint is no longer valid. The 1981–85 appreciation of the dollar was vital in breaking the inflation plaguing the United States at the beginning of the decade, but it also greatly reduced sales opportunities for a wide range of U.S. manufacturing industries. The recovery of the U.S. economy from the 1982 recession was made slower and more painful by the high value of the dollar and by its effects on U.S. export and import-competing industries. Imports and exports are now so important to this country that a large movement in the exchange rate can have very disruptive impacts on the U.S. macroeconomy.

U.S. monetary and fiscal policies used to be designed and implemented with little reference to their international impacts but that, too, has changed. The ability of the

(Average annual percentage change)

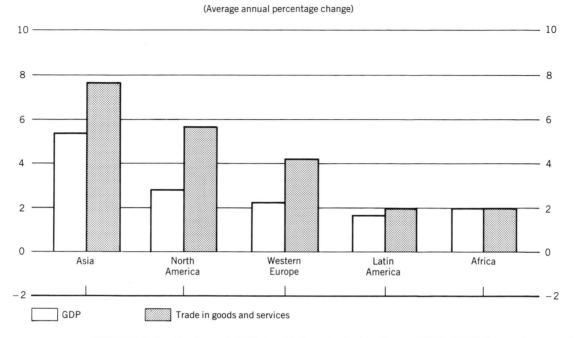

FIGURE 1-2 Trade and GDP growth in selected regions, 1979–1989 (average annual percentage change). *Source: GATT, International Trade, 1989–1990, Vol. 1 (Geneva, 1990), p. 9.*

Federal Reserve System to adopt an expansionary monetary policy to encourage a recovery from the 1990–91 recession, for example, has probably been constrained by the fear of an excessive depreciation of the dollar which would cause inflation to worsen. The desire to avoid the disruptive effects of large exchange rate changes has led the major industrialized countries to informally coordinate monetary and exchange market policies to avoid a repetition of the early 1980s. Increased ties to the world economy and vulnerability to shocks from abroad have meant that U.S. macroeconomic policies are not as independent as they were a few decades ago.

WHY INTERNATIONAL ECONOMICS IS A SEPARATE FIELD

In introductory macro- and microeconomics, students are taught a body of theory that is based on only two assumptions: namely, that economic agents maximize their self-interest and that such agents are rational. If those assumptions are universally valid, one might ask why a separate body of theory is needed for international transactions. If the forces that drive commerce between New York and Ontario are the same as those that determine transactions between New York and Massachusetts, and if standard macro- and microeconomics do an adequate job of explaining New York/Massachusetts transactions, why is a separate theory needed to deal with New York/Ontario transactions? Why is it impossible to view international transactions as being merely domestic transactions that cross an arbitrary and unimportant political border? It turns out that international trade theory is related to domestic microeconomics, but there are important differences between domestic and foreign transactions. The same situation exists on the macro side; international finance is closely tied to domestic macroeconomics, but political borders do matter, and international finance is far more than a modest extension of domestic macroeconomics.

The differences between international and domestic economic activities that make international economics a separate body of theory are as follows.

1. Within a national economy it is assumed that labor and capital are free to move among regions; this means that national markets for labor and for capital exist. Although wage rates may differ modestly among regions, such differences are reduced by an arbitraging process in which workers move from low- to high-wage locations. Because transportation costs for capital are far lower (the cost of a postage stamp), the arbitraging process in capital markets is more complete. As a result, domestic microeconomics operates on the assumption that firms competing in a market face the same, or at least similar, factor costs. General Motors, Ford, and Chrysler all pay about the same wage rates, and they also borrow money at the same or similar interest rates. Domestic microeconomics therefore deals with competition among firms facing very similar costs.

    International trade is quite different in this regard. Immigration laws preclude, or at least greatly limit, the arbitraging of wage rates among nations, so that wage rates differ sharply across the world. Labor can be hired in India for 75 rupees per day, which is about $4. Industrial wages in the United States, including fringe benefits, are typically over $10 per hour, implying a ratio of the U.S. to the Indian wage rate of about 20:1. Although labor does migrate among nations, immigration laws, high transportation costs, and other barriers are sufficient to prevent a complete arbitraging together of wage rates. Although capital flows among nations more easily than does labor, exchange controls, additional risks, costs of information, and other factors are sufficient to maintain sizable differences among interest rates in different countries. Whereas domestic microeconomics deals with competition among firms facing similar costs, international trade theory centers on competition in markets where firms face very different costs. Indian textile companies produce for the U.S. market on the basis of wage rates which are about one-twentieth of those paid by U.S. textile firms. This difference has major impacts on international trade flows and on the effects of trade on an internal economy, subjects that are dealt with in some detail later in this book.

2. There are normally no government-imposed barriers to the shipment of goods within a country. Accordingly, firms in one region compete against firms in another region of the country without government protection in the form of tariffs or quotas. Domestic microeconomics deals with such free trade within a country. In contrast, tariffs, quotas, and other government-imposed barriers to trade

are almost universal in international trade. A large part of international trade theory deals with why such barriers are imposed, how they operate, and what effects they have on flows of trade and other aspects of economic performance. Chapters 6 to 10 of this book all discuss various barriers to international trade.

3.   Domestic macroeconomics normally deals with a single nation having business cycles that affect all regions of the country. Such national cycles produce fiscal policy responses that are intended to affect the entire economy; monetary policy is similarly national in scope. Whatever fiscal and monetary policies exist in the eastern part of the United States also prevail in California, and domestic macroeconomics assumes that circumstance. International finance, or open economy macroeconomics, is about a very different situation. Different countries have different business cycles: Some may be in a recession while others enjoy periods of economic expansion. This means that fiscal policies will often differ among countries; some will have expansionary budgets at the same time that others are maintaining more restraint. Monetary policies can also differ among countries; for example, money supply growth may be far more rapid in one country than among its major trading partners. These differences in macroeconomic conditions and policies among countries have major consequences for trade flows and other international transactions. Much of the latter half of this book discusses these issues.

4.   A country normally has a single currency, the supply of which is managed by the central bank operating through a commercial banking system. Because a New York dollar is the same as a California dollar, for example, there are no internal exchange markets or exchange rates in the United States.

   International finance involves a very different set of circumstances. There are almost as many currencies as there are countries (a number of French-speaking African countries share a currency, and a few small countries, including Liberia, Panama, and some island nations in the south Pacific use the currencies of other countries), and the maintenance of a currency is typically viewed as a basic part of national sovereignty. International finance is concerned with exchange rates and exchange markets, and with what happens when the government decides to intervene in those markets.

   Most countries maintain fixed exchange rates; as a result, the exchange market is often out of equilibrium. Disequilibria are observed as balance-of-payments surpluses or deficits, which create a variety of problems for those managing domestic economic policies. In those countries, such as the United States, that do not maintain fixed parities but instead have floating exchange rates, exchange markets are often quite volatile. These countries have frequently experienced large exchange rate movements, such as when the U.S. dollar appreciated by over 60 percent between early 1981 and 1985. Exchange rate volatility creates another set of problems for policymakers. For a country that is heavily involved in international trade, the exchange rate may be the most important price in the economy. If it is volatile, the results can be highly disruptive. None of these problems exists within a closed domestic economy, but they become important as trade and other international transactions grow relative to the economy. The latter half of this book discusses these issues at some length.

THE ORGANIZATION OF THIS VOLUME

This book is divided into two broad segments, the first of which deals with international trade. Chapters 2 to 6 examine the theory of international trade, whereas Chapters 7 to 10 cover policy issues and debates. Chapter 11 discusses international factor mobility, that is, labor migration and international capital flows, and can be viewed as a transition from the trade to the finance sectors of the book.

The treatment of international finance begins with Chapter 12 and continues through the remainder of the book. It begins with a discussion of balance-of-payments accounting. Chapter 13 discusses foreign exchange markets, with a particular emphasis on the relationship between what is occurring in the balance-of-payments accounts and events in exchange markets.

Chapters 12 to 16 focus on the problem of balance-of-payments disequilibria, primarily under the assumption of a fixed exchange rate. This early emphasis on a regime of fixed exchange rates may seem strange since the United States maintains a floating exchange rate, but this organizational approach has been adopted for two reasons. First, the vast majority of the countries of the world do not have flexible exchange rates, but instead maintain some form of parity. Thus a discussion of a regime of fixed exchange rates remains relevant. The second and more important reason for this approach is pedagogical; our combined five decades of teaching international economics have made it clear that students find it much easier to understand a fixed exchange rate system than a regime of floating exchange rates. Since it is a general rule that the more accessible material should be taught before going on to more difficult topics, the discussion of a fixed exchange rate system should precede that of flexible exchange rates. Once students understand the problems of balance-of-payments disequilibria and adjustment under fixed exchange rates, they will find it much easier to learn how a flexible exchange rate system operates.

Chapter 17 discusses changes in otherwise fixed rates, that is, devaluations and revaluations. The theory of flexible exchange rates is then covered at some length in Chapter 18, which ends the theoretical discussion of international finance. Chapters 19, 20, and 21 are primarily historical, and are designed to apply the previously developed theory to events. The problems of the recent experience with flexible exchange rates and other current policy problems, such as the development of the European Monetary System and the Latin American debt crisis, are the topic of Chapter 21. A glossary follows Chapter 21. Readers encountering terms in the text which are unclear should refer to this glossary for help.

This book is designed for students whose previous exposure to economics has been limited to a two-semester principles course, but it also attempts to teach the theory of international economics with some rigor. As a result, some of the tools of domestic intermediate micro- and macroeconomics are taught within the text. Indifference curves are introduced in the trade theory chapters, and IS/LM curves are explained in Chapter 16 so that they can be modified to include the balance of payments. The IS/LM/BB version of this graphical approach is then used in Chapters 16, 17, and 18. The explanation of these graphs and their later use is placed in boxes that are separate from the main text, so that students and instructors who wish to do so can omit them entirely. The text is designed to be understood without necessary reference to the IS/LM/BB graphs, but the student will gain a fuller understanding of the theory of international finance or open economy macroeconomics if he or she works through those graphs.

A course in international economics will be both more enjoyable and better understood if an attempt is made to follow current events in the areas of international trade and finance. Both areas are full of controversies and are constant sources of news. Useful sources of current information include the following:

Business Week (largely business rather than policy coverage)

Finance and Development (quarterly, published by the International Monetary Fund and the World Bank)

Financial Times (expensive but extremely thorough)

IMF Survey (monthly)

The Economist (a British weekly)

The New York Times (financial section)

The Wall Street Journal (international news in section 1, data in section 3)

The Washington Post (a Washington perspective on current policy issues rather than international business coverage)

Current and historical statistics in the areas of international trade and finance can be found in the following sources:

Bank for International Settlements Annual Report

Directions of Trade (IMF)

Federal Reserve Bulletin

GATT (General Agreement on Tariffs and Trade), *International Trade* (annual)

IMF, *Annual Report*

IMF, *Balance of Payments Statistics Yearbook*

IMF, *International Financial Statistics* (monthly and available as a yearbook)

OECD, (Organization for Economic Cooperation and Development), *Main Economic Indicators*

Survey of Current Business (U.S. Department of Commerce)

UN International Trade Statistics Yearbook

UN Monthly Bulletin of Statistics

World Bank, *World Development Report* (annual)

World Bank, *World Tables* (annual)

Some of these sources, including the IMF's *International Financial Statistics* and the World Bank's *World Tables,* are available in forms that can be used by computer data banks. Citibank maintains an extensive data bank, named CITIBASE, which includes a wide range of international data and which is available in many college and university computer systems.

SELECTED REFERENCES

Adams, John, ed. *The Contemporary International Economy: A Reader*, 2nd ed. New York: St. Martin's Press, 1985.

Balassa, Bela, ed. *Changing Patterns in Foreign Trade and Payments*. New York: Norton, 1978.

Baldwin, Robert E., and J. David Richardson, eds. *International Trade and Finance: Readings,* 3rd ed. Boston: Little, Brown, 1986.

King, Philip, ed., *International Economics and Economic Policy: A Reader,* New York, McGraw Hill, 1990.

APPENDIX

TABLE 1-A1 Leading Exporters and Importers in World Merchandise Trade, 1989 (billion dollars and percentage)

Rank 1973	Rank 1989	Exporters	1989 Value	1989 Share	Rank 1973	Rank 1989	Importers	1989 Value	1989 Share
1	1	United States	364.0	11.8	1	1	United States	492.9	15.3
2	2	Germany, Fed. Rep.	341.2	11.0	2	2	Germany, Fed. Rep.	269.7	8.4
3	3	Japan	273.9	8.9	4	3	Japan	209.7	6.5
4	4	France	179.4	5.8	3	4	United Kingdom	197.7	6.1
5	5	United Kingdom	152.3	4.9	5	5	France	193.0	6.0
9	6	Italy	140.7	4.5	6	6	Italy	153.0	4.8
6	7	Canada	121.4	3.9	7	7	Canada	121.2	3.8
10	8	USSR[b]	109.4	3.5	10	8	USSR[a,b]	114.8	3.6
7	9	Netherlands	107.8	3.5	8	9	Netherlands	104.2	3.2
8	10	Belgium-Luxembourg	100.0	3.2	9	10	Belgium-Luxembourg	98.5	3.1
25	11	Hong Kong[c]	73.1	2.4	22	11	Hong Kong[d]	72.2	2.2
28	12	Taiwan	66.2	2.1	13	12	Spain	71.5	2.2
39	13	Korea, Rep.	62.3	2.0	29	13	Korea, Rep.	61.3	1.9
22	14	China	51.6	1.7	23	14	China	58.3	1.8
11	15	Sweden	51.5	1.7	11	15	Switzerland	58.2	1.8
13	16	Switzerland	51.5	1.7	31	16	Taiwan	52.5	1.6
33	17	Singapore[e]	44.7	1.4	25	17	Singapore[d]	49.7	1.5
24	18	Spain	44.5	1.4	12	18	Sweden	49.0	1.5
12	19	Australia	37.7	1.2	17	19	Australia	44.9	1.4
45	20	Mexico[f]	35.6	1.2	18	20	Austria	39.0	1.2

[a]Imports f.o.b.

[b]Figures are affected by severe difficulties in converting national currency data into dollars.

[c]Includes re-exports. In 1989 they amounted to $44.4 billion.

[d]Includes imports for re-export.

[e]Includes re-exports. In 1989 they amounted to $16.3 billion.

[f]Includes estimates of trade flows through processing zones.

[g]Estimates.

Source: GATT, *International Trade, 1989–1990*, Vol. 2 (Geneva, 1990), p. 3.

TABLE 1-A1 (continued)   Leading Exporters and Importers in World Merchandise Trade, 1989 (billion dollars and percentage)

Rank			1989		Rank			1989	
1973	1989	Exporters	Value	Share	1973	1989	Importers	Value	Share
19	21	Brazil	34.4	1.1	30	21	Mexico[f]	33.9	1.1
23	22	Austria	31.9	1.0	15	22	Denmark	26.7	0.8
15	23	German Dem. Rep.[b]	29.0	0.9	14	23	German Dem. Rep.[a,b]	26.5	0.8
17	24	Denmark	28.1	0.9	47	24	Thailand	25.1	0.8
14	25	Saudi Arabia[g]	27.5	0.9	27	25	Finland	24.4	0.8
26	26	Norway	27.1	0.9	19	26	Norway	23.7	0.7
41	27	Malaysia	25.1	0.8	42	27	Malaysia	22.5	0.7
21	28	Czechoslovakia[b]	23.5	0.8	21	28	Czechoslovakia[a,b]	22.4	0.7
30	29	Finland	23.3	0.8	48	29	Saudi Arabia[g]	21.9	0.7
20	30	South Africa	22.3	0.7	35	30	India	20.4	0.6
40	31	Indonesia	22.0	0.7	19	31	Brazil	20.0	0.6
46	32	Ireland	20.7	0.7	38	32	Portugal	18.8	0.6
51	33	Thailand	20.1	0.6	24	33	South Africa	18.0	0.6
50	34	United Arab Emirates[g]	16.5	0.5	40	34	Ireland	17.4	0.5
38	35	Bulgaria[b]	16.2	0.5	41	35	Indonesia	16.6	0.5
42	36	India	15.8	0.5	33	36	Greece	16.1	0.5
18	37	Iran, Islamic Rep.[g]	13.5	0.4	46	37	Turkey	15.8	0.5
43	38	Yugoslavia	13.5	0.4	28	38	Israel	15.5	0.5
16	39	Poland[b]	13.2	0.4	36	39	Bulgaria[a,b]	15.2	0.5
36	40	Venezuela	13.0	0.4	26	40	Yugoslavia	14.8	0.5
		Total	**2845.4**	**91.9**			**Total**	**2927.0**	**90.9**
		World	**3095.0**	**100.0**			**World**	**3220.0**	**100.0**

[a]Imports f.o.b.

[b]Figures are affected by severe difficulties in converting national currency data into dollars.

[c]Includes re-exports. In 1989 they amounted to $44.4 billion.

[d]Includes imports for re-export.

[e]Includes re-exports. In 1989 they amounted to $16.3 billion.

[f]Includes estimates of trade flows through processing zones.

[g]Estimates.

Source: GATT, *International Trade, 1989–1990*, Vol. 2 (Geneva, 1990), p. 3.

TABLE 1-A2   Network of World Merchandise Trade by Major Country Group, 1980 and 1989 (billion dollars and percentage share in world merchandise trade)

	Developed Countries			Developing Economies			Eastern Trading Area			World		
	Share		Value	Share		Value	Share		Value	Share		Value
Origin	1980	1989	1989	1980	1989	1989	1980	1989	1989	1980	1989	1989
Developed countries	45	55	1691	15	13	405	3	3	80	63	70	2176
Developing economies	20	14	435	7	6	171	1	1	44	28	21	650
Eastern trading area	3	3	83	2	2	59	4	4	126	9	9	269
World	**68**	**71**	**2210**	**23**	**21**	**635**	**9**	**8**	**250**	**100**	**100**	**3095**

Note: See Appendix Table A4.

Source: GATT, *International Trade, 1989–1990*, Vol. 2 (Geneva, 1990), p. 5.

TABLE 1-A3   Network of World Merchandise Trade by Region, 1989 (billion dollars)

	Destination								
Origin	North America	Latin America	Western Europe	Central/Eastern Europe/ USSR	Africa	Middle East	Asia	other	World
North America	164.5	51.4	112.5	6.1	8.7	12.4	126.2	3.7	**485.3**
Latin America	61.4	16.4	29.0	8.3	2.0	2.2	14.3	0.4	**134.0**
Western Europe	114.9	24.5	962.7	43.1	47.2	40.1	102.3	12.1	**1346.9**
Central/Eastern Europe/ USSR	2.5	8.4	56.0	109.3	3.7	3.6	19.9	9.1	**212.4**
Africa	11.2	1.3	40.8	3.0	5.9	2.7	8.0	8.4	**81.2**
Middle East	13.1	8.6	25.4	2.8	3.4	8.1	40.5	3.2	**105.0**
Asia	215.4	12.8	132.9	15.5	13.9	23.2	310.3	6.2	**730.1**
World	**583.0**	**123.5**	**1359.3**	**188.0**	**84.7**	**92.2**	**621.4**	**42.9**	**3095.0**

Note: See Appendix Table A5.

Source: GATT, *International Trade, 1989–1990*, Vol. 2 (Geneva, 1990), p. 9.

TABLE 1-A4 Shares of Regional Trade Flows in World Merchandise Trade, 1980 and 1989 (percentage share based on value)

Trade between:	1980	1989
North America and		
Latin America	4.1	3.6
Western Europe	6.3	7.3
Central and Eastern Europe		
and the USSR	0.4	0.3
Africa	2.1	0.6
Middle East	1.8	0.8
Asia	6.5	11.0
(Intra-North America)	4.0	5.3
Latin America and		
Western Europe	2.5	1.7
Central and Eastern Europe		
and the USSR	0.6	0.5
Africa	0.4	0.1
Middle East	0.7	0.3
Asia	0.9	0.9
(Intra-Latin America)	1.1	0.5
Western Europe and		
Central and Eastern Europe		
and the USSR	4.0	3.2
Africa	5.5	2.8
Middle East	6.3	2.1
Asia	4.7	7.6
(Intra-Western Europe)	27.1	31.1
Central and Eastern Europe and the USSR and		
Africa	0.4	0.2
Middle East	0.5	0.2
Asia	0.9	1.1
(Intra-Central and Eastern Europe and the USSR)	3.9	3.5
Africa and		
Middle East	0.2	0.2
Asia	0.9	0.7
(Intra-Africa)	0.2	0.2
Middle East and		
Asia	4.6	2.1
(Intra-Middle East)	0.6	0.3
(Intra-Asia)	6.5	10.0
Trade flows n.e.s.	2.2	1.4
World	**100.0**	**100.0**

Note: Trade of region A with region B is defined as the sum of A's exports to B and B's exports to A.

Source: GATT, *International Trade, 1989–1990*, Vol. 2 (Geneva, 1990), p. 10.

TABLE 1-A5 Developments in Regional Trade Flows, 1980–1989 (average annual percentage change in value)

	1980–89	1989
North America with Asia	11	9½
Western Europe with Asia	10½	9
Intra-Asia	10	10½
Intra-North America	8	7
Central and Eastern Europe and the USSR with Asia	7	3½
North America with Western Europe	6½	7½
Intra-Western Europe	6½	7
World trade:	**5**	**7½**
Latin America with Asia	4	12½
Intra-Central and Eastern Europe and the USSR	3½	−8
Latin America with Central and Eastern Europe and the USSR	3½	1
North America and Latin America	3½	11½
Intra-Africa	2½	14½
Africa with the Middle East	2½	18
Western Europe with Central and Eastern Europe and the USSR	2	11½
Africa with Asia	1½	6
North America with Central and Eastern Europe and the USSR	1½	16
Latin America with Western Europe	½	7
Central and Eastern Europe and the USSR with Africa	−1	−4½
Western Europe with Africa	−2½	7½
Latin America with Middle East	−3	22
North America with Middle East	−3½	14
Intra-Middle East	−3½	23
Intra-Latin America	−3½	½
Central and Eastern Europe and the USSR with the Middle East	−4	9
Middle East with Asia	−4	15½
Western Europe with the Middle East	−7	9½
North America with Africa	−8	8½
Latin America with Africa	−10½	11

Note: Trade of region A with region B is defined as the sum of A's exports to B and B's exports to A.

Source: GATT, *International Trade, 1989–1990*, Vol. 2 (Geneva, 1990), p. 10.

TABLE 1-A6 Shares of the Regions in World Exports, 1980 and 1988 (percentage based on value data)

	North America		Latin America		Western Europe		Central/Eastern Europe/USSR		Africa		Middle East		Asia	
	1980	1988	1980	1988	1980	1988	1980	1988	1980	1988	1980	1988	1980	1988
Merchandise	14	15	6	4	40	44	8	8	6	3	10	3	16	23
Commercial services[a]	12	17	5	4	62	55	—	—	4	3	3	2	13	18
Agricultural products	22	20	11	10	35	41	6	5	6	4	1	1	19	19
Mining products	7	10	10	10	17	24	8	17	14	10	35	18	9	11
Manufactures	16	14	2	2	54	49	7	6	1	1	1	1	19	27
Transportation[a]	11	16	5	4	58	52	—	—	5	4	3	2	18	22
Travel[a]	14	19	8	6	60	53	—	—	4	3	4	2	10	17
Other private services and income[a]	10	17	4	4	69	59	—	—	3	2	2	2	11	16

[a]Excludes Central/Eastern Europe/USSR.

Notes: 1. The commercial services figures used in preparing this table do not include the adjustment for the discrepancy in the shipment data.

2. In 1981, 1984, 1986–88, the United States improved its survey methods for trade in commercial services, which led to upward revision in the totals for each category.

Source: GATT, *International Trade, 1989–1990,* Vol. 1 (Geneva, 1990), p. 53.

TABLE 1-A7 Developed Countries' Merchandise Trade by Selected Product, 1989 (billion dollars and percentage)

Exports			Imports (f.o.b.)	
Value	Annual Change		Value	Annual Change
2176	**7**	**All products**	**2210**	**8**
		of which:		
197	5½	Food	205	2½
68	3½	Raw materials	74	5
84	14½	Ores, minerals, and nonferrous metals	98	14½
78	12	Fuels	200	19½
84	8½	Iron and steel	69	9
226	5	Chemicals	185	5
180	6½	Other semimanufactures	175	6½
897	8	Machinery and transport equipment	790	8
56	3½	Textiles	59	3½
38	5	Clothing	82	8½
194	9	Other consumer goods	212	9

Source: GATT, *International Trade, 1989–1990*, Vol. 2 (Geneva, 1990), p. 35.

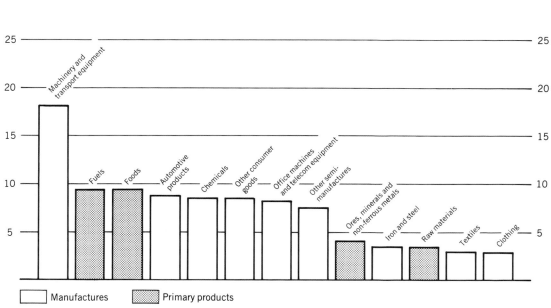

Note: Machinery and transport equipment excludes automotive products and office machines and telecom equipment.

FIGURE 1-A1 Shares of product groups in world merchandise trade, 1989. *Source:* GATT, *International Trade, 1989–1990*, Vol. 2 (Geneva, 1990), p. 35.

TABLE 1-A8 United States' Merchandise Exports by Product, 1989 (billion dollars and percentage)

	Value	Share	Annual Change
Office machines and telecom equipment	47.4	13	9 ½
Food	42.8	12	10
Chemicals	37.9	10 ½	16 ½
Other consumer goods	32.7	9	25
Other nonelectrical machinery	32.6	9	21
Automotive products	30.9	8 ½	4 ½
Other transport equipment	30.5	8 ½	13
Other semimanufactures	17.9	5	15
Raw materials	16.5	4 ½	9 ½
Electrical machinery and apparatus	14.7	4	11
Fuels	10.0	2 ½	22
Power generating machinery	9.9	2 ½	20
Ores and minerals	7.0	2	19 ½
Nonferrous metals	5.0	1 ½	30 ½
Textiles	4.4	1	12 ½
Iron and steel	3.7	1	53
Clothing	2.2	½	35

Source: GATT, *International Trade, 1989–1990,* Vol. 2 (Geneva, 1990), p. 12.

TABLE 1-A9 United States' Merchandise Imports by Product, 1989 (billion dollars and percentage)

	Value	Share	Annual Change
Automotive products	78.8	16	1
Office machines and telecom equipment	63.2	13	10
Fuels	56.1	11 ½	27
Other consumer goods	53.9	11	6
Other semimanufactures	36.2	7 ½	½
Other nonelectrical machinery	32.4	6 ½	9
Food	28.2	5 ½	3
Clothing	26.0	5 ½	13
Chemicals	21.8	4 ½	6 ½
Electrical machinery and apparatus	18.1	3 ½	−5 ½
Other transport equipment	11.9	2 ½	−8 ½
Iron and steel	11.4	2 ½	−7 ½
Nonferrous metals	11.0	2	5 ½
Raw materials	10.8	2	9
Textiles	6.4	1 ½	2
Power generating machinery	6.4	1 ½	22 ½
Ores and minerals	5.6	1	25

Source: GATT, *International Trade, 1989–1990,* Vol. 2 (Geneva, 1990), p. 12.

TABLE 1-A10   Merchandise Trade of GATT Contracting Parties, 1989 (million dollars and percentage)

	Value of Merchandise Trade		Trade as Percentage of GATT Contracting Parties' Trade		Share in CPS' Total Trade
	Exports	Imports	Exports	Imports	Exports & Imports
Antigua and Barbuda (1988)	20	230	0.0	0.0	0.0
Argentina	9,570	4,200	0.4	0.2	0.3
Australia	37,730	44,930	1.4	1.6	1.5
Austria	31,910	38,980	1.2	1.4	1.3
Bangladesh	1,310	3,650	0.0	0.1	0.1
Barbados	190	670	0.0	0.0	0.0
Belgium-Luxembourg	100,010	98,470	3.7	3.5	3.6
Belize	140	240	0.0	0.0	0.0
Benin (1987)	110	550	0.0	0.0	0.0
Bolivia	690	650	0.0	0.0	0.0
Botswana (1988)	1,420	1,030	0.1	0.0	0.0
Brazil	34,410	20,020	1.3	0.7	1.0
Burkina Faso (1988)	140	490	0.0	0.0	0.0
Burundi	80	190	0.0	0.0	0.0
Cameroon (1988)	930	1,270	0.0	0.0	0.0
Canada	121,360	121,160	4.5	4.3	4.4
Central African Rep. (1987)	130	210	0.0	0.0	0.0
Chad (1988)	140	420	0.0	0.0	0.0
Chile	8,190	6,500	0.3	0.2	0.3
Colombia	5,720	5,000	0.2	0.2	0.2
Congo (1987)	910	530	0.0	0.0	0.0
Costa Rica	1,400	1,740	0.1	0.1	0.1
Cote d'Ivoire (1987)	3,110	2,370	0.1	0.1	0.1
Cuba	5,810	7,330	0.2	0.3	0.2
Cyprus	790	2,290	0.0	0.1	0.1
Czechoslovakia[a]	23,450	22,400	0.9	0.8	0.8
Denmark	28,110	26,690	1.0	1.0	1.0
Dominican Rep.	930	2,280	0.0	0.1	0.1
Egypt	2,570	7,430	0.1	0.3	0.2
Finland	23,300	24,440	0.9	0.9	0.9
France	179,400	193,000	6.7	6.9	6.8
Gabon (1987)	1,290	730	0.0	0.0	0.0
Gambia, The (1987)	40	130	0.0	0.0	0.0
Germany, Fed. Rep.	341,230	269,700	12.7	9.6	11.1
Ghana (1988)	1,010	910	0.0	0.0	0.0
Greece	7,350	16,130	0.3	0.6	0.4
Guyana (1988)	230	190	0.0	0.0	0.0
Haiti	160	300	0.0	0.0	0.0
Hong Kong[b]	73,140	72,160	2.7	2.6	2.6
Hungary	9,590	8,780	0.4	0.3	0.3
Iceland	1,410	1,400	0.1	0.1	0.1

TABLE 1-A10 (Continued) Merchandise Trade of GATT Contracting Parties, 1989 (million dollars and percentage)

	Value of Merchandise Trade		Trade as Percentage of GATT Contracting Parties' Trade		Share in CPS' Total Trade
	Exports	Imports	Exports	Imports	Exports & Imports
India	15,820	20,440	0.6	0.7	0.7
Indonesia	22,030	16,570	0.8	0.6	0.7
Ireland	20,670	17,420	0.8	0.6	0.7
Israel	10,740	15,500	0.4	0.6	0.5
Italy	140,700	153,010	5.2	5.5	5.3
Jamaica	970	1,800	0.0	0.1	0.1
Japan	273,930	209,720	10.2	7.5	8.8
Kenya (1988)	1,070	1,980	0.0	0.1	0.1
Korea, Rep. of	62,330	61,300	2.3	2.2	2.3
Kuwait	11,480	6,300	0.4	0.2	0.3
Lesotho	70	460	0.0	0.0	0.0
Madagascar	310	340	0.0	0.0	0.0
Malawi	270	510	0.0	0.0	0.0
Malaysia	25,050	22,500	0.9	0.8	0.9
Maldives (1988)	40	110	0.0	0.0	0.0
Malta	840	1,480	0.0	0.1	0.0
Mauritania (1987)	430	240	0.0	0.0	0.0
Mauritius	990	1,330	0.0	0.0	0.0
Mexico[c]	35,640	33,940	1.3	1.2	1.3
Morocco	3,310	5,460	0.1	0.2	0.2
Myanmar	220	200	0.0	0.0	0.0
Netherlands	107,850	104,250	4.0	3.7	3.9
New Zealand	8,890	8,790	0.3	0.3	0.3
Nicaragua	300	690	0.0	0.0	0.0
Niger (1987)	320	370	0.0	0.0	0.0
Nigeria (1987)	7,370	3,910	0.3	0.1	0.2
Norway	27,060	23,670	1.0	0.8	0.9
Pakistan	4,710	7,140	0.2	0.3	0.2
Peru	3,640	2,330	0.1	0.1	0.1
Philippines	7,760	11,170	0.3	0.4	0.3
Poland[a]	13,160	10,460	0.5	0.4	0.4
Portugal	12,660	18,820	0.5	0.7	0.6
Romania[a]	11,850	10,200	0.4	0.4	0.4
Rwanda	100	330	0.0	0.0	0.0
Senegal (1987)	610	1,020	0.0	0.0	0.0
Sierra Leone	140	180	0.0	0.0	0.0
Singapore[b]	44,670	49,670	1.7	1.8	1.7
South Africa	22,320	17,950	0.8	0.6	0.7
Spain	44,490	71,470	1.7	2.6	2.1
Sri Lanka	1,550	2,190	0.1	0.1	0.1
Suriname (1988)	400	320	0.0	0.0	0.0

TABLE 1-A10 (Continued)   Merchandise Trade of GATT Contracting Parties, 1989 (million dollars and percentage)

	Value of Merchandise Trade		Trade as Percentage of GATT Contracting Parties' Trade		Share in CPS' Total Trade
	Exports	**Imports**	**Exports**	**Imports**	**Exports & Imports**
Sweden	51,550	48,980	1.9	1.7	1.8
Switzerland	51,530	58,190	1.9	2.1	2.0
Tanzania (1988)	280	800	0.0	0.0	0.0
Thailand	20,080	25,150	0.7	0.9	0.8
Togo (1988)	240	490	0.0	0.0	0.0
Trinidad and Tobago	1,560	1,220	0.1	0.0	0.1
Tunisia	2,930	4,370	0.1	0.2	0.1
Turkey	11,630	15,760	0.4	0.6	0.5
Uganda	270	650	0.0	0.0	0.0
United Kingdom	152,340	197,730	5.7	7.1	6.4
United States	363,990	492,920	13.5	17.6	15.6
Uruguay	1,500	1,170	0.1	0.0	0.0
Venezuela	12,950	8,730	0.5	0.3	0.4
Yugoslavia	13,460	14,830	0.5	0.5	0.5
Zaire	1,260	850	0.0	0.0	0.0
Zambia	1,350	870	0.0	0.0	0.0
Zimbabwe (1987)	1,430	1,210	0.1	0.0	0.0
Total contracting parties	2,694,540	2,799,250	100.0	100.0	100.0
Share in world	87	87			
World	3,095,000	3,220,000			

[a]Imports f.o.b.

[b]Includes re-exports and imports for re-export.

[c]Includes estimates of trade flows through processing zones.

Source: GATT, International Trade, 1989–1990, Vol. 2 (Geneva, 1990), Appendix.

TABLE 1-A11 Export Prices of Primary Commodities, 1980–90 (indices 1980 = 100)

Commodity	1981	1982	1983	1984	1985	1986	1987	1988	1989	1989 Q1	1989 Q2	1989 Q3	1989 Q4	1990 Q1	1990 Q2	1990 Q3
Food, Beverages, and Tobacco	94	84	90	93	80	75	70	85	84	89	88	80	80	80	80	70
Food:	97	82	89	89	75	66	67	86	89	91	91	86	87	85	84	79
Cereals	100	94	93	91	78	65	62	82	90	93	93	89	89	87	86	74
Wheat	101	93	91	88	79	67	65	84	98	101	100	96	95	94	86	69
Maize	104	86	108	108	89	70	60	85	89	94	92	83	86	85	95	87
Rice	111	68	64	58	50	49	53	70	74	64	74	83	74	72	67	63
Oilseed, oils and fats, oilseed cake, and meals	98	82	93	100	76	64	70	95	86	95	91	80	79	76	76	76
Meat	98	91	85	80	76	75	85	90	91	88	87	91	99	92	91	96
Beef	90	87	88	82	78	76	86	91	93	89	88	93	102	93	90	96
Lamb	95	83	67	67	64	71	75	83	80	80	80	80	81	87	93	95
Sugar	100	50	50	45	42	48	52	60	65	61	63	68	67	69	69	65
Bananas	107	100	114	99	101	102	101	128	146	128	157	131	139	158	144	150
Beverages:	79	80	86	100	88	102	73	73	61	74	68	52	49	50	54	53
Coffee	77	83	85	94	89	114	71	77	61	81	75	48	41	46	49	49
Cocoa beans	80	67	81	92	87	79	77	61	48	56	48	48	39	40	53	51
Tea	91	87	104	155	89	87	77	80	90	83	78	89	112	98	84	82
Tobacco	113	128	130	130	129	115	110	114	122	122	122	123	123	122	124	...
Agricultural Raw Materials	84	76	77	87	71	75	105	115	112	113	111	113	109	106	106	108
Logs	80	77	72	86	70	77	113	119	115	117	114	118	111	105	104	112
Cotton	85	71	78	89	69	58	83	77	95	84	95	101	99	96	101	101
Wool	100	92	84	85	78	77	109	159	131	146	129	124	126	125	117	108
Rubber	79	60	75	67	53	57	69	83	68	78	72	64	59	59	60	62
Hides and Skins	91	84	98	128	112	139	174	191	196	193	187	202	203	204	216	201
Jute	100	95	88	169	186	87	102	118	119	118	118	118	122	129	131	131
Sisal	84	78	75	76	69	67	67	72	85	77	83	90	92	92	94	94

TABLE 1-A11 (Continued)   Export Prices of Primary Commodities, 1980–90 (indices 1980 = 100)

	1981	1982	1983	1984	1985	1986	1987	1988	1989	1989 Q1	1989 Q2	1989 Q3	1989 Q4	1990 Q1	1990 Q2	1990 Q3
Minerals and Nonferrous Metals (excluding crude petroleum)	85	75	79	74	70	66	78	116	119	134	121	113	108	102	108	115
Copper	80	68	73	63	65	63	82	119	130	149	128	124	120	112	122	134
Aluminum	71	56	81	71	59	65	88	144	110	125	118	99	97	85	87	102
Iron ore	90	96	88	85	83	80	82	85	97	97	97	94	99	109	106	106
Tin	85	77	77	73	69	39	42	44	52	49	62	53	44	38	38	36
Nickel	91	74	72	73	75	60	75	211	204	273	209	186	148	119	133	159
Zinc	115	101	104	121	103	99	105	163	218	246	211	218	196	191	227	210
Lead	80	60	47	49	43	45	66	72	74	69	71	78	79	94	92	95
Phosphate rock	106	91	79	82	73	73	66	77	87	89	87	87	87	87	87	87
Total of above	90	80	85	87	76	73	79	98	98	104	100	94	92	90	91	88
Crude petroleum	96	89	80	80	76	39	50	40	49	46	50	49	51	53	43	70
All primary commodities	92	83	83	85	76	64	72	84	86	90	88	83	83	81	80	84

Note: The indices are computed in dollars.

Source: GATT, International Trade, 1989–1990 Vol. 2, (Geneva, 1990), Appendix.

PART I

INTERNATIONAL TRADE

2

WHY NATIONS TRADE: CLASSICAL THEORY

Nations (or firms in different nations) trade with each other because they benefit from it. Other motives may be involved, of course, but the basic motivation for international trade is that of the benefit, or gain, to the participants. The gain from international trade, like the gain from all trade, arises because specialization enables resources to be allocated to their most productive uses in each trading nation. Everyone recognizes the benefits of specialization and the division of labor in the case of individuals in a town, or between regions of a country, but we often fail to recognize that similar benefits exist in international trade. The political boundaries that divide geographic areas into nations do not change the fundamental nature of trade, nor do they remove the benefits it confers on the trading partners. Our task in this chapter is to establish and illustrate this basic truth, and to show briefly how it came to be perceived by the classical economists.

The reader who is not interested in the evolution of these ideas can move directly to Chapter 3, where a modern version of the theory of trade is presented. However, this chapter provides a useful background for, and introduction to, the modern theory.

The classical economists were searching for a way to deal with real and important issues of public policy, and their analysis, even though subject to severely restrictive assumptions, provides useful intuitive insights. As Haberler said of classical theory, "It will greatly facilitate analysis, and . . . deductions obtained with its aid do not depend for their validity upon its assumptions."[1]

ABSOLUTE ADVANTAGE

Adam Smith's original statement of the case for trade, contained in his epic *The Wealth of Nations* (1776),[2] was couched in terms of absolute cost differences between the countries. That is, Smith assumed that each country could produce one or more commodities at a lower real cost than its trading partners. It then follows that each country will benefit from specialization in those commodities in which it has an "absolute advantage" (i.e., can produce at lower real cost than another country), exporting them and importing other commodities that it produces at a higher real cost than does another country. A brief explanation of this conclusion is in order.

"Real cost," for Smith, meant the amount of labor time required to produce a commodity. His analysis was based on the labor theory of value, which holds that commodities exchange for one another in proportion to the hours of labor embodied in them, that is, the number of hours required for their production. For example, if 10 hours of labor are required to produce a shirt, and 40 hours to produce a pair of shoes, then four shirts will exchange for one pair of shoes. The labor embodied in four shirts equals the labor embodied in one pair of shoes. This argument holds for a given market area within which labor can move freely from one industry to another.

Economics has long since discarded the labor theory of value, but in this discussion of classical trade theory we will utilize it. Thus we will assume that labor is the only factor of production and labor time the only input, or cost, involved in the production of various commodities.

Within a single country, competition then ensures that commodities exchange in the market in proportion to their labor cost. In our example of shirts and shoes, no one would give more than four shirts for one pair of shoes because that would entail a cost of more than 40 hours of labor to obtain a pair of shoes, and we have assumed that one can obtain a pair of shoes directly by expending 40 hours of labor. No one would take fewer than four shirts for one pair of shoes for the same reason. Competition in the market, and the mobility of labor among industries within a nation, thus cause goods to exchange in proportion to their labor cost.

Money prices will simply reflect this result. Thus, in our example, if the price of shirts is $10, the price of shoes must be $40 (equal to the money value of four

[1]Gottfried Haberler, *The Theory of International Trade* (New York: Macmillan, 1936), p. 126.

[2]Adam Smith, *The Wealth of Nations,* Modern Library Edition (New York: Random House, 1937). (First published in 1776.)

shirts). Although they recognized the great benefits flowing from the use of money, the classical economists stated their analysis of international trade largely in real terms. This is sometimes confusing to modern students; most of us rarely think about the real exchange ratios between goods: the number of shirts that exchange for one pair of shoes, the pounds of sugar that are equal in value to one bushel of wheat. However, such real exchange ratios are implicit in our money prices. In our discussion of trade theory, we make much use of these real exchange ratios, or barter terms of trade, between two commodities.

This result—that within a given nation the exchange ratios between commodities will be determined by their real labor cost—requires the assumption that labor is mobile, that is, that workers can and do move freely from place to place and from industry to industry. Because of legal and cultural restrictions, however, labor cannot move freely between nations. To simplify the analysis, we will assume (as did the classical economists) that labor is completely immobile between nations.

The immobility of labor between nations obviously poses a problem for the labor theory of value when labor requirements vary from one country to another. The real exchange ratio of commodities moving in international trade need not be equal to the ratio of labor time embodied in their production. Thus a different theory is needed to explain or account for international exchange ratios. As we will see, that theory was first stated in fairly complete form by John Stuart Mill.

Adam Smith did not concern himself with this problem. He wished merely to show that a nation benefited from trade in which it exported those commodities it could produce at lower real cost than other countries, and imported those commodities it produced at a higher real cost than other countries.

An arithmetic example will help to illustrate the case of absolute cost differences. Suppose that, as shown in Table 2-1, in Scotland it takes 30 days to produce a bolt of cloth and 120 days to produce a barrel of wine, whereas in Italy it takes 100 days to produce a bolt of cloth and only 20 days to produce a barrel of wine. (Each commodity is assumed to be identical in both countries.) Clearly, Scotland has an absolute advantage in cloth production—it can produce a bolt of cloth at a lower real cost than can Italy—whereas Italy has an absolute advantage in wine production. Consequently, each country will benefit by specializing in the commodity in which it has an absolute advantage, obtaining the other commodity through trade. The benefit derives from obtaining the imported commodity at a lower real cost through trade than through direct production at home.

TABLE 2-1   Absolute-Cost Example

Country	Days of Labor Required to Produce	
	Cloth (1 bolt)	Wine (1 barrel)
Scotland	30	120
Italy	100	20

In the absence of trade, in Scotland one barrel of wine will exchange for four bolts of cloth (because they require equal amounts of labor); in Italy one barrel of wine will exchange for one-fifth of a bolt of cloth. Scotland will benefit if it can trade less than four bolts of cloth for one barrel of wine; Italy if it can obtain more than one-fifth of a bolt of cloth for one barrel of wine. Clearly, both countries can gain at an intermediate ratio such as one barrel of wine for one bolt of cloth. By shifting 120 days of labor from wine to cloth, Scotland could produce four additional bolts of cloth, worth four barrels of wine in trade with Italy. Scotland gets four barrels of wine instead of one. Italy obtains a similar gain through specialization in wine.

Adam Smith stated this argument in terms of an analogy with the behavior of an individual, treating the conclusion as self-evident. His famous passage deserves quotation in full:

> *It is the maxim of every prudent master of a family, never to attempt to make at home what it will cost him more to make than to buy. The taylor does not attempt to make his own shoes, but buys them of the shoemaker. The shoemaker does not attempt to make his own clothes, but employs a taylor. The farmer attempts to make neither the one nor the other, but employs those different artificers. All of them find it for their interest to employ their whole industry in a way in which they have some advantage over their neighbors, and to purchase with a part of its produce . . . whatever else they have occasion for.*

> *What is prudence in the conduct of every private family, can scarce be folly in that of a great kingdom. If a foreign country can supply us with a commodity cheaper than we ourselves can make it, better buy it of them with some part of the produce of our own industry, employed in a way in which we have some advantage. . . .*

> *The natural advantages which one country has over another in producing particular commodities are sometimes so great, that it is acknowledged by all the world to be in vain to struggle with them. By means of glasses, hotbeds, and hotwalls, very good grapes can be raised in Scotland, and very good wine too can be made of them at about thirty times the expense for which at least equally good can be brought from foreign countries. Would it be a reasonable law to prohibit the importation of all foreign wines, merely to encourage the making of claret and burgundy in Scotland? But if there would be manifest absurdity in turning towards any employment, thirty times more of the capital and industry of the country, than would be necessary to purchase from foreign countries, and equal quantity of the commodities wanted, there must be an absurdity . . . in turning towards any such employment a thirtieth, or even a three hundredth part more of either. Whether the advantages which one country has over another, be natural or acquired, is in this respect of no consequence.[3]*

This explanation certainly suffices to account for much international trade. Brazil can produce coffee at a lower real cost than can Germany; Florida can produce oranges at lower real cost than Iceland; Australia can produce wool at lower real cost than Switzerland. But what if a nation (or an individual) does not have an absolute advantage in any line of production? Does trade then offer it no benefit?

---

[3]Ibid., pp. 424–425.

COMPARATIVE ADVANTAGE

David Ricardo clearly showed, in his *Principles of Political Economy* (1817), that absolute cost advantages are not a necessary condition for two nations to gain from trade with each other.[4] Instead, trade will benefit both nations provided only that their relative costs, that is, the ratios of their real costs, are different for two or more commodities. In short, trade depends on differences in comparative cost, and one nation can profitably trade with another even though its real costs are higher (or lower) in every commodity. This point can best be explained with the aid of a numerical example.

Ricardo's own illustrative example is shown in Table 2-2. Note that Portugal has an absolute advantage in both commodities: It can produce a bolt of cloth in 90 days of labor compared to 100 days in England, and it can produce a barrel of wine in 80 days of labor compared to 120 days in England. Nevertheless, said Ricardo, Portugal can benefit from trading with the backward and inefficient English because of the fact that Portugal's cost advantage is relatively greater in wine than in cloth. That is, Portugal can produce wine for only two-thirds the cost in England, but its cloth costs nine-tenths as much as the cost in England. (Remember, we are assuming that labor is the only cost of production.) Portugal has greater superiority in wine than in cloth. This difference in comparative cost enables both nations to gain from specialization and trade, with each specializing in that commodity in which it has a comparative advantage.

The opportunity for gain can be seen immediately by comparing the real exchange ratios that will prevail in each country in the absence of international trade. In Portugal, in isolation 1 bolt of cloth will exchange for $9/8$ barrels of wine. (Why? Because 90 days of labor are required to produce both these quantities and, domestically, equal labor value in cloth will exchange for equal labor value in wine.) In England, on the other hand, 1 bolt of cloth will exchange for only $5/6$ of a barrel of wine. (One hundred days of labor can produce either a bolt of cloth, or $100/120 = 5/6$ of a barrel of wine.) Suppose now, as Ricardo did, that both countries are offered the chance to trade at the barter exchange ratio 1 cloth for 1 wine.

TABLE 2-2   Ricardo's Comparative Cost Example

Country	Days of Labor Required to Produce	
	Cloth (1 bolt)	Wine (1 barrel)
Portugal	90	80
England	100	120

---

[4]Scholars have disputed the origin of Ricardo's contribution, with some giving credit to Henry Torrens and others to James Mill. This argument need not concern us, but see J. Viner, *Studies in the Theory of International Trade* (New York: Harper, 1937).

Portugal will find such trade an attractive way to acquire cloth. Instead of giving up $9/8$ wine to obtain 1 cloth, it need give up only $8/8$ wine (i.e., 1 barrel). It saves $1/8$ barrel of wine on each bolt of cloth acquired. Consequently, Portugal will specialize in wine production and will obtain its cloth from England through trade. Similarly, England will benefit because for one cloth it can obtain a barrel of wine, instead of only $5/6$ of a barrel as in direct production. It will specialize in cloth, obtaining wine from Portugal through trade at less cost than it can be produced at home. Thus Ricardo showed that both countries gain, even though Portugal enjoys an absolute advantage in both commodities.

At this point, the reader may well be asking, "How did Ricardo know that the barter terms of trade between Portugal and England would be $1C : 1W$?" The answer is that he did not know precisely what that rate would be. All he knew was that the international exchange ratio had to lie somewhere in between the two domestic ratios, that is,

$$\text{Portugal} \quad 1C : 9/8W$$
$$\text{England} \quad 1C : 5/6W$$

Any ratio between these two limits will permit both countries to gain from trade. Ricardo chose the ratio $1C : 1W$ because it was a convenient one to use in making his point. He did not discuss the forces that would determine the exact ratio that would exist in the market. That was left for John Stuart Mill to explain, as we will see.

This demonstration, that the gain from trade arises from differences in comparative cost, has been hailed as one of the greatest achievements of economic analysis. It may seem, on first acquaintance, to be a rather small point to warrant such extravagant praise, but it has proved to have a great many applications in economics and in other fields of study as well. In some applications, as in considering the appropriate allocation of particular tasks to individuals, the principle of comparative advantage seems to be no more than common sense, and people no doubt act on it in their daily lives even though they do not analyze it and give it a special name. Ricardo appealed to this common-sense application in another of his own examples:

> *Two men can make both shoes and hats, and one is superior to the other in both employments, but in making hats he can only exceed his competitor by one-fifth or 20 per cent, and in making shoes he can excel him by one-third or 33 per cent;—will it not be for the interest of both that the superior man should employ himself exclusively in making shoes, and the inferior man in making hats?*[5]

Similar examples can readily be supplied: the engineer who is a better draftsman than anyone he can hire but who nevertheless finds it to his economic advantage to specialize in engineering and hire a draftsman; the surgeon who is also an expert auto mechanic but who maximizes his income by specializing in surgery, hiring a

---

[5]David Ricardo, *Principles of Political Economy and Taxation*, Everyman Edition (London: J.M. Dent, 1911), p. 83n. (First published in 1817.)

less skilled mechanic when he needs one; the farmer who has two fields, one of which is more productive in both soybeans and wheat than the other, but the first field yields three times as much soybeans per acre as the second, and only twice as much wheat, with the result that the first field is planted in soybeans and the second in wheat.

Basically, it is the principle of comparative advantage that underlies the advantages of the division of labor, whether between individuals, firms, regions, or nations. It causes us to specialize in those activities in which we have a relative advantage, depending on others to supply us with other goods and services. In this way real income can be increased along with economic interdependence.

RECIPROCAL DEMAND AND THE TERMS OF TRADE

As we have seen, Ricardo did not explain how a particular terms-of-trade ratio would be determined in international trade. He stopped with his demonstration that both countries would benefit from trade at any terms-of-trade ratio lying between the real exchange ratios in each country taken separately. Thus the exact ratio that would prevail was left undetermined.

This gap was filled by another great classical economist, John Stuart Mill.[6] Mill noted that the willingness of each country to offer its export good would depend on the amount of imports it could thereby obtain—that is, its exports would vary with the terms of trade (the price of its exports relative to the price of its imports). Thus he introduced demand considerations into the analysis. In addition, he stated that, at the final terms-of-trade ratio, trade must be in balance in the sense that the amount of exports offered by one country at that ratio must exactly equal the amount the other country is willing to purchase. Each country's supply of its export good must exactly equal the other country's demand for that good; this condition must be met for equilibrium to exist at that terms-of-trade ratio.[7] Mill said that this equilibrium would exist when "reciprocal demand" was equated in the two countries.

This point can also be made clear with the aid of an example. Suppose, as Mill did, that a given amount of labor (say, 10 man-days) will produce different outputs of two goods, broadcloth and linen, in two countries, as shown in Table 2-3. The

TABLE 2-3 Output Resulting from Given Labor Input		
Country	**Broadcloth (yd)**	**Linen (yd)**
England	10	15
Germany	10	20

[6]J.S. Mill, *Principles of Political Economy*, Ashley edition (London: Longman, Green, 1921), Book 3, Chapter 18.

[7]This condition of equilibrium assumes that only merchandise trade exists.

reader should note that Mill has changed the way of stating the relationship between cost and output. Instead of stating the amount of labor required to produce a given output, as Ricardo did, he states the output that can be produced by a given input of labor. In isolation, 10 cloth will exchange for 15 linen in England; 10 cloth will exchange for 20 linen in Germany. (This follows from the labor theory of value.)

With the opening of free trade between England and Germany, England will benefit from trade if it can obtain more than 15 linen for 10 cloth, while Germany will benefit if it can obtain 10 cloth for less than 20 linen. Thus the range within which the actual barter terms of trade may lie extends from $10C : 15L$ to $10C : 20L$. Mill then observed that the willingness or eagerness of each country to trade would depend on the barter terms of trade. For example, at a ratio very near $10C : 15L$, England would gain little and thus would not offer much cloth for export, whereas Germany would find that ratio attractive and would demand a large amount of cloth, thus offering much linen in exchange. Consequently, German demand for cloth imports would exceed the English supply of cloth exports, and the price of cloth in terms of linen would have to rise. As the real exchange ratio rises, to $10C : 16L$, $10C : 17L$, and so on, England will tend to offer more cloth and to demand more linen, whereas Germany will tend to demand less cloth and hence offer less linen.

Table 2-4 contains some hypothetical figures designed to illustrate the reciprocal demand relationship in the two countries. As the real terms-of-trade ratio rises (that is, more units of linen exchange for 10 cloth), England offers more cloth and demands more linen, whereas Germany demands less cloth and offers less linen. Equilibrium is reached at the ratio $10C : 17L$, where England's offer of cloth exactly equals Germany's demand for cloth, and England's demand for linen equals Germany's offer.

Mill thus showed that, within the terms set by the cost conditions in each country, the barter terms of trade will be determined by the demand in each country for the other country's export. In his chapter on international value, Mill analyzed the influence of elasticity of demand, size of country, changes in technology, and other factors on the terms of trade. His results have largely been confirmed by later writers, who developed geometric and other techniques to analyze these matters, as we will see in Chapter 3.

TABLE 2-4 Reciprocal Demand in England and Germany

| Real Terms of Trade | England | | Germany | |
	Cloth Offered (Supply)	Linen Demanded (Demand)	Cloth Demanded (Demand)	Linen Offered (Supply)
$10C : 15L$	0	0	20,000	30,000
$10C : 16L$	6,000	9,600	13,000	20,800
$10C : 17L$	10,000	17,000	10,000	17,000
$10C : 18L$	11,000	19,800	8,000	14,400
$10C : 19L$	13,000	24,700	4,000	7,600
$10C : 20L$	16,000	32,000	0	0

The reader will have observed that the classical economists had two theories of value. The labor theory of value explained domestic ratios of exchange, but reciprocal demand had to be brought in to explain the ratio of exchange in international trade. This dichotomy will be removed in Chapter 3.

▶ AN ILLUSTRATIVE EXAMPLE OF COMPARATIVE ADVANTAGE

Before we leave the classical analysis, with its simplifying assumption of the labor theory of value, it may be useful to work out an illustrative arithmetic example in some detail. Valuable insights can be derived from classical theory despite its severe abstraction, and it is often instructive to fix ideas by working through a concrete example, however contrived it may be.

Let us consider the following case, involving two countries, the United States and India, and two commodities, machines and cloth. Suppose that one day of labor produces outputs in the two countries as shown in Table 2-5. (Note that we are stating the cost and output in the same terms as Mill did.) On the basis of these figures, we can determine the following:

1. *Absolute advantage.* The United States has an absolute advantage in both products: one day of labor produces more machines and also more cloth in the United States than in India.

2. *Comparative advantage.* The United States' productivity advantage over India is relatively greater in machines (5 to 1) than in cloth (20 to 10, or 2 to 1). Consequently, the United States has a comparative advantage in machines, while India, being less disadvantaged in cloth than in machines, may be said to have a comparative advantage in cloth.

3. *Real exchange ratios in isolation.* Before trade, the real exchange ratio, or terms of trade, in the United States is 5 machines for 20 cloth, or 1 machine for 4 cloth. In India, it is 1 machine for 10 cloth. This result follows, as

TABLE 2-5   Comparative Cost Example

		Output of	
Country	**Input of Labor**	**Machines**	**Cloth**
United States	1 day	5	20
India	1 day	1	10

The ▶ denotes sections of greater than average difficulty or sections containing discussion that is more detailed than usual. These sections may be omitted without loss of continuity.

before, from the labor theory of value, in which products requiring the same amount of labor—one day in this case—will be equal in value in each country.

Since these ratios are different, traders in both countries will find it profitable at some intermediate terms-of-trade ratio to buy machines in the United States and ship them to India, and to import cloth from India. To show how an intermediate terms-of-trade ratio might be determined, let us assume that money wage rates are $20 per day in the United States and $5 per day in India.[8] With only one input, we can now calculate money prices in the two countries, as shown in Table 2-6. The U.S. price per machine, $4, is simply the wage cost ($20) divided by the output (5 units). The other prices are calculated in a similar fashion.

4. ***Real terms-of-trade ratio when trade takes place.*** As expected, the money price of machines is lower in the United States than in India, whereas the money price of cloth is lower in India. Since traders respond to money prices, when given the opportunity they will buy cloth in India for $0.50 per unit and machines in the United States for $4.00 each. However, the money prices at which trade takes place also imply a real terms-of-trade ratio between machines and cloth. Thus, when a machine costs $4.00 and a unit of cloth $0.50, 1 machine = 8 cloth in money value (8 × $0.50 = $4.00). For the assumed wage rates, this will be the real terms-of-trade ratio between the United States and India. We are assuming zero transport costs.

5. ***Limits on wage rates, or wage differences.*** At the wages rates we assumed, a flow of trade between the United States and India will occur. If that trade is balanced (i.e., if the money value of U.S. cloth imports just equals the money value of its machinery exports), then we have a stable equilibrium. If however, U.S. cloth imports have lower money value than Indian machinery imports, then India has a trade deficit. With fixed exchange rates, the classical specie-flow analysis (discussed in more detail in Chapter 16) calls for a flow of gold from India to the United States. The gold outflow would reduce the Indian money supply, putting downward pressure on prices and wages. As the Indian wage falls, Indian prices fall, encouraging the United States to buy more cloth and discouraging Indian purchases of U.S. machines. A falling price of Indian cloth also means that the real terms of trade are turning against India; that is, more units of cloth must be

TABLE 2-6 Comparative Cost Example (cont.)

Country	Labor Input	Wage Rate	Machines		Cloth	
			Output	Price	Output	Price
United States	1 day	$20	5	$4.00	20	$1.00
India	1 day	$ 5	1	$5.00	10	$0.50

[8]We use a dollar wage rate in both countries, implying a fixed exchange rate between U.S. dollars and Indian rupees. We also assume no transport costs.

given up to get one machine. This movement will tend to correct its trade deficit. If we assume for the moment that the U.S. wage remains constant at $20 per day, how low can the Indian wage go? The answer is that its lower limit is the level at which Indian machines become just as cheap as U.S. machines. Inspection of Table 2-6 shows this lower limit to be a daily wage of $4, since the Indian price of machines would then be $4. Indian cloth would cost $0.40, giving U.S. traders a strong incentive to import it, but Indian traders would no longer have any incentive to import U.S. machines. Consequently, there would no longer be a basis for profitable *two-way* trade. India would export cloth but import nothing; its trade balance would be in surplus; it would draw specie from the United States; and its wages and prices would tend to rise. Consequently, $4 is a lower limit that the Indian wage can approach but never quite reach.

Similarly, the upper limit on the Indian wage rate, given a constant U.S. wage of $20 per day, is the level at which the price of Indian cloth becomes equal to the price of U.S. cloth. From Table 2-6 we can see that the upper limit on the Indian wage is $10 (At that wage, what will be the Indian balance of trade? India will wish to import machines, but it can sell nothing to the United States. Hence it will have a trade deficit, a gold outflow, and downward pressure on its wage rate and prices.)

The reader should note that the ratio of U.S. wages to Indian wages can vary from $20 : $4 to $20 : $10, or from 5 : 1 to 2 : 1.[9] These ratios are equal to the United States' ratios of absolute advantage over India in the two products. The United States is five times as productive as India in machines and two times as productive in cloth. The moral is that wage differentials between nations reflect differences in productivity, and countries with higher wages can trade with low-wage countries to their mutual advantage.

6. *The influence of national currencies.* Let us now suppose that the facts in Table 2-6 remain the same except that Indian wages and prices are expressed in rupees and that the Indian wage rate is Rs 50 per day. We then have the situation portrayed in Table 2-7. Note that in the United States the price of machines is 4 times the price of cloth ($4 to $1) and in India 10 times (Rs 50 to Rs 5). That difference in relative prices is the signal that comparative advantage exists.

TABLE 2-7   Comparative Cost Example (cont.)

Country	Labor Input	Wage Rate	Machines		Cloth	
			Output	Price	Output	Price
United States	1 day	$20	5	$4	29	$1
India	1 day	Rs 50	1	Rs 50	10	Rs 5

[9]If we had held the Indian wage constant at $5 per day, then the limits within which the U.S. wage could vary would be $25 to $10, also between 5/1 and 2/1.

If we now assume that money wages remain unchanged in both countries, we can show that the rupee-dollar exchange rate must lie within certain limits in order for trade between the two countries to be in balance. Suppose, to begin with, that the exchange rate is $1 = Rs 8. Since U.S. traders can buy Indian cloth for Rs 5 per unit, they will offer dollars for rupees in the foreign exchange market and import Indian cloth for a dollar cost of $0.625 per unit. (Since 8 rupees cost $1, 5 rupees cost $\frac{5}{8} \times \$1 = \$0.625$, which is lower than the domestic price.) Similarly, Indian merchants can buy machines in the United States for Rs 32 ($4×8), compared to India's domestic cost of Rs 50. Thus India will export cloth and import machines, as expected, on the basis of comparative advantage.[10]

We have shown that at the assumed exchange rate, $1 = Rs 8, two-way trade will take place because cloth is relatively less expensive to produce in India and machines relatively cheaper in the United States. However, many other exchange rates also permit the two-way trade to occur. The limits within which the exchange rate can vary are set by the money prices in our two countries on our present assumption that money wage rates remain unchanged. From Table 2-7, money prices are as follows:

| | Price per Unit | |
Country	Machines	Cloth
United States	$4	$1
India	Rs 50	Rs 5

If India can buy a machine in the United States for less than Rs 50, it will import machines rather than produce them. As long as Indians can buy dollars for less than Rs 12.5 ($4 = Rs 50; $1 = Rs 50/4 = Rs 12.5), this condition is satisfied. Similarly, the United States will buy cloth from India as long as it costs less than $1 per unit, that is, as long as Rs 5 can be purchased for less than $1. This sets the other limit on the rupee-dollar exchange rate: $1 = Rs 5.

Just where between these two limits—$1 = Rs 12.5, $1 = Rs 5—the actual exchange rate will lie depends on the relative strength of demand in each country for the other country's product; that is, it depends on reciprocal demand. If, at the exchange rate we started with, $1 = Rs 8, the United States offers more dollars for Indian cloth than India demands to pay for its imports of machines, then there is an excess supply of dollars in the foreign exchange market. The dollar will fall in value—that is, the rate will move toward $1 to Rs 7.5, or $1 = Rs 7. This makes U.S. machines cheaper in

---

[10]Note that trade at this exchange rate also implies a real terms-of-trade ratio between cloth and machines. One machine costs India Rs 32 and one cloth costs Rs 5; therefore one machine is equal in money value to 6.4 cloth (32 ÷ 5 = 6.4). The real terms-of-trade ratio is 1 machine = 6.4 cloth.

rupees and Indian cloth more expensive in dollars, and it will tend to increase Indian imports of machines and decrease U.S. cloth imports.

With money wage rates fixed in both countries, variation in the rupee-dollar exchange rate permits the trade balance to be equilibrated. With exchange rates fixed, as in our previous example, variation in money wage rates provides the necessary flexibility.

7. *The gain from trade.* Finally, we will use this numerical example to show how trade can benefit the trading countries in the sense that it increases the real income level of the population. Let us assume that, in a given time period, the U.S. economy has 1.2 million man-days of labor available for productive use. According to the labor cost assumptions shown in Table 2-5, this means that if all its labor is devoted to machinery production, the United States can produce 6 million machines; and if all labor is devoted to cloth production, it can produce 24 million units of cloth. Furthermore, with constant costs the United States can produce any combination of machines and cloth lying on the straight-line production-possibility curve as shown in Figure 2-1. The slope of this line, $1M : 4C$, represents the real terms of trade between machines and cloth in the United States. To produce an additional 20 cloth, one day of labor must be withdrawn from machinery production, thus reducing output by five machines. Thus we can say that the opportunity cost of 20 cloth is represented by the five machines that must be foregone, or given up, when a day of labor is transferred from machinery to cloth production.

Basically, the production-possibility curve in Figure 2-1 portrays supply conditions in the U.S. economy.

When the United States is isolated, let us suppose that the population chooses to consume quantities of machines and cloth which require it to allocate one-half of the available labor supply to each commodity. That is, it produces at the point P in Figure 2-1, where total output is 3 million machines and 12 million cloth. Here we are bringing demand into the picture. The U.S. consuming public can choose any combination of machines and cloth lying along the production-possibility curve. We assume that consumer tastes are

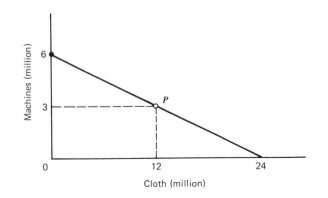

FIGURE 2-1   U.S. production-possibility curve.

such that the population actually prefers the combination represented by point P, where the ratio of machines consumed to cloth consumed is $\frac{1}{4}$ (3 million M:12 million C).

Now let us revert to the initial situation in our example, in which the opportunity arose for the United States to trade with India at the real terms-of-trade ratio, $1M : 8C$. As we saw in paragraphs 3 and 4, the United States has a comparative advantage in machines and will specialize in that commodity. Its production point will move from P to R in Figure 2-2. At R it is producing 6 million machines and zero cloth.

The next question is, How much cloth will consumers wish to consume now that cloth can be obtained from India at the terms of trade $1M : 8C$? U.S. consumers can choose any point along the trading-possibility curve, RT, the slope of which represents the real terms of trade, $1M : 8C$. Let us assume, as before, that U.S. consumers desire to consume one machine for each four units of cloth.[11] Thus our problem is to find the point on RT where the amounts of machines and cloth available for U.S. consumers are in exactly that ratio, $1M : 4C$. We can locate that point in three ways: arithmetically, geometrically, and algebraically.

Since the arithmetic method may be the most intuitive of the three, we will begin with it. Starting at point R, where output is 6 million machines and zero cloth, we can imagine merchants exchanging U.S. machines for Indian cloth in larger and larger amounts, thus moving along the trading-possibility curve RT. As such trade increases, the number of machines retained for U.S. consumption declines and the amount of cloth imports increases. The ratio of machines to cloth steadily falls. This process is illustrated in Table 2-8. When exports reach 2 million machines, the ratio of machines retained (4 million) to cloth imports (16 million) is exactly $1 : 4$. Hence, on our assumption about U.S. demand, the equilibrium position under free trade will be reached at that point, which is shown in Figure 2-2 as point S.

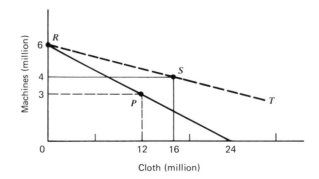

FIGURE 2-2   U.S. trading equilibrium.

[11]This assumption is quite arbitrary, but it does allow us to illustrate the new equilibrium and the gains from trade.

TABLE 2-8   U.S. Export Supply and Import Demand at Alternative Terms of Trade

Machines Produced	−	Machines Exported	=	Machines Retained for Consumption	Cloth Imports[a]	Ratio of Machines to Cloth
6,000,000		500,000		5,500,000	4,000,000	11 : 8
6,000,000		1,000,000		5,000,000	8,000,000	5 : 8
6,000,000		1,500,000		4,500,000	12,000,000	3 : 8
6,000,000		1,800,000		4,200,000	14,400,000	21 : 72
6,000,000		1,900,000		4,100,000	15,200,000	41 : 152
6,000,000		2,000,000		4,000,000	16,000,000	1 : 4

[a]Cloth imports = machine exports × 8.

The United States' gain from trade can now be clearly seen by comparing the amounts of goods retained for domestic use before and after trade:

	Before Trade	**After Trade**
Machines	3,000,000	4,000,000
Cloth	12,000,000	16,000,000

Trade enables the United States to move from P to S in Figure 2-2, and thus to obtain more of both goods for the same real cost in labor time.

Geometrically, the new equilibrium position, S, can be located simply by adding a line to Figure 2-2 to represent our assumption about the nature of U.S. demand. This is done in Figure 2-3, where the line OD indicates the assumed ratio of one machine to four cloth that U.S. consumers desire to consume. The line OD must pass through P, and it will intersect the trading-possibility curve RT at S.

Algebraically, we can find the point S simply by expressing RT and OD as equations and solving for the amounts of machines and cloth:

(1) $RT : M = 6,000,000 - \frac{1}{8}C$
(2) $OD : M = \frac{1}{4}C$

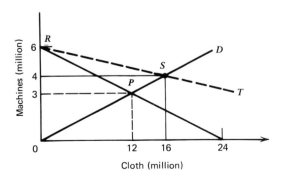

FIGURE 2-3   Determination of equilibrium trade position.

Substituting (2) in (1), we have:

$$\frac{1}{4}C = 6,000,000 - \frac{1}{8}C$$
$$\frac{3}{8}C = 6,000,000$$
$$C = 6,000,000 \times \frac{8}{3} = 16,000,000$$
$$M = \frac{1}{4}C = \frac{1}{4} \times 16,000,000 = 4,000,000$$

All three methods produce the same result and conclusions.

QUESTIONS FOR STUDY AND REVIEW

1. Distinguish between absolute advantage and comparative advantage.

2. Show that comparative cost differences lead to absolute price differences in a free market.

3. What is meant by the terms of trade?

4. If Country A can produce a certain product, say, shoes, with less labor and other inputs than can Country B, it follows that Country A has a comparative advantage in shoes. Do you agree? Explain.

5. Assume a classical world with a single factor, labor. One day of labor will produce the following amounts of the two goods in each of our two countries: (Show all your calculations and explain each part briefly.)

	Output	
Country	**Cloth (yds)**	**Wheat (bu)**
Togo	20	30
Ruritania	5	15

a. Which country has a comparative advantage in which product?

b. If the total labor time in Ruritania is 1000 man-days, construct that country's production-possibility curve. Label clearly.

c. If consumers in Ruritania wish to consume equal amounts of cloth and wheat (that is, just as many yards of cloth as bushels of wheat), how much of each good will be produced and consumed in isolation?

d. When international trade begins, assume that the equilibrium terms of trade are $1C : 2W$. If Ruritania still wishes to consume equal amounts of cloth and wheat, show on your diagram the production and consumption position in Ruritania after trade begins and the amounts of its exports and imports.

e. What is the gain from trade to Ruritania?

SELECTED REFERENCES

Allen, William R., ed. *International Trade Theory: Hume to Ohlin.* New York: Random House, 1965.

Haberler, Gottfried. *The Theory of International Trade.* New York: Macmillan, 1936. Chapter 10.

Mill, John Stuart. *Principles of Political Economy,* Ashley Edition. London: Longman, Green, 1921.

Ricardo, David. *Principles of Political Economy and Taxation,* Everyman Edition. London: J. M. Dent, 1911.

Smith, Adam. *The Wealth of Nations,* Modern Library Edition. New York: Random House, 1937.

Viner, Jacob. *Studies in the Theory of International Trade.* New York: Harper, 1937.

CHAPTER

WHY NATIONS TRADE: MODERN THEORY

Although the theory of comparative advantage, as stated by Ricardo, Mill, and other classical economists, became widely accepted in the nineteenth century, critics continued to attack its dependence on the labor theory of value. It was obvious to all that labor was not the only factor of production and that commodities required different proportions of capital, land, labor, and other factors in their production. To remain convincing, the theory of comparative advantage had to be freed from the restrictive and unrealistic assumption that commodities are exchanged for each other (in each country in isolation) in direct proportion to the labor time utilized to produce them. Our task in this chapter is to show how that was done.

The analysis that follows is not particularly difficult, but the argument is closely reasoned, and the reader should be careful to follow every step. We will make liberal use of diagrams to provide a visual picture of what is happening, but it is important to think through the economic processes that these diagrams portray. Although the analysis may seem a bit abstract and unrealistic, it has great significance for real-world policy issues. If readers will devote as much thought and care to this analysis, as, say, to the play of a three no-trump contract in bridge or to a seven-card stud poker hand, they will be repaid with an understanding of the concept of comparative advantage.

A number of assumptions underlie the analysis. Some of them can be dropped at a later stage, but it may be useful to list the main assumptions at the outset:

1. Perfect competition in both commodity and factor markets.
2. Given quantities of the factors of production (i.e., we abstract from population growth and capital formation).
3. A given, unchanging level of technology.
4. Zero transport costs and other barriers to trade.
5. Given tastes and preferences.
6. Factors of production that are perfectly mobile among industries within each country but completely immobile between countries.

SOME PRELIMINARY CONCEPTS

Opportunity Cost

One way to avoid the dependence on the labor theory was through the use of the now familiar concept of "opportunity cost."[1] As the reader may recall from an earlier course in economic principles, the opportunity cost of a unit of commodity A is simply the amount of another commodity, say, B, that must be given up in order to obtain it. We recognize that factors of production have alternative uses. (For example, if land, labor, and capital are withdrawn from B, they can be allocated to the production of A.) Thus, if just enough factors are withdrawn from B to permit the production of one unit of A, we can say that the opportunity cost of the additional (marginal) unit of A is the amount by which the output of B declines. The opportunity cost of a unit A is the amount of B that must be foregone in order to produce it. (Note that this definition implies that resources are fully employed, so that the production of an extra unit of A requires the withdrawal of productive resources from another use).

The concept of opportunity cost thus enables us to obtain real exchange ratios for each country, as in Chapter 2, but without making use of the labor theory of value. We can think of several factors of production combining to produce a unit of a commodity, but we need not measure the amount of each factor. Our measure of cost is simply the amount of another commodity that must be foregone. Thus we can drop out the labor theory of value but retain the real exchange ratio. A country has a comparative advantage in commodity A if it can produce an additional unit of A at a lower opportunity cost in terms of commodity B than can another country.

---

[1] One of the early applications of this concept to international trade theory was made by G. Haberler, *The Theory of International Trade* (New York: Macmillan, 1936), Chapter 12.

TABLE 3-1 Alternative Combinations of Wheat and Steel That Germany Can Produce (millions of tons)

Wheat	100	90	80	70	60	50	40	30	20	10	0
Steel	0	10	20	30	40	50	60	70	80	90	100

The Production-Possibility Curve

This view of cost leads directly to the concept of production-possibility curve. Suppose that Germany can produce only two commodities: wheat and steel. If it puts all its productive resources into wheat, let us suppose that it can produce 100 million tons. Suppose further that German conditions of production are such that the opportunity cost of a ton of steel is one ton of wheat. Starting from an initial position in which Germany is fully specialized in wheat, as resources are shifted into steel the output of wheat will drop by one ton for each additional ton of steel produced. When all German resources are devoted to steel production, its total output will be 100 million tons of steel and no wheat. We can now draw up a list (see Table 3-1) of a number of alternative combinations of wheat and steel that Germany can produce. In this example we assume that opportunity costs remain constant over the entire range of production possibilities.

These facts can also be shown in a diagram (Figure 3-1). The straight line *AB* represents the production-possibility curve for the German economy. Points along

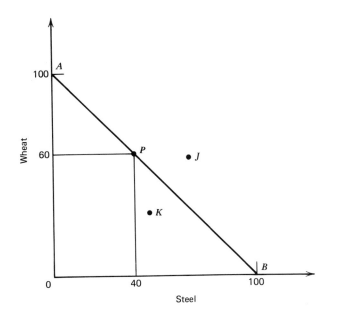

FIGURE 3-1 Germany's production-possibility curve.

the line *AB* represent alternative combinations of wheat and steel that Germany can produce at full employment. At *A*, it produces 100 million wheat and no steel; at *B*, 100 million steel and no wheat; at *P*, 60 million wheat and 40 million steel. The constant slope of *AB* represents the constant internal ratio of exchange (one wheat for one steel). The line *AB*, therefore, represents the highest attainable combinations of wheat and steel that the German economy can produce at full employment. All points above and to the right of *AB*, such as *J*, represent combinations of wheat and steel that are beyond the reach of German productive capacity. Points to the left of *AB*, such as *K*, involve unemployment or unutilized capacity.

The production-possibility curve *AB* thus provides a complete account of the supply side of the picture in our hypothetical German economy. To determine which one of all these possible combinations Germany will actually choose, we will have to deal with the demand side of the picture.

Community Indifference Curves

The use of "indifference curves" to represent consumption preferences and demand is most appropriate when one is considering an individual consumer. Suppose, for example, that a certain person has an initial combination (or bundle) of two commodities, food and clothing, as indicated by point *A* in Figure 3-2. These commodities yield him a certain level of satisfaction, or utility. Now suppose that one unit of food (*AR* in Figure 3-2) is taken away from our consumer, thus reducing his level of satisfaction or utility. The question is, How much additional clothing would it take to restore him to the same level of satisfaction or

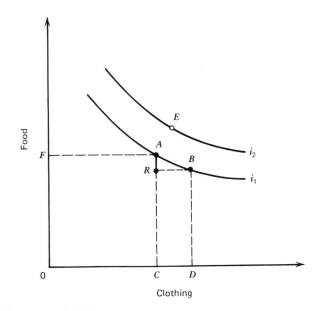

FIGURE 3-2   Consumer indifference curves.

utility that he enjoyed at point *A?* If that amount is two units of clothing (*RB* or *CD* in Figure 3-2), then at point *B* he is just as well satisfied as he was at *A,* and we can say that he is indifferent between the two commodity bundles represented by points *A* and *B.* These two points lie on the same indifference curve, i_1.

Proceeding in a similar way, we can locate other points on i_1. Conceptually, we wish simply to determine the amount of one commodity that will exactly compensate the consumer for the loss of a given amount of the other commodity.

Thus far we have derived only a single indifference curve, but it is easy to generate others. Starting back at point *A,* suppose we give the consumer more of both commodities, moving him to point *E.* Since both commodities yield satisfaction,[2] *E* represents a higher level of utility than does *A*—that is, it lies on a higher indifference curve, i_2. We can then proceed as before to locate other points on i_2. In this way, a whole family of indifference curves can be generated. The reader should be careful to note that movement to a higher indifference curve implies a higher level of welfare, utility, or real income. Note also that indifference curves are convex to the origin—that is, they bend in toward the origin. This curvature simply reflects the fact that, as the consumer gives up more food, it takes more and more clothing to compensate him, to maintain the same level of satisfaction. In other words, the marginal rate of substitution between food and clothing, which is the ratio of *AR* to *RB*, is falling as the consumer moves down the indifference curve. Finally, note that indifference curves do not intersect each other.

Before leaving the individual-consumer example, it may be useful to point out explicitly how indifference curves enable us to evaluate and determine preferences for commodity bundles that could not otherwise be unambiguously ranked. Consider points *A, E,* and *G* in Figure 3-3a. *E* is clearly preferred to *A* because the consumer has more of both commodities. But what about *G* and *A,* or *G* and *E?* At *G* the consumer has more food but less clothing than at A or E.

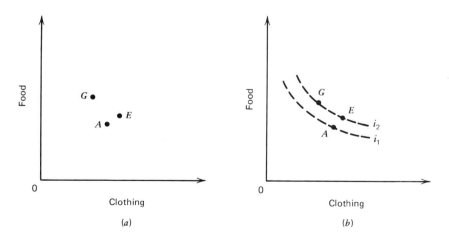

FIGURE 3-3   An illustration of the use of indifference curves.

Without more information about the consumer's willingness to substitute one of these commodities for the other, we are unable to determine which of these commodity bundles the consumer prefers. Consumption indifference curves supply precisely this needed information, as may be seen in Figure 3-3b. Once the indifference curves are drawn in, we observe that G and E lie on the same curve, i_2; hence the consumer is indifferent between them. G is preferred to A because it lies on a higher indifference curve than does A. Thus consumer indifference curves enable us, at least conceptually, to compare the levels of satisfaction or utility derived from alternative combinations of commodities available to a consumer.

To analyze the effect of international trade on a nation's welfare, it is extremely helpful to use indifference curves to represent the patterns of tastes and preferences of an entire nation. Such aggregate curves, or "community indifference curves," as they are called, are often used in international trade analysis despite the fact that they require highly restrictive assumptions in order to preserve their logical validity. This matter is much discussed in another branch of economics known as welfare theory; here we will briefly mention only two main points. First, the crucial difficulty in moving from individual to community indifference curves is that the utility or satisfaction enjoyed by one individual cannot be compared with the utility enjoyed by another. Utility is an ordinal concept and cannot be measured cardinally. Second, international trade is likely to increase the incomes of some individuals and reduce the incomes of others, as will be discussed in Chapter 4. It is then impossible to say how the welfare of the nation has been affected, because interpersonal comparisons between the gainers and the losers cannot be made.

One way to escape from these difficulties is to assume that every individual has exactly the same tastes and exactly the same factor endowments. Then the distribution of income remains unchanged and everyone is harmed or benefited in the same degree. Consequently, it is possible to conceive of community indifference curves just as we have described them for a single person.

Despite the unrealism of the necessary assumptions, we will make use of nonintersecting community indifference curves in our subsequent exposition in order to assess the effects that trade, and various policy actions affecting trade, will have on economic welfare. The reader should keep in mind the difficulties involved and remember that restrictive assumptions are required to justify use of this concept.

INTERNATIONAL TRADE: CONSTANT COSTS

We are now ready to bring supply and demand conditions together and to show how and why trade takes place. To begin, we show the initial equilibrium in a closed economy, before trade. Figure 3-4 contains community indifference curves for Germany superimposed on its production-possibility curve as developed earlier (Figure 3-1). Under competitive conditions, the German economy will be in equilibrium at point P, where 60 million tons of wheat and 40 million tons of steel are produced, and where Germany reaches the highest possible indifference curve (level of welfare) that it can attain with its given productive resources. At the point of tangency (P) between the production possibility curve (WS) and the community

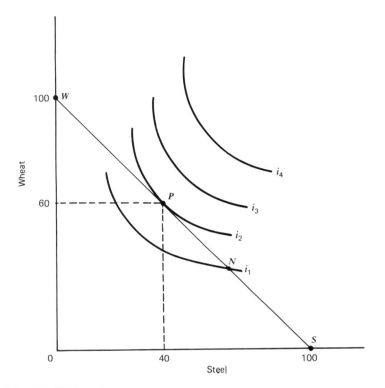

FIGURE 3-4 Equilibrium in a closed economy.

indifference curve (i_2), the slopes of the two are equal, which means that the opportunity cost ratio (one wheat for one steel) is exactly equal to the community's marginal rate of substitution in consumption. At any other production point, it is possible to reallocate resources and move to a higher indifference curve. At N, for example, Germany is on i_1. By shifting resources from steel to wheat, it can move to P and thus reach a higher indifference curve, i_2.

Although we speak of Germany shifting resources from steel to wheat, the reader should remember that in a competitive economy it is actually individual firms that are making these decisions and taking the necessary actions. Their motivation comes from the market. At N, the opportunity cost ratio facing producers is not equal to the slope of the indifference curve, i_1. Consumers are willing to swap, say, two steel for one wheat, whereas the opportunity cost in production is one steel for one wheat. When prices reflect this difference, producers are led to expand wheat production, and a move from N toward P occurs.

Given the initial closed economy equilibrium at P, now suppose that Germany has the opportunity to trade with the rest of the world (ROW) at a real exchange ratio different from its domestic opportunity cost ratio $(1S : 1W)$. Specifically, suppose the exchange ratio in ROW is $1S : 2W$, and suppose that Germany is so small relative to ROW that German trade has no effect on world prices. Comparing Germany's domestic ratio to the world exchange ratio, we can see that

Germany has a comparative advantage in steel. That is, its cost of steel (measured in foregone wheat) is less than the cost in ROW. Note that we do not need to know whether German labor is efficient or inefficient compared to labor in other countries. In fact, we do not know, or need to know, anything at all about the real cost in terms of labor hours, land area, or capital equipment. All that matters to Germany is that by transferring resources from wheat to steel, it can obtain more wheat through trade than through direct production at home. It will pay Germany to shift resources from wheat to steel, using the increased steel output to buy wheat from ROW. For every ton of wheat lost through curtailed production, Germany can obtain two tons through trade. Germany's gain from trade arises from its ability to obtain wheat at a smaller cost in resources than it would incur at home. An opportunity for a gain from trade will exist provided the exchange ratio in ROW differs from Germany's domestic ratio. That is, with a domestic ratio of $1S : 1W$, Germany can benefit provided it can get anything more than one ton of wheat for one ton of steel.[3] Only if the external exchange ratio is exactly equal to Germany's ratio will there be no opportunity for gainful trade.

This example can be given a useful geometric interpretation, as in Figure 3-5, in which we add to Figure 3-4 the "trading-possibility" line, *SB,* drawn with a slope equal to the exchange ratio in ROW ($1S : 2W$). Once they have the opportunity to trade at the ROW ratio, German producers will shift from wheat to steel. With constant opportunity costs, they will continue to shift until they are fully specialized in steel (at *S* in Figure 3-5). German firms will have an incentive to trade steel for wheat, moving along the trading-possibility line to reach the highest possible level of welfare, which will be found at the point of tangency between an indifference curve and the line *SB.* That is point *T* in Figure 3-5. At *T,* the price ratio is again equal to the marginal rate of substitution in consumption as represented by the slope of the indifference curve i_4 at that point.

In the final equilibrium position, Germany will produce at point *S* and consume at point *T.* It will produce *OS* of steel (100 million tons), keeping *OD* (55 million tons) for its own use and exporting *SD* of steel (45 million tons) in exchange for imports *DT* of wheat (90 million tons). Note what we will call the "trade triangle," *DTS,* where *DS* = steel exports, *DT* = wheat imports, and the slope of the third side, *TS,* represents the exchange ratio.

We can summarize the German position before and after trade in Table 3-2. Germany's gain from trade can clearly be seen by comparing the amounts of the two commodities that are available for domestic consumption before and after trade:

	Before Trade	**After Trade**
Wheat	60 million tons	90 million tons
Steel	40 million tons	55 million tons

Because population and resources employed remain the same, while more of both goods are available, Germany clearly can increase economic welfare in the sense

---

[3]If one ton of steel buys less than one ton of wheat in ROW, Germany will benefit from trading wheat for steel.

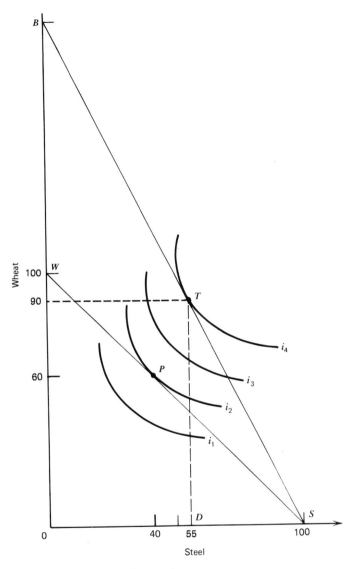

FIGURE 3-5   Equilibrium with foreign trade.

of providing its population with more material goods than they had before trade began.

Since we are using community indifference curves, however, the direct evidence that Germany has gained from foreign trade is provided by the fact that it reaches a higher indifference curve: the movement from i_2 to i_4. This point is important because it may well be that a country will end up with more of one commodity and less of another as a result of trade. As we have seen, indifference curves enable us to determine whether or not welfare has increased in such cases.

TABLE 3-2 German Production and Consumption

Before Trade			
Production (Net National Product)		**= Consumption**	
Wheat:	60 million tons	Wheat:	60 million tons
Steel:	40 million tons	Steel:	40 million tons

After Trade (millions of tons)						
Production (NNP)	**− Exports**	**+ Imports**		**= Consumption**		
Wheat:	0	−	0	+	90	=	90
Steel:	100	−	45	+	0	=	55

Up until this point, we have focused on the position of one country and have assumed that it has the opportunity to trade at a fixed world exchange ratio between steel and wheat. We assumed that Germany's offer of steel on the world market did not affect the world terms-of-trade ratio. We will now consider a case in which we have two countries of approximately equal size. This will enable us to show how the terms of trade are determined in the first place. We can also show that both countries can gain from international trade.

Our two countries are Germany and France. German supply and demand conditions remain the same as in Figure 3-4. We assume that France can produce 240 million tons of wheat or 80 million tons of steel if it specializes fully in one or the other. The French production-possibility curve, *HG,* drawn as a straight line to indicate a constant opportunity cost ratio of $1S : 3W$, is shown in Figure 3-6 along with community indifference curves to represent French demand. In complete isolation, the French economy is in equilibrium at point *K,* where $120W$ and $40S$ are produced and consumed.

Before trade, the domestic exchange ratios differ in our two countries: in Germany $1S : 1W;$ in France $1S : 3W$. As noted, the fact that these ratios are different is enough to show that comparative advantage exists. Steel is cheaper (in terms of foregone wheat) in Germany than it is in France; hence Germany has a comparative advantage in steel and France in wheat. Note that we need not compare the resources used in each country in order to determine comparative advantage; we need only to compare their opportunity cost ratios. If these are different, a basis for trade exists.

Germany will benefit if it can exchange $1S$ for anything more than $1W$, and France will benefit if it can obtain $1S$ for anything less than $3W$. Therefore, when trade begins between these two countries, the terms of trade may lie anywhere between the two domestic ratios: $1S : 1W$ and $1S : 3W$. Just where the terms-of-trade ratio will settle depends on the willingness of each country to offer its export commodity and to purchase imports at various ratios—that is, it depends on reciprocal demand in the two countries.[4] To explain this process, we will first

---

[4] As mentioned in Chapter 2, the phrase "reciprocal demand" was first used by John Stuart Mill. It involves not only the demand for imports but also the willingness to supply exports in exchange.

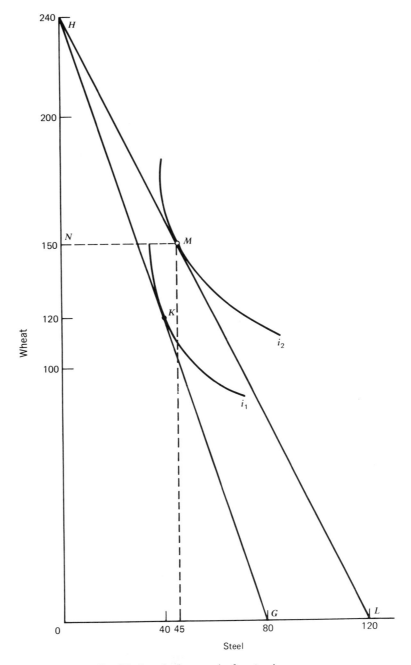

FIGURE 3-6   France: Equilibrium before and after trade.

show the conditions that must prevail for an equilibrium to exist in our illustrative example, and then we will present a more general approach.

We have already determined Germany's demand for imports ($90W$) and its offer of exports ($45S$) at the intermediate terms-of-trade ratio $1S: 2W$. Those amounts are shown in Figure 3-5. Now we will ask, How much wheat is France willing to export for how much steel at that exchange ratio? In Figure 3-6, we draw the line HL to represent France's trading-possibility curve. It originates at H because France will specialize in wheat production. We see that by trading wheat for steel, France can move along HL and attain higher levels of welfare than it can reach in isolation. At M, it reaches the highest possible indifference curve. At that point France will export $90W$ and import $45S$, as indicated by its trade triangle, NHM.

Thus it turns out that France is willing to export, at the exchange ratio $1S : 2W$, just the amount of wheat that Germany wants to import. And France wants to import just the amount of steel that Germany is willing to export. Geometrically, this equality can be seen by comparing the two trade triangles, DTS and NHM. They are congruent. Through a happy accident (though somewhat contrived, as the reader may suspect), we have hit upon the equilibrium terms-of-trade ratio in our very first attempt! Note carefully the conditions that are necessary for the exchange ratio $1S : 2W$ to be an equilibrium ratio: Each country must demand exactly the amount of its imported commodity that the other country is willing to supply.

Before proceeding to a more general explanation of the determination of an equilibrium exchange ratio, we pause to note that both France and Germany benefit from international trade. This is shown most directly by the fact that both countries end up on higher indifference curves in the trading equilibrium in Figures 3-5 and 3-6. The gain in this particular case can also be shown arithmetically in Table 3-3, which contains a summary of the world position before and after trade. Before trade, world outputs of wheat and steel were $180W$ and $80S$; post-trade outputs are $240W$ and $100S$. One may ask, By what magic has world output of both commodities increased without the use of any additional resources? The answer is that specialization—the use of each nation's resources to produce the commodity in which it possesses a comparative advantage—has made possible a larger total output than can be achieved under self-sufficiency.

The Offer Curve

The time has come to explain what determines the equilibrium terms of trade between two countries. We have seen that for an equilibrium to exist, each country must be willing to export just the amount of its export commodity that the other country desires to import at that price. That is, their reciprocal demands must be equal and opposite. Consider Figure 3-7a, which portrays a constant-cost production-possibility curve (WC) and indifference curves for Country A. The domestic opportunity cost ratio is equal to the slope of WC. We can now show how Country A's exports and imports change as the terms of trade change. Given the opportunity to obtain more wheat per unit of cloth through trade than it can produce at home, Country A will specialize in

TABLE 3-3 The Gain from Trade: Summary Showing Production and Consumption in Each Country Before and After Trade

	Wheat Production	– Exports	+ Imports	= Consumption	Steel Production	– Exports	+ Imports	= Consumption
Situation Before Trade								
France	120			120	40			40
Germany	60			60	40			40
Total World	180				80			
Situation After Trade								
France	240	– 90	+ 0	= 150	0	– 0	+ 45	= 45
Germany	0	– 0	+ 90	= 90	100	– 45	+ 0	= 55
Total World	240			240	100			100
Gain from Trade								
France				+ 30				+ 5
Germany				+ 30				+ 15
Total World				+ 60				+ 20

55

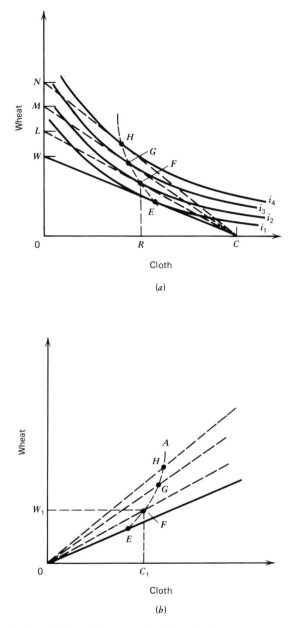

FIGURE 3-7 Derivation of the offer curve for Country A.

cloth and trade cloth for wheat until it reaches the highest possible indifference curve for that particular terms-of-trade ratio. Thus, when the terms of trade are given by *LC* in Figure 3-7*a*, it will export *RC* of cloth and import *RF* of wheat, thus reaching indifference curve i_2. As the terms of trade change, to *MC* and *NC*, Country A's volume of exports and imports change as indicated by the points of tangency between the terms-of-trade lines and indifference curves in Figure 3-7*a*. These points are alternative points of equilibrium for Country A. They show, for the various terms-of-trade ratios, how much cloth A is willing to export and how much wheat it wishes to import.

We can now transfer this information to another diagram and use it to construct A's "offer curve," or reciprocal demand curve. In Figure 3-7*b*, we measure A's cloth exports along the *X*-axis and its wheat imports along the *Y*-axis. The terms-of-trade ratios are now represented by the slopes of vectors from the origin—the line *OF* represents *LC* from Figure 3-7*a*, for example. The coordinates of point *F* in Figure 3-7*b*, therefore, represent Country A's exports of cloth (OC_1) and imports of wheat (OW_1) at the terms-of-trade ratio *OF*. Country A's offer curve, *OA*, is made up of straight-line segment *OE*, determined by its domestic opportunity cost ratio, and the curved segment *EFGH*, determined by its demand conditions.[5] [At the terms-of-trade ratio *OE* (= CW in Figure 3-7*a*), Country A is indifferent between domestic production and import of wheat. Thus it could be in a trading equilibrium anywhere along the straight-line segment of *OE*.]

In a similar way, we can obtain an offer curve for Country B. When we bring both countries' offer curves together, as in Figure 3-8, we observe that at only one

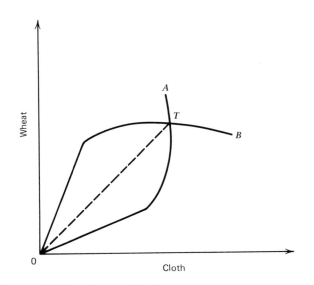

FIGURE 3-8 The equilibrium terms of trade.

[5]To make the transfer from Figure 3-7*a* to Figure 3-7*b*, the reader may find it helpful to think of shifting the origin from O to C in Figure 3-7*a*, and then rotating the figure 180° from left to right on its vertical axis so that the line *CEFGH* in Figure 3-7*a* becomes *OEFGH* in Figure 3-7*b*.

terms-of-trade ratio (*OT*) is A's offer of cloth (and demand for wheat) precisely matched by B's demand for cloth (and offer of wheat). Only at that terms-of-trade ratio are the equilibrium conditions satisfied. (In our preceding Franco-German example, the equilibrium exchange ratio was 1*S* : 2*W*, although we did not explain how that ratio was determined.)

A country's offer curve thus contains information about both supply and demand. Each point on it is a potential equilibrium position for that country in the sense that both producers and consumers would be in equilibrium at that exchange ratio. We will make use of offer curves in our subsequent analysis of commercial policy matters. However, we should keep in mind what lies behind these curves, which appear so simple at first glance.[6]

Before moving on, we pause to explain briefly the meaning of the elasticity of demand for imports as applied to an offer curve. The coefficient of elasticity is defined as the value of the ratio:

$$e = \frac{\text{Percentage change in quantity demanded}}{\text{Percentage change in the terms of trade}}$$

for very small changes in the terms of trade. When the offer curve is a straight line from the origin, as the segment *OS* of Country A's offer curve in Figure 3-9, its elasticity is infinite. With the slightest improvement in A's terms of trade, its offer of *X* for *Y* would increase without limit. (A reduction in the price of *Y* relative to *X* would be an improvement in Country A's terms of trade. This is shown geometrically by a steeper vector from the origin in Figure 3-9. Between points *S* and *T*, the offer curve is elastic (less than infinite but greater than unity); Country A will offer more *X* and *Y* as its terms of trade improve. When the offer curve is vertical, as at point *T*, its elasticity is equal to one; Country A offers a constant amount of *X* for *Y* as its terms of trade improve. Finally, when the offer curve is bending backward, as from point *T* to *V*, it is inelastic ($e < 1$); Country A offers less *X* for *Y* as its terms of trade improve.

The Role of Money Prices

In the modern world traders actually place their orders and strike bargains on the basis of money prices, not the barter ratios that we have examined thus far. Traders buy a foreign good when its price is lower than it is at home. (For the sake of simplicity we are still ignoring transport costs, but traders must allow for them and for all other costs—tariffs, insurance, commissions, legal costs, and so on—in comparing domestic and foreign prices.) German wheat importers pay no attention to the barter ratio between steel and wheat, and they may be oblivious to

---

[6]As Edgeworth remarked, the offer curve is a general equilibrium concept and does not require the assumption that other prices and outputs remain unchanged. "Rather a movement along an [offer curve] . . . should be considered as attended with rearrangements of internal trade; as the movement of the hand of a clock corresponds to considerable unseen movements of the machinery." F. Y. Edgeworth, "Theory of International Values," *Economic Journal,* September 1894, pp. 424–425.

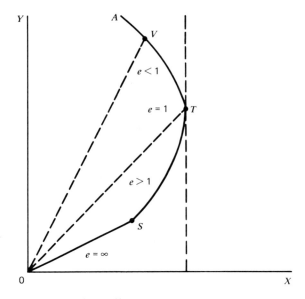

FIGURE 3-9   The elasticity of an offer curve.

opportunity cost as we have used it earlier. Nevertheless, the basic principles on which trade is based, principles laid bare in our simple barter examples, will still apply when we bring in money prices.

A barter exchange ratio, such as the one we have used in our example of trade between France and Germany, implies a ratio of money prices. For example, if one apple exchanges for two oranges, the price of an apple is twice the price of an orange. (If an apple costs $0.10 and an orange costs $0.05, then one apple is equal in value to two oranges.) Therefore, if barter exchange ratios differ in two countries, relative money prices will also differ.

We can use the French-German constant-cost example to illustrate this point. Before trade, the domestic (barter) exchange ratios were:

France: 1 ton of steel for 3 tons of wheat
Germany: 1 ton of steel for 1 ton of wheat

The money price in France of 1 ton of steel is therefore equal to the money price of 3 tons of wheat. That is, 1 ton of steel costs 3 times as much as 1 ton of wheat. In Germany, the money price of 1 ton of steel is equal to the money price of 1 ton of wheat. We assume the following actual money prices in the two countries:

	France	**Germany**
Steel (per ton)	Fr 300	DM 400
Wheat (per ton)	Fr 100	DM 400
Ratio $\left(\dfrac{\text{price of steel}}{\text{price of wheat}}\right)$	3 : 1	1 : 1

Note that the ratio of prices is different in the two countries (3 : 1 in France, 1 : 1 in Germany). This is what we mean by relative prices being different. Such relative price differences mirror the differences in opportunity cost ratios in our barter example, and they tell us that an opportunity for gainful trade exists.

These are the money prices prevailing before trade begins. When trade opens up, how can traders compare prices? Will German buyers wish to buy French steel at Fr 300 per ton? Or will French buyers find German steel a bargain at DM 400 per ton? Since the currencies used are different, we must know the exchange rate between francs and marks before meaningful price comparisons can be made. The exchange rate is a price, a rate at which we can convert one currency into another. If the exchange rate is Fr 1 = DM 2, French buyers can compare German prices with their own: German steel will cost them Fr 200 per ton (Fr 200 = DM 400) compared to Fr 300 at home; German wheat will cost Fr 200 per ton compared to Fr 100 at home. French traders will therefore import steel and export wheat. At the same time, German traders will find French wheat cheaper (Fr 100 @ DM 2 = DM 200) than domestic wheat. Thus a two-way trade, profitable to both sides, will spring up: German steel will exchange for French wheat, although each trader is simply pursuing his or her own individual interest in buying at the cheapest possible price.

The next question is, Will the money value of French imports of steel be equal to that of German imports of wheat? If so, we will have balanced trade; if not, the imbalance in trade will cause the exchange rate to shift.[7] In our preceding barter example, we had France import 45 million tons of steel and export 90 million tons of wheat. The money value of its trade, at the prices we have used above, would therefore be:

Wheat exports, 90 million tons @ Fr 100 = Fr 9 billion

Steel imports, 45 million tons @ Fr 200 = Fr 9 billion

Thus we have a position of balanced trade in money value, just as we did in barter terms.

If French exports did not equal imports in money value, the exchange rate would change. For example, if German traders wanted to buy 100 million tons of French wheat when the exchange rate was Fr 1 = DM 2, they would try to buy Fr 10 billion in the foreign exchange market, but French traders would be offering only Fr 9 billion for German steel. The excess demand for francs would drive up their price—that is, 1 franc would exchange for somewhat more than 2 marks, for example, Fr 1 = DM 2.5. If domestic money prices were kept unchanged in the two countries, the higher exchange value of the franc would make French wheat more expensive to German buyers (1 ton of wheat now costs DM 250 instead of DM 200), and German steel would now be cheaper to French buyers (1 ton of steel now costs Fr 160 [400/2.5 = 160] instead of Fr 200). These price

---

[7]In our analysis thus far we have assumed that commodity trade is the only form of economic transaction occurring between nations. Later we will allow for trade in services and for gifts, capital movements, and other transactions.

changes will tend to reduce German purchases of French wheat and increase French purchases of German steel. When exports become equal to imports in money value, the exchange rate will stop moving and equilibrium will exist. With fixed money prices in the two countries, the exchange rate thus plays the same role as the barter exchange ratio in our previous examples.

How far can the exchange rate go? Are there any limits on its movement? The answer is that profitable two-way trade can take place only at an exchange rate that makes wheat cheaper in France than in Germany. If *both* commodities were cheaper in Germany, trade would flow in only one direction: from Germany to France. In our example the prices in the two countries are as follows:

	France	**Germany**	**Ratio** $\left(\dfrac{\textbf{Price in Germany}}{\textbf{Price in France}} \right)$
Steel (per ton)	Fr 300	DM 400	4 : 3
Wheat (per ton)	Fr 100	DM 400	4 : 1

A little reflection will reveal that at exchange rates lying between Fr 1 = DM 1⅓ and Fr 1 = DM 4, wheat is cheaper in France and steel cheaper in Germany. Two-way trade will take place. At exchange rates outside these limits, both commodities are cheaper in one country. At Fr 1 = DM 5, for example, both commodities are cheaper in Germany: A French buyer can buy German steel for Fr 80 (80 × DM 5 = DM 400) and German wheat for Fr 80 compared with home prices of Fr 300 and Fr 100, respectively. French wheat would cost a German buyer DM 500 (100 × DM 5) compared to the home price of DM 400. Thus trade would go in only one direction. Consequently, when French traders offered to sell francs for marks in the foreign exchange market, no one would want to buy them. At the exchange rate Fr 1 = DM 5, there would be a demand for marks but no supply offered. French buyers would have to take less than 5 marks per franc in order to induce someone to sell marks. The money price of the franc would fall toward our limit of Fr 1 = 4 DM. In a similar way, we can show that at an exchange rate below our other limit of Fr 1 = DM 1⅓, for instance, Fr 1 = DM 1, both commodities are cheaper in France. Trade would again go in only one direction, this time from France to Germany. (The reader should compare the prices of French and German goods at the exchange rate Fr 1 = DM 1).

We conclude that the exchange rate must lie between the limits set by the money price ratios in the two countries: Fr 1 = DM 1⅓ and Fr 1 = DM 4. These exchange rate limits are analogous to the limits on the barter terms of trade noted earlier. (Remember that in our barter example the exchange ratio between steel and wheat could vary only within the limits set by the domestic exchange ratios before trade. In the constant-cost case, these limits were $1S : 1W$ and $1S : 3W$.) Thus the introduction of money does not change the fundamental basis for trade. Different relative money prices reflect relative differences in opportunity costs in the two countries. The existence of these differences constitutes the basis for comparative advantage and gainful trade.

On the other hand, if relative prices are the same in our two countries before trade, no basis for gainful trade exists. At no exchange rate can mutually profitable two-way trade take place. For example, suppose prices in France and Germany before trade were as follows:

	France	Germany
Steel (per ton)	Fr 200	DM 400
Wheat (per ton)	Fr 100	DM 200
Ratio $\left(\dfrac{\text{price of steel}}{\text{price of wheat}}\right)$	2 : 1	2 : 1

Relative prices are equal: 2 : 1 in both countries. At any exchange rate above Fr 1 = DM 2 (for instance, Fr 1 = DM 2.1), both commodities are cheaper in Germany and trade would move goods only to France. At any exchange rate below Fr 1 = DM 2 (for example, Fr 1 = DM 1.9), both commodities are cheaper in France and trade would move only from France to Germany. The foreign exchange market would be in equilibrium at Fr 1 = DM 2, and at this exchange rate prices are the same at home and abroad. Hence no basis for trade would exist.

INTERNATIONAL TRADE: INCREASING-COST CASE

So far, we have assumed that opportunity costs in each country remain unchanged as resources shift from one industry to another. We can now drop this assumption of constant costs and adopt the more realistic assumption of increasing costs. That is, we will now assume that as resources are shifted from, say, wheat production to cloth production, the opportunity cost of each additional unit of cloth increases. Such increasing costs could arise because factors of production vary in quality and in suitability for producing different commodities. Business firms, in their efforts to maximize profit, will be led through competition to use resources where they are best suited. Thus, when cloth production is increased, the resources (land, labor, and capital) drawn away from the wheat industry will be somewhat less well suited to cloth production than those already in the cloth industry. Hence, for a given increase in cloth output the cost in foregone wheat will be larger—that is, the marginal opportunity cost of cloth rises as its output increases. Other reasons could also be given, but it seems intuitively plausible to expect increasing costs to exist as a country moves toward greater specialization in a particular product.

Increasing costs give rise to a production-possibility curve that is bowed out (convex from above) as in Figure 3-10. At any point on the production-possibility curve, *WC,* the slope of the curve represents the opportunity cost ratio (real exchange ratio) at that point. As the production point moves along the curve from *W* toward *C,* the slope of the curve becomes steeper, which means that cloth costs more in terms of foregone wheat. In isolation, the country will seek to reach the highest possible indifference curve, which means that it will produce at point *P* in Figure 3-10. At *P,* the line *RR* is tangent to both the production-possibility curve, *WC,* and the indifference curve u_1. The slope of the tangent *RR* represents the real exchange ratio in isolation, and it is also equal to the marginal rate of substitution

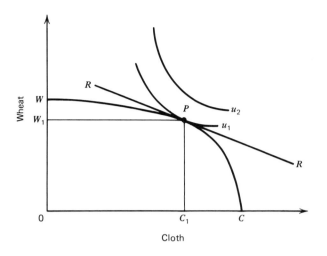

FIGURE 3-10 Increasing costs: Equilibrium in a closed economy.

in consumption.[8] At P, the country produces and consumes OC_1 of cloth and OW_1 of wheat.

Fortunately, most of the analysis just developed also applies to the case of increasing costs. The major difference is that we must allow for the changing internal exchange ratios in each country as trade begins to cause resources to shift toward the comparative advantage industry.

Let us consider a two-country, two-commodity example as depicted in Figure 3-11.

The Pre-Trade Equilibrium

In Country A, the pre-trade equilibrium is at point P in Figure 3-11a, with production and consumption of cloth and wheat represented by the coordinates of point P. A's domestic exchange ratio is represented by the slope of RR, and its level of welfare by u_1.

In Country B, the pre-trade of equilibrium is at point P^* in Figure 3-11b, with production and consumption of cloth and wheat represented by the coordinates of

[8]At P the following conditions prevail:

$$\frac{P_w}{P_c} = \frac{MC_W}{MC_C} = \text{Marginal rate of transformation} = \text{Slope of RR} = \text{Marginal rate of substitution} = \frac{MU_W}{MU_C}$$

where:

MC = marginal cost

MU = marginal utility

Both consumers and producers are in equilibrium at the real exchange ratio represented by the slope of *RR*.

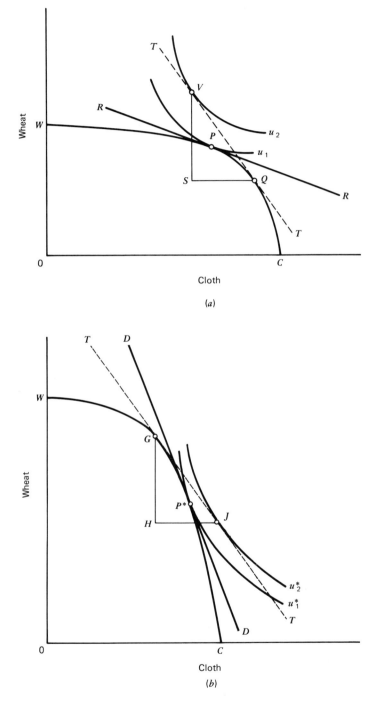

FIGURE 3-11 Equilibrium trade in a two-country case (increasing costs). (a) Country A. (b) Country B.

that point. B's domestic exchange ratio is represented by the slope of *DD,* and its level of welfare by u_1^*.

Because the slopes of the price lines are different in Countries A and B, it is clear that a basis for mutually beneficial trade exists. The proximate cause of trade is that relative prices differ in the two countries in isolation. In this case, cloth is relatively cheaper in A than in B, and wheat is relatively cheaper in B than in A. Hence A has a comparative advantage in cloth, and B in wheat.

The Post-Trade Equilibrium

When trade is opened up, producers in A will find it profitable to shift resources from wheat to cloth, moving along the production-possibility curve in Figure 3-11*a* from *P* toward *Q,* and exporting cloth to B for a higher price than they were getting at home, in isolation. How far this shift will go depends on the final terms-of-trade ratio. Similarly, producers in B find it profitable to shift resources from cloth to wheat, moving from P^* toward G in Figure 3-11*b,* and exporting wheat to A.

Trade will be in equilibrium at a terms-of-trade ratio at which the reciprocal demands are equal—that is, where A's exports of cloth precisely equal B's imports of cloth, and conversely for wheat. The equilibrium terms-of-trade ratio can be found, as shown earlier, by deriving the offer curves for A and B and determining the price ratio at their intersection. In Figure 3-11, the equilibrium terms-of-trade ratio is shown as the slope of the line *TT,* common to both countries. At this exchange ratio, the trade triangles *SVQ* and *HGJ* are identical. Thus A's cloth exports, *SQ,* exactly equal B's cloth imports, *HJ;* and A's wheat imports, *SV,* exactly equal B's wheat exports, *HG.* These equalities indicate that the two countries' offer curves intersect at the terms of trade, *TT.*

Country A produces at *Q* and consumes at *V;* Country B produces at *G* and consumes at *J.* Note that both countries are able to reach higher indifference curves than in isolation.

Given the opportunity to trade, each country tends to specialize in the commodity in which it has a comparative advantage, but this tendency is checked by the presence of increasing costs. Country A does not fully specialize in cloth; instead, it continues to produce much of the wheat its population consumes. Similarly, B retains part of its cloth industry—the more efficient part, in fact.

The Effects of Trade

We pause to review and summarize the effects of trade. First, trade causes a reallocation of resources. Output expands in industries in which a country has a comparative advantage, pulling resources away from industries in which it has a comparative disadvantage. Graphically, we see this effect as a movement along the production-possibility curve—for example, the movement from *P* to *Q* in Country A in Figure 3-11*a*. Under conditions of increasing costs, as resources move into the comparative advantage industry, marginal opportunity cost increases in that industry and falls in the industry whose output is contracting. The shift in resources will stop when the domestic cost ratio becomes equal to the world exchange ratio, as at Q in Figure 3-11a. Thus complete specialization normally will not occur. In the constant-cost case, however, where marginal costs do not change as resources move from one industry to another, complete specialization is likely.

This discussion of resource shifts throws into sharp relief the long-run nature of the theory we are discussing. Clearly, it will take much time for workers to be retrained and relocated and for capital to be converted into a form suitable for the new industry. The shift we show so easily as a movement from P to Q on a production-possibility curve may in fact involve a long and difficult transition period, with heavy human and social costs. These matters will be discussed more fully in later chapters; here we wish only to remind the reader to think about the real-world processes involved in the adjustment processes we are describing.

A second effect of trade is to equalize relative prices in the trading countries. (We are still ignoring transport costs.) Differences in relative pre-trade prices provide a basis for trade; they give traders an incentive to export one commodity and import the other. When trade occurs, it causes relative costs and prices to converge in both countries. In each country, the commodity that was relatively cheaper before trade tends to rise in price. Trade continues until real exchange ratios become equal in the two countries, as at the terms-of-trade ratio, TT, in Figure 3-11.

A third effect of trade is to improve economic welfare in both countries. Through trade, each country is able to obtain combinations of commodities that lie beyond its capacity to produce for itself. In the present analysis, the gain from trade is shown by the movement to a higher indifference curve.

The Division of the Gains from Trade

The division of the gains from this exchange between countries A and B depends on the ratio at which the two goods are exchanged, that is, on each country's terms of trade. The barter ratio is represented as the slope of the equilibrium trade line in the previous graphs. If that line (TT) in Figure 3-11 becomes steeper, cloth becomes more expensive relative to wheat and the gains for Country A increase while those for Country B decline. That figure shows that a steeper trading line allows Country A to consume both more cloth and more wheat, while the consumption opportunities for Country B become worse. Country B is better off if this trading line becomes flatter, meaning that less wheat is exchanged for more cloth. Each country would like its terms of trade (the price of exports over the price of imports) to be as high as possible, which is often a point of controversy in international trade. Underdeveloped countries (whose trade problems will be discussed in more detail later in this book) often feel that world prices for their exports are unfairly low and that they consequently get only small gains from international trade.

The determination of the barter ratio between the two goods was discussed in the earlier derivation of offer curves, but perhaps it can be seen more easily with simple supply and demand curves. The two graphs that follow in Figure 3-12 represent the markets for cloth in countries A and B where prices are denominated in terms of units of wheat; this means that we are still in a world of barter.

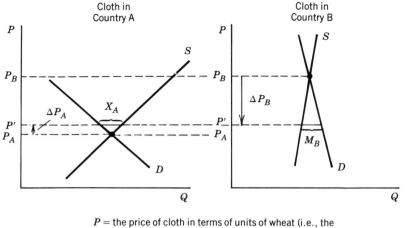

P = the price of cloth in terms of units of wheat (i.e., the number of bushels of wheat per yard of cloth)

FIGURE 3-12 Equilibrium price determination.

Equilibrium exists at a price (P') at which the volume of cloth which Country A wishes to export matches the volume that B wants to import. This graph shows that B gets most of the gains from trade, because its price of cloth falls sharply, whereas the price in A rises only slightly. B's import price falls much more than A's export price rises. Country B is able to purchase a great deal of imported cloth for a given amount of exported wheat, whereas Country A gains less because its exported cloth does not purchase a great deal of wheat. Country A must receive some gain from trade, however, or there would be no incentive for that country to export cloth in exchange for wheat. A's price of cloth rises slightly in terms of wheat, meaning that its price of wheat falls. Thus Country A does consume a combination of wheat and cloth which is superior to the combination it had without trade.

These graphs also reveal that Country B's enjoyment of particularly large gains from trade resulted from its relatively inelastic supply and demand functions. Country A gained less from trade because its supply and demand functions were more elastic. The general conclusion is that in trade between two countries, most of the gains go to the country with the less elastic supply and demand functions. The common sense intuition of this conclusion is that the existence of inelastic functions means that large price changes are needed to produce significant quantity changes. Country B would not export much wheat or import much cloth unless prices changed sharply, whereas Country A was willing to import a large volume of wheat (and export a large amount of cloth) in response to only modest price changes. As a result, large price changes and the larger gains from trade occur in Country B.

Comparative Advantage with Many Goods

In order to make the argument clear, thus far we have presented comparative advantage for only two countries and two goods, with the assumption of no transport costs. The real world, of course, includes thousands of goods, over one hundred countries, and significant transport costs. The next question concerns how a country's trade pattern is established in this more realistic situation.

A single country facing a multicountry rest of the world with many goods and with transport costs can be viewed as rank-ordering those products from its greatest comparative advantage to its greatest comparative disadvantage. It will export a number of goods at the top of the list and import a number of goods at the bottom of the list, with most small countries exporting large amounts of a few goods and importing smaller amounts of many goods. A country will tend to trade primarily with those countries that normally import its strongest comparative advantage goods and/or export its strongest comparative disadvantage goods. Trade volumes will be larger with countries that represent particularly large markets for exports or sources of imports, that is, countries with large populations and levels of GNP per capita.

Somewhere in the middle of a country's comparative advantage rank-ordering will be a number of goods that it will neither export nor import (nontradables) because its comparative advantage or disadvantage in these products is too slight to overcome transport costs. Such products will be produced domestically in sufficient volume for local consumption. The heavier or bulkier products are, the more likely they are to be nontradables; that is, very few countries export or import gravel and sand. Transport costs will also mean that a country will tend to trade more with its neighbors and somewhat less with more distant countries. In rare circumstances, countries which share a long border may trade commodities precisely because they are heavy or bulky. This occurs when transport costs between the two countries are lower than such costs within each country. This situation is known as border trade and is discussed in Chapter 5.

Additional Benefits from Trade

The discussion thus far has assumed perfect competition and has concluded that the only benefits from trade grow out of differences in comparative costs. Comparative advantage is the most important but not the only argument for, and source of benefit from, trade.

International trade can be a powerful antitrust policy, thus enabling countries to solve the dilemma of wanting both to promote active competition and to have companies that are large enough to gain all the available economies of scale.[9] Even in an economy the size of that of the United States, these two goals are often not reached internally, because economies of scale are sufficient in many heavy manufacturing industries to leave room for only a few companies if each is of minimum optimum size. Large economies of scale in research and development are often a source of this problem. The result is internal markets in the United States that would be dominated by a few oligopolistic firms if there were no competition from imports.

[9] See Richard E. Caves, "International Trade, International Investment, and Imperfect Markets," *Princeton Special Papers in International Economics*, No. 10, November 1974, for a discussion of the impact of trade and direct investment on the level of competition within an economy.

If the relevant market is no longer a single country, but rather the world, this problem is greatly eased. Although only a few companies manufacture automobiles or television sets in the United States, many firms sell those items in the U.S. market. If import competition does not make the automobile market perfectly competitive, the market does at least become much more competitive. Pressures to improve efficiency and to price aggressively are intense, and profit rates are not particularly high. Greater efficiency and lower profits are the expected results of competition. In contrast, before imported cars became common in the United States, profit rates were far higher, and the U.S. automobile industry was known neither for making technical advances nor for offering low prices.

Interestingly, the 30-year period (1960–1990) during which imports rose from about 4 percent of U.S. GNP to 11 percent was also the period during which profit rates in U.S. manufacturing declined significantly.[10] There may be other reasons for this decline, but increased import competition in the U.S. market is a likely contributor. Economists sometimes suggest that the antitrust division of the Department of Justice should not pursue U.S. industries that face heavy import competition, but should instead stress cases in the services sector or other areas in which imports do not create serious competition for U.S. firms.

Small countries such as those in Central America or parts of West Africa, have no possibility of developing competitive internal markets in manufactured goods, but international trade with neighbors at least gives them the possibility of establishing factories large enough to be reasonably efficient. If a country such as Honduras were to try to industrialize solely on the basis of its internal market, the result would be a set of very inefficient cottage industries. If regional trade were sufficiently free to make Central America a single market, firms in each country could be big enough to obtain most economies of scale.

International trade can also be a mechanism for transmitting knowledge about technology, alternative consumption possibilities, and even foreign societies from one country to another. Imported products can bring with them ideas about alternative life-styles and ways of running an economy. This knowledge-transmitting aspect of trade has sometimes been used as an argument against international commerce. It is contended that picturesque and beautiful cultures are debased by imported clothes, transistor radios, motor scooters, and the like, and that these imports should not be allowed in order to protect the local people from undesirable foreign ideas and influences. Economists usually respond by making the case for consumer sovereignty: that people are rational and can decide for themselves what to consume and what to avoid without the dictates of well-meaning academics or government officials. This process of choice may involve an element of trial and error in which people try new products and later discard those that are inadequate. Ultimately, however, people will be better off if their range of consumption options is widened through the availability of imported products.

Finally, the somewhat dubious argument is made that trade can be a force for peace. If two countries become mutually dependent on each other for important

---

[10]After-tax profits in U.S. manufacturing fell from 4.9 percent of sales in the 1960s to 3.6 percent of sales in the 1980s after allowance for a change in the manner of calculating these profit rates. See the 1991 *Economic Report of the President,* p. 391.

or even vital products, the argument states, it becomes more difficult for them to separate their economies sufficiently to go to war against each other. In addition, national prejudices that sometimes encourage conflict are often the result of too little contact with members of the other population. Because extensive trade relations require frequent personal contacts, it is hoped that ancient dislikes will be dispelled.

This is one reason why the United States supported the formation of the European Common Market in the mid-1950s. Having been involved in wars between the Germans and the French twice in less than 30 years, the United States hoped that tying these countries closely together in a common market would greatly reduce the likelihood of further conflict between them. No one can prove that this common market, which has evolved into the European Community, had this effect, but the fact remains that no armed conflict has occurred in Western Europe for more than 45 years.

If this argument were fully persuasive, there would never be a civil war; obviously then, the argument has its limitations. To whatever extent trade dependence is a force for peace, the dependence must be mutual rather than unidirectional. A situation in which one country is dependent on another for a vital product, but there is no reciprocal dependence, is not a force for peace. Instead, it becomes a powerful weapon in the hands of the exporter of the vital product. In the early 1970s a number of European countries were heavily dependent on the Middle East for oil, but there was no reverse dependence. That is, the Middle Eastern countries that exported oil were not dependent on Europe for anything of great short-term importance. As a result, the 1973 oil embargo, which curtailed these oil exports, was quite damaging to Europe.

If trade produces mutual dependence and extensive personal contacts between citizens of different countries, it can be a modest force for reducing international conflicts. Unfortunately, however, too many wars have been fought in eras of extensive trade for this argument to be a very powerful one.

Comparative advantage remains the dominant source of benefit from trade, but these additional arguments are worth remembering. The most important of these arguments is that trade can be a powerful tool in weakening monopolistic or oligopolistic power in domestic markets.

QUESTIONS FOR STUDY AND REVIEW

1. In a two-country, two-commodity case, what determines the exact terms of trade that will prevail in free trade? Explain. Be specific.

2. How do increasing-cost conditions affect the extent of international specialization and exchange? Explain.

3. "It is possible that Burma might not gain from trade with Japan because Japan has a comparative advantage in all goods." Do you agree? Explain.

4. Given two countries, A and B, and two products, cloth and wheat, state whether each of the following statements is true or false, and show why.

a. If Country A has an absolute advantage in cloth, it must have a comparative advantage in cloth.

b. If Country A has a comparative advantage in wheat, it must have an absolute advantage in wheat.

5. Suppose money prices of three goods are as follows in Japan and Burma:

Country	Cloth (yd)	Meat (lb)	Rice (bu)
Japan	Yen 100	Yen 200	Yen 300
Burma	Rupees 10	Rupees 40	Rupees 50

a. In what products, if any, can you be sure that Japan and Burma have a comparative advantage? Explain how you know.

b. Within what limits must the yen-rupee exchange rate settle in equilibrium? Why?

6. In isolation, Country A produces 12 million tons of rice and 8 million tons of beans. One ton of rice exchanges for 2 tons of beans, and there are constant costs.

a. Construct Country A's production-possibility curve, and label your diagram.

b. Suppose Country A now has the opportunity to trade with Country B. It can trade at the exchange ratio (terms of trade) $1R : 1B$, and in equilibrium Country A consumes 10 million tons of beans.

(1) What will Country A produce, with trade?

(2) What will Country A consume, with trade? Show its consumption point and its trade triangle.

(3) What is the gain from trade (in real terms) to Country A?

7. Show that if relative prices were the same in all countries in isolation, there would be no basis for trade.

8. "Trade theory assumes that resources are fully employed both before and after trade and that technology remains unchanged. But if the same amounts of resources are actually used, both before and after trade, world production must also be the same. There can be no gain to the world as a whole." Critically evaluate this statement.

9. Suppose Togo can produce 120 million bushels of wheat if it uses all its productive resources in the wheat industry, or 80 million yards of cloth if it uses all resources in the cloth industry. (Use a diagram to illustrate your answers to the following questions. Label the diagram and explain in words.)

a. Assuming constant opportunity costs, draw Togo's production-possibility curve.

b. With no trade, suppose Togo's consumers choose to consume 70 million bushels of wheat. How much cloth will Togo then be able to produce?

c. What is the real exchange ratio (terms of trade) in Togo?

    d.   Now suppose that Togo has the opportunity to engage in foreign trade and that the world terms-of-trade ratio is $1W : 1C$. What will happen to the allocation of resources in Togo? Explain why.

    e.   If Togo consumes 75 million bushels of wheat, after trade begins, how much cloth will it consume?

    f.   What is the gain from trade to Togo?

10.   Should the antitrust division of the U.S. Department of Justice evaluate the competitiveness of a U.S. market in order to approve or disapprove of mergers, in terms of the number of firms producing a product within this country? What alternative might it use?

SELECTED REFERENCES

Allen, William R., ed. *International Trade Theory: Hume to Ohlin.* New York: Random House, 1965.

Baldwin, Robert E., and J. D. Richardson, eds. *International Trade and Finance,* 2nd ed. Boston: Little, Brown, 1981.

Bhagwati, Jagdish, ed. *International Trade.* Baltimore: Penguin, 1969.

Caves, Richard, "International Trade, International Investment, and Imperfect Markets." *Princeton Special Papers in International Economics,* No. 10, 1974.

Caves, Richard, and Harry G. Johnson, eds. *Readings in International Economics.* Homewood, Ill.: Richard D. Irwin, 1967.

Ellis, Howard, and Lloyd Metzler, eds. *Readings in the Theory of International Trade.* Philadelphia: Blakiston, 1949.

Haberler, G. *The Theory of International Trade.* New York: Macmillan, 1936. Especially Chapters 10–12.

Jones, Ronald, and Peter B. Kenen, eds. *Handbook of International Economics,* Vol. 1. Amsterdam: North Holland, 1984.

Leamer, Edward E. *Sources of Comparative Advantage.* Cambridge, Mass.: MIT Press, 1984.

Meade, James E. *Trade and Welfare.* London: Oxford University Press, 1955.

A BASIS FOR TRADE: THE FACTOR PROPORTIONS HYPOTHESIS

In the preceding two chapters we have seen that if relative prices differ in two isolated countries, the introduction of trade between them will be mutually beneficial. Different relative prices of commodities reflect the fact that relative opportunity costs differ in the two countries. Thus each country has a comparative advantage in one or more commodities. Given the opportunity to trade, each country will specialize in those commodities in which it has a comparative advantage, exporting these in exchange for other commodities in which it has a comparative disadvantage.

Our next step is to ask why relative prices and costs differ in the first place. Classical theory did not really ask this question; Ricardo simply took it for granted that labor cost ratios (and hence prices) differed in the two countries before trade.

In our exposition of modern theory, we also took it for granted that opportunity cost ratios (and hence prices) differed in the two countries before trade, and we drew production-possibility curves with different shapes for the two countries.

THE FACTOR PROPORTIONS HYPOTHESIS: A GENERAL VIEW[1]

The central purpose of the factor proportions hypothesis is to provide one explanation as to why relative prices differ, before trade. It is not, however, the only view on this issue. Alternative theories as to why differences in relative prices occur will be discussed in Chapter 5.

The factor proportions or Heckscher-Ohlin theorem begins by explaining differences in the shapes of the production-possibility curves of different countries. The basic idea is very simple. It stems from the common observation that countries differ in the amounts of the various factors of production (land, labor, and capital) they possess. Moreover, they possess these productive factors in different proportions or ratios. When a particular factor is abundant in a country (such as land in Australia), the market price for that factor's services will tend to be low, and commodities that require large amounts of that factor for their production will tend to be cheap. If another productive factor is scarce (such as labor in Australia), the market price for its services will tend to be high, and commodities that require large amounts of the scarce factor for their production will tend to be expensive. Now, when we say that commodities are cheap or expensive, we mean in comparison to the prices in some other country whose resource endowment is different from that of the first country. That is, we are comparing relative prices, or price ratios, in the two countries.

Australia has such an abundance of land relative to its population that rents would be very low if the country had no trade with the rest of the world, because only the domestic demand for land-using commodities would then need to be satisfied, and that would entail use of only a small part of Australia's vast land area.

Thus Australia's abundance of land makes rents very low, and land-using commodities such as wool and meat are cheaper than they are in a small, densely populated country such as Belgium. On the other hand, a labor-intensive commodity such as cloth is relatively more costly in Australia than in Belgium. Each country has a comparative advantage in the commodity whose production requires relatively much of its abundant factor of production. Australia will export wool and meat; Belgium will export textiles and other commodities requiring a relatively large amount of labor. Through trade, the abundant Australian land is, in effect, made available to Belgians, and abundant Belgian labor is used to produce labor-intensive goods for Australians.

---

[1] Often referred to as the Heckscher-Ohlin theory, after its principal originators: Eli Heckscher, "The Effect of Foreign Trade on the Distribution of Income," in H. Ellis and L. Metzler, eds., *Readings in the Theory of International Trade* (Philadelphia: Blakiston, 1949); and Bertil Ohlin, *Interregional and International Trade* (Cambridge, Mass.: Harvard University Press, 1933).

For many commodities, the role of factor supply in determining the pattern of trade is obvious. Bolivia and Malaya export tin because they possess relatively abundant reserves of tin-bearing ore; Brazil and Colombia export coffee because they have an abundant supply of the soil and climatic conditions required for its production; Canada, Argentina, and the United States export wheat because they possess an abundance of temperate-zone land that is well suited for wheat production. Much trade in primary commodities (food, metals, raw materials) can readily be accounted for in this way—as a simple and obvious result of a given country's possession of specific productive resources and other countries' lack of or extreme scarcity of these resources.

The Heckscher-Ohlin theory says more than that, however. It asserts that the relative factor endowments of the trading nations can account for trade in all kinds of goods, including different types of manufactured goods. In general, it holds that the commodity composition or structure of the trade of nations can largely be explained on the basis of the quantities of the various productive factors they possess, relative to other nations. The theory predicts that a nation's export list will include commodities whose production requires relatively much of productive factors that it has in relative abundance, whereas its import list will include commodities whose production requires much of productive factors that are relatively scarce in that country. Thus it asserts that comparative advantage positions are basically determined on the supply side, that is, by the relative quantities of the various productive factors that each country possesses.

An important implication of the Heckscher-Ohlin theory is that trade tends to increase the price of the abundant factor of production in each country and to decrease the price of the scarce factor. The reason is simply that foreign demand for the export commodity causes its output to rise and thus increases demand for the abundant factor, which is heavily used in that commodity. Thus trade causes factor prices in the two countries to become more equal.

Before proceeding with a more detailed exposition of the Heckscher-Ohlin theory, we should note that demand conditions can conceivably overwhelm the influence of factor supply and cause a country to import a commodity even though it has an abundant supply of the factors required to produce that commodity. For example, if consumers in Country A are extremely fond of rhubarb, they may buy so much of it that the price stays high despite Country A's abundant supply of land (and other factors) suitable for growing it. Country A may then be a net importer of rhubarb, despite its resource endowment. Ohlin recognized the possibility that demand conditions could cause trade flows to go the wrong way, but he thought such cases would be rare and infrequent. In our subsequent discussion we will assume that demand conditions (tastes and preferences) are approximately the same in all countries. That is, we will assume that community indifference curves have about the same shape and position in all countries. This assumption is a common one in discussions of international trade theory, but the reader should note that it neutralizes demand conditions and leaves only supply conditions to determine the pattern of trade and to provide an explanation for the composition of a nation's exports and imports.

Note also that a nation's comparative advantage position is not permanently fixed. Because it depends on relative factor endowment, it changes as factor supplies change. A nation's labor supply depends on its population, and the supply of particular types of labor, such as technical and professional workers, depends on educational policy and other socioeconomic circumstances and, thus, can change through time. Similarly, capital can be accumulated through saving or borrowing; land can be altered through irrigation and reclamation. Consequently, a nation's comparative advantage position can change over time. The fact that Nigeria's principal exports in the 1960s were cocoa and peanuts does not mean that it will always specialize in these two products. We will return to this matter in a later chapter, for it is extremely important to many poor and underdeveloped countries that are trying to change their role in world trade.

► THE HECKSCHER-OHLIN THEORY: TWO COUNTRIES, TWO FACTORS, TWO COMMODITIES[2]

The factor proportions theory of trade requires a number of assumptions, some of which were not explicitly stated in our summary of the central idea. To provide a fuller explanation of the nature of this theory, we will analyze in some detail a highly simplified example involving only two countries (A and B), two commodities (cloth and wheat), and two factors (land and labor). This so-called $2 \times 2 \times 2$ case may seem too simple and abstract to be significant, but fortunately economists have shown that most of the conclusions drawn from the $2 \times 2 \times 2$ case continue to hold when the number of countries, commodities, and factors is increased.

We will make the following assumptions:

1. Perfect competition exists in commodity and factor markets in both countries. This implies, among other things, that price equals marginal cost in both industries and that full employment exists.

2. Factors of production do not move from one country to another. That is, we assume that factors are immobile internationally but perfectly mobile among industries within each country.

3. Demand conditions are everywhere the same. That is, consumer tastes and preferences are the same in the two countries, so that community indifference curves are identical.

4. Transport costs are zero, and no tariffs or other obstacles to trade exist in either country.

5. The state of technology is given and is everywhere the same. Therefore our two countries have identical production functions.

6. Constant returns to scale exist in both industries, cloth and wheat.

7. Commodities can be unambiguously ranked in terms of factor intensity. Specifically, we assume that wheat requires for its production a higher proportion of

---

[2] The foregoing explanation may suffice for some readers; others will want more proof. An elaborate analytical structure has been developed to demonstrate and prove the Heckscher-Ohlin theory. We will describe part of that structure. Readers not interested in the details of this analysis may skip to the next section without loss of continuity.

land to labor than does cloth, for any given ratio of factor prices. Thus wheat is (relatively) land intensive and cloth is labor intensive.

Assumptions 5 to 7 require some explanation. Their meaning can best be explained by introducing the production isoquant and the production function.

The Production Function

A production function defines the relationship between inputs of productive factors and the resulting output of a commodity. A commodity such as wheat can be produced with many different combinations, or proportions, of land and labor. For example, a given quantity of wheat, say, 5000 bushels, might be produced with 100 acres of land and 1 man-year of labor, or with 10 acres of land and 20 man-years of labor, or with many other combinations of land and labor.

This relationship can be illustrated by a production isoquant, such as the curve W_1 in Figure 4-1. Points on W_1, such as E and F, represent a constant, given output of wheat (5000 bushels). The coordinates of each such point (OT_1 and OL_1 for point E) show the inputs of land and labor required to produce that amount of wheat. As we move down and to the right on W_1, for example, from E to F, the proportion of land to labor decreases. The slope of the vector $OF(OT_2/OL_2)$ is smaller than the slope of $OE(OT_1/OL_1)$.

To show the input requirements for a larger output of wheat, we can draw another isoquant above and to the right of W_1. Thus W_2 in Figure 4-1 shows the alternative

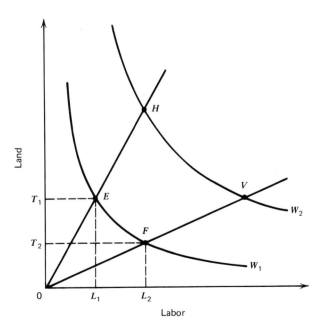

FIGURE 4-1 Isoquants for wheat production (W_1 = 5000 bu., W_2 = 10,000 bu.).

combinations of land and labor required to produce 10,000 bushels of wheat. Other isoquants can be drawn to represent other quantities of wheat production.

The whole set of isoquants that can be drawn in Figure 4-1 comprises the production function for wheat. It shows all alternative combinations of inputs required to produce all possible quantities of wheat.

Assumption 5, which states that the two countries have identical production functions, means that this entire set of isoquants is the same for countries A and B. Note carefully, however, that it does not say that countries A and B will actually use the same combination of land and labor to produce wheat. They are in fact likely to choose different points on the production function. We know very well, for example, that in India wheat is produced on tiny plots of land with highly labor-intensive methods, whereas in the United States a 1000-acre farm may be cultivated by a single farmer. These facts are consistent with our assumption that production functions are everywhere the same.

The meaning of assumption 6 (constant returns to scale) can also be explained with the aid of Figure 4-1. Suppose a given combination, or proportion, of factors is being used, as at point E. These inputs yield the output indicated by the isoquant W_1, namely, 5000 bushels. Constant returns to scale means that if the inputs of land and labor are both increased by a given proportion, then the output will also increase by that same proportion. For example, if the inputs at point E are doubled, the output of wheat will also double, as at point H, which lies on the isoquant W_2 representing an output of 10,000 bushels. This is a very strong assumption. It rules out both economies and diseconomies of scale.

Thus far we have concentrated on the production function for wheat. The production function for cloth is constructed in a similar way, but the position and shape of the isoquants will be different from those for wheat, reflecting our assumption that cloth is labor intensive relative to wheat.

Production isoquants can also help us to explain how a firm chooses the particular combinations of land and labor that it uses to produce its output. In making this decision the firm takes into account the prices it must pay for the services of land and labor (factor prices) and the technological data embodied in the production function. Its objective is to maximize the output it can produce for a given level of expenditure.

Geometrically, we can show the factor-price and budget information in a budget line such as MN in Figure 4-2. The firm's budget is just sufficient to purchase OM of land inputs (services) or ON of labor inputs, or any combination of land and labor inputs indicated by points lying on MN. The slope of MN represents the factor-price ratio. Given the budget constraint and the factor-price ratio represented by MN, a wheat-producing firm will maximize its output by producing at point E, the point of tangency between MN and W_1. Hence the firm will choose the land-labor ratio indicated by the vector OE. If it uses any other input ratio, such as B, it will find itself on a lower isoquant, W_0, meaning that it obtains a smaller output for the same expenditure.

We are now ready to explain the significance of assumption 7. In perfect competition, wage rates are equalized in all industries, and so are rents. Thus firms in both our industries face the same factor-price ratio. Assumption 7 means that for

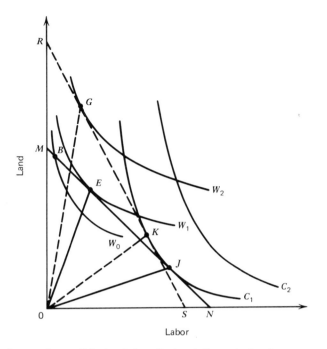

FIGURE 4-2 Comparison of factor intensity in cloth and wheat.

any particular factor-price ratio, the optimum ratio of land to labor will always be higher in wheat production than in cloth production.

In Figure 4-2 we have drawn isoquants W_1 and W_2 for wheat, and C_1 and C_2 for cloth to satisfy the condition in assumption 7. If the common factor-price ratio were given by the slope of MN, firms would choose factor proportions OE in wheat and OJ in cloth. If wages were higher, giving us a common factor-price ratio as indicated by the slope of RS, firms would choose factor proportions OG in wheat and OK in cloth. Note that in both cases the ratio of land to labor is higher in wheat than in cloth. This is what assumption 7 means—that within each country, for any given factor-price ratio, wheat will be land intensive relative to cloth. As wages rise, firms in both industries respond by economizing on labor, by using more land relative to labor.

Derivation of the Production-Possibility Curve

Given production functions for wheat and cloth, as just defined, once we know a country's resource endowment we can derive its production-possibility curve. To do so, we will make use of one more geometric device, the box diagram.

Let us first consider Country A, with its specific initial endowment of productive resources: land and labor. The amounts of these resources obviously place limits on the volume of output in Country A. Those limits are points on the production-possibility curve, and our present task is to show how the other points on that curve are obtained from the production functions and Country A's resource endowment.

In Figure 4-3, we again draw isoquants to represent the production functions for wheat and cloth. Note that wheat is land intensive relative to cloth. We wish to place these two industries in competition with each other for the given production resources available in Country A. We can do so by constructing a rectangular box diagram whose dimensions represent Country A's total endowment of land and labor, as in Figure 4-4a. From the origin in the lower left-hand corner, we draw the isoquant diagram for cloth, taken from Figure 4-3b. Then, by rotating the isoquant diagram for wheat, Figure 4-3a, in a counterclockwise direction, we move its origin to the upper right corner in Figure 4-4. From the new origin, O', the labor axis for wheat runs from right to left, and the land axis runs downward. Isoquants for the wheat industry emanate from the new origin, O'. Country A's total labor supply is measured by the horizontal dimension of the box, and its total land endowment by the vertical dimension.

Every point within the box represents a possible allocation of resources between wheat and cloth, but we are primarily interested in the "efficiency locus," the points at which the output of wheat is maximized, given the output of cloth. These efficient points turn out to be the points of tangency between wheat isoquants and cloth isoquants, such as points P, Q, and R in Figure 4-4. The reason for this result

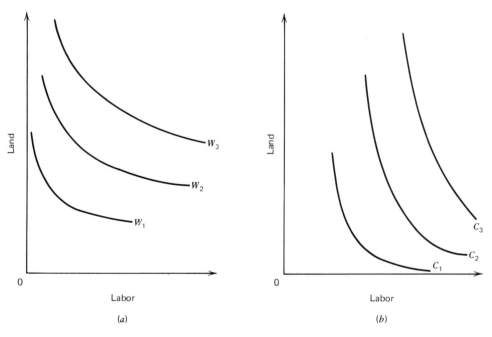

FIGURE 4-3   Production functions in wheat and cloth. (a) Wheat. (b) Cloth.

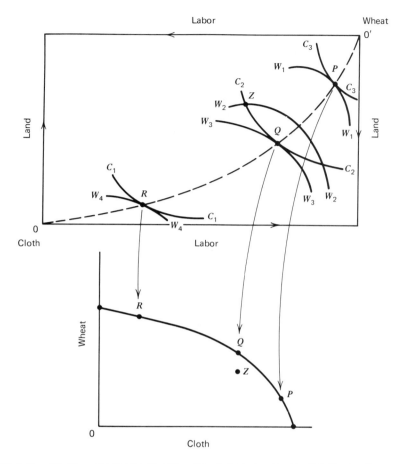

FIGURE 4-4 (a) Box diagrams for Country A (input space). (b) Production-possibility curve for Country A (output space).

can be seen as follows: Consider a point that is not on the efficiency locus, such as point Z in Figure 4-4a. Cloth output is indicated by isoquant C_2, and wheat output by isoquant W_2. However, we can hold cloth output constant, move along isoquant C_2 to point Q (i.e., produce the same amount of cloth with less land and slightly more labor), and thereby release resources that make it possible to produce more wheat. At point Q we have the same output of cloth, but we have increased the output of wheat by moving from isoquant W_2 to W_3. At point Q, however, we have maximized wheat production for the level of cloth output indicated by isoquant C_2. Point Q represents a combination of wheat and cloth outputs that lies on the production-possibility curve. P, R, and other points on the efficiency locus also correspond to points on the production-possibility curve.

Another way of seeing this point is to recall that firms in each industry are at a minimum cost optimum when the factor-price ratio equals the slope of the production isoquant. But at Z the slopes of the isoquants are different in wheat and cloth; this condition implies that wages and rents are not equal in the two industries. That situation indicates a disequilibrium situation in the market for productive factors because we know that in perfect competition factor prices are the same in both industries. Only when the isoquants for wheat and cloth are tangent to each other do we have the same factor prices in both industries. This equality is a condition of maximization of output.

To construct Country A's production-possibility curve, we must take note of the wheat and cloth outputs indicated by the production isoquants for each point on the efficiency locus. As we move along the efficiency locus from O to O', we record the output levels for wheat and cloth in the output space of Figure 4-4b. For example, point R in Figure 4-4a represents a small output of cloth but a large output of wheat for Country A; it appears as point R in Figure 4-4b. Point P represents a large output of cloth but a small output of wheat, whereas point Q is an intermediate position. (We also show point Z in Figure 4-4b; it lies within the production-possibility curve.)

We can now see how a country's resource endowment influences the shape and size of its production-possibility curve. If Country B has a relative abundance of labor compared to Country A, its box diagram will be elongated horizontally. The dimensions of the box diagram for each country reflect its resource endowment. Then, with identical production functions, the resources available in each country determine its production-possibility curve.

In Figure 4-5 we draw a box diagram for each country. Country A clearly has more land relative to labor than does Country B. In Ohlin's terms, Country A has a relative abundance of land, and Country B has a relative abundance of labor. These differences in resource endowment are reflected in the production-possibility curves for the two countries. Because wheat requires a higher proportion of land to labor than does cloth, Country A's relative abundance of land causes its production-possibility curve to be elongated, or biased, along the wheat axis. Country B's relative abundance of labor is similarly reflected in a greater relative capacity to produce cloth.

If these two countries do not engage in trade, but operate as closed economies, then their relative commodity prices will differ: Cloth will be cheaper in Country B than in Country A, relative to the price of wheat, as may be seen by the price lines (tangents to production-possibility curves) in Figure 4-5. This analysis now links up with that in Chapter 3, where we showed that, given different production-possibility curves and similar demand patterns, relative prices in the two countries will be different and each country will have a comparative advantage in its relatively cheaper commodity.

What the Heckscher-Ohlin theory has added is an explanation of the cause of the relative price differences, a basic reason for the existence of comparative advantage. In particular, we can now say that in each country price will be relatively low for the commodity that uses relatively much of that country's abundant factor of production. Hence the difference in relative factor endowments is the underlying basis of comparative advantage and the fundamental determinant of the pattern and composition of international trade.

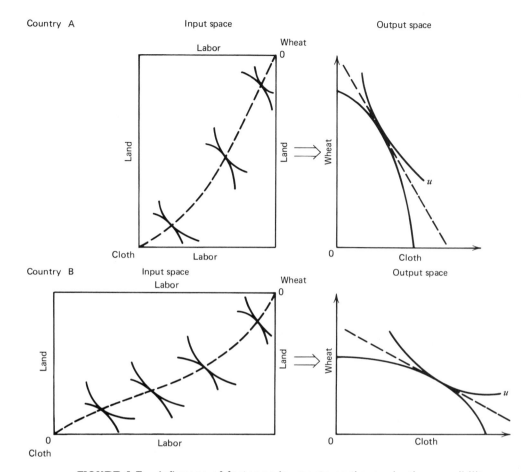

FIGURE 4-5   Influence of factor endowments on the production-possibility curves.

FURTHER IMPLICATIONS OF THE FACTOR PROPORTIONS THEORY

Equalization of Factor Prices

One important implication of the factor proportions theory is that the introduction of trade will tend to equalize factor prices in the trading countries. When trade begins, output of the comparative advantage good increases, thus increasing demand for the abundant factor of production and tending to raise its price. At the same time, output of the comparative disadvantage good decreases, which releases relatively much of the scarce factor of production and tends to reduce its price.

In the preceding example wages were originally relatively low in labor-abundant Country B. Therefore prior to trade we had:

$$\frac{W_A}{R_A} > \frac{W_B}{R_B}$$

where W stands for the wage rate and R is rent, the return to land. The introduction of trade causes the wage-rent ratio to rise in Country B and fall in Country A. Both these changes reduce the original inequality; that is, as W_A/R_A declines and W_B/R_B rises, the two ratios become more nearly equal.

Ohlin concluded that international trade will tend to equalize factor prices in the trading countries, but he recognized many practical obstacles that stand in the way of complete equalization. These obstacles include transport costs, imperfect markets, tariffs, and lack of knowledge.

Subsequent writers have proved that, as a matter of strict logic, factor prices will be completely equalized if all the assumptions we have made are satisfied.[3] Since they are unlikely to be satisfied in full, Ohlin's conclusion that a tendency toward equalization exists still seems a valid one.

Income Redistribution and the Welfare Economics of Trade

The income redistribution effect of international trade presents some serious problems for the earlier conclusion that free trade must increase economic welfare in both countries. Although total income (real GNP) in each country clearly rises with trade, some groups in society gain a great deal, whereas other groups lose. The relatively abundant factor of production wins, but the scarce factor loses. What happens to total welfare depends on how the gains of one group of people are evaluated relative to the losses of others.

Because total income rises, the winners must gain more income than the losers give up. If everyone can be assumed to have the same marginal utility for income (personal valuation of an extra dollar in income), then the earlier conclusion is maintained, because the winners must have received more additional utility than the losers gave up. It is unfortunate that there are losers, but because total utility rises with the increase in income, society is still better off. The problem is in making the assumption that everyone puts the same value on extra income.

There is no way to make interpersonal utility comparisons, that is, to compare one person's utility with the utility of another person for the same thing. As a result, we cannot be sure that total utility rises. If, for example, half the people in society gain $100 each, but each person in the other half loses $50, we cannot be certain that total utility rose just because average income rose by $25. What if each of those losing $50 happens to care much more about extra income than

---

[3]The proof of full factor-price equalization can be found in Wolfgang Stolper and Paul Samuelson, "Protection and Real Wages," *Review of Economic Studies* 9, 1941, pp. 58–73. See also Paul Samuelson, "International Trade and the Equalization of Factor Prices," *Economic Journal,* June 1948.

do the winners? What if they care three times as much about an extra dollar than do those gaining $100 each? Even though total income rises, utility or welfare falls. Because we cannot know how different groups evaluate income gains or losses, we can make no certain conclusion as to what happens to national welfare when free trade increases total income but redistributes enough income from the scarce to the abundant factor to leave owners of the scarce factor poorer than they were without trade.

One attempt to deal with this problem is known as the compensation principle; it argues that because the winners gain more income than the losers lose, the winners can fully compensate the losers and still retain net gains. Returning to the example of the preceding paragraph, we see that if each of those who gained $100 spent $50 to compensate the losers, they would still have a gain of $50 left and the previous losers would have returned to their original incomes. (If each winner spent $55 on compensation, everyone would gain something.) The problem is how to gather political support for, and then institutionalize, such compensation, particularly if those on the losing side of free trade are politically weak or do not trust the winners to continue the compensation payments after free trade is instituted. As a result, owners of the scarce factor (or factors) of production in any country tend to oppose free trade and to support protectionism.

This problem is particularly difficult for the United States, where the relatively scarce factor is unskilled labor. In this country the winners from free trade are owners of farm land, owners of human capital (highly educated people), and those with financial capital invested in export industries. The losers are a small number of owners of tropical land in Hawaii or Florida, and a large number of unskilled or semiskilled workers. Those who would gain from free trade are primarily people whose incomes are already above average, whereas the group being harmed consists overwhelmingly of those with below-average incomes. Free trade would increase total incomes in the United States but would make the distribution of income more unequal than it now is. It is not surprising that the AFL–CIO and others who represent the interests of U.S. labor are opposed to reducing barriers to more imports of labor-intensive products such as textiles, garments, and shoes. If compensation were offered through the tax system and if there were confidence that this compensation would be maintained after free trade was instituted, this opposition might decline, but with the lack of such confidence, protectionist sentiment in the U.S. labor movement will remain strong.

In a developing country such as Mexico, which has a set of relative factor endowments opposite that of the United States, the income distribution effects of free trade are reversed. Labor would gain, and owners of capital and land would lose. Most unions in labor-abundant countries will tend to support free trade but will hold the opposite views in labor-scarce countries.

Fixed Factors of Production in the Short Run

The conclusion that the abundant factor of production gains from free trade and that the relatively scarce factor loses is based on the assumption that the adjustment to free trade is complete, that is, that both factors of production have moved from the import-competing to the export industry and that full employment has been reestablished. In the short run, before this new equilibrium is reached, the results can be quite different. During the contraction of the import-competing industry, both capital and labor employed in that sector will experience declines in income, whereas both factors in the export sector are likely to be better off during its expansion.

If, for example, free trade means that the U.S. textile industry, which is labor intensive, contracts while the capital-intensive commercial aircraft sector expands, the income distribution effects will be quite different during the transition period than when adjustment is fully completed. While the textile sector is shrinking, both capital and labor in that sector will suffer as jobs are lost and factories are shut down. In the expanding aircraft industry both labor and capital will benefit as sales, employment, and profits all grow.

Only as labor and capital are able to move from the shrinking textile sector to the expanding aircraft industry will factor prices fully adjust. Wages will fall in the aircraft industry because of the inflow of large numbers of workers, and profits earned by owners of capital previously employed in the textile sector will rise as it is invested in the far more profitable aircraft sector.

The income distribution effects described by the Heckscher-Ohlin model occur as adjustment to free trade is completed, that is, as factors of production move from the import-competing to the export sector. Before that process is complete, all factors of production employed in the import-competing sector will suffer income losses.

This problem is exacerbated if these industries are concentrated in different regions of a country, which means that people have to move considerable distances to find new jobs or wait for new industries to come into their area. A contraction of the U.S. textile industry would largely affect North and South Carolina, whereas expansion of the commercial aircraft industry would occur primarily on the West Coast. The movement of large numbers of workers to the west and the arrival of new industries in the Carolinas would require time, and while adjustment was under way North and South Carolina would likely suffer sizable income losses.

Trade: A Substitute for Factor Movements

Another important implication of factor proportions theory is that international trade serves as a substitute for the movement of productive factors from one country to another. The actual distribution of productive factors among the nations of the world is obviously very unequal. One possible market response would be movements of labor and capital from countries where they are abundant and cheap to countries where they are scarce and more expensive, thus reducing the price differences and making factor proportions more equal throughout the world. Some such factor movements do take place, but powerful cultural and political obstacles prevent really large movements, especially the huge migrations of people that would be involved.

The factor proportions theory suggests that international factor movements are not necessary in any case, because the movement of goods in world trade can accomplish essentially the same purpose. Countries that have abundant labor can specialize in labor-intensive goods and ship these goods to countries where labor is scarce. Labor is in a sense embodied in goods and redistributed through trade. The same point applies to capital, land, and other specific factors. The economic effects of international factor movements can be achieved without the factors themselves actually having to move.

A major economic effect of an international factor movement is to alter the relative abundance or scarcity of that factor and thus to affect its price, that is, to raise the prices of abundant factors by making them less abundant relative to other factors. Thus, when Italian workers migrate to Germany, wage rates tend to rise in Italy because labor is made somewhat less abundant there, whereas wage rates in Germany tend to fall (or at least to rise less rapidly than they otherwise would) because the relative scarcity of labor is reduced. The same result is achieved when Germans buy Italian goods that are produced by relatively labor-intensive methods. More labor is demanded by Italian export industries, and Italian wage rates tend to rise.[4]

The fact that free trade and factor mobility are driven by parallel causes and have the same effects on the distribution of income has implications for the politics of immigration laws. In a labor-scarce country either free trade or liberal immigration policies will threaten the incomes of labor, whereas the opposite will be true in a labor-abundant country. Labor unions in relatively labor-scarce countries such as the United States oppose free trade or immigration for the same reason. Either policy will reduce the incomes of workers and increase those of owners of land and capital. The subject of international factor mobility will be discussed in more detail in Chapter 11.

EMPIRICAL VERIFICATION

For a long time, little empirical evidence could be brought to bear on the Heckscher-Ohlin theory. Most of the available evidence involved illustrative examples such as a labor-abundant India exporting lace, rugs, textiles, and other labor-intensive goods, or capital-abundant Germany and the United States exporting automobiles, machinery, and other capital-intensive goods, or land-abundant Canada, Australia, and Argentina exporting wheat, wool, meat, and other land-intensive goods. For some economists such examples were sufficient; indeed, they considered the Heckscher-Ohlin theory to be virtually self-evident. Its conclusions follow logically and inescapably from the assumptions made.

---

[4]See Robert Mundell, "International Trade and Factor Mobility," *American Economic Review,* June 1957, pp. 321–335, for an early version of this argument.

Then Wassily Leontief, a pioneer in input-output analysis, hit on the idea of using input-output data to test the Heckscher-Ohlin hypothesis for the United States. Using the interindustry matrix that had been developed for the United States, he calculated the amounts of capital and labor required to produce a $1 million basket of exports. Each export good counted in the $1 million basket in proportion to its share in total exports; for example, if agricultural machinery accounted for 5 percent of total U.S. exports, then 5 percent of the $1 million, or $50,000, was assumed to consist of agricultural machinery.

Similarly, Leontief calculated the amounts of capital and labor required to produce a $1 million basket of import-competing goods. Because he was measuring capital and labor used in the United States, Leontief had to exclude tin, coffee, and other imports that are not produced in the United States.

After all these calculations, Leontief ended up with four numbers: capital and labor inputs required to produce $1 million of exports, and capital and labor inputs required to produce $1 million of import-competing goods. It was generally believed (indeed, Leontief took it for granted) that the United States was a capital-rich country and that it had a greater abundance of capital relative to labor than did its trade partners. Consequently, the Heckscher-Ohlin theory predicted that U.S. exports would be more capital intensive than its import-competing goods—that is, that:

$$[C/L]_{\text{export goods}} > [C/L]_{\text{import-competing goods}}$$

To Leontief's great surprise, his results showed the opposite, namely, that U.S. exports were more labor intensive than its import-competing goods. The following table of inputs required to produce $1 million of exports and $1 million of import-competing goods shows Leontief's actual figures.[5] The capital/labor ratio in export industries ($14,011) was lower than the capital/labor ratio in import-competing industries ($18,182).

Inputs Required	Exports	Import-Competing Goods
Capital (1947 prices)	$2,550,000	$3,091,000
Labor (man-years)	182	170
C/L ratio ($ per man-year)	$14,011	$18,182

This result, which contradicted the Heckscher-Ohlin thesis, came to be known as the Leontief paradox. It stimulated many further studies, and a large number of books and articles have since been published on the subject. Comparable calculations have been made for other countries, and several of them also show paradoxical results. Many economists have sought to account for the apparent paradox, and

---

[5]Wassily Leontief, "Domestic Production and Foreign Trade," in J. Bhagwati, ed., *International Trade* (Baltimore: Penguin, 1969).

several explanations have been put forward to resolve it. We will mention only a few of the main results of this work.[6]

1. To consider only two productive factors, capital and labor, may introduce a bias. The United States imports many natural-resource–intensive commodities that happen to require relatively large amounts of capital in their production. When only capital and labor inputs are considered, these natural-resource–intensive imports show up as capital-intensive commodities. Actually, the United States is importing commodities that require relatively much of its scarce factor, natural resources. When a three-factor analysis is carried out, the results are more in accord with Heckscher-Ohlin predictions.

2. To treat labor as a homogeneous input, simply measured in man-years, does not take account of various degrees of skill. When labor inputs are differentiated by educational levels and other measures of skill, it appears that the United States exports goods that use relatively much capital and skilled labor and imports goods that use relatively much capital and unskilled labor.

3. Heckscher-Ohlin predicts what trade pattern would exist with free trade or with an unbiased commercial policy, that is, the same tariff rate on all imported goods. Instead, U.S. tariffs and other trade barriers provide high levels of protection for labor-intensive goods and much less protection for capital- or land-intensive goods. As a result, U.S. imports of labor-intensive goods are repressed relative to imports of other goods, helping to produce the Leontief results.

4. The accuracy of statistics used in the input-output calculations has been vigorously questioned. The margin of error in these statistics is large enough to raise doubts about the significance of the small difference in the two capital/labor ratios.

5. Finally, some economists have challenged our seventh assumption, given earlier, that industries can be ranked in order of capital intensity and that this ranking holds for all factor-price ratios. Some evidence has been presented to indicate that an industry's place in the capital-intensity ranking can change from one factor-price ratio to another. This is called a factor intensity reversal. The point is a subtle one and requires a word of explanation.

Industries may vary in the degree to which they can substitute capital for labor. Some industries, like petroleum refining, require a high ratio of capital for labor. Even if wages are very low, labor cannot be substituted for capital except in a limited way. Under these circumstances, isoquants for that industry have a "corner" in them, as the curve P_1 in Figure 4-6a. In other industries, such as textiles, there is much greater scope for the substitution of labor for capital as wages fall relative

---

[6]For a discussion of these and other explanations of the Leontief paradox, see E. Leamer, *Sources of International Comparative Advantage* (Boston: MIT Press, 1984), and W. P. Travis, *The Theory of Trade and Protection* (Boston: Harvard University Press, 1964).

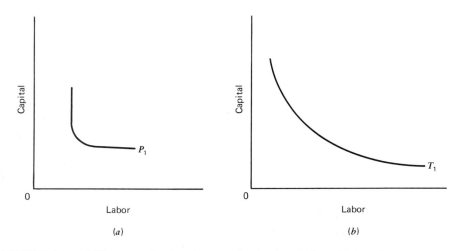

FIGURE 4-6   Differences in the degree of substitutability of labor for capital. (a) Low substitutability. (b) High substitutability.

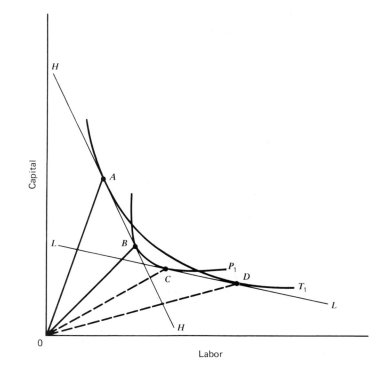

FIGURE 4-7   Factor intensity reversals.

to interest rates. For these industries the isoquants have a shape similar to that of the curve T_1 in Figure 4-6b.

Now suppose both types of industries exist, say, petroleum refining and textiles. When wages are very high relative to interest rates, textile production may be more capital intensive than petroleum refining. But when wages are very low, as in India, textile producers will substitute labor for capital, making textile production more labor intensive than petroleum refining. Such a reversal in factor intensity is illustrated in Figure 4-7. At the factor-price ratio *HH,* textiles are more capital intensive than petroleum refining (compare slopes of vectors *OA* and *OB*), but at factor-price ratio *LL,* textiles are labor intensive relative to petroleum refining (compare slopes of vectors *OC* and *OD*).

When such reversals occur, it follows that industries cannot be unambiguously ranked in order of capital intensity. Assumption 7 no longer holds, and the Heckscher-Ohlin prediction about the factor intensity of a nation's exports and imports is no longer valid.

Empirical research has not yet settled this question in a definitive way. Many economists still believe that the conditions necessary for the Heckscher-Ohlin analysis are satisfied for a wide range of industries and that this theory yields useful insights into the nature of, and basis for, international trade.

QUESTIONS FOR STUDY AND REVIEW

1. What is the effect of trade on relative factor prices in the trading nations, compared to a no-trade position? Explain why.

2. What does trade theory imply about the composition of a nation's exports and imports? Why?

3. "Alpha, a country with abundant labor and scarce capital, initially has completely free trade with the outside world. If Alpha imposes a tariff on imports, its ratio of wages to return on capital will rise." Do you agree? Why or why not?

4. Explain what is meant by the factor intensity of a product.

5. Suppose that Argentina has abundant capital and scarce labor compared with Brazil, that wheat is capital intensive relative to cloth, and that other Heckscher-Ohlin assumptions apply.

   a. Using appropriate diagrams, show that mutually beneficial trade between the two countries is possible. Label diagrams clearly, and explain in words the sequence of the argument.

   b. Once a free-trade equilibrium is reached, if Brazil imposes a tariff on imports, what will be the effect on its ratio of wages (W) to return on capital (R)? Explain why.

6. When trade begins, Country Z imports cloth, the labor-intensive commodity. What does this imply about Z's own factor endowment? Why? What is likely to be the effect of trade on wages in Z? Why?

7. What group in Country Z would you expect to support free trade? Why? Who would oppose it? How would you evaluate the claims by opponents that free trade reduced national welfare?

8. If the United States restricts imports from Mexico, what is the probable effect of such restrictions on the number of Mexican workers attempting to enter the United States? Explain why.

9. What exactly is paradoxical about the so-called Leontief paradox? What explanations have been offered to account for it or to resolve it?

SELECTED REFERENCES

Baldwin, Robert E. "Determinants of the Commodity Structure of U.S. Trade." *American Economic Review,* March 1971.

Heckscher, Eli. "The Effect of Foreign Trade on the Distribution of Income." In Howard Ellis and Lloyd Metzler, eds. *Readings in the Theory of International Trade.* Philadelphia, 1949.

Leontief, Wassily. "Domestic Production and Foreign Trade." In Richard Caves and Harry G. Johnson, eds. *Readings in International Economics.* Homewood, Ill.: Richard D. Irwin, 1967. Also in J. Bhagwati, ed. *International Trade.* Baltimore: Penguin, 1969.

Ohlin, Bertil. *Interregional and International Trade.* Cambridge, Mass.: Harvard University Press, 1933.

NEW APPROACHES TO TRADE THEORY

The factor proportions or Heckscher-Ohlin theorem, which was presented in the previous chapter, implies that trade should occur primarily between pairs of countries with very different relative factor endowments. That theory is quite successful in explaining trade between industrialized and developing countries; the industrialized countries import labor and tropical land-intensive products from less developed countries (LDCs), and export capital and temperate climate land-intensive goods to them.

A far larger volume of trade is not between industrialized and developing countries, however, but is instead among industrialized countries. The Heckscher-Ohlin theorem is less successful in explaining these trade flows. Some trade among industrialized countries may be based on Heckscher-Ohlin such as when, for example, France exports wine, which is based on an endowment of a particular type of land, to the United States. Because far more trade among industrialized countries does not appear to be based on differing factor endowments, alternatives to Heckscher-Ohlin are needed.

The new explanations of international trade flows, which will be discussed here, have been developed since the early 1960s. They are somewhat eclectic, occasionally overlap, and are far less rigorous or complete than Heckscher-Ohlin. They do not provide a fully developed theory of trade flows, but instead represent a set of useful insights as to why trade occurs.

THE PRODUCT CYCLE

One interesting hypothesis is that new products pass through a series of stages in the course of their development, and their comparative advantage position changes as they move through what is known as the Vernon Product cycle.[1] There are several variations on this theme, with different explanations for the movement for one phase, or stage, of the cycle to another. Most of these variations concentrate on U.S. trade patterns and on trade in manufactured, as opposed to primary, products.

Many new products are initially developed in the United States, with production and sales first occurring in its domestic market. After a new product has caught on in the United States, it attracts attention in other countries, and foreign merchants begin to place orders for it. Thus the United States starts off as an exporter of the new product.

As foreign demand grows, sales in some countries may eventually reach a threshold level, a level large enough to tempt foreign firms to undertake production for themselves. If foreign firms are able to acquire the technology necessary to manufacture the product, production in those countries begins, and U.S. exports decline. Foreign firms also begin to export to third-country markets, further reducing U.S. exports.

Finally, as foreign firms master the production process and as their costs fall with the increased scale of production, they may begin to export the product to the United States itself. This completes the cycle: The United States began as the exclusive exporter, then competed with foreign producers for export sales, and finally became a net importer of the new product. In terms of the U.S. trade position, the product cycle implies a change through time as illustrated in Figure 5-1 with the following four stages:

   I.   Product development and sale in U.S. market.
   II. Growth in U.S. exports as foreign demand springs up.
   III. Decline in U.S. exports as foreign firms begin to produce for their home markets.
   IV. United States becomes a net importer as foreign prices fall.

[1]Raymond Vernon was the originator of this view. See, R. Vernon, "International Investment and International Trade in the Product Cycle," *Quarterly Journal of Economics,* May 1966, pp. 190–207. See also R. Vernon, *The Technological Factor in International Trade* (New York: Colombia University Press, 1970).

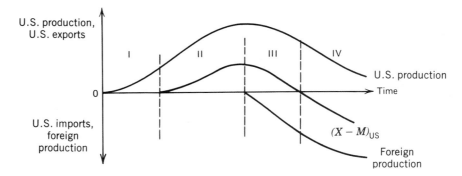

FIGURE 5-1 The product cycle.

This scenario seems to fit very well the observed experience with a number of new products in recent decades, such as radio, television, synthetic fibers, transistors, and pocket calculators. There is some evidence that the time span between stages I and IV may be getting shorter, although the length of the cycle probably varies from one product to another. A particular product might even move directly from stage I to stage IV, skipping stages II and III altogether. This appears to have happened in the case of the electric golf cart. Although it was developed in the United States and is little used elsewhere, a Polish firm began to produce it strictly as an export item for the U.S. market.

The product cycle hypothesis can be adapted and modified to take account of a variety of circumstances and explanatory factors. This gives it great flexibility but also weakens its power as a theory. For example, in explaining why the United States is frequently the first to develop and produce new products, some say that its high average income and enormous domestic market provide incentive and opportunity to innovators; others say that high wages give U.S. firms special incentives to develop labor-saving innovations; and still others claim that the United States simply has a relative abundance of scientifically trained persons and research facilities, and hence it has a comparative advantage in innovation.

All these variants of the product cycle hypothesis hold that the United States possesses certain features or characteristics that enable it to take a lead in the development and production of new products. Its lead is temporary, however. As demand grows for a product, as the new technology is learned and assimilated in other countries, and as the productive process is standardized, then the basic determinants of comparative advantage begin once again to dominate the location of production. Thus this theory is essentially short run, and it is explicitly dynamic. The United States, as the leader in innovation, has a temporary comparative advantage in the latest products, but it steadily loses that advantage and must continually develop other new products to replace those that are maturing and being lost to competitors.

Several empirical investigations have yielded results that lend support to this analysis. U.S. exports of manufactured goods turn out to require relatively large amounts of highly skilled labor: scientists, engineers, technicians. Another study showed that the five U.S. industries with the strongest export position were also the industries with the largest research and development (R&D) expenditures. These five industries accounted for 72 percent of U.S. exports of manufactures and for 89 percent of R&D expenditures. The authors of the study concluded that "all roads lead to a link between export performance and R&D."[2]

The length of time the U.S. lead will last also depends on a number of circumstances, such as the rate of growth in demand in foreign markets, the nature of the products developed, the speed with which foreigners acquire the new technology, the effectiveness of patent rights, and the extent of economies of scale. The organization of industry also plays a role. It is possible that the rise of multinational corporations will shorten or even eliminate the product cycle. Even though innovation occurs in the United States, a multinational firm might decide to locate initial production facilities in a foreign subsidiary.

We should note that the product cycle theory is not really in conflict with comparative advantage and factor proportions theory. The United States has a relative abundance of scientific and technical personnel, which gives it a comparative advantage in innovation. However, once a breakthrough is accomplished and a learning period has elapsed, production will gravitate toward the countries that have a relative abundance of factors required for routine production of the new product.

Of course, the United States itself might turn out to be the comparative advantage country. The likelihood of that outcome may be enhanced by a continuing flow of product improvements (as in computers), by pronounced economies of scale that serve as a barrier to entry, and by production processes requiring relatively large amounts of capital and highly skilled labor. However, the increased mobility of both capital and technology may make it difficult for the United States to establish a lasting comparative advantage in new products. In that event, maintenance of a strong research and development effort becomes even more important.

Recently, Washington has shown increased concern that stages I and II (see Figure 5-1) do not last as long for the United States as they did in the past and that this situation has seriously weakened U.S. export performance. This change may be partly the result of an acceleration in the rate of technical change, so that product monopolies are more short lived than they were in the past. It may also result from multinational firms moving production abroad, so that the company retains a monopoly but the inventing country does not. It has also become more common to license technology to foreign firms, particularly for inventions that are expected to have a short period of profitability. Allowing foreign firms to use technology in exchange for a fee is often the preferred way of maximizing profits over a brief economic lifetime.

Theft of intellectual property is another reason for the loss of U.S. exports, and this has become a major issue in trade policy. Some foreign countries either do not recognize U.S. patents or copyrights, or do not enforce their laws in this area. The result is the frequent use of U.S. technology or artistic property by foreign firms without compensation. Computer programs, movies, popular music, trademarks, and a variety of other forms of intellectual property have been affected by such

[2]William Gruber, Dileep Mehta, and Raymond Vernon, "The R&D Factor in International Trade and Investment of United States Industries," *Journal of Political Economy*, Vol. 75, February 1967, pp. 20–37.

theft. The United States has energetically pursued this issue with countries whose nationals have been accused of such activities; threats of retaliation against the exports of these countries have produced some progress in reducing this problem.

ECONOMIES OF SCALE IN IMPERFECTLY COMPETITIVE MARKETS

International trade can also be encouraged by economies of scale in the form of large fixed costs, which decline per unit of output as the volume of production increases. Research and development expenses are a particularly important source of such fixed costs.

If the costs of doing the research and development necessary to bring a new product to market are very large, firms may view exports as vital in order to spread those fixed costs across enough units of production to bring average costs down to acceptable levels. Firms with such research costs may vigorously pursue export sales, and if such sales are not possible because of foreign protectionist policies, the research may not be undertaken. For example, because the development of a new commercial airplane costs hundreds of millions of dollars, it is unlikely that Boeing would have brought its new generation of airplanes to market if it did not have confidence that large export sales were possible.

This approach to trade can be seen as an extension of the product cycle and perhaps as a way of forestalling stages III and IV of that process. In an industry in which technical change is ongoing (products are constantly being improved), an early investment in research and development can create a dominant competitive position for firms in one country, which will forestall entry by firms in other countries. Past research successes create current profits, which finance current research, and lead to future new products, profits, and financing for later research. Sufficient financial and research strength in an industry in one country may discourage firms in other countries from making the investments in research and development that would be necessary to challenge the status quo, thus perpetuating the first country's dominance of the industry. Such dominance is possible only for the country that gets into an industry first and creates a strong technical position.

As will be seen in Chapter 7, supporters of the industrial strategy approach have used this situation as an argument for protectionist policies. Protecting the home market may allow domestic firms sufficient sales to finance research costs and also discourage foreign firms from undertaking expensive efforts to enter the market.[3] Advocates of this approach to trade policy also suggest that, since the costs of research efforts have increased so sharply (the inexpensive inventions have long

---

[3] A summary of this argument can be found in Paul Krugman, "Is Free Trade Passe?" *Journal of Economic Perspectives*, (Fall 1987), pp. 131–144. A useful gathering of papers on the subject of strategic trade can be found in Paul Krugman, ed. *Strategic Trade Policy and the New International Economics* (Cambridge, Mass: MIT Press, 1986). See also Gene M. Grossman and J. David Richardson, "*Strategic Trade Policy: A Survey of Issues and Early Analysis,*" Princeton Special Papers in International Economics, No. 15 (April 1985).

since been exploited), the U.S. government should not use antitrust laws to stop U.S. firms from cooperating on major research efforts. Cooperative research efforts and protectionist policies should be used to enable U.S. industries to develop and maintain dominant positions in high-tech areas just as, it is suggested, Japan has done in many industries in recent years.

PREFERENCE SIMILARITY HYPOTHESIS

The preference similarity hypothesis, developed by Staffan B. Linder,[4] starts with the proposition that a nation will as a rule export only those products for which it has a large and active domestic market. The reason is simply that production for the domestic market must be large enough to enable firms to achieve economies of scale and thus to reduce costs enough to break into foreign markets.

Next, Linder argues that the most promising and receptive markets for exports will be found in other countries whose income levels and tastes are generally comparable to those of the exporting country. This is where the term *preference similarity* comes in. Linder believes that countries with similar income levels will have similar tastes. Each country will produce primarily for its home market, but part of the output will be exported to other countries where a receptive market exists.

An interesting aspect of this theory is its implication that trade in manufactured products will take place largely between countries with similar income levels and demand patterns. The theory also implies that the commodities entering into trade will be similar, though in some way differentiated. These two implications accord well with recent experience: The great majority of international trade in manufactured goods takes place among the relatively high-income countries: the United States, Canada, Japan, and European countries. Furthermore, a great deal of this trade involves the exchange of similar products. Each country imports products that are very much like the products it exports. Germany exports BMWs to Italy while importing Fiats. France imports both car brands, and exports Peugeots and Renaults to Germany and Italy. Similar patterns can be found in the U.S.-Canada trade.

These results about trade patterns are interesting because they are not predicted by the factor proportions theory. On the contrary, the theory suggests that trade will be most active between countries that are dissimilar in factor endowment and in tastes because such dissimilarities will give rise to large differences in relative prices. The theory also suggests that a country's exports will differ from its imports because different factor proportions will be required for the production of the two categories of products.

Linder emphasized that his theory was applicable only to trade in manufactured goods, in which tastes and economies of scale were deemed to be especially important. In his view, trade in primary products can be adequately explained by the traditional theory, with its emphasis on the supply of productive factors, including climate and natural resources.

[4]Staffan B. Linder, *An Essay on Trade and Transformation* (New York: John Wiley, 1961).

The Linder model does not explain why one country originates particular products or particular firms, and so these origins might be viewed as accidental. BMW happened to start producing cars in Bavaria, whereas Fiat began in Milan and Peugeot entered the car business from Paris. Each local economy had to be large enough to support a firm that was big enough to gain economies of scale, thus making competitive exports possible. Otherwise, there is no particular explanation of why various types of cars were produced in each country.

BORDER TRADE

Trade based on similarities in consumer preferences implies that similar products may cross a border in both directions, but that there should be some differences in product detail or brand reputation between those items entering a country and those leaving it. Occasionally the exact same product is shipped across a border in both directions, which seems to contradict both comparative advantage and common sense. This border trade occurs when two countries share a long border, so that shipping distances could be less across a border than they would be within a country. Canadian oil, for example, is produced primarily in Alberta, which is far from major markets in Ontario and Quebec but quite close to U.S. markets in the north central states. As a result, large amounts of Canadian oil are sold in Minnesota, Wisconsin, and neighboring states, whereas oil that arrives from abroad at Portland, Maine, is shipped through a pipeline to refineries in Montreal. Selling Canadian oil in the U.S. midwestern market and bringing oil through the United States to supply refineries in Quebec saves transport costs. Other heavy or bulky products are reportedly shipped in both directions across distant parts of the U.S.-Canadian border to save shipping costs.

EXTENSIONS AND APPLICATIONS

The Effects of Economic Growth on Trade: Changes in Factor Supplies

With a given endowment of resources and a given technology, a country's production-possibility curve depicts its capacity to produce various combinations of commodities. However, if its resources are growing over time (e.g., the labor force is increasing through population growth, or the stock of physical capital is being augmented by net investment from year to year), then the production-possibility curve is not fixed in one place. Instead, it is shifting to the right, indicating that the country's capacity to produce is expanding.

Many different patterns of growth can occur, depending on the rates at which different factors of production are growing and on the technological conditions that exist in the several industries. These patterns, in turn, will interact with demand conditions at home and abroad to determine the final effects on output, the quantities of exports and imports, and the terms of trade. A great many outcomes are possible, and economists have devoted much effort to their description and classification. We do not attempt an exhaustive discussion, but simply discuss a few examples in order to illustrate how various cases can be analyzed.

Neutral Growth

Perhaps the simplest case is one in which all of Country A's factors of production grow at the same rate over a certain time interval, while constant returns to scale exist in all industries and technology remains unchanged. In such a case of neutral growth in capacity, the production-possibility curve simply shifts outward in the same proportion throughout its length, as illustrated in Figure 5-2. The new curve, F_2C_2, is just a radial extension of F_1C_1, expanded outward in proportion to the growth in resources that has occurred. If Country A is small relative to the rest of the world, the terms of trade will remain unchanged, and Country A will continue to produce the two commodities in the same proportions as before, as indicated by the points P and P' on the vector OP'.

The effects on Country A's consumption and its volume of trade will then depend on its demand pattern, as shown in its community indifference curves. Country A may choose to consume food and cloth in the same proportions as before, in which case both its imports of food and its exports of cloth will rise in proportion to the increase in output. In this case, where A's income elasticity of demand for both goods is unity, Country A's consumption points (Q and Q') will lie on the

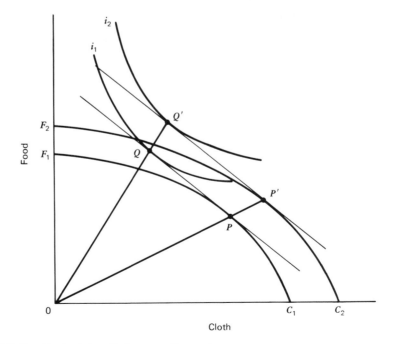

FIGURE 5-2   Neutral growth in a small country.

vector OQ', as shown in Figure 5-2, and consumption of both goods increases in proportion to economic growth. However, if Country A's demand for food (the imported commodity) rises more than proportionately to income, then its exports and imports will also increase by a larger proportion than does output. Growth is biased toward trade. On the other hand, if Country A's demand for food rises less than proportionately to income (i.e., it is income inelastic), then trade will rise less than output. Growth is biased against trade. The volume of trade could even shrink if Country A's demand for food had very low income elasticity.

Note that if Country A is large enough to influence the terms of trade, the situation is considerably more complicated. The terms of trade will tend to worsen whenever exports increase, whether or not growth is biased toward trade. Alternatively, if A's consumers spend their increased income primarily for A's export commodity (cloth), the terms of trade may improve.

The various possible outcomes may conveniently be analyzed with the aid of Figure 5-3 for this case of equiproportionate growth in factor supplies. Before growth, we have an equilibrium with production at P, consumption at Q, and a trade triangle SPQ representing cloth exports, SP, food imports, SQ. If the terms of trade remain unchanged when growth occurs (slope of $P'Q'$ = slope of PQ), the production of both commodities will rise in the same proportion and the outcome will depend on demand conditions in Country A. The various possibilities can be seen by considering the expansion path of consumption from point Q. The neutral path, with income elasticity of unity for both goods, is along the vector OQ': Consumption of both goods rises in proportion to income growth. If the demand for food rises more than in proportion to income (income elasticity

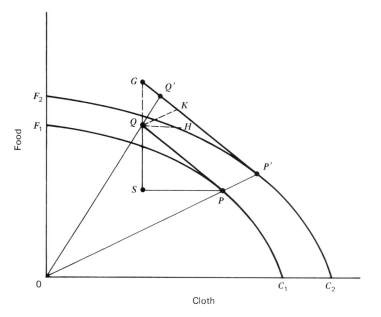

FIGURE 5-3   Effect of demand conditions on the volume of trade.

of demand for food is greater than one), then the expansion path will be steeper than QQ', falling in the angle GQQ', and exports will increase by a greater proportion than output. If the demand for food rises less than in proportion to income (income elasticity less than one), then the expansion path will be less steep than QQ', falling in the angle $Q'QH$, and exports will increase by a smaller, proportion than output, or they may even decline. (We exclude the case of inferior goods, in which consumption of one of the two goods actually declines when income rises.)

If we now drop the assumption that the terms of trade remain unchanged, we can see that increased exports from Country A will tend to reduce export prices and thus turn the terms of trade against Country A. In our example, this will occur for any expansion path steeper than QK. (We have drawn QK parallel to PP', so $QP = KP'$.) In general, the larger the income elasticity of demand for imports, the steeper the expansion path and the greater the adverse movement in the terms of trade. However, Figure 5-3 cannot be used to determine the new equilibrium position after the terms of trade have changed.

Growth in a Single Factor of Production

Let us now consider the case in which the supply of only one factor of production increases. As before, the production-possibility curve shifts outward to reflect the greater capacity to produce, but now the outward shift is biased toward the commodity that requires for its production relatively much of the factor whose supply has increased. To continue our preceding example, if cloth is labor intensive relative to food, then an increase in Country A's labor force will cause its production-possibility curve to shift outward but with a bias toward cloth output, as from F_1C_1 to F_2C_2 in Figure 5-4. Now if the terms

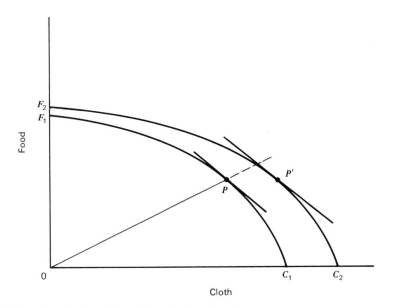

FIGURE 5-4   Growth in a single factor of production.

of trade remain unchanged, cloth output rises proportionately more than food output. This is indicated in Figure 5-3 by the fact that P', the new production point, lies below the point at which OP (extended) would cut the new production-possibility curve. In fact, under Heckscher-Ohlin assumptions, it can be shown that output of food will fall when Country A's labor supply increases, with constant terms of trade.[5] Thus we can see that growth in a country's relatively abundant factor tends to increase the volume of its exports; that is, such growth is export biased in its production effect. On the other hand, growth in Country A's relatively scarce factor would cause its production-possibility curve to shift with a bias toward food output. At constant terms of trade, such a shift would tend to reduce the volume of cloth exports. It does so because it reduces the disparity in factor endowments between Country A and the rest of the world; that is, it reduces the relative abundance of labor in Country A and thus makes Country A more like the rest of the world in its factor endowment. If the other factor, say, capital, grew enough, Country A would eventually develop a relative abundance of capital instead of labor, in which case its comparative advantage would lie in food instead of cloth. Such shifts in comparative advantage can be observed in many countries as economic growth proceeds. Comparative advantages are not permanent and immutable; instead, they change over time as circumstances change.

In this discussion of growth in one factor, we have concentrated on the production effect. For a complete analysis, we would have to consider the consumption effect as well. That involves, as before, the response of consumers in Country A to changes in incomes and prices. The key question we should want to ask is whether Country A offers more or fewer exports, at constant terms of trade, allowing for both production and consumption effects, as a result of growth in one factor, such as labor. If the outcome is that exports increase and Country A is large enough to influence world prices, then its increased offer of exports will tend to cause a fall in their price. The analysis must then allow for the effects of the change in the terms of trade.

This analysis can usefully be put in terms of the offer curves described in Chapter 3. Suppose Country A's original offer curve is OA, as in Figure 5-5. At the initial equilibrium, with terms of trade OT, Country A exports OC_1 of cloth and imports OF_1 of food. Then, as a result of growth in its labor force, Country A's offer curve shifts from OA to OA', indicating its willingness to export a larger quantity of cloth at each terms of trade. This is export-biased growth. If Country A is a small country, too small to affect the world price, then the rate of the world's (ROW) offer curve will be the straight-line OT and the new equilibrium will be at E_2, where Country A exports OC_2 of cloth and imports OF_2 of food.

On the other hand, if Country A is large enough to influence the world price, the ROW offer curve will be less than perfectly elastic, as indicated by the offer curve labeled ROW in Figure 5-5. The shift in Country A's offer curve will now

[5]We omit the proof of this result, which is known as the Rybczynski theorem. See T. M. Rybczynski, "Factor Endowments and Relative Commodity Prices," *Economica*, Vol. 22, November 1955, pp. 336–341.

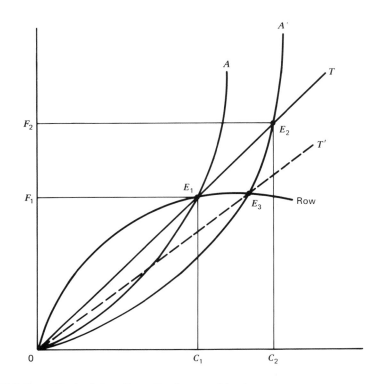

FIGURE 5-5 Effect of growth on the terms of trade.

cause a fall in the price of cloth relative to the price of food. The new equilibrium is at E_3, with the terms of trade indicated by OT'. (Note that the terms of trade have turned against Country A: It must offer more cloth per unit of food than before.)

The Case of Immiserizing Growth

We have seen that growth in a country's capacity to produce may increase its exports (shift its offer curve outward) and that as a result its term of trade may decline. By reducing economic welfare, such an adverse movement in the terms of trade offsets and counteracts the benefits derived from economic growth. It is even possible that the loss from an adverse change in the terms of trade will exceed the gain from increased capacity, thus leaving the country worse off than before. This rather extreme case, called "immiserizing growth," has attracted much attention in recent years, especially in connection with complaints of underdeveloped countries about their role in world trade. We will present more details about that in a subsequent chapter.

The theoretical possibility of immiserizing growth can easily be demonstrated with the analytical tools we have been using. Consider the example illustrated in Figure 5-6. Initially, Ruritania is producing at P_O and exporting primary products

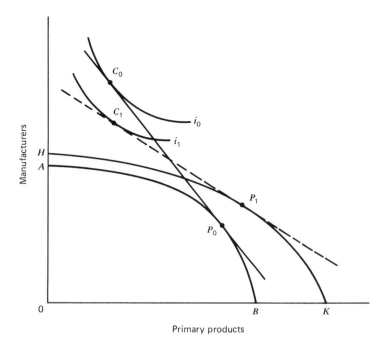

FIGURE 5-6 The case of immiserizing growth.

in exchange for manufactures at the terms-of-trade ratio indicated by the slope of $P_O C_O$. Through trade it can reach the welfare level represented by indifference curve i_O. Consumption is at C_O.

As a result of growth in the supply of factors used in the production of primary products, Ruritania's production-possibility curve shifts to the right, from AB to HK. It now offers larger quantities of exports, and its terms of trade decline to $P_1 C_1$ (slope of). At this exchange ratio, Ruritania continues to export primary products, but it can only reach the lower indifference curve, i_1. Thus growth in capacity has reduced economic welfare. Note that Ruritania now receives a smaller physical quantity of imports in exchange for a larger physical quantity of exports than it did before growth took place.

Although the theoretical possibility clearly exists, actual cases of immiserizing growth are hard to find and especially hard to prove. It requires a country large enough to have a significant effect on the world price of its export, and one whose growth is strongly biased toward exports. However, as we will see in Chapter 10, some economists believe that groups of underdeveloped countries have sometimes suffered losses as a result of expansion in their capacity to produce certain export commodities.

Technological Change
Changes in technology can be analyzed in a similar way. An improvement in technology means that a larger output can be produced with given inputs of the

factors of production. If the supply of these factors remains unchanged, such a technological change means that the production-possibility curve shifts outward to the right.

If the technological change increases productivity in all industries in the same proportion, we have another case of neutral growth, and the production-possibility curve shifts outward in the same proportion throughout its length. However, if the change in technique occurs in only one industry, or affects certain industries more than others, then the production-possibility curve shifts in a biased way toward the favored industry.

As before, such growth can be biased toward exports, tending to cause an expansion in world trade, or it can be biased toward expansion of import-competing goods, thus reducing the volume of trade. The outcome will depend on the nature of the technological change and on demand patterns at home and abroad.

Changes in Demand

Our discussion thus far has emphasized change that originates on the supply side, as a result of increased factor supply or an improvement in technique. It is also possible for shifts in comparative advantage to arise from changes in demand. Changes in the age structure of the population, or changes in tastes resulting from education, advertising, or passing fads and fashions, can alter the pattern of demand and thus cause relative prices to change. Geometrically, such changes would be shown as shifts in the shape and position of the community indifference curves. A country might begin to demand larger quantities of its own export commodity, thus increasing its price and eventually converting it into an import commodity.

In any event, it is clear that comparative advantage is not just a static concept. It is flexible enough to permit all sorts of changes over time. A nation's comparative advantage position reflects changes in factor supplies, technology, tastes, and many other variables.

Transport Costs

In our exposition of trade theory in Chapters 2 and 3, we generally assumed that transportation costs were zero. That convenient assumption simplified the analysis and enabled us to reach the important conclusion that international trade will equalize commodity prices at home and abroad. However, since freight, insurance, and other costs obviously do exist in transporting merchandise from one country to another, we should modify our analysis to allow for their influence in international trade. Fortunately, the modifications needed to take account of these costs are quite simple and straightforward, at least in principle.

The price of a commodity in the importing country will be higher than the price in the exporting country by an amount equal to the transport costs. (Note that we still assume perfect competition and no artificial barriers to trade, such as tariffs.) If Australian farmers sell wheat to Belgian importers for $4.00 per bushel, the price in Belgium will be $4.00 plus the cost of shipping the wheat to Belgium, say, $0.50 per bushel. Similarly, Belgium exports to Australia will sell at higher prices in Australia than in Belgium. Thus our previous conclusion that trade equalizes relative prices must be adjusted to allow for a differential caused by transport costs in both directions.

Starting from an equilibrium position with zero transport costs, provision for such costs means that the price of each country's import good rises. That is, the commodity terms of trade turn against both countries. The higher price for the imported commodity stimulates a larger production of import-competing goods in each country; hence the volume of trade is reduced.

Both countries continue to gain from trade, but the extent of the gain is reduced because trade itself is reduced by the presence of transport costs. In fact, for commodities that are low in value relative to bulk and weight, transport costs may be large enough to eliminate international trade altogether. For such commodities—for example, stone and gravel—large price differentials may exist between countries, but they remain because it does not pay to buy in the cheaper market and sell in the dearer one. These are in effect nontraded goods, just as many services such as haircuts are nontraded goods. (Except as an incidental aspect of foreign travel, it is not feasible for Americans to buy haircuts in India, even though they cost only $0.50 there compared to $10.00 at home.)

International transport costs clearly constitute an obstacle to trade. Part of the potential gain from specialization and exchange that exists when relative prices differ is used up in overcoming this obstacle. Consequently, transport costs reduce both the volume of trade and the extent of specialization and international division of labor, but they do not alter our previous conclusions concerning the basis and direction of trade, or the nature of the gain from trade.

According to International Monetary Fund data, transportation costs have fallen from about 9 percent of the value of trade to about 6 percent during the last four decades.[6] This is the equivalent of a tariff reduction of that amount and may be part of the reason for the rapid growth of world trade over that period.

Dumping

Dumping is usually defined as the sale of a commodity in a foreign market at a price below that charged in the domestic market. Our analysis of imperfect competition can be used to show why a particular firm might choose to engage in dumping.

Consider the position of the firm in Figure 5-7. If this firm has a protected domestic market and no foreign trade, it will produce Q_1 of output and charge the price P_1. Now suppose the firm has the opportunity to export its output at the world price P_2. If it can prevent the exported output from being brought back into the domestic market, to maximize its profit the firm will now (1) raise its domestic price to P_3 and reduce its domestic sales to Q_3 and (2) export the quantity Q_3Q_2 at the world price P_2.

At first glance it may seem paradoxical that the firm would reduce its sales in the higher priced market, but it turns out that the firm is simply following the

[6]International Monetary Fund, *International Financial Statistics Yearbook,* 1988, pp. 128–129.

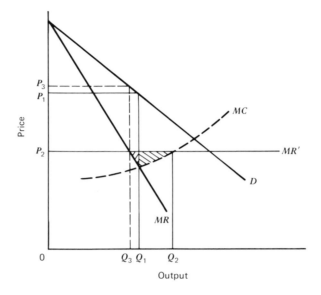

FIGURE 5-7   Dumping can increase profits—an example of price discrimination.

general rule of profit maximization: to equate marginal revenue and marginal cost, and to do so in each market. The marginal revenue curve for sales in the domestic market is downward sloping, but it becomes horizontal at P_2 for export sales, or MR'. Therefore no output will be sold in the home market that yields a marginal revenue less than P_2. On the other hand, exports are profitable out to the point at which $MR' = MC$. The opportunity to sell in foreign markets at the lower world price increases the firm's profits by the amounts indicated by the shaded areas in Figure 5-7—the difference between MR' and MC for the output that is exported. We should stress that this whole argument depends on the assumption that the two markets can be kept separated: The exported output cannot be returned to the home market. If it could be returned, the domestic price would fall to P_2 and the country would become a net importer, as in our previous example.

This result is a special case of a general proposition about price discrimination. A firm that sells its output in two or more distinct and separate markets will maximize its profits by equating MC and MR in each market. For the given MC, price will then be higher, the smaller the elasticity of demand in each market.

Dumping is generally regarded as an unfair trade practice, and nations frequently take action against it. Under U.S. law, dumping is defined as either selling in the U.S. market for less than in the home market, or as selling here for less than fair market value, which is usually based on average costs. If a charge of dumping is formally made, the Department of Commerce is required to investigate. If dumping is found to exist, the International Trade Commission investigates and determines whether the domestic industry is being injured by the dumping. If it is, retaliatory action can be taken. Several such investigations have been conducted in recent years, mostly in response to charges that

Japanese and European firms were dumping in the U.S. market. When American steel producers threatened to bring formal dumping charges in 1977, the United States established a so-called trigger price system. If foreign steel was offered below the stated trigger price, an official investigation would be automatically undertaken. With that threat hanging over the foreign steel-producers, it was hoped that they would refrain from selling below the trigger price because they would want to avoid retroactive penalty tariffs. For a time they did refrain, but U.S. firms continue to complain about the volume of steel imports.

One might think that importing countries would welcome the opportunity to obtain imports at bargain prices and that the exporting countries would be the ones to object. After all, trade improves consumer welfare by reducing the price of imported goods. However, it is usually the importing country that protests against dumping. The principal reason is that competing firms in the importing country recognize that low-priced imports are adversely affecting their sales and profits, and they are quick to claim that foreigners are engaging in unfair competition. Another popular argument is that dumping is a predatory activity; foreign firms will cut prices only temporarily in order to drive domestic firms out of business, after which they will raise prices to exploit a monopoly advantage. This argument certainly has some force in industries in which start-up costs are high or in which other barriers to entry of new firms exist. However, this is a short-run, temporary argument for dumping, unlike the static argument presented in Figure 5-7.

Cartels

Another important form of imperfectly competitive behavior results from the formation of cartels, the most important recent example of which is the Organization of Petroleum Exporting Countries (OPEC). A cartel is a collusive arrangement among producers of the same product in a number of different countries. These firms (or governments) act as a monopoly in setting prices and allocating markets. A cartel can then be viewed as an international version of a trust, and it has the same goal of earning monopoly profits by avoiding price competition.

Cartels were of considerable importance in world trade during the 1920s, but they largely disappeared during the depression. The topic received little attention from economists until OPEC began to dominate the world oil market in the early 1970s. Early examples of cartels can be found as early as 1301, and Adam Smith in 1776 noted the tendency of previously competing firms to collude to increase prices and profits, so this is not a new topic.[7]

Many developing countries that export other primary products thought OPEC would be a model that they could follow, but these hopes have been disappointed

---

[7]For an amusing history of cartels, see A. Gary Shilling, "Lessons in History from OPEC," *Wall Street Journal*, Op-Ed page, March 18, 1975. For a more detailed discussion of the rise of OPEC, see Raymond Vernon, ed., *The Oil Crisis* (New York: W. W. Norton, 1976). The World Bank *Annual Development Report* for 1986 deals at some length with the problems of agricultural cartels.

and even OPEC now has only a limited ability to affect prices. The requirements for creating a successful cartel are rather stringent, and cartels have a tendency to weaken the longer they are in operation. For a cartel to be successful in raising prices well above marginal costs, the following conditions must exist:

1. The price elasticity of demand for the product must be low, which means that it has no close substitutes. Otherwise the volume sold will shrink dramatically when prices are raised.

2. The elasticity of supply for the product from outside the cartel membership must be low, which means that new firms or countries are not able to enter the market easily in response to the higher price. If this condition does not hold, the cartel will discover that higher prices result in a sharp reduction in its sales as new entrants crowd into the business.

3. At least a few members of the cartel must be able and willing to reduce production and sales to hold the price up. If all members insist on producing at previous levels despite the higher price, there will almost certainly be an excess supply of the product, resulting in a price decline, often through secret price cuts by members competing for sales despite promises not to do so.

4. The membership of the cartel must be congenial and small enough to allow successful negotiations over prices, production quotas, and a variety of other matters. It would probably be impossible to manage a cartel of 50 members, particularly if some of them were historic adversaries.

From this list of conditions a reader can see why OPEC was temporarily successful and why this kind of success has been so rare in other markets. Most products do have substitutes and/or can be produced by new firms or countries if prices are increased sharply. Cartels have frequently failed when the market available to the members shrank, but none of them was willing to cut production sufficiently to support the price. Cheating in the form of secret price cuts to gain new customers followed, and the intended monopoly collapsed.

OPEC was temporarily successful in the 1970s because all four of the above conditions held for oil, but the longer high prices remained in effect, the weaker OPEC became. Efforts to conserve energy and the increased use of alternative energy sources reduced the demand for oil, and non-OPEC countries such as Mexico and the United Kingdom increased production sharply in the late 1970s. The results were a sharp reduction in the volume of oil that OPEC members could sell, unsuccessful attempts to get members to curtail production sufficiently, and an eventual decline in the price, as can be seen in Figure 5-8.

It is not clear, however, that OPEC is permanently weak. The low oil prices of the 1980s encouraged consumption and discouraged exploration in the United States and elsewhere, thus increasing their reliance on OPEC sources. Iraq's invasion of Kuwait in 1990 led to a temporary increase in the price of oil, but it is possible that increased dependence on OPEC during the 1990s will recreate the situation of the early 1970s when sharp price increases could be imposed and maintained for a considerable period of time.

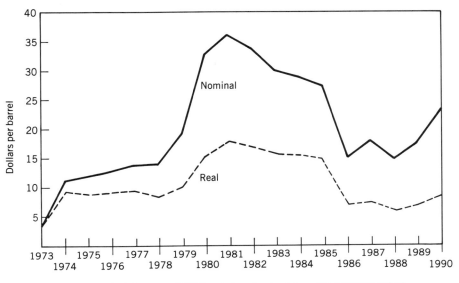

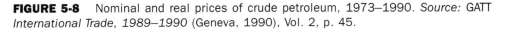

Note: The nominal price is the average of OECD import prices of crude petroleum. The real price is obtained by dividing the nominal price by the export unit value index of manufactures (base year 1973 = 100).

FIGURE 5-8 Nominal and real prices of crude petroleum, 1973–1990. *Source:* GATT *International Trade, 1989–1990* (Geneva, 1990), Vol. 2, p. 45.

QUESTIONS FOR STUDY AND REVIEW

1. Show how one can use offer curves to illustrate the case of immiserizing growth.

2. Name the several phases of the product cycle. Explain why each one gives way to the next.

3. Staffan Linder has argued that the Heckscher-Ohlin (factor endowment) theory does not explain much existing international trade, especially that in manufactured goods. What does Linder offer as an alternative theory? Explain.

4. Suppose that Country A, which has a relative abundance of capital, further expands its supply of capital. Explain how this expansion in capacity may affect the volume of trade and the terms of trade with Country B, its trading partner.

5. How might the product cycle theory help to account for the Leontief paradox? Explain.

6. "When a large domestic firm is exposed to competition from imported goods at lower prices, the firm will increase its output." Under what circumstances may this statement be true?

SELECTED REFERENCES

Grossman, Gene, and J. David Richardson. "Strategic Trade Policy: A Survey of Issues and Early Analysis." *Princeton Special Papers in International Economics,* No. 15 (April 1985).

Gruber, William, Dileep Mehta, and Raymond Vernon. "The R&D Factor in International Trade and Investment of United States Industries." *Journal of Political Economy,* Vol. 75, February 1967, pp. 20–37.

Johnson, Harry G. *Comparative Cost and Commercial Policy for a Developing World Economy.* Stockholm: Almquist & Viksell, 1968.

Keesing, Donald B. "Labor Skills and Comparative Advantage." *American Economic Review,* Vol. 56, No. 2, May 1966, pp. 249–258.

Krugman, Paul, ed. *Strategic Trade Policy and the New International Economics.* Cambridge, Mass.: MIT Press, 1986.

Linder, Staffan B. *An Essay on Trade and Transformation.* New York: John Wiley, 1961.

Vernon, Raymond. *The Technology Factor in International Trade.* New York: Colombia University Press, 1970.

Vernon, Raymond. *The Oil Crisis.* New York: W. W. Norton, 1976.

THE THEORY OF PROTECTION: TARIFFS AND OTHER BARRIERS TO TRADE

In our exposition of the theory of international trade, we started with countries that were initially operating as closed economies. We threw open these isolated countries and allowed them to trade freely with each other, and then we examined and analyzed the economic effects of trade. An important conclusion of this analysis was that countries, if not all individuals in the countries, generally gain from trade. When each country specializes in products in which it has a comparative advantage, exporting them in exchange for imports of other products in which it has a comparative disadvantage, the result is a gain in economic welfare.

This conclusion has long been a major tenet of trade theory. One of Adam Smith's principal objectives in his *Wealth of Nations* was to overturn and destroy the mass of mercantilist regulations that was hamstringing international trade. He argued that elimination of artificial barriers to trade and specialization would lead to an increase in real national income. David Ricardo shared this belief, as have most economists in subsequent generations.

This view has always been debated, however. Even if some trade is better than no trade, it does not necessarily follow that free trade is the best of all. Therefore we now need to turn the question around the other way: Starting from a position of full free trade, what is the effect of introducing an obstacle to, or restriction on, trade? Can a nation's welfare be improved by imposing tariffs or other barriers to trade, not necessarily to eliminate trade but at least to reduce it below the free-trade level?

In the past, tariffs (taxes on imports or, occasionally, on exports) were the dominant form of government regulation of trade, but that has changed. As average tariff levels have fallen owing to the successful completion of GATT (General Agreement on Tariffs and Trade) rounds, governments have sought ways to restrict trade without violating commitments to lower tariffs. As a result, nontariff trade barriers, widely known as NTBs, have proliferated and have become the most active means of interference with trade. A nontariff trade barrier is any government policy, other than a tariff, which reduces imports but does not similarly restrict domestic production of import substitutes. Quotas, which are limits on the physical volume of a product that may be imported during a period of time, are the most important NTB, but there are many others. Their range is limited only by the imagination of government officials seeking ways to restrict imports without violating GATT commitments. The following discussion deals first with tariffs, and then with quotas and other NTBs. Nations levy tariffs on both imports and exports, but the import tariff is by far the most important in practice, and it is the one we will emphasize. Import tariffs may be *ad valorem* (a percentage of the value of the imported article), specific (a given amount of money per unit, such as $0.50 per yard of cloth), or compound (a combination of *ad valorem* and specific, such as 10 percent *ad valorem* plus $0.20 per yard of cloth).

Ad valorem tariffs have the administrative advantage of rising automatically with inflation and of taxing different qualities of products at the same percentage rate. A tariff of 10 percent on wine produces proportionally more revenue as the price and quality of imported wine rise. A specific tariff will not have this effect. It will therefore decline in real terms in periods of inflation and will severely restrict imports of lower priced items within a product category while having little effect on expensive items. A tariff of $2 per bottle on wine would be prohibitive for inexpensive wines from developing countries, but would have very little impact on imports of high-priced wines from France. Such a tariff discriminates against producers and consumers of the cheaper wines.

The disadvantage of an *ad valorem* tariff is that it creates opportunities for cheating through what is called false invoicing or transfer pricing. If a misleading low price is shown on the shipping invoice, part of the tariff can be avoided. A 10 percent tariff on cars, for example, might encourage both car exporters and their customers to invoice the cars $1000 below their true value, thus saving $100, with a later fictitious transaction being used to move the $1000 as well as part of the $100 back to the exporter. A specific tariff of $500 per car would avoid this problem, because the customs officials would simply collect $500 times the number of cars driven off the ship and have no interest in the value of each car.

Some countries that believe they have been victimized by underinvoicing of imports refuse to accept normal documents showing the price of products being imported, and use their own customs valuation procedures to set the prices to which *ad valorem* tariffs will be applied. Such procedures are often arbitrary and result in tariff rates that are much higher than those that are supposed to apply. If the customs officials can simply decide that products are worth three times their actual value, a seemingly low tariff rate becomes very high. Customs valuation procedures are frequently a source of conflict in international trade, but there is a presumption that invoice prices will be accepted unless the government of the importing country has a clear reason to believe that those prices are not a fair representation of value. We now leave these practical problems and turn to the theory of tariffs.

TARIFFS: PARTIAL EQUILIBRIUM ANALYSIS

We begin by considering the effects of a tariff imposed on a single commodity, and we make the assumption that the industry involved is a very small part of the total economy. It is so small, in fact, that changes in this industry have negligible effects on the rest of the economy, and these effects can be ignored. That is, we will utilize partial equilibrium analysis.

The Small-Country Case

In Figure 6-1, we show Country A's domestic demand (D) and supply (S) curves for a particular commodity, say, oats. If trade is free, oats will be imported into Country A at the prevailing world price, P_W. At that price, Country A's total consumption will be OQ_4, its production will be OQ_1, and imports will make up the difference, Q_1Q_4. Total supply (OQ_1 of domestic output plus Q_1Q_4 of imports) equals total demand (OQ_4) at that price.

Now suppose that Country A imposes a tariff, equal to T per bushel, on imports of oats. The immediate result of the tariff is that the price of oats in Country A will rise by the amount of the tariff, to P_T. (Here we assume that the world price of oats remains unchanged when Country A imposes its tariff. That is, we assume that Country A is a small country whose actions will not affect the world market. We will relax this assumption later.) The increase in price has a number of effects that can conveniently be examined with the aid of Figure 6-1.

The first effect is that the consumption of oats is reduced from OQ_4 to OQ_3. The second effect is that domestic output rises from OQ_1 to OQ_2. Domestic producers

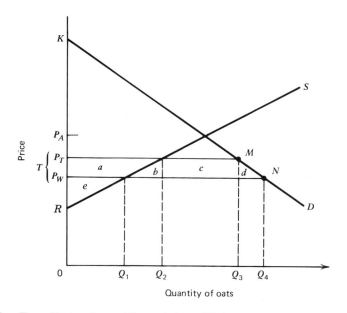

FIGURE 6-1   The effects of a tariff: partial equilibrium, small-country case.

do not pay the import tariff, of course, and the higher domestic price induces them to increase their output, as indicated by the supply curve. The third effect is that imports fall from Q_1Q_4 to Q_2Q_3. Both the fall in consumption and the rise in production cut into the previous level of imports of oats. (Note that if the tariff were large enough to raise the price to P_A, imports would fall to zero. Domestic producers would supply the entire demand. This would be a prohibitive tariff.)

We can also use Figure 6-1 to show the welfare gains and losses that result from the tariff. To show these gains and losses, we must recall that the area under the demand curve can be interpreted as a measure of the total welfare consumers obtain from consumption of the commodity. Part of this benefit must be paid for in the form of the price of the commodity, leaving a "consumer surplus" in the triangular area under the demand curve and above the horizontal line at the going price level. Conceptually, this is a benefit to consumers and does not have to be paid for in the commodity price. For example, in Figure 6-1, consumer surplus under free trade is the area of the triangle P_WKN, equal to the total area under the demand curve $OKNQ_4$, minus the rectangle OP_WNQ_4.

Imposition of the tariff reduces the consumer surplus to P_TKM, a reduction equal to the quadrilateral area P_WP_TMN. Some of this loss in consumer surplus is recouped by other segments of the economy, however. Area a accrues to domestic producers of oats as a kind of producer surplus.[1] Domestic producers receive the new price P_T for *all* the oats they produce, including the

---

[1] Consumer surplus is utility derived from a product for which the consumer does not have to pay. In Figure 6-1, someone was willing to pay a price of OK for a few units of the product, but only had to pay OP_w before the imposition of the tariff. Those units provided consumer surplus of P_wK. The total consumer surplus enjoyed by users of this product under free trade was triangle P_wNK, which

original output, OQ_1, that they had been willing to produce at the lower price, P_W. Thus they receive a windfall gain, or economic rent, on this output. Area a therefore represents a transfer from consumers to producers of this portion of consumer surplus. Similarly, area c represents the tariff revenue that accrues to government. The tariff revenue is equal to the tariff, T, times the imports on which the tariff is collected, Q_2Q_3. It is a transfer from consumers to government.

From a national point of view, therefore, areas a and c are not net losses; they are transfers from consumers to producers and to government, respectively. But the situation is different for the remaining pieces of the decreased consumer surplus. Areas b and d are lost to consumers, but they are not gained by any other sector. These areas therefore represent the net welfare loss resulting from the tariff, sometimes called the deadweight loss. Area b can be thought of as a loss resulting from inefficiency, as resources are drawn into oats production and paid higher returns than would be needed to obtain oats through free trade. Similarly, area d is the benefit consumers derive from the opportunity to consume the additional quantity, Q_3Q_4, at the world price, P_W. Consumers lose this benefit when a tariff is imposed because price rises to P_T.

Efforts have been made to estimate the amount of the deadweight loss for particular tariffs. If the demand and supply curves are approximately straight lines in the relevant range, then the deadweight loss is approximately equal to the reduction in imports times one-half the tariff.[2] Even if the deadweight loss were very small, consumers or other groups within an economy might strongly oppose a tariff. As we have seen, the loss in consumer surplus is the sum of areas $a + b + c + d$. It is small comfort to consumers to know that most of this loss is transferred to producers and to government. On the other hand, producers have reason to favor a tariff despite the fact that it inflicts a deadweight loss on the economy as a whole. This conflict of interest between consumers and producers is a common feature of the debate over tariff policy. In weighing the pros and cons of tariffs on particular

---

fell to triangle P_tMK when the tariff became effective. The common sense of consumer surplus can be seen through an example. If a person is extremely thirsty, a can of soft drink is worth far more to that person than the 50¢ it costs, the difference being consumer surplus.

Producer surplus is revenue received by those selling a product which is more than the absolute minimum they would have been willing to accept. In Figure 6-1 someone was willing to sell a few units for a price of OR, but actually received OP_w before the tariff was imposed. RP_w was producer surplus associated with those units. The domestic industry received producer surplus of triangle e before the tariff was put in place, which was increased by triangle a when the tariff began. The intuition of producer surplus can be seen with another example. If a student who is seeking a summer job is willing to accept a wage of $6.00 per hour but is fortunate enough to find a job paying $7.50, the student receives producer surplus of $1.50 times the number of hours for which he or she is paid $7.50 when $6.00 would have been acceptable.

[2]This result is obtained directly from the figure.

$$\text{Area } b = [Q_1Q_2] \cdot T \cdot \frac{1}{2}$$

$$\text{Area } d = [Q_3Q_4] \cdot T \cdot \frac{1}{2}$$

$$\text{Area } b + \text{Area } d = \frac{1}{2} \cdot T[Q_1Q_2 + Q_3Q_4]$$

products, one must evaluate the effects on consumers and producers and reach a judgment about where the balance lies. Political factors often play a prominent role in these debates.

This partial equilibrium analysis is extremely simple. Despite the many assumptions on which it rests, it is very powerful, and it yields some very strong and significant results. Before leaving the small-country case, we can modify our example to explain the effects of alternative techniques of intervention.

QUOTAS AND OTHER NONTARIFF TRADE BARRIERS

As was noted earlier, barriers to trade other than tariffs have become far more important in recent years as governments have looked for ways to restrict imports without raising tariffs that were reduced in GATT negotiations. As also noted earlier, quotas, which are limits on the physical volume of a product that may be imported per period of time, are the most common NTB, but there are many others. It is important to note the following: The mere fact that a policy reduces imports does not make it a trade barrier; it must discriminate against imports relative to domestic alternatives. Higher gasoline taxes would reduce imports of oil, but would equally discourage consumption of domestic oil and would therefore not be a trade barrier.

The restrictive effect of an NTB on imports is sometimes a secondary result of a policy directed at another objective, and may even be unintentional. Packaging and labeling requirements, for example, are easy for domestic firms to meet, because most sales will be in a market where they apply. They may be quite difficult or expensive for foreign firms, however, because only a small fraction of sales will be in this packaging or labeling format, and the cost of separate arrangements for these exports becomes prohibitive. For example, when Canada adopted rules requiring that all domestic labels be in both English and French, U.S. firms that sold small volumes of products in Canada faced high costs of compliance and a few may have decided to withdraw from the Canadian market. When the United States adopted automobile safety rules, Ford, General Motors, and Chrysler simply produced all domestic cars to meet the new specifications, but foreign firms faced a problem. For their local sales, no such rules held and the cars were not changed. To sell in the United States, however, the cars would have to be redesigned to meet U.S. rules. For firms such as Volkswagen, which had large sales volumes here, the cost per car of making the changes was acceptable, and they remained in this market. A few firms that had only small U.S. sales, however, decided that the redesign cost per car was excessive and withdrew from the U.S. market for a few years. These firms later returned with cars that met the U.S. rules, but for a few years these safety rules acted as an unintentional barrier to imports.

Most NTBs are decidedly intentional, but they are sometimes disguised to look like a policy directed at another goal. Product quality standards are sometimes designed to keep out foreign products while seeming to have another purpose. Countries sometimes have administrative reasons for slowing the passage of goods through customs. If the products are perishable or are directed at a seasonal market, such slowdowns can effectively keep imports out of a local market.

Governmental procurement rules are probably the most important NTB other than quotas. Such rules usually require that, whenever government money is being spent, domestic products must be purchased even if they are more expensive or less useful than imported alternatives. U.S. government employees or those on U.S. government grants, for example, must use U.S. flag carriers when flying to Europe, even if foreign carriers are cheaper or have more convenient schedules. Many governments have similar rules, although they may be eliminated within Europe in 1992, which would mean that a French firm would be able to compete equally with German firms in bidding on German government contracts.

Quotas

GATT supposedly outlawed quotas for manufactured goods decades ago, but they are in fact increasingly common in the form of so-called "Voluntary Export Restraints" (VERs). Under a VER arrangement, the importing country does not maintain a limit on the amount to be imported, but exporting countries voluntarily limit the volume being sent out to an agreed-upon level. Exporting countries often agree to maintain VERs out of fear that failure to do so will lead the importing country to adopt far more severe measures. The U.S. Office of the Special Trade Representative often negotiates VERs with exporting countries while the Congress is considering prohibitive limits on imports, and the successful negotiation of the VER is then used to convince the Congress that the more severe measures are not necessary. The VER system also has some particular advantages for exporting firms, which will become clear in the discussion of Figure 6-2.

This graph is quite similar to the earlier presentation (Figure 6-1) for a tariff. The line segment Q_1-Q_2 represents the volume allowed into the country, so the domestic supply curve begins again to the right of that volume. Areas a and a' are the increase in producer surplus for the domestic industry, and areas b and d

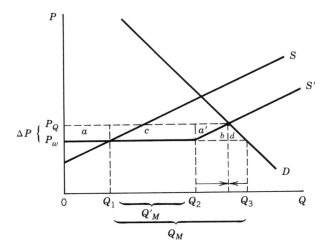

FIGURE 6-2 The effects of a quota: partial equilibrium, small-country case.

are the same deadweight losses that appeared earlier. The effects on the price of the product, domestic consumption, and domestic production are similar to those depicted in Figure 6-1.

Area c, however, is different. If a tariff is maintained, that area is government revenue that can be used to satisfy public purposes or to allow the reduction of other taxes. Under a quota, however, that money goes to whoever is fortunate enough to have the right to ship the product from the exporting to the importing country. If quota rights are allocated to importers, they receive the windfall profit. If, for example, oil can be purchased on the world market at $1.50 per barrel and shipped to the East Coast of the United States for $0.75 per barrel for a total landed cost of $2.25 when a U.S. quota is being used to protect an internal price of approximately $3.50, those allowed to bring oil into the United States receive a gift of $1.25 per barrel. They land oil here at a cost of $2.25, and it is immediately worth $3.50. This example is not accidental; it was the situation prevailing from the 1950s into the 1960s in this country, and it produced enormous monopoly rents for the major oil companies that were allocated quota rights by Washington.

In the case of a VER, however, it is the exporting country that limits the volume shipped, and it can allocate the rights and determine who gets the windfall profits. In this case the bonanza goes to exporting firms rather than to importers, which explains why exporting countries often accept VERs. The VER on Japanese cars that limited sales in the United States to 1.85 million cars per year during the early 1980s had the effect of raising U.S. car prices by almost $1000 per car.[3] That meant an additional profit of about $1.85 billion per year for the Japanese car companies. They were forced to reduce sales here but were compensated through a gift of almost $2 billion per year, with the Japanese government deciding how the money was to be divided among the firms.

If the U.S. government had auctioned the quota rights to the highest bidder, the Treasury would have recaptured the monopoly rents through the auction revenues. If the international market for cars and therefore the auction were competitive, firms would bid approximately the area of the windfall profit rectangle for the right to bring cars into this market. Such auctions are held in some countries, but it is much more common for governments to allocate these valuable rights arbitrarily, which creates obvious opportunities for graft and corruption. The allocation of quotas can be a source of bribery if importers (or exporters in a VER) offer money to government officials in charge of deciding who gets the rights. Political campaigns can be financed by promising later allocations to those who contribute now.

The Multi Fibre Arrangement (MFA) in textiles and garments is probably the world's largest quota system, and it allows exporting countries to decide which firms will sell what quantities in the U.S. market. During a recent visit by one of the authors to a cotton spinning mill in India, the owner said that a spool of yarn was worth $10 if it could be exported under an MFA quota, but only $8 if it had to be sold in the domestic market. Quota rights are extremely valuable, and it is hardly surprising

---

[3]Robert Crandall, "Import Quotas and the Automobile Industry: The Costs of Protectionism," *Brookings Review,* Summer, 1984, reprinted in Robert Baldwin and J. David Richardson, eds., *International Trade and Finance: Readings,* 3rd ed. (Boston: Little, Brown, 1986), pp. 62–73.

that their allocation can be the source of corruption. If the rights were auctioned in a competitive market, this problem would disappear and the operations of a quota would resemble those of a tariff, but such auctions are rare.

Quotas also create a problem of legal evasion, for exporters can resort to a number of strategies to reduce their protective effects. First, they can upgrade the product to sharply increase revenues and profits from a given volume that can be exported. During the period in which Japanese firms were limited to selling 1.85 million cars per year in the United States, for example, virtually all of the cars exported to the United States were top of the line models and had a variety of expensive options. U.S. firms were left with the less profitable lower end of the market. In addition, exporting firms can send major components for final assembly in the importing country, since such components are not subject to the quota. So-called screw driver factories are set up to do the final assembly of these products.

Finally, if quotas are assigned to an exporting country, products may be shipped to an intermediate stop, where they are relabeled and then sent on to the final market outside the quota. Indian manufacturers, for example, have been known to send 90 percent completed garments to Nepal or Mauritius, where the final work is done. They are then labeled as being from Nepal or Mauritius, and are sent to the United States outside of India's MFA quota. U.S. authorities eventually stop such imports, but by then the Indian exporters have found another small country from which to operate.

SUBSIDIES

Domestic production can also be increased and imports reduced through the use of a production subsidy. We show this case in Figure 6-3, which represents

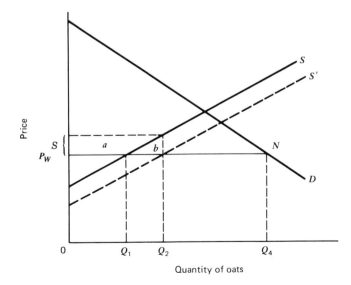

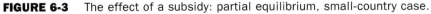

FIGURE 6-3 The effect of a subsidy: partial equilibrium, small-country case.

exactly the same initial situation as in Figure 6-1. If a subsidy equal to S (per unit) is paid to producers in Country A, their supply curve shifts from S to S' because the subsidy reduces average and marginal cost of production, and they will expand output to OQ_2. Since the price of oats in Country A remains at P_W, consumers continue to purchase OQ_4, and imports are Q_2Q_4. Because the price of oats remains unchanged at P_W, the loss of consumers' surplus does not occur. The subsidy to domestic producers must be included in government expenditures, however, and may be treated as a transfer payment to producers from the rest of the economy. The amount of the subsidy appears in Figure 6-3 as area a plus area b. Taxes in that amount must be levied to pay it. Area a is a pure transfer from taxpayers to producers, but area b involves the same inefficiency in resource use as before and can therefore be regarded as a deadweight loss. Since the subsidy does not reduce consumption, however, we avoid the other part of deadweight loss (area d in Figure 6-1). The conclusion is that a production subsidy is preferable to a tariff on welfare grounds: It has a smaller deadweight loss, and it leaves consumption unchanged.

Although subsidies are a less inefficient means of increasing domestic output, they are relatively uncommon because they are politically unpopular. A tariff raises money for the government, and a quota appears to be costless, but the taxpayers have to provide the funds for a subsidy. The benefits of a subsidy in the form of a lower price to consumers are frequently not understood by voters who instead object to the resulting expenditure of public funds. The domestic industry does not want to be seen as the recipient of a public handout and instead prefers a tariff or quota (particularly if it is allocated the import rights) which is a more indirect and less obvious form of public support. Subsidies are the least inefficient method of encouraging domestic output, but they are also the most unpopular.

THE LARGE-COUNTRY CASE

Returning to the subject of tariffs, we can extend the earlier partial equilibrium analysis to deal with the case in which Country A is large enough to influence the world price when it changes the amount of its imports of a given commodity, such as oats. To deal with such a case we will assume a two-country world in which both countries, A and B, are producing and consuming oats. We continue to ignore the effects of any change on the rest of the economy (i.e., outside of the oats industry).

In Figure 6-4 we show demand and supply curves for both countries, A and B. The only novel aspect of this diagram is that the quantity axis for Country B runs from right to left. The vertical axis representing price is the same for both countries. Country A's demand and supply curves are drawn in the conventional manner, but Country B's demand curve slopes downward from right to left, and its supply curve slopes upward from right to left. The reason for this construction is that we measure quantity for Country B from the origin, O, in a leftward direction. (To visualize

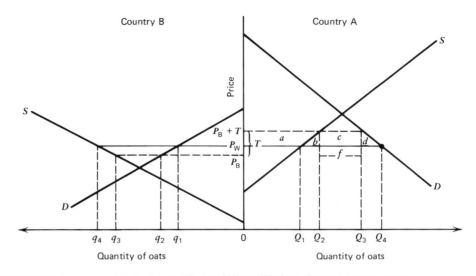

FIGURE 6-4 The effect of a tariff: partial equilibrium, large-country case.

the construction of this figure, the reader might imagine drawing Country B's demand and supply curves in the conventional manner and then, with a hinge along the vertical axis, flipping the figure over from right to left.)

Note that if no trade in oats were allowed, so that both countries were self-sufficient, the price of oats would be higher in Country A than in Country B. (The market-clearing price in each country would be the price at which the supply and demand curves intersect.) When trade is allowed, therefore, Country A will import oats from Country B.

In free-trade equilibrium, two conditions must be satisfied: Country A's imports must equal Country B's exports, and the price must be the same in the two countries. Graphically, we can visualize the determination of that equilibrium position by sliding a horizontal price line down the diagram until the point is reached at which Country A's excess demand exactly equals Country B's excess supply. In Figure 6-4, this free-trade equilibrium price is P_W. Country A's imports, Q_1Q_4, exactly equal Country B's exports, q_1q_4.

Now suppose that Country A imposes a specific tariff on its imports of oats, a tariff equal to T per bushel. What will be the effect on price in the two countries? We know that in the new equilibrium the price in Country A will exceed the price in Country B by the amount of the tariff. But to reach this new equilibrium the price will rise in Country A and fall in Country B. It is clear that we cannot simply add the tariff to the initial world price, because at such a price, $P_W + T$, Country A will import less than Country B is willing to export at the price P_W.

Once again, two conditions must be satisfied: Country A's imports must equal Country B's exports, and the price in Country A must exceed the price in Country B by exactly T. As before, we can graphically find that point by sliding a price line down the diagram (the price line now has a step in it, a differential equal to

T) until B's exports equal A's imports. In Figure 6-4, that point is reached at the price P_B in Country B and $P_B + T$ in Country A, with B's exports, q_2q_3, equal to A's imports, Q_2Q_3.

Using the right-hand side of Figure 6-4, we can now examine the effects of the tariff on Country A in the same way that we did for the small-country case. The price of oats has risen in Country A, but not by as much as the tariff, and it has fallen in Country B. The higher price in Country A stimulates domestic production, which rises from OQ_1 to OQ_2, and reduces consumption, which falls from OQ_4 to OQ_3. Imports fall from Q_1Q_4 to Q_2Q_3. The welfare effects are exactly the same as before, except that we must be careful to show tariff revenue in Country A as the tariff times the new level of imports (Q_2Q_3). Tariff revenue is larger than area c, representing the portion of consumers' surplus lost in Country A when the price of oats increased; it also includes area f. What this means is that the foreigner (Country B) is being made to bear some of the burden of the tariff.

How the tariff will be divided between a price rise in Country A and a price decline in Country B depends on the elasticities of demand and supply in the two countries, as the reader can verify by a little experimentation. We will consider a few polar cases to illustrate this relationship.

First, suppose that Country B's supply curve in Figure 6-4 is perfectly elastic. In that case, the price in Country B remains unchanged when Country A imposes a tariff, and the price in A rises by the full amount of the tariff. This is the case in which Country A is a small country, already discussed in the previous section. The tariff does not affect the price; the terms of trade remain unchanged.

Second, suppose that Country B's supply curve is perfectly inelastic (it is vertical in the relevant range) and that Country B has *no* domestic demand for the commodity it produces. This latter assumption may seem a bit odd, but it is a fairly close approximation to reality for a number of primary-product exporters. (For example, Malaya consumes a negligible amount of tin, its major export; Bolivia's domestic consumption of copper is a tiny fraction of its production.) Alternatively, we could assume that Country B's supply and demand are both perfectly inelastic. We show this case in Figure 6-5. Initially, with free trade, price is P_W and Country A imports Q_1Q_2. Now when Country A levies a tariff on its imports of the commodity, the price in Country B simply falls by the full amount of the tariff. The price in Country A remains unchanged. The reason for this result is that producers in Country B are unwilling to reduce the amount they export when the price falls. Since the price in Country A is unchanged, that country's imports are unaffected by the tariff. In effect, the entire tariff revenue collected by Country A (area f in Figure 6-5) is paid by Country B's producers, whose export proceeds are reduced by exactly that amount. This is called "making the foreigner pay the tax." and it means that the tariff has caused the terms of trade to turn against Country B.

We might expect countries in the position of Country B to object in this situation, and so they do, but oddly enough the loudest complaints often come from countries in the position of Country A. More specifically, producers in Country A complain because the tariff has had no protective effect: It has not reduced imports or

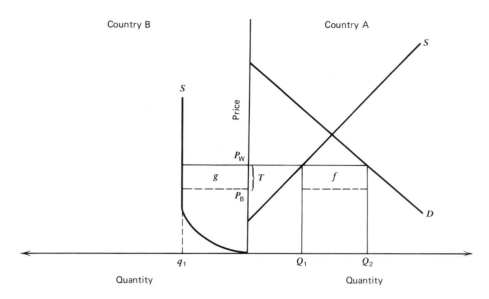

FIGURE 6-5   Making the foreigner pay the tariff: inelastic foreign supply.

increased the price in Country A; consequently, A's producers have not obtained any increase in producers' surplus.

In such circumstances, the producers in Country A are likely to advocate the use of a quota instead of a tariff. Because it sets a physical limit on the quantity of imports, a quota will reduce the supply of imports and cause the price in Country A to rise. The certainty of this result is a principal reason why many U.S. industries have urged the use of quotas instead of tariffs as a means of protecting them from import competition. Thus in this case we find that the effect of a tariff and a quota are not identical. It may be, however, that there exists a tariff large enough to reduce imports and thus to stimulate domestic output in Country A by the same amount as our quota.

Another interesting point to note about this example is that the tariff could be levied equally well by the exporting country, B. The only difference—an important one—is that the tariff revenue would then accrue to Country B's government instead of Country A's. Country B would be taxing away a part (area g) of the export proceeds. Such export tariffs are common in many developing countries where income taxes and other forms of taxation are difficult and costly to administer. It is often very easy and convenient to levy a tariff on a few highly visible export commodities, the trade in which is concentrated in one or two major seaports.

This point leads to our third example: the case of OPEC taxation of petroleum exports to the rest of the world. Let us treat this as a two-country case: oil exporters and oil importers. We will assume that the oil exporters' supply curve is perfectly inelastic, not because output cannot be increased at higher prices, but simply because the governments of oil-exporting countries are fixing the quantity of their production and export. We will ignore domestic demand in oil-exporting countries. (In many countries, such as Saudi Arabia and Libya, domestic demand is negligible.) Thus we show the position of oil-exporting countries in the left half of Figure 6-6.

Let us assume that both the demand for and the supply of petroleum in the oil-importing countries are perfectly inelastic. Obviously, neither of these assumptions is exactly right, but they are not far off the mark in the very short run. Higher prices will encourage exploration and stimulate output in oil-importing countries (North Sea oil, the Alaskan slope), but this response takes time and can be ignored for our present purposes. Similarly, demand in oil-importing countries may have some elasticity: Conservation measures have some effect as price goes up, and other energy sources may be sought to replace petroleum. But again, for simplicity we show in Figure 6-6 (right half) the polar extreme of zero elasticity for both demand and supply above the initial price.

Suppose the price initially is $3 per barrel, with exports (and imports) of 5 billion barrels. The export proceeds of oil-exporting countries amount to $15 billion. Then the oil exporters get together and agree to levy an export tariff of $9 per barrel. The price rises to $12 per barrel in oil-importing countries, yet imports remain unchanged at 5 billion barrels. Oil-exporting countries obtain an increase in their revenues of $45 billion. In effect, they have imposed a tax of this magnitude on the oil-importing countries (area g in Figure 6-6).

Although we have oversimplified the circumstances in this example, the analysis nevertheless captures some of the essential features of the oil price increase in 1973.

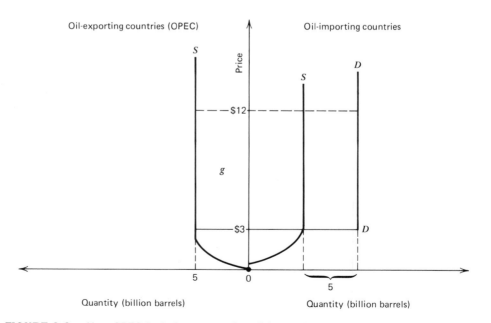

FIGURE 6-6 How OPEC levied a tax on the oil-importing countries.

GENERAL EQUILIBRIUM ANALYSIS

Although the foregoing analysis has enabled us to reach many useful conclusions about the nature and effects of tariffs, it is partial and it does leave out some significant aspects of the matter. For example, when a tariff causes the output of a particular commodity to rise in Country A, resources must be drawn into that industry, but we do not see what happens in other industries from which those resources must be taken. (Assuming full employment, output of other commodities must fall.) Similarly, when Country A's imports decline, other countries will themselves have less money to spend on imports; therefore Country A's exports will also decline. Import tariffs have many such effects that reverberate through the economy; to deal with these in a comprehensive way we must utilize a form of general equilibrium analysis.

One approach is to use the tools of analysis that we developed in Chapters 2 to 4: the production-possibility curve and community indifference map. These tools bring us back to the abstract world of two countries, two commodities, two factors, perfect competition, and all the other Heckscher-Ohlin assumptions. We will also assume that the tariff revenue is redistributed to consumers.

The Small-Country Case

As usual, it is convenient to start with a small country, so we can assume that the world terms of trade remain unchanged. The reader will recall that we reached the conclusion in Chapter 3 that in free-trade equilibrium, assuming only two commodities, food and cloth, Country A will maximize its welfare by producing at the point where its domestic ratio of marginal costs equals the world terms of trade, and then by engaging in trade in order to reach the highest possible indifference curve.

Such a free-trade equilibrium is shown in Figure 6-7, with the world price ratio shown by the slope of TT, production at point P_1, and consumption at point C_1, where TT is tangent to the indifference curve i_2. Country A exports cloth and imports food.

Now if Country A imposes a tariff on its imports of food, the first effect will be to increase the domestic price of food, thus causing a divergence between the domestic terms of trade and the world terms of trade. We show this effect in Figure 6-7; the domestic terms of trade become equal to the slope of DD, which is flatter than TT, indicating a higher relative price of food. It is said that the tariff drives a wedge between the domestic and external price ratios; geometrically, that wedge can be seen as the angle between the two price lines.

The higher price of food induces firms to expand food production and to reduce cloth production. The production point moves to P_2, where the domestic price line (DD) is tangent to the production-possibility curve.

Because we are assuming that the world price ratio remains unchanged, international trade takes place along the line P_2C_2 (parallel to TT). A new equilibrium in consumption is reached when two conditions are satisfied: (1) A domestic price

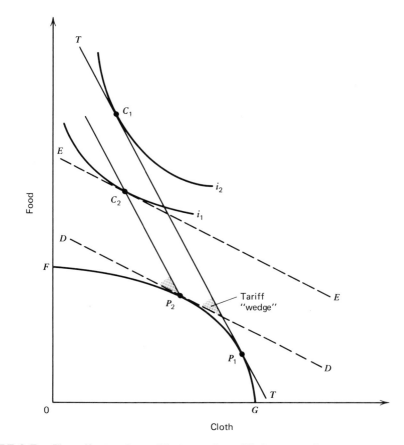

FIGURE 6-7   The effects of a tariff: general equilibrium, small-country case.

line, *EE,* whose slope is equal to the tariff-distorted domestic price ratio, is tangent to a community indifference curve; and (2) the world price line, P_2C_2, intersects the community indifference curve at its point of tangency with the domestic price line, *EE.* These two conditions are both satisfied at the point C_2 in Figure 6-7. Technically, the first condition guarantees that the marginal rate of substitution in consumption equals the domestic price ratio facing consumers; the second condition satisfies the requirement that the domestic price ratio diverges from the world price ratio exactly in proportion to the tariff.

In the new equilibrium, Country A continues to export cloth and import food but in smaller quantities than before. The tariff has stimulated domestic production of food, reducing Country A's dependence on food imports. It has also reduced domestic output and exports of cloth and reduced welfare, as indicated by the movement to the lower indifference curve, from i_2 to i_1. Thus we reach the same conclusion in both general and partial equilibrium analysis: In the small-country case a tariff reduces national welfare.

► **The Large-Country Case**

When the country imposing a tariff is large enough to influence the world price of what it buys, we must consider what effect a tariff will have on the world price ratio. To continue the same example, when Country A levies a tariff on food, the result may be that the world price of food falls relative to the price of cloth.

In that event, for a given *ad valorem* tariff, the domestic price of food will not rise as much as before. Thus the shift in production will be somewhat smaller. We illustrate this outcome in Figure 6-8, where conditions are the same as in the case just described except that the tariff now causes the world price ratio to change from the slope of the line TT to the slope of the line P_3C_3. Production takes place at P_3. (Note that the tariff is the same proportion as before, as measured by the size of the wedge.)

International trade now takes place at the world price ratio (i.e., along the line P_3C_3). A new equilibrium in consumption is reached at point C_3, where the tariff-distorted domestic price line is tangent to a community indifference curve, and the world price line also passes through this point of tangency. As drawn in Figure 6-8, Country A reaches a higher indifference curve as a result of the tariff. This result is not inevitable, however. It depends on the magnitude of the change in the world terms of trade. Intuitively, one can see that Country A benefits from the tariff when its gain from the improved terms of trade outweighs its loss from a less efficient use of domestic resources. How much its terms of trade will improve depends in turn on domestic and foreign elasticities of demand and supply.

The terms-of-trade effect of a tariff can also be seen with the aid of offer curves, although the welfare effect cannot be shown without further complicating the diagram. Suppose we have offer curves OA for Country A and OB for Country B, as portrayed in Figure 6-9. With free trade, equilibrium is at point E; the terms of trade are given by the vector OE; Country A exports OC of cloth and imports OF of food. If Country A imposes an *ad valorem* tariff on its food imports, its offer curve shifts from OA to OA'. The terms of trade turn in favor of Country A, from OE to OE'.

The less elastic Country B's offer curve, the more the terms of trade will shift in favor of Country A. If Country B's offer curve is perfectly elastic, the terms of trade will not change at all. For example, in Figure 6-9, if the vector OE represented Country B's offer curve, the tariff imposed by Country A would reduce its exports and imports, but would leave the terms of trade unchanged. The new equilibrium would be at E''. (This is the small-country case again.)

Thus we conclude that if a country faces an offer curve in the rest of the world that is less than perfectly elastic, it can improve its terms of trade by imposing a tariff on imports. The benefit from the improved terms of trade may be large enough to exceed the loss from less efficient resource use, leaving the country with a net gain in economic welfare. We should note, however, that this gain is at the expense of the rest of the world. If other countries act in concert, they can retaliate by imposing tariffs of their own, thus causing the terms of trade to shift back the other way.

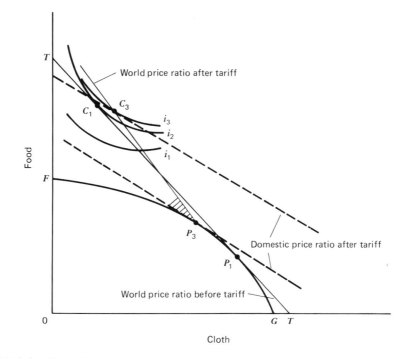

FIGURE 6-8 The effects of a tariff: general equilibrium, large-country case.

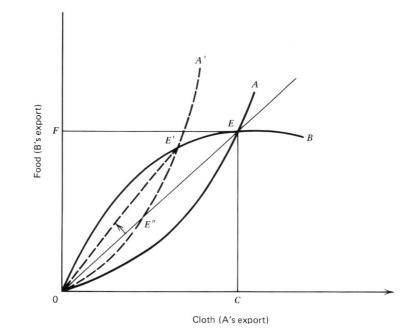

FIGURE 6-9 The effect of a tariff on the terms of trade.

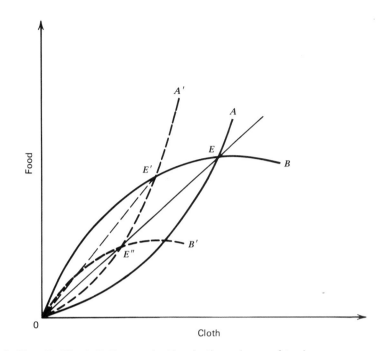

FIGURE 6-10   Tariff retaliation: reduction in the volume of trade.

For example, suppose that Country A levies a tariff and succeeds in shifting the terms of trade from OE to OE', as in Figure 6-10 (the same situation presented in Figure 6-9). Country B may resent this action and respond by imposing tariffs of its own, say, by shifting its offer curve to OB'. Now the equilibrium is at the intersection of the two tariff-distorted offer curves, that is, at point E''. In this case, the terms of trade are back to the free-trade ratio (not a necessary result), but world trade is greatly reduced and so is world welfare. A trade agreement for the mutual, reciprocal reduction of tariffs would be beneficial to both countries.

THE EFFECTIVE TARIFF

In the foregoing discussion of trade and protection, we have taken it for granted that a given commodity is wholly produced in one country. For example, a yard of cloth is the output that results from using a certain combination of inputs of primary factors of production (land, labor, capital) in that country. We have ignored the case in which some of the inputs, or some parts of the commodity, are imported. Thus we have ignored the large and important trade in intermediate products.

For many purposes, this omission is harmless. The essential aspects of the analysis are not affected by it. But for analysis of tariffs, and especially for measurement of their protective effect, the treatment of intermediate products makes a great deal of difference. The key point is that when a producer has the option of importing some of the material inputs required for the production of a given product, the *ad valorem* tariff on that product may not accurately indicate the protection being provided to the producer. A distinction needs to be drawn between the nominal tariff rate, which is just the usual *ad valorem* tariff or its equivalent, and the "effective tariff rate." The latter phrase, "effective tariff," is not particularly apt, but it is now generally accepted and we shall therefore use it.

The effective tariff rate refers to the level of protection being provided to a particular process of production by the given nominal tariffs on a product and on material inputs used in its production. It takes account of the fact that what is important to the producing firm is the size of the margin it has between its selling price and its materials costs. That margin, the firm's "value added," is what is available to cover primary factor costs, such as payments for the services of labor and capital, and also the net profit of the firm. Conceptually, a business firm purchases certain raw materials and intermediate products from other industries and transforms them into output, adding value to them in the process. The larger the margin of value added, the more leeway the firm has in which to work. Thus the question is, How is the value-added margin affected by nominal tariffs on the firm's output and on its material inputs?

This leads us to a definition: The effective tariff rate, or the effective rate of protection, is the percentage increase in an industry's value added per unit of output that results from a country's tariff structure. The standard of comparison is value added under free trade.

An example will help to explain the meaning of this definition. Suppose the world price of shoes is $20 and that it takes $12 worth of leather (also at the free-trade world price) to make a pair of shoes. In the manufacture of shoes, then, value added at world prices is $8. Now suppose Country A levies a nominal tariff of 30 percent on shoe imports but allows leather to be imported duty free. The price of shoes in Country A would rise to $26 (i.e., the world price plus the tariff), and consequently domestic shoe producers would have a margin of $14 for value added ($26 − $12). In other words, they could incur factor costs of $14 and still be competitive with a foreign firm whose factor costs were $8. Value added in Country A can be 75 percent larger than value added at the free-trade price [($14 − $8)/$8 = 75 percent]. Thus the effective tariff rate is 75 percent, and the nominal tariff is 30 percent. In summary, we have the following comparison between a shoe-producing firm in Country A and its free-trade competitor:

	Firm in Country A	Free-Trade Competitor
Shoe price	$26	$20
Leather input	$12	$12
Value added	$14	$ 8

$$\text{Effective tariff rate} = \frac{\text{value added in Country A} - \text{value added in free trade}}{\text{value added in free trade}}$$

$$= \frac{\$14 - \$8}{\$8} = 75 \text{ percent}$$

Note that a tariff on leather would reduce the effective tariff rate on shoes. The reason is obvious: A tariff on leather increases the price of leather in Country A and thus cuts into the value-added margin of a domestic shoe producer. In our example, a 20 percent nominal tariff on leather would lead to the following result (we assume the nominal tariff on shoes stays at 30 percent):

	Firm in Country A	**Free-Trade Competitor**
Shoe price	$26.00	$20.00
Leather input	$14.40	$12.00
Value added	$11.60	$ 8.00

$$\text{Effective tariff rate} = \frac{\$11.60 - \$8.00}{\$8.00} = 45 \text{ percent}$$

The effective tariff rate on shoes has fallen from 75 percent to 45 percent as a result of the tariff on leather. Clearly, shoe producers in Country A will tend to favor tariffs on shoes but oppose tariffs on leather.

A formula for calculating the effective tariff rate follows from the above discussion:

$$(1) \quad e_j = \frac{t_j - \sum a_{ij} \cdot t_i}{1 - \sum a_{ij}}$$

where e_j = the effective tariff rate in industry j
t_j = the nominal tariff rate in industry j
t_i = the nominal tariff rate in industry i
a_{ij} = the share of inputs from industry i in the value of output of industry j, at free-trade prices

The operation of the formula may usefully be illustrated with our second preceding numerical example, where we have:

t_j = 30% = the nominal tariff on shoes
t_i = 20% = the nominal tariff on leather
a_{ij} = 0.60 = share of leather in the value of shoes at free-trade prices ($12/20)

Therefore, the effective tariff rate for shoes is:

$$e_j = \frac{30\% - 0.60(20\%)}{1 - 0.60} = \frac{18\%}{0.40} = \frac{0.18}{0.40} = 45 \text{ percent}$$

In this example we had only a single intermediate input, leather. In actual practice, a given product may have many intermediate inputs, each having its own nominal tariff rate. The formula uses the share of each such input (a_{ij}) to weight the nominal tariff rates in forming the sum ($\sum a_{ij} t_i$).

In recent years, effective tariff rates have been calculated for many countries and a large number of industries. In most cases, effective tariff rates turn out to be higher than nominal rates, sometimes a great deal higher. The reason is that the tariff structures of most countries show a systematic pattern in which nominal tariff rates increase as the stage of production advances—that is, tariff rates are low (or zero) on raw materials, higher on semifinished products, and highest on finished manufactures. Such a pattern in nominal tariff rates produces an even greater escalation in effective tariff rates, with very high protection being accorded the higher stages of manufacture. Many advanced industrial countries, which used to point with pride to their very low tariffs on raw material imports, have been accused of using such a tariff structure to preserve their lead in manufacturing and to keep the underdeveloped countries from developing exports of finished manufactures. Needless to say, underdeveloped countries have seized on this point and used it to support their complaints about the operation of the system of international trade.[4]

Although effective tariff rates are usually higher than nominal rates, they can also be lower. In our shoe industry example, if the nominal tariff on leather were increased to 40 percent, then the effective tariff rate for shoes would be only 15 percent. The calculation is as follows:

$$e = \frac{30\% - 0.60(40\%)}{1 - 0.60} = 15 \text{ percent}$$

The effective tariff rate can also be negative. The economic meaning of such a rate is that a firm must pay such high nominal tariffs on its imported inputs that it is actually at a disadvantage in comparison to its free-trade competitors in the outside world. That is, its value-added margin is less than that of a free-trade competitor. In our shoe industry example, if the nominal tariff on leather were 60 percent, then the effective tariff on shoes would be -15 percent:

$$e = \frac{30\% - 0.60(60\%)}{1 - 0.60} = -15 \text{ percent}$$

The disadvantage of the domestic firm is shown in the following comparison:

	Firm in Country A	Free-Trade Competitor
Shoe price	$26.00	$20.00
Leather input	$19.20	$12.00
Value added	$ 6.80	$ 8.00

---

[4]For estimates of nominal and effective rates of protection for the United States, Japan, and the European Community both before and after the effects of the Tokyo GATT Round tariff cuts, see Alan Deardorff and Robert M. Stern, "The Effects of the Tokyo Round on the Structure of Protection," in R. E. Baldwin and Anne O. Krueger, eds., *The Structure and Evolution of Recent U.S. Trade Policy,* (Chicago: University of Chicago Press, 1984), pp. 370–375.

To compete with a foreign firm whose factor costs are $8.00, the firm in Country A must hold its factor costs to $6.80.

Because of the escalated tariff structure mentioned earlier, negative effective tariff rates are rather unusual in import-competing manufactured products, but they turn up more often among a nation's export products. The nominal tariff on an export product is zero because it is being sold in foreign countries at the world market price. Therefore, if firms producing the export item use any imported inputs at all that are subject to tariffs, their effective tariff rate is negative. Suppose, for example, that Thailand exports rice at the world market price, whereas rice production uses imported inputs such as fertilizer, water pumps, and tractors, on which nominal tariffs are levied. The result is that the value-added margin of Thai rice producers is lower, because of the nation's tariff structure, than it would be under full free trade. The effective tariff on rice is negative.

One of the benefits derived from recent discussion of the concept of effective protection has been a better understanding of the interindustry aspects of tariffs. In many countries, exports are severely handicapped by negative effective protection, and politicians are beginning to realize that the tariffs they impose on certain import-competing commodities may end up having a restrictive effect on the country's exports.

Before leaving this topic, we should note that thorny problems arise in the actual calculation of effective rates of protection. One needs a complete input-output table, or interindustry matrix, for the country concerned, but these are often not available. Sometimes the table of another country is used, and it is simply assumed that the input coefficients (a_{ij} in equation 1) are the same. A more fundamental problem is the assumption, made in all input-output analyses, that the input coefficients are fixed constants, unaffected by changes in prices. We know that international trade causes changes in relative prices and shifts in the allocation of resources. It seems likely that these changes will also affect the amounts of various inputs used to produce a particular product, but the concept of the effective tariff does not allow for this influence.

EXPORT SUBSIDIES

Thus far it has been assumed that government regulation of international trade is intended solely to restrict imports. Although that remains the dominant form of intervention, governments sometimes attempt to encourage exports through subsidies. This may occur because of a desire to improve a country's trade account, aid a politically powerful industry, or help a depressed region in which an export industry is located. The subsidy may be a simple cash payment to exporters, but frequently is more indirect or subtle. Research and development grants, favorable tax treatment, or a variety of other government benefits may be provided to encourage exports. In order to simplify this discussion, however, it will be assumed that the subsidy takes the form of a fixed cash payment for each unit of a product which is exported. It can therefore be viewed as a negative export tariff.

Figure 6-11 illustrates the effects of an export subsidy under the assumption that the exporting country is small and that it therefore faces an infinitely elastic demand in the rest of the world.

The subsidy has the effect of allowing exporting firms to receive revenues per unit of P'_d which equals the world price plus the subsidy. The subsidy is not available on domestic sales in the exporting company, so these firms are willing to sell to local customers only at a higher price (P'_d) than prevailed earlier. Export volumes rise from X to X', both because local consumers buy less and because the domestic industry produces more at the higher price. The cost to taxpayers in the subsidizing country is area b + c + d. In addition, domestic residents lose consumer surplus of area a + b. The local industry, however, receives benefits in the form of an increase in producer surplus of area a + b + c.

The dead weight losses are triangles b + d, the first of which is part of the loss of consumer surplus and the latter being a loss of productive efficiency which results from producing goods at a cost (the area under the supply curve) which is higher than the revenues which are received from foreign customers (the area under D_{row}). The interpretation of the dead weight loss triangle b deserves more explanation. It is an area that represents a loss by two parties and a gain for one party. It is part of the lost consumer surplus for domestic residents and part of the cost to taxpayers, but it is also part of the increased producer surplus benefits to the domestic industry. It is a dead weight loss because these units were previously being consumed by

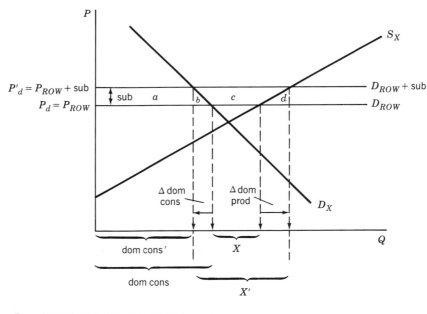

D_X = domestic demand in the exporting country
S_X = supply in the exporting country
D_{ROW} = demand in the rest of the world

FIGURE 6-11   The effects of an export subsidy provided by a small country.

local residents who valued them at the area under their demand curve (D_x), which includes triangle b, but these units are now consumed by foreign consumers who value them only at the area under their demand curve (D_{row}), which excludes this triangle. Benefits to foreign customers from the consumption of these goods are less than the lost benefits to local consumers by the amount of triangle b.

In Figure 6-11 it was assumed that the subsidizing country was small relative to its export market, and therefore that the world price was not affected by the subsidy, which was why the local price rose by the full amount of the subsidy. In the real world, exporting countries may not be small, and the world price may be driven down by the subsidy. Such price declines would provide obvious benefits to consumers in importing countries, but create understandable unhappiness among import competing firms. They face lower prices for their products, reduced profits, and the need to contract their operations. Export subsidies are widely viewed as an unfair competitive tool, and countervailing duties can be imposed on imports that can be proven to have been subsidized.

A major problem exists, however, in defining precisely what is a subsidy that allows a countervailing duty in response. Such a subsidy would obviously exist if a government made direct cash payments to firms in proportion to their export sales, but governments are seldom so obvious. A payment or benefit may exist which appears to be available to firms in an industry without regard to whether sales are domestic or foreign. If the vast majority of subsidized sales are in the export market, however, importing countries are likely to view the payment as an export subsidy and attempt to impose a countervailing duty.

The recent conflict between Canada and the United States with regard to softwood lumber illustrates this problem. British Columbia allows local firms to harvest lumber on provincially owned land in exchange for stumpage fees which are considerably lower than those prevailing in the United States. These cost savings are available on all lumber cut on this land, including that which is sold to Canadian buyers. The U.S. lumber industry, however, views the lower Canadian stumpage fees as an unfair cost advantage for British Columbia, and argues that a subsidy existed which called for a countervailing duty. The International Trade Administration of the U.S. Department of Commerce has supported the position of the U.S. industry, and a 6.4 percent countervailing duty has been proposed. The Canadian government and lumber producers in British Columbia feel that the U.S. decision is unfair, and an appeals process is being pursued.

If any government policy which benefits an exporting industry can be viewed as an export subsidy which allows a countervailing duty, conflicts such as the U.S.-Canada lumber case will be never-ending. This problem can be solved only if an export subsidy can be defined more precisely and if all of the major trading countries abide by that definition. This is an obvious topic for trade negotiations and export subsidies are one of the subjects of the current GATT round.[5]

---

[5]For a more detailed treatment of trade subsidies, see G. C. Hufbauer and J. S. Erb, Subsidies in International Trade, Washington, Institute for International Economics, 1984.

QUESTIONS FOR STUDY AND REVIEW

1. Compare the partial equilibrium effects of a tariff in the small-country case and in the large-country case. Explain what the difference is and why it exists.

2. The widget industry in Country A, a small underdeveloped nation, is calling for protection against imports of widgets. Raising the tariff is ruled out because of treaty commitments. You are asked to advise the government of Country A on whether to choose a quota or a subsidy as a means of assisting the domestic industry. State your recommendation and the case for it. (Assume that your boss understands economics! Diagrams are appropriate.)

3. At free-trade prices, a widget sells for $20 and contains $8 worth of tin and $6 worth of rubber. In Country A nominal tariff rates are:

Widgets	40 percent
Tin	20 percent
Rubber	10 percent

   What is the effective tariff rate on widgets in Country A? Explain briefly the economic meaning of your result.

4. How do tariffs affect the distribution of income within the tariff-imposing country?

5. You are given the following information about copper in the United States:

	Situation with Tariff	Situation without Tariff
World price (delivered in N.Y.)	$0.50 per lb	$0.50 per lb
Tariff (specific)	$0.15 per lb	0
U.S. domestic price	$0.65 per lb	$0.50 per lb
U.S. consumption	200 million lb	250 million lb
U.S. production	160 million lb	100 million lb

   Calculate:

   a. The gain to U.S. consumers from removing the tariff.

   b. The loss to U.S. producers from removing the tariff.

   c. The loss of tariff revenue to the U.S. government when the tariff is removed.

   d. The net gain or loss to the U.S. economy as a whole.

   Explain briefly the meaning of each calculation. In the case of (d), how might one challenge or dispute the result obtained in the calculation? (*Hint:* draw a demand-supply diagram, assuming linear functions, on the basis of the data given above.)

6. Draw the supply and demand graph for a product for which there is both a tariff and a quota, a situation that applies to most U.S. textile and garment products. (*Hint:* this graph can be derived from Figures 6-1 and 6-2 in this chapter.)

SELECTED REFERENCES

Baldwin, Robert, and Ann Krueger, eds. *The Structure and Evolution of Recent U.S. Trade Policy.* Chicago: University of Chicago Press, 1984.

Bhagwati, Jagdish. *International Trade: Selected Readings.* Cambridge, Mass.: MIT Press, 1981.

Corden, W. M. *The Theory of Protection.* London: Oxford University Press, 1971.

Corden, W. M. *Trade Policy and Economic Welfare.* London: Oxford University Press (Clarendon Press), 1974.

Ellis, H. F., and L. A. Metzler, eds. *Readings in the Theory of International Trade.* Philadelphia: Blakiston, 1949.

Meade, James E. *Trade and Welfare.* London: Oxford University Press, 1955.

7

ARGUMENTS FOR PROTECTION: GOOD AND BAD, MOSTLY BAD

Arguing for protection for different product areas has become one of the major subsectors of Washington lobbying. Many U.S. industries and labor unions want to limit or eliminate competition from imports, and the surge of imports into the United States during the 1980s has made them more active. Lawyers and public relations agents prosper by presenting all sorts of arguments to show why the industry they represent deserves special treatment in the form of a protected home market. Economists working as consultants sometimes turn their skills to proving that the deadweight loss triangles of the last chapter are so small as to be insignificant, and that as a result Americans do not really lose much from protection. The econometric techniques used in these proofs are sometimes tortured, but economists are not immune from the temptation to earn money by providing support for the dubious claims of their employers.

Protectionism versus free trade has always been a source of conflict in the United States, as will be seen in later chapters, but this argument has become more heated in recent years. A broad, if less than universal, consensus existed in Washington during the 25 years following World War II in favor of slow but steady reductions in tariffs and other trade barriers. Some elements of both political parties disagreed, but the leadership groups in both the Congress and the executive branch of government supported gradual trade liberalization. This consensus no longer exists, particularly in the Congress, where protectionist sentiment has become far stronger. U.S. policies have not become significantly more protectionist, but it is now harder to pass measures liberalizing trade and there is a stronger threat of measures being passed that would severely restrict imports. This chapter deals with the reasons for this change and with the various arguments that are being advanced in favor of protection.

It was easier for the United States to favor liberal trade in the era immediately after World War II because this country dominated world markets for a wide range of manufactured goods, ran steady trade surpluses, and faced little competition in its role as the world's strongest economy. The recovery of Europe and Japan and the more recent development of the newly industrialized countries (NICs) in Asia have changed this situation dramatically. Protectionism has become more popular in Washington in part because U.S. firms find the world economy to be a far more competitive environment than it was two decades ago and want relief from that competition. It is easy to advocate free competition when you dominate a market; it is harder when a number of foreign firms are sending attractive products into your domestic market at low prices.

As will be seen in the following discussion, protectionists offer a range of arguments, some of which are simply wrong and others which may be correct in narrow circumstances but which are often used where they are irrelevant. These arguments are sometimes put in very sophisticated forms, but often they are couched in cruder terms that rely on emotional appeals to patriotism. One end of the range of arguments is suggested by the following quotation from an actual congressional hearing.

> *Scissors and shears of all sizes and type are used in every school, retail establishment, office, factory, hospital, and home in the United States. They cannot be classified as a luxury, gimmick, or novelty.*
>
> *They are used to separate us from our mothers at birth, to cut our toe nails, to trim the leather in our shoes, to cut and trim the materials in the clothing we wear. They are used to cut our finger nails, to trim our mustache, the hair in our ears and nose, and to cut the hair on our head—even down to the end of the road when our best suit or dress is cut down the back so that the undertaker can dress us for the last ride. Scissors and shears are truly used from birth to death. They are essential to our health, education, and general welfare. I ask you, gentlemen, is this an industry that should be permitted to become extinct in this country?*
>
> *We request that the Committee report an Orderly Scissors and Shears Marketing Act of 1967 to the Senate.*[1]

---

[1]Statement by B. C. Deuschile, President, Shears, Scissors, and Manicure Implement Manufacturers Association, to the Senate Finance Committee in support of legislation to restrict the importation of foreign products. Published in *Import Quota Legislations, Hearings* before the Committee on Finance, United States Senate, 90th Congress, 1st Session, October 20, 1967, p. 1096.

MAJOR ARGUMENTS FOR RESTRICTING IMPORTS

Increasing Output and Employment

It is often argued that protectionism is a desirable way of increasing output, incomes, and employment because of the multiplier effect of reduced imports. If imports can be cut by $10 billion, it is argued, the resulting $10 billion increase in production of import substitutes will start a Keynesian multiplier process that will ultimately increase domestic output and incomes by far more than $10 billion. If the multiplier were 4, the ultimate increase in GNP would be $40 billion. This superficially attractive argument is simply wrong.

First, domestic output of import-competing goods does not increase by the amount imports decline. In the graphs for tariffs and quotas presented in the previous chapter, such protectionism produced only a partial increase in domestic output; the remainder of the import decline was caused by reduced consumption, with the associated deadweight loss of consumer surplus. If imports decline by $10 billion, domestic production may only rise by $5 billion as consumption falls by the other $5 billion. Recent estimates of the size of the multiplier are not in the range of 4, but are far lower, with some economists suggesting that there really is no predictable multiplier. The increase in output in the above example would not be $40 billion; it might even be less than $10 billion.

In addition, this argument assumes no retaliation by countries that lose export sales and output. Protectionism does not increase employment; rather, it merely shifts it from one country to another, and the country on the losing end of the process is very likely to respond by reclaiming the output and employment with protection of its own. If the United States were to adopt protectionist policies that did serious damage to production and employment in Japan, for example, it is unlikely that the government in Tokyo would remain passive. Retaliation in the form of protectionist policies directed at U.S. exports would follow, with the net result that neither country would gain any output or employment, and both would become less efficient. This sort of protectionism is often referred to as a "beggar my neighbor" policy, and the neighbor can be expected to react strongly to the losses imposed on it.

Finally, this argument for protection ignores the availability of alternative policies to increase output and employment. If a country's level of aggregate demand is insufficient to support acceptable levels of output and employment, expansionary fiscal and/or monetary policies are readily available as a remedy. It might be argued that such policies are inflationary, but protection is even more so. The first impact of a tariff or quota, as illustrated in the graphs in the previous chapter, is to raise prices of the imported good and of import substitutes. Expansionary domestic macroeconomic policies normally become inflationary only when capacity constraints are approached, but the first effect of a tariff or quota is to increase prices.

Under the regime of flexible exchange rates that currently prevails for most industrialized countries, protectionism is even less likely to increase domestic output than if exchange rates were fixed. Under flexible exchange rates, protectionist policies cannot be expected to significantly increase output and employment in the domestic economy because the exchange rate adjusts to largely cancel such an impact. This subject will be discussed in greater detail in the chapter on floating exchange rates in Part II of the book (Chapter 18), but to cover it briefly here, assume that the United States adopts a tariff that cuts domestic demand for Japanese goods by $50 billion. That means a reduction in the supply of dollars in the exchange market of $50 billion and a parallel reduction in the demand for yen. The yen will then depreciate and the dollar appreciate. U.S. goods will become more expensive in Japan and Japanese goods cheaper in this country. Japanese residents will buy fewer U.S. products, and American purchases of Japanese goods will recover. This response of trade flows to the exchange rate should leave the trade balance and the level of output and employment in the United States where it was before the tariff was adopted. Creating jobs and incomes is among the weakest of arguments for protection, but it remains surprisingly popular in Washington.

Closing a Trade Deficit

Countries with large balance-of-payments deficits sometimes view import restraints as a means of reducing or eliminating such problems. The causes and possible solutions for balance of trade problems will be discussed in Part II, but for now it is sufficient to note that such deficits are normally macroeconomic in cause and that solutions are typically to be found in exchange rate and other macroeconomic policies. When a deficit is large enough to threaten foreign exchange reserves, however, governments often seek any short-term policy available, and limits on nonessential imports are sometimes adopted as a stopgap measure.

Pauper Labor

One of the oldest arguments against free trade is based on a simple comparison between foreign wages and those prevailing in the home country. Domestic employers argue that it is impossible for their employees to compete against the pauper labor (i.e., low-wage labor) available abroad. It is frequently noted that U.S. minimum wage laws make it illegal for domestic firms to pay the wages that prevail in some foreign countries from which competing products are imported. If U.S. textile manufacturers are paying workers $8 per hour whereas firms in India are paying the rupee equivalent of $5 per day, it is hardly surprising that American firms feel that they are at an unreasonable competitive disadvantage. They are likely to argue for tariffs that offset these cost differences, thus putting them on a level playing field in competing with imports.

Despite its initial attractions, this is not a sound argument. First, it implicitly assumes that labor is the only cost of production. Capital, raw materials, and a variety of other inputs may be cheaper here, largely offsetting the differences in wage costs. Despite its high wages, the United States actually exports many textile products, particularly those using artificial fibers. Low U.S. prices for natural gas, which is the feedstock for these fibers, give U.S. firms a competitive advantage in this market. European textile firms sometimes claim that these U.S. exports are unfair precisely because our natural gas prices are so much lower than those paid by European producers of the same fibers.

Second, this argument implicitly assumes that there are no differences in labor productivity and that differences in wage rates are fully reflected in parallel differences in unit labor costs. U.S. wage rates have historically been higher than those prevailing abroad precisely because labor productivity was higher here than there. This productivity advantage for the United States may not be as large as it once was, but wage differences can still be expected to reflect parallel labor productivity differences, so unit labor costs diverge by less than wage rates.

Finally, there is the matter of the exchange rate through which wage rate comparisons are made. Because U.S. wages are paid in dollars and Japanese workers receive yen, any conclusion that American wages are higher than those in Japan must be based on the dollar/yen exchange rate, which changes frequently. When the dollar was overvalued in the early 1980s (a subject that will be dealt with later in this book), Japanese firms did have a large cost advantage in this market, but when the dollar depreciated sharply relative to the yen later in the decade, this disadvantage disappeared, and Japanese wages are now comparable to those in the United States. This experience is an argument not for protection, but for exchange rates that more accurately reflect the relative purchasing powers of national currencies.

Heckscher-Ohlin and Factor-Price Equalization

In Chapter 4 it was argued that international trade that is based on differences in factor endowments has the effect of reducing or, under extreme conditions, eliminating differences in factor prices among nations. Free trade then tends to produce a world labor market and a world market for capital, with wage rates and returns to capital that are similar among countries. In each country the relatively abundant factor gains from free trade, but the scarce factor loses. These losses are not temporary and may involve reductions in absolute as well as relative incomes. Since total income rises, those gaining from free trade could compensate the losers and still retain net increases in their incomes, but there is no certainty that compensation will be provided.

For the scarce factor of production this process provides a strong argument for protection. For unskilled and semiskilled laborers in the United States, the fact that free trade would increase total national income is irrelevant. Their incomes would fall relative to the incomes of others, and, in all probability, they would fall in real terms. Labor unions and others representing the interests of labor are understandably determined to restrict imports of labor-intensive products in order to preclude the effects of the factor-price equalization process. For the United States as a whole, the desirability of free trade depends on how the political system values the income losses of workers compared to the larger income gains accruing to other factors. If all dollars are valued equally, free trade retains its attractiveness, but if egalitarian attitudes mean that dollars lost by workers are more highly valued than those gained by other factors of production, free trade may not increase national welfare. Compensation remains an option, but if it is politically impractical or if voters believe it will not be provided, support for protectionism can be rational.

U.S. tariffs and other protectionist policies reflect this egalitarian attitude in that most labor-intensive products are more heavily protected than are capital- or land-intensive goods. The particularly stringent limits on imports of textiles and garments under the Multi-Fibre Arrangement are an example of the attempt to protect the incomes of unskilled and semiskilled workers. If such people were compensated for their losses through taxes and transfer payments that shifted part of the gains from trade from capital and land to labor, this problem could be solved and free trade would be consistent with the goal of protecting real wages. If such compensation is not provided, however, protection can be defended providing a sufficiently higher utility is placed on dollars earned by American workers than on those received by owners of capital and land. It ought to be noted here that only U.S. incomes are included in this calculation. In the developing world, which is relatively labor abundant, a decision by the United States to move to free trade would increase wages and therefore the incomes of low-income workers. Free trade would increase the total incomes of all workers across the world, but it would reduce the incomes of U.S. workers. An American decision to restrict imports on the basis of a desire to protect labor must consider only domestic workers rather than the interests of the world's labor force. The AFL-CIO, however, represents U.S. workers and not workers of the developing world; therefore, its support of tariffs and other restrictions on imports of labor-intensive goods is rational, as long as it believes that compensation will not be provided.

The Terms-of-Trade Argument

By imposing a tariff, a country may be able to turn the terms of trade in its favor, thus increasing the size of its gain per unit of export. This increase may outweigh the influence of a reduced volume of trade, thus increasing its net gain from trade. So runs the terms-of-trade argument, which is also known as the "optimum tariff" case, although it is optimum only for the country imposing the tariff and not for the world.

The analytical basis of this argument was presented in Chapter 6, where we showed that one effect of a tariff may be to reduce the demand for imports enough to cause a fall in the world price of the commodity. This implies that the importing country is large enough to exert an influence on the world price of what it buys and sells (see Figures 6-4 and 6-8 for geometrical illustrations of the partial equilibrium and general equilibrium analyses of the terms-of-trade effect.) That is, the importing country faces an offer curve that is less than perfectly elastic, as in Figure 7-1. The offer curve facing Country A is represented by OB. When Country A imposes a tariff, shifting its offer curve from OA to $OA\prime$, the equilibrium terms of trade move from OE to $OE\prime$ (slope of). Country A now gets a larger quantity of imports per unit of exports.

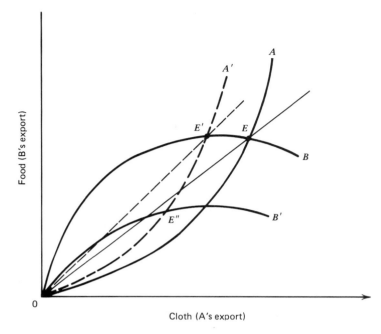

FIGURE 7-1 A tariff to improve a nation's terms of trade.

The gain to Country A is at the expense of the rest of the world. In fact, because the tariff reduces the degree of specialization in the world economy, the presumption is that world welfare is reduced. Thus the terms-of-trade argument takes a national perspective: It suggests that a nation may be able to use a tariff to take for itself a larger share of the gains from trade, thereby improving its welfare.

Although this argument is logically correct and consistent with the theory of trade, most economists have considered it to be a relatively unimportant exception to the general rule that free trade maximizes a nation's welfare. First, most of the over 150 nations in the modern world are not large enough to exert much influence on world prices. For them, the argument is irrelevant. Second, even for large countries, the benefit obtained through improved terms of trade may be lost if other countries retaliate by imposing tariffs of their own. If a tariff war breaks out, with successive moves by each side to escalate tariff rates, world trade will be progressively reduced, the gains from specialization lost, and world output reduced. Everybody loses. In Figure 7-1, for example, Country B might respond to Country A's tariff by imposing one itself, shifting its offer curve to OB' and moving the terms of trade back to OE'', where Country A is worse off than it was to start with.

In recent years, interest in the terms-of-trade argument has revived, particularly since the dramatic success of the oil-exporting countries (OPEC) in improving their terms of trade through the use of export tariffs. (As noted earlier, OPEC's collusive price and export controls are analytically equivalent to export tariffs.) Producers of many other commodities, from bauxite to bananas, have been inspired by the

OPEC example and been given hope that they could raise their prices in a similar way. Less developed countries have long suspected that world prices are influenced by market power and in particular that their terms of trade have been manipulated to their disadvantage by the advanced countries. OPEC's success during the 1970s in using monopoly power to produce drastic changes in its terms of trade is seen as a confirmation of that suspicion, and it has led to renewed demands for some kind of international action to improve the terms of trade of the LDCs. In fact, this was one of the most prominent features of the proposed new international economic order.

If a country can turn the terms of trade in its favor and improve its welfare by imposing a tariff, the question naturally arises, How large should that tariff be in order to obtain the maximum advantage? This question has led to attempts to define the optimum tariff. If we assume that retaliation will not occur, the optimum tariff for Country A turns out to be related to the elasticity of Country B's offer curve. If Country B's offer curve were perfectly elastic (the vector OE in Figure 7-1), a tariff imposed by Country A would have no effect on the terms of trade. Thus the optimum tariff is zero in this case. On the other hand, if the elasticity of Country B's offer curve were unity, Country B would supply a given quantity of its export commodity regardless of the price it received. In that case, Country A could keep raising its tariff without limit. To illustrate, in Figure 7-2, Country A could raise its tariff, shifting its offer curve successively from OA to OA' and OA''. Country B continues to export OF, whereas Country A need give up less and less of its export (OC_1 to OC_2 to OC_3). As Country A's offer curve shifts to the left, however, it must eventually reach a point on Country B's offer curve at which elasticity is greater than unity. The optimum tariff will be the tariff that enables Country A to reach the highest possible level of welfare (the highest community indifference curve, in terms of the analysis in Chapter 3). This optimum is not shown in Figure 7-2, but it will evidently be reached at a point on Country B's offer curve where elasticity is greater than one.

The Infant-Industry Argument

When production of a commodity first begins in a country, the firms producing it are often small, inexperienced, and unfamiliar with the technology they are using. Workers are also inexperienced and less efficient than they will become in time. During this breaking-in stage, costs are higher than they will be later on, and infant firms in the new industry may need temporary protection from older, established firms in other countries. So runs the infant-industry argument for tariff protection.

Thus stated, the infant-industry argument is analytically correct. It does not conflict with the principle of comparative advantage. In terms of our earlier analysis of trade, the argument is that the country's present production-possibility curve does not reflect its true potential. Given time to develop an industry that is now in its infancy, the production-possibility curve will shift and a potential comparative advantage will be realized.

Note that the infant-industry argument takes a global perspective: In the long run, world economic welfare is improved because tariff protection enables a po-

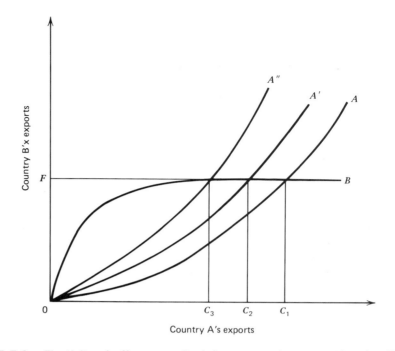

FIGURE 7-2   Elasticity of offer curve: Its influence on the terms-of-trade effect of a tariff.

tential comparative advantage to become realized and a more efficient utilization of resources to be achieved. Thus world output is increased.

This argument has great appeal for countries in an early stage of industrialization who are eager to develop a modern industrial sector. They fear that their attempts to develop new industries will be defeated by vigorous price competition from already established firms in advanced industrial countries such as the United States, Germany, and Japan. The infant-industry argument is now seldom used in the United States, but early in American history it was forcefully advanced by Alexander Hamilton in his *Report on Manufactures* (1791), and it was frequently used to support U.S. tariffs in the nineteenth century. Hamilton urged the necessity of tariff protection to shield the infant American industries from the ravages of competition with the then more advanced industries of Europe. His brilliant and eloquent statement of the case makes remarkably fresh reading even today, but its application is primarily to underdeveloped countries. These countries frequently assert their need for protection against the giant firms of the industrial nations.

The infant-industry argument also has a strong intuitive appeal. It seems to accord with common sense. Everyone knows that even a gifted beginner has trouble competing with a mature, experienced person, whether in sport, profession, or business. Societies acknowledge this disparity and deal with it in various ways: schools, training programs, apprenticeships, and others. Shielding infant firms from foreign competition during their most vulnerable stages seems to be an eminently fair and sensible thing to do.

Despite its analytical validity and its appeal to common sense, infant-industry protection encounters grave difficulties in actual practice. A country should use great care in extending such protection to its young industries. One key point is that it is difficult to determine in advance just which industries possess a potential comparative advantage. If protection is extended to the wrong industry, the cost to society can be heavy. Firms will expand their capacity, but costs per unit will remain high and continued protection will be necessary for their survival. Tariff protection involves a social cost in that consumers have to pay higher prices for the protected commodity than would be necessary with free trade. Such higher prices reflect the greater amount of scarce resources required to produce the commodity at home. If the industry eventually develops a comparative advantage, the extra costs incurred during its infancy may be recovered during its maturity. If a mistake is made, however, the nation is saddled with a continuing burden. The record is mixed, but infant industries have shown a distressing tendency to remain dependent on protection. A mistake, once made, is not easily corrected. Owners and workers in the new industry have a vested interest in it, and they will fight to preserve it.

In view of the extreme difficulty of selecting the correct industries to protect, many economists argue that a country should let the market decide. They doubt that government officials, no matter how dedicated, honest, and intelligent, can have the wisdom and foresight to pick out, in advance, exactly those industries in which a potential comparative advantage exists. If an industry is potentially profitable, private entrepreneurs will discover it, and they will bear the cost of its learning stage just as they bear the cost of construction, capital equipment, and training labor in any new venture. Here, the issue is joined, as other economists argue that special incentives may be necessary to induce entrepreneurs to undertake the new venture, especially in underdeveloped countries where entrepreneurs are timid.

Although it is difficult to identify potential comparative advantage industries, one useful rule is that infant-industry protection should be extended only when the country possesses an ample supply of the basic resources required in that industry. With no coal or iron ore, Costa Rica would be unwise to impose a tariff on steel imports in the hope that an efficient, low-cost steel industry would spring up in response. Possession of an adequate supply of raw materials and natural resources thus seems to be a necessary condition for infant-industry protection, but it may not be enough to assure efficient production and prices low enough to compete in world markets. When the protected home market is so small that it can support only one modern plant, there is no opportunity for a competitive struggle to determine which firms will survive. Everything depends on the efficiency of the single plant. Even in the United States, most new firms fail; thus the odds against success of an infant firm are high in an underdeveloped country, where entrepreneurs have many more unknown factors to cope with than in the United States.

Although a valid case can be made for giving temporary assistance to an infant industry, one can still question the merit of using a tariff for that purpose. We noted in Chapter 6 that a subsidy can provide the same protective effect as a tariff, but without distorting prices and causing a loss of consumers' surplus. Another advantage of the subsidy is that the social cost of protection is highly visible in the government's budget. On the other hand, in many countries where tax collection is a problem, a tariff may be preferred to a subsidy precisely because it does not involve government expenditure and the prior collection of tax revenue.

Industrial Strategy

A new argument for protectionism has recently been developed which can be viewed as an extension of the Vernon product cycle thesis and of the infant-industry position. Those who believe the United States has fallen behind Japan and various other countries in high-technology industries frequently attribute this loss of status to the federal government's failure to protect U.S. manufacturers against imports of products that require large research and development expenditures. Protectionism is advocated for new or emerging industries while expensive research is carried out and until sufficient economies of scale are gained to bring average costs down.[2] The Japanese government is frequently accused of following this approach, and U.S. advocates of such protectionism are suggesting that Washington adopt what they view as Tokyo's policy.

If, it is argued, the federal government can identify new product areas that require large research expenditures but promise large future profits, it should guarantee the U.S. market to domestic firms while this research is done and paid for, and until these firms become large and experienced enough to bring costs down. Once the research and development costs are recovered and large-scale production is underway, protection will no longer be needed and exports may be possible. To leave the U.S. market open to foreign firms during this start-up period, however, would make it impossible for domestic firms to get sufficient sales to pay for expensive research or become large enough to enjoy lower costs. Temporary protection is advocated during the period necessary to accomplish these goals.

Protection may even have the desirable effect of discouraging foreign firms from undertaking the research and development efforts that are necessary to enter the industry, thus creating the possibility of permanent dominance of the market by local firms. If, for example, Japanese firms are depending on exports to the United States to provide the revenues that are necessary to recapture huge research and development costs in a new product area, the imposition of a U.S. tariff which denies them these sales will discourage them from making the initial research efforts.

This creates the opportunity for U.S. firms to gain permanent dominance of the market; with the Japanese inactive in the industry, U.S. firms will have sufficient current sales and profits to finance the research costs necessary to develop future products, the profits from which will finance later research efforts for the following

---

[2]See Paul R. Krugman, "Is Free Trade Passe?" *Journal of Economic Perspectives,* Fall 1987, pp. 131–144, for a summary of this argument for protection. See also Elhanan Helpman and Paul R. Krugman, *Market Structure and Foreign Trade: Increasing Returns, Imperfect Competition, and the International Economy* (Cambridge, Mass.: MIT Press, 1985.

generation of products, and so on. A well-established U.S. technological and profits position will discourage or even frighten prospective foreign entrants, creating a self-sustaining U.S. market position.

The problem is how to finance the initial research efforts and then get sufficient domestic production volume to gain scale economies and bring costs down, while simultaneously discouraging foreign efforts to enter the business. Supporters of the industrial strategy, or "strategic trade," approach argue that providing temporary protection for the U.S. market will accomplish both goals, and they suggest that Japanese success in many high-tech product areas is the direct result of this policy being applied by the government in Tokyo.

An example may elucidate how a country might gain from such a protectionist policy. If Sony and RCA were both considering undertaking large research and development efforts to enter the high-definition television market, each would have greater sales and profits if the other did not compete. If either company, or its government, could somehow discourage the other firm from undertaking the research to develop such a television system, it would receive larger profits, or tax revenues. The "payoff matrix" facing the two firms might be as follows:

In this matrix, p stands for Sony producing, and n stands for Sony not producing; P stands for RCA producing, and N stands for RCA not producing. In each box, the number at the lower left is RCA's profits and the number to the upper right is Sony's profits. If both produce, each absorbs a loss of $5 million, because each would have a relatively low sales volume across which to spread large research costs. If only one firm produces, it earns $100 million because it will have a much larger volume of sales across which to spread these costs, thus bringing average costs down. In this case, whichever firm commits itself to a research effort first is likely to remain dominant, because the other firm will face a loss if it enters the business and will decide not to do so.[3]

The U.S. government, however, could adopt a policy that would shift this matrix in favor of RCA and make it very unlikely that Sony would enter the industry. If the United States adopted a tariff that was high enough to keep Sony out of the U.S. market, thus making the product profitable for RCA even if Sony produced the new television sets, the payoff matrix could become as follows:

[3]This example is adapted from Krugman, "Is Free Trade Passe?" pp. 131–144.

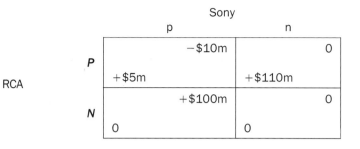

The U.S. tariff means that if both firms enter the market, Sony will lose $10 million, whereas RCA will receive profits of $5 million. This means that RCA will enter the market without regard to what Sony decides. Once the management of Sony understands this situation, it will be strongly discouraged from entering a market in which it faces certain losses of $10 million. Without competition from Sony, RCA earns profits of $110 million, some part of which accrues to the U.S. government as tax revenues.

This argument for protection has a superficial attraction, and the success of Japanese firms in technologically oriented industries makes it hard to argue against whatever Tokyo appears to be doing. This argument does, however, have at least two major problems. First, if a product is so promising and future profits so certain for the first firm into the industry, why is financing unavailable from private capital markets to cover research and start-up costs? Wall Street is in the business of picking future winners and providing financing for their growth, so why should the government need to do it? Second, how is Washington going to pick the particular emerging industries that are deserving of public help? If this is to be done by the Congress, politics and the desire of representatives and senators to protect their particular constituents will dominate the process. There is no reason to believe that the executive branch has the ability to pick prospective winners, and the question still remains, who makes the choices? Unless all industries are to be protected in the name of industrial strategy, this argument requires belief that Washington can do a better job of picking future winners than can private capital markets.

SECONDARY ARGUMENTS FOR PROTECTIONISM

A variety of other arguments have been advanced in support of protection on the grounds that it will enable a country to achieve some desirable social or economic objective. In nearly all these cases, an economist would argue that if society does indeed desire the stated objective, it can achieve it more efficiently in some other way. In other words, the economist would argue that a tariff is a second-best policy.

In fact, this point also applies to the infant-industry argument. We have observed that if a given industry were identified as a potential comparative advantage industry worthy of being assisted in its infancy, a subsidy would be a better method than a tariff to provide that assistance.

Even when it is correct, the argument that a tariff is a second-best policy may be irrelevant because no first-best policy can be used. It may be beyond the administrative capacity of the country, or there may be practical reasons why it is not feasible. Thus, in the infant-industry case, the country may be unable to collect enough taxes to pay subsidies, but it can protect the industry through use of import tariffs.

We will comment briefly on a few of the arguments that are often made to support the use of tariffs to achieve some objective, economic or noneconomic.

National Defense

A particular industry may be considered essential to maintain a nation's military strength. In order to preserve some capacity to produce this industry, the nation may choose to protect it. Economists have always recognized this exception to the case for free trade, and even Adam Smith observed that "defense is more important than opulence."

However, it is quite difficult to prove that a given industry is essential for national defense. Policymakers should cast a cool and skeptical eye on industry claims for protection on this basis, since producers of everything from garlic to clothespins have claimed it.

If the product can be stored, purchases in the cheapest foreign market would be a better way than domestic production to build up a stockpile. In any case, imposition of a tariff does not in itself lead to increased output for government use. That takes a separate act of government procurement.

If the product requires use of a depletable natural resource, tariffs will accelerate exhaustion of the national reserves. National security would seem to call for importing as much as possible to supply current consumption, thereby saving domestic reserves for future needs. It is a curious fact that the United States imposed quotas on oil imports during much of the post–World War II period on the ground that these restrictions were necessary to national defense. Import quotas do encourage domestic exploration, but they also increase production and thus use up domestic reserves.

The real issue concerning national security is maintenance of a domestic capacity to produce certain essential items. If that capacity is not maintained, skills and technological expertise may be lost, and the nation becomes dependent on foreign sources of supply. We know that trade means specialization. The other side of that coin is interdependence. The only real escape is to become self-sufficient, but self-sufficiency is extremely inefficient and its pursuit could weaken the nation by impoverishing it. Consequently, any serious use of the national defense argument for protection requires a careful calculation of the tradeoff between efficiency and defense essentiality. For most countries few, if any, industries qualify for protection on this score.[4]

---

[4] See T. N. Srinivasan, "The National Defense Argument for Intervention in Foreign Trade," in Robert M. Stern, ed., *U.S. Trade Policy in a Changing World Economy* (Cambridge, Mass.: MIT Press, 1987), pp. 337–376, for a discussion of the national defense argument for protection.

Cultural or Social Values

The specialization that results from international trade may also be opposed for cultural and social reasons. In a given country, people may have a high regard for a particular occupation or industry, and they may not want to see it knocked out by import competition. To preserve watchmaking, hand-blown glass, handwoven tapestries, or other activities threatened by lower priced imports, countries may choose to protect them, accepting the cost involved.

Similarly, countries may wish to protect a way of life: small-scale agriculture, a village system, a diversified structure of production. Some of the so-called romantic movements in the nineteenth century included attempts to prevent, or at least slow, the growth of industrialization, the migration from farm to city, and other manifestations of economic progress. Similar motives have been at work in many countries in more recent times, as traditional societies have been exposed to international trade and have seen its effects on resource allocation. Imports of manufactured goods, mass produced in large-scale factories, have often led to a decline in traditional small-scale handicraft industries, a decline that is resisted on cultural as well as economic grounds. In such cases trade restrictions are advocated precisely because the effects of trade are unwelcome. The society chooses to forego the gains from trade in order to retain its traditional way of life.

Protection to Correct Distortions in the Domestic Market

It is often argued that, because of various imperfections in the market, free trade does not lead to the results called for in theory. When some imperfection in the market causes a divergence between private and social costs of production, for example, a case can be made for a tariff or other trade restriction designed to offset or compensate for that divergence, thus bringing the economy closer to the free-trade outcome.

We can use partial equilibrium analysis to illustrate this basically simple idea. In Figure 7-3 we show for a particular commodity the domestic demand curve (D) and the domestic supply curve as perceived by private producers (S_p). The foreign supply curve is perfectly elastic at the world price, P_w. Consequently, with free trade, domestic production will be OA, domestic demand OF, and imports will make up the difference, AF.

Now let us suppose that the private supply curve (S_p) does not reflect certain external economies involved in the production of this commodity. When these are allowed for, the supply curve becomes S_s. That is, private marginal cost exceeds social marginal cost for any output by the vertical distance between these two curves.

Given the world price, P_w, domestic production would be equal to OB if the social marginal cost were being equated to price. That should be the outcome under free trade. However, because of the domestic divergence between private and social costs, output is actually OA.

To correct this divergence and encourage private producers to expand output to OB, a tariff can be levied to raise the domestic price to P_T.

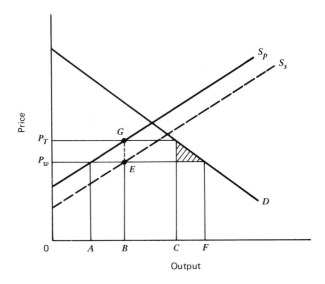

FIGURE 7-3 Use of a tariff to correct a domestic distortion.

This example enables us once again to show that the tariff is a second-best policy. Although it does correct the distortion in production, it introduces another distortion in consumption. That is, at the tariff-distorted price P_T, consumption is reduced from OF to OC, and there is a deadweight loss in consumer welfare (the shaded area in Figure 7-3). This consumption effect could be avoided if a subsidy were used instead of a tariff. A subsidy of EG per unit of output would induce domestic producers to expand output from OA to OB but would leave the price unchanged at P_w. Hence, consumption would remain the same. (As we have noted previously, however, the second-best policy may be the only one that is feasible.)

Domestic divergences between private and social costs (or benefits) may arise in many ways. The ones most frequently mentioned include monopoly elements in the economy, external economies or diseconomies, imperfect knowledge, and institutional rigidities. Developing countries frequently argue, for example, that their wage rates are higher in manufacturing than in agriculture, thus producing a bias against the production of manufactured goods. The imperfect labor market causes private marginal costs to be higher than the true social marginal cost. Whether or not the wage-rate differential constitutes a distortion that should be corrected to achieve the competitive outcome is a complex question. Some economists believe that most of the observed wage differentials can be accounted for on the basis of differences in skill or in urban living costs. This is a factual matter to be determined in each instance. Our point is simply that domestic distortions, when they do exist, may constitute a basis for protection, but that a subsidy is a far better option than a tariff or a quota.

Antidumping Tariffs

As explained in Chapter 5, dumping is a form of price discrimination that can occur when the seller can separate the foreign and domestic markets, charging a lower price for exports than for domestic sales. This is widely regarded as an unfair practice, and most countries have provisions for antidumping tariffs, that is, tariffs designed to offset or correct such price discrimination.

One might think that the country in which dumping occurs would welcome the chance to buy at bargain prices. U.S. consumers would be glad to learn that OPEC wished to dump oil at $5 per barrel instead of charging $30. Importing countries, however, are usually the ones to complain about dumping, for two principal reasons. First, dumping is often expected to be temporary. The reduced prices will be maintained until domestic competitors have been driven out of business, but then the bargains are over and the former dumper will begin to exploit its monopoly position. This is predatory dumping. Of course, there is no way to prove that a given case of dumping will result in such exploitation, but the accusation is commonly made whenever dumping occurs. The second reason is simply that workers and firms in industries competing with the dumped products will vigorously protest this practice. In fact, whenever imports undersell domestic products a charge of dumping is likely to be brought.

Dumping is generally considered to be an unfair practice in international trade. Other unfair practices also exist—such as discrimination in government procurement and administrative regulations imposed on importers—and it is often argued that tariffs should be used as retaliation against these measures, or perhaps as bargaining chips to secure their removal. For example, in recent years there have been many complaints about the difficulties U.S. firms face in exporting to Japan, and some have called for retaliatory restrictions on Japanese access to the U.S. market. The argument for a tariff as a bargaining chip is clearly a matter of political tactics, not a basic principle.

The Scientific Tariff

Finally, we should at least mention another hardy perennial, the so-called scientific tariff. It, too, appeals to a sense of fair play, calling for tariffs just high enough to equalize the costs of production at home and abroad, thereby enabling domestic and foreign firms to compete on an equal basis. As every reader will realize, such tariffs would destroy the whole basis for trade by equalizing relative prices at home and abroad. Although no one has advocated a thoroughgoing application of this principle, much solemn nonsense about the scientific tariff has been heard in U.S. political campaigns, and witnesses testify in its favor at every congressional hearing on tariff policy.

Revenues

Thus far, government restrictions on imports have been viewed solely as a means of protecting domestic producers, but tariffs are frequently a major source of revenue for the governments of developing countries. Rectangle c in Figure 6-1 in the previous chapter indicates the size of those revenues, and it is worth noting that they will be larger if the domestic demand and supply curves are inelastic. Tariffs on necessities that cannot be produced domestically can raise large sums of money. Tariffs designed to raise revenues can be applied to exports as well as imports, and such export taxes are common in developing countries. Import tariffs were a major source of revenue for the U.S. government until well into the twentieth century, and much of the developing world is simply following that pattern.

Tariffs are attractive as a source of revenues for a developing country because of the lack of alternative ways to tax efficiently. If much of an economy is subsistence farming or is based on barter, it is not clear how domestic taxes are to be applied. Even in that part of the economy that is monetized, most transactions may be through paper currency rather than check; therefore accurate records of transactions may be unavailable, making fair taxation impossible. International trade may be the only large sector of the economy for which good records of transactions are available, so it becomes an obvious target for taxation. If tariffs on imports (or exports) are high, however, smuggling becomes an attractive route for tax avoidance and revenues decline. Many developing countries that have high tariff rates also have serious problems with smuggling, particularly where long borders and limited police budgets make it difficult to apprehend people bringing illegal goods in or out of the country.

Ideally, better taxation systems would be developed in such countries, and considerable efforts are being made in this area by international agencies such as the International Monetary Fund and the World Bank. This is a slow process, however, and it is not surprising that governments of developing countries are resistant to reducing tariffs that have been a dominant source of operating revenues.

CONCLUSION

The debate over protectionism is often a matter of the general interest versus the interests of narrow groups, where the general interest is diffuse and badly organized, and group interest is concentrated and well organized. As a result, the Congress is typically faced with strong lobbying campaigns in favor of protectionism and almost no active opposition. It often appears that protectionist sentiment is strong and that nobody cares about the benefits from trade. The problem is that vast numbers of people gain modest amounts of real income from trade and may not even be aware of the gains, whereas far smaller groups lose quite a bit, are fully aware of their losses, and consequently are very active in promoting their interests. Well-organized groups with intensely held opinions frequently do very well in the U.S. political system, even if their memberships are small and their demands conflict with broader national interests.

In addition, there is the problem of unskilled labor and the distribution of income. Most members of the U.S. labor force are not unskilled and would benefit from free trade, but those who would be hurt disproportionately are people whose incomes are already relatively low. Free trade without compensation for losers would increase total incomes but would make the U.S. distribution of income more equal. Compensation is a potential solution to this problem, if a practical and politically acceptable way of providing it can be developed.

Many of the previous arguments for limits on imports can be viewed as examples of the "law of the second best," which argues that the existence of one distortion or problem often requires government intervention to minimize its costs.[5] The first best would be to eliminate the distortion, but if that proves impossible, government intervention in the form of a policy such as a tariff might be desirable. An external economy resulting from an industry's activities, or the inability of new industries to raise enough funds to cover losses during a start-up or infancy period, might be such distortions, and a tariff might be the government response designed to minimize the resulting losses. The problem is that protectionism is seldom the least costly form of intervention; therefore it is not second best but rather third or fourth best. In the previous chapter it was argued that domestic production subsidies encourage production with far smaller efficiency losses than do tariffs or quotas. A subsidy would be the second-best option, and a tariff or quota far worse. The problem is that second-best subsidies are viewed as impractical and unpopular; thus tariffs and quotas become acceptable alternatives.

Despite the almost universal support for free trade among economists, protectionism remains politically popular, especially in the case of labor-intensive manufactured goods, and this situation is unlikely to change. It is often said that death and taxes are the only certainties; debates over protectionism can be added to that list, as can be seen in the following column concerning the 1984 election campaign.

[5] R. G. Lipsey and K. Lancaster, "The General Theory of the Second Best," *Review of Economic Studies,* October 1956, represents the origin of this argument. For a discussion of various reasons for protectionist policies to accomplish their intended goals, see Robert E. Baldwin, "The Inefficacy of Trade Policy," *Princeton Essays in International Finance,* No. 150, December 1982.

Barriers to Trade

The White House decision on steel quotas illustrates a disturbing trend in the Reagan administration's foreign trade policy. It has refused to adopt formal quotas but instead will seek informal arrangements with steel-exporting countries to reduce their sales in this country to about $18\frac{1}{2}$ percent of the U.S. market. The administration avoids the appearance of open protectionism while actually moving in a protectionist direction.

The administration has talked about the desirability of free trade; it has opposed the domestic content bill for cars, and it has introduced a trade initiative for the Caribbean basin. Earlier this month it refused to limit imports of copper. But it also imposed quotas on Japanese cars that cost American

consumers about $1,000 per car. It further tightened limits on imports of textiles and garments from developing countries. And it imposed earlier restrictions on U.S. purchases of foreign specialty steel.

Inconsistency and an apparent desire to appear to favor open markets, while actually restricting imports, have characterized the last three years. For voters, the problem is that Walter Mondale's proposed alternatives are worse.

Mondale strongly supports the domestic content bill, which would drastically reduce U.S. imports of Japanese cars, and has also argued for strict quotas on steel imports. He has promised the Amalgamated Clothing and Textile Workers that imports of their products would be sharply restricted if he were elected, and a similar commitment has been made to shoe workers. For the first time in recent memory a major U.S. party has nominated a presidential candidate who is openly protectionist.

Our trading partners view the recent trends and prospects for U.S. trade policy with grave misgivings, and developing countries are particularly worried. Before the United States pursues Walter Mondale's thoroughly protectionist policies or continues with President Reagan's more inconsistent approach, the implications of increased U.S. protectionism should be thought out carefully.

The domestic content bill, for example, would sharply reduce U.S. demand for Japanese cars and therefore demand for yen to pay for these cars. Under the current regime of floating exchange rates, the yen would depreciate and the dollar would appreciate until the balance of payments was restored. The exchange rate for the dollar is already so high as to cause serious injury to U.S. export and import-competing industries.

The adoption of the domestic content bill would push the dollar considerably higher relative to the yen, worsening the problems of other U.S. industries. Every job saved in the auto industry would be offset by a job lost elsewhere. It does not appear that supporters of domestic content have informed these other industries and their employees what its adoption would mean for their futures.

As protectionism spreads from cars to steel, textiles and shoes, the target is no longer just Japan. The victims start to include a number of developing countries. U.S. policies that restrict imports from developing countries create at least two major threats to U.S. interests.

First, there is the matter of the massive debts owed to U.S. banks. Brazil, Mexico and the other less developed debtor countries cannot repay our banks in dollars; they do not have dollars. They can only repay in goods — that is, by exporting more to the United States

and other industrialized countries to earn the dollars with which to pay the banks.

If the United States makes it impossible for these countries to steadily increase their exports of goods such as steel, garments and shoes, it will also make it impossible for these countries to repay their debts or even make scheduled interest payments. A number of major U.S. banks have lent well over 100 percent of their net worth to developing countries and now face serious repayment problems.

For the stability of our banking systems, the implications of a U.S. shift toward protectionism are not pleasant. Major difficulties in the large banks mean financial losses for the Federal Deposit Insurance Corporation and ultimately for the U.S. Treasury. If Mondale's or Reagan's protectionism makes it impossible for Brazil to export more to earn funds to repay debts to U.S. banks, the resulting losses are going to be borne largely by the U.S. taxpayer.

Finally there is the broader issue of the basic development strategy pursued by developing countries and the U.S. role in the Third World. For a number of decades the United States has been encouraging developing countries to follow an export-led, market approach to economics, in opposition to those in Moscow, Havana, and elsewhere who have advocated non-market, inward-looking strategies. The results for the past two decades make it very clear that the United States was correct and that our opponents were dead wrong. The developing countries that have done well are overwhelmingly those that have used a market approach and that have pursued exports. The statistical evidence for the past 20 years has been widely understood among development planners in China and India, and there is a strong attempt in both countries and elsewhere to shift policies in the right direction.

The success stories among developing countries have been possible, however, only because the United States and its allies have been willing to purchase growing volumes of their exports. If this country now becomes protectionist, the successful strategy of the rapidly growing countries will become impossible for nations such as India and China, leaving them no choice but to move back toward an inward-looking, centrally planned approach to economic policy. The United States has won a major intellectual victory in the developing countries, but we may throw that success away and literally snatch defeat from the jaws of victory.

The choice between the trade policies of the two candidates is not easy, but Walter Mondale seems to be committed in principle to a series of protectionist measures, while the Reagan administration may be merely placating various groups of protectionist voters, and thus its policies might improve after the election. In addition, the domestic content bill would be a *permanent* change in U.S. trade law, while the car quotas are supposedly temporary and may be ended next April. We are offered a choice between a candidate who is consistently wrong and one who is inconsistent but often wrong. Perhaps inconsistency is better.

EXHIBIT 7-1   Barriers to Trade. Source: From *The Washington Post*, Robert M. Dunn, Jr., copyright ©1984 *The Washington Post*, (Op. Ed. page), September 20, 1984.

QUESTIONS FOR STUDY AND REVIEW

1. Under what circumstances is the terms-of-trade argument for a tariff valid for a single nation? Is this argument ever valid for the world? Why or why not?

2. If the United States raises tariffs enough to reduce its imports by $10 billion, what are likely to be the employment effects of this action? Discuss, considering as many aspects of this issue as you can.

3. Why does an industry seeking protection from imports sometimes prefer a quota to a tariff?

4. "A tariff is an attractive form of taxation because the tax burden falls on the foreigner." Do you agree? Explain.

5. Why exactly might foreign firms wish to engage in persistent dumping in the U.S. market?

6. "Higher tariffs don't increase employment; they just redistribute the unemployed." Do you agree? Explain.

7. "To show its support for underpaid workers in poor countries who are exploited in sweatshops and made to work in unsatisfactory conditions, the United States should restrict imports from countries where such conditions are allowed to exist." Critically evaluate this statement.

8. Discuss and evaluate the following arguments for tariffs. You should consider both theoretical and practical aspects as fully as possible.

    a. The infant-industry argument.
    b. The low-wage argument (i.e., high-wage countries require protection against imports coming from low-wage countries).

9. If West Virginia became a separate nation, would it be better able to solve its economic problems (high unemployment, depressed industries, etc.) through tariffs? Discuss, using economic analysis.

10. Under what circumstances might U.S. protectionist policies be intended to discourage foreign research and development efforts?

SELECTED READINGS

Adams, John, ed. *The Contemporary International Economy.* 2nd ed. New York: St. Martin's Press, 1985.

Adams, Walter, et al. *Tariffs, Quotas, and Trade: The Politics of Protectionism.* San Francisco: Institute for Contemporary Studies, 1979.

Baldwin, Robert. "The Inefficacy of Trade Policy." *Princeton Essays in International Finance,* No. 150, December 1982.

Baldwin, Robert E., and J. David Richardson, eds. *International Trade and Finance.* 3rd ed. Boston: Little, Brown, 1986.

Corden, W. M. *The Revival of Protectionism.* Occasional Paper No. 14, New York: Group of Thirty, 1984.

Helpman, E., and P. Krugman. *Increasing Returns, Imperfect Competition and the International Economy.* Cambridge, Mass.: MIT Press, 1985.

Jones, Ronald, and Peter B. Kenen, eds. *Handbook of International Economics.* Vol. 1. Amsterdam: North Holland, 1984.

King, Philip, ed. *International Economics and the International Economy: A Reader.* New York: McGraw–Hill, 1990.

Kravis, Irving. "The Current Case for Import Limitations." In Bela Balassa, ed., *Changing Patterns in Foreign Trade and Payments.* 3rd ed. New York: W. W. Norton, 1978.

Lawrence, Robert Z. *Can America Compete?* Washington, D.C.: Brookings Institution, 1984.

Stern, Robert, ed. *U.S. Trade Policy in a Changing World Economy.* Cambridge, Mass.: MIT Press, 1987.

REGIONAL BLOCS: DISCRIMINATORY TRADE LIBERALIZATION

To this point we have assumed that restrictions on imports are nondiscriminatory, that is, that all trading partners are treated equally in terms of market access. Such nondiscriminatory trade was a major goal of the GATT system, but it is far from universal. Many or perhaps most countries have different levels of protection, maintaining the lowest level for partners in trade blocs or friends, and less favorable circumstances for others. Most trading blocs, such as the European Economic Community, are regional, and GATT allows such arrangements. Colonial empires, such as those that existed in the nineteenth and early twentieth centuries, can be viewed as discriminatory trading blocs, because the colonial power frequently maintained a highly favorable situation for itself in selling in the colonies and for the colonies in selling in its markets. One reason for creating such empires was to guarantee export markets and sources of imports that could not be produced at home.

Even the United States, with its historic commitment to nondiscriminatory trade, maintains a number of levels of market access for different groups of foreign countries. At one extreme, a few countries such as Cuba and Libya are embargoed; that is, trade between the United States and those countries is illegal except for a few humanitarian goods such as medicine. On the next level are countries with whom the United States can legally trade but who do not enjoy most-favored-nation (MFN) status; their products consequently pay high tariffs. Russia has been in this situation but is eager to gain MFN status so that it can export more goods to the United States. Without MFN status it is impossible to build significant markets in the United States because the applicable tariffs are very high while competing countries pay low tariffs. MFN status means that any tariff cuts negotiated through GATT with any other country enjoying MFN treatment must be offered to the country in question. If, for example, the United States negotiates a tariff cut with the European Community, that offer must be extended to Japan and to all other countries with MFN status. Most U.S. trade is with countries on the MFN list.

Although it sounds impossible, a few arrangements allow some countries even better treatment than MFN allows. The U.S.-Canada free trade agreement, for example, which is currently being phased in, will mean no tariffs or other barriers to trade between the two countries, and there is discussion of extending that treatment to Mexico. In addition, under the Generalized System of Preferences (GSP) the United States permits some manufactured goods to come in from developing countries without tariffs, and it has a separate arrangement with a group of small countries under the Caribbean Basin Initiative. Although nondiscriminatory trade is supposed to be the norm, regional trade blocs and other discriminatory arrangements are becoming increasingly common and there is even some fear that they may be the dominant trading situation by the year 2000.

ALTERNATIVE FORMS OF REGIONAL LIBERALIZATION

Regional trading blocs exist at different levels according to how extensive the integration of national economies becomes. The first and easiest to negotiate is a free-trade area, under which tariffs and other barriers to trade among the members are removed (sometimes only for manufactured goods, owing to differing agricultural support programs), but each country retains its own tariff schedule and other commercial policies with regard to goods coming from nonmember countries. Such arrangements encourage the importation of goods into whichever member has the lowest tariffs and their subsequent reshipment to member countries with higher external tariffs. Certificates of origin are supposed to guarantee that products coming tariff-free from a member country really were produced there, but it is believed that false certificates are frequently used to allow such transshipment.

This problem can be avoided with the adoption of a customs union arrangement. A customs union is a free-trade area in which external tariffs and other barriers to imports coming from nonmembers are unified, that is, all member countries maintain the same restrictions on imports from non-members. A common market, the next step in regional integration, is a customs union that allows the free mobility of capital and labor among the member countries. This is a large additional step toward a single economy, and it is what the European Economic Community started to implement under the Treaty of Rome, which was signed in 1957. An economic union is a customs union that has a unified (or partially unified) taxation/expenditure system and perhaps a jointly managed monetary policy. The European Community can be viewed as a customs union that is moving toward becoming an economic union. If the European Monetary System and the other changes planned for 1992 are implemented, it will have made the transition. The current arrangement between the United States and Canada is a free-trade area, and there is no current discussion of its being moved toward one of the other forms.

EFFICIENCY GAINS AND LOSSES

The creation of a regional bloc or other form of discriminatory trading arrangement would appear to be a movement toward free trade and therefore toward greater economic efficiency. Because some barriers to trade are being eliminated and others are being left in place, the average tariff level for the world declines. This appearance of liberalization and of greater efficiency can be deceiving, however. Some regional blocs do increase efficiency, but others can represent a movement away from the allocation of resources that would occur under free trade and can therefore reduce world efficiency. The fact that the tariff cutting is discriminatory creates this possibility. There is no general rule as to whether discriminatory trade blocs increase or decrease efficiency; instead, each must be evaluated separately.[1] Whether a particular trade arrangement raises or lowers efficiency depends primarily on the relative strengths of two effects.

1. *Trade creation.* This is the beneficial effect of a discriminatory trading arrangement. It occurs when a member country was not previously importing the product and was instead consuming local goods that were produced inefficiently. As a result of the creation of the trading bloc, the product is imported from more efficient firms in another member country. Inefficient local production is displaced by more efficient output in another member country. Since the product was not being imported from a nonmember before the beginning of the arrangement, outsiders lose no exports and are unaffected.

[1] See Jacob Viner, *The Customs Union Issue* (New York: Carnegie Endowment for International Peace, 1953) for an early discussion of this topic. See also R. G. Lipsey, "The Theory of Customs Unions: A General Survey," *Economic Journal,* September 1960, and Tibor Scitovsky, *Economic Theory and Western European Integration* (London: Allen Unwin, 1958).

2. *Trade diversion.* This is the undesirable or efficiency-reducing effect of such a bloc. It occurs when a member country was previously importing a product from a country that does not become a member of the bloc. When the discriminatory tariff cutting occurs, other members have a large advantage over nonmembers; as a result, the previous trading pattern is destroyed as a member country takes the export sales from the nonmember. In a nondiscriminatory system, the nonmember would retain the sales, because it is the most efficient producer. Discriminatory tariff cuts mean that the nonmember country loses sales to less efficient producers in a member country, thus reducing world efficiency. Trade is diverted from low- to higher cost sources, and world efficiency suffers.

We can make the differences between these two effects clearer by the examples shown in Tables 8-1 and 8-2, the first of which represents trade creation and the second, trade diversion. As shown in Table 8-1, French consumers are purchasing local bicycles, even though the German bikes are more efficiently produced. The United States is the high-cost producer, has no market in France or Germany, and has nothing to lose. If France and Germany join the European Economic Community, as they did in the mid-1950s, the French tariff on German bicycles becomes zero, and French consumers substitute $70 bikes from Germany for local products that cost $80. Trade is created between France and Germany, thus increasing efficiency, and no trade is diverted from the United States because it did not have any previous bicycle sales in Europe to lose. In the next example, shown in Table 8-2, however, things are different.

As shown in Table 8-2, French consumers have been purchasing U.S. bicycles despite the tariff because their local costs ($120) exceed those in the United States ($90) by more than the tariff of $20. As long as the French tariffs are nondiscriminatory, the United States continues to sell in France because German bicycles cost $10 more to produce and the nondiscriminatory tariff of $20 makes them excessively expensive. When Germany and France enter the European Economic Community, however, the United States loses its market. German bicycles now only cost $100 in France, which is $10 less than the price of U.S. bikes. As a result of the discriminatory nature of the tariff cuts, the most efficient producer, the United States, loses its export market to higher cost German firms. World effi-

TABLE 8-1   The French Market for Bicycles

	Source		
	France	**Germany**	**United States**
Manufacturers' price	$80	$70	$100
Applicable tariff	0	$20	$ 20
French wholesale price	$80	$90	$120

TABLE 8-2 The French Market for Bicycles

	Source		
	France	**Germany**	**United States**
Manufacturers' price	$120	$100	$90
Applicable tariff	0	$ 20	$20
French wholesale price	$120	$120	$110

ciency declines by $10 times the number of bicycles whose production is diverted from the United States to Germany.

In these numerical examples unchanging costs have been assumed in each market, which implies horizontal supply functions. If upward-sloping local supply functions are introduced, it is possible to have both trade creation and trade diversion in the same market. This occurs where production from a member displaces that from a nonmember (diversion) but where lower local prices both discourage inefficient domestic production and increase consumption, thus raising total imports (trade creation). This situation can be seen in Figure 8-1.

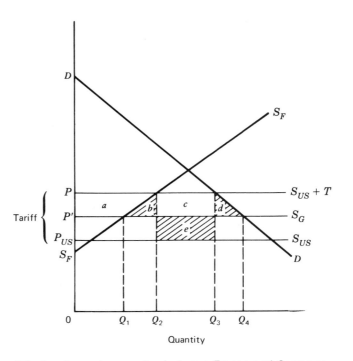

FIGURE 8-1 Effects of a customs union between France and Germany.

Prior to the creation of the customs union, France maintained a uniform tariff, which is shown as the vertical distance between S_{US} and $S_{US} + T$. German costs were higher, as shown by S_G, so with the uniform tariff, Germany sold no bicycles in France. The elimination of the French tariff on German bikes makes S_G the relevant import supply function; thus the United States loses export sales of Q_3Q_2, with a resulting efficiency loss of rectangle e which represents the difference between German and U.S. costs times the number of bicycles whose production is diverted. Since the French price of bicycles declines from P to P', however, consumption expands from Q_3 to Q_4 and French production declines from Q_2 to Q_1, thus increasing total imports from Q_3Q_2 to Q_4Q_1. The efficiency gains from this expansion of trade consist of the areas of triangles b and d. Whether efficiency increases or declines in this market depends on the relationship between the area of rectangle e (loss) and the sum of triangles b and d (gain). Total consumer surplus increases by areas $a + b + c + d$, with French manufacturers losing producer surplus of area a and the French government losing tariff revenues of area c. In addition, the government loses revenue in the amount of rectangle e, for a total of $c + e$.

Although the government loses revenues and manufacturers lose profits, French consumers gain a large amount of consumer surplus, and German firms gain sales. The only clear loser is the United States; it loses export revenues, and its firms lose sales to firms that are less efficient. Except for the impact on government revenues, regional blocs are generally beneficial to the members, but they can be decidedly harmful to nonmembers who find themselves on the losing side of a discriminatory trade arrangement.

As was noted earlier, a determination as to whether trade creation or diversion will dominate must be made on a case-by-case basis, that is, with reference to specific pairs or groups of members. There are, however, some general tendencies in such blocs. If the member countries are quite similar in terms of their factor endowments, levels of development, and industrial structures, trade creation will tend to dominate and the bloc will enhance efficiency. The important point is that before the bloc is created the potential members have similar or overlapping industries that will be forced to compete with each other after tariffs are eliminated. If both Germany and France have steel industries and have not been importing much steel from nonmembers, the beginning of the EEC will force the two industries to compete, creating efficient trade in which the country with the lower costs exports to the less efficient country.

Trade diversion will tend to dominate when the member countries are very different in terms of their factor endowments, levels of development, and industrial structures. If each country only produces goods that the other was already importing from a nonmember country, there are no obvious possibilities for trade creation, but trade diversion will take place. If, for example, the United States produces manufactured goods and temperate climate farm products, whereas Ecuador produces only tropical agricultural goods and minerals, a free-trade area consisting of the two countries will be overwhelmingly trade diverting. The United States was already importing all of its tropical product needs and much of its mineral consumption but was doing so on a nondiscriminatory basis from a wide range of countries. Ecuador was similarly importing most of its manufactured goods and temperate agricultural needs, again on a nondiscriminatory basis from a large number of countries based on who was more efficient in each market. The creation of a U.S.-Ecuador free-trade area will change this situation. U.S. requirements for tropical products and minerals will be diverted to Ecuador, whereas the United States will take over the Ecuadorian market for manufactured and temperate climate agricultural products. On both sides, this is trade diversion, and since the two countries started out with very few overlapping industries, almost no trade creation will occur. Such a trading bloc would clearly reduce economic efficiency.

From this standpoint, the evaluation of the welfare effects of a customs union comes down to a question of the relative importance of trade creation and trade diversion. There has been much interest in this question since the formation of the European Community, and many attempts have been made to measure the two effects. After reviewing a number of these studies, Professor Balassa concluded that "trade creation has been substantial in absolute terms and has exceeded trade diversion several times."[2] He also noted that increased specialization in manufacturing has been mostly intraindustry instead of interindustry. That is, business firms in a given industry—for example, metal products—did not leave that industry or go out of business; they simply began to concentrate in certain specialties within the metal products industry. This greatly eased the social tensions involved in the adjustment process; it minimized the dislocations of labor and capital.

Although trade creation appears to have exceeded trade diversion, the overall effects of trade diversion on particular outside countries may still be adverse. Some underdeveloped countries believe they have suffered from the preferential treatment enjoyed by some of the African countries (mostly former French colonies) that are associated with the European Community. Farmers in Canada, the United States, and Australia, faced with high common external tariffs for wheat and other agricultural products, have been displaced in European markets by French and other inside producers.

Thus far we have been concerned with analysis of the gains from the reallocation of existing resources as a result of the formation of a customs union. Empirical estimates of these static gains have generally been quite small: on the order of 1 percent of gross national product. These low estimates have led some economists to be skeptical about the value of membership in regional economic organizations, but other economists have argued that other, dynamic benefits will accrue to members. Unfortunately, these other benefits have proved to be difficult to measure, but they may nevertheless be quite important.

DYNAMIC EFFECTS

One source of potential benefits is the economies of scale. Just as developing countries argue that their home markets are too small to enable their producers to build plants large enough for greatest efficiency, so European countries used to argue that their national markets were too small to support firms as large as their competitors in the United States. This argument made a deep impression on

[2]Bela Balassa, ed., *European Economic Integration* (Amsterdam: North Holland, 1975), p. 116.

the popular mind. The average person was impressed by the fact that in many industries (before the European Community was organized) a single firm in the United States had a larger output than the entire industry in France, Germany, or Italy. It was said that the U.S. Constitution, by prohibiting any tariffs on trade between states, had created a large common market and enabled U.S. firms to achieve the economies of scale.

Prior to the formation of the European Community, industrial firms in the United States were much larger than their European counterparts. However, according to *Fortune*'s directory of industrial firms, European firms have now reached sizes comparable to, or larger than, their U.S. competitors in many industries.

The European Community now has a unified market large enough to enable it to obtain the benefits of size and large-scale production. In 1958, when it began, the combined gross national product of the six members was only one-third as large as the U.S. GNP. By 1990, however, the GNP of the original six members of the European Community was larger than that of the United States, and the full twelve members constituted a far larger economy than that of the United States.

A second source of benefits arises from the stimulus to competition provided by the Common Market. Firms that have grown fat and lazy in sheltered national markets are exposed to competition from rivals in all the other member countries. The hot winds of competition are a powerful stimulus to managerial efficiency. Firms become acutely cost-conscious and much more receptive to technological improvements than before. The efficient, low-cost firm sees its profits rise, and investment in additional capacity is encouraged. Such new investment naturally embodies the latest technological advances, and the high rate of investment in the European Community since 1958 has therefore brought a substantial modernization of its industrial plant. One of the main reasons for the United Kingdom's belated decision to join the European Community was its hope that competition would stimulate labor and management to increase productivity and generally shake them out of their lethargy.

Reduced international tensions and an increased likelihood of peace may be another benefit from a regional trading bloc. One of the reasons why the United States supported the formation of the European Economic Community, despite its prospective export losses from trade diversion, was a desire to tie Germany and France as closely together as possible. There had been three wars between these two countries in less than a century, and two of those wars involved the United States. It was thought that the integration of the two economies would make it difficult or even impossible for them to disentangle, and that the vast amount of personal and business contact that would occur across the border would dilute and ultimately destroy the negative images that each country sometimes had of the other.

THE 1992 PROGRAM FOR THE EUROPEAN ECONOMIC COMMUNITY

Although the European Economic Community has been successful in eliminating tariffs and some other barriers to trade among its members, a number of restrictions on trade and other transactions have remained in place. The Community is now committed to removing many of these during 1992, although it now appears that this schedule cannot be met and that 1992–95 is the more likely period during which a more complete economic union will be established.[3]

The barriers to be removed include the following:

1. Border controls on trade, which result from differing value-added tax (VAT) rates and other national rules or regulations.

2. Differing industrial standards, such as frequency standards for television sets, safety rules, or even what ingredients may be used to make beer. A representative of Philips, a large Dutch firm, said that his firm had to manufacture nine different types of television sets for various European countries.

3. Limitations of movements of workers, particularly in the professions. Differing licensing requirements for doctors, lawyers, and other professionals make it difficult or impossible for people to move among countries seeking employment.

4. Differing legal systems, which make it difficult to enforce contracts with firms or individuals in different member countries.

5. Capital controls which make it illegal for investors to move money from one member country to another.

6. Restrictions on trade in services such as banking, insurance, and air transport.

7. Government procurement policies which frequently make it impossible for a firm from one member country to bid on a contract being offered by a government agency in another member country.

If all, or even most, of these barriers were removed, Europe would have a far more unified and efficient market. It is extremely difficult to get the twelve member governments to give up their powers to regulate all of these matters, which is why 1992 now appears to be an unlikely date for completion of this program. Negotiations are continuing in Brussels, and considerable progress has reportedly been made in a number of important areas. Capital controls have now been largely removed within the Community, and the paperwork required for moving goods through border controls has been greatly simplified, which allows considerable savings in shipping costs.

Negotiations on the unification of industrial standards are reportedly progressing well. The United States has a particular interest in this topic because of a fear that new Community industrial standards might be designed to put U.S. products at a competitive disadvantage in the European market. U.S. industrial associations have reportedly been actively lobbying in Brussels to avoid that outcome. Progress

---

[3]For a discussion of the changes in the European Community that are planned for 1992, see Michael Calingaert, *The 1992 Challenge from Europe: Development of the European Community's Internal Market* (Washington, D.C.: National Planning Association, 1988). For a group of papers on the growing importance of regional blocs in international trade, see Richard Belous and Rebecca Hartley, eds., *The Growth of Regional Trading Blocks and the Global Economy* (Washington, D.C.: National Planning Association, 1990).

is reported in other areas, including the acceptance of one member country's professional licenses in other member countries and the reduction of barriers to trade in services.

Government procurement policies may turn out to be the most difficult issue. National governments can scarcely avoid favoring their own firms in awarding large contracts; it would be hard to imagine the government of France, for example, purchasing German Leopard tanks for the French Army or the British Royal Air Force flying Mirage fighter planes.

Despite these problems, it now appears that the European Economic Community will have a far more unified market for goods, services, and factors of production by the middle of the 1990s. If the European Monetary System (see Chapter 21) is successful in moving toward a single European currency by the end of the decade, Europe really will become similar to a single national economy.

OTHER REGIONAL GROUPS

The second most successful example of regional economic integration also appeared in Europe: the European Free Trade Area (EFTA). Its members now include Austria, Sweden, Norway, Liechtenstein, Switzerland, Iceland, and Finland. Unlike the European Community, it is a free-trade area: its members retain their own national tariff rates for nonmember countries, and they do not aspire to full economic union.

The more complete integration of the European Community economies, which is scheduled for 1992 or soon thereafter, was seen as threatening to some EFTA members, and has forced some of them to apply for full membership. In the fall of 1991, however, EFTA and the European Community reached an agreement for free trade (excluding agriculture because of complications created by the EEC Common Agricultural Policy) across all nineteen members. In addition, the EFTA countries will accept EEC industrial standards and other regulations, which will create a single market of nineteen countries and 380 million people. Turkey has applied for EEC membership, and the newly free countries of Eastern Europe are looking for ways to gain favorable access to EEC markets.

The most recent regional bloc, the Canada-U.S. free trade area, was negotiated in the late 1980s and began operation in 1989.[4] Tariffs were to be eliminated over a decade, but that process is now being accelerated and may be completed sooner. This agreement also includes provisions that allow financial institutions from each country to operate more easily in the other, to permit professional and managerial personnel to move freely across the border, and to eliminate export subsidies. The trade flow between the two countries was already the largest bilateral flow in the world (about $140 billion per year). Since the two countries are very similar and have many overlapping industries, the agreement should be overwhelmingly trade creating.

---

[4]Chapter 4 of the 1988 *Economic Report of the President* contains a discussion of the U.S.-Canada free-trade arrangement. See also J. Schott and M. Smith, eds., *The Canada-United States Free Trade Agreement: The Global Impact* (Washington, D.C.: Institute for International Economics, 1988). See also Peter Morici, ed., *Making Free Trade Work: The Canada-U.S. Agreement* (New York: Council on Foreign Relations Press, 1990).

The Canada-U.S. trade bloc is not, however, without problems. In Canada it has created a political split between Ontario and the western part of the country. The western provinces specialize in products that are exported to the United States, such as forest products, metals, oil, and gas, and therefore benefit from the pact. Ontario has a large manufacturing sector, much of which is of relatively small scale and high cost. Many Ontario residents, fearing that their manufacturing jobs will be lost as U.S. products arrive on a free-trade basis, strongly oppose the pact. Quebec is in an interesting situation, in that much of its textile, garment, and furniture sectors are threatened by U.S. products, but Quebec Hydro can earn enormous revenues if it can export electricity to the United States without any threat of trade barriers. As a result, the Quebec government, which owns Quebec Hydro, has favored the pact, despite the potential loss of some manufacturing jobs.

Ontario has experienced considerable job loss in manufacturing since the pact was first implemented, but the combination of an exchange rate that overvalues the Canadian dollar and a recession on both sides of the border is probably a more important cause of this job loss than lower barriers to U.S. goods. Ontario, however, remains very doubtful about the wisdom of the free-trade arrangement with the United States.

This pact has been debated far less in the United States, although the U.S. energy and forest products sectors opposed it. The U.S. coal industry will be injured if much larger volumes of electricity are imported from Canada, and the U.S. lumber industry understandably feels threatened, although the decline in new housing construction and environmental issues are probably more important problems for the U.S. lumber industry than the free-trade arrangement with Canada. Some of the controversies concerning the U.S.-Canada bloc are discussed in a newspaper column at the end of this chapter.

As noted earlier, the United States is now attempting to negotiate a free-trade area with Mexico, but that proposal is highly controversial because of its prospective income distribution effects within the United States, as discussed in Chapter 4. At present it is not clear whether negotiations will succeed or whether Congress would accept a pact with Mexico if negotiations were successful.

Regional economic integration has also been tried elsewhere. There is a Latin American Free Trade Area, and an association of Southeast Asian Nations, among others.

It was first thought that developing countries would benefit from regional economic integration, enabling them to overcome limitations imposed by the small size of national markets. But these hopes have not been realized. Regional economic integration has not been very successful among developing countries. When member countries export primary products, such as coffee or cocoa, their major markets are in the industrial countries, and regional integration does nothing to expand the market. When it is a matter of developing a new industry, conflicts arise about its location within the customs union. Which country will get the new industry? Member countries do not like to pay a higher price to import the commodity from a partner country than they would have to pay in the world market. They correctly see this as a welfare loss from trade diversion.

Political and administrative problems have also arisen. As a result, regional economic integration among LDC's has not proved to be very successful.

We Have a Big Stake in Canada's Choice

When Canadians go to the polls today, the outcome will have a major impact on the United States. The dominant issue in the campaign has been the Canadian-U.S. free trade agreement, which was signed earlier this year and recently ratified by the U.S. Congress.

If the Progressive Conservatives of Prime Minister Brian Mulroney get a parliamentary majority, this pact will also be ratified in Ottawa, and the elimination of tariffs and other barriers to trade between the two countries will begin in January. If they don't, the agreement is dead.

The importance of this agreement to the United States highlights the conflict between two views of how world trade should be expanded. For most of the post-war era, the dominant approach was through negotiations among all non-Communist countries that reduced trade barriers on a nondiscriminatory basis. These negotiations have occurred through the General Agreement on Tariffs and Trade, and have allowed all of the non-Communist world to benefit from trade growth. Another round of GATT negotiations is now underway in Geneva, but is reportedly progressing very slowly.

The alternative and increasingly dominant route to trade growth has been through regional blocs, the most important of which is the European Community. Trade liberalization through such blocs is discriminatory in that it occurs partially at the expense of reduced trading opportunities for non-member countries. When, for example, the formation of the European Community led to the elimination of French tariffs on German goods, U.S. firms discovered that German firms had a sizable competitive edge in France, and U.S. exports suffered.

The complete unification of European markets is now planned for 1992 and is advancing on schedule. The elimination of all remaining barriers to European trade in both goods and services will produce major economic gains for Europe, with some estimates suggesting a 7 percent increase in GNP. But there will also be trade diversion losses for the United States and other non-members. These costs will be increased if Austria, Norway and Sweden decide to join the European Community.

Losses for the United States would also rise if the unification of European markets is used as an opportunity subtly to increase barriers to goods coming from non-member countries. There are a number of ways in which this can be done, including the setting of European Community industrial standards in ways that discriminate against non-European products. There is a real concern in the United States about a possible Fortress Europe after 1992.

A larger and potentially inward-looking European Community does not offer very promising trading opportunities for the United States. Japan is becoming increasingly dominant in the far East and may be moving toward a regional trading bloc in that area. The debt crisis means that Latin America will not be a strong market for U.S. exports for the foreseeable future, which means that the Canada-U.S. free trade arrangement becomes vital if the United States is to become part of the trend toward regional trade growth.

Until a few weeks ago it appeared that the Conservative government of Mulroney would be reelected rather easily in Canada and that and the free trade pact with the United States would become effective in January. This agreement, however, has recently become extremely controversial among Canadian voters. Many Canadians understand that it would provide major economic benefits for Canada but are deeply fearful of becoming too closely tied to the United States.

Recent polls indicate that the election is very close. If the Liberals win or if there is a minority government, any prospects for the free trade pact would be dead.

In this event, the United States will be excluded from the possibility of trade growth through regional trade arrangements. A return to multilateral trade expansion through GATT then becomes the only U.S. option, and the success of the current negotiations in Geneva becomes critical. For the last few weeks, however, Americans with an interest in international economics have been watching the Canadian election campaign very closely, because the future of U.S. foreign trade may depend more on what happens today than on what happened Nov. 8.

EXHIBIT 8-1   We Have a Big Stake in Canada's Choice. Source: From *The Washington Post*, Robert M. Dunn, Jr. Copyright ©1988 *The Washington Post*, (Op. Ed. page), November 21, 1988.

QUESTIONS FOR STUDY AND REVIEW

1. Why is it much easier to negotiate a free-trade area than it is to arrange for a customs union or a common market, resulting in the fact that free-trade areas are far more common than either of the other two forms of regional bloc?

2. How can both trade creation and trade diversion effects occur in the same product market when a regional bloc is created? Explain carefully.

3. The European Economic Community was widely viewed as predominantly trade creating rather than diverting, except in the area of agriculture. What aspects of the European economies led to that conclusion? What happens to the trade creation and diversion effects of the EEC as more members, such as Greece and Spain, are added?

4. What will happen to Canada's gains from the free-trade arrangement with the United States if the U.S. Government negotiates a free-trade bloc with Mexico which does not include Canada? What would this imply about Canada's likely involvement in the current U.S.-Mexico talks?

5. If the regionalization of world trade continues through the formation of new trading blocs and the expansion of old ones, what will be the prospects for the success of future GATT rounds?

SELECTED REFERENCES

Balassa, Bela. *The Theory of Economic Integration.* Homewood, Ill.: R. D. Irwin, 1961.

Calingaert, Michael. *The 1992 Challenge from Europe: Development of the European Community's Internal Market.* Washington, D.C.: National Planning Association, 1988.

Commission of the EEC. *The Economics of 1992*. Brussels: Commission of the EEC, 1989.

Lipsey, R. G., "The Theory of Customs Unions: A Survey." *Economic Journal,* September 1961.

Schott, J. J., and M. G. Smith, ed. *The Canada-United States Free Trade Agreement*. Washington, D.C.: Institute for International Economics, 1988.

Scitovsky, Tibor. *Economic Theory and Western European Integration*. London: Allen Unwin, 1958.

Viner, Jacob. *The Customs Union Issue*. New York: Carnegie Endowment for World Peace, 1953.

9

COMMERCIAL POLICY

Regulation of external trade through tariffs, quotas, and other means has long been a prominent aspect of national sovereignty. A nation's position on such matters is commonly known as its "commercial policy." In this chapter we will describe the experience of the United States, after a brief account of world trends.

LONG SWINGS IN COMMERCIAL POLICY

Taking a long historical perspective, we can observe recurrent swings in commercial policy from protection toward free trade and then back again toward protection. The rise of nationalism in the Western world (c. 1500–1800) was associated with mercantilism and the close and detailed regulation of foreign trade. Under mercantilism, the national policy was to export much, import little, and thus acquire specie (gold and silver) through a favorable balance of trade. During the mercantilist period, all nations pursued highly restrictive commercial policies. They used tariffs, quotas, embargoes, state monopolies, and a variety of other measures to control and regulate their foreign trade.

The classical economists (Smith, Ricardo, et al.) were essentially attacking the whole edifice of mercantilist thought when they developed the theory of trade and comparative advantage. They stood mercantilist policy on its head: According to classical theory, imports are desirable, whereas exports are merely the necessary cost of obtaining them. As this theory gained ascendancy, the response in commercial policy was a swing from protection toward free trade. It did not go all the way and it was not universal, but there was a pronounced movement in the direction of free trade in the middle decades of the nineteenth century.

Great Britain was unmistakably the leader in this movement. After a protracted political struggle, the Corn Laws (which placed restrictions on grain imports) were repealed in 1846, and by 1850 virtually all British tariffs and other restrictions on imports had been swept away. Only a few revenue duties remained. Thus Great Britain, the leader in the Industrial Revolution, had unilaterally adopted a policy of free trade.

Other nations were influenced by the British example, and some of them moved significantly toward free trade in this period. Denmark, Holland, and Turkey accepted virtually full free trade, and many other European nations substantially reduced their tariff rates. For their part, the British pushed the cause of free trade with an almost evangelical fervor. Commercial treaties providing for tariff reductions and other measures to liberalize trade were negotiated with many European countries. Most of these treaties included a most-favored-nation clause, whereby the signatory countries agreed to extend to each other, automatically, the lowest tariff rates that might be granted to any third country in the future.[1] The resulting network of commercial treaties accomplished a substantial reduction in the level of protection in European trade.

British diplomacy also pushed the cause of free trade in other parts of the world. British colonies were perforce required to eliminate protective tariffs, keeping only a few revenue duties, although vestiges of preferential treatment for the mother country sometimes remained. In addition, British diplomacy and power combined to persuade a number of other countries to sign commercial treaties in which these countries agreed to open their economies to foreign trade and to fix very low tariff rates on such trade. In some of these unequal treaties, as they came to be called, the concessions were made almost entirely by the weaker country. Of course, it is true that Britain had already removed its trade restrictions, so it could claim that parity prevailed, but other Western powers quickly followed the British lead and asked for similar concessions even though they made none themselves.

For example, after Britain negotiated a treaty with Thailand in 1855 in which Thailand agreed to limit its import tariffs to 3 percent *ad valorem,* the same terms were obtained by other Western powers, including some nations that retained

---

[1]This clause has played an important role in U.S. tariff policy, as we will see.

high protective tariffs themselves (notably, the United States).[2] After the infamous Opium War (1839–42) in which Britain forced China to allow the importation of opium, China signed treaties that committed it to open certain port cities to foreign trade and fixed tariff rates at low levels. Other Western powers demanded and obtained the same terms.

The free-trade tide reached its peak in about 1870 but then began to ebb. In Germany, France, Italy, and other European countries, emerging industries called for protection against the established industries in England. The rapid expansion of American grain exports after 1870 led European agrarian interests to join with the industrialists in support of higher tariffs. As a result, tariff increases were frequent in the last quarter of the nineteenth century. Of the major nations, only Britain and Holland clung to free trade.

This swing toward protection was accompanied by a competitive scramble for colonies. Between 1875 and 1914, the entire continent of Africa was swallowed up, with the sole exceptions of Liberia and Ethiopia. In Asia and the Middle East, Western imperialism extended its sway over areas that had previously escaped. In all of Asia, only Japan and Thailand retained their sovereignty, and both of them had been forcibly opened to foreign trade in the 1850s. Colonies were seen as potential markets, as outlets for the new industrial capacity being created in the mother countries, and as sources of raw materials to supply the new industries. In many cases, preferential trading arrangements were set up between colony and mother country. Even Britain was not immune to this element of neomercantilism, and the dominions (such as Canada) began giving preferential treatment to imports from Great Britain in 1898.

The protectionist tide continued to swell after World War I, reaching its peak in the depression years of the 1930s. By that time, world trade was severely restricted by tariffs and other barriers to trade. Even in Britain, the citadel of free trade, protectionist tariffs were installed in the aftermath of World War I, with preferential rates for dominions and colonies of the British Empire.

Beginning in the 1930s, another swing toward free trade got underway, a movement in which the United States has played an important role.

THE U.S. TARIFF, 1789–1934

The United States did not participate in the free-trade movement during the nineteenth century. During the period from 1789 to 1934, tariff rates were set by acts of Congress, and the levels fixed in successive tariff acts reflected congressional preoccupation with domestic political and economic concerns. For most of the period, tariffs were quite high.

The first tariff, adopted in 1789, was designed primarily to provide revenue for the federal government. With a few exceptions, tariff rates were low: 5 percent *ad valorem*. Higher rates were fixed on a few selected manufactured goods, however, with the clear intent to stimulate and protect domestic production.

---

[2]It should be added that, to its credit, the United States took initiative in revising this treaty 75 years later. The first revision graciously allowed Thailand to increase tariffs to 5 percent.

The tariff issue remained dormant for the next 30 years, although tariff rates were steadily increased in a series of congressional tariff acts. The new nation, primarily agricultural, exported its raw materials and purchased a variety of manufactured goods from Europe. In the meantime, domestic manufacturing industries were beginning to emerge. These young industries received a sharp stimulus when foreign trade was interrupted by the Napoleonic War, Jefferson's embargo, and the War of 1812. These events, by cutting off the supply of foreign goods, provided total protection for domestic producers: the equivalent of a prohibitive tariff. Consequently, domestic output of manufactured goods increased greatly.

When the war ended in 1815 and normal trade resumed, these newly expanded industries were forced to curtail output and employment. They responded by demanding protection, and the tariff question moved onto center stage in American politics. A mildly protective tariff act was passed in 1816, but it did not satisfy the manufacturing interests, and political pressures for higher tariffs continued. A more protective tariff bill was hotly debated in 1820 but failed by a single vote to pass the Senate. The debate continued, and by the mid-1820s the tariff had become a major political issue. The tariff controversy reached the boiling point in the famous Tariff Act of 1828, known as the "Tariff of Abominations."

One reason why the tariff issue generated so much heat was that major geographic sections of the country were affected in different ways, and they clearly recognized that their interests were in conflict. Southern and western states produced agricultural surpluses and exported them to Europe. They wanted to be able to buy manufactured goods at the lowest possible prices; hence, they favored free trade. Manufacturing industries were located primarily in northern and mid-Atlantic states, on the other hand, and these states wanted high tariffs on imported manufactured goods to protect their industries, which were now hard-pressed by competition from European producers. In terms of our discussion in Chapter 6, the benefits of high tariffs accrued primarily to industrial states whereas the losses fell largely on agricultural exporting states. (Of course, the matter was further complicated by the fact that no state was wholly agricultural or wholly industrial.) Specifically, the real terms of trade of agricultural producers were adversely affected by tariffs on manufactured goods. Farmers sold their products at world market prices, but they had to pay tariff-inflated prices for the things they bought.

Members of Congress tended to vote in accordance with the interests of their constituents; consequently, much political maneuvering occurred each time a tariff bill was on the floor. In order to obtain a high tariff for an industry in his district, a congressman would agree to vote for high tariffs proposed for industries in other states. "I'll vote for your tariff if you'll vote for mine."

In such a bargaining atmosphere, free-trade advocates were at a disadvantage because they had nothing to offer. Appeals to the principle of comparative advantages did not influence many votes.

As a result, when the tariff came up for consideration by Congress in 1828, southerners tried a crafty maneuver. When the tariff bill was being prepared in committee, they loaded it with extremely high tariff rates on both raw materials and manufactured goods. Their purpose was to make the bill so unattractive and unpopular that it would be voted down on the floor. They took particular care to place high tariffs on a number of commodities that were imported by New

England states, such as hemp, sailcloth, molasses, and raw wool. The reason for this strategy was that New England had been ambivalent on the tariff issue. On the one hand, it had some manufacturing interests, especially textiles, that pulled it toward protection; on the other hand, it had an interest in trade and shipping and thus leaned toward free trade. The southern strategy was to levy such high tariffs on New England's import items that the bill would be unacceptable to New England congressmen. They would join the southerners in voting against it, thus producing the majority needed for its defeat.

The strategy nearly succeeded, but in the end the New England delegations split their votes, and to the surprise and consternation of the southerners, the bill was enacted into law. All those absurdly high tariff rates went into effect, and the Tariff of Abominations gave the United States a highly protectionist tariff structure. (South Carolina passed an ordinance declaring the Tariff of 1828 null and void in that state and threatened to secede over the issue, but this threat to the union was turned aside.)

Some of the worst abominations were soon removed, and in 1833 a new tariff act was passed in which a compromise was reached between the contending interests and tariff rates were reduced. Tariffs generally drifted down for the next 30 years, partly because they were generating too much revenue and had to be reduced to prevent an unwelcome surplus from piling up in the U.S. Treasury. By the time the Civil War broke out, U.S. tariffs had fallen to relatively modest levels (See Figure 9-1.)

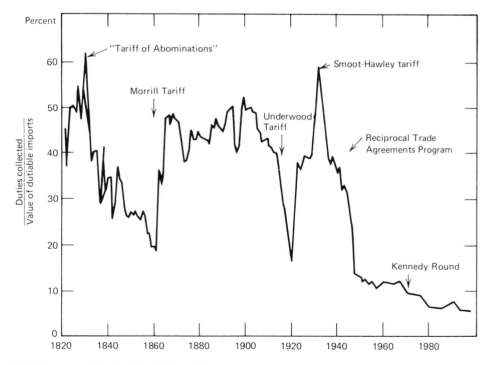

FIGURE 9-1 U.S. Tariff, 1821–1980. Duties collected as a percentage of the value of dutiable imports.

Tariffs were then sharply increased during the Civil War, and they remained at high levels for the rest of the nineteenth century. Southerners continued to favor free trade, but the South had little political weight after the Civil War. The Republican party, drawing its strength from the Midwest and the North, embraced protectionism and kept tariff rates at high levels. When the Democratic party came to power with the election of Grover Cleveland, an attempt was made to reduce tariffs, but it did not accomplish much. Not until the Underwood Tariff in 1913 was any significant reduction made.

The Underwood Tariff was a signal victory for the advocates of freer trade, but it had little actual effect because the outbreak of World War I in 1914 disrupted normal trade for several years. At the end of the war, the United States restored high tariffs in the Fordney-McCumber Tariff Act (1921). Finally, in the last tariff act passed by Congress, the Smoot-Hawley Tariff Act (1930), American tariff rates were raised to the highest level since the Tariff of Abominations in 1828.

The Smoot-Hawley Tariff Act has acquired considerable notoriety. It is often held up as a prime example of irresponsible economic policy and is blamed for aggravating world economic problems in the 1930s.

When Congress began its deliberations in 1929, the United States had experienced a decade of prosperity, unemployment was low, the balance of payments was strong, and no urgent demands for tariffs were being heard. Initially, the primary purpose of the new tariff legislation was to provide some relief and assistance to American farmers, but the stock market crash and early signs of a slide into an economic slump led to calls for protective tariffs on numerous products. Members of Congress began to trade votes with one another and finally produced a tariff bill that sharply increased the level of protection all around.

Even before its passage, this bill attracted much attention in the outside world. The United States had emerged from World War I in a strong economic position. Its economy had become a major market, and other countries had borrowed heavily from it both during and after the war. To pay their debts to us, other nations had to sell us their goods and services, but this bill would seriously impair their ability to do so. Strong protests were lodged with the United States, and other countries appealed to Congress to reject this course of action. Within the United States as well, many voices were raised against the pending bill. Over 1000 economists signed a petition opposing such an increase in tariffs and urging President Hoover to veto the bill.

All these protests were to no avail. The bill was signed, and the new tariff became effective. It established the highest level of tariff rates in U.S. history. Other countries soon retaliated with increases in their tariffs, and world trade steadily shrank as the world sank into depression. No one can say exactly how much the Smoot-Hawley Tariff Act was responsible for the economic woes of the 1930s, but it seems clear that it had a substantial effect. U.S. trade dropped 70 percent in value (50 percent in volume) from 1929 to 1932, and declining world trade contributed to the spread of depression throughout the world.

Thus, from 1861 to the 1930s the United States pursued a generally protectionist policy. It virtually ignored the swing to free trade that occurred in the outside world from 1850 to 1875.

A rough measure of the level of U.S. protection is provided in Figure 9-1, which shows the percentage ratio of tariffs collected to the value of imports subject to tariff. This is an imperfect measure of the average tariff: It has an upward bias because it ignored goods on the free list, and it has a downward bias because it gives no weight to goods subject to a prohibitive tariff (no duties collected and no imports). However, this measure, as depicted in Figure 9-1, probably indicated fairly accurately the level and direction of changes in the U.S. tariff from 1800 to 1980. Note the peak reached in 1828, the downward drift until 1860, the high level in the rest of the nineteenth century, and the high point registered after the Smoot-Hawley Act.

A great many tariff arguments were used during the period we have been discussing (1789–1934). At one time or another, virtually every argument mentioned in Chapter 7 was put forward. However, in the pre-Civil War period, the principal arguments used, aside from simple self-interest, were the revenue, defense, and infant-industry arguments. With no direct taxes available to it, the federal government relied on excise taxes and import duties for its revenue. The defense argument requires no further comment. For a young nation with vast undeveloped resources, the infant-industry argument was a natural. Ever since Alexander Hamilton's *Report on Manufactures* (1791), tariff advocates had pressed the case for protection of young industries. However, not until 1815 did the infant-industry argument become important as a basis for tariff legislation. Its influence was strengthened by the spectacle of fledgling industries being destroyed by import competition when trade resumed after the War of 1812, as well as by such speeches as that of Henry Brougham in the British House of Commons (1816), urging the need "to stifle in the cradle those rising manufacturers in the United States which the war had forced into existence."[3]

By the latter part of the nineteenth century, most American industries had grown too large to be called infants, and use of the infant-industry argument declined. Its place as the leading protectionist argument was taken by the cheap-labor argument. Indeed, that argument had always been heard, because American wages were consistently higher than those paid by their European competitors. It was often coupled with the fair play argument, a variant of the so-called scientific tariff. That is, it was said that tariffs should be just high enough to place foreign and domestic producers on an equal footing so that they could compete fairly. As noted in Chapter 7, such a policy would stifle trade.

Throughout the nineteenth century, the United States had been preoccupied with its own internal development, with the westward movement and the settlement of a continent. Its emergence after World War I as a world power and a major factor in world trade caught it unaware and unprepared. The angry response to the Smoot-Hawley Tariff Act in the rest of the world took the country by surprise. The U.S. tariff had not previously been taken all that seriously by other countries. Now the obligations of a world power began to make themselves felt.

---

[3]Cited in Edward Stanwood, *American Tariff Controversies in the Nineteenth Century,* Vol. 1 (New York: Houghton Mifflin, 1903), pp. 167–168.

A U.S. INITIATIVE: THE RECIPROCAL TRADE AGREEMENTS PROGRAM

As trade barriers rose after 1930 and the world slipped more deeply into depression, it became clear that something needed to be done to revive world trade and restore the gains from trade and specialization. In the United States the newly elected administration of President Franklin D. Roosevelt was urgently searching for ways to increase output and employment, and in 1934 Congress was persuaded to authorize a new approach to tariff policy that promised to help achieve both goals: revival of trade and expansion of employment.

In that year Congress passed the Reciprocal Trade Agreements Act, authorizing the president to negotiate bilateral trade agreements in which each signatory country would agree to reduce its tariff rates on specific commodities. The act authorized the president to reduce existing tariff rates by up to 50 percent. One of the remarkable features of this legislation was that Congress delegated to the executive the power to fix tax rates (i.e., tariffs), perhaps its most jealously guarded prerogative. There were restrictions and limitations, of course, and Congress could rescind the delegation any time it chose, but the fact is that since 1934 U.S. tariff rates have been set by the president. The Smoot-Hawley Tariff Act was the last one in which Congress itself set the actual rates of duty.

The reason for this approach was a simple, practical one: U.S. tariff reductions were to be made in exchange for reductions made by other nations, and there is no way the necessary bargaining could be done in Congress. As the program was explained to Congress, its primary goal was to increase U.S. exports in order to stimulate the domestic economy. Thus the tariff concessions made by other countries were vital, and they could only be obtained through negotiation. A certain guile, if not deception, seems to have been involved in this campaign to persuade Congress. It was made to sound as though the United States could, through clever bargaining, achieve an increase in exports without having to accept any more imports. In fact, President Roosevelt and Secretary of State Cordell Hull solemnly promised Congress that no tariff reduction would be made that would injure any American industry. Our earlier analysis of tariffs has clearly shown that tariff changes cause shifts in the allocation of resources, shifts that are favorable to some industries and harmful to others.

From 1934 to 1947, the United States negotiated bilateral trade agreements with 29 nations. These agreements provided for tariff concessions on 69 percent of all dutiable imports into the United States and reduced the average tariff by about one-third.[4] Two important principles were embodied in these trade agreements. First, every one of them included the unconditional most-favored-nation (MFN) clause. As noted earlier, this means that each of the signatory countries agreed to extend the tariff reductions covered in the agreement to all other countries that have MFN status, even though these other countries made no concessions themselves. For example, if France and the United States conclude an agreement in which

---

[4]*Trade Barriers,* Vol. 3 (Washington, D.C.: U.S. Tariff Commission, April 1974), Chapter 5.

France reduces its tariff on electrical machinery, the reduced tariff automatically applies to French imports from all MFN countries, even though the other countries give France no concession in return. Similarly, the U.S. concession to France, for example, a reduction in our tariff on wine, would automatically be extended to all other countries with MFN status.

The effect of the most-favored-nation clause is to keep a given country's tariff rates uniform and equal to all countries. Without it, bilateral trade agreements would produce a situation in which imports into a given country would be charged different tariff rates, depending on where the imports came from. Such tariff differentials are administratively awkward and economically inefficient. Thus the purpose of the most-favored-nation clause is to achieve a nondiscriminatory tariff structure.

The second negotiating principle, the "chief supplier" rule, was used to lessen the sense people had that third countries were getting something for nothing as a result of the inclusion of most-favored-nation clauses in these trade agreements. The point is simply that in each case the United States sought to bargain with the chief supplier of a given imported commodity. When the United States offered a tariff reduction on that commodity, it obtained, in return, tariff reductions on certain of its export commodities. That is the sense in which the agreements were reciprocal. By negotiating with the chief supplier of each commodity, the United States minimized the unearned benefit accruing to third countries to whom its tariff reductions were extended without any concession on their part. (Note that this whole discussion has a mercantilistic flavor. The implication is that exports are a good thing and should be encouraged, whereas imports are harmful to a country.)

By negotiating trade agreements with a large number of countries, the United States was able to achieve a significant reduction in the level of world tariffs. Even though each agreement was bilateral, the concessions they contained were generalized through the most-favored-nation clause.

In the original Reciprocal Trade Agreements Act, the delegation of power to the president was for only three years, but Congress renewed it for periods of one to three years until 1962, when the legislation was placed on a new footing in the Trade Expansion Act of 1962. In each renewal, Congress revised and restated the authority of the president to reduce tariffs. Over the whole period, Congress tended to tighten its reins on the executive: to authorize smaller tariff reductions, to place more restrictions on the terms of the agreements, and to provide more safeguards against injury to domestic industries. The main point, however, is that the extensions were approved, and the United States has maintained a generally liberal stance on tariff policy since 1934.

SHIFT TO MULTILATERALISM

During and after World War II, plans were drawn up for an International Trade Organization through which nations could regulate and coordinate their commercial policies. In 1945 the United States presented a draft charter for such an organization that would serve as a counterpart, in the field of trade and commercial policy, to the International Monetary Fund in the monetary field. However, this proposed charter ran into heavy opposition in several countries. When the U.S. Congress declined to approve it, it was quietly dropped.

In the meantime, under the authority contained in the Reciprocal Trade Agreements Act, the United States invited other nations to participate in multilateral negotiations for the reduction of tariffs and other trade barriers. At a conference held in 1947, a General Agreement on Tariffs and Trade was adopted. From this unlikely beginning, a permanent international organization by that name has emerged. It is commonly referred to by its acronym, GATT. The United States participates in GATT under the authority of the Reciprocal Trade Agreement acts and their successors. Formal congressional approval of GATT was not necessary.

GATT is a multilateral agreement whose articles constitute a code of conduct for international trade and a basis for multilateral negotiation of trade agreements. It seeks to reduce tariffs and other barriers to trade, and to place all countries on an equal footing in their trade relationships.

The principle of nondiscrimination in trade is central to the General Agreement. Article One incorporates the unconditional most-favored-nation clause, and all contracting parties are bound to grant to each other treatment as favorable as they give to any other country. This clause, which guarantees equality of treatment and rules out discriminatory trade barriers, is the most important single feature of GATT.

The crucial importance of nondiscrimination is underscored by the intense debate that has been generated by the exceptions made to the general rule contained in Article One. There are two important exceptions. First, when a group of countries forms a customs union or free-trade area, they may eliminate tariffs among themselves but retain tariffs against outside countries. Technically, such arrangements violate the most-favored-nation clause, but they are permitted in the General Agreement. A second exception was authorized in 1971 in response to demands made by developing countries for preferential treatment for their exports. A provision was made to allow countries to apply lower tariff rates to imports coming from developing countries than they apply to imports from other countries.

Another key feature of the General Agreement is its opposition to quantitative restrictions (quotas) on trade. The general position is that if trade barriers are to exist, they should take the form of explicit tariffs so that everyone can judge their severity and determine that they are being applied in a nondiscriminatory manner. Quantitative restrictions are almost unavoidably discriminatory, and their true protective effect is difficult to judge. Here too, however, exceptions have had to be made. Despite the general prohibition against quantitative restrictions in the Articles of Agreement, they continue to be widely used. One rather open-ended exception provides that quantitative restrictions can be applied by a country in order to safeguard its balance of payments. Another exception allows such restrictions if they are needed because of a country's economic development policies. In practice, it is the GATT's consultative machinery that enables these loosely worded exceptions to remain manageable. Another important exception allows quantitative restrictions on agricultural products when needed to permit the operation and enforcement of domestic agricultural support programs. The United States insisted on this provision. Its price support schemes, which had the effect of holding the domestic price above the world level, meant that imports had to be restricted, and quotas were used for this purpose.

Although GATT has compromised its general principles of nondiscrimination and opposition to quantitative restrictions, it has preserved a primary emphasis on these principles. The thrust of its influence and its policies has been toward equality of treatment among countries, simplification and reduction of trade barriers, and open discussions and negotiations. It has provided at least the beginnings of a code of conduct and a forum for the discussion of conflicts in the realm of commercial policy.

GATT's most important activity has been its sponsorship of a series of tariff negotiations in which member countries have engaged in bargaining to reduce their tariffs and other trade barriers. The procedure is that each country prepares lists of concessions it is willing to offer and of concessions it wants to obtain from other countries. Although these offers and requests are initially bilateral, they acquire a multilateral aspect because they are circulated to all other participating countries. Through the operation of the most-favored-nation clause, a concession to one country is a concession to all (at least to all members). By having all countries negotiating simultaneously, each country is able to evaluate the benefits it may obtain because of concessions made between any two other countries.

This negotiating process is complicated, cumbersome, and lengthy; some negotiations, or "rounds," have taken four or five years to complete. However, it has distinct advantages over the traditional bilateral negotiation, as the following passage makes clear:

> *The multilateral procedure for tariff negotiations, by contrast with the traditional methods, has the advantage of enabling participating countries to assess the value of concessions granted by other countries over and above the direct concessions negotiated. In traditional bilateral negotiations these indirect benefits could not be assessed with any accuracy and were generally disregarded. With the new approach the tendency is to strike a balance, not between direct concessions but between the aggregate of direct and indirect benefits; this enables negotiating countries to go much further in the way of tariff negotiation than would otherwise be possible.*[5]

Altogether, six rounds of multilateral negotiations took place between 1947 and 1967. They varied in scope and in the size of the tariff reductions accomplished, but their cumulative effect was a substantial reduction in tariff levels for manufactured goods, especially those levied by industrial countries. The average U.S. tariff on dutiable goods declined from 53 percent in 1933 (the peak level reached after the Smoot-Hawley Tariff Act) to about 10 percent in the 1960s. (See Figure 9-1.) However, this comparison exaggerates the influence of deliberate tariff reduction. Much of this reduction—perhaps as much as half—is the result of inflation. When prices rise, the *ad valorem* equivalent of specific tariffs is automatically reduced. Tariffs were especially low on raw materials, and many items were on the free list (except those competing with domestic producers).

[5]*GATT in Action*, Geneva, January 1952, pp. 20–21. Cited in Karin Kock, *International Trade Policy and the GATT, 1947–1967* (Stockholm: Almquist & Wiksell, 1969), p. 64.

Tariff averages conceal large disparities in tariff rates on individual items, however, and much room remained for further moves toward trade liberalization. We will describe the last three GATT rounds in some detail.

THE LAST THREE GATT ROUNDS

The first five rounds of tariff negotiations conducted under GATT auspices were essentially bilateral negotiations carried out simultaneously by all the participating nations. The first round, completed in 1947, achieved a substantial reduction in tariff levels (about 20 percent, on average), but the net effect of the next four rounds was much smaller. Bilateral bargaining for tariff cuts on specific commodities seemed to be running out of steam. Consequently, in the sixth session, known as the Kennedy Round, a new approach was used.

The Kennedy Round

The Trade Expansion Act of 1962 was the last important piece of legislation passed in President Kennedy's administration. It authorized the United States to engage in negotiations for across-the-board tariff reduction. After protracted bargaining, countries taking part in the Kennedy Round of GATT negotiations reached an agreement in 1967 providing for average tariff cuts of about 35 percent, with most reductions occurring across the board. Many exceptions were made, as each country had its list of sensitive items requiring special treatment, but for the great majority of specific tariff lines, existing tariffs were reduced by a uniform percentage.

One reason why this method was used was that the European Economic Community (the Common Market) had just agreed on a common external tariff schedule for its (then) six member nations. The EEC was bargaining as a single unit in the GATT negotiations, and agreement on across-the-board tariff cuts was much easier to achieve than tariff-reductions of varying size on different commodities. The latter procedure threatened to disturb the delicate balance of interests established among the member nations when the common external tariff had itself been negotiated.

Another innovative feature of the Trade Expansion Act of 1962 was its provision for "adjustment assistance" to U.S. workers and firms injured by tariff reductions. Injured parties could petition the U.S. Tariff Commission (a bipartisan agency, later renamed the International Trade Commission), and if the Tariff Commission found that injury had occurred as a result of import competition, various forms of relief and assistance could be given. For workers these included extended unemployment insurance, education and training allowances, and relocation allowances to enable them to move to places where jobs were available; for firms they included low-interest loans, technical assistance, or other benefits that would enable them to shift into other, more competitive lines of work. The idea is an excellent one: to use some of the gains from trade to compensate those who are adversely affected by tariff reductions, and thereby to lessen the frictional costs, the stresses and strains, of the resource reallocation that accompanies trade expansion. As we have seen in previous chapters, tariff reduction benefits some groups within a country and harms others. It seems sensible and equitable for society to take part of the gain in the form of taxes, and then to use these funds to ameliorate the losses suffered by those who must reallocate resources or otherwise bear the burden of adjustment.

Although analytically sound, adjustment assistance has not worked very well in practice. There are many administrative and operational difficulties. Forms must be filled out, hearings held, and proof of injury demonstrated. These procedures and routine formalities take time and money, especially for lawyer's fees, and only a few petitions were filed under the provisions of the 1962 act. Even if a petition is approved, it may be difficult for older workers to learn a new skill, and they may not wish to pick up and move to a new city, leaving friends and relatives behind. Another problem is that when a firm begins to experience difficulties, it is not easy to prove that import competition is the real cause. Domestic competitors may be underselling the faltering firm, or consumer demand for its product may have declined because attractive substitutes have been introduced by other industries. One might also question the logic of extending more assistance to firms and workers who have been displaced because of foreign competition than to those who are displaced because of technological change, shifts in consumer tastes, or other factors. For example, suppose two firms in the same New England city have fallen on hard times and have had to cut output and lay off workers. One firm—say, a shoe manufacturer—shows that it has been harmed by shoe imports from Brazil and Italy, and thus it and its workers qualify for adjustment assistance; the other firm—say, a hosiery mill—has been undersold by newly installed mills in Georgia and North Carolina, and thus it is not eligible for adjustment assistance. Such differential treatment seems difficult to justify. One approach is simply to recognize unemployment and underutilization of capacity as social problems and to provide some general programs for dealing with them, without regard for the specific cause of the dislocation. However, in the absence of such general programs, reductions of tariffs and other trade barriers will be resisted by those who bear the brunt of the costs of adjustment, and it may be necessary to fall back on an imperfect, second-best policy and attempt to extend adjustment assistance to those who suffer injury from increased imports.

Although the Trade Expansion Act of 1962 shifted emphasis toward adjustment in response to increased imports, it still retained an "escape clause": a provision for an industry that believes it has been injured by tariff reductions to petition for relief. Such clauses have been required in all U.S. trade agreements since 1947. They reflect a basic ambivalence in U.S. foreign trade policy: On the one hand, it seeks to reduce trade barriers and promote trade and specialization, but on the other, it seeks to avoid the reallocative effects of increased imports. To invoke the escape clause, the industry files a petition with the U.S. Tariff Commission, which then investigates and reports its findings to the president. If the Tariff Commission finds that injury has occurred, the president may provide relief in the form of an increase in the tariff or the imposition of some other restriction on imports. He may also authorize adjustment assistance to the affected workers and firms.

The specific terms and conditions for escape clause action have varied from one time to another, and so has the vigor of enforcement. The language of the

Trade Expansion Act was, comparatively speaking, unfavorable to the industries claiming injury. It even allowed the president to decline to provide tariff relief if he judged that to be in the national interest, and it allowed him to provide adjustment assistance instead of import restrictions. Escape clause petitions were also looked at with a critical eye in this period. From 1962 to 1969 only 13 new escape clause applications were filed, none of which was accepted.

Although the escape clause has not been heavily used, its existence has tended to restrain foreign exporters and has induced them to impose "voluntary" limits on their exports of certain commodities to the U.S. market. In some cases, several exporting countries have negotiated agreements among themselves to fix strict export quotas on their sales to the United States. Through such voluntary restrictions, they hope to avoid escape clause action to raise the U.S. tariff. In recent years voluntary quotas have been used to restrict exports of steel, textiles, meat, footwear, and other commodities. In the case of textiles, a multilateral agreement, known as the Multifibre Arrangement, was negotiated under GATT auspices in which several exporting countries accepted export restrictions. One of the stated purposes of this agreement was to avoid market disruption in the importing countries.

The Tokyo Round

A seventh round of GATT negotiations got underway in 1973, with U.S. participation authorized by the Trade Reform Act of 1974. This negotiation, popularly known as the Tokyo Round, was finally completed in 1979. We will briefly describe the main features of the Trade Reform Act and the attendant negotiations.

First, the president was authorized to reduce existing tariffs up to 60 percent, and to eliminate "nuisance tariffs" (those under 5 percent) completely. The final Tokyo Round agreement entailed a reduction by the major industrialized countries of about 33 percent on items included, although each country had its list of sensitive items that were excluded. The agreed-upon formula for tariff reductions had the effect of reducing high tariff rates more than low ones, thus tending to harmonize tariff levels around the world.[6] Similarly, tariff cuts on finished goods were deeper than those on raw materials, thereby tending to reduce the degree of tariff escalation: It lowers the effective tariff rates on finished goods.

Tariff cuts by developing countries were less extensive, but the overall result of the Tokyo Round was a substantial reduction in tariff levels. This was an impressive achievement in such a troubled period.

The magnitude of the cuts made, and the resulting low levels of average tariffs in industrial countries after the Tokyo Round, can be seen in Table 9-1. Tariffs are now so low that they do not constitute a major barrier to trade in industrial countries. Indeed, one study found that total elimination of all remaining tariffs would have minuscule effects on the world economy, an increase in welfare of

---

[6]The actual formula used was proposed by the Swiss. It is: Tariff reduction $= t/(t + 0.14)$, where $t =$ the existing tariff rate. Thus a 40 percent existing tariff would be cut by $0.40/(0.40 + 0.14) = 74$ percent, whereas a 10 percent existing tariff would be cut by $0.10/(0.10 + 0.14) = 42$ percent.

TABLE 9-1 Average Tariff Rates in Selected Countries

	Tariffs on Industrial Products (percent)		
	Before Tokyo Round	After Tokyo Round	Reduction
European Community	6.6	4.7	29
Japan	5.5	2.8	49
United States	6.4	4.4	31
All industrial countries	7.1	4.7	34

Source: International Monetary Fund, *Developments in International Trade Policy,* Occasional Paper No. 16, 1982.

only one-tenth of 1 percent.[7] However, as tariffs have come down, other forms of protection have come into greater use.

Second, the president was authorized to engage in negotiations for the reduction of nontariff barriers. Such negotiations were a prominent feature of the Tokyo Round. This reflects the growing recognition that as tariff walls have come down, nontariff barriers have become relatively more important. In many cases they now constitute the major obstacle to trade. Bargaining for the reduction of nontariff barriers is difficult, as we will explain, and in this case it was further complicated by a stipulation in the Trade Reform Act requiring congressional approval of the agreements on nontariff barriers.

Third, the Trade Reform Act extended, with modification, previous provisions for an escape clause and for adjustment assistance. The definition of injury was changed, making it somewhat easier for the International Trade Commission (ITC) to find that injury has occurred, but the ITC is now given the option of recommending tariff relief or adjustment assistance. (The president is not required to accept an ITC recommendation of tariff relief, but if he does not, Congress may override his decision.) The rules governing adjustment assistance were also modified to increase the benefits and to make it easier for injured parties to file petitions.

Fourth, the Trade Reform Act strengthened the hands of the executive branch in dealing with certain unfair trade practices sometimes employed by foreign firms and governments. These practices include dumping, subsidies, tax rebates, and various monopolistic practices. After hearings have been held and an investigation has been conducted, countervailing tariffs may be imposed or other action taken. This legislation has stimulated GATT to pursue more vigorously its efforts to define a code of rules for the conduct of international trade. The mere threat of U.S. action may be enough to cause foreign exporters to change some of their procedures.

[7]Alan V. Deardorff and Robert M. Stern, "The Economic Effects of Complete Elimination of Post-Tokyo Round Tariffs," in William R. Cline, ed., *Trade Policy in the 80s* (Cambridge, Mass.: MIT Press, 1983), Ch. 20.

Finally, the Trade Reform Act authorized preferential tariff treatment for developing countries. These countries had long sought such preferences, and many industrialized countries had already granted them, but the United States has resisted this idea. Tariff preferences meant a departure from the principle of nondiscrimination that had been a central feature of U.S. commercial policy ever since the Reciprocal Trade Agreements program had begun.

Under the authority provided in the Trade Reform Act, the United States accepted the Generalized System of Preferences in which tariff preferences are provided for developing countries subject to a number of restrictions and qualifications. For commodities on the approved list, the United States grants duty-free entry (a zero tariff) to imports from developing countries. The hope is that the competitive advantage provided by this preferential treatment will stimulate the production and export of manufactured goods in these countries. Eventually, as production expands and efficiency improves, the tariff preferences can be dispensed with. Thus, in a sense, the argument for tariff preferences is a variant of the infant-industry argument.

The American GSP contains a number of limitations. First, many commodities have been excluded from the list because of their political sensitivity and because imports have already threatened to disrupt domestic production or cause injury to domestic producers. These commodities include textiles, steel, footwear, glass, and watches. Furthermore, if import relief is approved for any commodity through an escape clause action, the president must withdraw preferential treatment under GSP. Second, the tariff preference is denied any developing country that supplies 50 percent or more of total U.S. imports of a given article, or that supplies more than $30 million worth of the article.[8] he effect of this provision, especially the $30 million ceiling, is to inhibit the expansion of exports from developing countries. If a country's exports exceed the stated limit, it loses the tariff preference on the full amount of its exports of that article. This gives a developing country a powerful incentive to restrain the expansion of its exports to the United States. Third, the benefits of GSP are denied to a number of countries for various reasons: some members of the Organization of Petroleum Exporting Countries (OPEC), countries that do not enjoy most-favored-nation treatment, countries that give reverse preferences to other developed countries, and countries that expropriate American investments without compensation.

In view of the restrictions and limitations surrounding GSP, some economists have concluded that developing countries would be well advised to forego preferential tariffs and focus their efforts on vigorous bargaining for nondiscriminatory tariff reductions on their principal exportable commodities. It has been estimated that only about 12 percent of the exports of developing countries to the United States qualify for GSP treatment. (European coverage is similar in magnitude.) However, tariff preferences have been one of the main objectives of developing countries, and they are unlikely to give them up. In fact, they secured an agreement in the Tokyo Round recognizing these preferential tariff systems as a permanent legal feature of the world trading system and not merely a temporary device, as originally intended.

---

[8]This particular limit is adjusted over time to allow for inflation and to permit some growth to occur.

The Uruguay Round

This GATT round began in 1986 in Punta del Este, Uruguay. The ongoing discussions are actually held in Geneva, Switzerland, and are focused on a wide range of nontariff trade barriers (N.T.B.s). Although it is hoped that sizable tariff reductions will also be part of the final agreement, the primary goal is to deal with trade in services, agricultural export subsidies, intellectual property rights, and Voluntary Export Restraints (VERs). All of these are sensitive issues, and at the time of this writing the formal talks have been suspended and it is not clear that they will be restarted. This may be the first GATT round to have failed to accomplish its goals.

Agriculture is a particularly difficult issue because the European Community support prices under its Common Agricultural Policy are high enough to generate huge surpluses. In an attempt to dispose of these excess supplies, the Community has exported them at low subsidized prices in competition with products coming from the United States, Argentina, Canada, and Australia. These four countries, and others with a comparative advantage in agricultural products, feel that these subsidized exports from Europe are unfair. Therefore they want binding agreements to limit them. Farmers are an extremely powerful political force in Europe, however, making it difficult for the Community representatives to agree to policies that would reduce European surpluses and the need to dump them on world markets. Food-importing countries, such as Egypt and Bangladesh, understandably prefer the present situation of competition through subsidies, because it sharply reduces the prices they pay for imported grain.

The discussions over trade in services include areas such as banking, insurance, construction, and data processing. Many developing countries keep foreign firms out of their markets for such services, and since the United States has, or believes it has, a comparative advantage in many such services, it is trying to negotiate increased access for U.S. firms in developing country markets for services. A proposed settlement of the remaining issues in this GATT round is discussed in an appendix to this chapter.

RECIPROCITY

In recent years a spate of new protectionist proposals have been put forward under the label "reciprocity." This is a new use of an old term. The original U.S. initiative for tariff reduction (in the 1930s) involved reciprocal concessions by the negotiating countries. So do the GATT negotiations. Starting from existing levels of tariffs, each country agrees to make certain reductions. The tariff reductions one country makes are balanced against the reductions made by the other country. All of these tariff changes are then generalized to third countries through the unconditional most-favored-nations clause.

The new reciprocity has a different thrust. One country, say, the United States, looks at its overall level of protection and compares it with that of another country. In the bilateral comparison, the goal is to secure equal access. If the other country has a higher level of protection than the United States has, we ask it to even things up by removing some of its barriers. If it declines, the United States is supposed to retaliate by imposing higher protection against that country's goods.

If such a policy were actually carried out, it would destroy the multilateral trading system built up in recent decades. As Cline has said: "Reciprocity enforced by retaliation would violate the fundamental principle of unconditional most favored nation treatment followed by the United States for the last sixty years, and would risk trade wars through counter-retaliation."[9]

The motive force underlying proposals for this kind of reciprocity seems to be frustration with the fact that despite low tariff levels we actually face high levels of protection in the form of nontariff barriers and various forms of administrative discretion and red tape. In the United States, there is a widespread belief that the U.S. market is more open than others, particularly the Japanese market. Existing trade practices are seen to be unfair, in some sense. People point to the large U.S. current account deficit with Japan, as if that alone was proof of unequal access. It is not. Bilateral current account balances are not expected to be zero. The large U.S. current account deficits of 1982–90 are primarily the result of U.S. macroeconomic policies and the dollar exchange rate, not protectionism in other countries.

INTELLECTUAL PROPERTY

As was discussed in Chapter 5, the United States tends to have a comparative advantage in research and development-intensive industries. Exports of Vernon product cycle products, however, are not permanent and only last until the technology becomes widely available in other countries. When patents expired and technology became generally known, the United States often became an importer of products that it had previously exported.

U.S. export success therefore depends on retaining technological monopolies as long as possible, through patents and copyrights, and on continuing technical advances by U.S. firms. The ability of companies to earn sizable profits on past inventions also determines their willingness to finance future research efforts, thereby affecting the speed at which science and technology advance. Because research has become far more expensive and because many projects do not produce a marketable product, the successful efforts must be quite profitable to recover the costs of those that did not succeed.

In recent years the misuse or theft of U.S. intellectual property in the form of patents and copyrights has become increasingly common. Copies of books, compact discs, videotapes, computer programs, and the like are made without compensation to their creators, and these pirated copies are sold internationally. Patent infringement is widespread, and foreign governments frequently refuse to stop it. Since the United States has a strong comparative advantage in these areas, its export revenues suffer and U.S. firms become hesitant to finance risky research or creative efforts.

The problem of misuse of intellectual property is particularly serious in the East Asian newly industrialized countries, although it is spreading elsewhere. An

[9]William R. Cline, "'Reciprocity': A New Approach to World Trade Policy," in William R. Cline, *Trade Policy in the 1980s* (Cambridge, Mass.: MIT Press, 1983), Ch. 4, p. 121.

English engineer told the following story of a visit to a factory in India which was jointly owned by his employers and local investors. The Indian firm had received permission to purchase one state-of-the-art machine from Germany which would produce and package a product in a fully automated manner. When the engineer visited the factory, he discovered five of the machines in operation. When he asked where the other four had come from, "the Indian engineers giggled." It is impressive that the engineers were able to copy this machine so successfully, but for the German firm whose technology was infringed upon and which lost what would have become four later sales, the outcome was less pleasant.

The U.S. Congress fully recognizes the need to protect U.S. intellectual property, both to increase export revenues and to encourage future research and development activities. The 1988 Omnibus Trade Act included provisions allowing retaliation against the exports of countries whose governments do not make reasonable efforts to enforce U.S. patents and copyrights within their borders.

Many developing countries feel that the U.S. attitude is unfair; they maintain that they are poor and cannot afford to purchase U.S. goods at full price or to pay the license fees required to use the technology. This is a particularly difficult issue in the area of pharmaceuticals, where the failure of a poor country to gain access to U.S. medicines at low prices may cost lives. U.S. pharmaceutical firms, however, face enormous costs in developing and gaining approval for new medicines, and have only a 17-year patent lifetime in which to recover those costs. If foreign countries can produce the medicines without compensating patent owners, recovery of these costs becomes far more difficult, and future research efforts are discouraged. As a result, medicines that could save other lives will not be developed. There is no easy answer to this problem, particularly in the medical area, and it is almost certain to remain a major point of contention between the United States and a number of developing countries for many years.

THE 1988 OMNIBUS TRADE ACT

A major effort to revise U.S. trade law was undertaken in the mid-1980s and produced the Omnibus Trade Act of 1988. Its early drafts were highly protectionist, and it was widely feared that it would be a major step backward in U.S. international commercial relations.[10] Most of the restrictive provisions were taken out before final passage, and what was expected to be a highly protectionist bill became a reasonable law. This act extended the power of the president to negotiate tariff and nontariff barrier (NTB) reductions through 1993, this extension being necessary for U.S. participation in the Uruguay Round. Because the import-competing industries believed that the International Trade Commission took too long to determine whether substantial injury from imports (which required temporary relief) had occurred, strict time limits were placed on the ITC and the White House. The act also provided for increased subsidies for U.S. agricultural exports unless

[10]A more detailed discussion of the provisions of the 1988 Trade Act can be found in "Senate Clears Trade Bill by Lopsided Vote," *Congressional Quarterly,* August 8, 1988, pp. 2215–2222.

the European Community reduced its competing subsidies; thus it strengthened the negotiating position of the United States in the Uruguay Round.

The most important provision of the 1988 act, however, was in the area of unfair trade practices by foreign countries. What has become known as Super 301 (named after Section 301 of the 1974 Trade Act that deals with such practices) provides for U.S. retaliation against the exports of countries that maintain a number of specified unfair trade practices. Export subsidies, discrimination against U.S. goods and services, and refusal to protect U.S. patents and copyrights are major items on this list. The United States Trade Representative (USTR) is required to identify publicly the countries that maintain such practices; retaliation is to follow if negotiations to reduce the problems are not successful. Japan, Brazil, and India were recently named as possibilities, but Brazil and Japan were eliminated from the list rather quickly, and the case against India was later dropped. Super 301 now appears to have been more bark than bite, but that may change if the Congress becomes convinced that U.S. trade performance continues to suffer from such unfair trade practices. Super 301 was in effect for a limited period of time and is no longer operative, but may be reintroduced as part of a 1992 trade act.

QUESTIONS FOR STUDY AND REVIEW

1. What are the basic principles on which GATT has operated? Are they appropriate for present-day conditions and circumstances? Discuss, drawing on any relevant analysis.

2. When tariffs are reduced, the nation as a whole may benefit, but particular individuals and firms may suffer. How has the United States tried to deal with this issue? What are the problems and difficulties involved?

3. How is the objective of nondiscrimination achieved in GATT tariff agreements? What are the two major exceptions that have been formally agreed on by GATT?

4. Why did the major regions or sections of the United States disagree about the tariff issue in the nineteenth century? What was the economic basis of this disagreement? Discuss.

5. Describe the main features of a U.S. foreign trade policy during the past 50 years.

6. What was the most distinctive (novel) aspect of the Tokyo Round of GATT negotiations?

7. What is the most-favored-nation clause? How exactly does it work, and why is it used in tariff agreements?

8. The United States has encouraged foreign producers to adopt Voluntary Export Restraints and orderly marketing arrangements to reduce our imports and protect domestic industries. Is this policy preferable to an ordinary tariff? Discuss.

9. Why did the Uruguay Round falter in late 1990? Why was the United States so forceful on the subject of EEC agricultural subsidies? What countries

might you have expected to have been allied with the United States on this subject? Allied with the EEC on this subject? Why?

10. What countries would you expect to support the U.S. position on intellectual property at the Uruguay Round discussions? Why?

SELECTED REFERENCES

Baldwin, Robert. "Trade Policies in the Developed Countries." In R. Jones and P. Kenen, eds., *Handbook of International Economics*. Vol. I. New York: North Holland Press, 1984.

Baldwin, Robert E., and Anne O. Krueger, eds. *The Structure and Evolution of Recent U.S. Trade Policy*. Chicago: University of Chicago Press, 1984.

Barfield, C. E., and J. H. Makin, eds. *Trade Policy and U.S. Competitiveness*. Washington, D.C.: American Enterprise Institute, 1987.

Benko, R. D. *Protecting Intellectual Property*. Washington, D.C.: American Enterprise Institute, 1987.

Bhagwati, J. N. *Protectionism*. Cambridge, Mass.: MIT Press, 1988.

Cline, William R., Noboru Kawanabe, T.O.M. Kronsjo, and Thomas Williams. *Trade Negotiations in the Tokyo Round: A Quantitative Assessment*. Washington, D.C.: Brookings Institution, 1978.

Frank, Charles R., Jr. *Foreign Trade and Domestic Aid*. Washington, D.C.: Brookings Institution, 1977.

Huffbauer, G. H., D. T. Berliner, and K. A. Elliott. *Trade Protection in the United States: 31 Case Studies*. Washington, D.C.: Institute for International Economics, 1986.

Lenway, Stephanie. *The Politics of U.S. International Trade*. Marshfield, Mass.: Pitman, 1985.

Moore, Michael. *Rules or Politics?: An Empirical Analysis of ITC Anti-Dumping Decisions,* Economic Inquiry, Vol. 30 No. 3, July 1992.

Morkre, Morris, and David Tarr. *The Effects of Restrictions on U.S. Imports: Five Case Studies*. Federal Trade Commission. Washington, D.C.: U.S. Government Printing Office, 1980.

OECD. *Costs and Benefits of Protection*. Paris: OECD, 1985.

URUGUAY ROUND UPDATE

Published by the Office of Multilateral Affairs
International Economic Policy
International Trade Administration
U.S. Department of Commerce 20230 April 1992

STATUS OF NEGOTIATIONS

The Uruguay Round of Multilateral Trade Negotiations is the most ambitious trade negotiation ever undertaken, involving 108 countries representing over 90 percent of world trade; the Uruguay Round was begun in 1986 in Punta del Este, Uruguay and is the eighth round of trade liberalization negotiations to be initiated under the auspices of the General Agreement on Tariffs and Trade (GATT). Negotiations were originally to have concluded by December 1990, but are continuing because of the inability of participants to reach agreement in key areas of the negotiations.

The Uruguay Round seeks to strengthen international disciplines in a number of trade areas. Benefits of an Uruguay Round agreement include:

- Lower tariff and non-tariff barriers to manufactured products and other goods;
- Rules to protect the intellectual property of U.S. entrepreneurs;
- New markets for U.S. services firms;
- An agreement opening world markets to investment;
- Fair competition and open markets in agriculture;
- Full participation of developing countries in the global trading system,
- Strengthened rules on dispute settlement, anti-dumping, subsidies, and trade remedy provisions.

The Uruguay Round negotiations fall into four broad categories:

(1) The "New Areas" (services, trade-related intellectual property rights (TRIPs), trade-related investment measures (TRIMs));

(2) GATT Rules (i.e., rules necessary to protect and guarantee market access and concessions negotiated: the non-tariff measure codes, including subsidies and anti-dumping, dispute settlement, safeguards, and GATT articles including balance-of-payments reform);

(3) Market Access (this includes tariffs and nontariff measures, natural resource-based products, tropical products, and textiles);

(4) Agriculture.

THE DRAFT FINAL ACT

The "Draft Final Act" (DFA) for the Uruguay Round, issued on December 20, 1991 by GATT Director General Arthur Dunkel, covers all issue areas being negotiated in the Round, except market access commitments in goods and services. The DFA is an important step in bringing the negotiations to conclusion. In cases where negotiating groups were unable to arrive at consensus, Director General Dunkel proposed his own compromise solutions in the DFA.

A Trade Negotiations Committee (TNC) meeting was held on January 13, 1992, at which participants discussed their initial reactions to the DFA. The DFA is not a legal text nor a final Uruguay Round agreement. It provides the basis for continued negotiations; Dunkel has proposed a four-track process aimed at concluding the Uruguay Round as expeditiously as possible:

I.   Negotiations on market access in goods;
II. Negotiations on market access in services;
III. Legal drafting,
IV. Efforts to refine the Draft Final Act, under Dunkel's direct supervision.

The United States is working to successfully conclude the Uruguay Round. However, the United States will not accept an agreement that does not meet its high standards. Final evaluation of the Uruguay Round agreements will have to await the results of market access negotiations in goods and services, as well as the conclusion of tracks III and IV. The remainder of this newsletter provides a factual summary of the major sections of the Draft Final Act (DFA).

DESCRIPTION OF SELECTED SECTIONS OF THE DRAFT FINAL ACT: (1) "NEW AREAS"

Services

The DFA includes a "framework" of rules setting out obligations (similar to those in the current GATT which covers only trade in goods) that would apply generally to all trade in services. The proposed services agreement is known as the General Agreement on Trade in Services (GATS).

Framework. The DFA includes a framework of universal obligations which apply generally to all trade in services. The framework includes the following obligations and disciplines: most-favored nation (MFN); transparency; disclosure of confidential information; increasing participation of developing countries; economic integration; domestic regulation; recognition; monopolies and exclusive service providers; business practices; emergency safeguard measures; payments and transfers; restrictions to safeguard the balance-of-payments; government procurement; general and security exceptions; subsidies; specific commitments on market access and national treatment, and institutional and dispute settlement provisions.

Annexes. The framework is augmented by annexes for financial services, labor mobility, telecommunications, and air transport services. These clarify and expand the framework provisions as they apply to specific sectors.

Market access. Taken together, the framework provisions and annexes of the DFA provide the legal basis on which to negotiate market access and national treatment commitments on a sector-by-sector basis. Market access negotiations, which are currently under way, are critical to the overall acceptability of the agreement.

MFN derogations. The DFA gives governments the opportunity to exempt themselves from the MFN obligation on a sector-by-sector basis. Derogations can be open-ended, but in principle should be for no more than 10 years, and are subject to review in 5 years.

Trade-Related Aspects of Intellectual Property Rights (TRIPs)

The DFA sets new and higher standards for the protection of a full range of intellectual property rights, including patents, copyrights, trademarks, trade secrets, and semiconductor chips. It also provides for strengthened enforcement of disciplines both internally and at the border.

Highlights:

• *Copyright* protection for computer programs as literary works; databases protected as compilations under copyright;

• 50-year term of protection for sound recordings;

• Exclusive rental rights for computer programs and sound recordings;

• *Patent* protection for product and process, including for pharmaceuticals and agricultural chemicals;

• Limits on compulsory licensing;

• 20-year term of protection from filing;

• *Trademark* protection is broadening by including protection for service marks and strengthened protection for internationally well-known marks;

• Mandatory linking of trademarks and compulsory licensing of marks is prohibited,

• Strong protection for *trade secrets.*

Trade-Related Investment Measures (TRIMs)

The DFA prohibits the use of local content requirements and trade balancing requirements (which require firms to export in order to import).

• These prohibitions are broad, and apply whether such measures are forced on a firm or if they are a condition for receipt of an "advantage";

• Transition periods for elimination of prohibitive TRIMs are 2 years for developed countries, 5 years for less developed countries (LDCs), and 7 years for least developed countries (LLDCs);

• In order to avoid disadvantaging established foreign investors abroad, the DFA permits equivalent TRIMs to be imposed on new entrants during the transition period.

(2) GATT RULES

Certain sections of the DFA dealing with specific articles of the GATT Agreement; Functioning of the GATT System (FOGs), and non-tariff measures (Pre-Shipment Inspection, Rules of Origin and Customs Valuation) have long been agreed by all Contracting Parties. Final acceptance and enactment of the provisions of these sections of the DFA is dependent upon their adoption by Contracting Parties as part of a final Uruguay Round package.

Anti-dumping

The Anti-dumping section of the DFA contains:

• Minimum due process and transparency requirements that would result in fairer treatment abroad for U.S. exporters charged with dumping;—Anti-circumvention provisions, giving welcome international recognition to a genuine problem in today's globalized manufacturing environment;

• Provisions for automatic adoption of panel reports;

• Sunset reviews with a difficult standard to meet in order to keep a remedy for more than five years,

• Tight restrictions on anti-circumvention determinations.

Subsidies and Countervailing Measures

The DFA appears to offer the prospect of obtaining a meaningful increase in international discipline over trade-distorting subsidies.

Prohibited subsidies. The DFA would prohibit *de facto,* as well as *de jure,* export subsidies and local content subsidies.

Domestic subsidies. The DFA makes it easier to challenge domestic subsidies under the GATT. In particular, large domestic subsidies (equal to more than 5 percent of the value of the product) would be presumed to cause adverse effects, thus greatly enhancing the prospect for successful challenge.

The DFA also creates a category of subsidies which may not be challenged, including:

• Certain regional subsidies;

• Basic industrial research subsidies up to 50 percent of the cost of the research,

• Applied industrial research subsidies (but not developmental subsidies) of up to 25 percent of the cost of the research.

The DFA also contains criteria and provisions for countervailing duty measures.

Dispute Settlement

The DFA makes significant improvements to the GATT dispute settlement system, which are expected to apply to all the Uruguay Round agreements. The new procedures prevent blockage and delay by building automaticity and time limits into the process.

• Appellate body: The DFA creates a standing appellate body to ensure consistency and coherence across-the-board in legal interpretations of the new Uruguay Round rules.

• Retaliation: The DFA would enable the United States, consistent with the GATT, to exercise promptly its right to retaliate when another country fails to live up to its GATT obligations.

• Cross-retaliation: The DFA also includes principles and procedures for cross-retaliation, across sectors and across agreements, providing greater leverage to enforce all the agreements.

The net result is a dispute settlement mechanism that would be far more effective than the GATT mechanism of the past.

Section 301 can be administered consistently under these new dispute settlement procedures. As now written, the DFA would require no change in Section 301, except for one technical adjustment:

• The time limit for 301 investigations involving the Subsidies Code would have to be changed from 12 months to 18 months in accordance with the new time limits for dispute settlement.

Multilateral Trade Organization

The section of the DFA establishing a Multilateral Trade Organization (MTO) would enable the new rules on trade in services and intellectual property protection to be brought under the same structural umbrella as the current GATT rules on trade in goods.

The MTO's membership would be open only to existing GATT Contracting Parties that agree to accept and implement *all* of the results of the Uruguay Round.

• Participants in the Round would not have the option of selecting among the results, but would be required to accept or reject the final package as a whole.

• Thus, the structure contemplated by an MTO would prevent the current problem of "free riders" that seek to take advantage of the benefits of some agreements while avoiding the obligations of others.

Safeguards

The DFA incorporates into the GATT concepts long included in U.S. law (Section 201), ensuring that all countries are using comparable rules for the provision of import relief, including:

• An 8-year maximum duration (some safeguard measures taken by other countries have been in effect for over 30 years);
• A requirement for a transparent, public process for determining whether increased imports caused or threatened to cause serious injury, including:

(a) a public hearing or comparable opportunity to present views and to challenge those presented by others;

(b) a published report by the investigating authority setting out, in detail, an analysis of the reasons for its decision.

• Progressive liberalization of safeguard measures each year they are in effect;
• Clearly defined criteria for making injury determinations,
• Recognition of the right to take special safeguard measures for perishable products.

The agreement prohibits any retaliation by affected exporting countries for the first 3 years. It also requires the phase-out of voluntary restraint agreements (VRAs) and similar measures over a reasonable period of time and prohibits their future use.

GATT Articles

Specific GATT articles dealt with in the DFA are: II:1(b) (Schedules of Concessions); XVII (State Trading Enterprises); XXIV (Territo-

rial Applications—Customs Unions and Free-Trade Areas); XXV (GATT Waivers); XXVIII (Modification of Schedules), and XXXV (Non-application Between Particular Contracting Parties). These sections of the DFA are not described in further detail in this newsletter. The DFA also contains a section on Articles XII and XVIII:b dealing with balance-of-payments exceptions (discussed below). This section of the DFA has not been agreed by all parties; it represents the GATT Secretariat's proposed text.

Balance-of-Payments

The DFA provides for increased transparency in the application of measures applied for balance-of-payments (BOP) purposes, including the requirement that specific information be provided by the invoking country to other Contracting Parties, and that countries announce, as soon as possible, a time schedule for the removal of restrictive import measures taken for BOP purposes.

The DFA also contains commitments that countries: give preference to price-based measures over use of quantitative restrictions; not apply more than one BOP measure to any one product, and apply BOP measures only to control the general level of imports and that these measures not exceed what is necessary to address the BOP situation.

The DFA also provides that the dispute settlement provisions of the General Agreement may be invoked with respect to any matters arising from the application of restrictive import measures taken for BOP purposes.

Pre-shipment Inspection

The DFA contains detailed provisions which require pre-shipment inspection (PSI) companies to: inform exporters of all PSI requirements; protect business confidential information; avoid inspection delays, and refrain from using price verification to arbitrarily lower a contract price.

The DFA also provides for a mechanism to resolve disputes between exporters and PSI companies. This program will be administered jointly by the International Chamber of Commerce and the International Federation of Inspection Agencies. The decisions of panels constituted under this dispute resolution mechanism would be binding upon the private parties to the dispute.

The DFA includes notification, review, consultation, and dispute settlement provisions with regard to PSI.

Rules of Origin

The rules of origin section of the DFA contains principles and disciplines that would apply to all non-preferential rules of origin (those used to determine most-favored-nation status, to apply antidumping or countervailing duties, and those used for government procurement purposes, etc.).

The DFA rules of origin section requires that new origin rules or changes to existing rules must be published at least 60 days before they take effect. In addition, the DFA would create a GATT Committee and a Customs Cooperation Council (CCC) Technical Committee on rules of origin.

The DFA specifies notification, review, consultation, and dispute settlement provisions with regard to rules of origin. The DFA sets out a harmonization work plan, which would be carried out by the GATT and the CCC within 3 years following the conclusion of the Uruguay Round. The results of this plan, containing common rules for all non-preferential purposes, would be put into a binding annex to the final GATT Uruguay Round agreement.

Specific disciplines on preferential rules of origin are outlined in an annex to the rules of origin section of the DFA.

Customs Valuation

The customs valuation section of the DFA addresses the concerns of less developed countries (LDCs) with regard to the burden of proof in cases of alleged fraud through a proposed Code Committee decision clarifying the obligations of both customs authorities and importers in establishing a "declared value" for an import.

LDC reservations concerning officially established minimum values were resolved in the DFA by providing that the Code Committee consider, sympathetically, LDC requests for reservations to retain officially established minimum values if an LDC is able to show good cause.

The DFA resolves the issue of how to treat importations by sole concessionaires by recommending that the Customs Cooperation Council (CCC) assist developing countries interested in studying areas of potential concern, including those related to sole concessionaires.

Standards

Multilateral agreement has been reached on the revisions to the Agreement on Technical Barriers to Trade ("Standards Code"). The DFA includes important improvements over the existing standards agreement, including coverage of regional standards bodies, strengthened disciplines on conformity assessment, and coverage of processes and production methods.

(3) MARKET ACCESS

Substantial negotiations remain to liberalize market access for goods and services before the Uruguay Round can be concluded. Negotiations are ongoing; the United States continues to push its sectoral and zero/zero initiatives.

Textiles

The DFA gradually phases out the Multifiber Arrangement (MFA) and integrates textile and apparel trade into a strengthened GATT regime over a 10-year period.

• Quota liberalization: The annual growth rate of U.S. quotas will be gradually increased in three stages from 3.9 percent to 4.5 percent in the first 3 years, 5.6 percent in the next 4 years, and 7.2 percent in the last 3 years;

• A major review will take place prior to each stage to assess the implementation of an agreement and to consider changes if appropriate;

• Improved safeguard: the DFA incorporates an improved safeguard mechanism based on the concept of cumulative damage, which will help importing countries respond to disruptive import surges;

• Anti-circumvention: The DFA would permit strong action, including the setting of unilateral quotas, to prevent illegal transshipments;

• Improved market access: The DFA requires all countries, developed and developing alike, to provide improved market access; tariff negotiations will continue in early 1992,

• Application: The DFA would apply only to current GATT members.

(4) AGRICULTURE

The proposed program for agriculture in the Draft Final Act (DFA) is a significant step in the process of meaningful agricultural reform consistent with the long-term objective of a fair and market-oriented agricultural trading system. The proposed text provides for reduction commitments over a 6-year period (1993–99) on internal supports, export subsidies, and barriers to market access.

Internal supports. Internal supports, other than those exempted, would be reduced by roughly 20 percent from a 1986–88 base, using product-specific aggregate measures of support (AMS). Exempted programs ("green box" category) include those with little or no effect on trade distortion or production; examples include government service programs (research, advisory activities, etc.), domestic food aid, decoupled income and income safety net programs, and environmental programs.

All domestic support not meeting the green box criteria would be subject to reduction commitments. Reductions are not required for support below a *de minimis* level.

Export subsidies. Export subsidies would be reduced by a quantitative reduction of 24 percent and a budgetary outlay reduction of 36 percent from a base period of 1986–90. Reduction commitments cover a wide range of current practices. Basic approach focuses only on subsidies contingent on export performance. Only budgetary disciplines will apply to export subsidies in primary products incorporated into processed agricultural products. Negotiations may be conducted regarding the extension of export subsidies to new markets.

Market access. The DFA calls for comprehensive tariffication (i.e., conversion of non-tariff barriers to trade (NTBs) into tariff equivalents) without exceptions. Tariffs (including tariff equivalents) would be reduced by 36 percent on an average basis from a base period of 1986–88. DFA section on agricultural market access also includes:

• 15 percent minimum tariff cut for each product (tariff line item);

• Where countries permit little or no access for a commodity, they must make minimum access commitments of 3 percent of domestic consumption, which will increase to 5 percent;

• Current access above 3 percent must be maintained and increased over the implementation period,

• Quantity-triggered and price-triggered safeguards.

One year before the end of the implementation period, negotiations will be initiated for continuing the reform process.

The DFA also requires participants to "exercise due restraint" in their application of rights under the GATT in relation to products covered in the reform package. Developing countries are granted a longer implementation period (up to 10 years), and are required to schedule reduction commitments of at least two-thirds of the rates for developed countries in each of the areas.

Provisions of the DFA Regarding Sanitary and Phytosanitary Measures

The DFA provides meaningful disciplines to ensure that countries do not erect protectionist trade barriers under the guise of health and safety measures.

At the same time, the DFA explicitly recognizes the rights of countries to protect human, animal, and plant life and health through sanitary and phytosanitary measures.

Government Procurement

While not technically part of the Uruguay Round, negotiations on expansion of the Government Procurement Code are proceeding in parallel with the Round. It is expected that a procurement agreement can be concluded at the same time as the Uruguay Round.

The DFA, however, contains negotiated text which clarifies existing Government Procurement Code accession procedures.

U.S. negotiators seek to open foreign procurement markets for services, public works, and telecommunications and heavy electrical equipment. Code signatories also seek to open subcentral procurement markets. The expanded Code will open multibillion-dollar procurement markets in signatory countries to U.S. suppliers.

The draft provisions for the new Code contain a prohibition of offsets for developed countries and provide for improved Code enforcement through the establishment of local bid challenge.

GATT MEMBERSHIP
Contracting Parties to the Gatt (103)
(Dates indicate accession)

Antigua and Barbuda	30 March 1987	Kuwait	3 May 1963
Argentina	11 October 1967	Lesotho	8 January 1988
Australia	1 January 1948	Luxembourg	1 January 1948
Austria	9 October 1951	Macau	11 January 1991
Bangladesh	16 December 1972	Madagascar	30 September 1963
Barbados	15 February 1967	Malawi	28 August 1964
Belgium	1 January 1948	Malaysia	24 October 1957
Belize	7 October 1983	Maldives	19 April 1983
Benin	12 September 1990	Malta	17 November 1964
Bolivia	8 September 1990	Mauritania	30 September 1963
Botswana	28 August 1987	Mauritius	2 September 1970
Brazil	30 July 1948	Mexico	24 August 1986
Burkina Faso	3 May 1963	Morocco	17 June 1987
Burundi	13 March 1965	Myanmar	29 July 1948
Cameroon	3 May 1963	Netherlands	1 January 1948
Canada	1 January 1948	New Zealand	30 July 1948
Central African Rep.	3 May 1963	Nicaragua	28 May 1950
Chad	12 July 1963	Niger	31 December 1963
Chile	16 March 1949	Nigeria	18 November 1960
Colombia	3 October 1981	Norway	10 July 1948
Congo	3 May 1963	Pakistan	30 July 1948
Costa Rica	24 November 1990	Peru	7 October 1951
Cote d'Ivoire	31 December 1963	Philippines	27 December 1979
Cuba	1 January 1948	Poland	18 October 1967
Cyprus	15 July 1963	Portugal	6 May 1962
Czechoslovakia	20 April 1948	Romania	14 November 1971
Denmark	28 May 1950	Rwanda	1 January 1966
Dominican Republic	19 May 1950	Senegal	27 September 1963
Egypt	9 May 1970	Sierra Leone	19 May 1961
El Salvador	22 May 1991	Singapore	20 August 1973
Finland	25 May 1950	Sweden	30 April 1950
France	1 January 1948	Switzerland	1 August 1966
Gabon	3 May 1963	South Africa	13 June 1948
Gambia	22 February 1965	Spain	29 August 1963
Germany	1 October 1951	Sri Lanka	29 July 1948
Ghana	17 October 1957	Suriname	22 March 1978
Greece	1 March 1950	Tanzania	9 December 1961
Guatemala	10 October 1991	Thailand	20 November 1982
Guyana	5 July 1966	Togo	20 March 1964
Haiti	1 January 1950	Trinidad & Tobago	23 October 1962
Hong Kong	23 April 1986	Tunisia	19 August 1990
Hungary	9 September 1973	Turkey	17 October 1951
Iceland	21 April 1968	Uganda	23 October 1962
India	8 July 1948	United Kingdom	1 January 1948
Indonesia	24 February 1950	U.S.A.	1 January 1948
Ireland	22 December 1967	Uruguay	6 December 1953
Israel	5 July 1962	Venezuela	31 August 1990
Italy	30 May 1950	Yugoslavia	25 August 1966
Jamaica	31 December 1963	Zaire	11 September 1971
Japan	10 September 1955	Zambia	10 February 1982
Kenya	5 February 1964	Zimbabwe	11 July 1948
Korea, Rep. of	14 April 1967		

THE TRADE OF LESS DEVELOPED COUNTRIES

Poor countries—those that we call less developed countries (LDCs)—have long been dissatisfied with their role in world trade. They believe that world markets have been biased against them, that they have not had a fair share of the gains from trade, and that trade theory is just a clever construction designed to keep them in a subordinate position vis-à-vis the more developed, industrial countries—those we call advanced countries (A-countries).

The theory of comparative advantage, as set forth in Chapters 2 to 4, is supposed to be a general concept, applicable to countries in every stage of development. Its central message is that every country, rich or poor, gains from specializing in those commodities in which it has a comparative advantage and then trading some of its output for the commodities offered by other countries. The gain from trade is shared by all participants. On the basis of their experience over several decades, the LDCs are deeply skeptical about their potential benefits of trade with A-countries. In this chapter we examine some of the reasons that have been offered to explain their skepticism and their hostility to this theory of trade.

Our division of the world into A-countries and LDCs is highly arbitrary, but it is convenient and widely used. A-countries are the economically advanced countries of Western Europe and North America, as well as Japan, Australia, and New

Zealand. LDCs include all the rest of the world except for the former Communist bloc, which we omit from our consideration.[1] Thus LDCs include all of Latin America, Africa, Asia (except China, Japan, North Korea, and Vietnam), and Oceania (except Australia and New Zealand).

The list of LDCs obviously includes countries that vary greatly in per capita income and other indices of economic development. Taiwan, South Korea, and Brazil may be economically closer to Germany and Japan than to Togo, Zaire, or Nepal. Kuwait and Saudi Arabia are now near the top of any ranking of countries by per capita income. However, all these LDCs have tended to think of themselves as part of the Third World, and they have shown a considerable degree of political solidarity, especially on issues involving trade and commercial policy. Thus it is useful to discuss the present issue in terms of a distinction between A-countries and LDCs.

Nevertheless, the reader should keep in mind the fact that economic development is a relative concept. Thirty years ago Japan was often classified as an LDC, and in the early nineteenth century the United States was an underdeveloped country par excellence. Some of the countries we classify as LDCs are already approaching or surpassing the economic status of some members of our A-country group. Oil-exporting nations are clearly a special case, and they are sometimes separated from other LDCs for analytical purposes. The World Bank has recently identified a group of least developed countries, sometimes referred to as the Fourth World.

TRADE GRUMBLES

The LDCs' attitude toward trade is intimately related to their concern about their economic development, or lack thereof. They seek both an explanation for their lack of development and a set of policies that will accelerate their pace of development. Thus the trade policy of LDCs is an aspect of the theory and strategy of economic development. This latter subject is too large to be dealt with in this chapter, and we will therefore focus on the role of trade. We begin with some of the complaints of LDCs about how they have fared in world trade.

Adverse Trend in the Terms of Trade

LDCs complain that the terms of trade have tended to turn against them during the past century or so: that the prices of their exports relative to the prices of their

---

[1] Russia, Poland, Czechoslovakia, and the other Eastern European countries might well be classified as intermediate if they were included, whereas China would be classified as a less developed country. Indeed, China constitutes about one-third of the underdeveloped world in terms of population. We omit what was the Communist bloc for most purposes simply because the nature of bloc trade has differed greatly from that of the rest of the world. Recent changes in Eastern Europe mean that many of these countries are becoming part of the rest of the world's trading system. What was East Germany, of course, became part of the European Community when it was merged with West Germany in October of 1990.

imports have persistently declined. This measure of the commodity terms of trade, T_C, is computed as the ratio of an index of export prices to an index of import prices, as follows:

$$T_C = \frac{P_x^t / P_x^0}{P_m^t / P_m^0}$$

where P_x^t is the export price index for year t, and P_x^0 is the export price index for the base year. P_m^t and P_m^0 are the corresponding import price indexes.

The allegation of an adverse trend in the terms of trade must ultimately rest on a factual base. That was originally provided by an influential report from the United Nations which showed that from 1876–80 to 1946–47 the prices of primary products relative to the prices of manufactured goods declined from 100 to 68.[2] This implies that in 1946–47 exporters of a given amount of primary products received, in return, only 68 percent of the amount of manufactured goods they had received 70 years earlier. Despite the growth in world population and great improvements in manufacturing technology, the real exchange ratio had turned sharply against the producers of primary products.

The principal author of this report, the Argentine economist Raul Prebisch, proceeded over the next several years to propose several theoretical explanations for the alleged secular decline in the terms of trade of LDCs. This work struck a responsive chord in others, and for three decades the Prebisch thesis has been widely accepted in the Third World and elsewhere. Even though serious doubts have been raised about the statistical basis for the alleged secular decline, policymakers in LDCs have acted on the belief or conviction that the decline did occur, and economists have constructed theories to account for it.

Prebisch later played a key role in the creation of the United Nations Conference on Trade and Development (UNCTAD) and became its first director general. UNCTAD has from its inception operated on the premise that the terms of trade are adverse to the LDCs. As Ian Little has said:

UNCTAD was founded on the mistaken view, which it has enshrined by constant repetition into the myth, that there is a trend in the terms of trade against developing countries as a result of an adverse trend in the terms of trade between manufactures and commodities. The mistake was originated by a League of Nations publication in 1945, and repeated by an early U.N. publication. Some more recent work suggests an improvement in the manufactures/commodities terms of trade for nearly a century before 1952–5, when there was a highly favourable and unsustainable peak in developing countries' terms of trade associated with the Korean War boom. Thereafter for at least seven years they worsened, but then improved for a decade, even excluding oil. Any reasonably objective observer would have been saying for many years now that the evidence cannot possibly be held to give grounds for maintaining that there is a trend in the terms of trade against developing countries. Theories have been

[2]United Nations Economic Commission for Latin America, *The Economic Development of Latin America and Its Principal Problems,* 1950.

invented to explain this non-existent trend: they are treated with respect even though they explain what does not exist.[3]

Much statistical work has been done in an attempt to resolve the controversy about trends in the terms of trade of LDCs, or of primary producers, but without success: "The most that can be said with conviction is that the evidence is insufficient to support any particular hypothesis about the nature of the long-term trend."[4] In some periods of time, the relative prices of primary products have fallen, and in other periods they have risen, but no clear long-run trend can be established. Advocates of the Prebisch thesis like to choose a base year such as 1953, the peak of the commodity boom associated with the Korean War, which enables them to show a subsequent deterioration in the relative prices of primary products. Opponents prefer a base year such as 1962, when commodity prices were depressed, which enables them to show a subsequent improvement in their relative prices into the 1970s, especially if petroleum is included.

Other statistical and conceptual difficulties include (1) the problem of making allowance in the price indexes for new products and for changes in quality, (2) the methods to be used in weighting the commodities included in the index, (3) the methods of valuing imports and exports,[5] and (4) the problem of making allowance for changes in technology and productivity.

Whatever the long-term situation for developing countries, the last decade has been difficult. Between 1977 and 1988 the terms of trade of nonoil-exporting LDCs deteriorated by 11.1 percent according to IMF data. As can be seen in Table 10-1, prices for commodities such as coffee and cocoa weakened, and even metals prices, which should have recovered in the economic expansion of the period after 1982, remained soft.

Although there is no fully convincing evidence of a long-term trend in the commodity terms of trade for LDCs as a whole, some economists have taken even the absence of such a trend as evidence that LDCs have not been treated fairly in the world market. The argument rests on the proposition that technological progress has been much greater in manufacturing than in primary production. Trade theory implies that the fruits of technological progress will be shared by all countries, consumers as well as producers, through the mechanism of downward relative

---

[3]"Economic Relations with the Third World—Old Myths and New Prospects," *Scottish Journal of Political Economy,* November 1975, p. 227.

[4]Kathryn Morton and Peter Tulloch, *Trade and Developing Countries* (London: Croom Helm, 1977), p. 27. Data providing support for the Prebisch hypothesis can be found in Enzo Grillo and Maw Cheng Yang, "Primary Commodity Prices, Manufactured Goods Prices, and the Terms of Trade of Developing Countries: What the Long-Run Shows," *World Bank Economic Review,* January 1988, pp. 1–47.

[5]In the data that Prebisch originally used, British exports of manufactured goods were in f.o.b. value, whereas British imports of primary products were valued c.i.f. Consequently, the great reduction in ocean transport rates after 1876 shows up as a decline in the prices of primary products. See P. T. Ellsworth, "The Terms of Trade between Primary Producing and Industrial Countries," *Inter-American Economic Affairs,* Summer 1956.

TABLE 10-1 Trends in Prices of Selected Primary Products, 1970–89 (index, 1980 = 100)

Commodity	1970	1989	Peak Value	Peak Year
Food	38	89	100	1980
Wheat	36	98	104	1974
Maize	46	89	108	1983
Rice	33	74	125	1974
Beef	47	93	105	1979
Oilseeds and oils	43	83	111	1984
Oil cake	40	95	100	1980
Fish Meal	39	81	100	1980
Sugar	19	65	100	1980
Bananas	44	146	146	1989
Beverages	32	61	149	1977
Coffee	31	61	152	1977
Cocoa	26	48	146	1977
Tea	49	90	155	1984
Agricultural raw materials	30	113	113	1989
Cotton	32	95	100	1980
Wool	31	131	159	1988
Rubber	29	68	100	1980
Hides and skins	28	196	196	1989
Logs	23	115	119	1988
Minerals and metals	45	119	119	1989
Crude petroleum	5	59	101	1981
Manufactures	*34*	*120*	*121*	*1988*

Notes: All indices are based on U.S. dollar prices.

Source: GATT, *International Trade, 1989–1990* (Geneva, 1990), vol. 1, p. 52.

price adjustments on manufactured products. Therefore the commodity terms of trade, unadjusted for productivity changes, should show a pronounced trend in favor of LDCs. The statistical finding that no clear trend can be established is thus treated as evidence that A-countries have largely retained the fruits of technological progress for themselves.

The positive statistical basis for this argument is also quite weak. Data on technical progress by industry and country are scarce and unreliable. To assume that technical progress has been greater in manufacturing than in primary products is to assume what needs to be demonstrated. Furthermore, the issue of quality changes would still remain to obscure the result.

Nevertheless, because of the general belief that technical progress has been much greater in A-countries than in LDCs, this argument suggests that LDCs have not enjoyed a fair share of the fruits of that progress. The amount of imports obtained in exchange for a given input of productive factors (e.g., labor) has risen less for LDCs than for A-countries. Here a different concept, the single factoral terms of trade, is used. It involves adjusting the commodity terms of trade to take account of productivity changes in the export industries, as follows:

$$T_F = T_C \cdot \left(\frac{F_x^t}{F_x^0}\right)$$

where T_F is the single factoral terms of trade, T_C is the commodity terms of trade, as defined above, and F_x stands for an index of productivity in export industries.

Suppose, for example, that there is no change in the commodity terms of trade in a given period of time, that productivity does not change in LDCs, and that productivity rises 50 percent in A-countries. Then the commodity terms of trade, steady at 100, would be adjusted by the relative change in productivities, to obtain the single factoral terms of trade for each group of countries, as follows:

$$\text{LDCs} : T_F = 100 \cdot \left(\frac{100}{100}\right) = 100$$

$$\text{A-countries} : T_F = 100 \cdot \left(\frac{150}{100}\right) = 150$$

The economic interpretation of this result is that the LDCs receive the same amount of imports for a given factor input as in the base year, whereas A-countries receive 50 percent more imports for a given factor input than in the base year. Thus A-countries have captured all the benefits of their technical progress. It is true that, in our example, the LDCs are no worse off than before, but their point is that the theory of trade implies that the benefits of technical progress will be shared by the trading nations, as explained in Chapters 3 and 5. The prices of A-country exports (LDC imports) should fall, thus causing an improvement in the commodity terms of trade of LDCs. Instead, say the critics, A-countries keep their prices up and increase their domestic factor incomes (wages, etc.).

The Widening Gap

This point is related to the observation that per capita incomes have risen far more in A-countries than in LDCs during the past century or two, and that the income gap is steadily widening. In 1750 per capita incomes in Europe and North America were not greatly different from those in Asia, Africa, and Latin America, although they may have been somewhat higher. Since then, however, the Industrial Revolution and technological advances have raised per capita incomes in A-countries to levels far above those in LDCs. According to World Bank statistics, in 1987 per capita income in A-countries averaged $14,600 compared to only $290 in the 33 countries with the lowest incomes or to $1570 in another 55 countries classified as middle-income countries.[6] Even though these estimates may overstate the disparity in incomes, this disparity is certainly very large and it is growing in absolute terms.

For LDCs, the significant point about the income disparity is that it emerged during a time when they were actively engaged in world trade, specializing in accordance with comparative advantage, and importing a large part of their manufactured goods requirements. The widening income gap seems flatly to contradict a key proposition derived from the theory of trade—namely, that trade will tend to equalize factor prices across nations and regions. LDCs consider the large and increasing disparity of wage rates and per capita incomes to be yet another indication that international trade has not worked as it is supposed to work and that the market is biased against them in a systematic way.

These complaints (adverse terms of trade and widening income disparities) are often linked together, and common explanations are offered. Prebisch originally argued that A-countries exercised monopoly power through labor unions, oligopolistic business firms, and various social institutions (minimum-wage laws, social security schemes) which tended to cause productivity increases to be taken in higher wages rather than lower prices. Prices in A-countries were sticky and did not fall when demand was slack, but they did increase during the upswing of the business cycle. Consequently, the prices of manufactures exported by A-countries tended to rise over the long run. In LDCs, on the other hand, markets were more competitive, labor was less well organized, and wages tended to be held down by the presence of a large excess supply of labor in the agricultural sector. Prices and wages might rise in boom periods when the demand for primary products was strong, but they would fall in the slack periods. There was no upward trend in prices and wages, as in A-countries. The result was rising per capita incomes in A-countries but little change in LDCs, and the factoral terms of trade turned against the LDCs.

It is also argued that the price elasticity of demand for primary products was low. When LDCs expanded their output and their exports of these products, specializing in accordance with the principle of comparative advantage, the result was a fall in price and, if price elasticity in the world market were less than unity, a fall in export proceeds as well.[7] Statistical evidence indicates that demand elasticities for primary products are quite low. See Table 10-2 for some estimates.

In the same vein, Prebisch argued that the income elasticity of demand was higher for manufactured goods than for primary products. Income elasticity of demand refers to the proportionate change in quantity demanded relative to the proportionate change in income: $\Delta Q / Q \div \Delta Y / Y$. (See Table 10-2 for statistical estimates.) Thus he suggested that a given rise in world income caused the demand for manufactured goods (the exports of A-countries) to increase more rapidly than the demand for primary products (the exports of LDCs). This tendency was

---

[6] *World Tables, 1988–89* (Washington, D.C.: World Bank, 1989).

[7] The terms of trade could fall so much that a country would be worse off than before its expansion of output. This is what was referred to as immiserizing growth in Chapter 5.

strengthened by technological progress, particularly the development of industrial substitutes for primary products, such as synthetic rubber, synthetic fibers, and plastics. (What would the price of natural rubber now be if synthetic rubber had never been invented?) Demand for LDC exports was also dampened by the tariffs, quotas, and other protective measures that A-countries used to assist their own primary producers.

These various points are essentially reasons why the terms of trade might have turned against primary products and therefore against LDCs, although the existence of such an adverse long-term trend has not been fully established.

TABLE 10-2 Estimates of Elasticities of Demand for Selected Products in A-Country Markets

Commodity	Price Elasticity (negative)	Income Elasticity
Bananas	0.5–1.0	0.2–0.7
Cocoa	<0.5	0.5
Coffee	<0.5	0.8
Fibers (jute, sisal)	<0.5	0.7
Oilseeds, oils	0.5–1.0	0.4–0.7
Rubber (natural)	0.5–1.0	n.a.
Sugar	<0.5	0.4
Tea	0.5–1.0	0.1

Source: G. K. Helleiner, *International Trade and Development* (Baltimore: Penguin, 1972), p. 39.

Trade Patterns in Developing Countries

The geographical pattern of trade flows shows that the majority of world trade takes place among the A-countries themselves. A smaller but still quite large amount of trade flows between A-countries and the LDCs, and only a small (but growing) amount of trade occurs among developing countries.

The majority of developing country exports are primary products, including oil. As of 1987, 51 percent of LDC exports were such primary products, whereas 18 percent were engineering products and 31 percent were other manufactured goods (GATT, *International Trade,* annual). The growth of manufactured goods exports by developing countries, however, has been quite striking. Exports of engineering products (machinery, automobiles, electronics, and other complex products) rose from virtually zero in the early 1960s to 18 percent of LDC exports in the late 1980s, whereas other manufactures (within which textiles, garments, and shoes would be major entries) rose from 16 percent to 31 percent of such exports over the same period. Nonfuel primary products accounted for 54 percent of total LDC exports in the early 1960s and fell to 21 percent by the late 1980s, whereas fuel exports remained unchanged at 30 percent, having risen sharply from 1974 through the early 1980s before falling later in the decade.[8]

The growth of manufactured goods exports by developing countries might appear to be highly encouraging evidence of a reduced reliance on primary products with stagnant markets and volatile prices. The problem is that most of the manufactured goods are coming from a few newly industrialized countries (NICs) such as Taiwan, South Korea, Hong Kong, and Singapore. Brazil, Mexico, Thailand, and India have also experienced considerable growth of manufactured goods exports, but the majority of the countries in the developing world (particularly in Africa) remain heavily dependent on exports of primary products. It could even be argued that the strongest of the NICs should no longer be viewed as LDCs and instead should be graduated to the status of the A-countries, which would lead to the conclusion that the remaining developing countries have experienced much less growth in exports of manufactured goods than the data in the previous paragraph would suggest.

The structure of their trade is one reason why many of the poorer developing countries remain skeptical about the validity of traditional trade theory. Following the prescription of that theory, they have specialized in primary products, and they now believe this specialization has adversely affected their economic development. In addition to the complaint about adverse terms of trade, LDCs believe that their industrial development has been hampered and that they have not enjoyed nearly as many benefits from economies of scale and technological progress as they could have had. They think that in assigning to them the role of hewers of wood and drawers of water, the world market was reflecting biases and subtle monopolistic controls exercised by A-countries.

These suspicions are strengthened by other circumstances, such as (1) the pattern of escalation in the tariff structures of A-countries, with nominal tariffs rising with the stage of manufacture, thus leading to high effective tariff rates on finished manufactures; (2) the great sensitivity in A-countries to imports of labor-intensive manufactures, and their propensity to resort to escape clauses, quotas, and other extraordinary measures in order to protect domestic industries; and (3) the widespread use of protective devices, including price support schemes, to stabilize their own agricultural sectors, while urging the virtues of free competitive markets to the LDCs. LDCs also charge that GATT negotiations for tariff reductions have concentrated on products exported by A-countries, and have systematically avoided any substantial concessions on the labor-intensive manufactures exported by LDCs. (It should be noted, however, that LDCs are partly responsible for GATT's neglect of their export products because they have declined to participate in parts of the GATT negotiations. By refusing to accept the principle of reciprocity, they were unable to bargain for tariff reductions on their export products.)

The U.S. response to increased imports of instant coffee is a good illustration of the kind of behavior that makes LDCs skeptical of the sincerity of A-countries and dubious about their commitment to competitive markets. In the 1960s Brazil began to install plants to produce instant coffee. These plants were able to compete with U.S. producers because they could buy broken beans at prices well below the

[8]GATT, *International Trade* (annual), 1990–1991.

world price for regular coffee beans, because they saved transport cost (two-thirds of weight is lost in the manufacturing process), and because they could pay lower wage rates. Before long, Brazilian producers had captured some 14 percent of the U.S. instant coffee market, and U.S. producers were demanding relief. After negotiations between the two governments, Brazil agreed to impose an export tax on instant coffee large enough to offset the advantage its producers enjoy through the low prices they pay for broken beans. This agreement, forced on Brazil by the United States, denies the principle of comparative advantage and prevents the development of a resource-based manufacturing industry that seems obvious and natural for Brazil. Such episodes do not increase the LDCs' confidence in A-countries' dedication to the economic principles they espouse.

Instability of Export Prices and Proceeds

LDCs maintain that their primary product exports are subject to large fluctuations in price and volume and that the high degree of concentration in exports makes their economies vulnerable to external disturbances. This greater instability, compared to A-countries, is another complaint that LDCs have had about their role in world trade.

Although exceptions can be found, "it is now generally agreed that export prices, quantities, and total earnings are all more unstable in the average poor country than in the average rich one."[9] Fluctuations tend to be even greater for individual commodities than for indexes, and it is the individual commodity that matters for a country that depends on one or two exports. Table 10-3 contains some data showing price and export value fluctuations for 13 important primary commodities during the period 1953 to 1972. These fluctuations are substantial, especially when we allow for the fact that the period covered includes the decade of the 1960s, when commodity price indexes were unusually stable. Since 1973 commodity prices have fluctuated even more widely.

Recent studies lend support to the view that export concentration is significantly related to export instability and that LDCs have experienced greater instability in their export proceeds than have A-countries. One of the main objectives of LDCs in international conferences has been to establish schemes to stabilize the prices of their primary product exports. This was one of the goals of the new international economic order agenda during the 1970s and early 1980s.

TRADE STRATEGY FOR LDCs

The suspicions of LDCs concerning their role in world trade have been accompanied by considerable debate about the trade strategy they should adopt. The issue is often posed as a choice between an inward-looking strategy in which industries are developed largely to supply the domestic market, with foreign trade assigned a minimal role, and an outward-looking strategy of concentrating on industries in which the country has a comparative advantage, with heavy reliance on the world

[9]G. K. Helleiner, *International Trade and Economic Development* (Baltimore: Penguin, 1972), p. 78.

TABLE 10-3 Fluctuations in Price and Export Valued of Selected Commodities, 1953–1972

Commodity	Average Annual Percentage Change from Trend[a]	
	Market Price	Value of Exports
Sugar	33.4	9.2
Cocoa	23.0	13.4
Copper	21.5	17.1
Beef and veal	20.8	15.4
Sisal	18.0	26.3
Coffee	17.0	11.1
Rubber	13.2	14.7
Jute	11.9	12.2
Wool	11.4	10.2
Rice	11.3	12.9
Iron ore	8.3	10.8
Cotton	8.2	9.1
Tin	7.9	18.8

[a]Average over the period of absolute differences between annual observations and calculated trend values, expressed as percentages of the trend value.

Source: Jere Behrman, Development, The International Economic Order, and Commodity Agreements (Reading, Mass.: Addison-Wesley, 1978), p. 49.

market as a source of demand for the expanded output of exportable products. We will briefly discuss these alternative strategies, beginning with the inward-looking strategy of import substitution.

Import Substitution

A rationale for import substitution readily emerges from the LDCs' view of world trade. They cannot expand their exports of primary products, it is argued, because of low price and income elasticities of demand for these products in world markets. Nor can they initiate exports of new types of manufactured products because they cannot compete with the established producers in A-countries, especially in view of the barriers that exist in A-country markets. Consequently, given the imperative need to accelerate their economic growth and development, LDCs have no alternative but to produce for themselves some of the products they now import. The very fact that imports exist is proof that domestic demand exists. Through the use of tariffs, quotas, and other barriers, imports can be restricted and the domestic market reserved for domestic producers. In this way, domestic manufacturing output can be substituted for imports.

This rationale is often coupled with the infant-industry argument. The hope is that the newly created industries will become more efficient as they gain experience and that external economies will be generated as more industries are installed. Eventually, the need for protection will diminish, and some of the new industries may even begin to export their products.

Import substitution was very popular in the 1950s and 1960s, especially in Latin America, and it is still widely used in LDCs. However, things did not work out as expected in certain respects, and a number of criticisms have been leveled against this strategy.

In many instances, the largest imports and the first candidates for import substitution were finished consumer goods. When imports of these goods were curtailed, domestic production often began with the "final touches." That is, component parts and semifinished articles were imported, and only the last steps in the production process were performed in the protected domestic firms. Many assembly plants were constructed. Advocates of import substitution hoped and expected that industrialization would proceed by stages, working its way backward from the final touches stage to the intermediate-product stage, and finally to the production of basic materials so that the LDC would acquire a full range of industries. However, this progression frequently did not occur. The final touches industries were installed, but they depended for their survival on a continued high level of effective protection. That is, they had to have high nominal tariffs on the finished articles and low (or zero) tariffs on the component parts and semifinished articles that they imported from abroad. Any attempt to encourage production of these intermediate products through tariff protection would adversely affect the final touches industry and perhaps drive it out of business. In the meanwhile, consumers had to pay higher prices. All that was accomplished was the substitution of intermediate-product imports for finished imports.

Furthermore, it has come to be recognized that import substitution has a number of undesirable side effects. First, the higher domestic prices of the protected products mean higher costs for other industries which use these products as inputs. If these other industries are exporters, they become less able to compete in world markets. In this case, protection to promote import substitution ends up reducing exports of the LDC. For example, Egypt placed a heavy tariff on fertilizer imports in order to encourage domestic production, but high fertilizer prices caused farmers to use less fertilizer per acre. Consequently, farm output declined and exports decreased, and the prices of food and other agricultural products increased. The policy, undertaken to save foreign exchange by reducing fertilizer imports, ended up reducing export proceeds and thus losing more foreign exchange than it saved.

When tariffs are imposed on inputs into an export industry, the effective rate of protection for the export industry is negative. This follows directly from the definition of the effective tariff rate:[10]

$$e_j = \frac{t_j - \sum a_{ij} \cdot t_i}{1 - \sum a_{ij}}$$

[10]The reader may wish to refer to the discussion of the effective tariff in Chapter 6.

The nominal tariff on the export product, t_j, is zero because the export must be sold in the world market at the going world price. Any nominal tariffs on inputs, t_i, will therefore cause the numerator in the above equation to be negative. The point is a simple one, but policymakers often overlook it in their preoccupation with partial equilibrium analysis of a single industry: Tariffs on inputs into export industries increase the costs of those industries and handicap them in competitive world markets.

A second side effect of import substitution has been the use of inappropriate technology in the new plants that have been constructed in LDCs. In most cases the capital equipment installed in these plants has been imported from A-countries, and the tendency has been to utilize the latest, most modern technology available. However, this equipment was designed for use in A-countries, and it tends to be highly capital-intensive. Capital-intensiveness is appropriate for A-countries, where capital is relatively abundant and therefore cheap, and where the emphasis is on labor-saving techniques. It is not appropriate for LDCs, where capital is scarce and labor abundant.

This problem is exacerbated by a set of policies that tends to encourage the use of capital. These policies essentially reduce the price of capital relative to wage rates. To promote import substitution, LDC governments may offer loans at low rates of interest, and international lending agencies such as the World Bank also make loans at favorable rates of interest. Governments provide tax incentives and even outright subsidies. Imports of capital equipment are often admitted duty free, and sometimes foreign exchange is made available below the market rate to encourage such imports.

The result has been the development of manufacturing sectors in LDCs that are not only inefficient and dependent on continued tariff protection, but that also employ very little labor. Despite the rapid growth in manufacturing output, employment in manufacturing industry has risen very little. High rates of urban unemployment are now a major social problem in many LDCs.

Import-substituting industries often remain dependent on imports of components, intermediate products, and other materials. They do not solve the problem that motivated their creation.

Export-Led Growth

These considerations have led many economists to advocate an outward-looking strategy for LDCs, a strategy that places greater emphasis on the principle of comparative advantage as a guide to the allocation of resources. This is not an argument for specialization in primary products by LDCs, but neither does it rule out the continuation of such exports as long as prices are attractive. It does, however, put considerable emphasis on export diversification, particularly toward manufactured goods, as a way to reduce risk.

The crucial issue is the allocation of new productive capacity, and advocates of an outward-looking strategy recognize that expansion of traditional primary-product exports may not be desirable because of unfavorable trends in the terms of trade. In that event, they say, LDCs should allocate new productive capacity to manufacturing industries that are capable of competing in world markets. If such potential comparative advantage industries can be identified and their production undertaken, a number of advantages accrue. First, there is no limitation on size and scale of plant because the world market is very large. Production plans can be based on considerations of cost and efficiency. Adam Smith's dictum that the division of labor is limited by the extent of the market can be set aside. (However, the industrializing LDC must be concerned about maintaining access to external markets; thus it has an interest in GATT trade negotiations, as well as in the various schemes for tariff preferences that were discussed in Chapter 8.)

Second, manufacturing industries that can successfully compete in world markets are likely to be industries that utilize the LDCs' abundant factors of production. These industries tend to be relatively labor intensive. Thus they provide employment and economize on scarce capital. The expansion of exports permits the country to expand its imports, and backward linkages may stimulate the development of manufacturing capacity in related industries.

Obviously, the crucial question is how to select the potential comparative advantage industries in the first place. There is no magic answer, but advocates of an outward-looking strategy argue that competitive market prices should be relied on to guide the allocation of resources. Subsidies, tax incentives, and other devices may be used to promote the export industries, but the acid test is the eventual ability of these industries to produce and sell their products at market prices. Instead of sheltering the new industries and permitting them to charge high prices in the small domestic market, the outward-looking strategy confronts them with the world market price. To survive, they must be able to get their costs down and meet that price.

In the 1950s and 1960s, LDCs widely adopted the strategy of import substitution, but a few countries chose an outward-looking, export-oriented strategy. The experience of both groups of countries has been carefully studied in recent years, most notably in two major research projects on foreign trade regimes and their effects on economic development that were done under the auspices of the Organization for Economic Cooperation and Development (OECD) and the National Bureau for Economic Research (NBER).[11] These and other studies have been closely scrutinized by economists in search of lessons for policymakers in LDCs.

[11] In addition to numerous country studies, there are three volumes that synthesize and summarize the overall results of this research:

Ian Little, T. Scitovsky, and M. Scott, *Industry and Trade in Some Developing Countries: A Comparative Study* (Oxford: Oxford University Press, 1970).

Jagdish Bhagwati, *Foreign Trade Regimes and Economic Development: Anatomy and Consequences of Exchange Control Regimes* (New York: Columbia University Press, 1976).

Anne Krueger, *Foreign Trade Regimes and Economic Development: Liberalization Attempts and Consequences* (New York: Columbia University Press, 1976).

A recent survey of the literature on trade policy and development can be found in Oli Havrylyshyn, "Trade Policy and Productivity Gains in Developing Countries," *World Bank Research Observer,* January 1990, pp. 1–24.

Debate continues, but a strong consensus is that the economic performance of outward-looking countries has been superior to that of import-substituting countries. Import substitution seems to have had many disadvantages, as noted earlier. Above all, it tends to erode the export capacity of the country using it. It does so by increasing the costs of inputs into the export industries, as well as by setting up price incentives to pull capital, skilled labor, and other resources into import-substituting industries and away from the export industries. Inducements given to the protected firms encourage them to use capital-intensive techniques, yet their plants are often designed on a relatively small scale to fit the small domestic market. Thus their costs per unit are high, and they remain dependent on continued protection. When the first, easy stage of import substitution is finished, many countries find it difficult to go on to the next stage.

A few LDCs following an export-oriented strategy have achieved substantial increases in their exports of manufactured goods, and they have also achieved high rates of economic growth. Examples include South Korea, Taiwan, Thailand, Malaysia, and Brazil. Their experience seems significantly different from (and superior to) that of such import-substituting countries as Argentina, Egypt, and the Philippines.

Not everyone agrees with this assessment. Some argue that the successful export expansion in these countries was preceded by a period of import-substituting industrialization in which the necessary groundwork was laid. This point is made, for example, about Brazil, India, and Mexico, all of whom now export manufactured goods. Furthermore, a small group of LDCs accounts for the great bulk of the increase in manufacturing exports that has been achieved. If all LDCs had tried to promote exports, could all of them have done so? This question reminds us again of the critical importance of access to A-country markets. If more LDCs adopt an outward-looking strategy, complaints about market disruption and the need for safeguards will undoubtedly increase.

The LDCs have an obvious comparative advantage in labor-intensive manufactures such as garments and shoes, and the pressure on the A-countries to reduce or eliminate import barriers on such products is becoming stronger. The problem in doing so goes back to our earlier discussion of the Heckscher-Ohlin theorem and of factor-price equalization. Total incomes in the A-countries would clearly rise as a result of trade liberalization, but incomes would be redistributed from unskilled and semiskilled labor toward capital and technical/professional labor. Such a redistribution of income is not popular in most industrialized countries; labor unions and other representatives of industrial workers are especially opposed to it. Most citizens of the A-countries are not unskilled or semiskilled and would clearly gain from free trade with the developing world, but those who would lose understandably oppose such trade liberalization.

The compensation principle appears to offer an obvious solution; since the winners from free trade gain more income than the losers lose, they could compensate unskilled and semiskilled labor and still retain net gains. If some of the income gains were taxed away and the resulting revenues were used to compensate those who are injured, free trade with the developing world would be an arrangement in which nobody loses.

This approach is theoretically simple but politically and administratively difficult. It implies more active income redistribution policies from the governments of A-countries, an approach which may not be popular. It is also not easy to measure the gains and losses from free trade; thus compensation would be approximate at best. In any event, this approach has received very little serious attention in the legislatures of the A-countries.

Unless the compensation approach becomes part of trade policy, it will be very difficult for A-countries to completely open their markets to textiles, garments, shoes, and other labor-intensive goods from the developing world. Instead there is likely to be slow, halting progress toward more open markets, with occasional threats of slippage back toward protectionism.

The industrialized countries face a difficult dilemma in designing policies for trade with the developing world. On the one hand, they want the gains in total income that would come from free trade, and they would like to encourage the growth of the economies of the developing world. On the other hand, they do not want the income redistribution effects which the Heckscher-Ohlin theorem tells them will result from this trade unless a compensation plan is devised. The result is trade policies in A-countries that are sometimes contradictory and slow to evolve.

QUESTIONS FOR STUDY AND REVIEW

1. Analyze and evaluate the several complaints that LDCs have made about international trade and their participation in it.

2. Nominal tariff rates in industrial countries commonly increase with the stage of processing. Why exactly do LDCs object to such a tariff structure?

3. Explain how it is that economic growth can be immiserizing.

4. In a country with tariffs on a wide range of imported products, what can be said about the effective rate of protection in the country's export industries? Explain why.

5. What are the pros and cons of tariff preferences for LDCs? Are such preferences in the best interests of the LDCs themselves? Discuss.

6. Discuss the issues (pros and cons) in the debate over import substitution and export substitution as a strategy for LDCs to follow. Which strategy do you favor? Explain, bringing in specific arguments as far as possible.

7. "LDC tariffs intended to promote industry may in fact inhibit development of the LDCs' most efficient industries." Do you agree? Explain.

8. Industrial countries generally have low or zero tariffs on raw materials and primary products that are the principal exports of LDCs. Do you think this is economically advantageous for the LDCs? Explain why or why not.

9. What interest groups within the United States would you expect to support a U.S. policy of allowing more products to be imported from emerging industrialized countries such as Thailand, Taiwan, and Mexico? Why? Who

within the U.S. political system would oppose such a liberal trade policy? Why?

SELECTED REFERENCES

Adams, F. G., and Jere Behrman. *Commodity Exports and Economic Development.* Alderholt: Gower, 1982.

Balassa, Bela. *Development Strategies in Semi-industrial Countries.* Baltimore: Johns Hopkins University Press, 1982.

Behrman, Jere. *Development, the International Economic Order, and Commodity Agreements.* Reading, Mass.: Addison-Wesley, 1978.

Corden, W. M. "The NIEO Proposals: A Cool Look." Reprinted in Robert Baldwin and J. Richardson, eds., *International Trade and Finance.* Boston: Little, Brown, 1981.

Corea, Gamaine. *Need for Change: Towards the New International Economic Order.* Elmsford, N.Y.: Pergamon Press, 1981.

Grilli, E., and M. C. Yang. "Primary Commodity Prices, Manufactured Goods Prices, and the Terms of Trade of Developing Countries: What the Long Run Shows." *World Bank Economic Review,* January 1988, pp. 1–47.

Krueger, Anne O. *Trade and Employment in Developing Countries: Synthesis and Conclusions.* Vol. 3. Chicago: University of Chicago Press, 1983.

Krueger, Anne O. "Trade Policies in Developing Countries." In R. Jones and P. Kenen, eds., *Handbook of International Economics.* Vol. I. New York: North Holland, 1984.

Michaely, Michael. *Trade, Income Levels, and Dependence.* Amsterdam: North Holland, 1984.

Reidel, J. "Trade as an Engine of Growth in Developing Countries, Revisited." *Economic Journal,* March 1984.

Reubens, E. P., ed. *The Challenge of the New International Economic Order.* Boulder, Colo.: Westview, 1981.

UNCTAD. *New Directions and New Structures for Trade and Development.* Report by the Secretary General of UNCTAD. Nairobi, May 1976.

World Bank. *World Debt Tables.* Washington, D.C.: World Bank, 1990.

World Bank. *World Development Report* (annual), particularly the 1987 edition.

INTERNATIONAL MOBILITY OF LABOR AND CAPITAL

The previous chapters have assumed that goods were internationally mobile (i.e., that merchandise trade occurred) but that factors of production were not mobile. The basis of Heckscher-Ohlin trade was precisely that large differences in relative factor endowments produced parallel differences in factor prices; these in turn led to the differences in relative goods prices, which made comparative advantage trade possible. A country with a relative abundance of labor, for example, would have low wages that would give it a comparative advantage in labor-intensive goods such as garments and shoes. The fact that differences in factor prices existed before trade began must imply that labor and capital were internationally immobile; otherwise the abundant factor in each country would have simply moved elsewhere to earn higher returns. Labor would have migrated to capital-abundant countries, and capital would have moved in the opposite direction, roughly equalizing relative factor endowments and prices, thus eliminating the basis for Heckscher-Ohlin trade.

Although trade theory assumes factor immobility, some labor and capital movement occurs among countries. Labor migrates, legally or otherwise, from low to higher wage countries, whereas international capital flows seeking higher returns are a major element of international finance. Capital and labor are not perfectly free to move because immigration laws, transportation costs, lack of information about job availability, and even language differences make it difficult for people to migrate, whereas international investors face other problems such as exchange rate risk. (This subject will be discussed briefly later in this chapter and in more detail in Part II of this book.) There is sufficient mobility of capital and labor, however, to make it useful to discuss the subject, especially since pressures from residents of developing countries who want to come to the United States or other industrialized countries have become intense in recent years and are likely to become more so.

ARBITRAGE IN LABOR AND CAPITAL MARKETS

The international migration of capital and labor can be viewed as an arbitraging process that is similar to the movement that occurs among regions of a country. People living in low-wage and/or high-unemployment areas of the United States, for example, move to states where wages and job opportunities are better. This movement reduces wage differentials by reducing the supply of labor where wages are low and by increasing the number of people seeking work in high-wage areas. Transportation costs, preferences for remaining in one's home region, and lack of information about job availability mean that this arbitraging process is not perfect, for it does not produce a single wage across all parts of the United States. It does, however, limit the range of wage differentials, because low-wage states consistently lose working-age residents and higher wage states gain them.

The international movement of workers reflects the same arbitraging process, except that the barriers to migration are higher than in the case of domestic migration. Transportation is more costly, information about job availability is harder to obtain, and differences in language, culture, and even climate make preferences for remaining in one's home country stronger. Most important, however, virtually every country maintains immigration laws that strictly limit the number of people who are allowed to enter from abroad in order to seek employment. These laws may be stricter in high-income countries that face heavier pressure from potential immigrants, but poor countries also maintain them in order to protect job markets for citizens, to control population growth, and to limit the number of people in the country from foreign cultures.

It was argued in Chapter 4 that free trade reduces international wage differentials and, under some unlikely assumptions, could eliminate them. The factor-price equalization process produced similar effects in capital markets. Free trade would then appear to produce the same effects as free international mobility of factors. If free trade prevailed, factor prices would become sufficiently similar to greatly reduce the pressure for labor or capital migration. It is precisely because merchandise trade is not free (or even close to free) that international differences in factor prices persist and thus create incentives for migration.

Heckscher-Ohlin trade and international factor mobility can then be viewed as close substitutes in terms of both causes and effects. Both result from differences in factor prices that reflect differences in relative factor endowments, and both would reduce or eliminate those price differences. Either process would sharply narrow international differentials in wage rates. If the United States had either free trade or the lack of any barriers to people moving here from abroad, domestic wage rates would fall and returns to capital and land would rise.[1]

This parallelism between Heckscher-Ohlin trade and factor mobility extends to politics. Because the relatively scarce factor of production absorbs income losses from either free trade or factor mobility, it tends to support both protectionism and strict limits on factor movements, whereas the abundant factor of production gains from both processes, and therefore favors free trade and more factor mobility. The AFL-CIO favors strict immigration laws and firm enforcement efforts for the same reason that it supports protection. Both will maintain or increase U.S. wage rates. Although it has not been an active issue in recent years, American labor has also favored limits on the ability of U.S. firms to move capital abroad, most recently in the case of the unsuccessful Burke-Hartke bill of the early 1970s. U.S. farmers and owners of businesses, who want readily available low-wage labor, tend to favor much less strict limits on immigration. U.S. vegetable and fruit farmers have been particularly unhappy with laws that restrict their use of temporary workers from Mexico and the Caribbean. The similarity between the forces behind, and the effects of, Heckscher-Ohlin trade and international factor mobility is striking.

Factor mobility increases efficiency and total output because it involves the movement of scarce productive assets from less productive to more productive locations and uses. Any such movement should increase output by the difference in marginal products times the amount of the factor that moves. If rates of return, and therefore marginal products, are equated through arbitrage, the efficiency gains become a bit more complicated, but they can be seen, along with the income distribution effects in Figure 11-1. This graph uses the movement of capital from the United States to Canada as its example, but it applies equally to the movement of labor from low-wage to higher wage countries. The marginal product of capital (MP_k in the figure) is the increase in total output that results from adding one unit of capital while holding inputs of other factors unchanged. In this case marginal product is measured as an annual percentage. The marginal product lines slope down because of the law of diminishing returns, that is, because adding more capital to unchanging amounts of labor and land reduces the marginal product of capital.

[1]The effects of immigration on the U.S. labor market are discussed in some detail in Michael Greenwood and John McDowell, "The Factor Market Consequences of U.S. Immigration," *Journal of Economic Literature,* December 1986, pp. 1738–1772. An earlier treatment of the welfare effects of labor mobility can be found in R. A. Berry and R. Soligo, "Some Welfare Aspects of International Migration," *Journal of Political Economy,* September/October 1969, pp. 778–794. See Clark Reynolds and Robert McCleary, "The Political Economy of Immigration Law: The Impact of Simpson-Rodino on the U.S. and Mexico," *Journal of Economic Perspectives,* Summer 1988, pp. 117–131 for a discussion of the effects of a recent tightening of U.S. immigration law. An early discussion of the similarity of Heckscher-Ohlin trade and factor mobility can be found in R. Mundell, "International Trade and Factor Mobility," *American Economic Review,* June 1957.

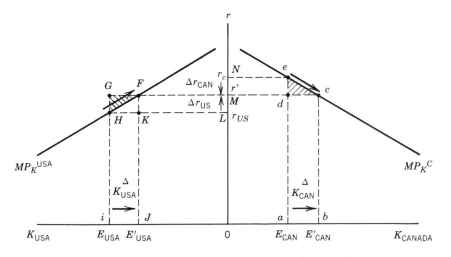

FIGURE 11-1 Effects of U.S. Capital Flows to Canada. *Source:* Adapted from Peter B. Kenen, *The International Economy*, 2nd ed. (Englewood Cliffs, N.J.: Prentice Hall, 1989), p. 137.

In this graph, the difference in interest rates, which represent differences in the marginal productivity of capital, causes capital to flow from the United States to Canada in the amount ij which equals ab. As a result, interest rates in Canada fall from r_c to r' while yields in the United States rise from r_{us} to r'. Output in Canada rises by the area under the marginal product function, area $ecbade$, whereas output in the United States falls by area $fhijkf$. The increase to total output, which is the result of reallocating scarce capital to a more productive location, is the area of the two triangles, dec and fgh. Canadians make interest payments to Americans in the amount of the rectangle $abcd$ per year, which means that the net gain in income for Canada is the triangle dce. The income received by Americans is rectangle $abcd$, which equals rectangle $ijfg$. Given the loss of U.S. output of area $ijkfh$, the net gain in income for the United States is triangle fgh. Capital moves from less to more efficient uses, interest rates are arbitraged together, and total income in both countries increases.

Sizable income redistribution effects exist however. Canadian-owned capital (distance Oa) was earning an interest rate of r_c for a total income shown by the rectangle $Onea$. As a result of the inflow of U.S. funds, this yield falls to r' which produces total income of only the rectangle $Omda$, meaning a loss of area $mden$. This income is shifted to Canadian labor in the form of higher wages resulting from a higher capital-to-labor ratio in Canada and a higher marginal product of Canadian labor. Canadian-owned capital loses and labor gains. The same income redistribution process occurs in the United States but in the opposite direction. U.S.-owned capital was previously earning r_{us} for a total income of rectangle $OLHi$. The increase of U.S. interest rates to r' means that American capital that remains behind (does not go to Canada) gains rectangle $lmfk$. This income is extracted from labor as U.S. wages fall owing to a lower capital-to-labor ratio in the United States and a resulting decline in the marginal product of U.S. labor. U.S. capital gains and labor loses.

International factor mobility produces the same dilemmas as does free trade. Total output and incomes clearly rise, but income is redistributed in ways that may be painful and politically controversial. From the perspective of Canadian labor and U.S. capital, the process described here should be encouraged, but U.S. workers and Canadian owners of capital will have the opposite view. Political conflicts over immigration laws and policies affecting international capital movements are likely to reflect these differing interests.

In addition, taxes can affect the conclusion that total incomes in both countries rise as a result of these factor movements. If, for example, the capital that flowed from the United States to Canada in the previous example was equity in a subsidiary rather than debt, the resulting profits would have been taxable in Canada rather than the United States, resulting in a loss for the Internal Revenue Service (IRS) and a gain for its counterpart in Ottawa. To see how the United States as a whole could lose from this investment, assume that both countries have 40 percent corporate tax rates in the following example:

	Profit Rates in:	
	United States	Canada
Gross or pre-tax	10.0%	12.0%
Tax Paid	4.0%	4.8%
Net to investors	6.0%	7.2%

If a U.S. firm invests domestically, the net return to its investors is only 6 percent, but the IRS gets 4 percent which can be used for public purposes. Thus the United States as a whole gets a return of 10 percent. If instead the firm invests the capital in its Canadian subsidiary, its investors earn 7.2 percent, but the IRS gets nothing because the 4.8 percent goes to tax collectors in Ottawa. The total return to the United States is 7.2 percent, meaning a loss of 2.8 percent. Total output is up by the 2 percent difference in gross yields, and the Canadian government and U.S. private investors certainly gain. However, the U.S. government loses 4 percent of the investment per year, and the American economy as a whole loses 2.8 percent. International capital flows do increase efficiency, but when taxes are allowed for, it is not clear that the flows benefit both the investing and the host country.

The same problem can arise with regard to labor if governments have high marginal income tax rates and highly skilled or professional labor moves from a developing to an industrialized country. This so-called brain drain can mean that the government of a country such as India can suffer sizable tax revenue losses when scientists, whose education was largely provided at public expense, move from India to the United States or Great Britain, taking tax revenues with them. A large number of scientists from Asia have come to the United States in recent years, creating some frustration over lost tax revenues in New Delhi, Hong Kong, and Taipei. It has been argued that the IRS ought to return some of the resulting tax revenues to the governments that provided education for scientists now employed in the United States.

IMMIGRATION PRESSURES
FROM DEVELOPING COUNTRIES

The dominant problem facing the United States in the area of international factor mobility does not involve scientists. Rather, it results from the tremendous desire of unskilled workers to migrate from poor countries in Latin America and the Caribbean region to this country. Differences in wage rates are often in the excess of 5 to 1, producing a huge incentive to move, legally or otherwise. It is becoming increasingly difficult for U.S. authorities to control the nation's borders. Moreover, many governments, such as that in Mexico, view emigration to the United States as a safety valve for excess population pressures, and therefore oppose U.S. attempts to tighten immigration controls. European countries are feeling similar pressures as people try to emigrate from Asia and Africa in search of higher incomes. If high rates of population growth continue in the developing world, this problem could prove extremely difficult for the industrialized countries.

Although immigration into the United States increases total incomes in the nation, it does not necessarily increase per capita incomes, because the population grows. If the immigrants are unskilled and bring little or no capital with them, they are likely to lower U.S. per capita output, although their departure will cause it to rise in the country from which they emigrate. The effect of such immigration on U.S. output per person can be seen most easily through a standard classical growth model:

$$Y = F(\overset{+}{K}, \overset{+}{LB}, \overset{+}{LN}, \overset{+}{T})$$

where Y = gross national product

K = capital stock

LB = labor force

LN = land stock

T = technology

This equation states that potential output is a positive function of the size of the capital stock, the labor force, the availability of land, and technology.

Capital is defined as including education and training, which is often referred to as human capital.

If $LB = a$(population)

where a = the labor force participation rate

and Y/c = output per capita

then $Y/c = F(\overset{+}{K/LB}, \overset{+}{LN/LB}, \overset{+}{T})$

This equation says that output per capita is positively related to the capital-to-labor ratio, the land-to-labor ratio, and technology. Technology does not have to be divided by the amount of labor because it is knowledge that can be used by more workers at no additional cost. The last equation makes the common-sense argument that output per capita will grow if the amount of capital per worker rises, if the amount of land per worker increases, or if technology advances. Increases in the population of a country, without corresponding increases in the stocks of capital and land, will cause GNP per capita to fall. This would not be true if a country were underpopulated to the extent that useful land was idle and markets were too small to get economies of scale. The United States may have faced this situation during much of the nineteenth century, but certainly not today.

The arrival of large numbers of immigrants without significant amounts of financial or human capital in the United States will reduce the capital-to-labor ratio and the land-to-labor ratio, thereby decreasing potential per capita GNP. The arrival of a few such people will not be sufficient to affect these ratios, and so no noticeable impact on GNP per capita will be expected. The effects of such emigration in overcrowded countries such as Mexico are, of course, exactly opposite in that potential GNP per capita increases with the reduced population and the increased capital-to-labor and land-to-labor ratios. This explains the unavoidable conflict between the government of this country and the governments in Mexico City, Kingston, San Salvador, and similar cities. They want their people to be able to leave for the United States, and they may even view such emigration as crucial for economic development, but it is not in the interests of the United States to allow them to come here. This is becoming a major issue in relations between industrialized countries and the developing world.

When immigrants bring significant amounts of capital (financial or human), the situation described above changes because the capital-to-labor ratio can rise rather than fall with their arrival. That is why countries such as Canada maintain immigration preferences for people who arrive with sufficient capital to start new businesses. Education and training is the more typical form of capital that makes immigrants a potentially important source of economic growth. The United States benefited enormously from the arrival of large numbers of scientists and engineers fleeing Europe before World War II, as it is benefiting today from the people migrating here from a variety of developing countries. Scientists from east and south Asia have become a major force is U.S. high-technology industries; businessmen from Cuba and elsewhere in Latin America have also been very successful here.

The unavoidable, if unpleasant, conclusion is that it is in the interests of the United States to allow highly educated and talented immigrants into this country, but that it is not in the economic interest of the existing U.S. population to allow large numbers of unskilled people to immigrate.

CAPITAL FLOWS AND MULTINATIONAL FIRMS

As was argued above, flows of capital between countries seeking higher yields can basically be viewed as an arbitraging process. It is similar to the movement of labor, except that transportation costs are much lower and legal prohibitions are usually less stringent in the country into which capital is flowing. Foreigners may have great difficulty getting permission to move to the United States, but they are usually welcome to invest here. To the extent that capital flows are regulated, it is usually by the country of the investor, and such regulation is the result of balance-of-payments constraints. Many developing countries do not allow their residents to invest abroad on the grounds that foreign exchange is needed for more important purposes, such as importing food or machinery.

Capital flows also involve some particular risks for investors; information on creditworthiness may be unreliable, and it may be almost impossible to enforce contracts in a foreign court system. In addition, political risks may arise if foreign governments decide to discriminate against foreign investors. Expropriation is an extreme possibility; discriminatory taxes are more common. There is the further problem of exchange rates; foreign securities may be purchased at one exchange rate, but a devaluation or depreciation of the foreign currency can mean that large losses are absorbed when funds are brought back. If, for example, an American bought British securities when the British pound was worth $2.80, holding those securities over the 1967 weekend when the parity was changed to $2.40 would have cost the investor 15 percent of the money measured in dollars. Since such changes in exchange rate are difficult or impossible to forecast, investment in foreign securities involves a risk that does not exist in domestic investment. This problem, as well as the use of institutions such as the forward exchange market to deal with it, will be discussed in Part II of this book.

One of the most important routes through which capital flows among countries is the multinational corporation (MNC), which is also known as a transnational corporation. Such firms have become a major element in the world economy since World War II. A multinational corporation operates in a number of countries through affiliates or subsidiaries over which it has effective control. The firm may be the sole owner of such subsidiaries, or it may merely have a sufficient equity interest to determine management policies.

Such firms have existed for a long time. For early examples we could go back to the Muscovy Company (1555), the East India Company (1600), the Hudson's Bay Company, and other large firms that operated in more than one country. But what is new and even revolutionary about the recent growth of MNCs is their rapid spread throughout the world and their growing dominance in a wide range of industries and activities. It is estimated that between one-fourth and one-third of all manufactured goods now moving in world trade are being shipped from one branch to another of a multinational corporation—that is, they are intracompany shipments. MNCs have played a significant role in the integration of the world economy, in creating what might be viewed as a global shopping center. A report of the U.S. Tariff Commission asserted that "the spread of multinational business ranks with the development of the steam engine, electric power, and the automobile as one of the major events of modern history."[2]

---

[2]*Implications of Multinational Firms for World Trade and Investment and for U.S. Trade and Labor*, Report to Senate Finance Committee, 93rd Cong., 1st Sess. (Washington, D.C.: U.S. Government Printing Office, 1973).

As MNCs have grown, their domain expanding far beyond the nation-state, they have been perceived as a threat to the power and authority of national governments. The social and political tensions arising from this conflict have figured prominently in several notable books written about them in recent years: *Sovereignty at Bay, Global Reach, The American Challenge, Storm over Multinationals*.[3] The sheer size of the largest MNCs, as well as their ability to operate in many locations around the world, makes it difficult for any single nation to control them effectively. This has led to calls for some kind of international supervisory body, or at least some multilateral agreements on essential aspects of their operations. So far, little progress has been made in this direction.

For a time, the multinational corporation was considered to be largely an American institution. Its spread was seen as an aspect of American power, and (by some) as a manifestation of American imperialism. In recent years, however, European and Japanese MNCs have grown in number and importance, and now MNCs are originating in less developed countries as well. The U.S. role is still large, but it has declined in relative terms.

It is of the essence of the MNC that it moves resources. It can survey alternative sites for productive facilities and locate them wherever it is most profitable. Capital, managerial talent, and skilled scientific and technical personnel can often be moved from one country to another, as required for optimal results. A U.S. firm may decide to supply the European market by locating a plant in Belgium, or in India, for that matter. The decision involves what is called "direct investment," a term that implies provision of a combination of capital, management, and technology for the new venture.

Traditional trade theory presumes that many small firms are operating in each industry, so that the model of perfect competition can be used. Each firm is a resident of a single country, and no one firm is large enough to have a discernible influence on the price of the product. MNCs, on the other hand, are large—sometimes very large. They are simultaneously residents of several countries, and they have considerable influence on price. Many international transactions are between the various parts of a single company.

The Debate over MNCs: Some Global Issues

The emergence of multinationals as a major force in the world economy has been accompanied by vigorous and intensive debate about virtually every aspect of their operations. The debate involves both source countries and host countries, and both developed and less developed countries. It ranges widely over economic and noneconomic factors, and involves many political and cultural elements that lie outside the purview of economics. It also involves instinctive and perhaps

---

[3]Raymond Vernon, *Sovereignty at Bay* (New York: Basic Books, 1971); Richard Barnet and Ronald Muller, *Global Reach* (New York: Simon & Schuster, 1974); J. J. Servan-Schreiber, *The American Challenge* (New York: Atheneum, 1968); Raymond Vernon, *Storm over Multinationals* (Cambridge, Mass.: Harvard University Press, 1977).

irrational attitudes. Many of the specific issues in this debate may be conveniently classified under three main headings: efficiency, equity, and sovereignty. We will discuss the broader aspects of these issues in this section and then consider some specific issues in the following section.

Efficiency

By moving resources from countries where they are relatively abundant to countries where they are relatively scarce, MNCs tend to bring about a more efficient allocation of world resources and an increase in world output. This is simply a variation of the principle of comparative advantage. In Chapter 4 we concluded that if factors of production were immobile between nations, trade in goods could serve as a substitute for factor movements. Each country could specialize in products requiring a relatively large amount of its abundant factor and export those products, thus indirectly making its abundant factors available to consumers in other nations.

Now we simply reverse that argument. If obstacles to trade exist, then factor movements can serve as a substitute for trade in goods. The world can achieve the gains from a more efficient allocation of resources by moving capital, technology, management, and skilled labor from places where they are abundant (and relatively cheap) to places where they are scarce (and relatively expensive). That is exactly what MNCs do.

National tariff barriers often provide a motive for direct foreign investment. For example, the common external tariff of the European Economic Community was a major stimulus to the large direct investments made by U.S. firms in Europe during the 1960s. Instead of building plants in the United States and exporting the output to Europe, these firms found it economically advantageous to leap the tariff wall and build the plants inside the EEC. They could then supply the same customers duty free. High tariffs in less developed countries still attract "tariff factories" to those countries. However, as tariff barriers have fallen in recent years, MNCs have been increasingly free to consider the global market and to plan production accordingly. Their objective is to move factors of production and locate wherever cost conditions are most favorable.

Of course, these factor movements are not perfectly free and costless, and they do not take place in sufficient volume to equalize the marginal returns throughout the world, but their tendency is in that direction. Aggregate world output is increased, although the division of the gains becomes a contentious issue.

Through its direct investment activity, the MNC moves a package of resources (capital, technology, and management) across national boundaries. Actually, direct investment may not involve the movement of much capital from the source country to the host country. MNCs are often able to tap supplies of capital in host countries, and they have increasingly made use of the world capital market to obtain the funds needed to construct or acquire their foreign plants. Sometimes host countries insist on the participation of local investors, or even the retention of a majority interest in the joint venture. (IBM withdrew from India in the 1970s because of India's insistence on a share in ownership and control.)

Equity

That direct investment through MNCs can improve the allocation of world resources is a widely accepted view, although it is subject to many qualifications in practice. But even when an increase in world output is acknowledged, there is much controversy about the division of that increased output, both within and between countries. This controversy raises questions of equity and the sharing of gains and losses.

When direct investment moves from a source country to a host country, our expectation is that it will increase the return to capital relative to labor in the source country (capital becomes less abundant, relative to labor) and reduce the return to capital relative to labor in the host country. This is simply an application of the Heckscher-Ohlin analysis, explained in Chapter 4. The distribution of income is affected in both countries, and it is easy to see why special interests in each country might oppose direct investment. This is one explanation for the recent opposition of U.S. labor unions to direct foreign investment by U.S. corporations. It tends to reduce U.S. wages relative to the return on capital. Such investment is also seen as an export of jobs, a decision to supply export markets through production in foreign subsidiaries instead of in U.S. plants.

In host countries, on the other hand, the owners of existing capital may oppose the inflow of direct investment because it tends to reduce the rate of return on capital (the scarce factor), and thus reduces their share of total income.

There is also much debate about how the increase in world output is shared between source countries and host countries. Host countries complain that the profits earned by MNCs are excessive. They also suspect that these huge foreign-owned corporations can manipulate prices to their own advantage, and thus keep most of the gains for themselves.

Taxation of MNCs plays a large role in this debate. Under U.S. law, profits earned by the foreign subsidiaries of U.S. corporations are not subject to U.S. income tax until they are remitted to the home office. Even then, the tax liability to the U.S. Treasury is reduced by the amount of foreign income taxes that have been paid. The purpose of this provision is to avoid double taxation of income, but its practical effect is virtually to eliminate U.S. income tax revenue on foreign-based profits. With a U.S. corporate-profits tax rate of 34 percent, if the tax rate in the host country is also 34 percent, the tax liability to the United States is zero. If the host country has a low tax rate, perhaps designed to encourage an inflow of foreign investment, a U.S.-based multinational can avoid (or postpone) the payment of U.S. taxes simply by reinvesting its profits in the host country, or elsewhere.

The result has been that the United States derived very little tax revenue from the foreign operations of its MNCs. In 1972, for example, U.S.-based MNCs generated $24 billion of taxable income abroad, paid $13 billion in taxes to foreign governments, but paid only $1 billion of taxes to the U.S. Treasury.[4]

[4]G. C. Hufbauer and J. R. Nunns, "Tax Payments and Tax Expenditures on International Investment and Employment," *Columbia Journal of World Business,* Summer 1975, pp. 12–20.

These tax laws have been criticized in recent years, and several proposals have been made to modify them. The Burke-Hartke bill in the early 1970s, which was supported by the AFL-CIO, made foreign income taxable when earned and allowed foreign taxes as a deduction, not as a credit against taxes due. We have noted that if the host country tax rate is 34 percent, the same as the U.S. rate, under present law no tax is payable to the United States. Under the Burke-Hartke proposal, if $100 million were earned abroad, the foreign tax would be a deduction, leaving $54 million of taxable income, on which the U.S. tax would be about $25 million (46 percent of $54 million). Total taxes would rise from $46 million to $71 million on $100 million of foreign income. The Burke-Hartke bill did not pass, but there is still dissatisfaction with the present tax treatment of foreign income.

Although host countries appear to have the advantage with respect to taxation of MNC profits, they also have complaints. They believe that MNCs can manipulate their accounts and cause profits to appear whenever it is to their advantage, that is, in countries with the lowest tax rates. This is one aspect of the problem of "transfer pricing." Many transactions are intrafirm (goods shipped from one subsidiary to another, or services provided by the home office for the entire corporation). The prices charged in these intrafirm transactions contain a large element of arbitrariness, yet the decision made by the MNC can substantially affect the amount of profit reported in each country.

Transfer pricing is a thorny problem; it concerns source countries as well as host countries. When income is switched from a U.S. parent company to a foreign affiliate—for example, by charging overhead costs to the parent company and not allocating it among affiliates—the U.S. Treasury loses tax revenue. Tax authorities in all countries scrutinize corporate records and try to prevent improper practices, but it is a difficult task. The allocation of some costs is essentially arbitrary, and there is no way to establish a true market price for some components and intracompany services because no competitive market exists for identical items.

All the countries in which MNCs operate are competing for tax revenues from them. The more taxes one country gets, the less others will get. If the United States requires its MNCs to allocate a share of their research and development expenses to foreign affiliates, host countries object. The allocation is arbitrary, and they could charge that the United States was artificially diverting profits from host countries to itself. To avoid conflict, some kind of international agreement is needed on the terms of an equitable division. Some tax treaties have been negotiated, but for the most part these matters must be worked out between the MNC and each national government that has the power to levy taxes on it.

Sovereignty

By definition, the domain of a multinational corporation extends beyond the boundaries of any nation-state. Many MNCs operate in dozens of nations. They truly have a global reach. Some are so large and powerful that they may be able to evade the political and economic controls of the nations in which they operate. If any single government tries to impose its will on an MNC, the corporation can simply leave and locate in another country where the authorities are more accommodating.

Much of the controversy surrounding MNCs is related to this fundamental issue of their challenge to the power and sovereignty of the nation-state. Some observers see this struggle as an unequal one and have predicted that "the long-run trend will be toward the dwindling of the power of the national state relative to the corporation."[5] It may be, but nations have won many of the battles.

Aside from their challenge to national sovereignty, MNCs also tend to break down the isolation of individual economies and to integrate them into the world economy. They serve as a vehicle for the transmission and diffusion of technology; they spread information about new products, influence consumer tastes, and even alter cultural values. They undermine the power and position of local monopolists, and, despite their size, they may increase the degree of competition in national markets.

The Debate over MNCs: Some Specific Issues

Because they are large, powerful, and highly visible, MNCs have generated much controversy. They are hailed by their supporters as an instrument of economic progress, but blamed by their critics for everything that goes wrong, for every flaw in the economy.

Both source countries and host countries are ambivalent about multinationals. Many host countries, developed and underdeveloped, have encouraged MNCs to locate plants within their borders. They have courted them, given them tax breaks and other incentives, and competed with each other for them. At the same time, these countries have complained about exploitation, external control, loss of national autonomy, and unfair competition. They often charge that MNCs are harmful to them on balance, and sometimes they forbid any new ventures and heavily tax existing firms.

Source countries have a similar ambivalence. For years the U.S. government encouraged direct foreign investment by U.S. business firms. It gave them incentives in the form of favorable tax treatment of foreign income, favorable credit terms, and insurance against certain risks. Later, restrictions were imposed on direct foreign investment for balance-of-payments reasons. More recently, labor unions and other groups have been strongly critical of direct foreign investment, claiming that it exports jobs and that in other ways it is harmful to the U.S. economy.

Whatever MNCs do, someone can and does object. If they bring in outside capital, they are taking unfair advantage of local firms; but if they raise capital locally, they reduce the amount available to domestic entrepreneurs. If they pay the prevailing wage, they are exploiting cheap labor; but if they pay higher wages, they are draining off the best workers. If they repatriate profits, they are depriving the host country of newly created wealth; but if they reinvest profits, they are expanding their control of the economy. If they install modern machinery, they are

[5]Harry G. Johnson, *Technology and Economic Interdependence* (London: Macmillan, 1975), p. 83.

introducing inappropriate technology and failing to expand job opportunities; but if they rely on a simpler technology, they are withholding modern methods and discriminating against the host country. If they are encouraged by high tariff barriers to set up plants to serve the local market, they are criticized for not exporting their output. So goes the litany.[6]

This is a very large subject, and it remains highly controversial. Many political, social, and emotional issues are involved in the debate. Even on the more narrowly economic aspects, no definitive appraisal of benefits and costs can be made, for either host or source countries. We will discuss some of the specific issues that have been raised, but without attempting a final judgment on the balance of costs and benefits of MNCs.

Mainly Source Country Issues

1. For the source country, the main benefit from direct foreign investment is that the MNC earns a higher rate of return than it can make on an alternative domestic investment. This higher return accrues to the owner of capital, and questions immediately arise about the effect on income distribution. As we have seen, foreign investment may adversely affect the share of labor (and other factors). The outflow of capital reduces the ratio of capital to labor in the source country, and that tends to reduce wages relative to the return on capital.

2. Taxes levied on the foreign income of MNCs can, in principle, capture some of the benefits of the higher income for the entire society. Such taxation would allow the gains to be shared by other groups in the source country. But, as was noted earlier, the host country has the first opportunity to tax the profits generated within its borders, and, to avoid double taxation, its taxes are usually deductible against source country taxes. The U.S. Treasury does not collect much revenue from taxes on the foreign income of its MNCs.

   In fact, an MNC may have incentive to invest abroad even when its before-tax return is lower than the return on an alternative domestic investment, simply because the tax rate is lower on foreign than on domestic profit. A foreign return of 12 percent, on which it pays a tax rate of 10 percent, is more attractive to the MNC than a domestic return of 15 percent, with a tax rate of 48 percent, as long as the foreign profits are reinvested. Such differences in tax rates may lead to *over*investment by MNCs—that is, expansion of foreign investment beyond the point at which the marginal rates of return are equalized at home and abroad.

3. Organized labor often opposes direct foreign investment on the ground that it involves an export of jobs. U.S. corporations go abroad and build plants that could be built in the United States. Even when the output is destined for foreign markets, production could take place in the United States. We could simply export the output of domestic plants. This is another complicated

[6]Isaiah Frank, *Foreign Enterprise in Developing Countries* (Baltimore: Johns Hopkins University Press, 1980), p. 29.

issue, one that is especially sensitive when unemployment is high in the source countries.

One question, with many facets, is whether the market is sufficiently competitive to produce an accurate and objective evaluation of the choice between home and foreign investment. Is it a fair game, so to speak? Since the players are giant corporations and national governments, many observers doubt that the competitive model has much relevance. Are U.S. firms being induced by foreign tariffs or quotas to invest abroad despite a U.S. comparative advantage? Are their decisions based on tax incentives and loopholes? Are MNCs using transfer pricing to make foreign plants appear more profitable than they really are? Are they even investing abroad to escape U.S. regulations: pollution, safety standards, and so on? In short, does the foreign location really possess genuine advantages, or are they artificial?

There is no general answer to these questions. Circumstances vary from country to country and over time. However, there is a lively suspicion among the MNC critics that improper practices are not uncommon and that the private interest of the MNC is often quite different from the national interest of the source country.

Another aspect of this issue concerns the real alternative to direct foreign investment. Critics often assume that the MNC is simply deciding whether to build a given plant at home or abroad. Actually, the alternative to foreign investment may be to do nothing, in which case direct foreign investment involves no loss of jobs in the source country. Furthermore, if the capital is raised in the host country, or in the world capital market, there is no capital outflow from the source country. It is providing technology and management.

If the foreign market for a given product cannot be supplied through exports from the United States because of tariffs or other trade barriers, a decision not to use a foreign affiliate would mean that U.S. firms are excluded from the market. This could result in loss of a foreign market for components, equipment, and complementary products.

4. Source countries often argue that they experience trade balance losses because host countries pressure MNCs to distort trade flows. Host countries sometimes agree to allow MNCs to operate within their borders only if the MNCs promise to export at least a certain percentage of their production or to strictly limit imports of parts and components. Such trade-related investment measures (known as TRIMs in Washington) can distort trade in an inefficient manner, and are viewed as an unfair trade practice in Washington. Elimination of TRIMs is a current goal of the United States in trade negotiations.

5. Confiscation is one of the obvious risks of direct investment. Even if compensation is paid, it may be less than the true value of the confiscated assets.

A related issue is the renegotiated contract. Any investment entails a risk of loss, and it is well known that a large proportion of ventures turns out badly. When the loser is an MNC, it is expected to bear the loss and nobody sheds any tears. But when a venture turns out well and begins to earn large profits, the host country often has second thoughts about the terms of the contract. Demands are made to renegotiate, that is, to reduce the share of the MNC. This practice has been dubbed the "obsolescing bargain." The motivation of the host country is clear enough, and it is usually claimed that the MNC somehow took unfair advantage of its knowledge and expertise, as it may well have done. But hindsight is 20/20, as they say. It is easy to spot the one investment out of 30 that is a big success. If the payoff for that success is removed through renegotiation, the incentive to take risk is greatly inhibited.

Mainly Host Country Issues

1. For host countries, the main benefits of direct foreign investment come from the additional resources made available, including capital, technology, management, and the training of labor. Output and income are increased. This package of capital, knowledge, and entrepreneurship may also impart a stimulus to the domestic economy, and accelerate its growth and development. To support its own operations, the MNC may assist and encourage local suppliers, thereby stimulating domestic enterprise and spreading the effects of technological change more widely through the economy.

   The potential for such benefits to exist is generally accepted, but host countries have many reasons to doubt whether the actual direct investments they receive are realizing that potential. The issue often depends on the terms of the bargain between the MNC and the host country, on whether it is a fair deal.

2. MNCs may improve the export capability of the host country. As we discussed in Chapter 10, expansion of manufactured exports is a major objective in less developed countries. By introducing new products and modern technology, MNCs may be able to export part of their output. (However, MNCs sometimes specifically forbid their foreign affiliates to export to certain markets.)

3. Critics say that MNCs transfer technology to host countries that is inappropriate for their economies. This point is usually made with respect to less developed countries. They have large supplies of labor, and they need industries that will provide employment and training of large numbers of workers. What they often get is a plant designed for the labor-scarce, high-wage economy of the source country. These capital-intensive industries do not provide much employment, and they may have few linkages into other sectors of the host country's economy.

   The problem is exacerbated by the common practice in MNCs of centralizing their research and development activities at the home office. Research activities tend to be conditioned by the circumstances prevailing in the source country, but the new technology developed in these centers is then inappropriate for many host countries.

4. Host countries also object to the fact that they do not have a share of the research and development activity, with its stimulus to scientific training, education, and innovation. Source countries, on the other hand, want MNCs to allocate a share of research and development expenses to their foreign affiliates. The argument is that the affiliates benefit from the research and

development activities, and that they should bear part of the expenses. Because the effect would be to reduce foreign profits and increase home office profits, host countries tend to object. If the allocation is made, there is likely to be further conflict about its size, since any allocation is essentially arbitrary.

5. Host countries say that MNCs manipulate prices on intrafirm transactions in order to understate profits and evade taxes. This is the familiar issue of transfer pricing, seen from the other side. The very nature of the process makes it impossible to obtain comprehensive data on the extent of the problem, but many specific examples have been cited.[7] A Swiss pharmaceutical firm, Hoffman-La Roche, sold two drugs to its U.K. affiliate for £370 and £922 per kilogram, when the open-market prices were £9 and £20 per kilogram, respectively. The purpose of the higher prices was simply to reduce the amount of profit reported by the U.K. subsidiary.

   Another well-known case involved a ceiling imposed by the Colombian government on the repatriation of profit. The MNCs operating in Colombia evaded this attempt at governmental control by simply increasing the prices charged to Colombian affiliates for goods imported from the home office. Over a period of three years, it was estimated that import prices to Colombian affiliates were 87 percent above the world price in pharmaceuticals, 44 percent above in rubber, 54 percent in electrical goods, and 25 percent in chemicals. Not much profit then needed to be repatriated.

   This practice is extremely difficult to control. Many host countries simply do not have enough qualified accountants, lawyers, and other skilled personnel capable of auditing corporate records and enforcing compliance with the spirit of the tax laws.

6. Several quasi-political issues often arise in the middle ground, where the interests of host countries, MNCs, and source countries converge or overlap. These issues touch on sovereignty, political control, legal jurisdictions, and the fairness of contracts. Since direct investment implies managerial control by the parent company over the foreign affiliate, there is ample scope for jurisdictional conflicts between the source country, whose laws govern the parent company, and the host country, whose laws govern the affiliate.

   One such jurisdictional conflict has involved the U.S. insistence that foreign subsidiaries of U.S. firms are subject to certain U.S. laws and regulations. These laws may run into conflict with the laws of the host country, which claims the right to regulate the activities of firms operating within its borders. For example, in the 1970s the United States required Canadian subsidiaries of U.S. firms to abide by a U.S. ban on exports to foreign countries such as Cuba. Canada had no such ban, and Canadians were incensed about the infringement on their sovereignty when this U.S. law was applied to firms operating in Canada. A similar jurisdictional problem arises when the United States enforces its antitrust regulations against foreign affiliates of U.S. firms.

---

[7]Neil Hood and Stephen Young, *The Economics of Multinational Enterprise* (London: Longman, 1979), pp. 209–210.

These conflicts are difficult to resolve. From the U.S. point of view, its laws would be made ineffective if U.S. firms could evade them simply by setting up a foreign subsidiary. But from the host country point of view, the extension of U.S. laws into its geographical domain is an unacceptable violation of national sovereignty.

7. Host countries also have conflicts with the MNCs themselves. Decisions made by the MNC may be seen as harmful to the national interest of the host country. For example, when an MNC has plants in several countries to produce a given product, a fall in demand means that it must cut back output. But where? The decision made by the MNC may cause severe economic distress in a particular host country. Some MNCs forbid foreign affiliates to export to certain markets; some allow only a limited transfer of technology.

Individual nations are often in a weak position in their negotiations with MNCs. If the government in a given country tries to strike a hard bargain with an MNC that is selecting a site for a new facility, the MNC can simply choose another country where the authorities are more malleable. This inequality in bargaining power applies even to a large industrial nation such as France. The French government has found its ability to keep MNCs under tight control seriously undermined because the MNCs could simply locate in another European country. If the alternate host was within the Common Market, its goods could even be shipped into France duty free.

One result of the rise in power and scope of the multinational corporations has been a widespread perception that they have the upper hand in their dealings with nation-states. They are a challenge to the sovereignty of nations. They transcend national boundaries and tend to integrate the world economy. There is a potential for benefit in all this, and it has been argued that the global, cosmopolitan stance of MNCs is one of their strengths. But a critic has said, "Cosmopolitanism is the favorite fig leaf of the imperialist,"[8] implying that MNCs are just an instrument of national power, even if in a new form.

Attitudes toward MNCs in developing countries appear to have gone through a full cycle; during the 1950s and early 1960s they were viewed as engines of development and therefore as highly desirable. During the latter half of the 1960s and throughout the 1970s, they were widely viewed as agents of capitalism, imperialism, and of every ill to afflict an LDC other than bad weather. During the 1980s, however, opinions appeared to have come back to the center. Most leaders in developing countries now view MNCs as desirable elements in their economies but want to bargain over how the benefits of their activities will be divided. MNC investments are actively sought, but governments want promises that the firms will export guaranteed proportions of their output, employ and train at least so many local people, pay taxes in reasonable proportion to the local business they do, and so on.

[8]Carlos Diaz-Alejandro, "North-South Relations: The Economic Components," in C. Fred Bergsten and Lawrence B. Krause, *World Politics and International Economics* (Washington, D.C.: Brookings Institution, 1975), p. 221.

Particularly since borrowing from New York and London banks has become difficult or impossible for them, developing country governments have realized that MNCs are a vital source of external capital. They can also boost exports and provide a range of external benefits. The LDC governments merely want to make sure that these benefits occur, and they are now inclined to bargain with MNCs over details of export plans, employment and training policies, and potential tax receipts. MNCs are quite clearly going to be a growing part of the world economy, and they are the source of an ongoing argument as to how their benefits are to be divided among the host government, the source country government, stockholders, and employees.

QUESTIONS FOR STUDY AND REVIEW

1. What is the relationship between Heckscher-Ohlin trade and free factor mobility? Explain.

2. What groups in the United States gain from allowing immigrants to enter this country? Who is harmed? How does this affect the politics of the immigration issue?

3. If the United States were to implement a free-trade arrangement with Mexico, what would you expect to happen to the number of Mexican residents trying to come to the United States? What would be the impact of this bloc on those Mexicans who have already come to this country?

4. What are the economic effects, positive and negative, of direct foreign investment in the investing and receiving countries? Explain.

5. "U.S. tax treatment of direct foreign investment tends to cause too much investment by American MNCs in other countries." Do you agree? Explain why or why not.

6. What is transfer pricing? Why is it a problem for national tax authorities? Who is harmed by this practice?

7. When U.S. firms make direct foreign investments in other countries, what is likely to be the employment effect in the United States?

SELECTED REFERENCES

Bergsten, C. Fred, Thomas Horst, and Theodore Moran. *American Multinationals and American Interests*. Washington, D.C.: Brookings Institution, 1978.

Ethier, W. J. "Illegal Immigration." *American Economic Review,* May 1986, pp. 258–263.

Frank, Isaiah. *Foreign Enterprise in Developing Countries*. Baltimore: Johns Hopkins University Press, 1980.

Greenwood, M., and J. McDowell. "The Factor Market Consequences of U.S. Immigration." *Journal of Economic Literature,* December 1986, pp 1738–1772.

Grunwald, J., and K. Flamm. *The Global Factory: Foreign Assembly in International Trade.* Washington, D.C.: Brookings Institution, 1985.

Mundell, R. "International Trade and Factor Mobility." *American Economic Review,* June 1957.

Rubin, Seymour J., and Gary C. Hufbauer. *Emerging Standards of International Trade and Investment.* New York: Barnes & Noble, 1984.

Streeten, Paul. "Multinationals Revisited." *Finance and Development,* June 1979.

United Nations. *Transnational Corporations in World Development: A Reexamination.* New York, 1980.

Vernon, Raymond. *Storm over Multinationals.* Cambridge, Mass.: Harvard University Press, 1977.

Wells, Louis, Jr. *Third World Multinationals.* Cambridge, Mass.: MIT Press, 1983.

PART II

INTERNATIONAL FINANCE AND OPEN ECONOMY MACROECONOMICS

CHAPTER

BALANCE-OF-PAYMENTS ACCOUNTING

The balance-of-payments accounts discussed in this chapter form the basic accounting system for all international commercial and financial transactions. Their relationship to international economics is analogous to that of national income accounts to domestic macroeconomics.

Balance-of-payments accounting is, to be sure, a less than fascinating topic, but it must be understood if the more interesting parts of international finance are to make any sense. Just as domestic macroeconomics would mean very little without an understanding of gross national product and related accounting concepts, so international finance requires an understanding of the payments accounts. People who work in the area of international economics are usually assumed to understand balance-of-payments accounting, and they often spend significant amounts of time interpreting these accounts for countries in which they are interested.

A nation's balance of payments is a summary statement of all economic transactions between residents of that nation and residents of the outside world which have taken place during a given period of time. Several aspects of this definition require further comment and emphasis. First, "resident" is interpreted to include individuals, business firms, and government agencies. Second, the balance of payments is supposed to include *all* economic transactions with the outside world, whether they involve merchandise, services, assets, financial claims, or gifts. Whenever a transaction is between a resident and nonresident, it is to be included. Third, the balance of payments measures the volume of transactions that occur during a certain period of time, usually a year or a quarter. Thus it measures flows, not stocks. In the case of transactions in assets, the balance of payments for a given year shows the changes that have occurred in, say, assets held abroad, but it does not show the stock of such assets.

The term "balance of payments" is itself a misnomer, because some of the transactions included do not involve any actual payment of money. For example, when an American firm ships a drill press to Canada for installation in its branch plant or subsidiary, no money payment will be made, but an economic transaction with the outside world has taken place and should be included in the balance of payments. Similarly, if the United States donates wheat to India, no payment will be made, but the shipment should be included in our balance of payments. Most transactions do involve a money payment, but whether or not a transaction involves payment, it is included in the balance of payments. A more appropriate name for this account might therefore be "Statement of International Economic Transactions," but we will use the conventional name, which has the sanction of long-established usage.

A nation's balance of payments is of interest to economists and policymakers because it provides much useful information about the nation's international economic position and its relationships with the rest of the world. In particular, the accounts may indicate whether the nation's external economic position is in a healthy state, or whether problems exist which may be signaling a change or a need for corrective action of some kind. An examination of the balance of payments for a period of time should enable us to determine whether a nation is approximately in external balance, or whether it suffers from a disequilibrium in its balance of payments. Much of international monetary economics is concerned with diagnosis of deficits or surpluses in balance of payments for countries with fixed exchange rates, and especially with analysis of the mechanisms or processes through which such disequilibria may be corrected or removed, which suggests why these accounts are so important.

Balance-of-payments accounts are not analogous to a balance sheet, because they represent flows of transactions during a year, whereas the balance sheet represents stocks of assets and liabilities at a moment of time, such as the close of business on December 31. This might suggest that balance-of-payments accounts are somehow like a corporate profit and loss statement, but here too the analogy is not a close one. A sources and uses of funds account for a business, which can be found in some corporate annual reports, would be a closer fit because the balance-of-payments accounts show flows of funds in and out of a country during a given time period.

DISTINGUISHING DEBITS AND CREDITS IN THE ACCOUNTS

Items in the balance-of-payments accounts are given positive or negative signs, and they are therefore labeled credits or debits, depending on whether the particular transaction causes a resident of a country to receive a payment from a foreigner or to make a payment to a foreign resident. If a payment is received, the transaction is a credit and carries a positive sign, and vice versa. Because every transaction that is a payment into one country is a payment out of another, each transaction should sum to zero for the world. The world's trade balance, for example, should be zero. In fact, the published data total to a negative number, in part because imports are normally valued on a basis that includes shipping (c.i.f., cost, insurance, and freight), whereas exports are shown without these costs (f.o.b., free on board or f.a.s., free along side). In addition, many sources of errors in the numbers (discussed later in this chapter) result in the published data not totaling zero.[1]

The assignment of pluses and minuses is fairly straightforward for trade and other current account transactions; exports are a plus and imports are a minus. Foreign tourist expenditures in this country are a plus in our accounts, whereas our payments of dividends or interest to foreigners are a minus. When a good or service is being exchanged for money, ascertaining what is a credit and what is a debit is fairly obvious.

International capital flows can be more difficult, because what is being exchanged for what is sometimes not clear. If an American deposits funds in a Canadian bank, that transaction is a minus for this country and a plus for Canada. If the American later writes a check on that account to pay for imports from Canada, there are two transactions of opposite sign. The American is withdrawing short-term capital from Canada, which is a plus for the United States and a minus for Canada, and the merchandise imports are a minus for the United States and a plus for Canada. When the American wrote the check on the Canadian bank to pay for the imports, the process was shortened, but actually two offsetting accounting transactions occurred.

Long-term capital flows, such as the purchase of foreign bonds or the movement of direct investment funds, are less complicated. If an American purchases German bonds, that is a minus for this country and a plus for Germany, because it is clear which way the money moved. If a British firm purchases a U.S. business, that is a plus for this country and a minus for the United Kingdom, and again the direction in which funds moved is clear.

Matters can become more confusing for movements of foreign exchange reserves, which are funds held by central banks. These funds are used to finance deficits in the remainder of the accounts, and payments are made into these reserves when there is a surplus in the other items.

The central bank of a country can hold foreign exchange reserves in a number of forms. Financial claims on foreign governments or central banks is one particularly

---

[1]For a discussion of various sources of errors in the world's current account data, see Nawaz Shuja, "Why the World's Current Account Does Not Balance," *Finance and Development,* September 1987, pp. 43–45.

important form, but gold and financial claims on the International Monetary Fund (IMF) are alternatives. Many countries hold U.S. dollars as their primary reserve currency, and their central banks have accounts at the New York Federal Reserve Bank as well as holdings of U.S. Treasury securities, for which the New York Fed typically acts as custodian. The United States holds reserves in the form of financial claims on the governments or central banks of Germany, Japan, and other industrialized countries, as well as in the form of gold and the U.S. reserve position at the IMF.

Foreign exchange reserves are analogous to an individual's holdings of cash; they increase when the individual has a surplus in his or her other transactions, and they decrease when he or she has a deficit. If a country's foreign exchange reserves rise, that transaction is a minus in that country's payments accounts because money is being sent out of the country to purchase a foreign financial asset. If, for example, U.S. holdings of such reserves in the form of Swiss francs increased, the New York Federal Reserve Bank would be required to purchase those francs in the New York foreign exchange market and then send them to Switzerland in exchange for a financial claim on the Swiss government or central bank. Money would leave this country, and the ownership of a financial claim on foreigners would come back in exchange. Many foreign governments and central banks hold their reserves in the form of dollar claims on the U.S. Treasury or the New York Federal Reserve Bank. If Canada reduces its holdings of such dollars, thereby reducing our official reserve liabilities to foreigners, that transaction is a minus for this country and a plus for Canada, because funds flow out of the United States. As counter-intuitive as it seems, increases in a country's reserve assets or reductions in its reserve liabilities are a minus, whereas reductions in its assets or increases in its liabilities are a plus.

ANALOGY TO A FAMILY'S CASH FLOW ACCOUNTS

The balance-of-payments accounts can be viewed as analogous to a cash statement that might be maintained to keep track of a family's financial affairs. In such an account, any transaction that brought money into the family would be a plus, and vice versa. Items would normally be separated into current and capital account classifications, with the current segment including all current income (+) and all current living costs (−), with the balance in that account representing the change in the family's financial net worth. The capital account would include all purchases of financial assets, such as common stocks or bonds, and repayments of previous borrowings as debits, because they result in money flowing out of the family. Sales of assets or new borrowings by the family would be credits because they bring money in. The monthly mortgage payment would have to be split between the current and capital accounts, with interest being current and repayment of the principal being put in the capital account. Because the current and capital accounts together represent all transactions bringing money into or out of the family, the number at the bottom of the account should equal the change in the family's holdings of cash during the period.

If cash balances were checked at the beginning and end of the period, and if the change in cash did not match the total in the account, it would be clear that errors or omissions existed. Since offsetting errors could occur, the gross errors can never be known. Therefore the difference between the change in cash predicted by the account and what actually happened to cash holdings would be the net error. Such errors would probably be the result of cash expenditures for current living costs. Hence an error and omission item would be put in the current account with an entry that would make the number at the bottom of the account match actual changes in cash holdings.

This family account is analogous to the balance-of-payments account of a country, with foreign exchange reserves playing the role of cash. The current account includes all international purchases and sales of goods and services (including the services of capital; dividend and interest payments are included), and its net balance represents the change in a country's net investment position relative to the rest of the world. A current account surplus means that the country either increased its net creditor position or reduced its net indebtedness by that amount during the year, which makes it quite analogous to the current account in the family account discussed above. The capital account includes all purchases and sales of financial claims (except foreign exchange reserves), in which one participant in the transactions is a local resident and the other is not. This account is frequently divided into long-term and short-term segments on the basis of whether asset maturities are more or less than one year. Long-term capital flows include direct investments by multinational firms, purchases or sales of bonds and common stocks, as well as loans with maturities of over one year.

Short-term capital includes money coming into or going out of asset forms such as Treasury bills, commercial paper, and bank accounts, as well as the short-term financing of export sales. If, for example, IBM exports a computer to France in November with 90-day payments terms, the U.S. balance-of-payments accounts for that year will show an export (+) in the current account and a short-term outflow (−) in the capital account. During the following year, when payment is received from France for the computer, the U.S. short-term capital account will show an inflow (+), thus completing the earlier transaction.

If a country's current and capital accounts sum to a positive number, its foreign exchange reserve assets should increase (or its reserve liabilities decrease) by that amount. Thus the following should hold:

$$CA + KA - dFXR = 0$$

where : CA = the current account

KA = the capital account

$dFXR$ = the change in the country's foreign exchange reserve position (i.e., an increase in reserve assets or a decline in liabilities)

Since increases in reserve assets (or reductions in liabilities) represent a minus in the payments accounts, the total for all items in the accounts must sum to zero. This is an important point in understanding balance-of-payments accounting; the accounts must sum to zero because foreign exchange reserve movements just offset or cancel the total of the rest of the items.

CALCULATION OF ERRORS AND OMISSIONS

The fact that the accounts must total zero provides the basis for calculating net errors and omissions, or the statistical discrepancy, as it is sometimes known. All the items in the current and capital accounts are estimates, and they are subject to sizable mistakes, usually because actual transactions are not recorded for some reason. Some of the omissions are innocent, as when an American travels to Canada with currency, spends it there on vacation services, and the records for the transactions are incomplete. Often, however, the omissions are not innocent. Illegal drug traffic is the source of sizable errors (unrecorded "imports"), as is the international movement of funds that result from criminal activity. Gross errors and omissions are unknown, because offsetting errors occur; the number reported in the accounts represents net errors and omissions.

The errors and omissions entry is calculated by adding up everything in the current and capital accounts and comparing the total to the known change in a country's foreign exchange reserve position. The errors and omissions number is whatever figure is necessary to make the two totals match. If, for example, the current and capital accounts total +$3,155 million, whereas foreign exchange reserve assets actually increased by $2,955 million, the net error and omission number must be −$200 million. That entry frequently appears in the short-term capital accounts, because it is thought that most of the unrecorded transactions are of that type. If −$200 is entered in the capital account for errors and omissions, the current and capital accounts will then total +$2,955, which matches what actually happened to foreign exchange reserves.

The fact that the balance-of-payments accounts must sum to zero means that they can be described as a double-entry bookkeeping system. If one number changes, another number must change in the opposite direction by the same amount to maintain the total at zero. A transaction sometimes has a clear offset, so it is obvious what both changes are; if General Electric sells turbines to a foreign firm on two-year credit terms, U.S. exports rise (+) as do U.S. long-term capital outflow (−), and the two entries just offset. If, however, the sale had not been on credit, and instead the foreign customer had sold foreign exchange and bought U.S. dollars to make payment to General Electric, it would not be clear what the offsetting transaction was. That transaction would be carried out by the agent who sold the dollars to, and bought the foreign exchange from, General Electric's customer. If that person was buying foreign goods to be imported into the United States, the U.S. import would be the offset. If, instead, an American was buying foreign exchange to make a foreign investment, the offset would be in the capital account. Since it is not known who sold the dollars and bought the foreign currency, it is not obvious what the offset is. All that is known is that because the items in the accounts must sum to zero, every transaction must have an offsetting transaction in the opposite direction.

ORGANIZING THE ACCOUNTS FOR A COUNTRY WITH A FIXED EXCHANGE RATE

Exhibit 12-1 is designed for a country that maintains a fixed exchange rate; it was published in this form for the United States until the mid-1970s. The vast majority of the world's countries still maintain fixed parities and publish payments accounts that are very similar to this one. A somewhat different accounting format is used for a country with a floating exchange rate; it will be discussed later in this chapter. Current account items are lines 1 through 14, with the total as line 15. Most of the items are self-explanatory, but remittances are payments by workers back to their families in another country, and U.S. government grants represent foreign aid expenditures. The long-term capital account begins with line 16 and ends with line 25, with line 26 being the total of current and long-term capital transactions. Short-term capital flows begin with line 27 and continue through line 41, with line 42 being the total of all current and capital account transactions. Lines 43 through 46 represent movements of foreign exchange reserves, and the total of these lines exactly matches line 42 with the opposite sign, which means that the table then totals zero. Lines 43 through 45 represent changes in U.S. foreign exchange reserve liabilities to foreign central banks and governments. These transactions exist because many foreign countries hold the U.S. dollar as a reserve currency. These lines would not occur in the accounts of a country whose currency did not play this role. Line 46 is the change in U.S. foreign exchange reserve assets.

Line 32 is net errors and omissions, and it was calculated by starting with the estimates for all the items totaled in line 42. That total was compared to the total for lines 43 through 46. Line 32 is whatever number is necessary to make a recalculated line 42 match the total for lines 43 through 46 so that the account can total zero. The memoranda items at the bottom are not part of the account and can be viewed as statistical footnotes.

Since the balance-of-payments accounts as a whole must total zero, surpluses or deficits obviously cannot be measured as the total of everything in the accounts. Rather, they are measured as the total of some items, with others being excluded. For countries that maintain fixed exchange rates, payment disequilibria are measured as the sum of the autonomous items in the accounts, with accommodating or residual items being excluded.[2] Autonomous transactions are those undertaken for ordinary commercial motives, without regard for their effect on the balance of payments. Accommodating transactions, on the other hand, occur in response to other transactions. They are not undertaken for their own sake, so to speak, but because other transactions leave a gap to be filled. Thus we may say that autonomous transactions are gap-*making*, and accommodating transactions are gap-*filling*.

Given this distinction, we place autonomous items above the line and accommodating items below, and we define a deficit in the overall balance of payments as a debit balance above the line. That is, a deficit exists when autonomous debits

---

[2]James C. Meade, *The Balance of Payments* (New York: Oxford University Press, 1951), Chapter 1.

U.S. Balance of Payments Summary

[Millions of dollars, seasonally adjusted]

Line	(Credits +; debits −)	Reference lines (table 2)	1973	1974p	Change 1973-74	1973 I	1973 II	1973 III	1973 IV	1974 I r	1974 II r	1974 III r	1974 IV p	Change 1974 III-IV
1	Merchandise trade balance [1]	2	471	−5,881	−6,352	−954	−363	578	1,210	−175	−1,674	−2,474	−1,558	916
2	Exports	16	70,277	97,081	26,804	15,230	16,679	18,152	20,216	22,212	23,921	24,731	26,217	1,486
3	Imports	3, 17	−69,806	−102,962	−33,156	−16,184	−17,042	−17,574	−19,006	−22,387	−25,595	−27,205	−27,775	−570
4	Military transactions, net	4, 5, 6	−2,266	−2,099	167	−833	−763	−547	−123	−500	−668	−473	−458	15
5	Travel and transportation, net	18, 19, 20	−2,710	−2,435	275	−686	−781	−613	−630	−531	−726	−566	−612	−46
6	Investment income, net [2]	11	5,291	9,679	4,388	1,447	1,208	1,257	1,378	3,104	1,870	2,282	2,422	140
7	U.S. direct investments abroad [2]	12, 13	9,415	18,240	8,825	2,194	2,210	2,323	2,688	4,650	4,546	4,824	4,220	−604
8	Other U.S. investments abroad		4,569	7,703	3,134	1,000	1,098	1,179	1,292	1,499	1,836	2,197	2,170	−27
9	Foreign investments in the United States [2]	25, 26, 27.	−8,693	−16,263	−7,570	−1,747	−2,100	−2,245	−2,602	−3,045	−4,512	−4,739	−3,968	771
10	Other services, net [2]	7, 8, 9, 10, 21, 22, 23, 24.	3,540	3,926	386	841	815	984	901	918	992	984	1,032	48
11	Balance on goods and services [3]		4,327	3,191	−1,136	−185	116	1,659	2,736	2,816	−206	−247	826	1,073
12	Remittances, pensions and other transfers	31, 32	−1,943	−1,775	168	−404	−411	−412	−717	−390	−467	−456	−463	−7
13	Balance on goods, services and remittances		2,383	1,416	−967	−589	−295	1,247	2,019	2,426	−673	−703	363	1,066
14	U.S. Government grants (excluding military grants of goods and services)	30	−1,933	−5,441	−3,508	−357	−645	−485	−447	[7] −2,561	−1,435	−772	−673	99
15	Balance on current account		450	−4,025	−4,475	−946	−940	762	1,572	[7] −135	−2,108	−1,475	−310	1,165
16	U.S. Government capital flows excluding nonscheduled repayments, net [4]	34, 35, 36.	−2,938	408	3,346	−699	−565	−608	−1,066	[7] 1,297	311	−186	−1,014	−828
17	Nonscheduled repayments of U.S. Government assets	37	289	1	−288	111	174	4	(*)	(*)		(*)	(*)	(*)
18	U.S. Government nonliquid liabilities to other than foreign official reserve agencies	48	1,111	634	−477	217	485	206	204	53	273	189	119	−70
19	Long-term private capital flows, net	39	62	−7,598	−7,660	309	−324	1,527	−1,451	504	−1,039	−2,402	−4,661	−2,259
20	U.S. direct investments abroad	49	−4,872	−6,801	−1,929	−1,815	−973	−710	−1,374	−627	−1,527	−2,047	−2,600	−553
21	Foreign direct investments in the United States	40	2,537	2,308	−229	351	588	886	712	1,281	1,677	−89	−561	−472
22	Foreign securities	50	−807	−951	−1,144	51	−124	−209	−525	−646	−313	−306	−686	−380
23	U.S. securities other than Treasury issues	41, 53	4,051	1,199	−2,852	1,718	489	1,173	670	687	419	168	−75	−243
24	Other, reported by U.S. banks	44, 51	−647	−1,186	−539	−120	−248	225	−504	−21	−902	68	−331	−399
25	Other, reported by U.S. nonbanking concerns		−200	−1,167	−967	124	−56	162	−430	−170	−393	−196	−408	−212
26	Balance on current account and long-term capital [4]		−1,026	−10,580	−9,554	−1,008	−1,170	1,891	−741	1,719	−2,563	−3,874	−5,866	−1,992
27	Nonliquid short-term private capital flows, net		−4,276	−12,955	−8,679	−1,663	1,457	97	−1,253	−3,994	−5,296	−1,427	−2,238	−811
28	Claims reported by U.S. banks	42	−3,940	−12,223	−8,283	−1,644	−1,399	222	−1,119	−2,817	−5,311	−1,653	−2,442	−789
29	Claims reported by U.S. nonbanking concerns	45	−1,240	−2,453	−1,213	−57	−59	−460	−664	−1,591	−695	−207	40	247
30	Liabilities reported by U.S. nonbanking concerns	52	904	1,721	817	38	1	335	530	414	710	433	164	−269
31	Allocations of special drawing rights (SDR)[3]	63												
32	Errors and omissions, net	64	−2,303	5,197	7,500	−3,943	850	−336	1,125	1,305	1,463	838	1,592	754

Line	Item	Ref												
33	Net liquidity balance †		−7,606	−18,338	−10,732	−6,614	−1,777	1,652	−869	−970	−6,396	−4,463	−6,512	−2,049
34	Liquid private capital flows, net		2,302	10,268	7,966	−3,581	2,063	290	3,530	2,016	1,874	4,143	2,235	−1,908
35	Liquid claims		−1,944	−5,464	−3,520	−1,853	923	−521	−493	−2,732	−1,197	133	−1,668	−1,801
36	Reported by U.S. banks	43	−1,103	−5,445	−4,342	−1,171	996	−456	−472	−2,368	−1,261	−431	−1,385	−954
37	Reported by U.S. nonbanking concerns	46	−841	−19	822	−682	−73	−65	−21	−364	64	564	−283	−847
38	Liquid liabilities	54	4,246	15,732	11,486	−1,728	1,140	811	4,023	4,748	3,071	4,010	3,903	−107
39	To foreign commercial banks		2,982	12,655	9,673	−1,673	729	699	3,227	4,663	2,161	2,896	2,935	39
40	To international and regional organizations		377	151	−226	11	32	−50	384	−530	297	221	163	−58
41	To other foreigners		887	2,926	2,039	−66	379	162	412	615	613	893	805	−88
42	Official reserve transactions balance †		−5,304	−8,070	−2,766	−10,195	286	1,942	2,661	1,046	−4,522	−320	−4,277	−3,957
	Financed by changes in:													
43	Liquid liabilities to foreign official agencies	55	4,452	8,253	3,801	8,816	−729	−1,488	−2,145	−557	4,255	1,263	3,295	2,032
44	Other readily marketable liabilities to foreign official agencies [5]	56	1,118	596	−522	1,202	259	11	−354	−277	182	61	630	569
45	Nonliquid liabilities to foreign official reserve agencies reported by U.S. Government	57	−475	655	1,130	−43	167	−452	−147	−2	443	−1	215	216
46	U.S. official reserve assets, net	58	209	−1,434	−1,643	220	17	−13	−15	−210	−358	−1,003	137	1,140
	Memoranda:													
47	Transfers under military grant programs (excluded from lines 2, 4, and 14)		2,772	1,790	−982	693	833	758	487	393	542	352	504	152
48	Reinvested earnings of foreign incorporated affiliates of U.S. firms (excluded from lines 7 and 20)	14, 28	8,124	n.a.	n.a.	n.a.	n.a.	n.a.	n.a.	n.a.	n.a.	n.a.	n.a.	n.a.
49	Reinvested earnings of U.S. incorporated affiliates of foreign firms (excluded from lines 9 and 21)		945	n.a.	n.a.	n.a.	n.a.	n.a.	n.a.	n.a.	n.a.	n.a.	n.a.	n.a.
50	Gross liquidity balance, excluding allocations of SDR	54,55,56, 57,58, 63.	−9,550	−23,802	−14,252	−8,467	−854	1,131	−1,362	−3,702	−7,593	−4,330	−8,180	−3,850
	Not seasonally adjusted													
51	Balance on goods and services		---	---	---	494	228	−195	3,800	3,948	−45	−3,030	2,317	5,347
52	Balance on goods, services and remittances		---	---	---	116	−187	−623	3,077	3,584	−514	−3,502	1,848	5,350
53	Balance on current account		---	---	---	−259	−872	−1,071	2,653	1,005	−1,990	−4,239	1,199	5,438
54	Balance on current account and long-term capital [4]		---	---	---	−1,054	−1,193	222	999	2,120	−2,539	−6,441	−3,719	2,722
55	Net liquidity balance†		---	---	---	−6,050	−2,104	637	−89	−144	−6,784	−5,773	−5,637	136
56	Official reserve transactions balance†		---	---	---	−9,994	769	939	2,982	1,495	−4,105	−1,609	−3,851	−2,242

r Revised.   p Preliminary.   * Less than $500,000 (±).   n.a. Not available.   † See table A.

1. Adjusted to balance of payments basis; excludes exports under U.S. military agency sales contracts and imports of U.S. military agencies.

2. Fees and royalties from U.S. direct investments abroad or from foreign direct investments in the United States are excluded from investment income and included in "other services".

3. Conceptually, line 11 is equal to net exports of goods and services, and the sum of lines 15 and 31 is equal to "net foreign investment" in the national income and product accounts of the United States. Beginning with 1973-IV however, these components in the product accounts exclude the shipments and the financing of extraordinary military orders placed by Israel. The balance of payments accounts include these transactions as follows in billions of dollars (line references are to tables 2 and 3): 1973-IV, line 3, 0.6; line 35, −0.6; 1974-I, line 3, 0.1, line 35, −0.1; line 3, 0.1, line 35, 0.5, line 30, −0.6; 1974-III, line 3, (*), line 35, 0.1, line 30, −0.1; 0.2, line 30, −0.2; 1974-IV, line 3, (*), line 35, 0.1, line 30, −0.1.

4. Includes some short-term U.S. Government assets.

5. Includes changes in nonliquid liabilities reported by U.S. banks and in investments by foreign official agencies in debt securities of U.S. Government corporations and agencies, private corporations, and State and local governments.

6. Includes return import into the United States, at a depreciated value, of aircraft originally reported as transfers under U.S. military agency sales contracts under long-term lease in 1970-III.

7. Includes extraordinary U.S. Government transactions with India. See "Special U.S. Government Transactions" in June 1974 SURVEY, p. 27.

NOTE.—Details may not add to totals because of rounding.

Source: U.S. Department of Commerce, Bureau of Economic Analysis.

EXHIBIT 12-1 U.S. balance of payments summary. *Source: U.S. Department of Commerce, Bureau of Economic Analysis.*

(payments) exceed autonomous credits (receipts), with the excess debits offset by accommodating credits. A surplus exists when the opposite condition holds true.

The most commonly used definition of a balance-of-payments disequilibrium is the total of lines 1 through 41 in Exhibit 12-1. All current and capital account items are viewed as autonomous, and only foreign exchange reserve flows (lines 43–46) are classified as accommodating. This is known as the "official reserve transactions balance" and is shown as line 42. It is sometimes referred to as the overall balance or the official settlements balance. If a country is described as having a balance-of-payments deficit without further comment, it can be assumed that the official reserve transactions definition is being used.

It has sometimes been argued, however, that some short-term capital transactions are accommodating in nature. In addition, the short-term capital account is volatile and unpredictable, so it might be excluded from a long-term view of a country's payments position. The "basic" balance-of-payments approach measures surpluses or deficits as the sum of the current account and of the long-term capital account, and both foreign exchange reserve flows and the short-term capital account are put "below the line" as accommodating items. The basic balance of payments is the sum of lines 1 through 25, totaled as line 26, in the table.

BALANCE-OF-PAYMENTS ACCOUNTING WITH FLEXIBLE EXCHANGE RATES

For countries such as the United States that maintain a flexible exchange rate, the concept of a payments deficit ceases to have much meaning, and the accounts are organized differently. In a country with a clean float, no transactions occur that involve foreign exchange reserve movements, so the official reserve transactions accounts is zero by definition. If the accounts must total zero and there are no movements of reserves, then the current and capital accounts must total zero. The balance of payments is kept in equilibrium in the same way that the market for General Motors common stock is kept in balance: through constant and occasionally large price changes. In this case it is the foreign price of the domestic currency that changes when payments shocks occur. If clean floats were in operation, the payments accounts could be published with only the current and capital accounts, and these would sum to zero. The actual world of floating exchange rates is more complicated, however.

The United States and a number of other industrialized countries such as Japan maintain what are commonly called "dirty" or managed floats. No parity is maintained, but foreign exchange reserves do move when central banks engage in foreign exchange transactions because they are displeased with the direction or speed of exchange rate movements. If, for example, a currency is declining in the exchange market, that country's central bank may sell foreign exchange and purchase the local currency to stop or slow its fall. As a result, foreign exchange reserves decline despite the existence of a floating exchange rate.

The U.S. balance-of-payments accounts have been published since 1976 in a format that reflects this situation of managed floating exchange rates.[3] (See Exhibit 12-2.) Current account items appear in considerably more detail (lines 1 through 32) than in the earlier format. No current account balance is shown in the table, although it does appear in the memoranda at the bottom (Line 69). The capital account, which begins with line 33, is reorganized into two broad categories: changes in U.S. assets abroad (lines 33 through 47) and changes in foreign assets in the United States (lines 48 through 61). Changes in U.S. foreign exchange reserve assets (lines 34 through 38) appear as a subcategory of changes in U.S. assets abroad. Changes in foreign holdings of reserves in the form of U.S. dollars are treated similarly and appear as lines 49 through 55 minus line 53. No official reserve transactions or basic balances appear, and the accounts end with the statistical discrepancy (line 63) which is merely a new name for errors and omissions. The structure of the accounts published for the United States is quite different under the two exchange rate regimes and is summarized in the accompanying listing.

Fixed Exchange Rates	**Floating Exchange Rates**
Current Account	Current Account
(balance shown)	(no balance shown)
Capital Account	Capital Account
Long-term capital	Changes in U.S. assets abroad
Basic payments balance	Changes in U.S. reserve assets
	Other changes in U.S. claims
	on foreigners
Short-term capital	Changes in foreign assets
(including errors and omissions)	in United States
Official reserve transactions balance	Changes in dollar FXR claims
	Other changes in claims
	on United States
Changes in foreign exchange reserves	Statistical Discrepancy (E&O)
Changes in foreign holdings	
of U.S. dollar reserves	
Changes in U.S. Foreign Exchange	
Reserve Assets	

[3]For the rationale for the mid-1970s reorganization of the U.S. balance-of-payments accounts, see "The Report of the Advisory Committee on the Presentation of the Balance of Payments Statistics," *Survey of Current Business,* June 1976. See also Donald Kemp, "Balance of Payments Concepts: What Do They Really Mean?," *Federal Reserve Bank of St. Louis Review,* July 1975, and Robert Stern et al., "The Presentation of the Balance of Payments: A Symposium," *Princeton Essays in International Finance,* No. 123, August 1977. Balance-of-payments data in abbreviated form for most countries can be found in the International Monetary Fund, *International Financial Statistics.* More detailed data can be found in the *Balance of Payments Yearbook,* which is also published by the IMF.

U.S. International Transactions

Line	(Credits +, debits −)¹	1989	1990ᵖ	Not seasonally adjusted 1990				Seasonally adjusted 1990			
				I	II	IIIᵖ	IVᵖ	Iᵖ	IIᵖ	IIIᵖ	IVᵖ
1	Exports of goods, services, and income	603,169	648,738	158,042	162,465	159,198	169,033	158,984	159,136	161,101	169,517
2	Merchandise, adjusted, excluding military²	360,465	389,286	96,275	99,588	92,888	100,535	96,093	96,585	96,152	100,456
3	Services³	115,169	130,623	30,374	31,466	35,602	33,180	31,341	31,860	33,060	34,361
4	Transfers under U.S. military agency sales contracts⁴	8,331	10,180	2,339	2,310	2,665	2,866	2,339	2,310	2,665	2,866
5	Travel	34,432	39,253	8,361	9,804	11,831	9,257	9,395	9,704	9,884	10,272
6	Passenger fares	10,101	11,850	2,573	2,951	3,697	2,629	2,984	2,904	2,903	3,058
7	Other transportation	20,416	22,011	5,366	5,412	5,583	5,650	5,425	5,347	5,516	5,723
8	Royalties and license fees⁵⁶	11,815	14,795	3,121	3,477	3,609	4,588	3,314	3,590	3,840	4,051
9	Other private services⁶	29,461	31,846	8,468	7,313	8,030	8,036	7,723	7,827	8,092	8,205
10	U.S. Government miscellaneous services	613	688	147	200	187	154	179	179	160	186
11	Income receipts on U.S. assets abroad	127,536	128,829	31,393	31,412	30,708	35,317	31,550	30,691	31,889	34,700
12	Direct investment receipts	53,617	54,137	13,170	13,610	12,593	14,763	13,234	12,885	13,839	14,179
13	Other private receipts	68,377	64,796	16,236	16,024	16,078	16,458	16,236	16,024	16,078	16,458
14	U.S. Government receipts	5,542	9,897	1,986	1,778	2,036	4,096	2,080	1,782	1,972	4,063
15	Imports of goods, services, and income	−698,483	−726,961	−172,813	−179,314	−185,854	−188,981	−177,864	−177,447	−183,483	−188,167
16	Merchandise, adjusted, excluding military²	−475,329	−497,966	−120,219	−120,731	−125,152	−131,864	−122,902	−119,810	−125,937	−129,317
17	Services³	−94,706	−107,699	−23,047	−26,901	−31,069	−26,682	−25,416	−25,956	−27,913	−28,415
18	Direct defense expenditures	−14,651	−16,593	−3,625	−3,691	−4,370	−4,908	−3,625	−3,691	−4,370	−4,908
19	Travel	−34,977	−38,376	−7,085	−10,339	−12,523	−8,429	−8,939	−9,464	−10,021	−9,952
20	Passenger fares	−8,522	−9,529	−1,920	−2,467	−3,020	−2,122	−2,222	−2,372	−2,517	−2,417
21	Other transportation	−20,791	−23,520	−5,477	−5,741	−6,114	−6,188	−5,657	−5,729	−6,000	−6,135
22	Royalties and license fees⁵⁶	−2,245	−2,703	−600	−613	−727	−762	−600	−613	−727	−762
23	Other private services⁶	−11,481	−14,756	−3,805	−3,493	−3,739	−3,719	−3,805	−3,513	−3,739	−3,699
24	U.S. Government miscellaneous services	−2,040	−2,222	−535	−557	−577	−553	−568	−574	−539	−541
25	Income payments on foreign assets in the United States	−128,448	−121,296	−29,546	−31,681	−29,633	−30,435	−29,546	−31,681	−29,633	−30,435
26	Direct investment payments	−14,004	−4,771	−1,190	−2,462	−683	−435	−1,190	−2,462	−683	−435
27	Other private payments	−78,489	−79,063	−19,173	−19,776	−19,620	−20,494	−19,173	−19,776	−19,620	−20,494
28	U.S. Government payments	−35,955	−37,462	−9,183	−9,443	−9,330	−9,506	−9,183	−9,443	−9,330	−9,506
29	Unilateral transfers, net	−14,720	−21,073	−3,556	−4,139	−4,016	−9,362	−3,440	−4,422	−4,099	−9,112
30	U.S. Government grants⁴	−10,963	−16,972	−2,403	−3,501	−2,993	−8,075	−2,403	−3,501	−2,993	−8,075
31	U.S. Government pensions and other transfers	−2,432	−2,948	−658	−583	−659	−1,048	−740	−740	−731	−737
32	Private remittances and other transfers	−1,326	−1,153	−496	−55	−364	−239	−298	−181	−375	−300

Line	Item	(1)	(2)	(3)	(4)	(5)	(6)	(7)	(8)	(9)	(10)
33	U.S. assets abroad, net (increase/capital outflow (−))	−127,061	−61,251	31,934	−34,208	−32,683	−26,294	32,905	−31,694	−31,894	−30,568
34	U.S. official reserve assets, net [1]	−25,293	−2,158	−3,177	371	1,739	−1,091	−3,177	371	1,739	−1,091
35	Gold										
36	Special drawing rights	−535	−192	−247	−216	363	−93	−247	−216	363	−93
37	Reserve position in the International Monetary Fund	471	731	234	493	8	−4	234	493	8	−4
38	Foreign currencies	−25,229	−2,697	−3,164	94	1,368	−995	−3,164	94	1,368	−995
39	U.S. Government assets, other than official reserve assets, net	1,185	2,971	−745	−775	−331	4,821	−659	−808	−360	4,797
40	U.S. credits and other long-term assets [4]	−5,513	−6,929	−1,580	−1,849	−1,347	−2,153	−1,580	−1,849	−1,347	−2,153
41	Repayments on U.S. credits and other long-term assets [5]	6,548	9,955	909	1,061	1,039	6,947	995	1,028	1,010	6,922
42	U.S. foreign currency holdings and U.S. short-term assets, net	151	−56	−74	13	−23	28	−74	13	−23	28
43	U.S. private assets, net	−102,953	−62,063	35,857	−33,804	−34,091	−30,024	36,741	−31,257	−33,273	−34,273
44	Direct investment	−31,722	−36,371	−10,202	−7,368	−20,004	1,204	−9,318	−4,821	−19,186	−3,045
45	Foreign securities	−21,938	−26,785	−7,496	−11,247	−11,223	−6,819	−7,496	−11,247	−1,223	−6,819
46	U.S. claims on unaffiliated foreigners reported by U.S. nonbanking concerns	1,391	n.a.	1,202	−1,550	625	n.a.	1,202	−1,550	625	n.a.
47	U.S. claims reported by U.S. banks, not included elsewhere	−50,684	816	52,353	−13,639	−13,489	−24,409	52,353	−13,639	−13,489	−24,409
48	Foreign assets in the United States, net (increase/capital inflow (+))	214,652	87,545	−32,988	25,496	56,131	38,907	−32,988	25,496	56,131	38,907
49	Foreign official assets in the United States, net	8,823	30,778	−8,203	5,541	13,588	19,851	−8,203	5,541	13,588	19,851
50	U.S. Government securities [9]	1,716	29,371	−6,418	2,788	12,192	20,809	−6,418	2,788	12,192	20,809
51	U.S. Treasury securities	333	28,704	−5,897	2,442	12,058	20,101	−5,897	2,442	12,058	20,101
52	Other [10]	1,383	667	−521	346	134	708	−521	346	134	708
53	Other U.S. Government liabilities [11]	332	1,486	−381	1,089	−202	979	−381	1,089	−202	979
54	U.S. liabilities reported by U.S. banks, not included elsewhere	4,940	1,495	−1,278	1,918	1,871	−1,016	−1,278	1,918	1,871	−1,016
55	Other foreign official assets [12]	1,835	−1,574	−126	−254	−273	−921	−126	−254	−273	−921
56	Other foreign assets in the United States, net	205,829	56,767	−24,786	19,954	42,543	19,055	−24,786	19,954	42,543	19,055
57	Direct investment	72,244	25,709	5,537	7,236	11,885	1,050	5,537	7,236	11,885	1,050
58	U.S. Treasury securities	29,951	1,144	−835	3,614	312	−1,947	−835	3,614	312	−1,947
59	U.S. securities other than U.S. Treasury securities	39,568	4,096	2,486	2,890	−1,670	390	2,486	2,890	−1,670	390
60	U.S. liabilities to unaffiliated foreigners reported by U.S. nonbanking concerns	2,867	n.a.	290	1,317	4,425	n.a.	290	1,317	4,425	n.a.
61	U.S. liabilities reported by U.S. banks, not included elsewhere	61,199	19,786	−32,264	4,897	27,591	19,562	−32,264	4,897	27,591	19,562
62	Allocations of special drawing rights										
63	Statistical discrepancy (sum of above items with sign reversed)	22,443	73,002	19,381	29,699	7,224	16,698	22,404	28,932	2,244	19,424
63a	Of which seasonal adjustment discrepancy							3,023	−767	−4,980	2,726
	Memoranda:										
64	Balance on merchandise trade (lines 2 and 16)	−114,864	−108,680	−23,944	−21,143	−32,264	−31,329	−26,809	−23,225	−29,785	−28,661
65	Balance on services (lines 3 and 17)	20,463	22,923	7,327	4,564	4,553	6,499	5,925	5,904	5,147	5,946
66	Balance on investment income (lines 11 and 25)	−913	7,533	1,846	−270	1,074	4,882	2,004	−990	2,256	4,265
67	Balance on goods, services, and income (lines 1 and 15 or lines 64, 65, and 66) [13]	−95,314	−78,224	−14,771	−16,849	−26,656	−19,948	−18,880	−18,311	−22,382	−18,650
68	Unilateral transfers, net (line 29)	−14,720	−21,073	−3,556	−4,139	−4,016	−9,362	−3,440	−4,422	−4,099	−9,112
69	Balance on current account (lines 1, 15, and 29 or lines 67 and 68) [14]	−110,034	−99,297	−18,327	−20,987	−30,672	−29,310	−22,320	−22,733	−26,481	−27,762

(Handwritten marginal notes:) −116,034 CA; 87,597 + 22,443; (33 + 48)KA (63)ST

EXHIBIT 12-2 U.S. international transactions. *Source:* U.S. Department of Commerce, Bureau of Economic Analysis.

THE INTERNATIONAL INVESTMENT POSITION TABLE

In addition to the balance-of-payments accounts discussed earlier in this chapter, many countries publish tables showing their net creditor or debtor situation relative to the rest of the world. This account is analogous to a balance sheet in that stocks of foreign assets are shown along with stocks of liabilities to foreigners to reach a net international investment position which is similar to the concept of net worth. A country's net investment position should change each year by the amount of its current account balance. A current account surplus of $1 billion means an increase in that country's net investment position of that amount. Consequently, either its foreign assets increase and/or its liabilities to foreigners fall by that amount. A recently published table for the United States is presented in Exhibit 12-3.

The decline in the U.S. investment position during the 1980s is rather striking. At the end of 1981 the United States was a net creditor in the amount of $141 billion. As a result of a series of current account deficits totaling $509 billion over six years, this country became a net debtor of $368 billion. The circumstances and policies that caused these enormous current account deficits will be discussed in later chapters.

The way in which real assets such as direct investments are valued in this table presents a problem. Such investments are carried at book or historic value, that is, purchase price minus depreciation. In a period of rapid inflation or common stock price increases, such valuation would be far less than market value for long-lived direct investments. William DeWald and Michael Ulan of the U.S. Department of State have argued that, if market rather than book values are used, the United States is not a net debtor but instead remains a creditor.[4] This change results from the fact that this country has large and longstanding direct investments abroad, whereas foreign direct investments in the United States by foreigners are smaller and more recent in origin. Therefore accrued but unrealized capital gains are much smaller. Any method of valuing such direct investments is open to question, and this proposed change in the account would complicate its relationship to the current account of the balance of payments. Since unrealized capital gains on foreign direct investments are not shown as a current account credit, there would no longer be a match between a country's current account results and the change in its net investment position.

All that can be said at present is that this valuation question has become quite controversial, that U.S. direct investments abroad are certainly worth more than their book value, and that as a result the United States is not as heavily indebted to the rest of the world as the published investment table indicates. The Bureau of Economic Analysis at the Department of Commerce, which is responsible for the methodology and data in these tables, is reportedly considering a change in valuation procedures that would enter direct investments on the basis of estimated

[4]Michael Ulan and William DeWald, "The U.S. Net International Investment Position," in James Dorn and William Niskanen, eds., *Dollars, Deficits, and Trade* (Norwell, Mass.: Kluwer Publishing Co., 1989).

[Billions of dollars]

Type of investment	1980	1981	1982	1983	1984	1985	1986	1987
Net international investment position of the United States...	106.3	141.1	136.9	89.4	3.5	−110.7	−269.2	−368.2
U.S. assets abroad	607.1	719.8	824.9	873.9	896.1	950.3	1,071.4	1,167.8
U.S. official reserve assets	26.8	30.1	34.0	33.7	34.9	43.2	48.5	45.8
Gold	11.2	11.2	11.1	11.1	11.1	11.1	11.1	11.1
Special drawing rights	2.6	4.1	5.3	5.0	5.6	7.3	8.4	10.3
Reserve position in the International Monetary Fund	2.9	5.1	7.3	11.3	11.5	11.9	11.7	11.3
Foreign currencies	10.1	9.8	10.2	6.3	6.7	12.9	17.3	13.1
U.S. Government assets, other than official reserve assets	63.8	68.7	74.6	79.5	84.8	87.6	89.5	88.4
U.S. loans and other long-term assets	62.0	67.2	72.9	77.8	82.9	85.8	88.7	87.6
Repayable in dollars	59.8	65.0	70.9	76.0	81.1	84.1	87.1	86.0
Other	2.2	2.2	1.9	1.8	1.8	1.7	1.6	1.6
U.S. foreign currency holdings and U.S. short-term assets	1.7	1.5	1.7	1.7	2.0	1.8	.8	.8
U.S. private assets	516.6	621.1	716.4	760.7	776.3	819.5	933.4	1,033.6
Direct investment abroad	215.4	228.3	207.8	207.2	211.5	230.3	259.6	308.9
Foreign securities	62.7	63.4	75.5	83.8	89.1	112.8	133.2	146.7
Bonds	43.5	45.8	56.7	57.7	61.8	73.0	81.8	91.0
Corporate stocks	19.2	17.6	18.8	26.1	27.3	39.8	51.4	55.7
U.S. claims on unaffiliated foreigners reported by U.S. nonbanking concerns	34.7	35.9	28.6	35.1	30.1	29.1	33.3	30.1
U.S. claims reported by U.S. banks, not included elsewhere	203.9	293.5	404.6	434.5	445.6	447.4	507.3	547.9
Foreign assets in the United States	500.8	578.7	688.1	784.5	892.6	1,061.0	1,340.7	1,536.0
Foreign official assets in the United States	176.1	180.4	189.1	194.5	199.3	202.6	241.7	283.1
U.S. Government securities	118.2	125.1	132.6	137.0	143.0	143.4	177.3	219.1
U.S. Treasury securities	111.3	117.0	124.9	129.7	135.5	135.7	170.6	211.2
Other	6.9	8.1	7.7	7.3	7.5	7.7	6.7	7.9
Other U.S. Government liabilities	13.4	13.0	13.6	14.2	15.0	15.7	17.8	15.0
U.S. liabilities reported by U.S. banks, not included elsewhere	30.4	26.7	25.0	25.5	26.1	26.7	27.9	31.8
Other foreign official assets	14.1	15.5	17.9	17.7	15.2	16.7	18.8	17.3
Other foreign assets in the United States	324.8	398.3	498.9	590.0	693.3	858.4	1,098.9	1,252.9
Direct investment in the United States	83.0	108.7	124.7	137.1	164.6	184.6	220.4	261.9
U.S. Treasury securities	16.1	18.5	25.8	33.8	58.2	83.6	91.5	78.4
U.S. securities other than U.S. Treasury securities	74.1	75.1	93.0	113.8	127.3	206.2	308.8	344.4
Corporate and other bonds	9.5	10.7	16.7	17.5	32.7	82.5	142.1	171.0
Corporate stocks	64.6	64.4	76.3	94.5	94.6	123.7	166.7	173.4
U.S. liabilities to unaffiliated foreigners reported by U.S. nonbanking concerns	30.4	30.6	27.5	26.9	31.0	29.5	26.6	28.8
U.S. liabilities reported by U.S. banks, not included elsewhere	121.1	165.4	228.0	278.3	312.2	354.5	451.6	539.4

Source: Department of Commerce, Bureau of Economic Analysis.

EXHIBIT 12-3   International investment position of the United States at year-end, 1980–87. *Source:* Published in Economic Report of the President, 1989.

market values, but the means of making such market estimates is still unclear and controversial.[5]

TRADE ACCOUNT IMBALANCES THROUGH STAGES OF DEVELOPMENT

The emphasis on balanced barter trade in the first half of this book may lead to the conclusion that it is normal or good for exports to equal imports so that the trade and current accounts are in balance. Trade and current account imbalances are actually more normal, and such disequilibria play a critical role in moving real capital from one country to another. If a country has a current account deficit, for example, its domestic investment exceeds domestic saving, with the net inflow of real goods and services filling the gap between investment and saving. A current account surplus necessarily implies an excess of saving over investment, as can be seen through the standard national income accounting identities, first with the simplifying assumption of no government sector.

$$Y = C + I + (X - M)$$
$$Y = C + S_p$$

$$
\begin{aligned}
\text{where} \quad Y &= \text{GNP} \\
C &= \text{consumption} \\
I &= \text{investment} \\
S_p &= \text{private saving} \\
X &= \text{exports} \\
M &= \text{imports}
\end{aligned}
$$

It then follows that

$$I + (X - M) = S_p$$

and that

$$I - S_p = M - X$$

[5]The history of this debate begins with Sarah Hooker, *The International Investment Position of the United States*, (Santa Monica, Calif.: Rand Corporation, 1988). See also Michael Mann and Henry Townsend, "Methodology and Assumptions Used for Market Revaluation of Direct Investment," U.S. Department of Commerce, Bureau of Economic Analysis, mimeo, April 2, 1991. As this volume was being completed, the Bureau of Economic Analysis of the Department of Commerce concluded that, if assets and liabilities are carried at market values, the United States was a net debtor in the amount of $281 billion at the end of 1989, compared to $664 billion on the basis of the traditional valuation procedure. See J. Steven Landefeld and Anne Lawson, "Valuation of the U.S. Net International Investment Position," *Survey of Current Business*, May 1991, pp. 40–49.

A country must invest more than it saves if it has a current account deficit. Adding the government sector,

$$Y = C + I + G + (X - M)$$
$$Y = C + S_p + T$$

where G = government expenditures
T = taxes

It then follows that

$$I + (X - M) = S_p + (T - G)$$

and that

$$I - (S_p + (T - G)) = M - X$$

If $T - G = S_g$
and $S_t = S_p + S_g$

which simply says that total domestic savings equals private saving (S_p) plus government savings $(T - G)$, where the government can have negative savings.

It then follows that

$$I - S_t = M - X$$

Investment will now exceed total domestic savings (including the government) if the country has a current account deficit. Since world exports equal world imports, world investment equals world savings, so this is not a way of increasing the world's volume of investment above savings. Instead it is a way of allowing saving to take place in one country and the resulting investment to occur in another.

In recent years, for example, the United States has had gross private investment levels of about 18 percent of GNP despite gross savings (including depreciation charges) of only about 15 percent of GNP. The difference has been made up through current account deficits of about 3 percent of GNP. Japan and Germany have been in a mirror-image situation, saving more than they invest and running current account surpluses. Savings originating in Japan and Germany have financed a large volume of investment in the United States; current account imbalances have served as the mechanism through which real resources were moved from Germany and Japan to the United States. German and Japanese lending to the United States provided the necessary financing for U.S. current account deficits, allowing the overall balance of payments to be in approximate equilibrium.

The only unusual aspect of this situation is that a country as highly developed as the United States should be saving so little and therefore become dependent on large capital inflows. This is the more normal circumstance for a country that is beginning the development process.

An underdeveloped country typically has a small stock of capital relative to the size of its labor force; this situation implies a high marginal product of capital, which should be reflected as a high interest rate, high profit rates, or both. Such countries are natural magnets for external capital, unless the government adopts tax or other policies that destroy this underlying attractiveness for investors. As a result, well-governed developing countries have typically experienced large financial capital inflows that allowed parallel current account deficits and overall payments equilibrium. This situation allows domestic investment well in excess of savings levels, thus breaking the longstanding cycle of poverty argument that says that poor countries remain poor because they cannot save much, therefore cannot invest much, and can never increase their capital to labor ratios. As a result, labor productivity remains low, and poverty persists. With external capital inflows financing current account deficits, investment is no longer limited to the level of domestic savings, and the capital stock can grow more rapidly than would be possible with only domestic resources.

During the early decades of development, sometimes known as the early debtor stage, countries normally run current account deficits to provide real resources so that they can invest more than they save, and they borrow the necessary funds abroad. During these years the country's net indebtedness to the rest of the world increases each year by the amount of its current account deficit.

This process is self-limiting or reversing, however. As the capital stock grows rapidly relative to the labor force (and relative to a fixed stock of land), the marginal product of capital falls and the marginal product of labor rises. As a result, interest and profit rates fall, but local labor incomes increase. The attractions for foreign capital decline, but local savings rates increase as incomes rise. Investment needs decline somewhat, because a large capital stock has already been put in place. The combination of rising savings rates and declining needs for massive investment levels allows the country to export more and import less, which is helpful because lower profit and interest rates mean that less foreign capital is flowing in.

When the trade and then the current account cease to be in deficit (the current account lags the trade account because it is necessary to make interest payments on previously accumulated indebtedness), and instead become positive, net indebtedness reaches its peak and begins to decline.[6] This period is known as the late debtor stage. Net indebtedness declines each year by the amount of the current account surplus, and eventually it reaches zero. The country then becomes a net creditor. This is known as the early creditor stage. The current account remains in surplus, domestic savings exceeds investment by the amount of this surplus, and the country accumulates net financial claims on the rest of the world. The only difference between the late debtor and early creditor stages is that the dividend and interest item within the current account should be positive in the early creditor

---

[6]A discussion of the stages model of the balance of payments can be found in Dragaslov Avramovic, *Economic Growth and External Debt* (Baltimore, Md.: Johns Hopkins University Press, 1964).

stage. In theory, this stage could go on indefinitely, but economists do not like permanent disequilibria and seek ways to return to equilibrium.

The late creditor stage is a theoretical abstraction, but it could be considered the model for some OPEC countries after their oil reserves are depleted. In this situation, a country has accumulated large net financial claims on the rest of the world, from which it earns sizable dividend and interest payments. This income is used to pay for a trade deficit, so that both the current and capital accounts are in equilibrium. Such a country is analogous to a trust fund beneficiary who lives on income from capital. When countries such as Saudi Arabia and the United Arab Emirates have extracted all of their oil, they may be in this situation. These countries do not appear to have other resources, and they now have high standards of living. When the oil is gone, the accumulated financial claims on the world will need to be sizable if the resulting income is to maintain current living standards.

The United States was an early debtor during much of the nineteenth century, borrowing heavily in London and elsewhere to finance investments and a westward expansion. It became a late debtor near the end of the century, and it reduced its net indebtedness early in the twentieth century, becoming a net creditor sometime in the interwar period. It accumulated a sizable net creditor position after World War II and during the 1960s. It had an approximate balance in its current account in the 1970s and might be viewed as a mature creditor during that decade. Then, of course, this country turned the stages model of the balance of payments on its head by becoming a large debtor during the 1980s because of massive current account deficits. A sharp decline in the domestic savings rate, caused in large part by massive public dis-saving in the form of federal budget deficits, left the United States dependent on foreign saving to maintain normal investment levels. The mechanism through which this occurred will be discussed later in this book.

QUESTIONS FOR STUDY AND REVIEW

1. What sign would each of the following transactions have in the U.S. balance-of-payments accounts, and in what section of the account (current, private capital, or foreign exchange reserves) would it appear?
   a. IBM of Canada remits dividends to IBM of the United States.
   b. The Bank of Japan purchases U.S. dollars which are added to the foreign exchange reserves of Japan.
   c. A Japanese corporation sells machinery to a U.S. firm, with payment to be received one year after delivery. Delivery is this year.

2. "An increase in foreign-owned balances in U.S. banks is equivalent to a short-term loan to the United States" True or False? Explain.

3. Distinguish between the reserve settlements balance and the current account balance.

4. Explain why both a foreign asset acquired and a foreign liability reduced give rise to a debit entry in a nation's balance of payments.

5. Distinguish between autonomous and accommodating transactions in the balance of payments. What is the purpose of the distinction. *in Accounting bc3 they must offset each other*

6. If a country is an exporter of long-term capital, what do you expect its current account balance to be? Why? *positive*

7. What is the essential distinction between the current account and the capital account in the balance of payments? *Current → net creditor or debtor nation* *Capital → purchases & sales of L.T. financial claim*

8. If the U.S. net creditor/debtor table is now to be published on a market value rather than historic value basis, what changes will have to be made to the published version of the U.S. current account to make it match changes in the new creditor/debtor table?

SELECTED REFERENCES

Advisory Committee on the Presentation of the Balance of Payments Statistics. "Report." *Survey of Current Business,* June 1976, pp. 18–27.

International Monetary Fund. *Balance of Payments Yearbook.*

International Monetary Fund. *International Financial Statistics* (monthly).

Landefeld, J. Steven, and Anne Lawson. "Valuation of the U.S. Net International Investment Position." *Survey of Current Business,* May 1991, pp. 40–49.

13

MARKETS FOR
FOREIGN EXCHANGE

Foreign exchange markets appear to be rather exotic, but the basic idea behind them is simple. In order to complete the international transactions described in the previous chapter, people need to sell one currency and buy another. Foreign exchange markets are merely the institutional arrangements through which such purchases and sales are made.

If Americans purchase foreign goods or financial assets, they begin with dollars and need foreign exchange to complete the transactions. British exporters will expect to be paid in pounds sterling, so a U.S. importer must sell dollars and purchase sterling to buy British goods. Even if the U.K. exporter were to accept payment in dollars, he or she would be selling them for sterling. Thus no matter which currency is used for payment, someone will be selling dollars and purchasing sterling. U.S. purchases of British financial assets would result in the same requirement that someone sell dollars for sterling. Even an increase in U.S. holdings of official foreign exchange reserves has this result. The New York Federal Reserve Bank sells dollars and purchases sterling to increase such reserves.

If foreigners purchase U.S. goods or financial assets, they face a parallel need to sell their currencies and buy dollars. This also applies to foreign central banks that accumulate foreign exchange reserves in the form of dollars; they sell their currencies and purchase dollars in their exchange markets to add to such dollar reserves.

Balance-of-payments transactions that are debits and carry a minus sign in the U.S. accounts cause sales of dollars and purchases of foreign exchange, whereas credits that carry a plus sign produce sales of foreign currencies and purchases of dollars. The only exception to this conclusion occurs when the same individual is simultaneously involved in two international transactions of the same size and the opposite sign. Such a set of transactions would be self-canceling in terms of its balance-of-payments effect. If, for example, a U.S. newspaper purchased Canadian newsprint and paid for it with a Canadian dollar check drawn on the Bank of Montreal, there would be no purchase or sale of either currency in the exchange market. The U.S. balance-of-payments accounts would show two entries: a short-term capital flow from Canada to the United States that would be a credit (+) and the importing of the newsprint, which would be a debit (−). There would be no net impact on the U.S. official reserve transactions balance and no use of the exchange market.

Except for such paired and offsetting transactions, there is a parallel or mirror-image relationship between what occurs in the balance-of-payments accounts and in the exchange market. Since credit (+) transactions represent demand for dollars, and vice versa, a balance-of-payments deficit means an excess supply of dollars in the exchange market, whereas a surplus would imply an excess demand for dollars. Disequilibria in the balance-of-payments accounts produce parallel disequilibria in the exchange market. In a regime of flexible exchange rates, a subject to be dealt with in detail later in this book, the price of foreign exchange adjusts to clear the market. Under fixed exchange rates, which will be discussed before flexible rates, it becomes the obligation of the central bank to intervene in the exchange market to absorb the excess demand or supply, so that the market can clear despite a lack of balance in the autonomous transactions. Foreign exchange reserves rise or fall through such intervention.

SUPPLY AND DEMAND FOR FOREIGN EXCHANGE

The operations of the exchange market can be represented by a standard supply and demand graph (see Figure 13-1). The demand for foreign exchange is derived from the domestic demand for foreign goods, services, and financial assets, whereas the supply of foreign exchange is similarly derived from the foreign demand for

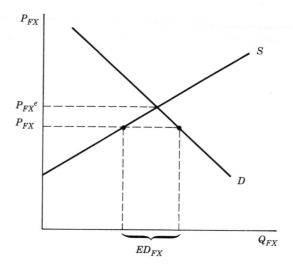

FIGURE 13-1   Supply and demand in the market for foreign exchange.

goods, services, and financial assets coming from this country. Foreigners sell their currency in order to purchase U.S. dollars for the purpose of completing purchases of U.S. goods, services, or financial assets.

If the United States had a fixed exchange rate and a payments deficit, as shown in the figure, there would be an excess demand for foreign currencies in the exchange market. The New York Federal Reserve Bank and/or its counterparts abroad would then be obligated to buy up the excess dollars and sell the foreign currencies that were in excess demand. Such transactions would either reduce U.S. foreign exchange assets (if the New York Fed acted) or increase foreign official holdings of dollar reserves (if foreign central banks intervened). If the central banks failed to intervene to purchase the excess dollars, the price of foreign exchange would rise to the equilibrium level shown in Figure 13-1, and a fixed exchange rate would no longer exist. It is the willingness of central banks to maintain a commitment to purchase or sell foreign currencies as needed to maintain unchanging exchange rates that differentiates a fixed parity system from a world of flexible exchange rates.

If the United States had a payments surplus, there would be an excess supply of foreign exchange (an excess demand for dollars), and central banks would need to provide the required dollars and absorb the excess foreign currencies. In this case, either U.S. reserve assets would increase or foreign official reserve assets in the form of dollars would decline, depending again on which central bank acted. It is possible, of course, that both central banks would act and that the U.S. surplus would be offset by a combination of an increase in U.S. reserve assets and a decline in foreign official holdings of dollars, with the total intervention by the two sides equaling the U.S. surplus.

Because all plus transactions (autonomous plus accommodating) represent purchases of dollars and all minus transactions are dollar sales, the balance-of-payments accounts including all transactions must total zero. For every dollar bought, one must be sold, or the transaction cannot be completed. Therefore the total of plus transactions must equal the total of the minuses, where foreign exchange reserve movements as well as autonomous transactions are included. Central bank intervention in the exchange market fills the gap between imbalances in total autonomous transactions and the need for all transactions to total zero. It may be useful briefly to discuss different regimes or arrangements for such intervention, beginning with the pre-1914 gold standard.

EXCHANGE MARKET INTERVENTION REGIMES

The Gold Standard

Under this system (discussed in more detail in Chapter 16), central banks set exchange rates indirectly by establishing relative prices of gold, and then by promising to buy and sell gold in unlimited amounts at those prices.[1] If, for example, the British government set the price of gold at 4 pounds sterling per ounce while the U.S. Treasury price was $20, as long as both governments or central banks maintained a willingness to buy and sell at those prices, the exchange rate would have to be about $5 equals 1 pound. If, for example, sterling fell significantly below that value, British residents would be unwilling to sell in the exchange market because they had the obvious alternative of selling their sterling to the British government for gold, shipping the gold to New York, and selling it for dollars to the U.S. Treasury. A British balance-of-payments deficit that produced an excess supply of sterling in the exchange market and downward pressure on the exchange value of sterling would automatically result in the loss of gold reserves by Great Britain and a gain in such reserves by the surplus country, in this case the United States.

If the United States had a payments deficit that produced an excess supply of dollars that drove the currency downward in the exchange market, Americans would not have to accept an unattractive price for their currency. The reason is that they would have the alternative of turning their dollars in for gold, sending the gold to London, and thereby transferring into sterling at an exchange rate of $5 for 1 pound. If transportation costs were zero, the exchange rate could not diverge even slightly from the 5 to 1 parity. Because such costs were not zero, a narrow range existed within which the exchange rate could move. When it hit the edge of that range, gold would start to flow between New York and London; the two edges of the range were therefore known as the gold points. More will be said about this system later, but for now it is important to note that fixed exchange rates were maintained indirectly by a willingness of both central banks to buy and sell the same commodity at fixed prices. Gold had no particular significance in

---

[1] For a discussion of gold points, see Leland Yeager, *International Monetary Relations: Theory and Policy* , 2nd ed. (New York: Harper & Row, 1976), pp. 20–21 and 317–318.

this arrangement. Any commodity (silver, wheat, or whatever) that could easily be shipped across the Atlantic could have been used.

The Bretton Woods Arrangements

The Bretton Woods system emerged from a summer 1944 conference at a resort of that name near Mount Washington in New Hampshire. The World Bank, the International Monetary Fund, and a variety of other postwar economic and financial arrangements were agreed to at that conference. One of its results was the exchange market intervention system that prevailed from the late 1940s until August 1971. The dollar was tied to gold at $35 per ounce, and the U.S. government promised to buy and sell at that price, doing business only with foreign central banks or governments. Other countries set fixed parities for their currencies in terms of the U.S. dollar and intervened in their exchange markets to hold market rates within a narrow range around those parities.[2] British sterling was, for example, $2.80 for many years, and the Bank of England (the British central bank) was committed to maintaining the market rate between $2.78 and $2.82. Whenever the United Kingdom had a payments deficit, the resulting downward pressure on sterling would drive the rate down toward $2.78. Before it got that low, the Bank of England would start selling dollars and buying sterling to slow its decline. If it fell significantly below $2.80, that is, if it approached $2.78, the sales of dollars/purchases of sterling would become sufficiently heavy to stop its decline. If Great Britain had a payments surplus, the resulting upward pressure on the currency would take it above $2.80 and the Bank of England would purchase dollars and sell sterling in sufficient volume to guarantee that it did not reach $2.82.

In the case of a British surplus, the dollars which the Bank of England bought in the London foreign exchange market would be deposited at the New York Federal Reserve Bank, thus adding to U.K. reserve assets and to U.S. reserve liabilities. Any such reserves that would not soon be needed would normally be switched into an interest-bearing form such as U.S. Treasury bills, with the New York Fed acting as custodian for the Bank of England. If the British accumulated more dollars than they wanted, they had the option of using them to purchase gold from the U.S. government. If British payments deficits depleted their reserves of dollars, gold could be sold to the United States to replenish the dollar holdings of the Bank of England. Reserves were held both as dollars and as gold, with countries being free to switch back and forth depending on their confidence in the dollar and the interest rates they could earn on U.S. Treasury bills.

This arrangement placed the United States in a unique and somewhat disadvantageous situation because it had no control over its exchange rate. If there are N currencies in the world, there are $N - 1$ dollar exchange rates. If $N - 1$ countries

---

[2] An extensive discussion of the Bretton Woods intervention system can be found in Yeager, Chs. 20 and 22. See also Robert Solomon, *The International Monetary System 1945–1976: An Insider's View* (New York: Harper & Row, 1977), Chs. 5–7 for a discussion of the problems of this system during the late 1960s. For a more recent analysis of exchange market intervention in this era, see B. Diane Pauls, "U.S. Exchange Rate Policy: Bretton Woods to Present," *Federal Reserve Bulletin,* November 1990, pp. 891–908.

peg their currencies to the dollar, the dollar exchange rate is automatically set relative to that of all other countries without U.S. involvement or control. The United States could change its price of gold, which would be of interest to South African and Russian mines, but it could not change any bilateral exchange rate. This turned out to be a significant disadvantage for this country in the late 1960s and early 1970s, but that subject will be dealt with in greater detail later.

Payments Arrangements in Developing Countries

Most developing countries had somewhat different arrangements throughout the Bretton Woods era. The system described above implies free currency convertibility; that is, private residents are free to buy and sell foreign exchange in order to carry out transactions in the current and capital accounts, although some industrialized countries did maintain restrictions on international capital flows. Many developing countries do not have such free convertibility in that virtually all transactions are subject to government regulation.[3] These legal arrangements are designed first to guarantee that foreign exchange revenues received by residents flow into official reserves immediately. Residents are required to sell any such funds, whether received from exports, tourism, or whatever, to the central bank promptly at the official exchange rate, inasmuch as the purpose of this system is to maximize foreign exchange reserve availability. Second, the government or central bank then licenses all transactions that require foreign exchange, granting approval only to those viewed as being important or at least useful. Investments abroad, imports of luxury goods, or foreign travel are not likely to receive permits and are therefore legally impossible. The goal of this part of the regulatory system is to allocate scarce foreign exchange to uses that the government considers vital for the country's development and to avoid use of such funds for less important expenditures. The underlying reason for such exchange controls is the constant threat of balance-of-payments deficits and a resulting shortage of foreign exchange reserves. Facing such shortages, governments decide to control the use of available funds to guarantee the availability of vital imports such as food, oil, medicines, and spare parts and to avoid expenditures on nonnecessities.

This approach to rationing scarce foreign exchange sounds reasonable, but it has a number of major disadvantages. Those residents who are denied legal access to foreign exchange will not only be displeased, but they will probably start looking for illegal sources of funds. In particular, they are likely to be willing to pay a premium for foreign exchange in an illegal or street market. If the legal exchange rate is 10 pesos per dollar, the street rate may be 15 or 20 pesos per dollar. The existence of this premium provides a strong incentive for exporters and other recipients of foreign exchange to divert their funds from the legal market at 10 pesos per dollar to the street market at 20 per dollar. Governments usually attempt

---

[3]The problems of such exchange control regimes are analyzed in J. N. Bhagwati, *The Anatomy and Consequences of Exchange Control Regimes* (Cambridge Mass.: Ballinger Publishing Co., 1978). See IMF, *Annual Report on Exchange Arrangements and Exchange Controls* for information on practices being maintained by various countries.

to enforce the requirement that such funds be sold only to the central bank, but such efforts are seldom very successful. Foreign tourists are likely to be approached by large numbers of people offering very attractive rates for local money on the street. It is extremely difficult to stop people from arbitraging between the two rates. As a result, the flow of foreign exchange into legal reserves is likely to stagnate or decline as more business is diverted to the illegal market. Officials of the central bank or finance ministry may be offered bribes to allow the purchase of foreign exchange at the legal rate for what should be illegal transactions. Such systems of exchange market control are frequently the source of graft and corruption.

The illegal or street market sometimes becomes so important to commerce and finance that its exchange rate is viewed as the most accurate barometer of what is happening to the balance of payments. If, for example, the legal rate stayed fixed at 10 pesos per dollar, but the street rate suddenly fell from 20 to 30 per dollar, that would be taken as evidence of a deteriorating payments situation, and perhaps of a growing desire of local residents to move capital out of the country and into foreign currencies. Because fear of accelerating inflation or of political instability would produce such a desire, the street or illegal exchange rate is often viewed as a measure of confidence in the future of the price level and the political system. A sudden decline in the value of the local currency in that market indicates a deterioration of such confidence.

The attractions of a regulated exchange market for a developing country facing payments deficits are obvious, but the record of such control systems is poor. Enforcement is difficult and frequently produces graft and corruption. Increasing volumes of export receipts (particularly from tourism) are diverted to an illegal market, so the availability of foreign exchange for important purposes stagnates or declines. Economics is about how rational economic agents maximize their self-interest, which means that it is about avarice and ingenuity. Few situations bring out the unattractive aspects of such maximizing behavior more quickly than a system of foreign exchange market controls that denies people the opportunity to purchase foreign exchange legally, thereby driving them to illegal alternatives. Such systems almost guarantee widespread law breaking and thereby undermine respect for the legal system. Despite the arguments of economists and a poor historical record, these systems of exchange market controls remain common in the developing world.

Exchange Market Intervention with Floating Exchange Rates

In theory, a flexible exchange rate system means that no central bank intervenes in the exchange market and that rates are determined the way prices of common stocks are settled: through shifts in supply and demand without official stabilization. In a clean or pure float, the exchange rate rises and falls with shifts in international payments flows, and these exchange rate movements keep the balance of payments in constant equilibrium (i.e., the official reserve transactions balance = 0). If the balance of payments and the exchange market were in equilibrium when a large surge of imports occurred, the local currency would depreciate to a level at which offsetting transactions were encouraged and the market again cleared, which is analogous to what happens to the price of General Motors stock if a sudden wave of selling hits the market. The price falls until enough buyers are attracted to clear the market. In a clean float, the exchange market operates in the same way, but countries do not maintain clean floats. Large or rapid exchange rate movements are seen as so disruptive that central banks instead operate dirty or managed flexible exchange rates.

There is no defense of a fixed parity, but instead discretionary intervention takes place whenever the market is moving in a direction or at a speed that the government wishes to avoid. If, for example, the dollar were depreciating beyond the wishes of Washington, the New York Federal Reserve Bank would purchase dollars and sell foreign currencies in an attempt to slow that movement. Such purchases might be coordinated with similar actions by central banks in Europe and Japan, creating a stronger effect on the market. Since the mid-1980s such intervention has increased, and more of it is being coordinated among the central banks of the major industrialized countries. Many economists remain skeptical, however, that such intervention can have more than temporary effects on exchange rates unless it is accompanied by changes in national monetary policies. Purchases of dollars by the New York Fed may temporarily slow a depreciation, but a reduction in the total dollar money supply, that is, a tighter U.S. monetary policy, would have a more lasting impact. Despite such doubts among economists, the central banks of countries with flexible exchange rates have become more active in exchange markets in recent years. The result seems to be some reduction in exchange rate volatility.[4]

EXCHANGE MARKET INSTITUTIONS

The foreign exchange market is maintained by major commercial banks in financial centers such as New York, London, Frankfurt, Singapore, and Tokyo. It is not like the New York Stock Exchange where trading occurs as a single location, but instead it is a "telephone market" in which traders are located in the various banks and trade electronically. Although trading occurs in other cities, the vast majority of the U.S. market is in New York, where it includes New York banks, foreign banks with U.S. subsidiaries or branches, and banks from other states that are allowed to do only international banking in New York. The banks typically maintain trading rooms that are staffed by at least one trader for each major currency.[5]

[4]For a discussion of official intervention in a regime of flexible exchange rates, see Victor Argy, "Exchange Rate Management in Theory and Practice," *Princeton Essays in International Finance*, No. 150, October 1982. See also Robert M. Dunn, Jr., "The Many Disappointments of Flexible Exchange Rates," *Princeton Essays in International Finance*, No. 154, December 1983, pp. 13–15, and the Working Group on Exchange Market Intervention, Report, March 1983. For a history of U.S. intervention policy under floating rates, see B. Diane Pauls, "U.S. Exchange Rate Policy: Bretton Woods to Present," *Federal Reserve Bulletin*, November 1990, pp. 891–908.

[5]The institutional arrangements through which foreign exchange is traded are covered in Michael Melvin, *International Money and Finance* (New York, Harper & Row, 1989). Also Roger Kubarych, *Foreign Exchange Markets in the United States*, Federal Reserve Bank of New York, 1983, and K. Alec Chrystal, "A Guide to Foreign Exchange Markets," *Federal Reserve Bank of St. Louis Review*, March 1984, pp. 5–18.

Orders come to the traders from large businesses that have established ties to that bank and from smaller banks around the country that have a correspondent banking relationship with that institution. The banks maintain inventories of each of the currencies which they trade in the form of deposits at foreign banks. If, for example, Citibank purchases yen from a customer, those funds will be placed in its account in Tokyo, and sales of yen by Citibank will come out of that account. Because these inventories rise and fall as trading proceeds, the banks take risks by frequently having net exposures in various currencies. If, for example, Citibank has sold yen heavily and consequently retains yen assets that are less than yen liabilities, the bank will have a short position in yen, and will lose if the yen appreciates and gain if it falls. Some banks try to impose strict limitations on such exposure by buying currencies to offset any emerging short or long positions, whereas others view such exposure as a way to seek speculative profits.

Currencies such as the Canadian dollar or the Deutsche mark (DM) would normally be quoted in hundredths of a penny or basis points, with bid/asked spreads being about ten basis points or one-tenth of a penny for large transactions. The Canadian dollar, for example, might be quoted at 83.42-52 U.S. cents; that is, the banks are prepared to purchase it for 83.42 cents or to sell it for 83.52 cents. Before the advent of flexible exchange rates in the early 1970s, bid/asked spreads were narrower, because exchange rate volatility and risk were smaller.

The current ten basis point spreads are for large transactions. For purchases of smaller amounts, the spreads become wider, and when tourists exchange money at airport banks or similar institutions, the spreads are much wider because the institutions need to cover their costs and make a profit on small transactions.

The ten basis point spread also operates in what is known as the interbank market, in which the banks trade among themselves. If, for example, Chase Manhattan had bought a large volume of Canadian dollars over a period of a few minutes and the traders became uncomfortable with the resulting long position, they would sell the excess Canadian funds in the interbank market, perhaps using a broker as an intermediary or perhaps dealing directly with another bank to save a brokerage fee. Information on interbank rates and spreads is provided electronically, primarily by Reuters, which supplies television monitors with the current rates for the major currencies. Reuters gathers information on current trades and on the willingness of banks to trade various currencies. The resulting spreads appear on its screens both in the major banks and in major industrial firms that have extensive international business dealings. As a result, virtually everyone in the market has the same information as to what rates are available.

Reduced cost and increased speed for international communications mean that during overlapping business hours, the European and New York markets are really a single market. Early in the day, New York banks can trade as easily in London or Frankfurt as in New York. Thus differences in exchange rates among these cities are arbitraged away almost instantly. Chicago and San Francisco continue trading after New York, and then Tokyo and Hong Kong open for business, so trading is going on somewhere in the world around the clock. Some New York banks are reportedly maintaining two shifts of traders, with one group arriving at 3 A.M. when London and Frankfurt open and the other group trading very late at night until Tokyo opens. The large New York banks have branches or subsidiaries in

Tokyo, Frankfurt, and London; therefore these banks are trading somewhere all the time during business days.

Foreign exchange transactions in the spot or current market are typically completed or cleared with a two-day lag, so that transactions agreed to on Monday will result in payments being made on Wednesday. This lag is partially the result of differences in time zones and is required to allow paperwork to be completed. Canadian/U.S. dollar business is normally cleared in one day because New York and Toronto are in the same time zone.

Payment is made by electronic transfer through a "cable transfer," which is simply an electronic message to a bank instructing it to transfer funds from one account to another. If, for example, General Motors bought 2 million DMs from Chase Manhattan on Tuesday, Chase would send such a cable transfer to its subsidiary or branch instructing it to transfer the funds from its account to that of General Motors on Thursday, and General Motors would transfer the required amount of dollars from its U.S. account to Chase Manhattan at the same time. The transaction that had been arranged on Tuesday would then be complete. The electronic arrangements through which these international transfers are made is known as CHIPS, the Clearing House International Payments System. In the late 1980s it was reportedly handling over $430 billion per day through New York, London, and Frankfurt.

ALTERNATIVE DEFINITIONS OF EXCHANGE RATES

In the past, exchange rates were measured only bilaterally and as the local price of foreign money. The U.S. exchange rate for sterling might be $2.80 or whatever. This practice had two disadvantages: (1) it did not provide any way of measuring the average exchange rate for a currency relative to a number of its major trading partners, and (2) it meant that if a currency fell in value or depreciated, its exchange rate would rise. A decline of the dollar would mean an increased U.S. cost of purchasing sterling and an increase in the U.S. exchange rate. Because this practice was found to be confusing, informal usage has now changed. An exchange rate now means the foreign price of our money, so the U.S. exchange rate for sterling might be 0.5610. That is, just over one-half of a pound is required to purchase a dollar. The newspaper table shown in Exhibit 13-1 presents bilateral exchange rates in both forms. With the new usage, reading that the exchange rate for the dollar fell tells us that the dollar declined in value relative to foreign currencies. Thus less foreign money is required to purchase a dollar but more U.S. money is needed to buy foreign currencies.

The Nominal Effective Exchange Rate

We still have to resolve the problem of how to measure the exchange rate for the dollar relative to the currencies of a number of countries with whom the United

EXCHANGE RATES

Thursday, January 2, 1992

The New York foreign exchange selling rates below apply to trading among banks in amounts of $1 million and more, as quoted at 3 p.m. Eastern time by Bankers Trust Co., Telerate Systems Inc. and other sources. Retail transactions provide fewer units of foreign currency per dollar.

Country	U.S. $ equiv. Thurs.	U.S. $ equiv. Tues.	Currency per U.S. $ Thurs.	Currency per U.S. $ Tues.
Argentina (Austral) ...	.0001010	.0001010	9905.01	9905.01
Australia (Dollar)	.7567	.7600	1.3215	1.3158
Austria (Schilling)	.09276	.09363	10.78	10.68
Bahrain (Dinar)	2.6525	2.6525	.3770	.3770
Belgium (Franc)	.03171	.03197	31.54	31.28
Brazil (Cruzeiro)	.00100	.00096	1002.30	1040.00
Britain (Pound)	1.8650	1.8695	.5362	.5349
30-Day Forward	1.8547	1.8587	.5392	.5380
90-Day Forward	1.8348	1.8388	.5450	.5438
180-Day Forward	1.8059	1.8098	.5537	.5525
Canada (Dollar)	.8688	.8654	1.1510	1.1555
30-Day Forward	.8665	.8632	1.1541	1.1585
90-Day Forward	.8624	.8590	1.1596	1.1642
180-Day Forward	.8572	.8538	1.1666	1.1713
Czechoslovakia (Koruna)				
Commercial rate	.0362845	.0366300	27.5600	27.3000
Chile (Peso)	.002750	.002743	363.68	364.50
China (Renminbi)	.185185	.185185	5.4000	5.4000
Colombia (Peso)	.001761	.001739	568.00	575.00
Denmark (Krone)	.1678	.1694	5.9610	5.9020
Ecuador (Sucre)				
Floating rate	.000804	.000804	1244.01	1244.01
Finland (Markka)	.24038	.24207	4.1600	4.1310
France (Franc)	.19120	.19305	5.2300	5.1800
30-Day Forward	.19022	.19205	5.2570	5.2070
90-Day Forward	.18838	.19015	5.3085	5.2590
180-Day Forward	.18576	.18742	5.3832	5.3357
Germany (Mark)	.6532	.6601	1.5310	1.5150
30-Day Forward	.6502	.6570	1.5379	1.5220
90-Day Forward	.6444	.6511	1.5518	1.5358
180-Day Forward	.6361	.6425	1.5721	1.5565
Greece (Drachma)	.005714	.005714	175.00	175.00
Hong Kong (Dollar) ..	.12861	.12858	7.7755	7.7770
Hungary (Forint)	.0132591	.0133156	75.4200	75.1000
India (Rupee)	.03876	.03876	25.80	25.80
Indonesia (Rupiah)	.0005040	.0005040	1984.01	1984.01
Ireland (Punt)	1.7345	1.7524	.5765	.5706
Israel (Shekel)	.4478	.4464	2.2329	2.2400
Italy (Lira)	.0008636	.0008715	1158.00	1147.50
Japan (Yen)	.008026	.008013	124.60	124.80
30-Day Forward	.008017	.008006	124.74	124.91
90-Day Forward	.007999	.007983	125.02	125.26
180-Day Forward	.007977	.007957	125.36	125.67
Jordan (Dinar)	1.4859	1.4859	.6730	.6730
Kuwait (Dinar)	3.5186	3.5186	.2842	.2842
Lebanon (Pound)	.001138	.001138	879.00	879.00
Malaysia (Ringgit)	.3674	.3676	2.7217	2.7205
Malta (Lira)	3.2000	3.2000	.3125	.3125
Mexico (Peso)				
Floating rate	.0003237	.0003237	3089.00	3089.00
Netherland (Guilder) .	.5797	.5858	1.7250	1.7070
New Zealand (Dollar)	.5390	.5400	1.8553	1.8519
Norway (Krone)	.1657	.1676	6.0345	5.9675
Pakistan (Rupee)	.0407	.0407	24.60	24.60
Peru (New Sol)	1.069	c1.05	.936	c.95
Philippines (Peso)	.03824	.03824	26.15	26.15
Poland (Zloty)	.00009259	.00009524	10800.00	10500.00
Portugal (Escudo)	.007543	.007485	132.58	133.60
Saudi Arabia (Riyal) ..	.26667	.26667	3.7500	3.7500
Singapore (Dollar)	.6141	.6171	1.6285	1.6205
South Africa (Rand)				
Commercial rate	.3651	.3648	2.7388	2.7413
Financial rate	.3153	.3153	3.1720	3.1720
South Korea (Won)	.0013180	.0013180	758.70	758.70
Spain (Peseta)	.010274	.010354	97.33	96.58
Sweden (Krona)	.1790	.1807	5.5865	5.5355
Switzerland (Franc) ..	.7321	.7372	1.3660	1.3565
30-Day Forward	.7297	.7349	1.3704	1.3607
90-Day Forward	.7248	.7298	1.3796	1..703
180-Day Forward	.7177	.7225	1.3934	1.3840
Taiwan (Dollar)	.039231	.039216	25.49	25.50
Thailand (Baht)	.03992	.03992	25.05	25.05
Turkey (Lira)	.0001985	.0001990	5037.00	5025.00
United Arab (Dirham) .	.2723	.2723	3.6725	3.6725
Uruguay (New Peso)				
Financial	.000407	.000407	2457.00	2457.00
Venezuela (Bolivar)				
Floating rate	.01647	.01645	60.73	60.80

SDR	1.43360	1.43043	.69754	.69909
ECU	1.34256	1.34093	....	....

Special Drawing Rights (SDR) are based on exchange rates for the U.S., German, British, French and Japanese currencies. Source: International Monetary Fund.

European Currency Unit (ECU) is based on a basket of community currencies. Source: European Community Commission.

c-Corrected.

EXHIBIT 13-1 Exchange rates. *Source: Wall Street Journal,* January 3, 1992.

States trades extensively. The "nominal effective exchange rate" is an index number of the weighted average of bilateral exchange rates for a number of countries, where trade shares are typically used as the weights. An effective exchange rate might be calculated for the dollar, for example, using January 1973 as the base, by calculating how much the dollar had risen or fallen since that time relative to the currencies of a number of other countries, as can be seen in Exhibit 13-2. If 20 percent of U.S. trade with that group was carried on with Canada, the Canadian dollar would get a 20 weight in that average; if 8 percent of that trade was with Great Britain, then sterling would get an 8 percent weight. Either U.S. or world trade shares could be used as weights, and published indices sometimes appear in both forms. U.S. trade shares would give the Canadian dollar the largest weight, whereas world trade shares would put the DM or the yen in that position.

Effective exchange rate indices can sometimes give an incomplete image of a currency's behavior if too few foreign currencies are included. Some of the early effective exchange rate indices for the dollar, for example, only included nine currencies of major industrialized countries. Although the majority of U.S. trade is still with those countries, the role of a number of developing countries, particularly the NICs, has grown rapidly. A moderately representative index for the

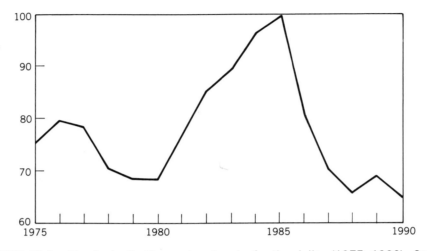

EXHIBIT 13-2 Nominal effective exchange rate for the dollar (1975–1990). *Source:* IMF *International Financial Statistics Yearbook,* 1991, pp. 750–751.

dollar would now have to include the currencies of South Korea, Taiwan, Hong Kong, Mexico, and Brazil, and an ideal index would include every country with whom the United States has significant trade.

The Real Effective Exchange Rate

In recent years a new exchange rate index has been developed which is designed to measure changes in a country's cost or price competitiveness in world markets. Such an index would begin with the nominal effective exchange rate but would adjust for inflation in the domestic economy and in the rest of the world. If, for example, the local rate of inflation was 8 percent whereas that country's trading partners had only 3 percent inflation, a fixed nominal effective exchange rate would imply a 5 percent deterioration of that country's competitive position in world markets. If the currency depreciated by 5 percent in nominal terms, just offsetting the difference in rates of inflation, the competitive position of the country would remain unchanged. The index of the real exchange rate is constructed as follows:

$$XR_r = \frac{XR_n \times P_{dom}}{P_{row}}$$

where XR_r = the real effective exchange rate

XR_n = the nominal effective exchange rate, measured as the
foreign price of local money

P_{dom} = the domestic price level, usually measured as wholesale prices.

Unit labor costs may be used as an alternative to wholesale prices.

P_{row} = the price level for the rest of the world, using the country's major trading partners as a proxy. Trade shares are used as weights.

Unit labor costs may be used as an alternative.

If the real exchange rate (XR_r) rises, the country's cost-competitive position has deteriorated because it has experienced more inflation than its trading partners after allowance for changes in the nominal exchange rate. Such a deterioration implies greater difficulty in selling exports and an increased volume of imports. Real exchange rate indices, calculated using prices and unit labor costs, can be found in the IMF, *International Financial Statistics Yearbook*. (See Exhibit 13-3.)

ALTERNATIVE VIEWS OF EQUILIBRIUM NOMINAL EXCHANGE RATES

Economists have had a variety of opinions as to how nominal exchange rates ought to be set, and the oldest of those views is implicit in the index of a real exchange rate. The Purchasing Power Parity (PPP) view is that nominal rates should move to just offset differing rates of inflation, that is, that the real exchange rate ought to be constant.[6] In a regime of floating exchange rates it was widely expected that the workings of the exchange market would produce that result, in that nominal exchange rates would naturally follow differences in rates of inflation. That has not been the case since 1963, and changes in real exchange rates were quite large during the 1980s.[7] The U.S. dollar appreciated by approximately 40 percent in real terms between 1981 and 1985, and then depreciated by a similar amount in the following four years. Some developing countries have had modest success with a "purchasing power parity crawl" in that they have adjusted otherwise fixed exchange rates by small amounts every month or so to offset the difference between local and foreign inflation. If, for example, Brazil was experiencing 40 percent inflation when the rest of the world had 4 percent inflation, a 3 percent devaluation of the Cruzado per month would maintain the ability of Brazilian firms to compete in world markets.

[6]The history of the purchasing power parity approach to exchange rate determination begins with Gustav Cassel, "Abnormal Deviations in International Exchanges," *Economic Journal,* September 1918. See also Bela Belassa, "The Purchasing Power Parity Doctrine: A Reappraisal," *Journal of Political Economy,* December 1964, pp. 584–596.

[7]The failure of market-determined exchange rates to follow purchasing power parity is analyzed in Pieter Korteweg, "Exchange Rate Policy, Monetary Policy, and Real Exchange Rate Variability," *Princeton Essays in International Finance,* No. 140, December 1980, and Jacob Frenkel, "The Collapse of Purchasing Power Parities in the 1970s," *European Economic Review,* May 1981, pp. 145–165.

Based on Relative Wholesale Prices (1985=100)

Industrial Countries

	1976	1977	1978	1979	1980	1981	1982	1983	1984	1985	1986	1987	1988	1989	1990
United States	80.8	78.8	72.8	73.0	73.7	83.9	90.3	92.9	98.9	100.0	79.8	71.7	69.0	73.5	69.6
Canada	112.4	104.7	96.6	96.0	95.6	97.8	100.9	104.7	103.0	100.0	94.6	96.0	101.8	106.0	103.1
Japan	97.2	101.0	113.3	100.7	98.1	103.3	93.8	99.1	101.4	100.0	116.8	119.0	126.6	119.8	104.9
Austria	104.3	107.3	105.5	104.5	105.4	102.5	102.1	101.4	100.3	100.0	100.7	102.3	99.4	96.9	100.0
Belgium	142.3	144.5	142.2	138.6	129.4	119.3	107.8	103.7	100.4	100.0	102.7	105.0	101.3	101.3	102.2
Denmark	112.1	110.1	111.0	108.1	100.1	99.4	98.7	100.0	99.4	100.0	102.1	105.7	104.7	103.2	108.0
Finland	103.5	99.4	89.1	90.0	95.9	102.0	103.7	97.1	99.2	100.0	94.6	95.3	97.9	102.4	102.8
France	103.9	98.0	100.6	104.0	108.9	104.1	100.0	97.7	96.3	100.0	105.3	107.5	104.4	101.7	106.7
Germany	108.8	111.4	111.8	112.5	108.7	100.3	104.1	104.8	101.1	100.0	107.4	109.8	107.6	105.6	109.6
Ireland	99.0	101.4	104.2	106.6	101.7	98.8	102.0	100.5	98.9	100.0	105.5	104.2	102.9	102.2	103.0
Italy	99.6	101.5	99.8	100.5	102.7	99.2	99.1	101.2	101.8	100.0	101.8	104.2	103.2	102.8	111.6
Netherlands	108.9	112.9	111.8	107.8	104.7	105.7	104.5	104.1	102.0	100.0	105.4	109.3	107.1	106.8	107.8
Norway	118.8	117.0	108.9	104.5	107.9	104.4	105.2	103.2	100.9	100.0	100.3	102.6	105.6	104.8	104.4
Spain	104.8	100.5	98.0	111.0	107.5	104.4	103.2	93.7	98.4	100.0	98.9	98.3	101.7	106.4	110.5
Sweden	114.9	106.6	101.4	104.3	105.5	99.2	98.4	92.9	98.5	100.0	100.2	100.8	103.9	108.6	108.2
Switzerland	107.5	101.5	116.2	110.7	101.1	99.2	103.8	105.6	102.3	100.0	108.8	112.8	111.1	104.5	110.1
United Kingdom	81.4	87.0	90.6	98.2	109.9	111.4	107.7	101.6	98.5	100.0	97.4	99.2	107.2	105.0	107.1

Based on Relative Unit Labor Costs (1985=100)

Industrial Countries

	1976	1977	1978	1979	1980	1981	1982	1983	1984	1985	1986	1987	1988	1989	1990
United States	76.9	75.0	68.6	69.4	70.1	79.1	88.6	90.7	97.1	100.0	77.1	64.7	59.9	63.0	56.6
Canada	113.9	103.6	92.8	89.6	93.9	96.5	106.2	108.8	103.2	100.0	95.9	103.7	116.0	128.6	138.2
Japan	106.9	114.2	127.6	109.0	93.4	102.6	90.4	98.0	100.1	100.0	125.7	126.9	137.4	131.3	116.1
Austria	103.6	107.1	105.1	100.9	100.2	96.7	97.0	90.7	98.5	100.0	104.5	97.5	100.9	98.0	95.1
Belgium	142.5	149.1	145.6	142.5	134.0	121.4	102.1	94.2	95.2	100.0	103.7	102.5	98.4	96.8	100.2
Denmark	112.4	111.9	113.7	113.6	99.4	93.6	92.8	93.8	95.5	100.0	109.3	120.4	118.2	115.0	118.0
Finland	111.8	105.2	89.6	88.4	89.9	93.6	96.7	94.6	99.0	100.0	96.8	96.0	97.8	102.8	110.6
France	121.1	112.2	112.1	114.1	120.0	116.4	114.3	112.0	114.1	100.0	101.9	102.2	99.4	95.8	100.8
Germany	97.2	102.8	106.2	106.6	105.2	96.4	98.6	100.1	98.7	100.0	111.3	126.0	126.3	122.6	126.8
Ireland	99.2	98.1	99.1	101.3	107.1	98.2	103.4	104.3	99.5	100.0	104.0	96.6	90.8	88.3	91.4
Italy	101.3	101.2	95.8	96.0	94.1	92.6	94.5	100.9	98.8	100.0	101.5	102.5	102.0	109.2	117.2
Netherlands	129.0	131.4	128.5	125.5	118.7	106.3	110.5	109.9	100.2	100.0	106.3	111.9	109.3	104.0	104.3
Norway	97.3	132.6	92.6	90.3	92.6	96.2	98.9	100.1	99.0	100.0	99.9	101.9	104.0	98.8	95.7
Spain	94.7	97.4	100.8	122.7	116.1	108.5	107.1	94.6	95.9	100.0	97.4	99.5	106.9	115.4	124.8
Sweden	133.3	131.7	121.1	113.4	113.6	114.7	100.5	90.5	94.1	100.0	99.7	100.8	106.7	115.3	118.8
Switzerland	109.3	100.7	116.9	109.4	98.8	99.7	107.5	109.5	100.1	100.0	104.3	108.5	99.0	93.3	96.7
United Kingdom	74.0	73.5	80.0	94.7	117.3	120.0	111.6	101.0	97.5	100.0	93.0	90.7	96.8	95.0	98.4

EXHIBIT 13-3 Real effective exchange rate indexes. *Source:* IMF *International Financial Statistics Yearbook,* 1991, pp. 110–111.

This view of equilibrium exchange rates is entirely tied to international trade in that it makes no allowance for capital account transactions as determinants of the exchange rate. In recent years exchange rates for the industrialized countries have frequently been modeled in an "asset market" context.[8] Since capital flow transactions have increasingly dominated the exchange markets in such countries, the equilibrium exchange rate is that which allows international markets for financial assets to clear. Borrowers and lenders are assumed to operate in both domestic and local markets, and therefore to move funds through the exchange market. The exchange rate then becomes an element in supply and demand functions for such assets, and the equilibrium exchange rate is determined by the clearing of these financial markets. This approach has the problem of ignoring trade. Although a majority of exchange market transactions are for capital accounts, it does seem a bit extreme to determine an equilibrium exchange rate without reference to differing rates of inflation or other factors affecting trade flows.

Finally, there is the somewhat tautological view that the equilibrium exchange rate is that which produces a zero official reserve transactions account balance. It is therefore the rate that would be observed in a regime of clean floating exchange rates. Such a view implies little permanence and instead a great deal of volatility. Large swings in short-term capital flows, in part driven by speculation, have produced large and frequently reversed changes in exchange rates during recent years. This approach therefore implies that the equilibrium exchange rate is likely to change from one month to another for reasons as ephemeral as speculative moods.

FORWARD EXCHANGE MARKETS

Forward exchange markets allow the purchase or sale of foreign exchange today for delivery and payment at a fixed date in the future. Contracts typically have maturities of 30, 60, or 90 days to match payment dates for export sales and the maturities of short-term money market assets such as Treasury bills, commercial paper, and certificates of deposits (CDs). If, for example, a U.S. importer is committed to pay 500,000 DM for German exports in 90 days, a forward purchase of DM is a convenient way to avoid the possibility that the currency may appreciate over that time, which would impose higher dollar costs on the importer.

Trading in forward contracts is carried on by the same banks and traders that do the spot trading described earlier in this chapter. The arrangements are similar

---

[8]For a discussion of the asset market approach to exchange rate determination, see William Branson, "Asset Markets and Relative Prices in Exchange Rate Determination," *Reprints in International Finance* No. 20, 1980, International Finance Section, Princeton University. See also Polly Allen and Peter Kenen, *Asset Markets, Exchange Rates, and Economic Integration* (New York: Cambridge University Press, 1980). For a survey of empirical results in tests of alternative models of exchange rate determination, see Richard Levich, "Empirical Studies of Exchange Rates: Price Behavior, Rate Determination, and Market Efficiency," in Ronald Jones and Peter Kenen, eds., *Handbook of International Economics,* Vol. II (Amsterdam: North-Holland Press, 1985), Ch. 19.

to those for spot trading, except that settlement takes place in 30, 60, or 90 days rather than in 2 days. For a few major currencies trading is common at 180- and 360-day maturities, and longer contracts are sometimes done on a negotiated basis. Forward exchange rates for a number of currencies can be found in Exhibit 13-4.

As can be seen below, forward rates frequently differ from prevailing spot rates. If a currency is worth less in the forward than in the spot market, as is the case for sterling in this table, it is said to be at a forward discount. A forward premium exists in the opposite situation. Although those involved in these markets on a day-to-day basis frequently quote such discounts or premiums in terms of pennies, economists usually refer to annual percentages. This is done to make such discounts or premiums directly comparable to annual interest rates. If, for example, sterling were trading at $2.00 in the spot market and at $2.01 in the 90-day forward market, the premium would appear to be one-half percent (1/200), but that is for only 90 days or one-quarter of a year. The premium measured as an annual rate is four times one-half percent, which is 2 percent. The reasons for using annual rates rather than monetary units to measure this premium will become more apparent when we discuss the factors determining forward rates.

The forward market is similar to the futures market for commodities such as corn or soybeans, but there are small differences between the two types of arrangements. All futures contracts close on the same day of the month, whereas forward contracts close a fixed number of days after they are signed, which can be any day of the month. Futures contracts are relatively liquid, in that they can be resold in commodity exchanges before maturity, whereas forward contracts usually

EXCHANGE RATES

Thursday, January 2, 1992
The New York foreign exchange selling rates below apply to trading among banks in amounts of $1 million and more, as quoted at 3 p.m. Eastern time by Bankers Trust Co., Telerate Systems Inc. and other sources. Retail transactions provide fewer units of foreign currency per dollar.

Country	U.S. $ equiv. Thurs.	U.S. $ equiv. Tues.	Currency per U.S. $ Thurs.	Currency per U.S. $ Tues.
Britain (Pound)	1.8650	1.8695	.5362	.5349
30-Day Forward	1.8547	1.8587	.5392	.5380
90-Day Forward	1.8348	1.8388	.5450	.5438
180-Day Forward	1.8059	1.8098	.5537	.5525
Canada (Dollar)	.8688	.8654	1.1510	1.1555
30-Day Forward	.8665	.8632	1.1541	1.1585
90-Day Forward	.8624	.8590	1.1596	1.1642
180-Day Forward	.8572	.8538	1.1666	1.1713
France (Franc)	.19120	.19305	5.2300	5.1800
30-Day Forward	.19022	.19205	5.2570	5.2070
90-Day Forward	.18838	.19015	5.3085	5.2590
180-Day Forward	.18576	.18742	5.3832	5.3357
Germany (Mark)	.6532	.6601	1.5310	1.5150
30-Day Forward	.6502	.6570	1.5379	1.5220
90-Day Forward	.6444	.6511	1.5518	1.5358
180-Day Forward	.6361	.6425	1.5721	1.5565
Japan (Yen)	.008026	.008013	124.60	124.80
30-Day Forward	.008017	.008006	124.74	124.91
90-Day Forward	.007999	.007983	125.02	125.26
180-Day Forward	.007977	.007957	125.36	125.67
Switzerland (Franc) ..	.7321	.7372	1.3660	1.3565
30-Day Forward	.7297	.7349	1.3704	1.3607
90-Day Forward	.7248	.7298	1.3796	1.3703
180-Day Forward	.7177	.7225	1.3934	1.3840

EXHIBIT 13-4   Spot and Forward Exchange rates. *Source: Wall Street Journal,* January 3, 1992.

have to be held to maturity. Although forward contracts are traded by banks in large transactions, futures are traded in commodity exchanges such as the Chicago Board of Trade in smaller transactions and with sizable brokerage commissions.

A futures market for foreign currency exists as the International Monetary Market (IMM) in Chicago (data for which can be found in Exhibit 13-5) where trading is carried on just as it would be for commodities such as copper or wheat. It is used both to hedge risks arising from relatively small trade transactions and to provide a vehicle for speculation.[9]

	Open	High	Low	Settle	Change	Lifetime High	Low	Open Interest
JAPAN YEN (IMM)—12.5 million yen; $ per yen (.00)								
Mar	.8045	.8058	.7997	.8010	+ .0019	.8058	.7000	53,127
June	.8025	.8033	.7979	.7987	+ .0020	.8033	.7015	2,897
Sept	....	....		.7972	+ .0021	.7945	.7265	1,317
Dec	....	....		.7964	+ .0022	.7940	.7512	1,623
Mr93	....	....		.7965	+ .0022	....	....	910

Est vol 22,562; vol Tues 8,189; open int 59,874, +2,103.

DEUTSCHEMARK (IMM)—125,000 marks; $ per mark								
Mar	.6520	.6545	.6442	.6474	− .0037	.6563	.5353	52,486
June	.6438	.6455	.6360	.6389	− .0036	.6478	.5322	1,607
Sept	....	....		.6311	− .0036	.6385	.5685	367

Est vol 46,664; vol Tues 10,950; open int 54,472, +910.

CANADIAN DOLLAR (IMM)—100,000 dlrs.; $ per Can $								
Mar	.8624	.8639	.8617	.8631	+ .0029	.8857	.8253	18,578
June	.8570	.8586	.8565	.8575	+ .0031	.8820	.8330	1,802
Sept	....	....		.8522	+ .0033	.8774	.8348	106

Est vol 3,243; vol Tues 1,355; open int 20,540, −253.

BRITISH POUND (IMM)—62,500 pds.; $ per pound								
Mar	1.8528	1.8574	1.8360	1.8434	−.0014	1.8646	1.5560	20,172
June	1.8220	1.8280	1.8060	1.8142	−.0006	1.8346	1.6410	381

Est vol 9,951; vol Tues 3,105; open int 20,576, −70.

SWISS FRANC (IMM)—125,000 francs; $ per franc								
Mar	.7325	.7370	.7232	.7279	− .0021	.7394	.6225	25,880
June	.7257	.7295	.7165	.7208	− .0020	.7325	.6546	390

Est vol 16,801; vol Tues 6,622; open int 26,301, −144.

AUSTRALIAN DOLLAR (IMM)—100,000 dlrs.; $ per A.$								
Mar	.7511	.7523	.7503	.7523	− .0042	.7880	.7540	861

Est vol 177; vol Tues 63; open int 868, −4.

U.S. DOLLAR INDEX (FINEX)—500 times USDX								
Mar	84.47	85.28	84.20	84.96	+ .27	98.90	84.20	4,997
June	85.75	86.39	86.39	86.25	+ .28	100.15	85.78	143

Est vol 2,637; vol Tues 631; open int 5,144, −196.
The index: High 84.06; Low 83.12; Close 83.83 +.18

—OTHER CURRENCY FUTURES—

Settlement prices of selected contracts. Volume and open interest of all contract months.

British Pound (MCE) 12,500 pounds; $ per pound
Mar 1.8434 −.0014; Est. vol. 110; Open Int. 256
Japanese Yen (MCE) 6.25 million yen; $ per yen (.00)
Mar .8010 +.0019; Est. vol. 125; Open Int. 219
Swiss Franc (MCE) 62,500 francs; $ per franc
Mar .7279 −.0021; Est. vol. 275; Open Int. 205
Deutschemark (MCE) 62,500 marks; $ per mark
Mar .6474 −.0037; Est. vol. 500; Open Int. 835
BP/DM Cross Rate (IMM) US $50,000 times BP/DM
Mar 2.8475 +.0145; Est. vol. 5; Open Int. 30
DM/JY Cross Rate (IMM) US $125,000 times DM/JY
Mar .8082 −.0066; Est. vol. 4; Open Int. 58
FINEX—Financial Instrument Exchange, a division of the New York Cotton Exchange. IMM—International Monetary Market at the Chicago Mercantile Exchange. MCE—MidAmerica Commodity Exchange.

EXHIBIT 13-5 Foreign Exchange Futures. *Source: Wall Street Journal,* January 3, 1992.

[9]The Chicago futures market for foreign exchange is discussed in Normal Fieleke, "The Rise of the Foreign Currency Futures Market," Federal Reserve Bank of Boston, *New England Economic Review,* March 1985.

Foreign Exchange Options

Futures or forward contracts obligate the holder to complete the transaction at maturity, unless it is sold in the meantime or offset by a contract in the opposite direction. A 90-day forward purchase of sterling, for example, could be canceled after 30 days through a sale of 60-day sterling. Otherwise the contract goes to maturity, whether or not the outcome is favorable. In contrast, an option contract provides the opportunity to purchase or sell a fixed amount of a currency or a common stock during a fixed period of time at a guaranteed or strike price, but the holder of the option has the alternative of not completing the purchase or sale.[10] A "put" gives the buyer of the contract the right to sell the asset, and a "call" provides the opportunity to buy. Because an option is a one-sided bet, an often sizable fee is required to purchase such a contract as can be seen in Exhibit 13-6. Options markets for common stocks have been active for some time, but such arrangements have only recently developed for foreign currencies.

Purchases of puts or calls can help minimize risks of loss on a speculation while providing the possibility of making a large profit. If, for example, a sterling call is purchased, the possible loss is limited to the fee or price of the call. If sterling rises by more than that price, the call is profitable. If sterling falls, the option is not exercised, and the loss is limited to that price. Options are also a means of hedging risks from transactions that may not be completed. If, for example, a U.S. firm were in the midst of negotiations to buy a German business and knew approximately what the DM price would be, an options contract could be used to guarantee the availability of the DM at a known price if the negotiations succeeded, but would still allow the firm to escape any commitment to purchase DMs if the negotiations were not successful.

Reasons for Forward Trading

The forward exchange market has three separate, but related, roles in international commercial and financial transactions. First, it is a way of hedging risks arising from typical credit terms on export/import business. If Montgomery Ward agrees to pay 50 million yen for television sets to be sold from its U.S. stores, it will not make that payment when it becomes committed to the transaction or even when the sets are delivered. It will normally have 30-, 60-, or 90-day payment terms. Consequently, it faces the risk that the yen may appreciate during that period, resulting in higher dollar costs for the television sets. The yen might, of course, fall instead, which would save Montgomery Ward money, but if the company does not view itself as being in the business of speculating on the future exchange rate for the Japanese currency, a forward contract to purchase yen becomes a convenient way to avoid any uncertainty as to the dollar cost of the sets. As soon as the commitment to purchase the television sets is binding, an immediate purchase of

---

[10]Foreign exchange options are discussed in Robert Feldman, "Foreign Currency Options," *Finance and Development,* December 1985.

OPTIONS
PHILADELPHIA EXCHANGE

Option & Underlying	Strike Price	Calls—Last			Puts—Last		
		Jan	Feb	Mar	Jan	Feb	Mar
50,000 Australian Dollars-cents per unit.							
ADollr.....	75	r	0.98	1.18	r	r	r
75.99	76	0.19	0.49	r	r	r	r
75.99	77	0.02	r	0.38	r	r	r
75.99	78	r	r	r	2.42	r	3.00
31,250 British Pounds-cents per unit.							
BPound ..	177½	r	r	r	r	0.50	1.50
186.98 ..	180	6.65	r	r	r	r	2.25
186.98 ..	182½	r	r	r	r	2.01	3.08
186.98 ..	185	r	3.15	3.80	0.85	3.20	3.75
186.8 ..	187½	0.82	2.45	r	r	r	5.75
186.98 ..	190	0.33	1.50	1.80	3.00	5.50	r
186.98 ..	192½	r	r	1.16	r	r	r
186.98 ..	195	r	r	0.84	r	r	r
50,000 Canadian Dollars-European Style.							
CDollar....	86½	r	r	r	0.12	r	r
50,000 Canadian Dollars-cents per unit.							
CDollr.....	84½	r	r	r	r	0.10	0.18
86.54	85½	r	r	r	r	r	0.40
86.54	86	r	r	0.93	r	0.33	0.57
86.54	87	r	r	0.38	r	r	r
1,000,000 cross.				GermanMark-JapaneseYen			
62,500 German Marks-cents per unit.							
DMark	61	r	r	r	r	0.16	r
65.90	62	r	r	r	r	r	0.58
65.90	63	r	2.54	3.26	r	r	0.87
65.90	64	r	1.70	r	0.13	0.83	1.28
65.90	65½	0.44	0.98	r	0.75	1.12	1.71
65.90	66	0.30	0.79	0.96	0.92	r	r
65.90	67	0.14	0.49	0.75	r	r	r
6,250,000 Japanese Yen-100ths of a cent per unit.							
JYen......	76	r	r	4.50	r	r	0.16
80.12	76½	4.18	r	r	r	r	r
80.12	77	r	r	r	r	0.15	0.32
80.12	77½	r	r	r	r	0.20	r
80.12	78	r	r	2.69	r	0.24	0.46
80.12	78½	1.85	r	r	r	r	r
80.12	79	1.47	r	2.16	0.07	0.44	0.83
80.12	79½	1.00	r	r	0.14	r	r
80.12	80	0.82	1.40	1.45	0.42	0.84	r
80.12	80½	0.38	1.15	r	0.60	1.12	r
80.12	81	0.41	0.88	1.16	r	r	r
80.12	81½	0.13	r	r	r	r	r
80.12	82	0.14	0.52	0.66	r	r	0.71
80.12	82½	0.07	r	r	r	r	r
80.12	83	r	0.31	0.53	r	r	r
6,250,000 Japanese Yen-European Style.							
JYen......	74	r	r	r	r	r	0.06
80.12	78	r	r	2.88	r	r	0.48
80.12	82	r	r	0.70	r	r	r
62,500 Swiss Francs-European Style.							
SFranc....	72½	r	r	r	0.32	r	r
73.59	73	r	r	r	0.24	r	r
62,500 Swiss Francs-cents per unit.							
SFranc....	69	r	r	r	r	0.16	r
73.59	70	r	r	r	r	r	0.73
73.59	72	1.45	r	r	r	0.99	1.44
73.59	73	r	1.65	r	0.53	r	r
73.59	74	0.50	r	r	r	1.90	r
73.59	75	r	0.59	r	r	r	r
Total Call Vol	19,735				Call Open Int	346,834	
Total Put Vol	13,362				Put Open Int	512,763	

EXHIBIT 13-6 Foreign Exchange Options. *Source: Wall Street Journal,* January 3, 1992.

50 million yen in the forward market means that Montgomery Ward has eliminated the exchange risk arising from its delayed payment to the Japanese manufacturer.

When fixed parities existed under the Bretton Woods system and market exchange rates fluctuated only within a narrow band, many firms did not worry about such risks, and they frequently left accounts payable or receivable denominated in a foreign currency uncovered. The introduction of flexible exchange rates in the early 1970s greatly increased the perceived risk of such behavior and reportedly resulted in a sharp increase in the volume of forward contracts being traded as firms sought to eliminate such exposure.

The second major role of the forward market is to cover risks arising from interest arbitrage. When banks or other financial institutions seek to take advantage of higher interest rates available in foreign markets, they typically seek to avoid the risk that the currency in which they invest may depreciate. Undertaking a "swap" in which a currency is simultaneously bought spot and sold forward, is a way of covering such risk. New York banks, for example, might hope to observe the following situation:

U.K. Treasury bill yield	14 percent
U.S. Treasury bill yield	10 percent
Uncovered differential	4 percent favoring the U.K.
Forward discount on sterling	2 percent
Covered differential	2 percent favoring the U.K.

U.K. interest rates are 4 percentage points above those in New York, but switching into sterling for 90 days involves a sizable risk that the currency could depreciate by enough (or more than enough) to destroy the transaction's profitability. If, however, sterling is bought in the spot market (in order to purchase the 14 percent bills) and simultaneously sold forward, the cost is only 2 percent (measured as an annual rate), leaving a net profit of 2 percent. For reasons that will be discussed soon, this situation would be extremely unlikely, and banks would normally face a situation such as the following:

U.K. Treasury bill yield	14 percent
U.S. Treasury bill yield	10 percent
Uncovered differential	4 percent favoring the U.K.
Forward discount on sterling	4 percent
Covered differential	0

Finally, forward contracts are used to take on risk as well as to avoid it. If speculators believe, for example, that a currency will depreciate during the next 90 days to a level below the existing forward exchange rate, a forward sale of that currency is a convenient way to gamble on that outcome without investing large sums of money. If sterling were trading at $1.86 in the spot market and at $1.85 in the 90-day forward market when a speculator believed that a depreciation of the spot rate of considerably more than 1 cent was likely during the next three months, he or she could sell forward sterling at $1.85 and wait. If the exchange rate was, for example, $1.83 at the end of the contract, the speculator would purchase the currency spot at that rate and deliver it on the forward contract, for a net profit of 2 cents times the number of pounds sterling in the contract. If, of course, sterling were $1.88 at the end of the contract, he or she would absorb a loss of 3 cents per pound. Since this is not an option, the speculator is obligated to complete the losing transaction, and the bank with which he or she did business would normally have required that the speculator provide enough money as "margin" at the beginning of the contract to protect it against the possibility of an attempt to evade that obligation.

Factors Determining Forward Rates

The determination of forward exchange rates can be viewed in two separate ways, but the differences are more apparent than real. The two approaches can be reconciled and finally regarded as a single approach under reasonable assumptions. First, forward rates are set through the interest arbitrage process described earlier. If New York banks faced the 2 percent covered interest rate spread that appears in the first set of numbers on page 288, they would purchase spot sterling in enormous volumes, driving the currency up, and they would simultaneously sell forward sterling in the same volumes, driving it down. The 2 percent forward discount on sterling would widen to 4 percent in the twinkling of an eye, eliminating the profitability of the swap transaction.[11] The arbitraging process will normally produce the following outcome, when forward rates are measured as annual percentage discounts or premiums:

$$\text{Sterling forward discount} = r_{uk} - r_{us}$$

Or, making the same statement for the opposite situation:

$$\text{Sterling forward premium} = r_{us} - r_{uk}$$

Sterling should trade at a forward discount that equals the difference between British and U.S. interest rates, and vice versa. Any time this is not true, the possibility for arbitrage profits exists and money can be expected to move in sufficient volume to force the forward rate to the level at which such profits are eliminated. This adjustment of the forward rate should be instantaneous. When covered interest arbitrage profits have appeared to exist, it has often been because (1) the two assets were not of the same perceived risk, so that a risk premium existed on one of them, or because (2) investors feared the imposition of exchange controls within 90 days that would make it impossible to complete the arbitrage transactions. Sometimes the appearance of such profits has been created when interest and exchange rate data were not collected for the exact same times. Using average daily interest rates and daily closing exchange rates, for example, could produce the appearance of arbitrage profits when none actually existed.

---

[11]The first presentation of the interest parity model of forward rate determination appears in J. M. Keynes, *A Tract on Monetary Reform* (London: Macmillan, 1923), pp. 113–139. See also Paul Einzig, *The Dynamic Theory of Forward Exchange* (London: Macmillan, 1967), and S. C. Tsaing, "The Theory of Forward Exchange and Effects of Government Intervention on the Forward Exchange Market," *IMF Staff Papers,* April 1959.

The second approach to the forward rate is that it represents the exchange markets' consensus prediction of what will happen to the spot exchange rate over the period of the forward contract. If, for example, spot sterling is trading at $1.86 and the 90-day forward rate is $1.84, the market expects spot sterling to depreciate by 2 cents during the next three months. If this were not the case, speculators would undertake transactions that would move the forward rate to a level that would represent their consensus expectation. If, for example, forward sterling were $1.84 when most market participants thought it would be no lower than $1.86 in 90 days, speculators would buy it heavily at $1.84 in expectation of a sizable profit. The volume of such purchases would be large enough to push the rate to the expected spot rate, when the buying pressure would end. It is not necessary that everybody have the same expectation, for that is obviously impossible. It is only necessary that the average expectation match the forward rate so that speculative purchases and sales roughly match. If, for example, 20 percent of the market participants expect the spot rate to be $1.86 in 90 days, whereas 40 percent think it will be lower and 40 percent think it will be higher, the forward market should clear at $1.86 because the number of people speculating that it will be higher will equal the number of people betting on the opposite outcome, and the market will clear. (For the sake of simplicity, this example assumes that each market participant is prepared to gamble the same amount of money.) To use an inelegant analogy, the forward rate is like the point spread on a basketball game; it represents the consensus prediction of how the game will end. Otherwise, bets on one team will greatly exceed those on the other, and the spread will be adjusted.

These two approaches to forward rate determination seem different, but they can be reconciled; both are dominated by differences in expected rates of inflation. If British interest rates exceed those in the United States by 4 percentage points, it strongly suggests that investors expect 4 percentage points more inflation in the United Kingdom than in the United States. Real interest rates are thought to be arbitraged together because if people expect more inflation in one currency than another, a higher nominal interest rate will be required to attract them to hold assets in that currency. The following statement represents the arbitraging together of real interest rates:

$$r_{uk} - r_{us} = \text{expected UK inflation} - \text{expected US inflation}$$

The forward discount on sterling, which superficially reflects differing nominal interest rates, more fundamentally reflects the fact that more inflation is expected in Britain than in the United States.

Speculators can be viewed as forming exchanging rate expectations on the basis of inflationary predictions. If national monies are ultimately claims on real goods and services, exchange rates should reflect the relative purchasing powers of those monies, which is to say that they should reflect purchasing power parity, as discussed earlier. If speculators expect nominal exchange rates to follow purchasing power parity, indicating that they expect a constant real exchange rate, they will form expectations of future spot rate behavior on the basis of forecasts of differences in rates of inflation. Trading forward sterling at a discount of 4 percent (annual rate) indicates the speculators' belief that Great Britain will experience 4 percentage points more inflation than will the United States and therefore that spot sterling will have to depreciate at a 4 percent annual rate to maintain purchasing power parity.

Both the interest arbitrage and the expected-spot-rate approaches to forward rate determination can be traced back to the same origins—expectations with regard to relative rates of inflation. The following statements summarize this conclusion:

Expected UK inflat. – Expected US inflat. $= r_{UK} - r_{US} =$ Fwd. discount on sterling

Expected UK inflat. – Expected US inflat. = Expected spot sterling depr. = Fwd. discount sterling

Therefore:

Expected UK inflat. – Expected US inflat. = Fwd. discount sterling

This might be visualized more easily in Figure 13-2. The forward rate reflects both differences in nominal interest rates and expected changes in the spot exchange rate, both of which result from differences in expected rates of inflation. The way inflationary expectations are formed is a more complex matter. It might begin with differences in the rates of growth of national money supplies, but that subject is beyond the scope of this chapter.

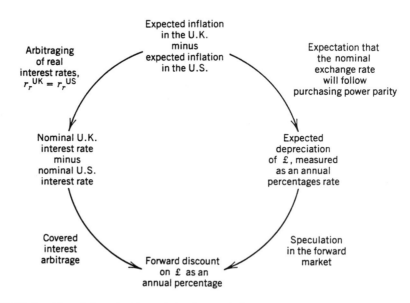

FIGURE 13-2 The determination of the forward discount on sterling.

QUESTIONS FOR STUDY AND REVIEW

1. Suppose you are a bicycle dealer. You have signed a contract in which you agree to import 1000 bicycles from an English manufacturer and to pay £100,000 for them six months from today. How exactly can you use the forward exchange market to protect yourself against exchange rate risk?

2. Where does one look in a nation's balance of payments for items that give rise to a demand for foreign exchange? For a supply of foreign exchange?

3. What is the essential difference between a hedger and a speculator in the foreign exchange market?

4. How will each of the following tend to affect the foreign exchange rate for Country A's currency (the peso)? Also state why in each case.
   a. An increase in foreign demand for Country A's exports.
   b. A rise in the rate of inflation in Country A.
   c. A rise in foreign interest rates.
   d. A fiscal stimulus to GNP in Country A (e.g., via tax reductions).

5. Suppose one-year U.S. Treasury bills yield 10 percent, and one-year German Treasury bills yield 6 percent. If the spot exchange rate is $0.50 = DM 1.00, what will be the forward exchange rate? Explain why.

6. Under what circumstances will the supply curve of foreign exchange become backward sloping?

7. "If the spot exchange rate is DM 4.00 = $1.00, and short-term interest rates are 10 percent in Germany, 6 percent in the United States, the forward exchange rate will probably be more than 4 DM for $1.00." Do you agree? Defend your answer.

8. If French demand for imports from Germany has zero elasticity, what does this imply about the supply curve of francs in the foreign exchange market?

9. When a nation chooses to peg its currency at a given exchange rate vis-à-vis another currency, what exactly must its central bank do?

10. Explain how the elasticity of demand for foreign exchange is influenced by the elasticity of home demand for imports and by the elasticity of home supply of import-competing goods.

11. If U.S. short-term interest rates are 12 percent and Japanese rates are 9 percent and the Japanese yen is trading at a 3 percent (annual rate) discount in the forward market, what does that imply about the market's expectations with regard to U.S. and Japanese inflation? Why?

SELECTED REFERENCES

Aliber, Robert. *The International Money Game,* 5th ed. New York: Basic Books, 1987.

Chrystal, K. Alec. "A Guide to Foreign Exchange Markets." *Federal Reserve Bank of St. Louis Review,* March 1984, pp. 5–18.

George, Abraham M., and Ian Giddy. *International Finance Handbook.* New York: John Wiley, 1983.

Kubarych, Roger M. *Foreign Exchange Markets in the United States,* rev. ed. Federal Reserve Bank of New York, 1983.

Melvin, Michael. *International Money and Finance.* New York: Harper & Row, 1989.

Pauls, B. Diane. "U.S. Exchange Rate Policy: Bretton Woods to Present." *Federal Reserve Bulletin,* November 1990, pp. 891–908.

Walker, Townsend. *A Guide for Using the Foreign Exchange Market.* New York: John Wiley, 1981.

Weismeiller, Rudi. *Managing a Foreign Exchange Department.* Cambridge, Eng.: Woodhead-Faulkner, 1985.

14

THE IMPACT OF TRADE ON THE DETERMINATION OF NATIONAL INCOME

Most of the latter half of this book deals with exchange rates and the balance of payments, but it is now necessary to turn briefly to the effects of international trade on the workings of a domestic macroeconomy. This chapter seeks to add international trade to the typical Keynesian national income determination model that is taught in introductory economics courses in order to see how the macroeconomic behavior of an economy is affected. It turns out that the effects are sizable, particularly for an economy in which exports and imports play a large role. Macroeconomic shocks that originate within an economy have somewhat milder domestic impacts because the Keynesian multiplier is smaller, but business cycles can be transmitted from one economy to another through trade flows. Before dealing with the impacts of trade, however, it may be useful to review briefly the closed economy Keynesian model.

A CLOSED ECONOMY

We begin with the case of a closed economy. Our economy is assumed to have two sectors: a business sector and a household sector. We assume that it has no government and no transactions with the outside world, and that prices remain unchanged.

Determination of the Level of Income

The gross national product of our economy is defined as the money value of all final products (goods and services) produced in a period of time, usually a year. This product can be divided into two categories, consumption (C) and investment (I). Thus we have the following definitional equation:

(1) $Y = C + I$

where Y stands for GNP.

In the production of goods and services making up the GNP, an equal amount of income is generated in the form of wages, rent, interest, and profit. All income earned is either spent for consumption or saved. Thus we have another definitional relation to state the disposition of income:

(2) $Y = C + S$

Setting equations 1 and 2 equal to each other, we obtain:

$$C + S = Y = C + I$$

and thus $C + S = C + I$

Subtracting C from both sides yields the important identity which states that saving equals investment:

(3) $S = I$

Equations 1, 2, and 3 express ex post, or realized, relationships. They hold true, by definition, for any past period. I is actual investment, which may contain an unintended component in the form of the accumulation of unsold inventories. Intended investment equals savings only when the economy is in equilibrium.

The amount of investment expenditure is assumed to be exogenously determined (i.e., it is independent of the level of income).

Consumption, on the other hand, is a function of income: When income increases, consumption also increases, but not by as much as the increase in income. This gives us a relationship (a "consumption function") such as the following:

(4) $C = C_a + cY$

where C_a is the amount of consumption expenditure that is not a function of income, and c is the fraction of income $(0 < c < 1)$ that is spent for consumption. This fraction (c) is the marginal propensity to consume, defined as

$$(5) \quad c = \frac{\Delta C}{\Delta Y}$$

the *change* in C divided by the *change* in Y. For convenience we will assume that the marginal propensity to consume is a constant fraction.

We can obtain an expression for the equilibrium level of income by substituting equation 4 into 1, as follows:

$$(1) \quad Y = C + I$$
$$(4) \quad C = C_a + cY$$
$$Y = (C_a + cY) + I$$
$$Y - cY = C_a + I$$
$$Y(1 - c) = C_a + I$$
$$(6) \quad Y = \left(\frac{1}{1 - c}\right)(C_a + I)$$

Equation 6 states that the equilibrium level of income is equal to a *multiplier* $[1/(1 - c)]$ times autonomous consumption plus investment.

A numerical example can be used to illustrate the determination of the equilibrium level of income. We assume the following consumption function:

$$(7) \quad C = 50 + 0.60Y$$

where $C_a = 50$, and $c = 0.60$. Thus we assume that 60 percent of any increase in income will be spent for consumption.

This relationship is depicted in Figure 14-1a, which also shows the determination of Y for a given amount of investment. The consumption function, $C = 50 + 0.60Y$, shows how much is spent for consumption (vertical axis) at various levels of income (horizontal axis). The slope of the consumption function represents the marginal propensity to consume, $c = \Delta C/\Delta Y = 0.60$.

The 45° line in Figure 14-1a is a guideline representing points that are equidistant from the vertical and horizontal axes; thus the level of income can be measured either horizontally or vertically. Since all income is either spent for consumption or saved, the vertical difference between the consumption function (labeled C) and the 45° line represents the amount of saving at any level of income. At point B, where the two lines intersect, all income is spent for consumption; hence saving equals zero. At lower levels of income, saving is negative—that is, people are dis-saving, or dipping into past savings in order to spend more than their current incomes.

Given the amount of planned investment expenditures, which is assumed to be the same for all levels of income, we can now draw a line representing total expenditures $(C + I)$ for every level of income. In Figure 14-1a, we assume

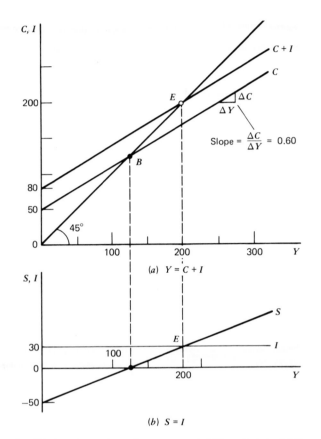

FIGURE 14-1   Equilibrium in a closed economy. (a) Y = C + I. (b) S = I.

$I = 30$, and that amount is added vertically to the consumption function to give us the $C + I$ line, also called the aggregate demand function.

The equilibrium level of income is that level at which aggregate demand just equals the level of income as indicated by the 45° line. In Figure 14-1a, the $C + I$ line intersects the 45° line at E, indicating an equilibrium level of income of 200. It is clear that only one such point exists: At lower levels of Y, aggregate demand $(C + I)$ is above the 45° guideline; at higher levels of Y, aggregate demand is below the 45° guideline.

The solution can also be obtained by substituting equation 7 into equation 1, setting $I = 30$, and solving, as follows:

(1) $Y = C + I$
(7) $C = 50 + 0.60Y$
      $Y = (50 + 0.60Y) + I = (50 + 0.60Y) + 30$
      $Y = 0.60Y + 80$
      $Y - 0.60Y = 80$
      $Y(1 - 0.60) = 80$
      $Y = \left(\dfrac{1}{1 - 0.60}\right)80 = 200$

The equilibrium level of income may also be defined as the level at which intended investment just equals the amount of saving people are willing to take out of income. In Figure 14-1b, we show the saving function (S), obtained from the upper part of the diagram by taking the vertical difference between consumption at the 45° line at each level of income. The saving function can also be obtained by substituting equation 7 into equation 2, as follows:

(2) $Y = C + S$
(7) $C = 50 + 0.60Y$
$Y = (50 + 0.60Y) + S$
(8) $S = -50 + 0.40Y$

The saving function shows that saving increases as income increases. Equation 8 indicates that 40 percent of any increase in income will be saved. The fraction, 0.40, is the marginal propensity to save, defined as

(9) $s = \Delta S/\Delta Y$

As noted earlier, we assume that there are no taxes so that all income is either spent for consumption or saved. Thus it is clear that the marginal propensities to consume and save add up to 1.00, that is:

(10) $c + s = 1$

In our example, of each $1.00 of additional income, $0.60 will be spent for consumption and $0.40 will be saved.

The level of planned investment is shown in Figure 14-1b by a horizontal line at $I = 30$. The equilibrium level of income, at which $S = I$, is indicated by point E, where $Y = 200$.

Algebraically, this solution entails substituting equation 8 into equation 3 and setting $I = 30$, as follows:

(3) $S = I$
(8) $S = -50 + 0.40Y$
$-50 + 0.40Y = 30$
$0.40Y = 80$
$Y = \left(\frac{1}{0.40}\right)80 = 200$

The two parts of Figure 14-1 contain the same information and thus yield the same outcome, although the lower part is especially useful for the case of an open economy, as we will see.

The Multiplier in a Closed Economy

We are now in a position to explain how a change in investment expenditure (actually, any autonomous change in expenditure) will affect the level of income, consumption, and saving. To continue the given example, suppose planned investment increases by 10. This change appears as an upward shift in the aggregate demand function (to $C + I'$) in Figure 14-2a, and as an upward shift in the horizontal investment line (to I') in Figure 14-2b. In both diagrams we see that the equilibrium level of income rises by 25, from 200 to 225. Thus income rises by a multiple of $2\frac{1}{2}$ times the initial increase in investment ($25 \div 10 = 2\frac{1}{2}$).

The size of this multiplier is determined by the division of an increment of income between consumption and saving—that is, the value of the marginal propensities to consume and save. In this case, with $c = 0.60$, when investment rises by 10, thus generating an initial increase in income of 10, 60 percent of that increase in income is spent for consumption. Therefore the first-round increase in consumption is 6. That increase in consumer expenditure is income to those who produce and sell consumer goods, and they in turn spend 60 percent of their increased income, so in the second round $\Delta C = 6 \times (60\%) = 3.6$. This process generates a sequence:

$$\Delta Y = 10 + 10(0.60) + 10(0.60)^2 + \cdots$$

$$\Delta Y = 10(1 + 0.60 + 0.60^2 + \cdots)$$

$$\Delta Y = 10\left(\frac{1}{1 - 0.60}\right) = 10(2.5) = 25$$

More generally:

$$\Delta Y = \Delta I \left(\frac{1}{1 - c}\right)$$

where c is the marginal propensity to consume.[1] The multiplier is the expression in parentheses:

$$(11) \quad k = \frac{1}{1 - c}$$

Since $c + s = 1$, we can replace $(1 - c)$ in the denominator and write the multiplier as

$$(12) \quad k = \frac{1}{s}$$

This last formulation focuses on the so-called leakage from the circulator flow of income. When people use their income to buy goods and services, their expenditure represents income to the seller and is thus returned to the income stream. That part of income which is not spent, namely, the part saved, causes subsequent increments to income to be smaller, and thus reduces the size of the multiplier. In equation 12, the larger the value of s, the smaller is the multiplier, k.

[1]The sum of an infinite sequence, where $0 < c < 1$, is

$$1 + c + c^2 + c^3 + \cdots = \frac{1}{1 - c}$$

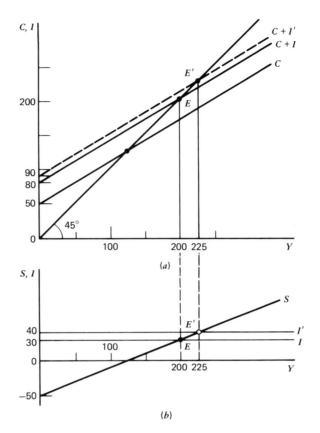

FIGURE 14-2   The multiplier in a closed economy.

AN OPEN ECONOMY

To extend this analysis to an economy that is engaged in trade with the outside world, we must allow for an additional sector, the foreign sector. Thus we will now include a third category of final product—exports of goods and services—and a third use of income—imports of goods and service.

Determination of the Level of Income

The gross national product is still defined as the money value of all final products produced in a given period of time. Since we are still omitting the government sector, the gross national product can be divided into three categories, and we have the following definitional equations for the product:

(13) $Y = C_d + I + X$

and for the disposition of income:

(14) $Y = C_d + S + M$

where X and M represent exports and imports of goods and services, respectively, and C_d is consumption of domestically produced goods and services.

In equation 13, we define Y as the value of final product produced domestically — that is, net of imports. In the case of consumption, this is denoted by C_d, with the subscript d serving as a reminder that we mean consumption of domestically produced goods and services. However, we are also assuming that I and X are net of imports.[2]

Now we can set equations 13 and 14 equal to each other and subtract C_d from both sides, as before:

$$C_d + S + M = C_d + I + X$$
(15) $S + M = I + X$

Equation 15 states that, ex post, saving plus imports (leakages) must equal investment plus exports (the exogenous injections of expenditure). Although this relationship is a definitional one, it has interesting and useful interpretations. For example, when written in the form:

$$S - I = X - M$$

it indicates a necessary relation between the trade balance and domestic saving and investment. If domestic investment exceeds saving in any period, imports must exceed exports. Similarly, if a country has an export surplus, its domestic saving must exceed investment; it is making savings available to the rest of the

---

[2]If C, I, and X include imported components, then we should subtract M in order to obtain domestically produced final product:

$$Y = C + I + X - M$$

M is then equal to the sum of imports in all three categories:

$$M = C_m + I_m + X_m$$

We can thus subtract these items from each category separately; thus

$$Y = (C - C_m) + (I - I_m) + (X - X_m)$$

This gives us a statement for Y that is net of imports:

$$Y = C_d + I_d + X_d$$

where $C_d = C - C_m$, and so on. This net concept is the one used in the present text.

world, or acquiring claims on the rest of the world in exchange for the excess exports.

Note that this relationship can also be written as

(16) $S = I + (X - M)$

In Chapter 12 we observed that the balance of trade in goods and services $(X - M)$ is equal to the change in this country's net creditor/debtor position relative to the rest of the world, which can also be regarded as net foreign investment.[3] Consequently, the familiar identity between saving and investment still holds, with investment including both domestic and foreign investment. That is:

$$S = I_d + I_f, \qquad \text{where } I_f = X - M$$

Now we are ready to explain how income is determined in an open economy. We assume that exports, like investment, are exogenous—that is, the level of exports does not depend on domestic income. Imports, on the other hand, are a function of income; an increase in income leads to an increase in imports. This gives us a relationship (an import function) such as the following:

(17) $M = mY$

where m represents the "marginal propensity to import," the fraction of additional income that is spent for imports. That is:

(18) $m = \Delta M / \Delta Y$

For the purposes of this example, we will assume that m is 0.20. The import function is then simply:

(19) $M = 0.20Y$

It is depicted in Figure 14-3, which shows how much is spent for imports (vertical axis) at various levels of income (horizontal axis). If it is assumed that exports are determined externally (on the basis of foreign levels of foreign GNP) and that the exchange rate is fixed, the graph shown in Figure 14-3 leads to Figure 14-4. Figure 14-4 shows how the trade balance behaves as domestic GNP increases. With given exports and with imports rising by the marginal propensity to import times any increase in income, there is an inverse relationship between GNP and the trade balance. As can be seen, a trade surplus exists at low levels of income, but the surplus declines and becomes a deficit as the economy expands.

Returning to Figure 14-2, we observe that we can derive Figure 14-5 by deducting the fixed level of investment from the savings line.

---

[3] Strictly speaking, it was the current account balance that we found equal to net foreign investment. Here we assume no unilateral transfers.

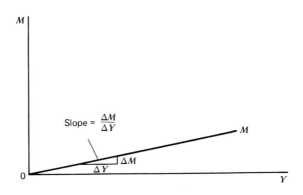

FIGURE 14-3 The propensity to import, and the marginal propensity to import.

Equation 16 on page 303 expressed the following identity:

$$S - I = X - M$$

That expression can be presented graphically by combining two graphs derived previously (see Figure 14-6). Figure 14-6 shows an equilibrium level of national income at which $S = I$ and $X = M$; that is, the trade account is in balance so that domestic savings equals domestic investment. Figure 14-7 illustrates what would occur if the economy were to experience an internal shock in the form of an increase in domestic investment.

The Multiplier in an Open Economy

If the economy had been closed, national income would have increased to Y'', but because trade exists and imports increase with income, the resulting increase in national income is considerably smaller, as shown at Y'. An expansionary domestic

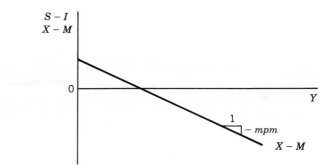

FIGURE 14-4 The trade balance as income rises.

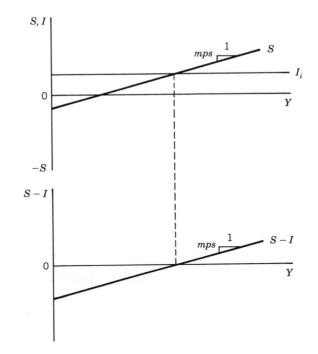

FIGURE 14-5 Domestic savings, investment, and the $S - I$ line.

shock produces both a trade deficit and a smaller increase in GNP than would have occurred in a closed economy or in an economy with barter trade where exports always equal imports. The smaller increase in GNP implies a smaller multiplier, inasmuch as imports are an additional leakage from the income stream. In a closed economy without a government sector, savings are the only leakage, so a marginal propensity to save of 0.20 implies a multiplier of 5. With an open economy and a marginal propensity to import of 0.20, total leakages become 0.40 and only 60 percent of marginal income is spent on domestically produced goods, so the

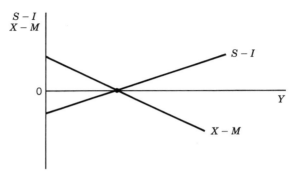

FIGURE 14-6 Savings minus investment and the trade balance with both at equilibrium.

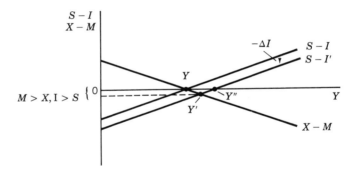

FIGURE 14-7   The impact of an increase in domestic investment.

multiplier falls to 2.5. The multiplier is now defined as follows:

$$K = \frac{1}{mps + mpm} = \frac{1}{1 - mpc_{dom}}$$

mps   = marginal propensity to save, which would include the marginal tax rate
               on income if government were included.
mpm   = marginal propensity to import.
mpc_{dom} = marginal propensity to consume domestic goods and services.

The marginal propensity to import in the United States is slightly in excess of 0.10.
Thus its impact on the multiplier is not large, but in a country such as Belgium,
where the marginal propensity to import could be 0.40 or more, the multiplier
would become very small. The more open the economy, that is, the larger the
marginal propensity to import, the smaller the multiplier.

Another effect of trade in this model is that the domestic economy becomes
vulnerable to external macroeconomic shocks that affect export sales. A recession
abroad, for example, will reduce foreign demand for imports, which means declining exports for this economy. A decline in export sales has the same effect on
national income as does a decline in domestic investment (see Figure 14-8).

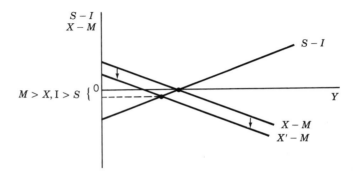

FIGURE 14-8   Impact of a decline in exports.

The decline in exports, which resulted from a foreign recession, caused domestic GNP to decline. Therefore this economy imported the recession. The trade balance did not deteriorate by as much as the decline in exports because the domestic recession caused imports to fall. A shift in export sales will be partially offset by a parallel change in imports, resulting from changes in domestic national income. Hence the trade balance will not fluctuate as sharply as export sales.

THE INTERNATIONAL TRANSMISSION OF BUSINESS CYCLES

An important conclusion of this chapter is that business cycles of major trading partners tend to be linked through trade under the assumption of fixed exchange rates. A recession that begins in one large importer will tend to spread to its trading partners through declines in their exports. Small countries do not export cycles, because exports to them are not sufficiently important in the other countries' economies to produce such an impact, but big importers such as the United States, Germany, and Japan certainly do export cycles.[4]

The short-term business cycle prospects of the large trading countries are therefore of intense interest around the world. A cyclical turn in any of the largest importers brings the likelihood of a parallel cycle in many other countries; accordingly, the large countries are expected to manage their economies in such a way as to avoid destabilizing other economies. When such a country does a poor job of managing its cycles, as when, for example, the United States had an excessively expansionary set of policies during the Vietnam War, other affected countries become displeased. In such cases considerable diplomatic pressure is brought to bear on the country that is causing the problems to improve its performance. The United States has frequently been the target of such pressure, which is often exerted through international organizations such as the Organization for Economic Cooperation and Development (OECD) or the Bank for International Settlements (BIS).

Governments often try to predict the cyclical behavior of their major trading partners in order to adopt timely domestic macroeconomic policies to offset their impacts. If, for example, the Canadian government believes that the United States will enter a recession within a year, it will prepare to adopt more expansionary fiscal or monetary policies to maintain GNP despite the loss of export sales. If Canada were to use a more expansionary monetary policy to increase domestic investment expenditures, the situation depicted in Figure 14-9 would occur.

---

[4]A great deal of econometric research has been done on foreign trade multipliers, linkages among business cycles of countries, and other macroeconomic ties among national economies. Much of this work has been done through Project Link and Eurolink. For a review of this literature and of its main conclusions, see J. Helliwell and T. Padmore, "Empirical Studies of Macroeconomic Interdependence" in R. Jones and P. Kenen, eds., *Handbook of International Economics,* Vol. II. (Amsterdam: North-Holland Press, 1985), pp. 1107–1151.

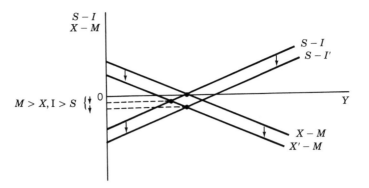

FIGURE 14-9   Impacts of a decline in exports and an increase in domestic investment.

Although Ottawa was successful in avoiding the U.S. recession, it did so at the cost of a larger trade deficit. A recession that originates in the United States can produce a difficult choice for Canada in a world of fixed exchange rates; it can avoid the recession at the cost of a serious deterioration of the trade account, or it can limit the trade balance deterioration by accepting the recession.

FOREIGN REPERCUSSIONS

This discussion has avoided one complication in its discussion of multipliers and of the transmission of business cycles from one country to another. That complication is bounce-back effects or repercussions. A recession in the United States, for example, will reduce Canadian exports and therefore Canadian GNP. The recession in Canada will reduce that country's demand for imports, which means a decline in U.S. exports, which is a repercussion back to this country from its original recession working through Canada. This secondary loss of U.S. export sales would deepen the U.S. recession, which would further reduce imports from Canada, adding to the Canadian recession, cutting Canadian imports from the United States, and so on. These repercussions tend to be fairly small, and the rounds decline in size because each country has a positive marginal propensity to save. Thus only part of each repercussion is passed back to the trading partner.

The size and nature of the foreign repercussions depend on the values of the marginal propensities to save and import in both countries. Formulas can be derived for the foreign trade multiplier with allowance made for foreign repercussions, but they are cumbersome and complex. The interested reader can find examples in more advanced textbooks. Here we wish only to provide an intuitive grasp of the role of foreign repercussions in the adjustment process.

Any multiplier formula rests on a number of assumptions, including assumptions about the influence of economic policy. Thus when U.S. imports rise, inducing a rise in Canada's exports and income, authorities in Canada may take action to stabilize its national income. Then the repercussive chain is broken, because, with no change in income, there is no change in Canada's imports and thus no subsequent effects flowing back to the United States.

These alternative policy stances cannot be easily encompassed in multiplier formulas, except arbitrarily, but they are extremely important in practice. In an interdependent world, economic changes in one country can be and are transmitted to others. Economic policy in any one country must take account of these external influences.

SOME QUALIFICATIONS

In the preceding discussion we have concentrated on the relationship between national income and the balance of trade. In the attempt to isolate that one relationship, we have made the simplifying assumption, common in economic analysis, that a number of other things remain unchanged. But in the real world, some of these other things do not remain unchanged when income changes, and we need to take note of the implications of that fact for our analysis. We will mention only two qualifications of this kind.

First, we have made no allowance for the effect of a change in income on money market conditions, especially the effect on the rate of interest. We have implicitly assumed that the interest rate remains unchanged. Actually, an increase in income is likely to lead to an increase in the demand for money and a rise in the interest rate. A rising interest rate would tend to check or restrain expenditure (for investment, consumer durables, housing) and thus constrain the rise in income. In omitting this influence, we have implicitly assumed that the money supply is being increased just enough to leave interest rates unchanged.

If the money supply were held constant, an increase in autonomous expenditure would lead to a rise in interest rates and thus tend to hold down the resulting increase in income. With a smaller increase in income, the induced rise in imports would also be smaller than we have shown.

Second, we have assumed that prices (and exchange rates) remain unchanged. In our analysis an increase in aggregate demand simply brings about an increase in output. This implies that idle resources exist and that supply is perfectly elastic at the existing price. In the real world, an expansion of aggregate demand is likely to lead to some upward pressure on prices and wages. For a given stimulus, such price increases will mean a smaller rise in real output, but they may make foreign prices more attractive and thus lead to a larger increase in imports than we have allowed for in our analysis. Here, too, conditions in the money market become important, as does the nature of expectations at home and abroad. The interaction among all these factors becomes extremely complex. Our only recourse is to simplify and deal with two or three variables at a time.

Despite these simplifying assumptions, the central conclusions of this discussion do operate in the real world. Foreign trade does have the effect of reducing the size of domestic Keynesian multipliers, and the more open an economy is, the larger the reduction. Trade also links the business cycles of countries, with large countries that import a great deal tending to pass their domestic cycles on to their smaller trading partners. As will be seen later, in Chapter 18, the adoption of flexible exchange rates weakens, but does not end, this linkage.

QUESTIONS FOR STUDY AND REVIEW

1. If a country has a deficit on current account, what must be the relation between domestic saving and investment?

2. In Country X, the marginal propensity to save = 0.10, and the marginal propensity to import = 0.15. If only the income effect is operating, what would be the effect on X's balance of trade of an increase in domestic investment of $200 million? Explain.

3. State the national income identity for an open economy.

4. Why is the multiplier different in an open economy from what it is in a closed economy?

5. What is meant by the foreign repercussion, and how does it affect the adjustment process in the balance of payments?

6. Given an initial equilibrium level of GNP of $2000, with the following breakdown:

Consumption	$1500
Investment	200
Exports	300

   a. If Saving = $250, what is the initial trade balance?

   b. Given $m = 0.25$, $s = 0.15$, suppose an autonomous increase of $200 occurs in investment. What will be the new equilibrium level of GNP? The change in imports? The new trade balance?

SELECTED REFERENCES

Heller, H. Robert. *International Monetary Economics*. Englewood Cliffs, N.J.: Prentice-Hall, 1974.

Machlup, Fritz. *International Trade and the National Income Multiplier*. Philadelphia: Blakiston, 1943.

Meade, James E. *The Balance of Payments*. New York: Oxford University Press, 1951.

Rivera-Batiz, Francisco, and Luis Rivera-Batiz. *International Finance and Open Economy Macroeconomics*. New York: Macmillan, 1985.

Stern, Robert. *The Balance of Payments*. Chicago: Aldine, 1975.

ALTERNATIVE MODELS OF BALANCE OF PAYMENTS OR EXCHANGE RATE DETERMINATION

What causes changes in the sum of the autonomous items in the balance of payments, which in turn causes either payments disequilibria or alterations in exchange rates? Those factors that would cause a balance-of-payments deficit for a country maintaining a fixed parity would instead cause a depreciation of the currency if a floating exchange rate existed. Accordingly, we are seeking to explain exchange market pressures that can result in changes either in the balance of payments or in the market exchange rate.

Why are some countries frequently in deficit (or have depreciating currencies), whereas others experience constant surpluses (or long-term appreciations)? There is no single cause of such disequilibria; rather, several factors can produce such outcomes. There are also different theories, which sometimes overlap but sometimes conflict, in this area. First, we discuss these factors and theories in order to provide a broad understanding of what drives the balance of payments or the exchange rate. Next, we examine payments adjustment, that is, how payments disequilibria are resolved, and, finally, how flexible exchange rates operate.

The ordering of this discussion may seem odd in that the treatment of fixed exchange rates and payments disequilibria precedes that of flexible exchange rates, despite the fact that the United States and many other industrialized countries maintain floating exchange rates. This ordering has been chosen primarily because of pedagogical reasons, but also because most countries of the world maintain parities rather than having floating exchange rates. With regard to the pedagogical argument, the experience of teaching international economics has led to the conclusion that students find a system of fixed exchange rates to be far easier to understand than a regime of floating exchange rates. The concepts of international finance will then be better understood if the less complicated system is presented first and if the more difficult arrangements follow.

Since this chapter is long and rather complicated, we want to indicate at the outset where it is going and how it is organized. The presentation of alternative models of the balance of payments is preceded by a section on why the balance of payments or the exchange rate matters, that is, why governments are concerned about payments disequilibria and frequently adopt various policy measures to bring about payments adjustment. This section is followed by a discussion of balance-of-payments determination which views the current and capital accounts separately. The current account is modeled in a traditional or Keynesian framework. The capital account is then discussed as responding first to differences in levels of interest rates or risks in what is known as a flow-adjustment model.

A more current view of the capital account, which is known as the portfolio balance or stock-adjustment model, is the next topic. In this view of the capital account, international flows respond to recent changes in yields and risks rather than to differences in levels.

This item-by-item approach is followed by the more recent monetarist model, which views the balance of payments as a whole as responding to differences between the domestic demand for money and the supply of money being created by the central bank. The monetarist model of the balance of payments and the portfolio balance model of the capital account are related in that both can be viewed as subcategories of the asset market approach to balance-of-payments or exchange rate determination. The presentation of the monetarist model is followed by a discussion of some limitations or criticisms of that approach.

WHY THE BALANCE OF PAYMENTS (OR THE EXCHANGE RATE) MATTERS

Before beginning a discussion of causes of balance of payments disequilibria, we might ask why anyone cares. That is, why are deficits or surpluses seen as a policy problem that requires attention, or if a parity is not being maintained, why are large changes in exchange rates undesirable?

Balance-of-payments deficits, especially if they continue for long periods, present a variety of problems, some obvious and others more subtle. First, there is the question of the adequacy of foreign exchange reserves and of what happens if reserves approach exhaustion. A payments deficit normally means that reserve assets decline, and such reserves are finite. If these reserves approach zero, the country becomes unable to make payment for imports, and deliveries may cease. It might be thought that no country would allow reserve depletion to continue to such an extreme, but it does happen and the results are not pleasant. If vital imports, such as petroleum, spare parts, or raw materials, become unavailable, the domestic economy slows dramatically. A few years ago Tanzania was in such a situation, and the operating rule for the delivery of imports was that ships did not come into Dar es Salaam to unload until the captain had received a radio message to the effect that payment had been received. There are no 30- or 60-day payment terms for such countries. As a result, imports are available only when export receipts arrive, and the modern economy barely operates. Sometimes this means a lack of imported medicines or insecticides, with obvious consequences for public health.

Countries that face the exhaustion of foreign exchange reserves often find themselves dependent on lenders such as the International Monetary Fund. The typical result is emergency loans extended under rather stringent conditions. The country's ability to manage its own economic and financial affairs can be compromised by such conditions, a situation that is politically embarrassing.[1]

In addition to the budgetary constraint implied by finite foreign exchange reserves and a limited ability to borrow, there is the problem of trade deficits as a recessionary factor in a Keynesian view of a macroeconomy. A loss of export sales that shifts the trade or current account toward deficit reduces aggregate demand in the economy (as discussed in the previous chapter) and reduces total output and incomes through the multiplier process. If the economy was in an inflationary state at the time of the export decline, such a reduction in total demand might be desirable. If, however, the economy was already weak or tending toward recession, such a deficit would be harmful. Expansionary fiscal or monetary policies could be used to offset such an impact, but the trade deficit would still be a complicating factor in the domestic macroeconomy. The more open the economy of a country is, the more vulnerable it is to macroeconomic shocks from abroad through shifts in the trade balance.

Balance-of-payments deficits also affect the domestic money supply which may not match the desires of the central bank, thus complicating the management of monetary policy. A payments deficit requires that the central bank sell foreign

---

[1]The often demanding terms under which the IMF is willing to lend large sums of money to chronic deficit countries are discussed in various works on the subject of conditionality, that is, on IMF loans being conditional upon certain policy changes. See Paul Mosley, "Conditionality as Bargaining Process: Structural Adjustment Lending 1980–1986," *Princeton Essays in International Finance*, No. 168, October 1987. Also Sydney Dell, "On Being Grandmotherly: The Evolution of IMF Conditionality," *Princeton Essays in International Finance*, No. 144, October 1981. See also J. Sproas, "IMF Conditionality: Ineffectual, Inefficient, and Mistargeted," *Princeton Essays in International Finance*, No. 166, December 1986.

[handwritten margin note: Gov't needs to obtain the foreign currency to purchase the goods (import)]

currency in the exchange market, with payment being made to the central bank in domestic money. The result is a reduction in the member bank reserves of domestic commercial banks. It is exactly as if the central bank had sold domestic treasury bills in a standard contractionary open-market policy, except that foreign money replaces the treasury bills and the transaction was not voluntary. The central bank is required to sell foreign exchange reserves, thus reducing the stock of member bank reserves or base money, by its commitment to maintain a fixed exchange rate. The reduction in the stock of base money works through the coefficient of monetary expansion or money multiplier (one over the reserve ratio) to further reduce the domestic money supply and the availability of credit. Assuming a 20 percent reserve requirement and a payments deficit of $10 million, we can expect the banking system to be affected as shown in the balance sheets in Table 15-1.

The money supply has fallen whether or not such a decline matches the wishes of the central bank. This effect could be canceled through a practice known as "sterilization," namely, the open-market purchase of sufficient domestic treasury bills (or other domestic assets) to return the stock of member bank reserves to its original level. In this case a purchase of $10 million in such domestic assets would be called for, as shown in the balance sheets in Table 15-2.

Sterilization is any open-market purchase or sale of domestic assets which has the effect of canceling or offsetting the monetary effects of a balance-of-payments disequilibrium. In the case of a payments deficit, an open-market purchase of domestic assets produces this effect; that is, it returns the money supply to the level prevailing before the payments disequilibrium. Although central banks widely practice sterilization, payments deficits still significantly complicate the management of a domestic monetary policy.

Balance-of-payments surpluses present fewer and less pressing problems than deficits, but even surpluses are not without disadvantages. First, a trade surplus is a source of aggregate demand, and the sudden emergence of such a surplus can be inflationary. Countries with open economies often find sharp increases in export sales to be a mixed blessing at best. The resulting increases in domestic incomes can work through the multiplier process to cause serious inflation, particularly if the economy was close to full employment when the export increase began.

A balance-of-payments surplus also increases the domestic money supply through the same process described earlier for a deficit. The central bank's purchases of foreign exchange are paid for with domestic money which is deposited in commercial banks, thus adding to the stock of member bank reserves. The

TABLE 15-1 Impact on the Domestic Money Supply of a Balance-of-Payments Deficit Shown Through Balance Sheet Changes

Central Bank		One Commercial Bank		All Commercial Banks	
−$10m FXR	−$10m MBR	−$10m MBR	−$10m demand deposits	−$10m MBR −$40m loans	−$50m demand deposits

TABLE 15-2   The Sterilization of Effects of a Payments Deficit

Central Bank	One Commercial Bank			All Commercial Banks	
+$10m Treasury bills	+$10m MBR	+$10m MBR	+$10m demand deposits	+$10m MBR +$40m loans	+$50m demand deposits

transactions are the same as those shown in the balance sheet summaries on page 314, except that all the signs are reversed. Sterilization is possible, but in this case domestic treasury bills would be sold rather than purchased. If the central bank sells off all its domestic assets, control of the money supply might be threatened, but an increase in the reserve ratio would remain available as a way to control the money supply despite a payments surplus. The point remains that a payments surplus increases the money supply unless sterilization is pursued and that large payments imbalances of either type complicate the management of monetary policy.

A balance of trade surplus means that the country is producing more than it is using or absorbing domestically, which may not be in the interests of the local population. Let us return to the national income accounting identities of the previous chapter:

$$(1) \quad Y = C + I + G + (X - M)$$
$$(2) \quad (X - M) = Y - (C + I + G)$$

where C, I, and G are totals rather than only goods and services of domestic origin. A trade surplus of $10 billion means that the country is producing $10 billion more real output than its residents are utilizing, with the difference being sent to the rest of the world in exchange for financial assets. Those assets presumably earn a rate of return that will allow even more resources to be used later, but such assets are also subject to the effects of inflation. The U.S. price level more than tripled between 1967 and 1987, and during many of those years ex post real interest rates on U.S. government securities were negative. Foreign governments that held dollar assets during that period did not do well. Balance-of-trade surpluses run during the 1950s and early 1960s were used to purchase such securities, only to have inflation reduce their value. If a government's purpose is to maximize the utility or welfare of its citizens, it may not be desirable to use continuing current account or balance-of-payments surpluses to finance the accumulation of foreign assets, which are vulnerable to inflation.

Finally, to the extent that some countries have chronic payments surpluses, they make it impossible for the rest of the world to eliminate deficits. The world's balance of payments totals zero; thus if some countries maintain and even defend surpluses, the rest of the world is necessarily in deficit. During the 1960s the United States sometimes found that its attempts to deal with payments deficits were frustrated by policies pursued by Japan, Germany, and other surplus countries which seemed designed to perpetuate their surpluses.

In a world of flexible exchange rates, the forces that would have caused large payments disequilibria instead produce exchange rate volatility, such as was experienced in the market for the U.S. dollar in the early 1980s. The dollar rose by over 60 percent (nominal) from early 1981 to 1985 and then fell by a similar amount in the next few years. More will be said about flexible exchange rates in Chapter 18, but for now let us note that such exchange rate volatility has decidedly disruptive effects on a nation's economy. For a relatively open economy, the exchange rate is probably its most important single price, in that it affects almost everything, including the price level, production, and the distribution of incomes. Exchange rate volatility of the type experienced by the United States during the early 1980s is certainly to be avoided. Either large payments disequilibria or large exchange rate changes are undesirable, and the next question is what causes them.

ALTERNATIVE VIEWS OF BALANCE-OF-PAYMENTS (OR EXCHANGE RATE) DETERMINATION

This chapter presents two broad views of the forces that drive the autonomous transactions in the balance of payments; these forces produce either payments disequilibria or exchange rate movements. The first approach is more traditional and views the payments accounts in an item-by-item format. The trade account is examined in a Keynesian framework, and the capital account is then analyzed separately as being driven by relative rates of return and risk variables. The second approach is considerably newer and looks at the accounts as a whole rather than at items within the accounts. It is the "monetarist model of the balance of payments," and it is an extension of the domestic neoclassical model for which the University of Chicago is so well known.

The Nonmonetarist View of the Trade Balance

The traditional view of the trade account begins with an accounting identity and then adopts a demand-driven or Keynesian approach to explain elements in that identity:

$$(3) \quad \text{BOT} = P_x \cdot Q_x - P_m \cdot Q_m$$

which says that the balance of trade is defined as the world price of exports times the volume exported minus the world price of imports times the volume imported. For most countries world prices of traded commodities can be taken as given, in that the country in question cannot be expected to affect these prices. With given prices of exports and imports (and hence given terms of trade), the question then becomes, what determines the quantities of goods exported and imported? Taking imports first in this Keynesian approach,

$$(4) \qquad Q_m = F(\overset{+}{Y_d}, \overset{+}{XR_r})$$

which says that imports are a positive function of domestic incomes and of the real exchange rate, measured as the foreign price of domestic money. Imports rise with local incomes and when the domestic currency appreciates in real terms.

The marginal propensity to import, as discussed in the previous chapter, provides the linkage from domestic incomes to imports, the idea being that when domestic incomes rise people will spend more on a variety of consumer goods and part of the marginal expenditures will be on imports. Imports tend to be cyclical, rising during domestic expansions and declining in recessions.

The real exchange rate reflects the attractiveness of foreign versus domestic goods in terms of relative costs. A real appreciation means that domestic goods have become more expensive relative to foreign alternatives, which encourages domestic residents to substitute toward imports. A real depreciation means that domestic goods become relatively cheaper, thus discouraging imports. To summarize, imports are determined by domestic incomes and relative prices, rising with incomes and falling as foreign goods become relatively more expensive. Other variables might be added, including some measure of tastes or fashion, as well as changing reputations for quality and prompt delivery, but those less important (and unmeasurable) factors will be ignored for the time being.

Turning to exports, we find that

$$(5) \qquad Q_x = F(\overset{+}{Y_f}, \overset{-}{XR_r})$$

which says that the volume of goods exported is positively related to foreign incomes and negatively related to the real exchange rate. An increase in foreign incomes causes rising purchases of a range of goods, some proportion of which will be exports from this country. Export volumes are then tied to foreign business cycles, rising with expansions and declining in recessions. Foreigners also make purchases on the basis of relative prices, purchasing fewer of this country's goods when its currency is overvalued and more when it is undervalued. Rapid inflation in this country, which is not offset by a nominal depreciation or devaluation, will make our products less price competitive and reduce export volumes.

Substituting equations 4 and 5 into equation 3:

$$(6) \qquad \text{BOT} = P_x \cdot F(Y_f, XR_r) - (P_m \cdot F(Y_d, XR_r))$$

or

$$(7) \qquad \text{BOT} = F(\overset{+}{P_x}, \overset{-}{P_m}, \overset{-}{Y_d}, \overset{+}{Y_f}, \overset{-}{XR_r})$$

which says that the balance of trade is positively related to this country's terms of trade (P_x/P_m), negatively related to domestic incomes (due to the impact of such incomes on import expenditures), positively related to foreign incomes (for the same reason), and negatively related to the real exchange rate. The last variable is an index of this country's cost and price competitiveness in world markets. When it is high, our currency is overvalued and our products are overpriced, resulting in depressed exports and a larger volume of imports, and vice versa.

A country's terms of trade are determined in world markets for its exports and imports. Such markets can be highly competitive and have volatile prices, or they can be oligopolistic and have more stable prices. Many developing countries export large volumes of a small number of primary products into highly competitive markets, and find that their terms of trade are unstable. A country such as Zaire or Zambia is dependent on the world price of copper, over which it has no control, whereas Sri Lanka is similarly dependent on tea prices. Diversifying exports makes a country's terms of trade more stable, but this is not easy for small developing countries. Highly industrialized countries, such as Japan, export a wide variety of products in largely oligopolistic markets with far more stable prices. The terms of trade of such countries can still be affected by particularly important import prices, such as the price of oil, but these countries have typically had far less unstable terms of trade than have developing countries. In the mid-1970s, however, many developed countries found their trade balances seriously worsened by terms-of-trade effects when the price of oil rose sharply. The year 1990 produced similar effects on a smaller scale.

The role of domestic incomes in this model suggests that a country's trade balance is negatively related to its own business cycle but positively related to foreign cycles. When the domestic economy is in a strong expansion, rapidly rising imports worsen the trade account, but when foreign economies are booming, rising exports improve trade results. If the business cycles of all countries were in phase—that is, they all had expansions and recessions at the same time—these effects would largely cancel, but such cycles are seldom in phase. The impacts of business cycles on trade flows occur rather quickly in that a strong increase in domestic incomes can be expected to cause a parallel rise in imports within a few months. Cost and price competitiveness, as measured by the real exchange rate, affects the trade balance with a longer lag. Consumers, being creatures of habit, do not immediately adjust to changing relative prices. Finding alternatives to previous purchases may take time, and trade in primary commodities is often managed through long-term contracts that set prices and quantities well into the future. The real exchange rate affects the trade account with a lag of as much as a year, or occasionally even longer. The U.S. dollar, for example, started to depreciate in 1985, but the trade balance did not start to improve significantly until 1987.

Many of the services items in the current account are determined by the same factors that are relevant for merchandise trade. Tourism, which is a major source of foreign exchange for many developing countries, is determined largely by price competitiveness and the business cycle in developed countries. When a developing country's currency is overvalued, it becomes an expensive place to visit, and tourism declines, and vice versa. When the United States is in an economic expansion, its residents have more funds for vacations, and Caribbean countries benefit from strong tourism receipts. When this country is in a recession, fewer Americans travel abroad and tourist receipts in the Caribbean decline.

Net dividend and interest transactions are determined first by whether a country is a net debtor or creditor, and second by prevailing interest rates. Brazil, for example, experienced a serious deterioration of its current account in the early 1980s because it was already a large net debtor when interest rates on that debt increased sharply. Some developing countries, such as India and Pakistan, have large current account receipts from remittances, which depend on the state of the economies that employ their workers. When countries along the Persian Gulf are prosperous and peaceful, India and Pakistan receive payments of as much as $1 billion per year from their citizens employed abroad. The Persian Gulf crisis of 1990–1991 seriously worsened the current account results for those South Asian countries.

The Capital Account

Chapter 11, which dealt with factor mobility in general and multinational corporations in particular, suggested that international capital movements were the result of a simple arbitraging process. Funds move from countries in which rates of return (interest or profit rates) are low to countries in which they are high. Risks are an additional problem in that investors are assumed to be averse to risk and therefore to avoid countries where political or other risks are high. Capital then flows from low yields or high risks toward higher yields or lower risks. Unattractive yield/risk combinations drive money out of a country and vice versa. This would suggest that capital flows during any period, which constitute the capital account within the balance of payments, should be a simple function of relative yields and risks:

$$(8) \quad KA = F(\overset{+}{r_d}, \overset{-}{r_f}, \overset{-}{\text{risk}_d}, \overset{+}{\text{risk}_f})$$

$$KA = \text{capital account}$$

where risks may be measured as the variability of past yields in particular countries and as probabilities of political instability. This is known as a flow-adjustment model of the capital account and suggests that constant yield differentials should produce a steady flow of funds from one country to another. If U.S. interest rates exceed those prevailing in Tokyo by two percentage points, a steady volume of funds should flow from Tokyo to New York; if the yield spread widens, the flow of funds should increase proportionally, and vice versa. This was the dominant view of international capital flows for many years, and it remains implicit in some simple graphical analyses of the balance of payments (the *IS/LM/BB* curves that will be introduced in Chapter 16), but it turns out to be based on an unrealistic and oversimplified view of how investment managers behave.

The Portfolio Balance Approach

More recent models of the capital account, which are known as stock-adjustment, or "portfolio balance," models, have grown out of Tobin and Markowitz's work on domestic financial behavior.[2] These models begin with the obvious point that an investment manager (banker or mutual fund director, for example) has a fixed stock of capital to invest at any time. That stock will hopefully grow as his or her institution attracts more funds, but investment behavior at any moment is based on the allocation of a fixed stock of funds with the goal of maximizing yield subject to a risk constraint. The investment manager knows the current yields on the alternative assets and forms expectations with regard to future yields, but he or she cannot know actual future yields. An unexpected increase in interest rates, for example, will impose sizable capital losses on that part of the portfolio that is held in the form of bonds, but will produce higher returns on short-term assets. The manager also has opinions about the riskiness of each of the assets, with those opinions probably being formed on the basis of the degree of instability in past or historic yields. On the basis of expected yields and perceived risks, the manager constructs an ideal portfolio that is designed to maximize the expected yield on the portfolio subject to a risk constraint. The risk constraint is important, because without it the manager would simply put all the funds under his or her management into the asset with the highest expected yield.

Risk is reduced through portfolio diversification, that is, by not putting all portfolio funds into one asset or one type of asset. If, for example, the portfolio is divided between long-term bonds and short-term money market funds, unforeseen increases in interest rates will produce a capital loss on the first half of the portfolio and an increased rate of return on the latter half. A decline in yields would produce the opposite result. As unexpected increases and decreases in interest rates occur, the portfolio as a whole will have a yield that is more stable than the return on either half of it. For this increase in yield stability to occur, the various parts of the portfolio must not have the same pattern of yield behavior. If, for example, the whole portfolio was invested in 30-year AT&T bonds and then half of it was shifted to 30-year IBM bonds, no significant reduction in yield instability would occur, because both assets would experience the same decline in value when interest rates rose, and vice versa. Default risk would be reduced by holding claims on two separate firms, but the more serious risk arising from unforeseen changes in interest rates would not be reduced. Reduction in yield instability requires that the portfolio contain assets that have performed quite differently over interest rate cycles and in response to other financial shocks. Dividing a portfolio between long- and short-term assets is one obvious way to reduce yield instability.

Another way to reduce risk is to diversify a portfolio internationally, that is, to hold claims denominated in more than one currency. Since changes in interest rates in various industrialized countries do not have the same timing, holding assets from a number of countries can be expected to reduce risk in the portfolio as a whole. The fact that business cycles have had quite different timing patterns in

[2]H. P. Markowitz, "Portfolio Selection," *Journal of Finance,* May 1952, and James Tobin, "Liquidity Preference as Behavior Toward Risk," *Review of Economic Studies,* February 1958.

various industrialized countries means that manufacturing corporations can reduce instability in profit rates by becoming multinational enterprises. When Europe is in a recession, the United States may be booming, so declining European profits are offset by higher profits here. In the early 1980s the Ford Motor Company was losing enormous amounts of money in the United States but had large profits in Europe, which may have been responsible for keeping the parent firm in business. As long as national business cycles do not follow the same timing pattern, foreign direct investments can be viewed as a form of portfolio diversification.

Returning to financial institutions such as mutual funds or banks, we can view the managers of such enterprises as facing different expected yields on classes of assets within their home country and abroad, as well as associating various degrees of risk with each of them.[3] Estimates of risk may be derived from the past behavior of each asset type. Based on the set of expected yields and perceived risks, the manager constructs a desired portfolio that reflects the institution's preference for yield versus risk, that is, its willingness to take higher risks to increase expected yields. A venture capital fund would presumably prefer a much riskier portfolio than would a commercial bank. The manager then compares the desired portfolio to that which the institution actually holds, and shifts funds among asset types to eliminate differences between the two. Once this portfolio adjustment process is complete—that is, the actual portfolio matches the desired portfolio—the manager has no further reason to shift funds among classes of assets despite the continuing existence of yield differentials. As long as the portfolio manager wants to limit risk and does not view foreign assets as perfect substitutes for domestic assets, the continued existence of international differences in interest rates will not cause a continuing or indefinite flow of funds from low- to high-yield markets. Once the actual portfolio matches the desired portfolio, where the desired portfolio reflects existing expected yields and risks, there is no reason to move funds from one country to another.

When expected yields change, the desired portfolio is affected and the manager moves funds in response. That process is completed fairly quickly, however, and then funds cease to flow. If, for example, expected rates of return rise in the United Kingdom and there are no changes in perceived risks, portfolio managers might conclude that an additional 5 percent of the funds under their control should be in sterling assets. Over the next few weeks or months, adjustments in the actual portfolio would be made until an extra 5 percent was in sterling claims. Then no further flows of funds to the United Kingdom would occur, despite the continuation of higher relative yields in that market.

If this is how managers of financial institutions behave, international capital flows, and therefore the capital account of the balance of payments, should respond

---

[3] Early work on the effects of portfolio balance considerations on international payments includes William Branson, *Financial Capital Flows in the U.S. Balance of Payments* (Amsterdam: North-Holland Press, 1968). See also Penti Kouri and Michael G. Porter, "International Capital Flows and Portfolio Equilibrium," *Journal of Political Economy,* June 1974. See also R. McKinnon and W. Oates, "The Implications of International Economic Integration for Monetary, Fiscal and Exchange Rate Policies," *Princeton Studies in International Finance,* No. 16, 1966.

to recent changes in interest rates and risks rather than to differences in the levels of such yields and risks. The capital account can then be viewed as follows:

$$(9) \quad KA = F(d\overset{+}{r_d}, d\overset{-}{r_f}, d\overset{-}{\text{risk}_d}, d\overset{+}{\text{risk}_f})$$

$$d = \text{change}$$

The actual modeling of the capital account for purposes of econometric estimation would be far more complicated, but the basic idea is that capital flows are responses to recent changes in yields and risks rather than to continuing differences in the levels of such yields and risks.

Combining Models of the Capital and Current Accounts

If the earlier model of the trade and current accounts is combined with the above view of capital account determination, the balance of payments is determined as follows:

$$(10) \quad \text{BOP} = F(\overset{+}{P_x}, \overset{-}{P_m}, \overset{-}{Y_d}, \overset{+}{Y_f}, \overset{-}{XR_r}, d\overset{+}{r_d}, d\overset{-}{r_f}, d\overset{-}{\text{risk}_d}, d\overset{+}{\text{risk}_f})$$

This rather lengthy algebraic expression says that a country's official reserve transactions balance of payments is

1. Positively related to its terms of trade, that is, positively related to world prices of its exported commodities and negatively related to world prices of its imports.
2. Negatively related to domestic incomes and positively related to foreign incomes, because rising local incomes cause a parallel increase in imports through the marginal propensity to import. Rising foreign incomes cause increased export sales, for the same reason.
3. Negatively related to the real exchange rate, which is measured as the foreign price of the local currency adjusted for differing rates of inflation. An increase in a country's real exchange rate reduces the cost and price competitiveness of its products in world markets. If, for example, U.S. inflation is 7 percent when foreign inflation averages only 3 percent, a constant nominal exchange rate means a 4 percent real appreciation, which worsens the cost and price competitiveness of U.S. firms by 4 percent a year.
4. Positively related to recent changes in domestic interest rates, and negatively related to recent changes in foreign yields. When U.S. interest rates rise relative to those prevailing abroad, capital will flow into this country while financial portfolios are being adjusted to the new relative yield situation. Once that adjustment is complete, such flows should cease.
5. Negatively related to recent changes in domestic risk and positively related to recent changes in risks abroad. An increase in the likelihood of political

instability in Latin America or elsewhere, for example, will typically cause large flows of capital into the United States as investors seek a safe haven.

Asset Market Approaches to the Balance of Payments and the Exchange Rate

As noted in Chapter 13, capital account transactions have become far larger than current account transactions as sources of supply and demand for foreign exchange in the United States. As a result, many economists have come to view the exchange market and the balance of payments solely as financial phenomena and largely (or totally) ignore real factors that determine trade and other current account transactions.

The exchange market is then viewed (and modeled) as reflecting the supply and demand for financial assets denominated in different currencies. Equilibrium in the balance of payments and the exchange market exists when these financial asset markets clear; payments deficits or depreciations occur when the relative demand for foreign financial assets rises, and vice versa.[4]

This broad class of asset market models of the balance of payments (or the exchange rate) includes two subsectors. In one group of models, domestic and foreign assets are viewed as imperfect substitutes in financial portfolios because of uncertainty and risk constraints. This is the portfolio balance approach to the balance of payments, which was discussed earlier in this chapter as a model of only the capital account. In the second group of asset market models, problems of risk and uncertainty are ignored, thereby allowing domestic and foreign assets to be viewed as perfect substitutes in portfolios. This is known as the monetarist approach to the balance of payments, a discussion of which follows.

The Monetarist Model of the Balance of Payments

The monetarist model of the balance of payments includes far fewer variables than do the models described earlier and is an outgrowth of the monetarist model of a domestic economy. It operates on the basis of that model's simplifying assumptions.

Markets are assumed to be perfectly competitive and therefore to move toward equilibrium rather quickly if they are shocked out of equilibrium. Money is neutral, meaning that purely monetary factors cannot have permanent effects on real variables. An increase in the money supply, for example, cannot permanently affect real output. The model has a long-run orientation in that short-run impacts of

---

[4]The asset market approach and alternative models are surveyed in Richard Levich, "Empirical Studies of Exchange Rates: Price Behavior, Rate Determination, and Market Efficiency" in R. Jones and P. Kenen, eds., *Handbook of International Economics,* Vol. II (Amsterdam: North-Holland Press, 1985), pp. 979–1040. See also William Branson, "Asset Markets and Relative Prices in Exchange Rate Determination," *Socialwissenschaftliche Annalen,* 1977. Also available as a National Bureau of Economic Research Reprint.

macroeconomic shocks receive less attention than in a Keynesian world. As was noted above, the monetarist model of the balance of payments adds the assumption that investors or portfolio managers view domestic and foreign financial assets as perfect substitutes. Therefore they are not constrained by portfolio balance considerations, and they can therefore move far larger amounts of money in response to changes in expected yields. It is not suggested that these assumptions are realistic; they are, however, necessary to construct the model in a rigorous fashion. The usefulness of the model is judged not by whether its assumptions are realistic (most economic theory would be abandoned if that were so), but instead by its ability to explain real-world payments flows. Although this model is not perfect in that regard, it does have a fairly impressive empirical track record.[5]

A monetarist view of macroeconomics operates through a general equilibrium framework and therefore requires an understanding of Walras Law, which was developed by a French mathematical economist in the 1870s. This law states that if an economy is defined as an all-inclusive set of markets (a supply function, a demand function, and a market-clearing identity for each good, financial asset, etc., in the economy), where one market is for money, net excess demands must total zero. That rather complicated statement means simply that if something is in excess demand, something else must be in a parallel excess supply. Since nobody expects to be given anything for free (there is no charity in this model), an excess demand for one item necessarily implies an excess supply of whatever people are willing to give up to get what is in excess demand. If, for example, goods are in excess demand, that means people are willing to reduce their holdings of money (or of something else, such as other financial assets) in order to get more goods at current prices. An excess supply of bonds means that people want to reduce their holdings of bonds in order to increase their holdings of something else. That something else, which may be money, is in excess demand.

This point is sufficiently simple that we may wonder why it is so important. It is important because it implies that an economy cannot experience a single disequilibrium. Disequilibria always come in offsetting pairs. If there is an excess supply of goods, there must be a parallel excess demand for something, and it is frequently important to discern what that something is. To think in Walrasian terms is to have a mental reflex of always looking for the offsetting disequilibrium. If one market is observed to be out of equilibrium, the Walrasian response is immediately to seek the offsetting disequilibrium elsewhere in the system. For a monetarist,

[5]A full listing of the important works in the monetarist approach to the balance of payments is impossible in the available space, but the J. Frenkel and H. G. Johnson (eds.) volume is a good place to begin: *The Monetary Approach to the Balance of Payments* (Toronto: University of Toronto Press, 1976). A very useful and reasonably nontechnical survey is M. Kreinin and L. Officer, "The Monetary Approach to the Balance of Payments: A Survey," *Princeton Studies in International Finance,* No. 43, 1978. See also Steven Magee, "The Empirical Evidence on the Monetary Approach to the Balance of Payments," *American Economic Review,* May 1976, pp. 163–170. See also A. Rabin and L. Yeager, "Monetary Approaches to the Balance of Payments and Exchange Rates," *Princton Essays in International Finance,* no. 148, November 1982. For the relationship between international and domestic monetarism, see Herbert Grubel, "Domestic Origins of the Monetary Approach to the Balance of Payments," *Princeton Essays in International Finance,* No. 117, June 1976.

problems in the markets for goods or financial assets usually have their origin in the market for money. That is, an excess demand for goods is caused by an excess supply of money, which in turn results from unwise decisions by the central bank.

In the monetarist model of a closed economy, an excessive rate of monetary expansion causes price inflation which returns the real money supply (the nominal money supply divided by the price level) to its original equilibrium level. The demand for money is a stable function of GNP. If real growth is 3 percent, any attempt to increase the money supply beyond that rate will merely produce offsetting inflation. A rate of monetary expansion of 10 percent would produce 7 percent inflation and a rate of growth of the real money supply of 3 percent, which matches the growth of real GNP.

In a monetarist model of the balance of payments, or in open economy monetarism, monetary growth has somewhat different effects. Under the assumption of fixed exchange rates, no tariffs or transport costs, and perfect competition, the domestic prices of tradable goods are constrained by international arbitrage. If the exchange rate is 5 francs to the dollar and the French price of wine is 40 francs, the U.S. price must be $8. This is known as the law of one price:

$$(11) \quad P_d = \frac{P_{\text{row}}}{XR_n}$$

The domestic price of tradable goods must equal the foreign price divided by the nominal exchange rate. If that were not true, profits could be made arbitraging between the two markets, assuming no transport costs or tariffs. There is significant evidence that in less than perfectly competitive markets the law of one price is frequently violated, but it is a necessary assumption if the monetarist model is to be understood.[6] The existence of nontradables (goods not involved in international trade) is ignored for the moment.

Since domestic and foreign bonds are perfect substitutes, the law of one price holds in the bond market as well as in the market for goods. Because the exchange rate is rigidly fixed (and confidently expected to remain fixed), prices of bonds and therefore interest rates are arbitraged together.

$$(12) \quad r_d = r_f$$

Both goods and bonds move freely among countries to maintain the law of one price in both markets. Any increase of U.S. prices above those prevailing in Canada would cause goods to flow south in sufficient volume to destroy that price difference. The same situation holds in the market for bonds. As a result, a disequilibrium in either the goods market or the bond market causes large balance-of-payments flows. An excess supply of goods quickly becomes a balance of trade

---

[6]For an early indication of the failure of the law of one price, see Robert M. Dunn, Jr., "Flexible Exchange Rates and Oligopoly Pricing: A Study of Canadian Markets," *Journal of Political Economy,* January/February 1970, pp. 140–151. For a more recent study that reaches the same conclusion, see Michael Knetter, "Price Discrimination by U.S. and German Exporters," *American Economic Review,* March 1989, pp. 198–210.

surplus as the goods that are unsold at home are exported, and an excess demand for bonds causes a capital account deficit as bonds are imported from abroad to fill the domestic shortage.

In the monetarist model, the balance of payments can be viewed as a mechanism through which domestic market disequilibria are ended and through which excess supplies or demands for money are eliminated. Imagine an economy consisting of three markets: goods, bonds, and money. Both the goods and the bonds are traded internationally. If the three markets started in equilibrium and then the central bank increased the money supply by 10 percent, an excess supply of money would be created. Walras law says that any such excess supply must create a mirror-image excess demand; hence the market for either goods or bonds (more likely, both) must be in excess demand. An excess demand for goods, with domestic prices that are fixed by the law of one price, must spill over into the trade sector as a balance of trade deficit. The shortage of goods is filled by imports without any significant increase in domestic prices. If the excess demand were in the bond market, it would be filled through an inflow of bonds from abroad, which would mean a capital account deficit. If the excess demand situation prevailed in both markets, both the trade and the capital account would go into deficit. In any of these cases, the official reserve transactions balance of payments moves into deficit.

If, starting from equilibrium in all markets, the central bank had reduced the money supply, the resulting domestic excess demand for money would have created an excess supply of goods and/or bonds, resulting in an outflow of the goods and/or bonds to foreign buyers and a balance-of-payments surplus. In the monetarist view, balance-of-payments disequilibria have a single dominant cause: disequilibria in the domestic market for money, usually caused by central bank errors, which cause mirror-image disequilibria in the domestic markets for goods and for financial assets such as bonds. These latter disequilibria spill over into the balance of payments, causing deficits or surpluses, depending on whether the money supply was too large or too small. If the law of one price does not quite hold in goods or bond markets, an excess supply of money may create some domestic inflation and/or declines in real interest rates, but these are not the ultimate causes of the resulting balance-of-payments deficit. Changes in the domestic price level or in interest rates are merely symptoms of the real cause of the payments deficit, which is an excess supply of money.

The balance of payments disequilibrium is not only a response to a nonequilibrium money supply; it is also the mechanism through which the market for money is brought back to equilibrium. Earlier in this chapter we noted that a balance-of-payments deficit automatically reduces the domestic money supply and that a surplus increases it. An excess supply of money causes a payments deficit, which reduces the money supply until equilibrium is restored. All that is required is that the central bank not sterilize the monetary impact of its loss of foreign exchange reserves. In the reverse case, an excess demand for money, caused by an excessively restrictive domestic monetary policy, causes a balance-of-payments surplus, which automatically increases the money supply as the central bank accumulates foreign exchange reserves. Again, all that is required is that the central bank not sterilize.

Balance-of-payments disequilibria are therefore both the result of monetary policy errors and the source of their reversal. An unwise increase in the money supply causes a payments deficit that drains the excess money out of the economy, and vice versa. All that is required for the system to be automatically restored to equilibrium is that the central bank avoid sterilization. If the central bank does sterilize, it merely recreates the original disequilibrium in the market for money and maintains the balance-of-payments disequilibrium. In the case of a balance-of-payments deficit, for example, sterilization means that the central banks purchase domestic assets, adding to the stock of the member banks' reserves and the money supply, thus avoiding the money supply reduction which is the normal result of a payments deficit. Since the money supply is not allowed to fall, the excess supply of money that caused the payments deficit cannot be eliminated. Therefore the market for money (and the markets for goods and bonds) cannot return to equilibrium.

The balance of payments will automatically return the markets for money, goods, and bonds to equilibrium if the central bank avoids interfering with the process. Sterilization is one form of such interference, and it merely maintains market disequilibria and the resulting balance-of-payments problems.

Modeling the Monetarist View of the Balance of Payments

A simple version of the monetarist model can be put in algebraic form, which makes it possible to understand how econometric tests can be run.

(13) $\quad MD = F(\overset{+}{Y}, \overset{-}{r})$

which says that the demand for money is positively related to domestic incomes (the transactions' demand for money) and negatively related to the cost of holding money, which is the interest rate.

(14) $\quad MS = 1/RR$ (base money stock)

$\quad RR$ = reserve ratio for commercial banks

which says that the money supply equals the coefficient of monetary expansion (1 over the reserve ratio) times the stock of base money. Since the stock of base money is the total liability side of the central bank's balance sheet (ignoring currency in peoples' pockets), and since the balance sheet identity holds:

(15) $\quad$ Base money $= DA + FXR$

which says that the stock of base money equals the sum of the domestic assets of the central bank and its holdings of foreign exchange reserves.

Substituting equation 15 into equation 14,

$$(16) \quad MS = 1/RR \cdot (DA + FXR)$$

Equating money supply with money demand

$$(17) \quad MS = MD$$

and therefore

$$(18) \quad F(Y, r) = 1/RR \cdot (DA + FXR)$$

This equation is then put in the form of changes or first differences. Since domestic interest rates cannot change (the law of one price in the bond market) and since the reserve ratio is assumed to be fixed, the above equation becomes:

$$(19) \quad F(dY) = dDA + dFXR$$
$$\text{where} \quad d = \text{change}$$

Because a balance-of-payments surplus causes an equal increase in foreign exchange reserves, and vice versa, the above can be reorganized as

$$(20) \quad dFXR = BOP = F(dY, dDA)$$

This equation, often in a more complicated form, can be estimated econometrically. The monetarist view of the balance of payments predicts a positive coefficient on the first independent variable and a negative coefficient on the second. Published econometric studies generally support this expectation, although the results are far from perfect.[a]

Criticisms or Limitations of the Monetarist Model

Although the model described in the previous paragraphs has impressive empirical support and is widely used in analyzing payments problems, it is not without problems. First, it results in central banks being blamed for payments deficits without questioning whether the central bank is actually an independent decision-making agency. Monetarists tend to assume that other countries have central banks that are similar to the Federal Reserve System in its independence from the executive

[a]For an empirical study that is highly supportive of the monetarist approach, see L. Girton and D. Roper, "A Monetary Model of Exchange Market Pressure Applied to the Post-War Canadian Experience," *American Economic Review,* September 1977, pp. 537–548. See also S. Magee, "The Empirical Evidence on the Monetary Approach to the Balance of Payments," *American Economic Review,* May 1976, pp. 163–170. For a more negative view of monetarism in a world of flexible exchange rates, see J. Boughton, "The Monetary Approach to Exchange Rates: What Now Remains?", *Princeton Essays in International Finance,* No. 171, October 1988. Boughton particularly questions the monetarist assumption that domestic and foreign assets are perfect substitutes; he argues that models that allow for imperfect substitutability provide better empirical results.

branch of the government. The Open Market Committee of the Federal Reserve System can decide how rapidly to expand its holdings of domestic assets, and therefore the U.S. stock of base money, without having to accept the "advice" of the White House or the secretary of the treasury. If the U.S. money supply is badly managed, it is reasonable to blame the Federal Reserve System.

Few other central banks enjoy such independence. It is far more common, particularly in developing countries, for the governor of the central bank to report to the minister of finance, and therefore to be unable to make independent decisions. The overriding concern of the finance ministry is the financing of budget deficits, and the central bank is often viewed as the obvious lender. If the finance ministry must borrow vast sums to cover a budget deficit, it is extremely tempting to order the central bank to purchase the required bonds and issue new money in exchange. When the government spends these funds, they enter the domestic banking system, and rapid monetary expansion results. It appears to be a typical expansionary open-market policy, except that the central bank purchases government debt directly from the finance ministry, and, more importantly, it does not do so voluntarily. The money supply expands, often at an inappropriate rate, not because the central bank decides on such a policy, but because it is forced to monetize large government budget deficits.

The resulting balance-of-payments deficits should be blamed not on the central bank, which has no policy independence, but on the fiscal authorities who allowed an excessive budget deficit that had to be financed by the central bank. In such a policy situation, the rate of growth of the central bank's domestic assets cannot be controlled unless the government budget deficit is constrained. Balance-of-payments deficits are therefore caused, not by unwise central bankers, but by excessively large government budget deficits that are monetized.[7]

This situation is particularly common in the less developed economies. Such countries typically have very limited private financial markets; thus the government has few, if any, alternatives to borrowing from the central bank. If the Federal Reserve System does not purchase the new securities being issued by the Department of the Treasury, they can be sold to private banks, insurance companies, pension funds, and so on, in New York, but the finance ministry of the typical developing country does not have such alternatives. In addition, developing country governments seem to have particular difficulties in controlling budget deficits. First, their economies make it difficult to collect a sizable percentage of total incomes as taxes. Much of the economy may be informal (subsistence hunting, fishing, and farming), which cannot be taxed easily. Even the market economy may be based in part on barter, which is hard to tax. When money is used, records may be incomplete, making it almost impossible to enforce an efficient income tax. Such countries often rely heavily on import and export tariffs, and have very limited tax revenues.

On the expenditure side, many developing countries have state-owned enterprises that lose vast sums of money with the necessary funds coming out of public

---

[7]For a model that includes the effects of budget deficits on the money supply in developing countries, see Ziba Farhadian and Robert M. Dunn, Jr., "Fiscal Policy and Financial Deepening in a Monetarist Model of the Balance of Payments," *Kyklos,* April 1986, pp. 66–84.

resources.[8] Subsidies for consumer goods such as food and fuel often result in large expenditures. When the costs of a sizable military and a large civilian bureaucracy are added, the result is total government expenditures that cannot be financed with a very limited tax system. The resulting deficit is often monetized, causing an excessively rapid rate of growth of the money supply, which in turn leads to large balance-of-payments deficits.

This suggests why balance-of-payments adjustment programs for developing countries usually contain requirements for reducing government budget deficits as well as for limiting the growth of the money supply. Little is accomplished by requiring the central bank to promise that it will restrain excessive growth of the money supply unless the government budget deficit is also controlled.

The next problem with the monetarist view of payments disequilibria involves the stability of the demand for money, which means the velocity of money. A stable relationship between GNP $(P \cdot Q)$ and the demand for money, in the form of a fixed or at least a predictable velocity of money, is central to both domestic and international monetarism, but that stability is not as apparent as it once was. As can be seen in Figures 15-1 and 15-2, the velocity of money for M1 followed a slow and steady upward trend until the late 1970s, but it has not been stable or predictable since then, while the velocity of money for M2 has also changed often. The phasing out of Regulation Q in the early 1980s, which means that elements of both M1 and M2 now can legally pay interest, is widely blamed for the changed behavior of the velocity of money. But whatever the cause, the monetarist view of a stable demand for money, which is closely tied to GNP, is now subject to large doubts.

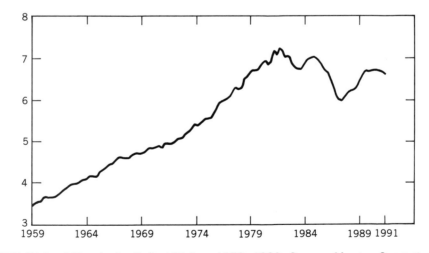

FIGURE 15-1 M1 velocity, United States, 1959–1989. *Source:* Morgan Guaranty Trust Company.

---

[8]For data on the size of state-owned enterprise losses in developing countries, see M. Gillis, D. Perkins, M. Roemer, and D. Snodgrass, *Economic Development,* 2nd ed. (New York: W. W. Norton, 1987), pp. 575–576.

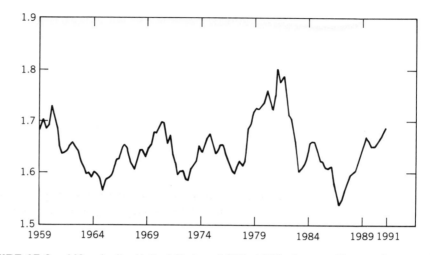

FIGURE 15-2   M2 velocity, United States, 1959–1989. *Source:* Morgan Guaranty Trust Company.

Another possible reason for the increased volatility of *V* involves what has become known as currency substitution.[9] The monetarist view that the demand for a national currency is a stable function of that country's GNP is based on the implicit assumption that each currency has a monopoly as the circulating money within its national borders, that is, that only dollars are used in the U.S. economy, only sterling is used in Great Britain, and so on. That may be true for paper currency but not for bank accounts. As barriers to international capital flows have declined and business has become more international, an increasingly large number of firms hold more than one currency in the form of bank deposits. They might hold each currency in proportion to the amount of business they do in that country, but if they observe that different interest rates are available on deposits in various countries and they form expectations as to likely exchange rate changes, they should make certain changes. Specifically, they should shift their portfolios of money balances toward currencies with high expected yields, after making allowance for likely exchange rate movements, and away from currencies where yields are low and/or a depreciation is expected. As a result, the demand for various currencies may be quite volatile as views change on likely exchange rate movements or other factors that affect expected yields.

Each company may have a demand for all monies that is a stable function of its total transactions volume, but it need not have a demand for any single currency that is a stable function of the amount of business it does in each country. Thus the total demand for a currency need not be a stable function of that country's GNP; instead, it can be far more volatile. This currency substitution argument may have

[9]Early elements in the discussion of currency substitution include C. Chen, "Diversified Currency Holdings and Flexible Exchange Rates," *Quarterly Journal of Economics,* 1973, pp. 96–111. See also L. Girton and D. Roper, "Theory and Implications of Currency Substitution," *Journal of Money, Credit, and Banking,* February 1981, pp. 12–30, and R. McKinnon, "Currency Substitution and Instability in the World Dollar Standard," *American Economic Review,* June 1982.

been the cause of the exchange rate volatility that plagued many industrialized countries in the 1970s and early 1980s. The total demand for the monies of the major industrialized countries may be a relatively stable function of the total GNPs of those countries, whereas the demand for each currency is far less closely related to the GNP of that country.

It is argued, for example, that the rapid appreciation of the U.S. dollar in the early 1980s was the result of currency substitution into the U.S. dollar. High nominal interest rates, combined with widespread confidence among foreign investors in the ability of the new chairman of the Federal Reserve Board, Paul Volcker, to reduce the U.S. rate of inflation, produced very high real interest rates on U.S. dollar holdings. As a result, desired dollar balances by multinational firms increased sharply, as did the demand for the dollar and therefore the exchange rate for this currency. The observed velocity for both M1 and M2 fell in the United States as more dollars were held per dollar of U.S. GNP, and monetary conditions may have been tighter than the Federal Reserve Board intended. If the Fed did not allow for increased foreign holdings of dollars, it would overestimate the volume of dollars held by Americans and underestimate the extent to which it had tightened domestic monetary conditions. The currency substitution argument remains controversial, but it is an interesting explanation for the increased volatility in the data for the velocity of money in the United States.

Despite these criticisms and problems, the monetarist model is widely used in analyzing balance-of-payments problems and in designing adjustment programs. It is particularly useful in developing countries that are suffering from serious inflation. Its emphasis on controlling the rate of growth of the money supply, which usually requires controlling the government budget deficit, is correct, and countries that are designing a payments adjustment program typically include a target for reduced growth in the money supply. That target may have been of their own choosing, or it may have originated with the International Monetary Fund. In either case, limiting the rate of growth of the domestic assets of the central bank is crucial to avoiding balance-of-payments deficits.

This discussion of monetarism has operated entirely under the assumption of a fixed exchange rate. The monetarist model includes views as to how devaluations affect the balance of payments and how a flexible exchange rate should behave. Those subjects are covered in later chapters. The next topic, however, is alternative views as to how balance-of-payments adjustment can occur within the confines of a fixed parity.

QUESTIONS FOR STUDY AND REVIEW

1. What is the effect of a balance-of-payments surplus on a country's domestic money supply? How does this effect occur? How can it be offset or canceled by the central bank of the payments surplus country?

2. If your employers asked you to explain why a particular country experienced a serious deterioration of its balance of payments, what aspects of that country's economy would you study in seeking to respond to that request?

3. If interest rates in Japan rise relative to those prevailing in the United States, would you expect a steady flow of capital into Japan? Why, or why not?

4. Real output and incomes rise in Country A. How and why would a Keynesian analysis of the likely effect of that event on the balance of payments of Country A differ from that of a monetarist?

5. Why is the role of the terms of trade in current account determination of more concern to small developing countries than to larger developed countries?

6. In a monetarist model of the balance of payments, assuming a fixed exchange rate and starting from equilibrium in all markets, how would Country A's balance of payments react to each of the following events:

   a. The central bank of Country A increases its domestic assets sufficiently to increase the stock of base money in the banking system by 10 percent.

   b. Central banks in the rest of the world increase their domestic assets sufficiently to increase the stock of base money in the banking system of the rest of the world by 10 percent.

   c. Because of a drought, GNP in the rest of the world declines by 10 percent.

SELECTED REFERENCES

Frenkel, J., and H. G. Johnson, eds. *The Monetary Approach to the Balance of Payments*. Toronto: University of Toronto Press, 1976.

Girton, L., and D. Roper. "A Monetary Model of Exchange Rate Pressure Applied to the Postwar Canadian Experience." *American Economic Review,* September 1977, pp. 537–548.

Kenen, P. "Macroeconomic Theory and Policy: How the Closed Economy Was Opened." In R. Jones and P. Kenen, eds. *Handbook of International Economics*. Vol. II. Amsterdam: North-Holland Press, 1985, pp. 625–678.

Kreinen, M., and L. Officer. "The Monetary Approach to the Balance of Payments: A Survey." *Princeton Studies in International Finance,* No. 43, 1978.

Levich, R. "Empirical Studies of Exchange Rates, Price Behavior, Rate Determination, and Market Efficiency." In R. Jones and P. Kenen, eds. *Handbook of International Economics*. Vol. II. Amsterdam: North-Holland, 1985, pp. 979–1040.

McKinnon, R. "Currency Substitution and Instability in the World Dollar Standard." *American Economic Review,* June 1982, pp. 320–334.

16

PAYMENTS ADJUSTMENT WITH FIXED EXCHANGE RATES

For most of the postwar era, the world operated with fixed exchange rates, and even today most developing countries still maintain fixed parities. It therefore seems useful to discuss possible routes to balance-of-payments adjustment with a fixed parity before going on to devaluations and then to floating exchange rates. As will be seen, payments adjustment without use of the exchange rate is frequently painful and/or unsuccessful. This situation may explain why devaluations are so common in the developing world and why many of the industrialized countries have flexible exchange rates.

DAVID HUME'S SPECIE FLOW MECHANISM

A payments adjustment system that David Hume described as early as 1752 operated for many countries before World War I and is still relevant for a few countries and situations.[1] It has the advantage of being automatic, that is, of not depending on fallible central bankers or politicians for prudent decisions, but it leaves a government with very little ability to manage its own monetary affairs. Although they were not followed precisely,[2] the formal system is based on two rules:

1. National currencies are to be backed rigidly by gold; that is, the stock of base money is determined solely by the stock of gold held by the government or the central bank. The central bank therefore has no monetary policy discretion; it must create a money supply that is based on its holdings of gold.

2. Gold is to be the only foreign exchange reserve asset; that is, payments deficits cause a parallel loss of gold, and vice versa.

These two rules mean that the domestic money supply is determined by the balance of payments (and by the gold mining industry). A payments surplus causes an inflow of gold and a parallel increase in the stock of base money. A deficit causes gold to flow out, and the money supply must fall proportionally. This is analogous to the monetarist world described in the previous chapter, except that sterilization does not occur. The money supply must be allowed to fall when a country has a payments deficit and to rise in the case of a surplus.

These changes in the money supply produce payments adjustment through three linkages. In the case of a payments deficit, the resulting decline in the money supply:

1. Raises domestic interest rates, which attracts capital inflows, thereby improving the capital account of the balance of payments.

2. Puts downward pressure on the price level, thereby improving price competitiveness. Exports should rise and imports fall, improving the current account.

3. Puts downward pressure on economic activity and on real incomes. Imports should fall by the marginal propensity to import times the decline in domestic incomes. A reduction in the money supply is recessionary and discourages imports, thereby improving the current account.

The first two of these linkages are not particularly difficult or painful; the third, however, is unpleasant or worse for deficit countries. To the extent that wages

[1]David Hume, "On the Balance of Trade," originally written in 1752, published in Hume, *Essays: Moral, Political, and Literary* (London: Longmans Green, 1898). Reprinted in R. N. Cooper, ed., *International Finance: Selected Readings*. Baltimore: Penguin Books, 1969.

[2]Robert Triffin, "The Myths and Realities of the So-Called Gold Standard," in R. Triffin, *Our International Monetary System: Yesterday, Today, and Tomorrow* (New York: Random House, 1968), Ch. 1. See also Barry Eichengreen, ed., *The Gold Standard in Theory and History* (New York: Methuen, 1985).

and prices are downward rigid or sticky, which appears to be the case in modern industrialized economies, the second linkage becomes largely inoperative, necessitating greater reliance on the third. This payments adjustment mechanism means that countries with payments deficits are likely to be forced into recessions and then be unable to use an expansionary monetary policy to escape such downturns.

For surplus countries, the same three linkages operate in the opposite direction. Interest rates fall, worsening the capital account, and prices rise, a condition that hurts the trade account. Output and incomes rise, thereby increasing imports. If the economy is fully employed, however, output and real incomes cannot rise. Thus inflation can become serious as the money supply rises without the central bank being able to control it.

This system means that the government and the central bank have no policy discretion in the management of the money supply. The recessionary implications for deficit countries, and the prospects for inflation in the case of a surplus, suggest why this system was abandoned. In the late 1970s and early 1980s a few "gold bugs" argued for a return to this approach, but this discussion has now largely ended. Some elements in that debate are discussed in Exhibit 16-1.

The pre-1914 gold standard has the additional disadvantage of being subject to shocks from the gold mining industry. When major ore discoveries are made, the government or the central bank is required to buy gold and to issue new money, resulting in inflation. Spain experienced disastrous inflation in the sixteenth century when its conquest of Latin America produced huge inflows of gold.

The specie flow mechanism may seem to be an historic relic, but it retains its relevance today. A few small countries do not have their own currencies but instead use the currency of another country. Panama and Liberia use the United States dollar, and a number of tiny South Pacific countries use the New Zealand or

Gold Won't Pan Out

The current debate over United States economic policy has developed a case of gold fever.

After decades as a subject of interest primarily to monetary cranks and owners of mining stocks, the gold standard has re-emerged as a topic of serious, or at least semi-serious, debate. Several popularly known economists have proposed tying the dollar rigidly to gold in order to end inflation, reduce interest rates, and solve a variety of other problems. Whatever ails the economy, gold will improve it, they say.

The only problem is that these are primarily the same economists who were recently telling us that sharp tax cuts would not reduce Government revenues and would instead help balance the budget, reduce inflation, and cure the same variety of problems. Partly as a result of their arguments, the United States has now adopted an excessive tax cut and faces the prospect of enormous Federal deficits, continuing high interest rates, and the resulting repression of badly needed investment in housing, new plant and equipment. Perhaps to cover their tracks on the previous debacle, these economists are now blaming our economic ills on the lack of a gold-based currency. When one dubious idea fails, think of another one.

The proponents of a return to the gold standard are suggesting that the United States set the price of gold by offering to buy or sell unlimited quantities of it at a fixed price. The effective result of such a policy would be that the Federal Reserve System could create only as much money as could be supported by the available gold stock. If the Fed printed too much money, for example, people would switch to gold, and the large Government sales of gold would take the money out of circulation. An attempt to reduce the money supply would produce the opposite result. The long-run growth of the United States money supply would be limited by the growth of the gold stock.

Such a change in the way American monetary policy is run would have several major disadvantages. First, it would provide a high guaranteed price for the two major producers: South Africa and the Soviet Union. Whether one is a rightist or a leftist, half of that result is undesirable, and most Americans would dislike both halves.

Second and most important, the ability of the United States to increase its money supply with the growth of the economy and to manage a counter-cyclical monetary policy would be severely limited. An attempt to decelerate monetary growth in inflationary times, for example, would probably lead to large amounts of gold being offered to the Government, which would have to buy with newly created money, thus canceling the intended monetary contraction. An expansionary monetary policy during a recession could be expected to lead to the opposite results. The Federal Reserve would simply be unable to use changes in monetary policy to deal with business cycles. Even if one thinks that the Federal Reserve has often erred in its policy shifts, ending all monetary discretion is a rather crude solution, particularly in light of the more conservative

and able management that the Fed has had since mid-1979.

Finally, the United States money supply could be destabilized by any market participant or event that sharply changed the supply of gold. The world's gold stock has grown slowly in recent decades, but a major gold discovery could change that and cause serious inflation. The Soviet Union apparently holds enormous stocks of gold but now sells cautiously to avoid depressing the price. An American return to the gold standard would end that risk, and the Soviet Union might decide to sell large amounts, causing an increase in the American money supply, and inflation. Alternatively, the Russians might withdraw from the market or even buy, which could have a deflationary effect in the United States. Any instability in South Africa that shut down the mines could produce similar results. It hardly makes sense to tie our currency to a commodity that an adversary holds in enormous quantities and that could be subject to large supply shifts because of mining discoveries or political instability in a major producing country.

The new "gold bugs" are suggesting that the United States give up discretionary monetary policy as a way to deal with business cycles and that the currency be tied to a commodity whose supply is potentially unstable and that might be subject to manipulation. A few popular economists have apparently been operating on the premise that if an idea sounds crazy, it must be right. First they gave us the idea that we should cut taxes to increase Government revenue, reduce the Federal deficit, and slow inflation. The New York financial markets have recently told us what smart money thinks of that idea and of the tax cut that it spawned. Now these people are trying to sell the gold standard. These ideas not only sound crazy, they *are* crazy.

EXHIBIT 16-1 *Source: The New York Times*, Robert M. Dunn, Jr., copyright ©The New York Times, Op. Ed. page, September 9, 1981. Reprinted by permission.

Australian currencies. A balance-of-payments deficit in such a country means that more money is flowing out of the country than is flowing in, and there is no central bank to restore the previous money supply. A payments deficit reduces the money supply by the amount of that deficit, producing payments adjustment through the three linkages described above. A payments surplus in such a country means a net inflow of money, with no domestic central bank to control it, and adjustment of the surplus through the same method.[3]

Specie flow is also the balance-of-payments adjustment mechanism that operates for countries that maintain a currency board rather than a central bank. A currency board resembles a central bank with one large difference: foreign exchange reserves are the only financial asset on the left side of the balance sheet. A currency board is usually prohibited by law from owning government debt or other domestic financial assets. This means that changes in foreign exchange reserves cannot be sterilized through purchases or sales of government debt. A loss of foreign exchange reserves, resulting from a payments deficit, must produce a parallel reduction in the stock of base money and the money supply. The money supply is regulated by changes in foreign exchange reserves that result from payments imbalances, and adjustment occurs through the specie flow mechanism.

Currency boards have typically been maintained by very small countries, such as emirates in the Middle East. A number of currency boards operated in British colonies or dependencies and held their reserves in the form of U.K. government bonds. A few developing countries with debt problems and a recent history of serious inflation are reportedly moving in the direction of currency boards by requiring that their central banks maintain at least partial backing for domestic base money in the form of foreign exchange reserves.

This same specie flow mechanism forces the balance of payments of a state or region within a country toward adjustment. We usually do not think of the balance of payments of Massachusetts, but there is one, and it must be adjusted when it is out of equilibrium. A deficit in the Massachusetts balance of payments means that residents of the state are making more payments to nonresidents than they are receiving from them. The stock of dollars held by Massachusetts residents must fall by the amount of that deficit. As checks are cleared against Massachusetts banks and in favor of out-of-state banks, the stock of member bank reserves in the local banking system declines, requiring a reduction of lending activity. A payments deficit reduces the money supply of a state, and imposes the same adjustment process as was described above for a country on the gold standard.

The implications of this mechanism are often quite severe. When a state or region suffers a major export loss, the resulting decline in output and incomes is not limited to the export industry. The resulting payments deficit drains money out of the local economy and banking system, deepening the resulting economic downturn. Eventually, local wages and other costs of doing business decline sufficiently to attract new businesses, and a recovery begins. The migration of unemployed

---

[3]For a discussion of balance-of-payments adjustment in a country or dependency that lacks its own currency, see James C. Ingram, *Regional Payments Mechanisms: The Case of Puerto Rico* (Chapel Hill: University of North Carolina Press, 1962), pp. 113–133.

people out of the state reduces both purchases of imports and the demand for local housing, which lowers real estate prices, making the state more attractive for incoming businesses.

A sharp decline in the textile and shoe industries in Massachusetts during the 1950s caused such an adjustment process, and the state economy did not fully recover for many years. Declining expenditures on national defense and soft markets for the state's computer industry produced a similar process in Massachusetts during the early 1990s.

THE *IS/LM/BB* GRAPH AS A ROUTE TO UNDERSTANDING BALANCE-OF-PAYMENTS ADJUSTMENT

A graphical technique that is widely used in domestic macroeconomics can be readily extended to an open economy framework.[a] It allows a somewhat more rigorous, if oversimplified, analysis of the effects of various policies designed to adjust payments disequilibria. For students who have had an intermediate macroeconomics course, the purely domestic portion of what follows will probably not be new, and even part of the international extension may be familiar. For those who have not been introduced to these graphs, an introduction follows.

The *IS/LM* Graph

The domestic economy is modeled on a real sector and a market for money. The real sector is in equilibrium when $I_i = S$, that is, when intended investment equals savings, which is the standard definition of equilibrium in a simple Keynesian model. The market for money is in equilibrium when $MD = MS$, that is, when the demand for money equals the supply. If both the market for goods and the market for money are in equilibrium, then Walras law implies that the market for bonds must also be in equilibrium. Thus to analyze equilibrium in the entire economy, we need consider only two markets, goods and money.

Returning to the real sector, which is to be represented by the *IS* line, we find that savings is a positive function of domestic income (Y) through the marginal propensity to save. Intended investment (I_i) is a negative function of the interest rate (r), so:

$$S = F(\overset{+}{Y})$$

and

$$I_i = F(\overset{-}{r})$$

[a]Readers who have already been introduced to *IS/LM* graphs can move immediately to page 345.

The situation in which $S = I_i$ can then be represented as shown in Figure 16-1. Along IS, intended investment equals savings; therefore GNP is at its equilibrium level. To the left of IS intended investment is greater than savings, so GNP tends to rise. Interest rates are too low (which increases investment) or incomes are too low (which represses saving), resulting in the excess of intended investment over savings. The opposite situation holds to the right of IS. The economy automatically moves toward IS when it is out of equilibrium through changes in output up to the level of full employment, beyond which there is inflation which raises nominal GNP. A movement from point A to point B illustrates the offsetting impacts of an increase in Y and a decline in the interest rate. Starting from equilibrium at point A, an increase in output and incomes causes an increase in savings, making it exceed previously intended levels of investment. If interest rates fell by dr, however, intended investment would rise to the new level of savings and the economy would be at point B.

The slope of IS reflects the relationship between the size of the marginal propensity to save and the impact of changes of the interest rate on intended investment levels. If the marginal propensity to save was high or if intended investment was insensitive to changes in the interest rate, IS would be steep because a large change in interest rates would be required to offset the effect of a small change in incomes. A flatter IS would imply the opposite situation: that investment is highly sensitive to interest rates and/or that the marginal propensity to save is low, so that a large change in incomes would be required to offset the effect of a small change in the interest rate.

Since this graph has only two dimensions, the effects of only two variables (Y and r) on the savings/investment relationship can be shown. If any other relevant factor shifts, the IS line moves. A more expansionary fiscal policy, for example, would shift it to the right, as would an increase in export sales caused by an economic expansion abroad. Either event would increase the level of GNP that was consistent with a given level of the interest rate because

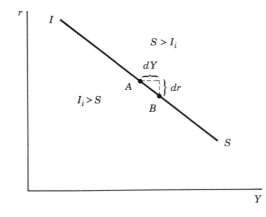

FIGURE 16-1   Equilibrium in the savings/investment relationship.

domestic savings would have to rise relative to private domestic investment to make room for the larger government budget deficit or the stronger current account. With a government sector and with international trade, the savings investment identity becomes:

$$I = S + (T - G) + (M - X)$$

It should be remembered that in this identity I is actual investment, including unintended changes in inventories. This identity must be true, but intended investment equals the sum of the items on the right side of the equation only when the economy is at equilibrium, that is, when intended investment equals actual investment, because there are no unintended changes in inventories.

The market for money is in equilibrium when $MD = MS$, where the money supply is determined by the central bank. The demand for money is a positive function of income (the transactions demand for money, stressed by monetarists) and a negative function of the interest rate under the assumption that money does not pay interest and that therefore the interest rate is the opportunity cost of holding money rather than bonds. This can be shown as

$$MD = F(\overset{+}{Y}, \overset{-}{r})$$

$MS = \overline{MS}$ meaning that the money supply is determined

$ = $ outside the model by the central bank

$MD = MS$ in equilibrium

With a given money supply, which has been determined by the central bank, equilibrium exists in the market for money along the LM line shown in Figure 16-2.

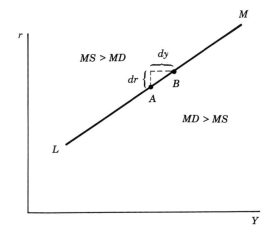

FIGURE 16-2   Equilibrium in the market for money.

Starting from point A, an increase in the interest rate reduces the amount of money people want to hold, creating an excess supply of money. An increase in incomes of dY would raise the transactions demand for money sufficiently to return the market to equilibrium with the preexisting money supply. The slope of LM reflects the relative sensitivity of the demand for money to changes in incomes and in interest rates. A monetarist would believe that the role of income is far stronger and that the line is therefore very steep. A Keynesian would argue for a stronger role for the interest rate and would therefore believe that the line was flatter, particularly at low interest rates.

Since only the level of national income and the interest rate are shown on the two axes, any other factors that affect the market for money cause the LM line to shift. An increase in the money supply, for example, would cause it to shift to the right, whereas a decision of people to hold more money at every level of GNP (a reduction in the velocity of money) would cause LM to shift to the left.

If the two lines derived above are put on the same graph, it is possible to see where the economy is in equilibrium and how it reacts to policy changes (see Figure 16-3). At the equilibrium levels of Y and r, the real economy is at rest, because intended investment equals savings, and the market for money is in equilibrium, because the demand for money equals the supply. If a more expansionary fiscal policy were adopted, the situation shown in Figure 16-4 would hold.

A more expansionary budget causes GNP to rise because a higher level of income is required to produce enough additional private saving to offset the decrease in government saving $(G - T)$. It also produces a higher interest rate owing to the effect of the higher level of incomes on the transactions demand for money. If the LM line were steeper, the expansionary effect on Y would

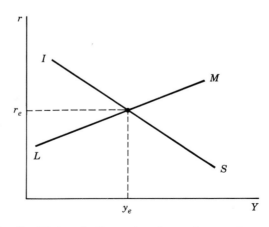

FIGURE 16-3   Equilibrium in the real and monetary sectors.

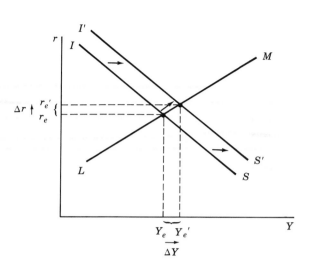

FIGURE 16-4 Impacts of fiscal expansion.

be smaller. If *LM* were vertical, as some monetarists would suggest, there would be no effect on *Y*; the expansionary fiscal policy is entirely crowded out through its effects on interest rates.

The central bank's decision to increase the money supply would have the effects illustrated in Figure 16-5. The expansion of the money supply causes the interest rate to fall, which increases intended investment. At the resulting higher level of output, savings rises to the new level of investment and the economy is again at equilibrium.

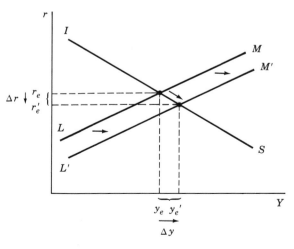

FIGURE 16-5 Impacts of an expansion on the money supply.

BALANCE-OF-PAYMENTS EQUILIBRIUM, AS AN ADDITIONAL LINE

If the balance of payments is added to this macroeconomy and if payments equilibrium is a goal or policy constraint, a new line is needed. If the balance of payments is viewed in the following oversimplified form:

$$CA = F(\overline{Y})$$

and

$$KA = F(\overset{+}{r})$$

with equilibrium where

$$CA + KA = 0$$

then the balance of payments is in equilibrium along the line shown in Figure 16-6.

The slope of BB represents the relationship between the impact of the interest rate on the capital account and the impact of domestic incomes on imports. If the marginal propensity to import is very high or if international capital flows are unresponsive to changes in local interest rates, BB is steep. If instead capital markets are closely integrated, so large amounts of capital flow in response to small interest rate differentials, and/or if the marginal propensity to import is low, BB becomes much flatter. It is worth noting that the capital account is positively related to the level of domestic interest rates rather than to recent changes in yields. A flow-adjustment model of the capital account, rather than a stock-adjustment approach, is implicit in the BB line. It would not be possible to define the IS and LM lines, and

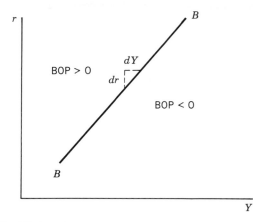

FIGURE 16-6   Equilibrium in the balance of payments.

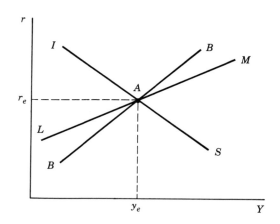

FIGURE 16-7   Domestic and international equilibrium.

therefore to combine the three functions, if changes in interest rates were on the vertical axis of this graph, as would be implied by a stock-adjustment or portfolio balance approach.

Since only the effect of interest rates and domestic income on the balance of payments can be shown directly on the graph, any other factor that shifts the payments situation causes BB to shift. An increase in foreign incomes, for example, that caused an increase in the demand for domestically produced exports would cause BB to shift to the right. A devaluation of the local currency, which strengthened the current account, would have the same effect.

If the BB line is added to the previously discussed IS/LM graph, equilibrium in all three sectors exists at point A (see Figure 16-7). There is no reason, of course, for the economy to be in such an equilibrium state. In Figure 16-8 an economy with a fixed exchange rate operates at point A and has a balance-of-payments deficit.

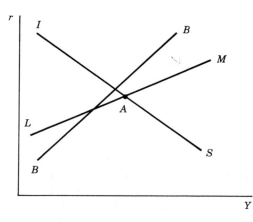

FIGURE 16-8   Domestic equilibrium with a balance of payments deficit.

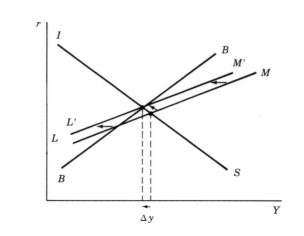

FIGURE 16-9   Balance-of-payments adjustment under specie flow.

PAYMENTS ADJUSTMENT THROUGH SPECIE FLOW

As was discussed in the main text, the specie flow mechanism requires that the domestic money supply be allowed to fall when a country has a balance-of-payments deficit until the deficit is fully adjusted. Such a decline in the money supply is shown as a leftward shift of *LM* (Figure 16-9). Balance-of-payments adjustment is automatic, but it produces higher interest rates and, more importantly, a lower level of GNP. If this exercise had begun with a payments surplus, *LM* would have shifted to the right until equilibrium was reestablished. Nominal income would have been higher, which might have meant considerable inflation. *LM* moves to the right or left as required to produce equilibrium, whether or not the resulting effects on national income are desirable.

THE BRETTON WOODS ADJUSTMENT MECHANISM: FISCAL AND MONETARY POLICIES

The post–World War II international financial system designed at the Bretton Woods conference in New Hampshire during the summer of 1944 was intended not only to avoid the rigidity and lack of policy autonomy of the specie flow system, but also to escape the relative chaos that resulted from the lack of a broadly accepted system during the interwar period. The result was a rather ingenious approach that functioned with varying degrees of success until the early

1970s.[4] The international financial history of that period is discussed later in Chapter 20.

For minor and presumably temporary payments imbalances, there was no expectation of active adjustment policies. Foreign exchange reserves would accumulate or be depleted, and their monetary impacts would be sterilized, until normal payments patterns returned. National macroeconomic policies were not to be diverted from their domestic goals by transitory and minor changes in balance-of-payments results.

If payments disequilibria were more serious, however, both monetary and fiscal policies were to be used to produce adjustment. Deficits called for a more restrictive set of policies, and payments surpluses were to be adjusted through more expansionary policies. The system was to be symmetrical in that both deficit and surplus countries were to bear the same responsibility for adjustment. Because the timing and mix of policies were to be determined by individual governments, the rigidity of specie flow was avoided. If, however, countries were in sufficiently serious payments deficits to require large loans (drawings) from the International Monetary Fund, the design of an adjustment program would involve the Fund through what became known as "conditionality"; that is, large drawings from the IMF are conditional on the imposition of a policy program that can be expected to make repayment possible. Although national governments were not put under the binding constraints implied by the specie flow system, those countries that rely heavily on IMF resources (primarily LDCs) often complain that conditionality requirements leave them with considerably less than full control over national macroeconomic policies.

Although Bretton Woods was a fixed exchange rate system, it did have provisions for parity changes. Countries facing particularly large and chronic payments disequilibria were expected to change their parities, with deficits calling for devaluations and vice versa. Large exchange rate changes, however, were to occur only after consultations with the International Monetary Fund in order to avoid competitive devaluations (Country A undertakes a large devaluation, which Country B feels to be threatening to its payments situation, so Country B devalues, threatening Country C's payments position, and so on) or otherwise disruptive exchange rate changes. Exchange rate changes will be covered in more detail in the next chapter.

With regard to payments adjustment through fiscal and monetary policies, the tighter policies required for deficit countries were to have the same effects described for the specie flow system: prices and incomes were to be held down, thus improving the current account, and higher interest rates that resulted from a tighter monetary policy were to attract capital inflows. The more expansionary policies adopted by surplus countries were to produce the opposite effects, the thought being that if both sides of the disequilibrium followed the rules, neither side would have to shift policies very far from those desired for domestic purposes.

[4]The academic history of balance-of-payments adjustment under the Bretton Woods system can be found in Peter Kenen, "Macroeconomic Theory and Policy: How the Closed Economy Was Opened," in R. Jones and P. Kenen, eds., *Handbook of International Economics,* Vol. II (Amsterdam: North-Holland Press, 1985, pp. 625–678. The history of international financial policy in this era is covered in Robert Solomon, *The International Monetary System 1945–1976: An Insider's View* (New York: Harper & Row, 1977), Chaps. 2 through 13.

IS/LM/BB ANALYSIS OF ADJUSTMENT UNDER THE BRETTON WOODS SYSTEM

If a country tightens its monetary policy to adjust a payments deficit, the *IS/LM/BB* representation is the same as for the specie flow system presented earlier. The only difference is that the central bank decides to tighten monetary policy rather than having a reduction of the money supply result automatically from a loss of gold reserves. (See Figure 16-10.)

The effects of fiscal policy on the balance of payments are more complicated and depend on the relative slopes of the *LM* and *BB* lines. The case in which *BB* is steeper than *LM*, which implies much less than complete international capital mobility, is shown in Figure 16-11. Tightening of fiscal policy eliminates the payments deficit, but it does so at the cost of a larger loss of GNP than occurred in the case of a tightening of monetary policy in Figure 16-11. The two policies are compared in Figure 16-12. Monetary policy is more efficient as a route to payments adjustment in the sense that the resulting loss of GNP is smaller. This is because tightening the fiscal policy reduces domestic interest rates, which worsens the capital account. Hence a larger reduction in GNP is necessary to produce the required current account improvement. Tightening the monetary policy both reduces incomes and raises interest rates. The latter effect improves the capital account, which means that the required current account improvement, and therefore the reduction in GNP, is smaller.

If the *BB* line is flatter than the *LM* line, implying a great sensitivity of international capital flows to small interest rate differentials, the effects of fiscal policy on the balance of payments become quite different (Figure 16-13).

A balance-of-payments deficit is adjusted, not by tightening the budget, but by a more expansionary fiscal policy. This odd conclusion results because *BB* is flatter than *LM*. Thus when the more expansionary budget increases the

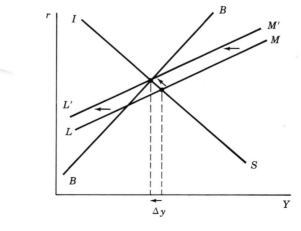

FIGURE 16-10 Payments adjustment through monetary policy.

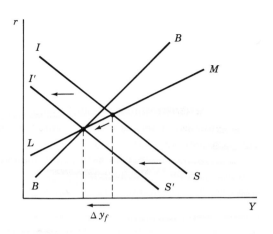

FIGURE 16-11   Payments adjustment through a tightening of fiscal policy.

interest rate, the result is a huge inflow of capital that more than offsets any negative impact of higher GNP on the current account. The capital account dominates the balance of payments, and so changes in interest rates are far more important to balance-of-payments results than are changes in income.

The Bretton Woods participants did not foresee this case because strict controls on capital flows were expected to remain in effect. This would make the capital account relatively unresponsive to interest rate differentials, causing the BB line to be much steeper than the LM line. In the 1960s and 1970s, however, controls on capital account transactions were eased or eliminated in most industrialized countries, creating the possibility that BB could be flatter than LM. Thus this seemingly perverse relationship between fiscal policy and the balance of payments could occur.

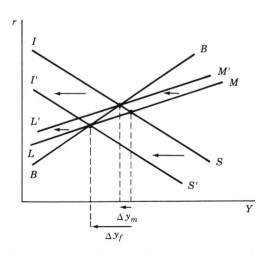

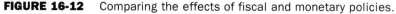

FIGURE 16-12   Comparing the effects of fiscal and monetary policies.

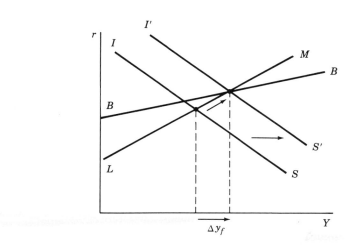

FIGURE 16-13   Adjustment of a payments deficit through expansionary fiscal policy.

This result would only be possible for a few highly industrialized countries such as the United States, Japan, and Germany, whose capital markets are highly integrated. During the early 1980s, for example, large U.S. budget deficits were accompanied by a sharp appreciation of the dollar, which would have been a payments surplus in a fixed parity system. A larger budget deficit appeared to strengthen rather than weaken the U.S. balance of payments. The conclusion is made uncertain by the fact that the U.S. monetary policy was very tight at this time, which means that either the more expansionary budget or the tighter monetary policy could have pushed the dollar up.

Critical Flaws in the Bretton Woods Adjustment Process

The use of monetary and fiscal policies to adjust payments disequilibria was not particularly successful, especially in the latter part of the Bretton Woods era. This failure helped to bring about the collapse of the system in the early 1970s. Many surplus countries believed that they should not have to adopt more expansionary policies than they desired for domestic purposes in order to adjust payments disequilibria that were caused by excessively expansionary policies in the deficit countries. Because the surplus countries were unwilling to adopt more expansionary macroeconomic policies, the whole adjustment burden fell on deficit countries. In such a situation payments adjustment required that they adopt very restrictive policies because they were getting no help from macroeconomic expansion in the surplus countries. The deficit countries found the required tightening of monetary and fiscal policies to be extremely painful and frequently resorted to protectionism or other distortions of international transactions as an alternative. Limits were put on the residents' ability to spend money abroad while traveling, exchange controls on capital transactions were reintroduced, and protectionism designed to reduce imports for payments purposes became more common.

In the 1950s a British economist, James Meade, described four situations in which a country could find itself.[5] Two of these cases, which are still widely known as the Meade conflict cases, suggest why many countries found balance-of-payments adjustment through fiscal and monetary policy changes to be unacceptable:

1. A balance-of-payments surplus and a domestic recession.
2. A balance-of-payments deficit and domestic inflation.
3. A balance-of-payments surplus and domestic inflation.
4. A balance-of-payments deficit and a domestic recession.

Cases 1 and 2 do not present obvious problems for those managing domestic macroeconomic policies. In case 1, both problems call for more expansionary policies. The more rapid growth of the money supply or larger government budget deficit that will adjust the payments surplus will also lead to recovery from the domestic recession. In case 2, the same situation holds, but the policies are to shift in the opposite direction. Tighter fiscal and monetary policies will both reduce domestic inflation and eliminate the payments deficit.

Cases 3 and 4, however, present problems for the management of macroeconomic policies. In case 3, the domestic economy calls for restrictive policies that would increase the payments surplus. Payments adjustment under Bretton Woods rules calls for expansionary policies that would exacerbate the domestic inflation. Whichever way the policies are shifted, one problem is eased while the other is aggravated. The choice between the two sides of the conflict is relatively easy, however. A balance-of-payments surplus may create annoying problems, but it is hardly a crisis. The domestic economy was typically viewed as far more important, and restrictive policies were used to stop the inflation at the cost of a larger payments surplus. The problems facing countries with payments deficits were, of course, made considerably worse, but that was of little concern to the surplus countries, for whom the dominant goal was the control of inflation.

Case 4 is the worst of the group. The balance-of-payments deficit calls for restrictive policies that would deepen the recession, whereas the domestic economy needs expansionary policies that would worsen the payments deficit. In this case, however, the balance of payments could not be ignored. If foreign exchange reserves were being depleted and confidence in the domestic currency was rapidly evaporating, the government could not risk the expansionary policies required for domestic recovery. In this situation the temptation to adopt protectionist policies, controls on capital account transactions, and a variety of other distorting interventions has often become irresistible. The United States was in case 4 when the Kennedy administration took office in early 1961. The result was the 1962 adoption of the Interest Equalization Tax (a tariff on imported securities) and great caution in the adoption of expansionary macroeconomic policies, which produced a very slow recovery in 1961–1963.

[5] James Meade, *The Balance of Payments* (London: Oxford University Press, 1951).

Cases 3 and 4 occurred with sufficient frequency in the Bretton Woods era to make the use of domestic macroeconomic policies for payments adjustment largely unworkable. By the end of the 1960s the system was almost inoperative, which led to its collapse in the early 1970s and the adoption of floating exchange rates by many major industrialized countries in 1973.[6]

THE POLICY ASSIGNMENT MODEL: ONE LAST HOPE FOR FIXED EXCHANGE RATES

During the 1960s Robert Mundell and J. Marcus Fleming produced an interesting attempt to salvage payments adjustment with fixed exchange rates.[7] The model was not successful, as indicated by the events of the early 1970s, but it remains intellectually useful. It is based on an older concept of the relationship between the number of policy goals being pursued by a government and the number of policy tools it has at its disposal. The idea is that if the government has at least as many policy tools as it has goals, it should be possible to design a set of policy positions that will reach all the goals simultaneously. The policy tools must have different relative strengths in affecting different goals, and it must be possible to run the policies separately or independently.

Each policy tool is directed at the goal on which it has the greatest relative impact, but allowance is made for the secondary effects of other policies on that goal. In theory it should be possible to maneuver the policies toward a set that reaches all the goals.

Mundell and Fleming argued that because monetary policy had a great relative impact on the balance of payments while fiscal policy was more powerful in affecting domestic output (as was shown in Figure 16-12) it should be possible to solve the Meade conflict cases. Fiscal policy would be directed at maintaining the desired level of domestic output while the central bank pursued balance-of-payments equilibrium, with each policy being so managed that allowance was made for the secondary effects of the other policy on its goal. Figure 16-14, which is adapted from an article by Robert Mundell on this model, indicates how this may work.[8]

The *DD* line represents all the combinations of fiscal and monetary policies that will produce the desired level of domestic output. It therefore indicates how

[6]Despite its problems, the system of fixed exchange rates retained some defenders. See Samuel I. Katz, "The Case for the Par Value System," *Princeton Essays in International Finance,* No. 92, March 1972.

[7]The literature on what became known as the Mundell–Fleming policy assignment model begins with Robert Mundell, "The Appropriate Use of Monetary and Fiscal Policy for Internal and External Stability," *IMF Staff Papers,* March 1962, pp. 70–77, and J. Marcus Fleming, "Domestic Financial Policies Under Fixed and Under Floating Exchange Rates," *IMF Staff Papers,* 1962, pp. 369–379. Mundell's work in this and related areas is gathered in a book of readings: Robert Mundell, *International Economics* (New York: Macmillan, 1968). For an important early discussion of the problem of the number of policy goals versus the number of policy tools, see Jan Tinbergen, *The Theory of Economic Policy* (Amsterdam: North-Holland Press, 1952), Chaps. 4–5.

[8]Robert Mundell, *International Economics* (New York: Macmillan, 1968), p. 235.

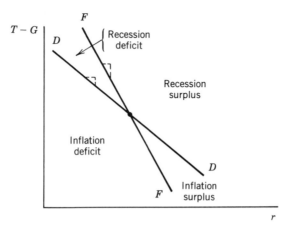

FIGURE 16-14 Internal and external balance

fiscal and monetary policy can be traded off against each other. The fact that *DD* is relatively flat indicates that a small adjustment of fiscal policy will have the same impact on the domestic economy as would a larger change in monetary policy. This point of view is decidedly Keynesian and would not be popular among monetarists. To the right of *DD* the policy set is too restrictive and the economy is in a recession, whereas to the left the policies are too expansionary and inflation results. *DD* can therefore be viewed as a frontier between two regions of the quadrant: inflation to the lower left and recession to the upper right, with the line representing sets of policies that will avoid either of these problems.

The *FF* line represents all the policy sets that will produce balance-of-payments equilibrium, and its slope again illustrates the manner in which the two policies trade off. The greater steepness of the line means that a small change in monetary policy will have the same impact on the balance of payments as a large change in fiscal policy. Hence monetary policy is powerful and fiscal policy less so in producing payments adjustment. To the left of *FF* the policies are too expansionary, creating a payments deficit, whereas to the right of the line the policies are too restrictive, producing a surplus. *FF* is also a frontier, in this instance between the lower left area of the quadrant where a payments deficit exists, and the upper right where a surplus results. The four areas of disequilibrium correspond to the four Meade cases discussed above. The recession/surplus case is to the right of both lines, the deficit/inflation case is to the left of both lines, and the two conflict cases are the smaller areas between the equilibrium lines.

Both policy goals are met where the lines cross. Thus just one policy set will produce both payments equilibrium and the desired level of domestic output. If a government starts from a disequilibrium situation, its ability to find the point where the lines cross depends critically on the correct assignment of policies to goals (Figure 16-15). As this figure shows, the incorrect assignment of policies to goals can produce a disaster. If, starting from Point *A*, fiscal policy is used to reach *FF* (payments equilibrium) and monetary policy is used to deal with the domestic economy (*DD*), things end badly. If, however, the correct assignment was made, the path reaches point *B* and the desired equilibrium for both goals fairly easily.

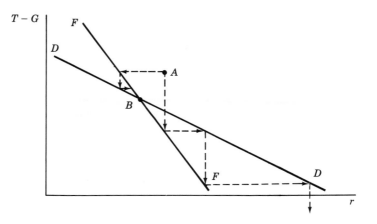

FIGURE 16-15   Balance-of-payments adjustment through policy assignment.

THE *IS/LM/BB* GRAPH
FOR THE POLICY ASSIGNMENT MODEL

The policy assignment approach to dealing with the two Meade conflict cases can also be seen with the *IS/LM/BB* graph that was introduced earlier. If, for example, a country faces a domestic recession and a balance-of-payments deficit (case 4), an expansionary fiscal policy is used to escape the recession, and tight money is used to adjust the payments deficit (Figure 16-16). The tightening of monetary policy shifts *LM* to the left, whereas the more expansionary budget moves *IS* to the right. The goal is to have them cross on the *BB* line above the desired level of GNP, represented in the figure as Y_{fe}.

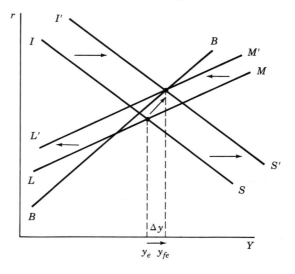

FIGURE 16-16   Balance-of-payments adjustments through policy assignment in the deficit recession case.

Problems with the Policy Assignment Model

Although the policy assignment model is ingenious, it contains flaws and was not the salvation of the fixed exchange rate regime of Bretton Woods. Some of the problems lie with the theory behind the model, whereas others are more practical. First, the modeling of the balance of payments is extremely simple, and the capital account is viewed in a pure flow-adjustment perspective. In a stock-adjustment world, the model would not work because high but unchanging interest rates would attract capital inflows for only a brief period. Constant increases in interest rates would be necessary to produce continuing capital inflows, and such repeated yield increases would be inconsistent with domestic macroeconomic equilibrium at a desired level of GNP. If a stock-adjustment model of the capital account is adopted, the definition of FF in the previous Mundell graph requires that the horizontal axis be labeled "change in the interest rate," which would make it impossible to define the DD line. The model is internally consistent only with a flow-adjustment model of the capital account.

The problem of the number of goals is more important. The model assumes that the government cares about only two things: balance-of-payments equilibrium and a desired level of current GNP. If additional goals are introduced, additional policy tools are required or the full set of goals cannot be reached. If, for example, the government is concerned about the long-term rate of economic growth, it will want to avoid excessively high interest rates that reduce the share of current GNP going into investment. A rate of growth of the capital stock that is sufficient to produce fairly rapid long-term economic growth may require a fiscal/monetary policy set that represses both private and public consumption sufficiently to make room for more investment in plant and equipment. That implies a tighter fiscal policy, to reduce consumption, and a more expansionary monetary policy, to encourage investment. Monetary policy can no longer be assigned solely to the balance of payments because it is needed to pursue a desired level of domestic investment. When a third goal of long-term growth is introduced, two policy tools are no longer sufficient.

If the problem of the number of goals is pursued further, the distinction between goals and tools starts to break down. Goals are what the government cares about, and tools are what it is prepared to manipulate to reach those goals. Fiscal policy, however, contains government expenditure programs, about which the voters care a great deal. It also includes taxes, about which people have strong opinions which they feel free to express on election day. Voters do not want programs from which they benefit to be turned on and off over the business cycle, and they want their taxes to be stable and therefore predictable. Fiscal policy contains large elements of 'goal,' and is often unavailable to deal with short-term business cycle problems.

The record of the U.S. federal budget during the 1980s does not suggest a fiscal policy that was based on the macroeconomic needs of the economy. Many have argued that the federal budget was (and remains) out of control. That leaves monetary policy as the only macroeconomic tool available for cyclical stabilization, but even the Federal Reserve System faces constraints. Monetary policy means interest rates, and voters care very much about sharp increases in yields, because large losses are taken on bond and stock portfolios, and because mortgage loans become impossible to arrange at monthly costs that families can afford. There is certainly far more flexibility in U.S. monetary policy than there is in the federal budget, but even the central bank must operate within limits.

The policy assignment model is based on the assumption that both fiscal and monetary policy are readily available for rapid adjustment to pursue only two goals. That is not the case. There are more than two goals, and fiscal policy is seldom available for short-run adjustment. The United States has only one powerful macroeconomic tool—monetary policy—and the country has a number of goals. Balance-of-payments adjustment requires another tool, which leads to the exchange rate. The next chapter, Chapter 17, deals with changes in otherwise fixed parities, that is, with devaluations and revaluations. The chapter that follows it discusses a regime of floating or flexible exchange rates.

QUESTIONS FOR STUDY AND REVIEW

1. Under the pre-1914 gold standard, Country A has a large gold strike: that is, it becomes able to produce far more gold. What happens to the balance of payments of Country A? Why? How is it returned to equilibrium? What is the effect of this process on the rest of the world?

2. Under the Bretton Woods system, a country with a balance-of-payments deficit is to make what changes in its domestic macroeconomic policies? Under what circumstances would these changes parallel the needs of the domestic economy? When would these policy changes conflict with those needs?

3. Why were payments surplus countries under far less pressure to adopt the domestic macroeconomic policies called for by the adjustment process than were deficit countries under the Bretton Woods system? What effect did this situation have on the problems facing deficit countries as they tried to adjust?

4. Under the Mundell/Fleming policy assignment approach, what policies are called for if a country experiences a payments surplus and a domestic inflationary boom?

5. Use the *IS/LM/BB* graph to show what happens in the situations described in questions 1, 2, and 4. Show the line-shifts, and explain why they occur.

SELECTED REFERENCES

Eichengreen, B. *The Gold Standard in Theory and History.* New York: Methuen, 1985.

Hume, D. "On the Balance of Trade (1752)." In R. Cooper, ed. *International Finance: Readings.* Baltimore: Penguin Books, 1969.

Kenen, P. "Macroeconomic Theory and Policy: How the Closed Economy Was Opened." In R. Jones and P. Kenen, eds. *Handbook of International Economics,* Vol. II (Amsterdam: North-Holland, 1985), pp. 625–678.

Meade, J. *The Balance of Payments*. New York: Oxford University Press, 1951.

Mundell, R. *International Economics*. New York, Macmillan, 1968.

Solomon, R. *The International Monetary System 1945–1976: An Insider's View*. New York: Harper & Row, 1977.

Stern, R. *The Balance of Payments*. Chicago: Aldine, 1968.

Yeager, L. *International Monetary Relations: Theory, History, and Policy*. 2nd ed. New York: Harper & Row, 1976.

17

BALANCE-OF-PAYMENTS ADJUSTMENT THROUGH EXCHANGE RATE CHANGES

A RETURN TO SUPPLY AND DEMAND

The argument for using the exchange rate as the primary tool for balance-of-payments adjustment goes back to the first week of elementary economics. When a market is out of equilibrium, a price change is the preferred solution; if a market remains in disequilibrium, it is typically because government intervention or some other rigidity has precluded the necessary price adjustment. If the market for foreign exchange is viewed as being analogous to the market for corn, the same argument holds, and exchange rate changes are the obvious answer for payments disequilibria. A supply and demand graph for foreign exchange may make this point clearer (see Figure 17-1).

The autonomous demand for foreign exchange is derived from the domestic demand for foreign goods, services, and financial assets. The autonomous supply of foreign exchange represents the foreign demand for the local currency, and

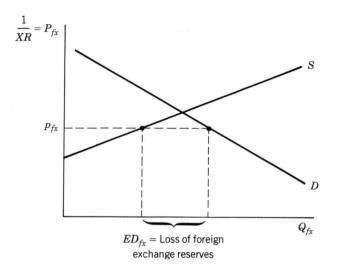

FIGURE 17-1 The market for foreign exchange with a balance-of-payments deficit.

it is similarly derived from the rest of the world's demand for this country's goods, services, and financial assets. (If the local demand for foreign goods, services, and assets exceeds the foreign demand for the same items in this country, the demand for foreign exchange exceeds the supply at the existing price, and a balance-of-payments deficit exists.) The excess demand for foreign exchange is absorbed through central bank intervention as the deficit country loses foreign exchange reserves.

All the adjustment mechanisms discussed in Chapter 16 represent attempts to force the demand function shown in Figure 17-1 to shift to the left and the supply function to shift to the right, producing equilibrium at the historic fixed parity. As was suggested in that chapter, the domestic effects of the policies required to produce such demand and supply shifts are painful and may not be politically acceptable. It might be wondered why a government would even consider imposing such difficulty on its economy, when the option of an exchange rate change is readily available. If there is excess demand for foreign exchange, then the best policy is to raise the price (lower the exchange rate) to a level at which the excess demand disappears.

Raising the price to clear the foreign exchange market, as indicated in Figure 17-2, and avoiding all the problems of payments adjustment discussed in the previous chapter, would seem to be an easy matter. Unfortunately, it is far from simple. Devaluations are difficult to impose and often fail, in the sense that improvements in the balance of payments are insufficient or so short-lived that the devaluation has to be repeated. The market for foreign exchange is not analogous to the market for corn. Merely adjusting a price to clear the market, which would succeed in the corn market, is not a guaranteed solution in the case of the market for foreign exchange, as will be discussed in this chapter.

For a country with a relatively open economy, the exchange rate can be its most important single price. The exchange rate directly or indirectly affects virtually

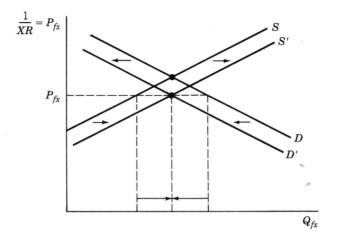

FIGURE 17-2 The market for foreign exchange in an adjustment of a payments deficit with a fixed parity.

everything in the economy, and many of the effects of exchange rate changes can be quite disruptive. Exchange rate changes have impacts on the level of aggregate demand, the price level, the interest rate, the distribution of income within the country, and many other aspects of the economy. Because changing an exchange rate in either direction will be unpopular with at least one major group in the economy, elected governments usually prefer to avoid such changes whenever possible.

For the sake of simplicity, the following discussion stresses devaluations but it should be remembered that revaluations are also possible, if less frequent, and that the resulting impacts are in the opposite direction.

REQUIREMENTS FOR A SUCCESSFUL DEVALUATION

For a devaluation to succeed in adjusting a chronic payments deficit, a number of conditions must be met. Devaluations have both microeconomic and macroeconomic effects that can complicate the payments adjustment process. The microeconomic requirements for a successful devaluation, which are typically less serious, will be discussed first. Macroeconomic problems, which are often much more demanding, follow.

The Marshall-Lerner Condition: The Desirability of High-Demand Elasticities

The primary objective of a devaluation is to change relative prices in ways that will encourage exports and discourage imports. To devalue a currency is to increase the local price of foreign money, thereby raising local prices of imports. If the U.S. dollar were devalued by 10 percent, the price of British sterling would rise from, for example, $1.80 to $1.98, thereby causing U.S. prices of British goods to increase proportionally. A British car with a price of £10,000 would have previously cost $18,000; now it will cost $19,800, which it is hoped will discourage U.S. buyers of such vehicles, who will instead shift to domestic models. The U.S. price increase would be smaller only if the British manufacturer decided to absorb some of the effects of the devaluation in the form of a lower sterling price.

The effect of these increases in domestic prices on the volume of imports depends on the elasticity of demand. If that elasticity is high, a relatively large decline in import volumes occurs, and the devaluation has its intended effect. If the elasticity is less than one, however, the volume reduction will be insufficient to offset the price increase, and the local currency value of imports will rise. The higher the demand elasticity, the better the prospects for the success of the devaluation.

That elasticity depends on the strength of substitution and income effects. If domestic substitutes for imported goods are readily available, the substitution effect will be strong, suggesting a large decline in imports. If, however, imports consist largely of necessities for which domestic substitutes are not available, import reductions will be smaller, implying poor prospects for the success of the devaluation. This situation is more likely in developing countries, although even a highly developed nation such as the United States does not have obvious substitutes for some imported products such as oil.

The income effect will be powerful if imports are a major part of the typical citizen's budget; it is easy to see, then, why devaluations are unpopular in this circumstance. If a devaluation raises the domestic prices of major items in consumer budgets, such as food and fuel, real incomes decline, which necessitates reduced purchases of imports and other goods. Devaluations reduce real incomes in relatively open economies, which makes both devaluations and the governments that impose them unpopular.

With regard to exports, a devaluation will produce some combination of a reduction in the foreign currency price and an increase in the local currency price, with relative elasticities of supply and demand determining the outcome. If the local currency price of exports is fixed, implying an infinitely elastic supply function, the foreign currency price falls by the full percentage of the devaluation, which should encourage foreigners to purchase more of this country's goods. Returning to the earlier example, we see that when British sterling was $1.80, a U.S. product priced at $100 carried a price of £55.55 (100/1.80). The devaluation of the U.S. dollar by 10 percent produced a U.S. cost of sterling of $1.98. Therefore the U.S. product carrying a price of $100 would now cost British residents only £50.5, which should encourage U.K. purchases of American products.

If, instead, foreign currency prices of exports are fixed, implying an infinitely elastic foreign demand for such goods, the local currency price of exports rises by the percentage of the devaluation, which should encourage domestic firms to make greater efforts to sell abroad. Returning to the above numerical example, we find that if a product carries an unchanging British price of £100, the $1.80 exchange rate means a U.S. price of $180, and the 10 percent devaluation to $1.98 means a U.S. price of $198, which both earns U.S. firms more revenue for the same volumes of exports and encourages them to make greater efforts to increase those volumes.

If neither the demand nor the supply curve for exports is infinitely elastic, the foreign price of exports will fall by less than the full percentage of the devaluation, and the local price will rise by the rest of that percentage. The result will be an incentive for foreigners to purchase more of these goods and for exporters to make greater efforts to sell them. In all these cases, however, higher elasticities of demand for both imports and exports increase the desired impact of the devaluation on the balance of trade.

If the elasticities of demand for exports and imports are extremely low, a devaluation can worsen the trade balance rather than improve it. If prices are always fixed in exporters' currencies, which means that both elasticities of supply are infinite, the condition for the desired response of the trade account to the exchange rate is relatively simple: the two elasticities of demand (for imports and exports) must sum to more than one, that is, average more than 0.5. If they sum to exactly one, the trade account does not change when a devaluation occurs. The perverse trade account response to the exchange rate occurs only if they sum to less than one. This is known as the Marshall-Lerner condition.[1]

The effects of a devaluation on the trade balance can be seen in Figure 17-3. Prices are in the local currency; thus the devaluation causes a vertical shift in the foreign functions (demand for exports and supply of imports). A case in which

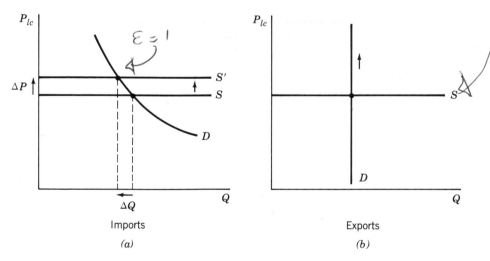

FIGURE 17-3 The Marshall-Lerner case.

[1]The discussion of the problem of elasticities of demand begins with Alfred Marshall, *Money Credit and Commerce* (London: Macmillan, 1923) and Abba Lerner, *The Economics of Control* (London: Macmillan 1944). See also G. Haberler, "The Market for Foreign Exchange and the Stability of the Balance of Payments," *Kyklos* 1949, pp. 193–218. The mathematical derivation of the more complicated cases in which supply elasticities are not infinite can be found in Jaraslav Vanek, *International Trade: Theory and Economic Policy* (Homewood, Ill.: Richard D. Irwin, 1967). For a survey of much of the recent research on this topic, see M. Goldstein and M. Khan, "Income and Price Effects in International Trade" in R. Jones and P. Kenen, eds., *Handbook of International Economics,* Vol. II (New York: North-Holland Press, 1985), pp. 1041–1106. For more recent econometric estimates, see Jaime Marquez, "Bilateral Trade Elasticities" *Review of Economics and Statistics,* Vol. 72, No. 1, February 1990, pp. 75–76.

the elasticities sum to exactly one is presented first. Since the foreign demand for exports is vertical, its shift upward means that it slides along itself, that is, that there is no change. Since the elasticity of demand for imports is one, the vertical shift of the supply function means that total expenditures on imports are the same before and after the devaluation, the decline in import volumes being just offset by the price increase. Neither export revenues nor import expenditures change, demonstrating that the trade balance is unaffected by the devaluation.

If the elasticity of demand for exports exceeds zero, which indicates that the elasticities sum to more than one, the results shown in Figure 17-4 will occur. Import expenditures remain unchanged, but export receipts have clearly increased. Thus the trade balance improves by the amount of the export revenue growth. The Marshall-Lerner condition is met, and a devaluation has its intended effect. If the elasticities sum to less than one, however, the outcome is quite different (see Figure 17-5). In this case, the trade account deteriorates. The vertical foreign demand for this country's products means that export revenues do not change, and the fact that the domestic elasticity of demand for imports is less than one means that total expenditures rise. The decline in the volume of imports is insufficient to offset the price increase, so the local currency cost of imports increases. The trade account worsens by the amount of the import expenditure growth.

The assumption of infinitely elastic supply functions is unrealistic, but it makes possible the simple version of the Marshall-Lerner condition. (The demand elasticities must sum to more than one.) If the elasticities of supply are less than infinite, the Marshall-Lerner condition becomes far more complicated. It remains true, however, that the higher the demand elasticities, the better the prospects that a devaluation will improve the trade balance. If these elasticities sum to more than one, the prospects that the devaluation will produce the desired change in the trade account are quite good.

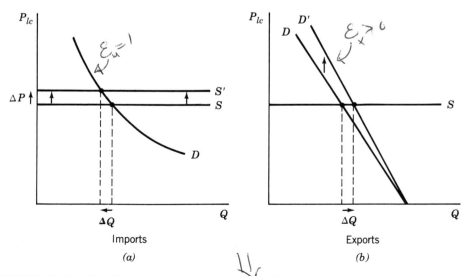

FIGURE 17-4 The Marshall-Lerner case where a devaluation succeeds.

$$\varepsilon_M + \varepsilon_x > 1$$

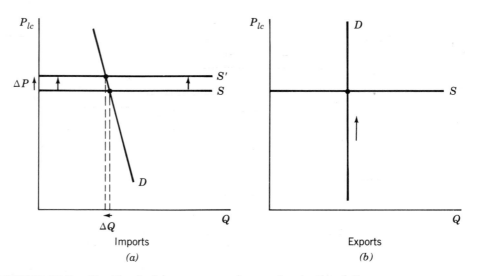

FIGURE 17-5   The Marshall-Lerner case where a devaluation fails.

It may be useful to show two somewhat more realistic cases. First, a small country is one that is a perfect competitor in both export and import markets (Figure 17-6). It has neither monopoly nor monopsony power, and it takes world prices of exports and imports as given. Imagine, for example, the role of Honduras in world trade. A dollar price of coffee exists in New York, over which Honduras has no control. Honduras can export as much or as little coffee as it chooses, without affecting that dollar price. The Honduras price of coffee is then the dollar price times the exchange rate, expressed as the number of Honduran lempiras per dollar. A 10 percent devaluation of the lempira leaves the dollar price of coffee

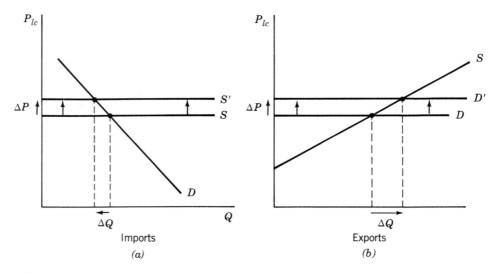

FIGURE 17-6   The small-country case.

*on export
pide* (handwritten margin note)

unchanged and therefore raises the lempira price by 10 percent. Honduras faces an infinitely elastic demand for coffee at the world price translated into lempiras at the current exchange rate. On the import side, Honduras faces a similar situation. Dollar prices are fixed, and the Honduras price is simply the dollar price times the number of lempiras per dollar. Honduras faces an infinitely elastic supply of imports at the world price translated into lempiras at the existing exchange rate. Since both export and import prices, measured in lempiras, rise by the percentage of the devaluation, there is no change in Honduras' terms of trade.

Many, or perhaps even most, countries in the world are in this situation, particularly when we allow for the large number of small island countries that have become independent in recent years. In this case, a devaluation is almost certain to improve the trade account.

On the export side, both quantity and price rise, producing a large increase in revenues. With regard to imports, the volume falls, which helps, but prices rise, which does not. Import expenditures rise if the elasticity of demand is less than one, and they fall if it is more than one. Whatever happens to import expenditures, export revenues rise sharply. In this case the trade account fails to improve, and instead is unchanged, only if both the domestic demand for imports and the supply of exports are vertical. If either of the domestic elasticities exceeds zero, the trade account improves.

The second case is that of a country that is somewhat larger in the sense that it has some market or monopoly power in one or more export markets but has no monopsony power as an importer. Many of the larger developing countries export large volumes of a few goods and import smaller amounts of many things. In their major export markets, they have significant market power and face sloping demand curves, but as importers they have no market power and face infinitely elastic supply curves. Brazil is such a country because it is far from a perfectly competitive seller of coffee and a few other major commodities, but it has no ability to control or influence its import prices. Sri Lanka and India would be in a similar situation with regard to exports of tea, whereas Zaire, Chile, and Zambia probably export enough copper to have some potential influence over prices. For such countries, the supply and demand curve shifts depicted in Figure 17-7 occur.

Again, there is a strong presumption that the balance of payments improves. On the export side, both price and quantity increase, implying significantly larger local currency revenues. It is worth noting, however, that the export price does not rise by the full percentage of the devaluation. World prices, denominated in foreign exchange, fall by the reminder of that percentage. Because import prices do rise by the percentage of the devaluation, there is a modest deterioration of this country's terms of trade. With regard to import expenditures, the outcome depends solely on the elasticity of demand. If it is more than one, expenditures fall, and vice versa, which repeats the small-country case. Because export revenues clearly rise, whereas import expenditures rise or fall slightly depending on whether the elasticity of demand is greater or less than one, the balance of trade should improve. That would fail to be the case only if the elasticities of demand for both exports and imports were very low.

During the 1950s and 1960s "elasticity pessimism" was fairly common. Many economists feared that the relevant demand elasticities were sufficiently low for

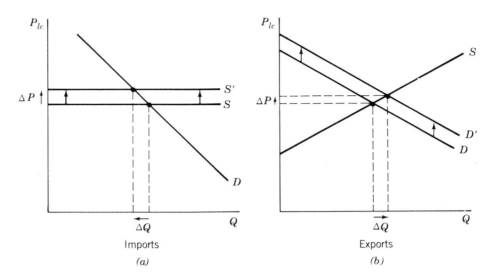

FIGURE 17-7 The larger country case.

many countries to make devaluations an unlikely solution for payments deficits. Improved econometric estimates of these elasticities and ongoing studies of de-valuations have made it clear that such pessimism is typically unjustified. Over reasonably long periods of time, demand elasticities are almost certain to be high enough to produce the desired effect of a devaluation on the trade account.[2]

Over short periods, however, there can be problems. Buyers of imports are creatures of habit, in the sense that they are accustomed to dealing with the same suppliers and need time to find alternatives. In addition, trade in raw materials often involves contracts that set prices and quantities to be purchased per month for considerable periods. Buyers cannot respond to exchange rate changes until such contracts expire and new arrangements can be made. If, for example, a Japanese steel company is committed by contract to purchase its iron ore requirements from Australia when another country devalues and offers iron ore at a lower yen price, the Japanese firm can make no response until its contract with the Australian mines expires.[3]

[2]Econometric estimates of the relevant elasticities can be found in H. Houthaker and S. Magee, "Income and Price Elasticities in World Trade," *Review of Economics and Statistics,* May 1969. See also E. Leamer and R. Stern, *Quantitative International Economics* (Boston: Allyn & Bacon, 1970). More recent estimates can be found in J. R. Artus and M. D. Knight, "Issues in the Assessment of Exchange Rates for Industrial Countries," *Occasional Paper No. 29,* International Monetary Fund, July 1984. For a review and summary of work in this area, see M. Goldstein and M. Khan, "Income and Price Effects in Foreign Trade," in R. Jones and P. Kenen, eds., *Handbook in International Economics,* Vol. II (Amsterdam, North-Holland Press, 1985), pp. 1041–1106.

[3]The J-curve problem is discussed in Steven Magee, "Currency Pass Through and Devaluation," *Brookings Papers in Economic Activity,* No. 1, 1983. See also Steven Magee, "Contracting and Spu-rious Deviations from Purchasing Power Parity," in H. Johnson and J. Frenkel, eds., *The Economics of Exchange Rates* (Boston: Addison-Wesley, 1978).

The effect of the time required to find new sources, and of such contracts, is to produce what is widely known as the "J-curve effect." After a devaluation, the trade balance follows a pattern that resembles a "J"; that is, it declines slightly for a brief period and then rises sharply. The period of worsening trade results may be six months or a year, but the trade account does respond in the intended manner if sufficient time is allowed to pass. Hence countries need enough foreign exchange reserves at the time of a devaluation to finance continuing trade deficits for that period, which suggests why IMF drawings often accompany such parity adjustments. Borrowing from the IMF is arranged to provide the foreign exchange needed to cover the period before the trade balance can be expected to improve.

Another complication is created if a country has maintained severe restrictions on imports during the period before the devaluation. Such import controls are quite common for countries with severe payments deficits which necessitate later devaluations. If these imports restraints are removed or eased at the time of the devaluation, imports will rise, or at least not fall as much as normally would be the case, partially offsetting the intended effect of the exchange rate change on the trade account. If a parity change is to be accompanied by the easing of previous import controls, the devaluation will have to be larger, and it is likely to take somewhat longer to have its intended effect on the trade balance than otherwise would be the case.

Macroeconomic Requirements for a Successful Devaluation

Devaluations typically fail not because of the microeconomic issues discussed in the previous section, but because of macroeconomic effects. As a result, the success of a devaluation generally depends on the adoption of appropriate fiscal and monetary policies.

Devaluations often seem to self-destruct, in the sense that the exchange rate change causes macroeconomic effects within the economy which cause the devaluation to fail. There are two views of these issues, Keynesian and monetarist; the Keynesian analysis is widely known as the absorption model of the trade account.[4]

The Absorption Approach to Devaluation

The absorption approach begins with the fact that a devaluation is expected to have effects that sharply increase aggregate demand for domestic output. Production of exports and import substitutes rises, which leads to higher incomes and

---

[4]The discussion of the absorption condition for the success of a devaluation begins with Sydney Alexander, "The Effects of a Devaluation on the Trade Balance," *IMF Staff Papers,* 1952, pp. 263–278. A combination of the elasticities and the absorption approach can be found in Sydney Alexander, "Effects of a Devaluation: A Simplified Synthesis of Elasticities and Absorption Approaches," *American Economic Review,* March 1959, pp. 22–42. The savings/investment relationship is discussed in J. Black, "A Savings and Investment Approach to Devaluation," *Economic Journal,* June 1959, pp. 267–274.

more consumption expenditures through the multiplier effect. Export- and import-competing industries become more profitable, which should encourage increased plant and equipment investment in those sectors. These expansionary forces may become excessive, particularly if the economy is close to full employment at the time of the devaluation, and result in inflation that destroys the effectiveness of the devaluation. These effects can be seen through simple national income identities:

$$Y = C + I + G + (X - M)$$

Therefore:

$$(X - M) = Y - (C + I + G)$$

where $C + I + G$ = absorption, which is the total domestic use of goods and services. Therefore:

$$d(X - M) = dY - d(C + I + G) \text{ or } dY - dA$$
$$\text{where } d = \text{change.}$$

The trade account can improve [$d(X - M)$ exceeds zero] only if domestic output grows by more than the growth in domestic absorption. This is a simple but important point. If an economy is producing $10,000 in output and is absorbing $11,000, the current account must be in deficit by $1,000. If, as a result of a devaluation, output increases to $12,000 but domestic absorption rises to $13,000, nothing has been accomplished. The trade account remains in deficit by $1,000. The $2,000 growth of output must be accompanied by sufficient restraint on domestic absorption to hold its growth to $1,000, thus producing output and absorption that are equal at $12,000 and a current account that is in balance. In this case the growth of absorption must be restricted to 50 percent of the growth of output, which implies a considerable tightening of fiscal and monetary policy.

In this case there is no suggestion that absorption must fall in absolute terms, but merely that its growth must be held well below the growth of output and incomes to allow the trade account to improve. If, however, the economy had been fully employed at the time of the devaluation, the implications of the absorption model would be more demanding. If output cannot rise, absorption must fall in absolute terms for the trade account to improve:

$$d(X - M) = dY - d(C + I + G)$$

If $dY = 0$, then

$$d(X - M) = -d(C + I + G) = -dA$$

In this case the trade account can improve only if absorption falls in absolute terms. Returning to the previous example, we see that if a country is producing its maximum potential output of $10,000 and absorbing $11,000 so that the current account is in deficit by $1,000, balance-of-payments adjustment requires that absorption fall to $10,000, which means extremely restrictive macroeconomic policies. It is much easier to devalue when the economy has excess capacity, because in that case the growth of absorption merely has to be held below the growth of output. If a devaluation is undertaken when an economy is fully employed, the implications for domestic absorption are unpleasant at best.

Many developing countries find the implications of this model to be particularly painful. They often face severe output bottlenecks in the form of limited transport and electricity-generating capacity, so that large numbers of unemployed workers do not represent additional potential output in the short run. Their absorption levels are already low enough to imply real suffering, and balance-of-payments adjustment means reducing absorption further. If full-capacity output, allowing for bottlenecks, is $350 per person and absorption has been $400 per person, returning the current account to balance requires squeezing $50 per person out of an already low level of absorption. Unless this country can find sources of foreign aid or loans, however, it faces the same budget constraint that applies to a poor family; it cannot absorb more than it can produce, no matter how miserable the standard of living implied by that level of income. It can easily be seen from this discussion, however, why the governments of poor countries find the requirements of standard balance-of-payments adjustment programs to be distasteful and why they often fail to adopt policies that make a devaluation successful.

IS/LM/BB ANALYSIS OF A DEVALUATION

Returning to the graphical analysis of the previous chapter, we observe that a devaluation shifts both the BB and the IS lines to the right. The IS line shifts because the current account improves, thus increasing the level of GNP so that domestic savings rise relative to intended domestic investment. Domestic savings must rise relative to domestic investment by the amount of the current account improvement in order to maintain the identity that

$$S_T - I = X - M$$
$$\text{where} \quad S_T = S_p + (T - G)$$

Since $X - M$ has risen, S_T must rise relative to I, and it is the increase in GNP that produces that increase in savings. The BB line shifts to the right because the balance of payments improves, thereby increasing the level of GNP that is consistent with payments equilibrium. (See Figure 17-8.)

The devaluation increases the equilibrium level of GNP, which may create capacity problems. If the new level of equilibrium GNP is above that which the economy can easily produce, the result will be worsening inflation, which is likely to undermine the effectiveness of the devaluation. The rightward shift of IS must be limited to where BB and LM cross. If the IS line shifts too far

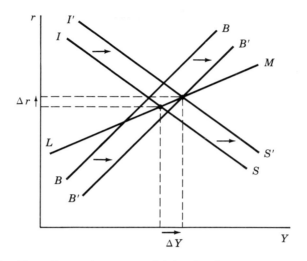

FIGURE 17-8 The effects of a successful devaluation.

to the right, the result is a return to payments deficit. Fiscal policy must be sufficiently restrictive to avoid that outcome. It is also worth noting that the devaluation increases the interest rate; this results from an increase in GNP, which raises the demand for money.

The Monetarist View of a Devaluation

Monetarists, it was argued earlier, view balance-of-payments deficits as being caused by excessively expansionary monetary policies. An excess supply of money creates a parallel excess demand for goods or financial assets, which spills over into the balance of payments as a deficit. Since deficits have a single cause, they can be remedied only by a reversal of that problem.

The elasticity analysis is irrelevant because monetarists believe that all prices in the devaluing country will ultimately rise by the percentage change in the exchange rate. Although they would not disagree with the desirability of budgetary restraint, the Keynesian analysis holds little attraction for monetarists. Balance-of-payments deficits can be adjusted only if the fundamental problem of an excess supply of money is remedied.

In the monetarist view, a devaluation has only one important effect on the balance of payments: it raises the price level and thereby reduces the real money supply. Put in nominal terms, a devaluation raises nominal GNP because of an increase in the price level, and it thereby increases the demand for nominal money balances. In either form, the conclusion is the same; the problem of the excess supply of money is solved. Short-term elasticities of demand and Keynesian absorption conditions are unimportant. The only important role of a devaluation is to raise the price level, thereby reducing the real money supply (or increasing the demand for nominal money balances) and eliminating the excess supply of money that caused the deficit.[5]

According to this model, devaluations fail when they are followed by further increases in the nominal money supply that recreate the original disequilibrium. Repetitive cycles of balance-of-payments deficit, devaluation, price increases, money supply growth, payments deficit, and devaluation are the common result. Some Latin American countries, for example, often face huge payments deficits and have to devalue. The prices of imports, and then of other goods and services, rise, thereby reducing the real money supply and moving the balance of payments toward equilibrium. The central bank, however, then allows the money supply to grow too rapidly, recreating the excess supply of money and the excess demand for goods and financial assets. The balance of payments returns to deficit, and soon another devaluation is needed, starting the cycle all over again. Only when the central bank sustains a restrictive monetary policy, which typically means when the government no longer forces the central bank to monetarize large budget deficits, can any balance-of-payments adjustment program be successful. With or without exchange rate adjustments, fiscal and monetary austerity is necessary if payments deficits are to be resolved, which again suggests why stabilization programs are so unpopular in developing countries. The medicine may be necessary, but that fact does not make it pleasant.

Effects of the Exchange Rate on the Capital Account

The discussion thus far has stressed the response of the current account to the exchange rate, and it may have created the incorrect impression that there are no additional effects of the exchange rate on the capital account. Since a devaluation increases nominal GNP, it should increase the demand for money and raise interest rates. The result should be an inflow of capital and an improvement in the balance of payments.

In addition, the devaluation was probably preceded by a period of speculative capital outflows, creating the possibility of large reverse flows after the parity change. If investors had suspected that a devaluation would occur, they would have shifted large sums of money into foreign financial assets before that event. When the devaluation is complete, they might be expected to return these funds to the home market. This reflow of speculative capital will occur, however, only

---

[5]The monetarist view of the impacts of the exchange rate on the balance of payments can be found in M. Kreinin and L. Officer, "The Monetary Approach to the Balance of Payments: A Survey," *Princeton Studies in International Finance,* no. 43, 1978, pp. 20–26. The effects of price-level changes on the real money supply, which became known as the real balances effect, was brought back to the attention of economists by Don Patinkin in *Money, Interest, and Prices* (New York: Harper & Row, 1956 and 1965). An early application of the real balances effect to the balance of payments can be found in Per Meinich, *A Monetary General Equilibrium Theory for an International Economy* (Oslo: Universitetsforlaget, 1968). See also Michael Michaelly, "Relative Prices and Income Absorption Approaches to Devaluation: A Partial Reconciliation," *American Economic Review,* March 1960, pp. 144–147.

if the devaluation is large enough,and if macroeconomic policies are sufficiently restrictive, to convince investors that the devaluation will not be repeated soon. If, for example, the market consensus is that a 20 percent devaluation is needed, an announcement of a 10 percent parity adjustment will not cause a return of speculative funds. Investors will suspect that another 10 percent devaluation will occur relatively soon, and so they will merely wait. A devaluation that is followed by a continuation of inflationary monetary and fiscal policies will also fail to attract speculative capital reflows, because investors will see such a parity change as the first of a potentially endless series.

Direct investment will also be affected by a devaluation, but again this reaction depends critically on strict control over later inflation. Direct investment is based to a considerable degree on relative production costs in different countries, and a devaluation improves a country's cost competitiveness as a location for factories or other production facilities.

A 10 percent devaluation of the dollar, for example, lowers the cost of hiring U.S. labor by 10 percent compared to the cost of hiring labor elsewhere. This should encourage both U.S. and foreign firms to locate more factories in this country, but this effect will occur only if U.S. wages and other costs do not rise sufficiently to offset the devaluation. A 10 percent increase in U.S. dollar wages and other costs, relative to such costs elsewhere, would fully offset the devaluation, and leave the competitive situation of the United States unchanged. The devaluation must be real, rather than merely nominal, to have the effect of attracting direct investment funds.

POTENTIALLY UNDESIRABLE SIDE EFFECTS OF DEVALUATIONS

As noted earlier, devaluations are unpopular; the restrictive fiscal and monetary policies that must accompany such parity changes are only part of the reason for this public response. Devaluations produce a range of disruptive side effects across an economy that add to this reaction. First, the prices of a wide range of imports and exportables rise, lowering the real incomes of domestic residents who purchase them. In an open economy, this decline in real incomes can be sizable.

Second, the local currency required to service foreign debts increases, imposing large losses on anyone with outstanding liabilities that are denominated in foreign exchange. Any resident who has borrowed abroad, and whose debt is denominated in a foreign currency, will find that the local currency cost of paying the interest and the principal on such a loan will have increased by the percentage of the devaluation. People suffering such losses will be unhappy about the decision to devalue.

In many developing countries, the largest such debtor is the government, and so the budgetary cost of servicing public debts to foreigners increases by the percentage of the devaluation. The government of Brazil, for example, owes almost $100 billion to foreign banks and governments, and virtually all of that debt is denominated in dollars or other foreign currencies. Whenever the cruzeiro is devalued, the cost to the Brazilian government budget of servicing that debt increases proportionately. That cost increase makes it more difficult to maintain the restrictive fiscal policy that is necessary to make the devaluation succeed.

Although those who have debts denominated in foreign exchange lose, those who hold assets abroad gain; this situation creates another political problem. Private speculators, who suspect that a devaluation is coming, frequently move large sums of money into a foreign currency in anticipation of the parity change. When the devaluation occurs, they receive large capital gains in terms of local currency. Such speculators, who make large profits while the rest of the economy is suffering, are likely to be unpopular. As a result, the decision to devalue, which allows such profits, may not be popular. A government can minimize such problems by devaluing as soon as it believes the payments deficit is serious rather than waiting to be forced to devalue. If such a decision can be made and implemented before investors suspect what is underway and move large sums of money, large speculative profits can be avoided.

In addition to capital gains and losses, devaluations also produce more long-lasting income redistribution effects. Those industries that produce exports and import substitutes gain, and the rest of the economy loses. As was noted at the beginning of this chapter, the first effect of a devaluation is to raise the local price of imports, which allows price increases for competing domestic goods. Export prices denominated in the local currency are also likely to increase, as was discussed in the small- and larger-country cases described earlier in this chapter.

If the economy is viewed as containing two sectors, one of which produces tradables (exports and import-competing goods), with the other producing nontradables (mostly services, including government, along with highly protected goods-producing industries), a devaluation increases the real incomes of those in the first sector and imposes losses on those in the second. These losses occur through an increase in the prices that must be paid for tradable goods and the lack of an offsetting increase in nominal incomes. Eventually, prices and incomes in the nontradables sector may rise to match the increase in the prices of tradables, which is the monetarist prediction, but that final equilibrium may be long in coming.

In the meantime, these effects can sometimes have regional implications. In Canada, for example, the western part of the country specializes in the production of exports, while Ontario has a heavier concentration of service and other nontradables industries. Whenever the Canadian dollar has depreciated (depreciation is the same as a devaluation but in a flexible exchange rate regime), western Canada has prospered at the expense of Ontario, creating considerable unhappiness in a province with a huge population and considerable political power.

In many developing countries the tradables/nontradables distinction exists between the rural and the urban sectors. Rural areas in such countries typically produce agricultural products that are exported (coffee, tea, cocoa, jute, etc.) and food products that compete with imports. In addition, export-oriented mineral extractive industries are generally located in rural areas. In contrast, urban areas typically have a far heavier concentration of nontradables. Government, banking, insurance, and a range of other urban service industries are usually nontradables.

Because manufacturing industries are often highly protected by tariffs and other import barriers, they are not greatly affected by the exchange rate. A devaluation in such a country raises the prices of tradables (including food) relative to the prices of nontradables and shifts real incomes from the cities to the rural areas. Such income shifts, particularly in the form of sharp increases in the local prices of food, sometimes result in civil disturbances in the cities of developing countries.

Finally, devaluations are unpopular because they are a public admission that the policies of the government or central bank have not been successful in defending the value of the currency. The creation and maintenance of a currency is one of the basic roles of a national government, and the announcement that that currency is being reduced in value relative to foreign currencies suggests that the government and the central bank have not managed that role prudently. Governments, preferring to avoid such admissions, often delay devaluations as long as possible.

A BRIEF CONSIDERATION OF REVALUATIONS

Thus far this discussion has stressed devaluations, in part because they are far more frequent than revaluations. Even so, revaluations do occur, and they have the same effects that have been presented above but in the opposite direction. Assuming that the relevant elasticities of demand are high enough, the trade balance declines as imports rise and exports fall. The decline in the trade account works through the Keynesian multiplier to produce potentially large recessionary effects, which may have to be offset with expansionary fiscal and monetary policies. If the economy is fully employed and threatened by rising prices, a revaluation helps reduce aggregate demand and contain inflation. If the economy is in a recession, however, a revaluation worsens the situation. Revaluations are easier to impose on a fully employed economy, and are very painful if the economy is already operating at less than full capacity. In this case, macroeconomic policies would have to be strongly expansionary to avoid a serious recession.

Revaluations also reverse the pattern of capital gains and losses discussed above. Those who own assets denominated in foreign exchange lose, whereas those with foreign debts discover that the local currency costs of repaying such obligations decline. Such gains or losses for an individual have to be measured, of course, on the basis of a net foreign exchange position. If a firm has $10 million in foreign assets and $7 million in foreign liabilities, its net foreign exchange position is $3 million and it will lose if the local currency is revalued. Companies frequently try to maintain roughly equal volumes of assets and liabilities in each foreign currency so that their net position in each is close to zero. Hence they do not face such exchange rate risks.

A revaluation results in a decline in the internal prices of tradable goods. Imports are less expensive, and the local currency prices received for exports typically decline. This results in a decline in incomes received from the production of tradables, but an increase in real incomes in the nontradables sector. This real income increase takes the form of lower prices for tradables paid by those working in the nontradables sector. Revaluations are extremely unpopular with export- and import-competing industries.[6] Such industries often argue that the decline in local currency prices that they receive for their output will force them into bankruptcy. Owners and managers of firms producing tradables, together with their labor unions, can be expected to argue forcefully against any consideration of a revaluation. As a result, changes in exchange rate are often delayed until long after it is apparent that a country's balance of payments is in fundamental and chronic surplus.[7]

THE MEADE CASES AGAIN

In Chapter 16 we argued that fiscal and monetary policies can deal with combinations of inflation/deficit or recession surplus quite successfully, but that they encounter serious conflicts in the recession/deficit or inflation/surplus situations. In this chapter we have suggested that devaluations are much more likely to succeed in adjusting a payments deficit if the economy is in a recession at the time the exchange rate change is undertaken and that revaluations are more likely to succeed at reasonable domestic cost if the economy is fully employed. Returning to the four Meade cases listed on page 352, an apparent solution to each situation now exists:

	Set of Problems	*Policy Response*
1.	Balance-of-payments surplus and a domestic recession	Expansionary fiscal and monetary policies
2.	Balance-of-payments deficit and domestic inflation	Restrictive fiscal and monetary policies
3.	Balance-of-payments surplus and domestic inflation	Revaluation of the local currency
4.	Balance-of-payments deficit and a domestic recession	Devaluation of the local currency

[6]For a discussion of the income redistribution effects of a revaluation, and of the resulting political obstacles for governments considering revaluations, see R. Dunn, Jr., "Exchange Rate Rigidity, Investment Distortions, and the Failure of Bretton Woods," *Princeton Essays in International Finance*, No. 97, February 1973.

[7]For papers on a wide range of effects of exchange rate changes, see P. Clark, D. Logue, and R. Sweeney, eds., *The Effects of Exchange Rate Adjustment* (Washington, D.C., U.S. Department of the Treasury, 1974). See also Leland B. Yeager, *International Monetary Relations: Theory, History, and Policy,* 2nd ed. (New York: Harper & Row, 1976), Chs. 6, 8, 9, 10, and 11. For a study of the effectiveness of a large number of devaluations, see Steven B. Kamin, "Devaluation, External Balance, and Macroeconomic Performance: A Look at the Numbers," *Princeton Studies in International Finance,* No. 62, August 1988. For a review of the effects of IMF stabilization programs, which typically include a devaluation, see Mohsin S. Kahn, "The Macroeconomic Effects of Fund-Supported Adjustment Programs," *IMF Staff Papers,* June 1990, pp. 195–231.

Real-world policy choices may not be as simple as this list would suggest. For example, the degree of domestic policy tightening which the balance of payments calls for in case 2 may differ from that required by the domestic business cycle, and fiscal policy may simply be unavailable as a short-run macroeconomic policy because of political constraints, but the direction of suggested policies is clear. Countries facing deficits and recessions should devalue, but they may have to adjust domestic macroeconomic policies to produce the desired level of aggregate demand. In the deficit/inflation case, the primary emphasis must be on restrictive domestic policies. If a devaluation is necessary, the fiscal and monetary tightening will have to be quite severe. The surplus cases are somewhat easier because there is no threat of foreign exchange reserves being exhausted. If the surplus is combined with a recession, there should be no thought of a revaluation; instead, the adoption of more expansionary domestic policies should be pursued. If inflation is a problem, however, a revaluation will both adjust the surplus and put downward pressure on prices, thus easing both difficulties.

This chapter has dealt with discrete changes in otherwise fixed parities. The next topic to be discussed is the regime of flexible exchange rates that many of the industrialized countries have maintained since the early 1970s.

QUESTIONS FOR STUDY AND REVIEW

1. Draw the supply and demand graphs for exports and imports for a small country that revalues. Do the same for a larger country. Explain the shifts in the lines that occur.

2. Why might a typical poor developing country be more worried about whether the price elasticities of demand for its exports and imports will be high enough to meet the Marshall-Lerner condition than would an industrialized country?

3. Explain why it is easier for a country to revalue its currency if it has a fully employed economy and faces inflationary pressures than if it is in a recession. Why is it similarly easier for a country to devalue if it has a recession than if it is fully employed?

4. Why do developing countries often find the macroeconomic policy requirements for the success of a devaluation to be particularly painful and politically unpopular?

5. From the perspective of a monetarist, what is the only really important effect that a revaluation has on a surplus country? How does this affect the surplus? What must the central bank do in order to avoid interfering with the intended effects of the revaluation?

6. "One problem with achieving balance-of-payments equilibrium through devaluation is that the therapy may be addictive. That is, additional devaluations become necessary." Why might this be true? How can a country avoid such an outcome?

SELECTED REFERENCES

Alexander, S. "The Effects of a Devaluation on the Trade Balance." *IMF Staff Papers,* 1952, pp. 263–278.

Alexander, S. "Effects of a Devaluation: A Simplified Synthesis of Elasticities and Absorption Approaches." *American Economic Review,* March 1959, pp. 22–42.

Clark, P., D. Logue, and R. Sweeney, eds. *The Effects of Exchange Rate Changes.* Washington, D.C.: U.S. Department of the Treasury, 1974.

Goldstein, M., and M. Khan. "Income and Price Effects in International Trade." In R. Jones and P. Kenen, eds., *Handbook of International Economics.* Vol. II. New York: North-Holland Press, 1985, pp. 1041–1106.

Kamin, S. "Devaluation, External Balance, and Macroeconomic Performance: A Look at the Numbers." *Princeton Studies in International Finance,* No. 62, August 1988.

Khan, M. "The Macroeconomic Effects of Fund-Supported Adjustment Programs." *IMF Staff Papers,* September 1990, pp. 195–231.

Kreinin, M., and L. Officer. "The Monetary Approach to the Balance of Payments: A Survey." *Princeton Studies in International Finance,* No. 43, 1978.

Solomon, R. *The International Monetary System 1945–1976: An Insider's View.* New York: Harper & Row, 1977, Chaps. 6, 9, 11, 12, and 13.

Yeager, L. *International Monetary Relations, Theory, History and Policy.* 2nd ed. New York: Harper & Row, 1976, Chaps. 6–11.

 18

THE THEORY OF FLEXIBLE EXCHANGE RATES

In recent decades, one of the most important debates in international finance has been between those favoring flexible exchange rates and those advocating fixed parities. Bankers and others directly involved in international transactions have often had a strong preference for fixed exchange rates, whereas academic economists typically have supported floating exchange rates.[1] In 1973 many of the major industrialized countries decided to adopt floating rates. This was not a victory of the professors over the men of affairs, but rather it followed the collapse of the previous system and the lack of a feasible alternative. At the time it was thought that floating exchange rates would be replaced by a return to parities within a few months, but the OPEC price shock and other sources of financial turmoil made that return impossible.

Flexible exchange rates have been retained not because they performed as well as academic supporters predicted they would, but in spite of many unforeseen problems which they have created. They are still in operation simply because there are no attractive alternatives. Fixed parities still pose the major problems that became apparent in the late 1960s and early 1970s, and none of the proposals for new or reformed systems has thus far seemed feasible. Academic and other supporters of exchange rate flexibility would now have to be described as "sadder but wiser," but no likely replacement for this system is on the horizon.

This chapter emphasizes the theory of a floating exchange rate system; the experience of the last two decades is discussed in Chapter 21.

Since this chapter is probably the most demanding of the book, it may be useful to indicate at the outset how it is organized and what it is intended to accomplish. This chapter begins with three brief sections that deal with the contrast between a clean and a dirty or managed float, factors determining the volatility of exchange rates, and the impacts of introducing floating rates on how international business is done. These sections lead to the dominant topic of the chapter: the effect of a regime of floating exchange rates on a domestic macroeconomy, which might be referred to as open economy macroeconomics under alternative exchange rate regimes.

The first topic within the open economy macroeconomics discussion is the mechanism through which business cycles are transmitted from one economy to another, which was introduced in Chapter 14. That linkage is significantly weakened by the existence of floating exchange rates; therefore this exchange rate regime may make a national economy less closely tied to its trading partners and more independent. This material is followed by a discussion of the impacts of floating exchange rates on the management of monetary policy. Domestic monetary policy shifts have more powerful effects on aggregate demand under floating than under fixed ex-

---

[1]Milton Friedman produced one of the most influential early defenses of a flexible exchange rate system in "The Case for Flexible Exchange Rates," in *Essays in Positive Economics* (Chicago: University of Chicago Press, 1953). An early discussion of the balance-of-payments adjustment process under floating exchange rates can be found in Joan Robinson's "The Foreign Exchanges," in her volume, *Essays in the Theory of Employment* (Oxford: Basil Blackwell, 1947). A 1970 conference volume contains a wide range of articles summarizing both sides of this debate at that time; see George Halm, ed., *Approaches to Greater Exchange Rate Flexibility: The Burgenstock Papers* (Princeton, N.J.: Princeton University Press, 1970), particularly the paper by Harry Johnson (pp. 91–111). See also Egon Sohmen, *Flexible Exchange Rates* (Chicago: University of Chicago Press, 1969). A recent and extensive study of flexible exchange rates, with references to most of the published work on the topic, can be found in Ronald MacDonald, *Floating Exchange Rates: Theory and Evidence* (London: Unwin Hyman, 1988).

change rates, but this strengthening of the ability of central bankers to manage the domestic macroeconomy depends upon their willingness to accept a large increase in exchange rate volatility.

Floating exchange rates also affect the management of fiscal policy, although the nature of the effects will vary from economy to economy. *IS/LM/BB* graphs are used throughout the discussion of monetary and fiscal policies under alternative exchange rate regimes to illustrate the main conclusions, but these graphs are placed in boxes so that they can be avoided by readers wishing to do so. The effect of floating rates on a protectionist policy designed for mercantilist purposes is also discussed. Using protection to increase aggregate demand is unwise under any exchange rate regime, but it is particularly foolish with a floating exchange rate. The exchange rate can be expected to respond to policies designed to restrict imports in ways that will exactly cancel the intended effects on aggregate demand and output. The chapter concludes with a brief discussion of the expectation (which ultimately proved mistaken) among many economists that floating exchange rates would follow purchasing power parity, thus producing relatively constant real effective exchange rates.

CLEAN VERSUS MANAGED FLOATING EXCHANGE RATES

A floating exchange rate supposedly eliminates any central bank intervention in the exchange market. Since, as was discussed in Chapter 12, all items in the balance of payments must sum to zero, the lack of any transactions that result in the movement of foreign exchange reserves means that the official reserve balance of payments must be in equilibrium. Balance-of-payments surpluses or deficits simply become impossible. The exchange market, and therefore the balance of payments, clears the same way the market for copper clears—through constant price changes. The academic literature and the existing theory of flexible exchange rates typically discuss such a clean or pure float.

The real world of floating exchange rates, however, is quite different. Because managed or dirty floats do exist, central banks retain the option of intervening in the exchange market when the exchange rate moves too rapidly or in a direction the government does not like. There is considerable debate over whether such intervention accomplishes much, but it does mean that the balance of payments is not kept in exact equilibrium by the exchange rate.[2] The United States and other large industrialized countries exist in a sort of halfway house, in that exchange rates are allowed to move roughly to adjust the balance of payments, but intervention occurs whenever rates become volatile or move beyond what is considered a reasonable

---

[2]An influential study of official intervention that grew out of the 1982 Versailles G-7 economic summit can be found in Working Group on Exchange Market Intervention, *Report*, 1983. See also Marsha Shelburn, "Rules for Regulating Intervention under a Managed Float," *Princeton Essays in International Finance,* No. 155, December 1984. Also J. A. Artus and A. Crocket, "Floating Rates and the Need for Surveillance," *Princeton Essays in International Finance,* No. 127, May 1978.

range. The goal of such intervention has been to produce not fixed exchange rates but less volatile rates.

For the sake of simplicity, the theoretical discussion of this chapter assumes a clean float; accordingly, it is assumed that the exchange rate moves sufficiently to maintain equilibrium in the payments accounts. These assumptions permit rather clear distinctions between the workings of a flexible and a fixed exchange rate system. The broad conclusions of this theory hold for the real world, though in a less precise way.

THE STABILITY OF THE EXCHANGE MARKET

The volatility of the exchange rate depends on how items in the payments accounts react to shocks in the form of major transactions shifts. If, for example, a $500 million capital inflow occurs, how far will the exchange rate have to rise to produce offsetting transactions totaling $500 million? If trade flows and other transactions respond weakly to the exchange rate, a large appreciation might be necessary to absorb the $500 million, while a strong responsiveness implies a small or even infinitesimal rise.

The trade account's response to the exchange rate depends on the same elasticity conditions that were discussed in Chapter 17. Low-demand elasticities imply a weak or perhaps even perverse response of the trade account to the exchange rate, which would make the rate more volatile. As was implied in the J-curve discussion earlier, the short-term response of the trade account to the exchange rate is unlikely to be very stabilizing. Thus other items in the payments accounts will have to be the primary source of stabilizing reactions to transactions shifts.

Stabilizing flows of capital, based largely on speculative motives, are the most likely source of such payments response. If market participants believe that the currency is basically sound (because the central bank is prudently managed), they will typically view any sizable exchange rate movements as temporary and as likely to be reversed. If, for example, the market viewed British sterling as being worth approximately $1.80 and had confidence that the policies of both the Federal Reserve System and the Bank of England were stable, any significant movement of the market away from $1.80 would be resisted by speculative capital flows. A rate of $1.83, for example, would be viewed as too high, encouraging sales of sterling that would drive it back toward $1.80. If a large flow of capital out of the United Kingdom pushed the rate down to $1.77, speculators would view sterling as likely to rise, generating flows of short-term funds into the currency, thereby stabilizing the rate. As long as market participants have confidence in the future of the exchange rate, speculation will be stabilizing. Accordingly, shocks to the market, such as large capital flows, will be absorbed with only modest exchange rate movements.

If, however, speculators lack such confidence and instead fear that rates may face large unpredictable changes, speculation can be destabilizing. A decline in sterling from $1.80 to $1.77, for example, might create fears that this was the beginning of a trend, setting off a speculative bandwagon effect in the form of sales of sterling, thereby driving the currency lower. If such uncertain expectations exist, the exchange rate can be quite volatile.

How such expectations are formed by market participants is uncertain, but the degree of confidence in the relevant central banks is a critical factor. If speculators view monetary policy in one or both countries as unpredictable and subject to large changes, their behavior is likely to be destabilizing. They may view small exchange rate changes as the result of monetary policy shifts, and move out of the currency that is depreciating, thereby encouraging further changes in the same direction. Confidence in the soundness of monetary policy is important in any exchange rate regime, but particularly in a floating rate system. If the market fears the adoption of an unsound expansionary monetary policy, any sign of weakness in the currency will be seen as a reason to move to alternatives. Confidence in the stability of monetary policy produces the opposite result; a depreciation is seen as an opportunity to make profits by moving funds into that currency before it recovers to its normal exchange rate.

In a managed float, central bank intervention can be a source of stabilizing capital flows. A depreciation may encourage the central bank to support the weakening currency, and vice versa. If private participants in the exchange market believe that the central bank will behave in such a stabilizing way, they may be encouraged to follow the same pattern, that is, to support a declining currency in expectation that the central bank will push it back up, thus making their transactions profitable. Central bank intervention is sometimes intended to encourage such stabilizing behavior by other investors.

IMPACTS OF FLEXIBLE EXCHANGE RATES ON INTERNATIONAL TRANSACTIONS

Opponents of flexible exchange rates have frequently expressed the fear that the abandonment of fixed parities would discourage trade and other international transactions. Additional transactions costs (wider bid/asked spreads in exchange markets) and risks would encourage businesses to emphasize domestic activities and avoid international business. Studies of international trade during the period since 1973 provide little support for these fears. Some studies show no reduction in trade volumes, whereas others show very small impacts.[3] Capital flows have become so enormous that they appear to dominate exchange markets; consequently, additional risks do not appear to have discouraged international investors.

Despite the increased risks implied by flexible exchange rates, trade and other transactions have continued to grow, in part because it is possible to hedge or cover such risks through the forward market and other routes. Conversations with

[3]Rachel McCulloch, "Unexpected Real Consequences of Floating Exchange Rates," *Princeton Essays in International Finance*, No. 153, August 1983, p. 6. See also D. O. Cushman, "The Effects of Real Exchange Rate Risk on International Trade," *Journal of International Economics*, August 1983, pp. 44–63.

exchange traders and other market participants indicate that the volume of forward contracts increased sharply after the adoption of flexible exchange rates in the early 1970s. Firms that were previously willing to accept the risks implicit in the narrow band within which spot exchange rates were allowed to move decided that these risks became too large when rates could move over an indefinite range. Rather than reduce or abandon their international business, however, they made heavy use of the forward market and other hedging techniques to avoid unacceptable increases in exchange risks.[4]

The adoption of flexible exchange rates had far less impact on the management of international business than many people had feared. Such business continued normally and has grown. Opportunities for speculation certainly increased as exchange rates moved over ranges that provided large opportunities for profits or losses on uncovered positions. For those wishing to avoid such risk, forward markets and other hedging techniques made such avoidance possible for many transactions.

OPEN ECONOMY MACROECONOMICS UNDER ALTERNATIVE EXCHANGE RATE REGIMES

Some of the most interesting aspects of the economics of floating exchange rates involve the domestic economy rather than international transactions. Many important relationships in macroeconomics are altered by the adoption of flexible exchange rates, including the effectiveness of policy shifts. The mechanisms through which fiscal and monetary policies affect aggregate domestic demand, for example, are quite different under a flexible exchange rate regime, as will be discussed later in this chapter.

The critical difference between a system of fixed versus flexible exchange rates that generates these impacts is the absence of balance-of-payments disequilibria in the flexible system. Any economic relationship or process that is dependent on shifts of the balance of payments to surplus or deficit is eliminated or changed because there are no such shifts. Since a clean float is assumed for this discussion, the balance of payments on official reserve transactions is always zero. That is, it is always in equilibrium, which means that movements in that balance cannot affect anything.

Since the exchange rate, rather than the balance of payments, moves constantly, domestic prices of traded goods are affected. As argued in Chapter 17, a devaluation increased local currency prices of tradable goods, whereas a revaluation reduced them. A depreciation has the same effect on prices as a devaluation, whereas an appreciation replicates the price effects of a revaluation. The domestic prices of tradables should rise when the local currency depreciates, and vice versa. If the markets for these goods are oligopolistic, however, these price changes may

[4]Michael Duerr, *Protecting Corporate Assets under Floating Currencies* (New York: The Conference Board, 1975). Also S. I. Katz, "Exchange Risk Under Fixed and Flexible Exchange Rates," New York University *Bulletin,* No. 83–84, June 1972. See also R. Dunn, Jr., *The Canada-U.S. Capital Market* (Washington, D.C.: National Planning Association, 1978), pp. 95–102.

be smaller than the exchange rate movements and may occur with a considerable lag, because, as noted in Chapter 15, the law of one price often does not hold in less than perfectly competitive markets.

Business Cycle Transmission with Flexible Exchange Rates

As shown in Chapter 14, international trade provides a mechanism through which business cycles are transmitted from one country to another. For example, a recession in the United States reduces U.S. demand for Canadian exports, which reduces output in Canada, thus transmitting the recession to the north. This argument assumes a fixed exchange rate. With a flexible exchange rate this process becomes more complicated, and the transmission process is weakened, because the exchange rate absorbs at least some of the macroeconomic shock that would otherwise be passed through to Canada.

The decline in U.S. demand for Canadian exports, which results from a U.S. recession, causes a parallel decline in the exchange market demand for Canadian dollars to pay for those exports. With a fixed exchange rate, Canada would have a payments deficit and incur a loss of foreign exchange reserves. With a floating exchange rate, however, the Canadian dollar would depreciate sufficiently to return the balance of payments to equilibrium. Canada does not have a balance-of-payments deficit, but instead a lower exchange rate. The depreciation of the Canadian dollar should encourage exports and discourage imports, producing a recovery of the trade account. Low short-term demand elasticities may delay this response, but after the J-curve lag has passed, Canada's trade account should recover to approximately its previous position. In the meantime, if speculators view the U.S. recession and its impact on the exchange rate as temporary, they can be expected to support the Canadian dollar. The contrast between macroeconomic linkages under the two systems can be seen in the following diagrams:

Fixed Exchange Rates

$$\downarrow dY_{us} \rightarrow \downarrow dM_{us} \rightarrow \downarrow dX_{cn} \rightarrow \downarrow dY_{cn}$$

Flexible Exchange Rates

$$\downarrow dY_{us} \rightarrow \downarrow dM_{us} \rightarrow \downarrow dX_{cn} \rightarrow \downarrow dXR_c \rightarrow \uparrow dX_{cn} \rightarrow \uparrow d(X-M)_{cn}$$
$$\hookrightarrow \downarrow dM_{cn} \hookrightarrow$$

(In this and similar diagrams to follow in this chapter, the horizontal arrows are lines of causation; the vertical arrows indicate the direction of change; d means change; Y is GNP; M is imports; X is exports; XR is the exchange rate defined as the foreign price of local money; and the subscripts refer to the country, the United States or Canada.)

If the trade account were the sole source of adjustment to the exchange rate, the improvement in the Canadian current account that completes the diagram should exactly match the original loss of Canadian exports, leaving the current account and Canadian aggregate demand unaffected by the U.S. recession. If stabilizing speculative capital flows, or central bank intervention under a managed float, support the Canadian dollar, the current account reaction to the exchange rate will be less than the original loss of export sales, leaving a current account deterioration and some recessionary impacts in Canada. The exchange rate and the resulting response of the current account, however, will still absorb part of the macroeconomic shock from the United States, leaving Canada somewhat less vulnerable to recessions that originate in the United States.

If international trade were the only source of supply and demand in the market for foreign exchange, a clean float would mean that the trade account was always in balance. Such a situation would completely isolate total demand in a domestic economy from foreign business cycles transmitted through the trade account. In a more realistic world which includes speculative capital flows and central bank intervention, floating exchange rates reduce the extent to which business cycles are passed from one country to another but do not eliminate the mechanism. It should be noted that the price effects of foreign business cycles are passed through the exchange rate. In the previous example, the depreciation of the Canadian dollar, which resulted from the U.S. recession, could be expected to increase the Canadian prices of tradable goods.

The greater the extent to which stabilizing speculation and/or central bank intervention stops the exchange rate from moving in response to shifting trade flows, the closer we are to the fixed exchange rate situation in which such cycles are fully transmitted. If countries such as Canada wish to avoid the aggregate demand impacts of U.S. cycles, they must be willing to allow their currencies to depreciate in response to a U.S. recession and appreciate when this country has an expansionary boom. Any attempt to stabilize the exchange rate over the business cycle will increase Canadian vulnerability to U.S. recessions.

Monetary Policy with Fixed Versus Flexible Exchange Rates

One of the most striking macroeconomic effects of the introduction of flexible exchange rates is an increase in the independence and effectiveness of monetary policy. A regime of fixed exchange rates means that the central bank is constrained by balance-of-payments considerations (it cannot adopt an expansionary policy that would result in the exhaustion of foreign exchange reserves) and often finds that payments disequilibria tend to offset its intended changes in the money supply. In contrast, under flexible exchange rates the balance of payments is no longer a constraint, and movements of the exchange rate tend to enhance the impacts of monetary policy on aggregate demand.[5]

[5]Much of the original theoretical work on this topic was done by Robert Mundell. See his "The Monetary Dynamics of International Adjustment under Fixed and Floating Exchange Rates," *Quarterly Journal of Economics,* May 1960, and "Flexible Exchange Rates and Employment Policy," *Canadian Journal of Economics,* November 1961, and "Capital Mobility and Stabilization Policy under Fixed and Flexible Exchange Rates," *Canadian Journal of Economics,* November 1963. These articles can also be found in Robert Mundell, *International Economics* (New York: Macmillan, 1968). See also Ahira Takayama, "The Effects of Fiscal and Monetary Policies under Flexible and Fixed Exchange Rates," *Canadian Journal of Economics,* May 1969.

In a fixed exchange rate regime, the adoption of an expansionary monetary policy reduces interest rates and encourages capital outflows. If international capital market integration is close, these capital outflows can be quite large. The resulting balance-of-payments deficit results in a loss of foreign exchange reserves. As was argued in Chapter 15, a loss of foreign exchange reserves automatically reduces the money supply, which reverses the original monetary policy, raising interest rates and returning the economy to its situation before the attempted monetary expansion. If capital market integration is extensive, the central bank has very little ability to manage its own monetary policy. This is particularly true for a relatively small economy, such as that of Canada, which is closely tied to a much larger economy such as that of the United States. The following diagram indicates how an attempted monetary expansion by the Bank of Canada would be frustrated by balance-of-payments flows under fixed exchange rates.

$$\uparrow dMS_{cn} \rightarrow \downarrow dr_{cn} \rightarrow \uparrow dI_{cn} \rightarrow \uparrow dY_{cn}$$
$$\hookrightarrow \downarrow dKA_{cn} \rightarrow \downarrow dBOP_{cn} \rightarrow \downarrow dFXR_{cn} \rightarrow \downarrow dMBR_{cn} \rightarrow \downarrow dMS_{cn} \rightarrow$$
$$\hookrightarrow \uparrow dr_{cn} \rightarrow \downarrow dI_{cn} \rightarrow \downarrow dY_{cn}$$

(In this and later diagrams MS represents the money supply, BOP the balance of payments, FXR foreign exchange reserves, MBR member bank reserves, r the interest rates, I intended investment, and KA the capital account.)

The balance-of-payments impacts of the Bank of Canada's expansionary policy largely cancel its intended effects on the money supply, interest rates, and domestic output.

In a regime of flexible exchange rates, however, these conclusions change. An expansionary monetary policy still lowers interest rates and encourages capital outflows, but a balance-of-payments deficit and a loss of foreign exchange reserves no longer occur. Instead, the domestic currency depreciates, which improves the trade balance, thus increasing domestic output of exports and import substitutes. This depreciation also increases domestic prices of tradable goods. Since there is no loss of foreign exchange reserves, there is no decline in member bank reserves or of the money supply. The original increase in the domestic money supply remains intact, and the depreciation of the local currency adds to the intended expansionary effect on domestic output and incomes. The following diagram, which again represents a monetary expansion by the Bank of Canada, illustrates these impacts under the assumption of a "clean flexible exchange rate":

$$\uparrow dMS_{cn} \rightarrow \downarrow dr_{cn} \rightarrow \uparrow dI_{cn} \rightarrow \uparrow dY_{cn}$$
$$\hookrightarrow \downarrow dKA_{cn} \rightarrow \downarrow dXR_{cn} \rightarrow \uparrow dX_{cn} \rightarrow \uparrow d(X-M)_{cn} \rightarrow \uparrow dY_{cn}$$
$$\hookrightarrow \downarrow dM_{cn}$$

The international effects of monetary policy shifts enhance rather than undermine the intended effects of such policy changes. Flexible exchange rates have frequently been seen as a way of increasing the power and influence of the central bank in managing domestic aggregate demand as can be seen in Exhibit 18-1. Consequently, flexible rates are more popular among those who have strong confidence in the management of that institution. In contrast, fixed exchange rates are seen as a mechanism for restricting the power of the central bank and are therefore supported by those who distrust the central bankers. If the governor of a country's central bank is thought to be sensible and prudent, flexible exchange rates are acceptable; if that governor is thought to be incompetent and given to unwise policy shifts, fixed exchange rates are a better option.

Why Is the Fed Suddenly So Important?

The question of Paul Volcker's reappointment generated controversy beyond anything in the history of the Federal Reserve Board. William McC. Martin was reappointed chairman a number of times with a minimum of fuss. Arthur Burns and William Miller arrived and departed without great debate. But suddenly the chairmanship had become President Reagan's most important appointment since he put Sandra Day O'Connor on the Supreme Court—and that term is for life, not a mere four years.

One reason for this extraordinary rise in interest in the Fed is that the constant acrimony between the two ends of Pennsylvania Avenue on the subject of the budget has produced chaos in the form of unmanageable deficits, and the widespread view here and abroad that the United States merely has a fiscal result rather than any policy. This makes the Federal Reserve Board the only source of thoughtful macroeconomic planning in Washington. With the federal budget out of control, monetary policy is the only game in town, and the chairmanship of the Fed becomes correspondingly more critical to the future of the economy.

A more interesting but less widely understood reason for the increased importance of the Federal Reserve chairmanship is that the existence of a regime of flexible exchange rates during recent years has made monetary policy a far more powerful tool for the management of the economy then it was in the previous era of fixed exchange rates.

With flexible exchange rates, the adoption of a restrictive monetary policy, which raises interest rates and attracts foreign capital inflows, will cause an appreciation of the dollar. This increase in the exchange rate for the dollar makes imports cheaper in the United States and American products more expensive abroad. As domestic and foreign consumers respond to these shifts in relative prices, U.S. imports rise and exports fall, reducing aggregate demand and production in this economy.

The decline in the price of imports also forces U.S. firms that compete with imports to restrain their prices, and U.S. exporters are under strong pressure to reduce U.S. dollar prices to remain competitive abroad. Flexible exchange rates make monetary policy an awesome macroeconomic tool. Tight money produces an appreciation of the dollar that literally forces a reduction in a wide range of prices of traded goods, and sharply reduces aggregate demand through a decline in the trade balance.

If a fixed exchange rate for the dollar had been maintained, the effects of tight money would have been less impressive. Higher interest rates would have had restrictive impacts within the economy through their effects on investment expenditures, but the foreign capital inflows that resulted from higher yields would not have caused an appreciation of the dollar, which forced down prices and reduced production and employment in the export and import-competing sectors.

Instead, the U.S. balance of payments would have been pushed into surplus by the inflow of foreign funds, and this surplus would have increased the U.S. money supply, partially cancelling the Fed's original tightening. Although this undesired increase in the money supply could be reversed through domestic monetary policy shifts, it remains true that a tightening of monetary policy would not directly affect the exchange rate, the domestic prices of traded goods or the trade balance. A fixed exchange rate makes monetary policy a far more limited tool for the management of the economy.

Flexible exchange rates have the additional effect of reducing the expansionary impacts of federal budget deficits and of thus weakening fiscal policy. An increase in government expenditures that raises federal borrowing and interest rates, for example, will attract foreign capital inflows and lead to an appreciation of the dollar. As the trade balance responds to the exchange rate, the expansionary effect of the government expenditure is largely offset by the loss of output in the export and import-competing sectors. The intended effects of the expansionary fiscal policy are "crowded out" through the exchange rate and the trade balance. In any conflict between an expansionary budget and a restrictive monetary policy, the central bank will win easily.

The success of the Federal Reserve System in dramatically reducing the U.S. rate of inflation during the last three years is largely the result of a 35 percent appreciation of the dollar during 1981 and 1982. This exchange rate change was also a major cause of the huge costs of this disinflation in terms of output and employment. The appreciation had particularly harsh impacts on export sectors such as agriculture and heavy machinery.

The recovery of these sectors depends on a depreciation of the dollar that has been expected for some time by many economists but that has not yet occurred.

Whether one supports or opposes the "cold shower" approach to fighting inflation of the last three years, it is clear that the great importance of Federal Reserve policy to the economy results in large part from the nature of the exchange rate regime. If the United States maintained a fixed exchange rate, the impacts of shifts in Fed policy would be far less dramatic, and there would probably have been far less interest in whether Paul Volcker was reappointed.

EXHIBIT 18-1 Source: From *The Washington Post*, Robert M. Dunn, Jr., copyright ©1983, Op. Ed. page, October 28, 1982. Reprinted with permission.

IS/LM/BB Analysis of Monetary Policy under Alternative Exchange Rate Regimes

Returning to the graphical analysis of the previous two chapters, we find that a monetary policy expansion shifts *LM* to the right (Figure 18-1). With a fixed exchange rate, the result is a balance-of-payments deficit that results in a loss of foreign exchange reserves and a reduction of the money supply, which is shown as a leftward shift of *LM*. Equilibrium is reestablished at

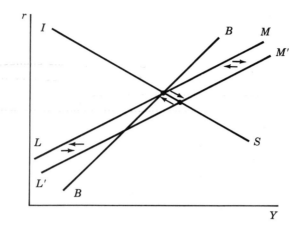

FIGURE 18-1 Effects of an expansionary monetary policy with fixed exchange rates.

the original level of GNP, which means that the monetary policy shift was unsuccessful in increasing output and incomes.

If a flexible exchange rate is being maintained, however, the rightward shift of *LM* does not create a payments deficit; instead it produces a depreciation that shifts *BB* and *IS* to the right (Figure 18-2). *IS* shifts to the right because the depreciation improves the trade account, thereby increasing the level of GNP at which domestic savings equals intended investment.

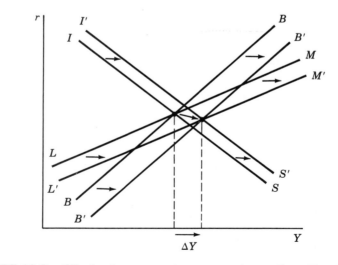

FIGURE 18-2 Effects of an expansionary monetary policy with a floating exchange rate.

The conclusion that a flexible exchange rate greatly enhances the independence and power of the central bank in its management of domestic aggregate demand is not without problems. First, it requires that the government be willing to accept the implications of potentially large exchange rate changes. It was argued in Chapter 17 that such exchange rate movements can be very disruptive, and that remains true in a regime of flexible exchange rates. If the government concludes that these disruptions are unacceptable, the central bank will have to design its policies to stabilize the exchange rate rather than produce an ideal level of GNP. If the avoidance of exchange rate volatility becomes a dominant goal, monetary policy may not be much more independent in a regime of flexible exchange rates than it would be with fixed parities.

Monetarists argue that the adoption of flexible exchange rates will have no more than short-run impacts on the effectiveness of monetary policy in managing GNP because price-level changes will return the real money supply to its equilibrium level.[6] An expansionary monetary policy, for example, will create an excess supply of money which causes a parallel excess demand for goods and bonds. These excess demands spill over into international transactions, creating an excess demand for foreign exchange. The local currency depreciates, which increases domestic prices of tradable goods. Eventually, all prices rise by the percentage of the depreciation, reducing the real money supply to its previous level. Real output and incomes are unaffected. The following diagram illustrates this argument for an expansionary monetary policy pursued by the Bank of Canada.

$$\uparrow dMS_{cn} \rightarrow \uparrow ESM_{cn} \rightarrow \uparrow EDG\&B_{cn} \rightarrow \downarrow dXR_{cn} \rightarrow \uparrow dPt_{cn} \rightarrow \uparrow dP_{cn} \rightarrow \downarrow \frac{dMS_{cn}}{P_{cn}}$$

(ESM is an excess supply of money, $EDG\&B$ an excess demand for goods and bonds, and Pt the price of tradables.)

Any effects on output are temporary. When prices have fully adjusted to the exchange rate, the real money supply returns to its original level, leaving all real variables unaffected by the central bank's policy change. Rudiger Dornbusch maintains that, to the extent that prices adjust to the exchange rate with a significant time lag, the exchange rate will "overshoot" its long-term equilibrium. When prices do adjust fully, the rate will return to that equilibrium, but in the meantime the exchange rate will be quite volatile.[7]

---

[6]R. Dornbusch, *Open Economy Macroeconomics* (New York: Basic Books, 1980), Chs. 11 and 12. See also L. Girton and D. Roper, "A Monetary Model of Exchange Market Pressure Applied to Postwar Canadian Experience," *American Economic Review,* September 1977, pp. 537–548.

[7]R. Dornbusch, "Expectations and Exchange Rate Dynamics," *Journal of Political Economy,* December 1976, pp. 1161–1176. Also see R. Dornbusch, *Open Economy Macroeconomics* (New York: Basic Books, 1980), Ch. 12. For alternative sources of overshooting, see R. Dunn, Jr., "The Many Disappointments of Flexible Exchange Rates," *Princeton Essays in International Finance,* No. 154, December 1983, pp. 19–23. See also J. Levin, "Trade Flow Lags, Monetary and Fiscal Policy, and Exchange Rate Overshooting," *Journal of International Money and Finance,* December 1986.

An example may clarify the process of overshooting. Assume that 50 percent of the weights in the Consumer Price Index are assigned to tradable goods and that 50 percent are assigned to nontradable goods and services. Starting from equilibrium in all markets, assume that the central bank increases its domestic assets by a sufficient amount to increase the money supply by 10 percent, creating an excess supply of money of that amount. According to Walras Law, there is an excess demand for goods and bonds, which creates an excess demand for foreign money in the exchange market. The domestic currency starts to depreciate.

If the law of one price holds, prices of tradables should rise quickly when the currency falls, but nontradables prices will not respond quickly. If the currency has depreciated by 10 percent, prices of tradables will have risen by 10 percent, but nontradables prices will not have changed, producing a 5 percent increase in the average price level and a 5 percent decline in the real money supply. This leaves the real money supply 5 percent above its equilibrium level, creating further downward pressure on the domestic currency in the exchange market. When the currency has depreciated by 20 percent, as shown in Figure 18-3, domestic prices of tradables will have risen by 20 percent, prices of nontradables will still not have changed, and the average price level will have risen by 10 percent, returning the real money supply to its equilibrium level. There is no longer an excess supply of money, so there is no longer an excess demand for goods and bonds, and a temporary equilibrium is established.

Eventually, this equilibrium is disturbed by an increase in the price of non-tradables. This increase occurs for two reasons. First, tradables and nontradables are gross substitutes, which means that the 20 percent increase in the price of tradables causes consumers to substitute toward nontradables, driving their prices up. Second, the production of tradables and nontradables uses the same factors of production. Firms that produce tradables respond to increased prices by attempting to expand production; thus they must bid for more land, labor, and capital. Because

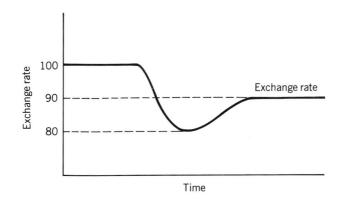

FIGURE 18-3   Exchange rate overshooting after a monetary expansion.

full employment is assumed, the prices of these inputs increase, putting upward pressure on costs in all sectors of the economy. The prices of nontradables rise as the costs of inputs increase.

The increase in the price of nontradables moves the average price level more than 10 percent above its original equilibrium. If nontradables prices rise by 10 percent while tradables prices are still 20 percent above their original level, the average price level has risen by 15 percent, reducing the real money supply 5 percent below its equilibrium level. The earlier excess supply of money is replaced by an excess demand for money and by a parallel excess supply of goods and bonds. There is now an excess demand for the local currency in the exchange market, and an appreciation begins. Prices of tradables start to fall. Eventually, the currency rises by 10 percent from its lowest level, leaving a net depreciation of 10 percent from the original level, as shown in Figure 18-3. The prices of both tradables and nontradables have risen by 10 percent from their original level, the real money supply returns to its equilibrium level, and the system is at rest.

Dornbusch overshooting is based on the fact that, although tradables prices may respond to the exchange rate quickly (and even that assumption is doubtful because the law of one price may not hold, as was noted in Chapter 15), nontradables prices will respond with a considerable lag. Thus the overall price level moves by less than the exchange rate in the short run. This requires a larger movement of the exchange rate to produce an adjustment of the average price level which will return the real money supply to a temporary equilibrium. Eventually, prices of nontradables adjust, producing a partial reversal of the earlier exchange rate movement and a permanent equilibrium.

This is the best known explanation of exchange rate volatility, but there are other explanations, including the responses of capital flows to interest rate changes in the portfolio balance model of Chapter 15. During the time in which preexisting portfolios are being adjusted to recent changes in expected yields or risks, large capital movements will occur which will cause large exchange rate changes. When the adjustment of portfolios is largely completed, capital flows will become far smaller, and the exchange rate will move back toward its original level.

Fiscal Policy under Alternative Exchange Rate Regimes

The effect of the introduction of flexible exchange rates on the management of fiscal policy is both complicated and uncertain. It depends on the relative strength of two economic relationships (the sensitivity of the capital account to interest rates and the sensitivity of imports to domestic incomes), which will vary among countries. One relationship may dominate for the United States, while another may be stronger for a developing country.

The traditional argument depends on the extensive integration of capital markets and leads to the conclusion that fiscal policy is effective in managing domestic output under a fixed exchange rate, but is much weaker with a flexible exchange rate.[8] A larger budget deficit, for example, raises GNP in the standard Keynesian manner, but an increase in the transactions demand for money follows. Without a supportive increase in the money supply by the central bank, the result is an increase in interest rates that might be expected to crowd out domestic investment, making the fiscal expansion largely ineffective. The higher interest rates, however, attract capital inflows, shifting the capital account toward surplus. With a fixed exchange rate, the result is a payments surplus and an increase in the central bank's foreign exchange reserves. This accumulation of foreign exchange reserves has the effect of increasing the money supply, thus bringing interest rates back down and eliminating the "crowding out" problem. Fiscal policy is effective because the balance of payments shifts in a manner that provides the money supply change that is necessary to make it successful.

If a flexible exchange rate exists, however, this line of causation is changed. A fiscal expansion still increases GNP, the demand for money, and the interest rate. The resulting capital inflows, however, now cause the local currency to appreciate. The money supply does not increase, which would have supported the fiscal expansion; instead, the appreciation worsens the trade account, reducing domestic output and incomes. Higher interest rates not only crowd out domestic investment; they also cause an appreciation of the local currency which lowers exports and increases imports, producing an additional form of crowding out in the economy. The following diagrams, which are similar to those used earlier in this chapter, illustrate the situation in which fiscal expansion is adopted when international capital market integration is close.

Fixed Exchange Rate

$$\uparrow d(G-T) \rightarrow \uparrow dY \rightarrow \uparrow dr \rightarrow \downarrow dI \rightarrow \downarrow dY$$
$$ \hookrightarrow \uparrow dKA \rightarrow \uparrow dBOP \rightarrow \uparrow dFXR \rightarrow \uparrow dMBR \rightarrow \rceil$$
$$ \hookrightarrow \uparrow dMS \rightarrow \downarrow dr \rightarrow \uparrow dI \rightarrow \uparrow dY$$

Flexible Exchange Rate

$$\uparrow d(G-T) \rightarrow \uparrow dY \rightarrow \uparrow dr \rightarrow \downarrow dI \rightarrow \downarrow dY$$
$$ \hookrightarrow \uparrow dKA \rightarrow \uparrow dXR \rightarrow \downarrow dX \rightarrow \downarrow d(X-M) \rightarrow \downarrow dY$$
$$ \hookrightarrow \uparrow dM \rceil$$

The top line represents the traditional crowding out argument for both exchange rate systems. With a fixed exchange rate, the second line largely reverses the crowding out, making the fiscal policy effective. Under flexible exchange rates,

---

[8]R. Mundell, "Flexible Exchange Rates and Employment Policy," *Canadian Journal of Economics,* November 1961, and "Capital Mobility and Stabilization Policies under Fixed and under Flexible Exchange Rates," *Canadian Journal of Economics,* November 1963. See also Takayama, "The Effects of Fiscal and Monetary Policies under Flexible and under Fixed Exchange Rates." For a gathering of econometric studies of the problem of coordinating macroeconomic policies among countries with flexible exchange rates, see Ralph Bryant et al., eds., *Empirical Macroeconomics for Interdependent Economies* (Washington, D.C: Brookings Institution, 1988).

however, the second line shows an appreciation of the currency and a worsening of the trade account which, rather than reversing the earlier crowding out, enhances it. Flexible exchange rates tend to weaken fiscal policy, unless it is accompanied by a cooperative monetary policy. If the central bank had increased the money supply sufficiently to preclude an increase in interest rates, both types of crowding out would have been avoided. If the central bank refuses to cooperate, however, the adoption of a flexible exchange rate greatly weakens fiscal policy.

These seemingly strong conclusions become quite uncertain when an additional linkage between fiscal policy and the balance of payments is introduced. That linkage is to the trade account, and it is the Keynesian argument that an increase in domestic incomes will cause a parallel rise in imports and a worsening of the trade balance.

An expansionary fiscal policy will increase GNP, which causes an increase in imports. Under a fixed exchange rate, the result is a balance-of-payments deficit that reduces foreign exchange reserves, thereby reducing the domestic money supply. There is no increase in the money supply that supports the fiscal expansion, but instead a money supply reduction that frustrates it. If increased income has a stronger impact on imports than on interest rates and the capital account, so that an expansionary fiscal policy worsens rather than strengthens the balance of payments, the conclusion that a fixed exchange rate makes fiscal policy effective in managing domestic aggregate demand is reversed. Balance-of-payments effects weaken rather than strengthen fiscal policy if a fixed exchange rate is maintained.

A strong linkage from income to imports means that the introduction of a flexible exchange rate makes fiscal policy more effective. An expansionary budget increases domestic output and incomes, thereby attracting more imports, causing the currency to depreciate. With a time lag, the decline in the exchange rate will improve the trade balance, adding to domestic output and strengthening the intended impact of the fiscal expansion. The introduction of a flexible exchange rate strengthens fiscal policy if income growth has a stronger effect on imports than on interest rates and capital flows. The following diagrams illustrate these linkages:

Fixed Exchange Rate

$$\uparrow d(G-T) \rightarrow \uparrow dY \rightarrow \uparrow dM \rightarrow \downarrow dBOP \rightarrow \downarrow dFXR \rightarrow \downarrow dMS \rightarrow \uparrow dr \rightarrow \downarrow dI \rightarrow \downarrow dY$$

Flexible Exchange Rate

$$\uparrow d(G-T) \rightarrow \uparrow dY \rightarrow \uparrow dM \rightarrow \downarrow dXR \rightarrow \downarrow dX \rightarrow \uparrow d(X-M) \rightarrow \uparrow dY$$
$$\longrightarrow \downarrow dM \longrightarrow$$

There is no clear theoretical conclusion as to whether flexible exchange rates strengthen or weaken the fiscal policy's ability to manage domestic aggregate demand. It depends on the relative strengths of the two linkages described here, which will differ among countries. If there is close international integration of capital markets, the first of the two linkages is likely to be stronger. The implication is that fiscal policy is more effective if a fixed exchange rate is maintained and is weakened by the introduction of a flexible exchange rate. Such financial market integration requires free convertibility for capital account transactions, which is common for the industrialized countries but not in the developing world. This suggests that the traditional argument that fiscal policy is stronger with fixed exchange rates is more likely to hold for the industrialized countries. The opposite conclusion should hold for developing countries that maintain exchange controls that limit the responsiveness of the capital account to interest rate changes.

IS/LM/BB Graphs for Fiscal Policy under Alternative Exchange Rate Regimes

Changes in fiscal policy are represented by shifts in the *IS* line because an expansionary budget increases the level of GNP at which total savings (private plus government) would equal intended investment. GNP must rise sufficiently to generate increased private savings to offset lower government savings $(G - T)$. The slope of the *BB* line relative to that of the *LM* line indicates whether international capital market integration is sufficiently close to make fiscal policy stronger under fixed exchange rates and weaker with a flexible exchange rate regime. Perfect capital market integration (where the *BB* line is horizontal), meaning that fiscal policy is effective only with a fixed exchange rate, is depicted in Figure 18-4.

With a fixed exchange rate, the fiscal expansion tends to raise interest rates, but that causes large capital inflows, producing a payments surplus that

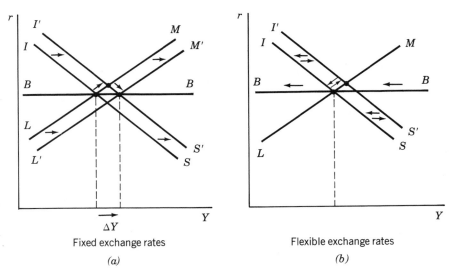

Fixed exchange rates

(a)

Flexible exchange rates

(b)

FIGURE 18-4   Effects of fiscal policy expansion with perfect capital mobility.

increases the money supply, shifting *LM* to the right and reversing the increase in interest rates. The result is a large increase in GNP. Increases in imports resulting from the higher level of GNP are similarly offset by capital inflows. If a flexible exchange rate is in operation, however, the capital inflows cause the currency to appreciate, shifting *BB* and *IS* to the left. *BB* shifts along itself, and *IS* returns to its previous position. Fiscal expansion has no effect on output.

If capital market integration is less than complete but sufficient to make *BB* flatter than *LM*, international repercussions still make fiscal policy more effective in a fixed exchange rate regime than under a float (Figure 18-5). Under fixed exchange rates, the fiscal expansion still produces higher interest rates and a balance-of-payments surplus that increases the money supply, thus supporting the intended effects of the larger budget deficit. With a flexible exchange rate, the currency appreciates, shifting *BB* and *IS* to the left and reducing the impacts of fiscal expansion.

The case in which capital market integration is weaker than the current account linkage to imports is represented as the *BB* line being steeper than the *LM* line. Fiscal policy is more effective with a flexible exchange rate, as can be seen in Figure 18-6.

Under fixed rates, a payments deficit results from fiscal expansion, shifting *LM* to the left and reducing the impact of the budget deficit on GNP. In the floating exchange rate graph, however, the worsening of the current account dominates any capital account response. The currency depreciates, shifting *BB* to the right and *IS* further to the right, making fiscal expansion more effective in raising GNP.

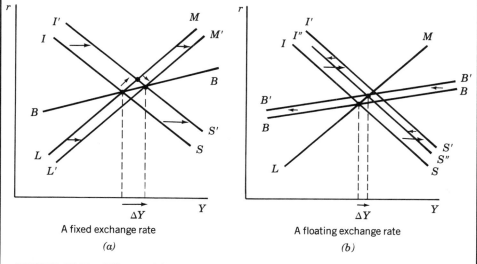

FIGURE 18-5   Effects of fiscal policy expansion when *BB* is flatter than *LM*.

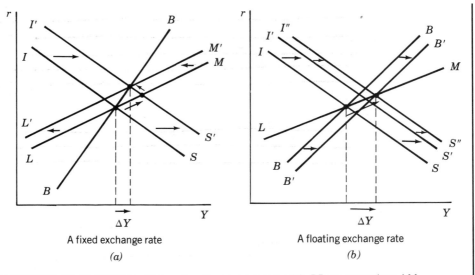

A fixed exchange rate
(a)

A floating exchange rate
(b)

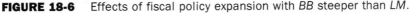

FIGURE 18-6   Effects of fiscal policy expansion with *BB* steeper than *LM*.

These figures and the accompanying discussion may seem confusing; therefore it may be useful to summarize the conclusions with regard to the effectiveness of fiscal policy in changing domestic output and incomes under alternative exchange rate regimes (see Table 18-1).

TABLE 18-1   Strength of Fiscal Policy in Affecting GNP Under Alternative Exchange Rate Regimes

	BB **flatter than** *LM* (extensive capital market integration)	*BB* **steeper than** *LM* (only limited capital market integration)
With:	Fiscal policy is:	
Fixed rates	Powerful	Weak
Flexible rates	Weak	Powerful

MERCANTILISM AND FLEXIBLE EXCHANGE RATES

One of the arguments for protectionism that was discussed in Chapter 7 is that domestic output and incomes may be increased by replacing imports with domestic products. It was suggested that this is a weak argument under any circumstances, but flexible rates make it even weaker. The introduction of a tariff that reduces imports, for example, produces a parallel reduction in the domestic demand for foreign exchange needed to pay for those imports. The local currency appreciates and foreign currencies depreciate until balance-of-payments equilibrium is reestablished. The appreciation of the local currency reduces exports and increases other imports, leaving the trade balance and the level of domestic aggregate demand largely unaffected. Any benefits received by domestic producers of the protected goods occur at the cost of losses in production and employment in other domestic industries that produce tradables goods.[9] The following diagram outlines this process, where T represents the tariff rate:

$$\uparrow dT \rightarrow \downarrow dM \rightarrow \uparrow d(X - M) \rightarrow \uparrow dY$$
$$\qquad\qquad \longmapsto \uparrow dXR \rightarrow \uparrow dM \rightarrow \downarrow d(X - M) \rightarrow \downarrow dY$$
$$\qquad\qquad\qquad\qquad \longmapsto \downarrow dX \rightharpoonup$$

The decline in domestic output with which the diagram ends should largely cancel the increase in output on the top line, leaving domestic production and output unaffected.

Some supporters of flexible exchange rates believed that the widespread understanding of this argument might eliminate much of the political pressure for protectionist policies, because those who would be injured by the adoption of restrictions would argue forcefully against them. If, for example, the U.S. textile and garment industries asked the Congress for sharp reductions in the quotas for textile and garment imports, other U.S. industries that produce tradables would understand that the dollar would appreciate and they would be injured if this policy was adopted. These industries could then be expected to offer strong opposition to the demands of the textile and garment interests, making it much less likely that the quota proposal would become law. This argument is discussed in Exhibit 18-2.

[9]H. Johnson, "The Case for Flexible Exchange Rates," in G. N. Halm, ed., *Approaches to Greater Exchange Rate Flexibility: The Burgenstock Papers* (Princeton, N.J.: Princeton University Press, 1970), pp. 100–101.

Save an Auto Worker's Job, Put Another American Out of Work.

People who support domestic-content (or "local-content") laws for imported automobiles argue that they would reduce unemployment in the United States. They are wrong.

As long as the United States maintains a floating exchange rate, the adoption of protectionist measures to help one industry will merely shift jobs from elsewhere in the economy to the favored sector, with no significant effect on total employment. Changes in the exchange rate for the dollar are the mechanism through which output and jobs are lost in the unprotected industries. Protectionism is never a sensible way to increase domestic employment, but it is wholly self-defeating for a country with a floating exchange rate.

Under fixed exchange rates, it might be possible to view the short-term effects of a tariff solely in terms of impact on the protected industry, because there would be no exchange rate movement to cause undesirable effects elsewhere in the economy. If foreign countries did not retaliate against U.S. restrictions on car imports, for example, employment would increase in Detroit without loss of jobs elsewhere in the United States.

But since the exchange rates began to float in 1973, this is no longer true. A decision to apply domestic-content rules to cars sold in the United States, for example, would greatly reduce imports from Japan, causing a parallel decline in the U.S. demand for yen to pay for those cars. The yen would then depreciate and the dollar would appreciate until the balance in international transactions was restored. As consumers in the United States and abroad responded to this change in relative prices by purchasing fewer U.S. goods and more foreign products, sales and employment would be lost in a range of U.S. industries. The U.S. car industry might gain from the imposition of domestic-content rules, but other domestic industries that must compete in world markets would lose. Total employment in the U.S. economy would not increase.

With fixed exchange rates among currencies, the worldwide employment effects of U.S. protectionism would be a "zero-sum game," in that job gains in the United States would be offset by job losses abroad. Under the existing system of floating exchange rates, the effects of protectionism on employment are a "zero-sum game" *within* the United States. Job gains in Detroit are matched by job losses in Boston and Seattle, with exchange rate changes imposing the losses on unprotected parts of the U.S. economy.

A statistical study has recently been completed in the Labor Department supporting this argument. It concludes that the original form of the domestic-content bill would create about 300,000 jobs in automobile manufacturing and related industries, but that about the same number of jobs would be lost elsewhere in the U.S. economy as the exchange rate for the dollar rose. The study indicates that the apparel and electronic components industries would be particularly injured by the exchange rate change, and that computers and commercial aircraft would also be seriously affected. The study suggests that because the U.S. auto industry uses fewer workers per million dollars in sales than do many other affected industries, the adoption of the domestic-content bill for cars might actually cause a slight net loss of employment in the United States.

It is surprising that industries such as apparel and computers have not realized that protectionism for automobiles would hurt them, and entered the lobbying battle against the domestic-content bill. The late Harry Johnson of the University of Chicago argued many years ago that floating exchange rates were a good idea precisely because they would destroy the traditional arguments for tariffs and encourage an era of free trade. He optimistically assumed that politicians and lobbyists would understand that protection for one industry was merely a tax on other domestic industries under floating exchange rates. But it doesn't seem to be working out that way. Walter Mondale's conversion to protectionism is a particularly unfortunate example.

If Washington wants to help U.S. industries compete against foreign firms, the first goal must be to reverse the sharp increase in the exchange rate for the dollar that has occurred during the last 18 months. A decline of the dollar to more realistic levels would be expensive for American tourists abroad, but it would greatly help U.S. industries that compete against imports, such as cars and apparel, and those that export, such as computers and aircraft.

Bringing down the exchange rate for the dollar requires a continuing decline in U.S. interest rates. Although interest rates are determined by a number of factors, predictions of huge federal deficits have been a dominant element in maintaining high U.S. yields since early 1981. Gaining permanent control over federal deficits requires decisions that are painful and politically risky. It is far easier for politicians to promise help for U.S. workers and industries through domestic-content rules and other protectionist policies. Such an approach will actually produce no increase in employment or any other help for the economy, but that result would be apparent only in the long run. Election results are always in the short run.

EXHIBIT 18-2   Source: From *The Washington Post*, Robert M. Dunn, Jr., copyright ©The Washington Post, Op. Ed. page, October 28, 1982. Reprinted with permission.

PURCHASING POWER PARITY AND FLEXIBLE EXCHANGE RATES

Finally, many supporters of flexible exchange rates predicted that nominal exchange rates would move roughly to offset differing rates of inflation, leaving real exchange rates relatively constant. If U.S. inflation continued at 4 percent while the rest of the world's price level rose at an average annual rate of 7 percent, the dollar would appreciate by about 3 percent per year, leaving the cost- and price-competitive position of U.S. producers of tradables largely unchanged. The adoption of flexible nominal exchange rates would then be a route to relatively constant real exchange rates.

As will be seen in Chapter 21, the experience with flexible exchange rates since 1973 has differed in a number of ways from the theory presented here. Nominal exchange rates have not moved to offset differences in rates of inflation, and large changes in real exchange rates have been quite frequent and persistent. Such changes in real exchanges rates have been very disruptive, and recently the governments of the major industrialized countries have tried to limit such changes. As a result, national monetary policies are not as independent or powerful as the theory discussed in this chapter would imply. In addition, pressures for protectionism in the United States have not disappeared but seem to have become stronger. As was stated earlier, academic and other supporters of flexible exchange rates have to be described as "sadder but wiser."

QUESTIONS FOR STUDY AND REVIEW

1. When a country has a floating exchange rate, the domestic money supply is not affected by shifts in its international payments. Is this statement true or false? Why?

2. Starting from an initial position of payments equilibrium, suppose that foreign demand for Country A's exports suddenly rises. If a flexible exchange rate exists, explain what would happen and how equilibrium would be restored.

3. How does the existence of a flexible exchange rate affect the impact of monetary policy shifts on a domestic economy? Explain, and illustrate for a tightening of monetary policy using the *IS/LM/BB* graph.

4. What effect does the adoption of a flexible exchange rate have on the impacts of fiscal policy shifts in a country whose capital markets are closely integrated with those of the rest of the world? Use the *IS/LM/BB* graph to illustrate for a fiscal tightening.

5. Why is the mercantilist argument for protection weakened by the adoption of a flexible exchange rate?

6. In what sense does a flexible exchange rate encourage national macroeconomic independence as opposed to the macroeconomic interdependence implied by a fixed parity?

7. A Keynesian views an appreciation as deflationary, whereas a monetarist views the same appreciation as expansionary. Why?

SELECTED REFERENCES

Dornbusch, R. *Open Economy Macroeconomics*. New York: Basic Books, 1980.

Dreyer, J., G. Haberler, and T. Willett, eds. *Exchange Rate Flexibility*. Washington, D.C.: American Enterprise Institute, 1978.

Dunn, R. "The Many Disappointments of Flexible Exchange Rates." *Princeton Essays in International Finance,* No. 154, December 1983.

Friedman, M. "The Case for Flexible Exchange Rates." In *Essays in Positive Economics*. Chicago: University of Chicago Press, 1953.

Halm, G., ed. "Approaches to Greater Exchange Rate Flexibility: The Burgenstock Papers." Princeton, N.J.: Princeton University Press, 1970.

MacDonald, R. *Floating Exchange Rates: Theory and Evidence*. London: Unwin Hyman, 1988.

McCulloch, R. "Unexpected Real Consequences of Floating Exchange Rates." *Princeton Essays in International Finance,* No. 153, August 1983.

Mundell, R. *International Economics*. New York: Macmillan, 1968, Chs. 17, 18, and 19.

Sohmen, E. *Flexible Exchange Rates*. Chicago: University of Chicago Press, 1969.

INTERNATIONAL MONETARY EXPERIENCE, 1880 TO 1940

In this chapter and the next we will describe the main features of about 90 years of international monetary experience, from 1880 to 1973. We will draw on the analytical framework developed in previous chapters to explain and interpret the course of events. Knowledge of this historical background and experience will facilitate our later discussion (in Chapter 21) of current international monetary problems and proposals to reform the system. However, there is such a wealth and variety of experience in this period and such a plethora of interpretations of it that we can attempt to provide only a "broad-brush" treatment of the subject. Thus these chapters present a synopsis, not a detailed history. The chapter's aim is twofold: to show how analysis can be used to explain and interpret events, and to show how current issues and problems unfold from those of previous periods.

The full period under review is divided into three subperiods by the two world wars, during each of which normal monetary and trade arrangements gave way to special wartime measures and government controls. The chronology of the international monetary system during these periods is shown in Figure 19-1. During

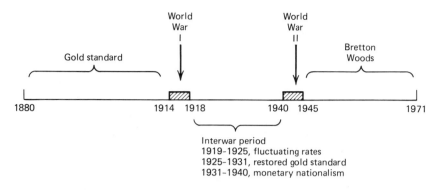

FIGURE 19-1 A chronological sketch: The international monetary system, 1880 to 1971.

the first subperiod, from about 1880 to 1914, the gold standard reached its fullest flower; during the second subperiod, 1918 to 1940, considerable monetary turmoil existed, and a number of different monetary arrangements were tried; and during the third subperiod, 1945 to 1971, a formal international agreement, embodied in the International Monetary Fund, was adopted to regulate international monetary arrangements.[1] In this chapter we will discuss the first two subperiods, 1880 to 1940. The post–World War II experience is described in Chapter 20.

THE GOLD STANDARD, 1880 TO 1914

The gold standard had no precise date of origin. It gradually emerged in the latter part of the nineteenth century, although some countries could be said to have been on the gold standard at a much earlier date. It reached its heyday in the two decades before the outbreak of World War I, when most of the leading industrial nations had linked their currencies to gold and were generally abiding by the so-called rules of the game of the gold standard. Many writers have thought of this period before World War I as an idyllic period, a true golden age, and they have hankered to restore the conditions that then existed.

When a nation went on the gold standard, it entered into no formal agreements with other nations. No treaty was signed, nor was any other kind of written commitment made to other nations. The nation simply began to operate in accordance with the unwritten rules of the game. That is, the nation defined its currency in terms of gold; its treasury or central bank was required by law to buy and sell gold without limit at that stated price; and it allowed gold to be freely imported and exported. The crucial factor was that the public should have complete confidence

---

[1]The Articles of Agreement of the International Monetary Fund were worked out at a wartime conference held at Bretton Woods, New Hampshire, in 1944. Hence the articles are known as the Bretton Woods agreement.

that the nation would abide by these rules. Given such confidence, the results were that actual market exchange rates between currencies were fixed within narrow limits and, more important, that a mechanism was provided through which disturbances to the flow of international payments between countries would be both financed and corrected. Broadly speaking, this mechanism of adjustment worked in the manner already described in Chapter 16, but conditions and circumstances existing in the pre-1914 period facilitated its operation.

The Process of Adjustment

In Chapter 16 we showed that the process of adjustment under a fixed exchange rate system involved three elements: interest rate effects, income effects, and price effects. Under gold standard conditions, the interest rate (or lending) effect played an important role. It was highly sensitive to disturbances in the balance of payments, and thus its influence was quickly felt in foreign exchange markets.

If the public had complete confidence in maintaining the value of a currency in terms of gold, short-term capital tended to move to support the gold parity of that currency whenever it came under pressure as a result of a disturbance in the balance of payments. Private firms and individuals would buy the currency when its value in the foreign exchange market dropped below its mint par, and sell it when its value rose above mint par. These short-term capital flows thus tended to be stabilizing in the sense that they caused the market exchange rate to move toward, or stay very close to, the mint par value. The sensitive response of short-term capital also reduced the need for actual shipments of gold from one country to another.

For example, the mint par exchange rate between the British pound sterling and the U.S. dollar was $4.866 = £1.00. This value is obtained by taking the ratio of the gold content of the pound to the gold content of the dollar, as defined by British and U.S. law. The gold content of the pound sterling was fixed by the Coinage Act of 1816 at 113 grains of pure gold. (Actually, the pound was defined in terms of gold of 11/12 purity, but we have adjusted to pure gold content.) One dollar was defined by U.S. law to be equal in value to 23.22 grains of pure gold.[2] Therefore the mint par exchange rate between the dollar and the pound was $113 \div 23.22 = \$4.866494 = £1.00$.

Since the cost of shipping gold from London to New York was about $0.026 per pound sterling equivalent,[3] the market exchange rate was constrained between the limits of $4.893 = £1 and $4.840 = £1 (i.e., $4.866 ± 0.026). These were

---

[2]With 480 grains in an ounce, these currency definitions imply prices of $20.67 per ounce of pure gold in the United States and £4.4s. 11 1/2d. in Great Britain. (Again, British law actually stated a price in terms of gold of 11/12 purity, that is, a selling price of £3.17s.10 1/2d; and a buying price of £3.17s. 9d.

[3]This figure includes freight, insurance, and handling charges. The figure is an average cost per pound for a fairly large shipment, for example, £10,000 worth of gold. No one would ship a small sum this way.

the gold points, as described in Chapter 13. When the spot exchange rate moved toward the gold export point for Great Britain, namely, $4.84 = £1, U.S. traders and businesspeople who had payments to make in pounds, perhaps against contracts to buy British goods, would regard the pound as cheap. After all, its price could not fall below $4.84, while it might rise in the future by as much as $0.05 per pound. Consequently, they would step up their purchases of pounds as the price moved toward its lower limit of $4.84.

Short-term capital also tended to flow into sterling assets when the pound fell in terms of dollars. Banks, insurance companies, and other financial institutions with large holdings of short-term securities would see in the low pound price an opportunity to increase the effective interest rate on their assets. For example, if the short-term interest rate were 4 percent in both New York and London, a New York insurance company could convert $4,840,000 into £1,000,000 and buy three-month sterling treasury bills in London. Three months later, when the bills matured, the exchange rate might be higher, say, $4.88 = £1. In that case, the New York insurance company could convert the sterling proceeds back into dollars and realize an annual yield of 7.3 percent in terms of dollars, a substantial improvement over the 4 percent available in New York. In addition to the straight interest earned, it would make a profit of $0.04 per pound on the exchange rate change.[4]

Of course, the dollar price of the pound might not be higher when the treasury bills matured, in which case no improvement in yield would be achieved. However, if gold parities are maintained for the dollar and pound, the insurance company can be certain that the exchange rate will not drop below $4.84 and therefore it cannot earn less than 4 percent on this transaction. With no chance of loss and some chance of gain, the incentive to short-term capital flows is very strong when the exchange rate approaches the gold points.

The reader may have noticed the close similarity between these short-term capital movements and the flows of funds involved in interest arbitrage as described in Chapter 13. One difference is that, in the example above, the New York insurance company did not cover its initial purchase of spot pounds by selling forward pounds. The reason it did not was that it had perfect confidence in the gold parities and thus had no need to protect itself against the risk of a fall in the pound (below $4.84). However, if the spot exchange rate were somewhere between the gold points, so that it could move in either direction, forward cover would typically be obtained by a financial institution seeking to maximize its interest yield but unwilling to take exchange rate risk.[5]

The effect of these responses by traders, financial institutions, and individuals was to make the demand and supply of pounds highly elastic as the market exchange

---

[4]$4,840,000 converted into £1,000,000 and invested in 4 percent treasury bills will amount to £1,010,000 in three months (£1,000,000 × 1.04 × ¼). At $4.88 = δ1, £1,010,000 is equal to $4,928,800. The effective yield on an annual basis is ($4,928,800 − $4,840,000) ÷ $4,840,000 × 4 = 7.3 percent.

[5]For an expert discussion of short-term capital movements in the pre-1914 gold standard, see Oscar Morgenstern, *International Financial Transactions* (Princeton, N.J.: Princeton University Press, 1959), Chap. 5.

rate approached the gold points. Consequently, many small, temporary disturbances in the balance of payments could be and were accommodated by such equilibrating flows of funds, without need for an actual shipment of gold or for any positive action by monetary authorities. This point is illustrated in Figure 19-2, in which the demand for pounds(D) becomes highly elastic as the exchange rate approaches the lower gold point of $4.84 = £1. The initial equilibrium at point E, where the exchange rate is at the mint par value, $4.866 = £1, is disturbed by a shift in the supply curve of pounds from S to S'. This increased supply of pounds causes the exchange rate to drop, but the demand curve is so elastic that the rate does not reach the gold export point and therefore no gold flow occurs. The increased supply of pounds is taken up by traders and financial institutions who stand ready to buy pounds as the price falls, producing a new equilibrium at E'.

This sensitive response of short-term capital to exchange rate changes provides a partial explanation of a fact that puzzled many observers of the gold standard mechanism, namely, that so little gold actually moved from one country to another. Balance-of-payments adjustment occurred, but gold movements, the ostensible motive force in accomplishing that adjustment, appeared to be quite small in absolute magnitude. We can now see that one reason the gold shipments were small is that short-term capital moved in an equilibrating direction and thus prevented the exchange rate from reaching the gold export point.

So far we have assumed that the monetary authorities remained passive, as indeed they often did in the case of small changes in demand and supply of foreign exchange. However, the central bank had a sensitive and powerful instrument

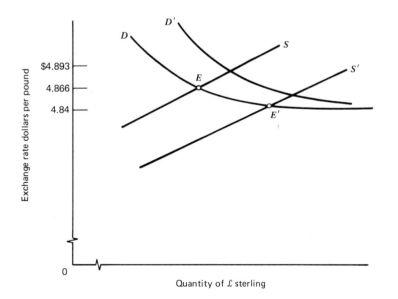

FIGURE 19-2 Increase in demand for pounds, resulting from a rise in interest rates in London.

that it could use to influence the flows of short-term capital just described. That instrument was called the bank rate in British usage. The bank rate is a rate of interest (comparable to the discount rate of the Federal Reserve System in the United States) that the central bank charges when it makes loans to commercial banks (or advances funds to them by discounting their notes). In the pre-1914 period, when the Bank of England raised the bank rate, that tended to cause the whole structure of interest rates to rise in London financial markets. Therefore a rise in bank rate increased the incentive for traders and financial institutions to shift short-term funds from New York (and other centers) to London because it would increase the interest rate they could earn on sterling assets. In short, a rise in bank rate tended to cause the demand for pounds sterling in the foreign exchange market to increase. In Figure 19-2 this increase in demand would appear as a shift to the right in the demand curve, say, from D to D', and it would tend to cause the dollar-pound exchange rate to rise.

Therefore if the bank rate were increased before the dollar-pound price reached $4.84, the gold export point for England, no gold flow might ever occur. If the bank rate were increased after gold had begun to move, then the increased demand for pounds would quickly check the outflow of gold by raising the dollar-pound price above $4.84.

Contemporary observers were well aware of the interrelationships between bank rate, exchange rates, and gold movements. They described many episodes in which the Bank of England used its bank rate to influence gold movements. In fact, it was reported that a rise in bank rate sometimes caused gold that was already loaded onto ships for export to be unloaded and sold back to the British Treasury. A sufficiently high bank rate could even push the exchange rate to the gold import point and draw gold from other countries. This is reflected in the old saying, "Seven per cent will bring gold from the moon."[6]

Small, temporary balance-of-payments disturbances might be accommodated by the lending effect alone, but larger, more lasting disturbances required a more basic process of adjustment involving changes in prices, wages, and national incomes in deficit and surplus countries. This adjustment process was explained in Chapter 16; here we will describe its application under conditions existing in the pre-1914 gold standard.

Through the fixed exchange rates between their currencies, and through trade in goods and services, prices in the various nations were rather tightly linked together. Tariffs existed, of course, but otherwise governments allowed private merchants to buy goods in the cheapest markets they could find and sell in the dearest. Free enterprise and a laissez-faire ideology generally prevailed in the world economy. Wages and prices possessed a high degree of flexibility, rising or falling in response to shifts in demand and supply.

Under these circumstances, if a country developed a payments deficit and gold flowed out, the consequent rise in its interest rates and decline in its money supply

---

[6]P. T. Ellsworth, *The International Economy* (New York: Macmillan, 1950), p. 316. There are many variations on this saying.

would tend to cause a fall in aggregate demand and put downward pressure on wages and prices. Investment expenditures would be reduced, bringing about a multiplier effect (decline) in national income. Such deflationary pressure in the deficit country, by checking imports and stimulating exports, would tend to correct the payments deficit and thus stop the gold inflow.

Similarly, a tendency toward a payments surplus would be checked by an inflow of gold, which would bring a rise in money supply, easier credit conditions, an expansion of aggregate demand, and a rise in prices and wages. Such increases in income and prices would tend to stimulate imports, depress exports, and thus reduce the payments surplus.

Flexibility of wages and prices in each country, and some tolerance for swings in income and employment as well, were essential to the operation of the gold standard adjustment process. In the pre-1914 period, the social and political climate permitted such flexibility to exist. Economic changes were accepted almost as natural phenomena.

In this generally laissez-faire climate, a remarkable degree of economic integration occurred. The spread of industrialization, the expansion of markets for both raw materials and finished goods, developments in ocean transportation that sharply reduced freight rates, and freedom from major wars were all accompanied by a rapid expansion in total world trade. World merchandise exports tripled from 1876–1880 to 1911–1913.[7] The climate of political stability and economic optimism also encouraged foreign investment, and British long-term capital flowed abroad to develop raw material sources and to finance industrial development.

These close connections between the economies of major nations, lubricated by trade and capital flows at fixed exchange rates and encouraged by acceptance of internal economic adjustments necessary to make the system work, at once instilled confidence in the maintenance of fixed gold parities and prevented the emergence of disparate trends in wages and prices that would make those parities untenable. Because economic conditions in each nation were closely attuned to those elsewhere, deviations tended to be small and to be corrected quickly. They were not given time to grow into large deviations. Consequently, a nation was not confronted with the necessity of accepting a heavy and prolonged internal deflation in order to restore equilibrium in its external accounts. A small deviation could be corrected by a small dose of "classical medicine," as it came to be called. Furthermore, with wage and price flexibility, the ravages of unemployment were less severe than in later periods. A fall in demand, which might cause output to be reduced and workers laid off, would lead to lower wages and lower prices, but lower prices would stimulate exports and tend to restore the level of output and employment.

Thus, in pre-1914 conditions, the world economy had a cohesiveness and a degree of harmonization of national monetary and credit policies that linked wage and price levels closely together. By accepting the adjustment process signaled by small divergences in national price trends, large divergences were prevented from developing. As Triffin stated, the harmonization of national policies that existed

---

[7]P. Lamartine-Yates, *Forty Years of Foreign Trade* (London: Allen & Unwin, 1959), p. 28.

depended far less on ex post *corrective action, requiring an extreme flexibility, downward as well as upward, of national price and wage levels, than on the* ex ante *avoidance of substantial disparities in cost competitiveness and in the monetary policies which would allow them to develop.*[8]

Triffin also said that "national export prices remained strongly bound together among all competing countries" and "national wage and price levels . . . remained closely linked together," while Morgenstern emphasized the "solidarity of international capital markets,"[9] meaning that competition kept prices of comparable securities approximately the same in different national capital markets.

Our discussion thus far has concerned the process of adjustment through which national balances of payments were supposed to be kept in equilibrium under the international gold standard. There is another important aspect of the gold standard that we should explain briefly, that is, its role in regulating the long-run relationship between world prices and the world supply of money (especially the stock of gold).

If all national currencies were tied to gold, and if each nation maintained a fairly stable ratio between its gold reserves and the supply of national money, then the rate of growth in the world money supply (i.e., the sum of all national money supplies, expressed in terms of gold) clearly would depend on the flow of newly mined gold into the world economy. Since gold mining is an economic activity that is undertaken for profit, the output of mines will depend on the price of gold relative to other goods and services. This relationship provides a mechanism that will tend to stabilize world price levels. Thus if worldwide deflationary pressures develop—that is, the money prices of goods and services fall—while the money price of gold remains fixed, the real value of gold will rise. An ounce of gold commands a larger quantity of goods and services than before. Hence gold mining becomes more profitable, and the flow of new gold increases. This permits a more rapid expansion of the world money supply and thus tends to check and reverse the tendency toward deflation. Inflationary tendencies would be checked in a similar way, by causing a reduction in the flow of new gold.

Thus the "discipline" of the gold standard operates at two levels, the national and the global. Any single nation's ability to expand its money supply is limited by its balance-of-payments position; excessive expansion would cause it to lose gold, which would set off internal deflation. For the world as a whole, growth in the money supply is regulated by the flow of newly produced gold, a matter that depends partly on providence or the state of nature (the amount and distribution of gold-bearing ore in the earth's surface) and partly on the price of gold relative to other goods and services.

This analysis leads to a view of the gold standard system as a kind of natural order. Nations are subject to a discipline that lies beyond human control. World money supply and world trends in prices will be regulated by natural forces.

---

[8]Robert Triffin, "The Evolution of the International Monetary System," *Princeton Studies in International Finance,* No. 12 (Princeton, N.J.: Princeton University Press, 1964), p. 10.

[9]Ibid, p. 10; Morgenstern, *International Financial Transactions,* p. 166.

Many people have found this view of gold standard discipline very appealing. They like the idea that these matters are outside the control of governments or human institutions because they instinctively mistrust the management of money. They fear that anyone in authority—politicians, rulers, or central bankers—will make mistakes or succumb to the temptation to inflate the currency, or otherwise mismanage it. They prefer to take their chances with an impersonal, automatic mechanism that is beyond human control. The strong preference for gold and silver coins and ornaments on the part of peasants in many parts of the world reflects this same distrust of paper money and its managers.

Despite the appeal and apparent logic of this thesis, it does not fit the facts very well, even in the century ending in 1914. The largest changes in gold production occurred, not in response to changes in relative prices, but as a result of major new discoveries of gold-bearing ore (California, 1849; South Africa, 1890s) and changes in technology that made possible deeper shafts and economical refining of lower grade ores. Since we have no reason to believe that these events were related in any systematic way to price trends (they appear to have been random), it seems unlikely that a growing world economy could avoid deflationary pressure if it relied on gold production to determine the pace of growth in the money supply. We will return to this issue in the next section.

Some Qualifications and Amendments

The prewar gold standard evolved over a considerable period of time; it was not a deliberate, conscious creation of the participating nations. In fact, during its heyday its operation was not fully understood, and even now there is much that remains unclear about the nature of the gold standard and its role in the world economy. Much of the analysis and study of the gold standard mechanism was formulated after World War I, when it was no longer in operation or had ceased to function as effectively as in the pre-1914 period.[10] Many later writers have tended to view the gold standard period through rose-colored glasses and to idealize it as a period in which adjustment occurred quickly, smoothly, and painlessly. A kind of stereotype developed; some would say a gold standard mythology emerged. For years after World War I, the prime objective of public policy for many people was to return to the gold standard, to restore the conditions and the kind of world economy that existed in that halcyon period.

Recent studies have tended to deflate some of the more extravagant claims made for the gold standard and to modify the simple, stereotyped view of its adjustment process. Since our account of that process is itself rather close to the conventional stereotype, we will briefly mention a few of the qualifications and amendments that have been stressed in recent studies.

---

[10]However, we should note that the central relationship between gold flows, price levels, and external balance was worked out in the eighteenth century by David Hume and further elaborated in the early nineteenth century by David Ricardo and others.

1. First, the relatively satisfactory and successful operation of the world economy in the pre-1914 decades, and the smooth and generally effective process of international economic adjustment may have been the result of other conditions and circumstances prevailing in that period. Perhaps the gold standard has been given more credit than it deserves. The pre-1914 decades comprise an expansive period characterized by economic growth, scientific and technological advances, freedom from major wars, a widespread (though not complete) acceptance of trade and specialization, spreading industrialization, and rapid development of mineral and other natural resources in many parts of the world not previously linked closely into the world economy.

   In such a context of growth and development, many economic adjustments became easier to accomplish than they would have been in a static context. A country with a balance-of-payments deficit might be able to remove it, not by deflating its economy, but simply by reducing its rate of growth relative to growth rates in the other countries. In that case, wage rates need not fall; they simply rise less fast or stay about the same. Imports need not be reduced in absolute value; they simply rise less rapidly than exports. This point is a simple one, but allowance for it helps to explain some apparent discrepancies between our account of the gold standard process of adjustment and economic statistics for this period which do not show prolonged internal deflation or money-wage cuts in countries undergoing adjustment to correct a payments deficit.

2. Second, the pre-1914 gold standard system worked much more satisfactorily in the so-called center countries, the leading industrial nations of Europe and North America, than in the less developed, nonindustrial nations in the periphery. The principal center country was, of course, Great Britain, and some writers assert that the world was really on a sterling standard in this period and that the adjustment process was largely managed by the British. It is a fact that many nations in the periphery frequently depreciated their currencies against gold (and sterling), which is at least an indication that severe adjustments were being required of them.

   Triffin and others have argued that the gold standard mechanism operated in such a way that cyclical fluctuations fell heavily on suppliers of food and raw materials in the peripheral areas. For one thing, a rise in the British bank rate would tend to check British demand for imported raw materials (the exports of peripheral nations) and thereby cause their prices to fall. Since inventories of these raw materials were largely financed by borrowing in London, the rise in interest rates also tended to be accompanied by a selloff of inventories, further reducing raw material prices. Consequently, these prices tended to fall sharply—more sharply than the prices of British industrial exports, which were less volatile and less sensitive to interest rate changes. Consequently, Britain's export prices would fall proportionately less than its import prices, a result contrary to what one would expect on the basis of the gold standard stereotype.[11]

[11] When a deficit country raises the bank rate, its prices are supposed to be depressed relative to those in the outside world. See Robert Triffin, "The Evolution of the International Monetary System," pp. 2–20, for a very interesting discussion of this and other aspects of the gold standard mechanism.

A second aspect of this argument involves foreign investment, especially British investment in raw material production in peripheral countries. When the British economy was booming, its demand for raw material imports would be rising and British capital would flow abroad to develop additional sources of supply. In the peripheral countries, these capital inflows would increase their capacity to import, which was already swollen by favorable prices for their exports of raw materials. But when Britain's boom gave way to recession, the capital flows would dry up and, at the same time, prices of raw material exports would fall. Thus the peripheral countries would face a sharp reduction in their capacity to import goods and services from the outside world. In this way, the system tended to exaggerate economic instability in the peripheral countries. This instability was evidently too severe to be accommodated through internal price and wage adjustment, and the peripheral countries responded by allowing their currencies to fluctuate against gold.

Even aside from this instability argument, long-term capital movements played a large role in the operation of the world economy in the pre-1914 period. These flows occurred on a large scale and sometimes continued for a long time, even for decades. Consequently, nations did not necessarily have to balance their merchandise imports and exports, or even their current accounts, as implied by the gold standard stereotype. A borrowing nation could run an import surplus for several years, and some did so.

The large flows of long-term capital are a striking feature of the close world economic integration that developed in the decades before World War I. The magnitudes involved in these flows were impressive even by modern standards, and on a relative basis they dwarf present-day capital flows. Britain was the largest supplier of capital, although other European countries also played important roles. Foreign investment amounted to about 4 percent of British national income in 1880, 7 percent in 1905, and 9 percent in 1913.[12] At its peak in 1913, foreign investment absorbed about one-half of British savings. The earnings generated by this foreign investment formed a significant part of the British national income (10 percent toward the end of the period) and enabled Britain simultaneously to enjoy an import surplus on merchandise account and to make additional investments abroad. Indeed, it is a remarkable fact that throughout the whole of the period 1880 to 1913, when British foreign investment reached its fullest flow, British imports of goods and services exceeded exports of goods and services. Earnings on foreign investments financed both the import surplus and the net new foreign investment.

For our present purpose, the main point is that long-term capital movements lessened or postponed the need for corrective adjustments in prices and wages in order to restore the current account balance. Instead, as Triffin said:

[12]Arthur Salter, "Foreign Investment," *Essays in International Finance,* No. 12 (Princeton N.J.: Princeton University Press, February 1951). Other figures in this paragraph come from A. K. Cairncross, *Home and Foreign Investment, 1870–1913* (Cambridge, U.K.: Cambridge University Press, 1953).

> *. . . international capital movements often did cushion—and even stimulate—vast and enduring deficits, or surpluses, on current account without calling for any correction whatsoever, except in a very long run indeed.*[13]

3. Additional qualifications concern the actual importance of gold movements in the operation of the world economy and the extent to which countries actually followed the so-called rules of the game. On both points, doubts have been expressed about the validity of the conventional view of the adjustment process.

   Despite the crucial role attributed to gold movements in theory, statistical evidence indicates that actual gold shipments from one country to another were quite small. It is hard to see how small gold flows could be responsible for producing the rapid and effective adjustments in national balances of payments that were observed. Not only were gold flows small, but, in addition, prices changes seemed to be much smaller than one would expect on the basis of theory. Taussig ruefully acknowledged "that here we have phenomena not fully understood."[14] Our previous discussion provides a partial explanation: highly sensitive short-term capital movements cushioned the shock of disturbances to equilibrium, and, to some extent, they took the place of gold flows; long-term capital movements also lessened the need for current account adjustments that would require price changes. Furthermore, much of the adjustment was accomplished by the income effect, an aspect not explicitly allowed for in early accounts of the gold standard process.

   In addition, some countries held their reserves in the form of sterling balances in London. They covered payments deficits by drawing down their sterling balances, not by shipping gold.

   Modern studies have also indicated that, even in center countries, central banks did not strictly follow the gold standard rules of the game.[15] Many of them occasionally changed their buying or selling prices for gold in order to influence gold movements. Others sometimes interfered directly with the supposedly free movement of gold, for example, by temporarily prohibiting its export. But most important, central banks did not determine their monetary policies in a mechanical way as an automatic response to gold flows, that is, tighten money supply when gold flows out, or loosen it when gold flows in. Instead, they used some discretion in these matters and took other factors into consideration. For example, when a central bank was gaining gold, it did not always lower its discount rate and reinforce the effect of gold inflows on commercial bank reserves. They usually did so, but exceptions were numerous.

---

[13] Triffin, "The Evolution of the International Monetary System," p. 7.

[14] F. W. Taussig, *International Trade* (New York: Macmillan, 1927), p. 239.

[15] The key reference is Arthur I. Bloomfield, *Monetary Policy Under the International Gold Standard* (New York: Federal Reserve Bank, 1959). Bloomfield notes that the concept of the rules of the game was itself a post–World War I invention, apparently first used by J. M. Keynes in the 1920s.

Furthermore, in a fractional-reserve system, when the gold reserves of central banks changed, they were supposed to use discount and credit policy to bring about changes in their domestic asset holdings: to increase them when reserves rise and reduce them when reserves fall. These changes would further affect commercial bank reserves and thus tend to magnify the effects of gold flows. Bloomfield found that leading central banks did not play by these rules in the majority of cases. Using annual data, he found that, more often than not, central banks' domestic assets and reserves moved in opposite directions.[16] Bloomfield is cautious about his results, but he does conclude (p. 61) that "the evidence presented here, somewhat inconclusive though it is, suggests . . . that the 'rules of the game' were of much less importance and influence than the usual stereotype would have it."

4. Finally, the role of gold in determining the world's supply of money has been challenged. We mentioned above that gold production fluctuated greatly, reflecting new discoveries and developments in mining technology. However, the world money supply grew steadily at a rate of 3 to 4 percent from 1870 to 1913, and exchange rates remained largely stable, at least in most leading nations. How are these facts to be reconciled with the marked variability of gold-mining output? One answer is that credit money (paper currency and bank deposits) grew rapidly in this period and provided the growth in money supply that was needed to finance the growth in output and trade. Triffin estimates that increases in credit money accounted for over 90 percent of total monetary expansion from 1873 to 1913, and credit money comprised nearly nine-tenths of the world's money supply by 1913.[17] This was a period of innovation in financial institutions, of a displacement of gold and silver coins by paper currency, and of a spectacular growth in the use of deposit money. Without these developments, money supply growth would have been heavily dependent on the output of newly mined gold, in which case considerable deflationary pressure would have existed.

As it was, much concern was expressed about the scarcity of gold, and a few preliminary measures were taken to pull existing gold into central banks and treasuries and thus to economize on its use in domestic circulation. As we will see, this concern grew stronger after World War I and finally led to the virtual elimination of gold as a circulating hand-to-hand money.

THE INTERWAR PERIOD, 1918 TO 1940

During World War I the international gold standard ceased to function. Some countries maintained some of its forms, but for all practical purposes its operation was suspended with the outbreak of war in August 1914. An important consequence

[16]Bloomfield, *Monetary Policy,* pp. 48–50.

[17]Triffin, "The Evolution of the International Monetary System," p. 15.

followed—namely, that national economies were no longer kept in close alignment with one another with respect to prices, wages, and other conditions. Countries whose economics had become interlocked, integrated, and closely attuned to each other in the decades leading up to 1914 were suddenly cut free from the connective mechanisms and the unifying discipline of the gold standard. They could now diverge and develop in different directions, and they did so to a considerable extent during the war years.

By the end of the war, in 1918, substantial divergences in economic circumstances had developed in the several countries. Internal rates of inflation varied greatly as nations resorted to inflationary methods of war finance, and wages and prices rose at different rates. The closely knit fabric of the prewar world economy had also been ripped and torn by the political and economic consequences of the war. Some countries had suffered great destruction of productive capacity, whereas others had developed new industries under the spur and incentive of wartime shortages and high prices. Creditor nations had liquidated many of their foreign assets to finance the war, and some debtor nations (notably the United States) emerged in 1918 as creditors, on balance.[18] Political borders were redrawn: The Austro-Hungarian Empire was dismantled and the Russian Revolution had occurred. The structure of the world economy had been profoundly altered by 1918.

Such drastic changes in political and economic circumstances made it difficult to resume normal activity after the war. In particular, wartime changes and distortions made the prewar pattern of exchange rates inappropriate for postwar conditions. It was not possible for all countries simply to go back on the gold standard at prewar parities and pick up where they had left off in 1914. Prewar exchange rates no longer represented equilibrium rates in the sense that they would produce approximate balance between market demand and supply of foreign exchange. To have suddenly restored the prewar mint parities would have caused huge deficits in some countries and surpluses in others; drastic internal adjustments would have been necessary in a short period of time.

1919 to 1926: An Episode of Fluctuating Exchange Rates

Recognition that prewar exchange rates could not be easily restored caused most countries to temporize, to delay in fixing an official par value in terms of gold, and thus to postpone their return to the gold standard. In the meantime, many countries removed wartime controls and allowed their currencies to float more or less freely in the foreign exchange market.

This episode of fluctuating exchange rates was generally regarded as a temporary expedient, however, for the almost universal expectation was that national currencies would once again be linked to gold and the gold standard restored in its prewar form. People had fond memories of the smoothly functioning prewar system, and they wanted above all to escape from postwar problems and to return to normalcy.

---

[18]The United States became, on balance, a creditor nation by the end of the war, but only if its wartime loans to the Allies are counted. Most of these loans were never repaid.

The main question was not whether to restore the gold standard but at what parities to restore it. Some urged that the prewar parities be restored; they saw the floating episode as a transitional device to allow countries to take actions and pursue policies necessary to enable them to go back on gold at their prewar parities. Others argued that changed economic conditions had changed the equilibrium exchange rates between national currencies and that gold parities should be adjusted to allow for the changed conditions.

Both groups made use of the theory of purchasing power parity.[19] This theory started from the assumption that prewar exchange rates had been equilibrium rates and that, as such, these rates had reflected an equality of purchasing power of the currencies traded. For example, in 1913, when the mint parity was $4.866 to £1.00, $4.866 would buy about the same amount of goods and services in the United States as £1.00 would buy in Great Britain. Given this assumption, the central idea of the purchasing power parity theory was that a new set of exchange rates should reflect relative changes in purchasing power, as indicated by relative changes in price levels. Furthermore, if exchange rates were allowed to float freely in the market, they would tend to settle at levels indicated by purchasing power parity. Thus, if British prices had doubled while U.S. prices remained unchanged, £1.00 would buy half as much as before while $1.00 would buy the same amount as before; hence the new exchange rate would be $2.433 = £1.00. As Cassel put it, "When two currencies have undergone inflation, the normal rate of exchange will be equal to the old rate multiplied by the quotient of the degree of inflation in the one country and in the other."[20]

Since prices rose more during the war in France and Britain than in the United States, purchasing power parity implied that the franc and the pound sterling were worth less in 1918 than in 1914, relative to the U.S. dollar. If 1914 is taken as the base (= 100), wholesale prices in December 1918 were as follows:[21]

United States	202
France	355
Great Britain	246

This implies that compared to its prewar parity of $4.866, the pound was worth about $4.00 (202/246 · $4.866) in 1918, and compared to its prewar parity of 19.3 cents, the franc was worth about $0.11 (202/355 · $0.193).

---

[19]This is an old idea that was revived by the Swedish economist Gustav Cassel. See his *Money and Foreign Exchange after 1914* (New York: Macmillan, 1923).

[20]Cassel, *Money and Foreign Exchange,* p. 140. Thus in our example above we have:

$$\$4.866\left(\frac{\text{U.S. Price Index}}{\text{British Price Index}}\right) = \$4.866\left(\frac{100}{200}\right) = \$2.433$$

[21]J. P. Young, *European Currency and Finance* (Washington, D.C.: U.S. Government Printing Office, 1925). Purchasing power parity calculations were also made on the basis of Consumer Price Indexes. Neither method is free of criticism.

With such a gap between the prewar gold parity and the estimate of present worth of their currencies, it was clear that Britain and France could not immediately return to the gold standard at their prewar parities, especially since the United States immediately announced its intention to maintain the dollar price of gold at its prewar level and resumed free export of gold at $20.67 per ounce. Both countries decided to let their currencies float while they decided what to do. We will briefly describe the contrasting experience of these two countries with fluctuating exchange rates, an experience that influenced attitudes toward exchange rate policy for years to come. (Actually, many other countries had similar experiences; we are simply using Britain and France as examples.)

The Pound Sterling, 1919 to 1925

Although a return to the gold standard at the prewar parity was out of the question immediately after the war, the British government made it plain that its objective was to restore the prewar parity as soon as feasible. This policy was endorsed in the report of the famous Cunliffe Committee, and, indeed, it seems to have been simply taken for granted as an ethical and moral imperative.[22] National honor was at stake. Everyone who had acquired sterling assets in the prewar period had the right, it was argued, to have them redeemed in pounds worth the same weight of gold as when acquired. Failure to honor that commitment would damage London's position as the world's financial center and undermine confidence in the pound.

In the meantime, the pound was allowed to float. When the wartime peg was removed in March 1919, the pound fell in value against the dollar, dropping to $3.81 by December 1919. A burst of postwar inflation drove it down even more in 1920, to a low of $3.38 (monthly average basis). Its value in the foreign exchange market was approximately equal to the value implied by purchasing power parity, although the two sometimes differed temporarily.

The policy prescription was clear. To lift the exchange value of the pound back to $4.86, British prices and wages had to be reduced relative to those elsewhere. Internal deflation was the order of the day. That meant keeping money tight and interest rates high, restraining investment, raising taxes, and cutting government expenditures. It also meant unemployment. Wages and prices were not as flexible as had been expected, for much social change had occurred during the war, including a strengthening of labor unions. They stoutly resisted cuts in money wages, and much labor strife ensued.

Nevertheless, the government clung to its objective and kept the pressure on. It was determined "to look the dollar in the face," that is, to make the pound worth $4.86, as before. To oversimplify a complex period, Britain continued to pursue deflationary policies from 1920 to 1925. The pound inched its way upward, though not without occasional setbacks. Figure 19-3 depicts the course of the fluctuating

---

[22]Committee on Currency and Foreign Exchanges after the War, *First Interim Report* Cond. 9182 (London, 1918). W. A. Brown says that he was told by leading monetary officials in London that "the British decision to return to the old parity with the dollar was taken on the day when sterling first deviated from it," namely, at the outbreak of war. *The International Gold Standard Reinterpreted, 1914–1934,* Vol. 1 (New York: National Bureau of Economic Research, 1940), pp. 221–222.

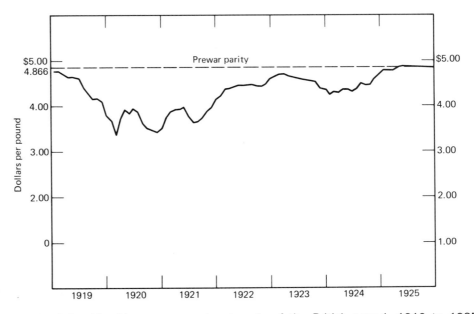

FIGURE 19-3 Monthly average exchange rate of the British pound, 1919 to 1925 (U.S. dollars per pound). *Source:* Federal Reserve Board, *Banking and Monetary Statistics* (Washington, D.C., 1942).

dollar-pound exchange rate from 1919 to 1925. In general, it moved in accordance with changes in purchasing power parity and thus reflected Britain's success in bringing down its price level relative to the outside world, especially relative to the United States.

Britain paid a heavy price to deflate its economy. Unemployment remained uncomfortably high throughout this period; indeed, it did not drop below 10 percent of the labor force. Major industries, including traditional export industries, remained depressed. Since trade unions resisted cuts in money wages, costs of production did not fall enough to make these industries competitive in world markets, and the gradual appreciation of the pound acted as a deterrent to export expansion. (Remember, for given world market prices, an appreciating pound means lower prices in terms of pounds for British exporters.) Output was cut back, with consequent effects on employment and income. Some of Britain's traditional export industries also faced fresh competition in world markets from new industrial capacity that had developed during the war in other parts of the world. The British economy needed to make adjustments, to develop new lines of export specialization, and to introduce new, cost-reducing technology. But such a response was inhibited by the deflationary policy, which tended to restrain investment in new plant and equipment.

U.S. monetary policy put additional pressure on the British economy in this period. As mentioned earlier, the United States had resumed its commitment to buy and sell gold at the prewar price, $20.67 per ounce. Its balance-of-payments position was strong in the early 1920s, and gold flowed into the United States in substantial quantities. According to conventional rules of the game, a gold standard country with a gold inflow was expected to increase its money supply, expand credit, and experience a rise in prices. Such a response in the United States would have lessened the need for deflation in Great Britain. But the Federal Reserve Board, facing its first major test since its creation in 1914, began to question the wisdom of letting gold flows determine the U.S. price level. It stressed the desirability of a stable domestic price level, and it began to offset, or neutralize, the monetary effects of gold inflows by open-market operations.[23] That is, it sold government securities in the open market in order to reduce the reserves of commercial banks—or, rather, to prevent a rise in those reserves as gold flowed in. The Federal Reserve Board was essentially asserting the primacy of domestic economic objectives; it was unwilling to accept instability at home in order to obtain external equilibrium. As observed in Chapter 16, there is a lack of symmetry in a fixed-exchange rate system such as the gold standard; a surplus country has more scope to avoid adjustment than has a deficit country.

Nevertheless, Britain persevered. As British prices gradually fell relative to U.S. prices, the pound rose in value on the foreign exchange market. This experience, coupled with the clearly expressed official determination to restore the pound to its prewar parity, had an influence on capital movements. Speculators and others were induced to buy pounds and to hold sterling securities, because if the pound rose to par, they would make a capital gain. Such capital inflows gave a kind of fillip to the pound, especially in 1925, when rumors spread that restoration of parity was at hand.

A diagram may help to illustrate this point. In Figure 19-4, D_1 and S_1 represent the original market demand and supply curves of pound sterling, with the free market price at \$4.25, well below the prewar parity. Deflationary policies in Great Britain tend to lower British prices and cause the demand for pounds to rise (to D_2), the supply to fall (to S_2), thus increasing the exchange rate to \$4.50. Now the rising exchange rate encourages people to believe the government will be successful in its campaign to restore the pound to its prewar parity, and speculators and others rush in to buy pounds in anticipation of its continued rise in value. These purchases shift the demand curve to D_3, causing a further rise in price to \$4.75. The expectation of a rise in price has led people to take action that in fact brought about a rise in price. This is a case of what is called self-realizing expectations. Such expectations occasionally appeared to exist in the foreign exchange market, and they could cause the exchange rate to diverge temporarily from purchasing power parity.

Finally, in April 1925, after having obtained dollar credits and raised the bank rate to strengthen sterling, the Chancellor of the Exchequer, Winston Churchill, announced that the Bank of England would again redeem its notes in gold and permit gold to be freely exported. Britain was back on the gold standard.

Unfortunately, this triumphant return did not mean an end to deflationary pressure on the British economy. For one thing, the exchange rate had been raised to this level (\$4.86) through internal deflation, and it could be sustained at

---

[23]This policy was enunciated in the famous *10th Annual Report of the Federal Reserve Board* (Washington, D.C.: U.S. Government Printing Office, 1923).

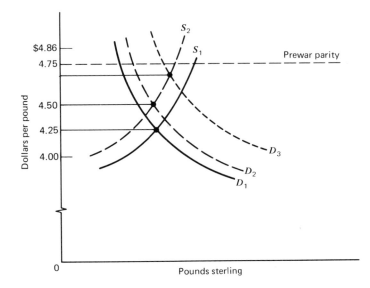

FIGURE 19-4   The approach to prewar parity for the pound.

that level only by making certain that British prices did not rise relative to those in other countries (i.e., by maintaining the deflationary pressures). For another, the capital that had flowed into London in anticipation of capital gains from exchange rate increases now tended to flow out again as speculators took their profits. Such outflows put downward pressure on the exchange rate and threatened British gold reserves. Thus deflationary pressure had to be maintained and even intensified to preserve confidence. Restoration brought no respite to the British economy.

We should not leave this episode without at least mentioning the vigorous, even strident, opposition to the official policy by some economists, most notably by J. M. Keynes. Keynes deplored a policy that inflicted such hardships on the domestic economy in order to achieve an external objective that he thought was of little real value. He warned that the new parity would require continued deflation and unemployment. Echoing the Federal Reserve Board, he urged the primacy of domestic economic objectives and said that Britain should not allow "the tides of gold to play what tricks they like with the internal price level." Keynes was arguing that the gold standard was no more, that it had been replaced with a managed (paper) currency system, and that the attempt to restore it would inevitably fail. One eloquent passage deserves quotation here:

In truth, the gold standard is already a barbarous relic. All of us, from the Governor of the Bank of England downwards, are now primarily interested in preserving the stability of business, prices, and employment, and are not likely, when the choice is forced on us, deliberately to sacrifice these to the outworn dogma . . . of £3.17s 10 1/2d per ounce. Advocates of the ancient standard do not observe how remote it now is from the spirit and the requirement of the age. A regulated non-metallic standard has slipped in unnoticed. It exists. Whilst the economist dozed, the academic dream of a hundred years, doffing its cap and gown, clad in paper rags, has crept into the world by means of the bad fairies—always so much more potent than the good—the wicked ministers of finance.[24]

The French Franc, 1919 to 1926

The effects of the war were more serious in France than in Great Britain. Wartime disruption and destruction were greater, and wartime inflation was more severe. Consequently, when the French government removed its controls and allowed the franc to float freely in the foreign exchange market, it dropped sharply in value. From March to December 1919, the franc dropped from $0.183 to $0.092, somewhat below its purchasing power parity at that time.

At first many people believed the franc would eventually be restored to its prewar value ($0.193), and this conviction led them to buy francs at what they regarded as a bargain price. Such purchases slowed the fall of the franc and sometimes even caused it to rise in value.

France, however, was plagued with political instability at this crucial time, and the French government was unable or unwilling to formulate and carry out a sound and realistic fiscal policy. Heavy expenditures were required in the reconstruction period, but taxes were not raised enough to cover these outlays. Much reliance was placed on reparations payments to be received from Germany. "Taxpayers need not worry, Germany will pay," said the French Finance Minister Klotz.[25] In the meantime, the government's current deficit was financed in an inflationary way, thus adding to pent-up inflationary pressures carried over from the war years. These deficits were financed in large part by the issue of short-term government securities. To facilitate the treasury's financing operations, interest rates were held down. They remained appreciably below interest rates on comparable securities in London and New York. France thus pursued an easy-money policy despite the presence of inflationary pressures. This policy also encouraged business expansion. Banks could obtain funds for loans to businesses simply by letting their short-term treasury securities mature. In these circumstances, the central bank had practically lost its power to control credit.

In the immediate postwar years, a fall in the franc tended to evoke the orthodox response. That is, franc depreciation stimulated exports, checked imports, and improved the balance of trade. It also encouraged capital inflows in anticipation of an eventual return to parity. These responses sometimes even caused the franc to rally on the foreign exchange market. As may be seen in Figure 19-5, the franc rallied in 1920, 1921, and 1922, and it rose nearly 50 percent from April 1920 to April 1922.

---

[24]J. M. Keynes, *Tract on Monetary Reform* (London: Macmillan, 1924), p. 138. The earlier quote in this paragraph is from the same source. See also his *The Economic Consequences of Mr. Churchill* (London: Macmillan, 1925).

[25]Quoted in Eleanor Dulles, *The French Franc, 1914–1928* (New York: Macmillan, 1929), p. 114. In addition to the Dulles book, two other detailed accounts of the French experience are available: Martin Wolfe, *The French Franc Between the Wars, 1919–1939* (New York: Columbia University Press, 1951); and James H. Rogers, *The Process of Inflation in France* (New York: Columbia University Press, 1929).

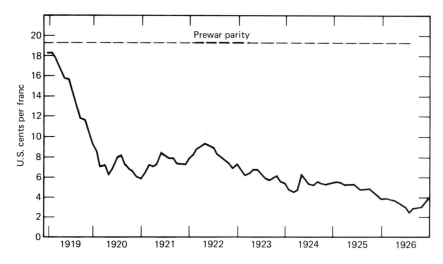

FIGURE 19-5 Monthly average exchange rate of the French franc, 1919 to 1926 (U.S. dollars per franc). *Source:* Federal Reserve Board, *Banking and Monetary Statistics* (Washington, D.C., 1942).

Despite this recovery and the steady growth in French output, the franc remained vulnerable. Government budget deficits continued to add to inflationary pressures, and prices resumed their upward climb. The reparations discussion temporarily broke down in 1922, and after the abortive French occupation of the German Ruhr in 1923, it became clear that actual reparations payments would fall far short of French hopes and expectations. The "phantom of reparations" had to be exorcised.[26]

As time went on, expectations of an eventual recovery of the franc tended to weaken. Doubts increased that the government could check the downward trend in the franc, much less restore it to prewar parity. This shift in mood and expectation was reflected in the foreign exchange market. A fall in the franc no longer evoked the orthodox response; it might instead be regarded as a harbinger of further weakness, in which case importers would accelerate their purchases from abroad (buy now before the price goes up even more) and exporters would hold their sale proceeds in dollars or pounds (wait for a more attractive rate of exchange before converting back into francs). Similarly, holders of franc assets, expecting a further fall in the value of the franc, were induced to liquidate them and buy foreign exchange. All these actions in anticipation of a fall in the franc tended to bring about that result: They were self-realizing in the sense described earlier.

Furthermore, changes in the exchange rate began to have direct effects on domestic prices and wages. Movements of the franc became a matter of lively interest to the general public, a subject of constant conversation and attention, and a signal for action. Changes in the value of the franc became an index of the rate

[26]Space does not permit an adequate discussion of the extremely important role and influence of the reparations issue in French policy in the postwar period. See Roger Haig, *The Public Finances of Postwar France* (New York: Columbia University Press, 1929).

of inflation, and merchants began to mark up the franc prices of their goods in proportion to a fall in the franc. Exporters began to quote prices in dollars, which meant that their prices in terms of francs rose in proportion to a depreciation of the franc. Workers began to demand higher wages when the franc fell. In these circumstances, an exchange rate change itself may cause shifts in the demand and supply curves of foreign exchange, and these shifts in turn may cause a further change in the exchange rate.

This sequence is illustrated in Figure 19-6. Suppose that, initially, the foreign exchange market is in equilibrium at E_1, as determined by the supply curve (S_1), and demand curve (D_1) of francs. The exchange rate is r_1. Now suppose the supply of francs shifts to S_2, perhaps because of a rise in French prices and wages. The conventional analysis is depicted in Figure 19-6a: The exchange rate falls to r_2, inducing increased purchases of francs (a movement along the new supply curve, S_2), thus producing a new equilibrium at E_2. However, when we allow this fall in the franc to affect expectations and behavior, additional consequences follow, as shown in Figure 19-6b. If importers fear a further fall in the franc, they increase their orders of foreign goods, causing the supply curve to shift to the right, for example, to S_3, and reducing the exchange rate to r_3. If exporters begin to hold their sale proceeds in New York bank accounts instead of converting them into francs, the demand curve shifts to the left, for example, to D_2, and the exchange rate falls further, to r_4. If this continued fall causes French prices and wages to rise, as suggested earlier, demand and supply curves both shift again, for example, to D_3 and S_4, and the franc continues to drop. Holders of francs, franc deposits, and other franc assets, seeing their real value steadily falling, may try to divest themselves of francs. A flight of funds from francs means still another shift of the supply curve to the right, for example, to S_5. In this way a cumulative, self-reinforcing movement in the exchange rate may get underway.

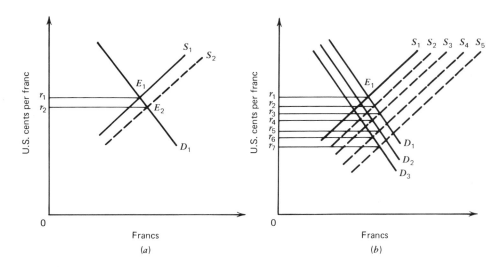

FIGURE 19-6 The fall of the franc. (a) Initial shift in the supply of francs. (b) Subsequent shifts in supply and demand for francs.

Such a sequence depends heavily on the state of expectations, on a psychological mood. Confidence in the currency is a crucial, highly fragile element; once lost, it is difficult to restore. Keynes's comment in the preface to the French edition of his *Tract on Monetary Reform*, written in March 1924, was remarkably prophetic:

> ...*if Frenchmen get it into their heads...that their national...money...[is] a depreciating asset, then there is no near limit to the fall in the value of the franc.... Moreover, the process will be cumulative, for each successive liquidation of franc assets..., by provoking a further fall, will seem to justify the prescience of those who fled first from the franc and will thus prepare the way for a second outburst of distrust.*[27]

This cumulative process, with exchange rate changes, price changes, expectations, and capital flight mutually reinforcing each other, is essentially a short-run process. It cannot continue for very long unless expansion of the money supply is also occurring. In the French case, many writers have emphasized the fact that the money supply was steadily increased during the phase of cumulative depreciation of the franc.[28] The large short-term debt of the French Treasury had to be redeemed in cash when presented at maturity, and the central bank was forced to expand the supply of credit. Moreover, as prices rose, the treasury's need for cash to meet its obligations also increased and, in the absence of new taxes, it could only be met by further increases in the money supply. The general public began to closely watch statistical reports on the money supply, such as the Bank of France's statements showing the amount of currency in circulation. According to Eleanor Dulles, "The number of notes in circulation [currency] came to be a decisive factor to those considering purchase of foreign currencies. In fact, this one item in the Bank of France statement was capable of precipitating a panic."[29]

Psychological influences played an important role in the course of the franc-dollar exchange rate from 1924 to 1926, although they continued to be supported, or validated, by monetary and fiscal expansion and by political unrest. In November 1923, a severe flight of funds got underway (a so-called bear attack). Contemporary observers agree that heavy speculative sales of francs occurred, and the franc dropped from about $0.06 in October 1923 to $0.035 in March 1924, well below its purchasing power parity. In the face of this crisis, a new government was formed by Raymond Poincaré, a fiscal conservative, and strong measures were proposed to put the government's finances on a sound basis. The government borrowed $100 million from J. P. Morgan and Company and threw this money into the foreign exchange market to buy francs. The purpose of this action was to change the market psychology and to punish the speculators—that is, to push up the exchange rate by sudden heavy buying and thus to force speculators who had sold francs

---

[27]Keynes, *Tract on Monetary Reform,* p. xix. This preface accurately previewed the events that were to take place in France during the next two and a half years.

[28]See especially S. C. Tsiang, "Fluctuating Exchange Rates in Countries with Relatively Stable Economies," *IMF Staff Papers,* November 1959, pp. 259–273.

[29]Dulles, *The French Franc,* p. 46.

short to take losses. The ploy was successful, at least temporarily, and the franc rose to $0.065 in April 1924 as short-sellers frantically bought spot francs to cover their contracts.

In May 1924, however, the Poincaré government was toppled in a general election. Fiscal reforms were set aside—the new tax measures were never put into operation—and the government continued to borrow heavily. As seen in Figure 19-5, the franc resumed its downward drift.

In the next two years no fewer than six changes in government occurred, and finance ministers changed even more frequently than governments did. The cumulative depreciation sequence again operated, fed not only by deficit financing and monetary expansion but also by political instability and financial scandal. (At one point the venerable Bank of France was forced to admit that it had issued false reports, understating the amount of notes in circulation.) Finally, in July 1926, a wave of selling hit the foreign exchange market, sending it into a state of virtual panic. The franc dropped to a daily low of $0.0205 on July 21. The specter of the collapse of the German mark was on everyone's mind.[30]

At this critical juncture Raymond Poincaré was again asked to form a government, and this time the French legislature supported his fiscal and monetary proposals. New taxes were levied, the budget was balanced, and the floating short-term debt was funded and controlled. Poincaré deliberately set out to restore confidence in the franc, and his success was quickly reflected in a steady rise in the value of the franc on the foreign exchange market. By December 1926 it had risen nearly 100 percent, to $0.0392, and the Bank of France announced that it would stabilize the franc at that rate—that is, it would buy and sell francs in order to maintain the exchange value of the franc at that level. The experiment with fluctuating exchange rates was over; de facto stabilization existed.

For all practical purposes, France went back on the gold standard with de facto stabilization, although it did not officially return to the gold standard until 1928.

The final frenzy of speculative panic in July 1926 had again driven the franc well below its purchasing power parity. Indeed, with domestic inflation largely halted, the franc remained somewhat undervalued even at its new fixed rate of $0.0392. This fact proved to be important in the next few years, as we will see.

For the moment, we should note that the strong measures taken by the Poincaré government, including de facto stabilization, did convince the market that the long decline of the franc was over. As a consequence, capital that had fled from a depreciating franc now returned. A speculative flight of capital toward the franc developed, partly in anticipation of a rise in its value, but the Bank of France resisted any such rise and simply purchased the excess supply of foreign exchange offered at the newly fixed rate. As its foreign currency balances (especially pounds sterling) grew, the Bank of France converted them into gold, thus draining gold from Britain and forcing the British to take deflationary measures to defend their slender gold reserves.

---

[30]In June 1923, German hyperinflation went out of control and the mark fell to zero. The currency was declared worthless and a new mark currency was created.

Before concluding our discussion of this episode, we should note that their experience with fluctuating exchange rates left bitter memories with the French, Belgians, Italians, and others whose currencies greatly depreciated. The sharp decline in the value of money wiped out the savings of large numbers of people, and the seemingly erratic fluctuations of the currency caused uncertainty and fear. Whether correctly or not, those who lived through this experience placed much of the blame for their discomfort and distress on the system of fluctuating exchange rates. They wanted no more of such a system. It has been said that if you met a middle-aged Belgian in the 1940s, when international monetary plans were being formulated for the postwar period, he or she would almost certainly have been vehemently opposed to allowing much flexibility in exchange rates.

On the other hand, significant elements of British public opinion were similarly dissatisfied with their forced return to a fixed exchange rate. They objected to the economic hardships and social distress associated with a commitment to maintain a fixed gold parity. Whether correctly or not, they placed much of the blame for their problems on the rigid link to gold. This view was widely held in other countries that followed the British pattern and returned to gold at prewar parities. The British mood was not improved by the realization that they, who had chosen the path of financial rectitude and virtue, were suffering unemployment and chronic recession, while the French, who had taken the primrose path of inflation and financial irresponsibility, were enjoying full employment and expanding output.

The Gold Standard Restored, 1925/ 1926 to 1931

In our discussion of the period 1919 to 1926, we have focused on the experience of Britain and France, culminating in their return to the gold standard at fixed exchange rates. Although the details of other countries differ, nearly all of them found their way back to the gold standard in the mid-twenties. There was general agreement that restoration of the pre-1914 system was a desirable goal. Figure 19-7 shows, year by year, the parade of countries back to gold.

It soon became apparent, however, that putting Humpty Dumpty together again was to be no easy task. We will briefly describe some of the difficulties that attended this effort, and then examine the course of events in Britain and France under the new gold standard.

The first difficulty in restoring the pre-1914 system was that the new exchange rates did not comprise an equilibrium set. Some countries found that the gold value of their currencies was too high, causing them to have a tendency toward deficits in their balances of payments; others had the opposite problem—undervalued currencies and a tendency toward surpluses in their balances of payments. Such errors in the new exchange rates were unavoidable because there was no way to determine in advance the equilibrium rate for any currency, especially in view of the drastic social and economic changes during and after the war. Purchasing power parity was at best a rough guide, and it was not heeded in some cases. Furthermore, exchange rates were not set all at once. Thus one country, having fixed its new gold parity

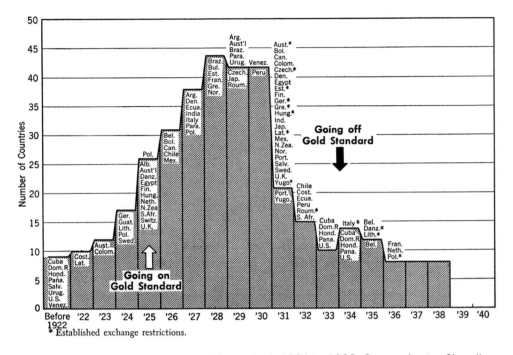

FIGURE 19-7 Countries on the gold standard, 1921 to 1938. *Source:* Lester Chandler, *The Economics of Money and Banking*, rev. ed. (New York: Harper, 1953), p. 135.

in 1925, might find that the parities chosen by other countries in 1926 or 1927 were incompatible with its already fixed rate. Ideally, all exchange rates should have been simultaneously set, but no mechanism existed to do that. Consequently, the new system had to face immediately the strains and tensions of adjustments needed to correct balance-of-payments disequilibria in many countries.

A second difficulty was that there was much concern about the adequacy of the world supply of gold. The problem was that the output of newly mined gold had not kept pace with the growth of world income and trade. It was feared that the use of traditional ratios of gold reserves to money supply would constrain the growth of national money supplies and thereby exert an all-around deflationary pressure on the world economy. Indeed, such fears had been expressed even in the pre-1914 period. They were taken more seriously in the 1920s because of the sharp rise in money prices in all countries during and after the war and because of the decline in gold production. The value of gold, expressed in dollars or pounds sterling, was unchanged, but prices of goods and services were much higher than in 1914. Therefore the real value of gold was much reduced, which tended to discourage gold mining and thus reduce the output of new gold. The classical solution was to let price levels decline, thereby increasing the real value of gold, but such deflationary pressure is precisely what people were worried about and trying to avoid.

A number of schemes were proposed to economize on gold; we will mention two that were widely used.[31] First, it was urged that existing stocks of gold be concentrated in the coffers of central banks and treasuries, and thus used primarily as an international monetary reserve. To accomplish this end, gold coins were withdrawn from circulation in many countries, and the obligation to sell gold against national currency was restricted to transactions of a certain minimum size. For example, after 1925 the Bank of England was required to sell gold ingots of not less than 400 ounces—that is, a minimum value of about £1700 ($8272). This is what came to be called the gold bullion standard. The public could easily use paper currency and checks for domestic transactions, it was argued; gold should be conserved for official use in the important business of managing the international economy.

Second, nations were urged to keep part or all of their international reserves, not in gold itself, but in the currency of a major gold standard country such as Great Britain or the United States. Since dollars and pounds were freely convertible into gold, other countries could hold their reserves in dollar or pound bank deposits (or short-term securities) just as well as in gold itself. In this way, a given world stock of gold could be made to support a larger total amount of national money surpluses. In this scheme, called the gold exchange standard, the dollar and pound were regarded as the most appropriate currencies to be held as reserves. Thus they came to be treated as reserve currencies. Indeed, the pound sterling was being used as a reserve currency even before World War I.

Although the logic of the gold exchange standard was sound enough, the scheme required great confidence in the ability of the reserve-currency countries to maintain the gold value of their currencies. It also put additional burdens on the gold reserves of those countries; they now had to be ready to cope not only with disturbances in their own balances of payments, but also with gold movements resulting from changes in other countries' economic circumstances. The state of confidence—that fragile element in financial stability—became increasingly important.

A third difficulty encountered in operating the new gold standard was a reluctance, or inability, of the countries involved to play the game according to the traditional rules. A surplus country, gaining gold, often chose to offset or neutralize its gold inflows. It did not want to let the gold inflow cause an expansion of its money supply and a rise in its price level. Memories of wartime inflation were too vivid. Similarly, a deficit country often tried to avoid the deflationary consequences of a gold outflow. Even if it did not deliberately offset the gold outflow, the deficit nation might find that prices and wages did not fall in response to deflationary pressure. Changes in social attitudes and institutions had made the price system less flexible than before. Labor unions, long-term wage contracts, social insurance schemes, agricultural support prices, and other such devices now made it difficult to reduce wages and prices. The attempt to do so led to unemployment.

At the same time, there was an upsurge of nationalism, and governments tended to concentrate on finding solutions to their own internal economic problems; they

[31] See Ragnar Nurkse, *International Currency Experience* (Geneva: League of Nations, 1944), Chap. 2, for a discussion of this matter.

had less regard for their responsibilities to an international economic system. One aspect of this preoccupation with national economic objectives concerns monetary policy—an example is the Federal Reserve Board's avowed goal of a stable domestic economy in the United States. Another aspect is the use of tariffs and other restrictions on trade and commerce to shield a country's economy from unwelcome influences emanating from the world economy. Compared to the prewar period, economic autarky was much more prevalent in the 1920s. Instead of integrating their economies into a world system, nations tended to be aloof, to draw apart.

Finally, large amounts of short-term funds now existed, funds that could be shifted from place to place on very short notice. The funds were highly sensitive to changes in economic circumstances and to rumors of impending political or economic events that might cause changes in exchange rates. Heavy flows of "hot money," as it came to be called, could be very disturbing to external balance, but governments disliked having to let such capricious flows of funds affect their domestic economies in fundamental ways. They tried to insulate themselves against these effects.

Britain and France

As we have seen, the British pound was somewhat overvalued at its restored parity of $4,866 = £1.00, whereas the French franc was somewhat undervalued at $0.0392 = Fr 1.00. Consequently, Britain had a chronically weak balance of payments in the late 1920s, and it had to maintain constant deflationary pressure on the domestic economy to avoid losing gold. Unemployment remained uncomfortably high (it dropped below 10 percent only in 1927, when it was 9.6 percent), and prices were gradually forced down. Labor was bitterly opposed to the deflationary policy, and labor strife continued. The general strike in 1926 was partly a response to the decision to go back on gold at the old parity. The overvalued pound hampered exports and encouraged an outflow of speculative short-term capital, especially to France, where speculators had some hope of an appreciation of the franc, at least until formal stabilization in 1928. Both tendencies aggravated the balance-of-payments position.

In France, on the other hand, pegging the franc at a low value both stimulated exports and encouraged an inflow of capital, producing a surplus in the French balance of payments. The Bank of France rapidly built up its holdings of gold and foreign exchange, especially in pounds sterling. However, France did not want to jeopardize its newfound stability by expanding its money supply enough to drive up domestic prices. In this matter, France took essentially the same position that the United States had taken—that is, it placed a higher priority on domestic stability than on external balance. Surplus countries have the luxury of that choice in a fixed exchange rate system. On the other hand, France did not much like the idea of holding its reserves in pounds sterling. Consequently, it began to convert its sterling balances into gold, thus putting pressure on Britain's slender gold reserves.

Just when nations were being urged to economize on gold and to cooperate in developing a gold exchange standard, France began to draw large amounts of gold from London, New York, and elsewhere. Since these gold flows were largely sterilized, they were not automatically self-limiting as contemplated in the traditional gold standard stereotype. In fact, the French price level actually declined while the gold inflow was occurring, from 1926 to 1931.

In response to appeals from officials in the Bank of England and the Federal Reserve Board, the Bank of France slowed its conversion of foreign exchange into gold, but it did not change its basic policy toward gold.[32] France never much liked a gold exchange standard in which it held dollars and sterling, while Britain and the United States held gold.

When France formally returned to the gold standard in 1928, the Bank of France was forbidden to issue currency against foreign exchange, which meant, in effect, that any subsequent balance-of-payments surpluses would have to be covered by gold inflows. Nurkse says that this French action "sealed the fate of the gold exchange standard."[33] Thereafter, when British and American monetary authorities pleaded with the Bank of France not to take in more gold, the Bank simply replied that it was bound by the terms of the 1928 law. French gold reserves rose sharply in 1929, 1930, and 1931.

This gold drain, combined with the reduced output of new gold, greatly increased concern about the scarcity of gold. Price levels in many countries were under severe deflationary pressure, the more so because the two largest gold-holding countries (France and the United States) were not allowing gold inflows to push up their prices. These two countries also hampered adjustment by restricting imports by high tariffs and other measures.

The Crisis of 1931

By the end of the 1920s a number of influences converged to place overwhelming pressure on the world's financial system. Deflation had spread and had led to heavy unemployment in many countries. It was clear that a severe depression was spreading around the world. The Wall Street crash in 1929 undermined confidence and had its echoes in other countries. Political conflicts, particularly in Europe, made people nervous about the safety of their money and other assets in various financial centers. Agricultural and raw-material-producing countries had been hit hard by the drop in their export prices. Some of these countries, unable to meet their foreign debt obligations, had already been forced to abandon the gold standard.

In this climate of fear and uncertainty, owners of liquid funds were poised and ready to flee from any currency that showed signs of weakness. Thus, in May 1931, when rumors spread that the biggest bank in Austria, the Credit Anstalt, was in trouble, a run on that bank took place. Funds were transferred to Berlin and London, and the Credit Anstalt was declared insolvent. Then a capital flight from Germany began. The German authorities, fearing a repetition of their 1923 experience with hyperinflation, were determined to maintain the gold value of the mark. The discount rate was increased to 15 percent, an extraordinarily high rate

---

[32]See Stephen V.O. Clarke, *Central Bank Cooperation, 1924–31* (New York: Federal Reserve Bank of New York, 1967), for an interesting description of the negotiations that took place among the central bankers.

[33]In Ragnar Nurkse, *International Currency Experience*, Chap. 2.

for that time, in order to defend the mark, and other stern measures were taken, including a freeze on funds owed to foreigners by German banks.

In these and other cases of capital flight, central banks tried to support each other. The Bank of England made a loan to Austria in an attempt to save the Credit Anstalt, for example. The Bank of France, Bank of England, and Federal Reserve System all joined in extending credit to the German central bank. However, the hot money movements continued to erupt.

To make a long story short, in the summer of 1931 foreign holders began to withdraw funds from British banks, and Britain's gold reserves came under renewed pressure. In an attempt to calm the market and maintain confidence, the Bank of England announced that it had arranged to borrow $250 million from the Bank of France and the Federal Reserve System. Withdrawals continued, however. Meanwhile, the British government was divided on the wisdom and desirability of further doses of deflationary medicine for the domestic economy. Unemployment was already high.

In September 1931, when some British sailors demonstrated to protest cuts in their pay, widespread reports of a naval mutiny led to heavy outflows of short-term capital. France and the United States declined to extend any more credit, and on September 20, 1931, the British government announced the suspension of gold payments. Britain was off the gold standard a little over six years after having restored it. The British action was taken, even though the bank rate was only $4\frac{1}{2}$ percent and British gold reserves had declined very little. The truth is that the government simply had no stomach for another dose of classical medicine. To deflate an economy that had been under constant deflationary pressure for ten years seemed too much to endure.

An immediate result was a sharp fall in the value of the pound in the foreign exchange market. It fell to $3.46 = £1.00 (compared with the gold parity of $4.86) within a week, but it later recovered part of this fall. Holders of pound deposits thus suffered substantial losses. Among the losers were the central banks that had held their reserves in sterling, as urged by advocates of the gold exchange standard. They were not happy to take such heavy capital losses. Even the Bank of France took losses. It still had some sterling balances that had been acquired before 1928, and on these its loss was about 30 percent. Although the loss comprised a small proportion of total assets, it was considerably larger than the net capital funds of the bank, and it had a traumatic effect on French opinion.[34] Central bankers have long memories: The French passion for gold in the 1960s may be traced in part to this episode.

When Britain suspended gold payments, it put an end to the vain attempt to restore the gold standard as a worldwide system on the pre-1914 model. Some countries clung to gold, but more as a symbol than as a system. Many countries

---

[34]W. A. Brown, *The International Gold Standard Reinterpreted,* Chap. 2, pp. 1176–1178. Perhaps the most embarrassing case from the British point of view was that of the Netherlands. Only two weeks before the final crisis, the Netherlands Bank was assured that its sterling deposit was safe and that Britain's gold reserve would be used to defend the pound. Yet when Britain left the gold standard, its gold stock was scarcely touched (pp. 1170–1173).

followed Britain's lead and abandoned the link to gold; indeed, some countries had already done so. Figure 19-7 shows the time pattern of countries leaving the gold standard.

In retrospect it seems clear that the restored gold standard failed because nations were never able to reestablish the closely knit, highly integrated world economy that had evolved in the prewar period. This failure resulted, in part, from the technical difficulty of fixing a set of exchange rates that would properly reflect the drastically changed economic situation of the various countries. But the most important cause of failure was probably the change in social and political attitudes that had occurred. Nations were no longer willing to let their domestic economic conditions be determined by the dictates of external influences. It is significant that in the pre-1914 period gold movements were small and adjustment was surprisingly quick and effective, whereas in the postwar period gold movements were large but adjustment slow and ineffective. The reason for this change is that nations deliberately blocked the adjustment mechanism called for by gold standard theory. The United States was a leader in this practice, starting with the Federal Reserve Board's policy of offsetting (sterilizing) gold inflows immediately after World War I. From that moment gold standard theory was "dead as mutton," as Keynes remarked. The whole effort to reestablish the gold standard was doomed to failure. Thus Winston Churchill had profoundly misread the political and economic climate when he led Britain back on gold in 1925, introducing the bill in the House of Commons with these words:

> *All the countries related to it [the gold standard] will vary together, like ships in a harbour whose gangways are joined and who rise and fall together with the tides.*[35]

After World War I, countries rejected that interdependence and sought in various ways to go it alone.

Monetary Nationalism, 1931 to 1940

The decade of the 1930s was a troubled time for the international monetary system. Indeed, it can hardly be said that a system existed in any meaningful sense. This was a period of experiment and improvisation, with each country looking out for its own interests as best it could. All countries felt the impact of the depression and lived in the shadow of political disturbances and threats of war. Under these circumstances, that delicate but essential element of monetary order and stability, confidence, had little chance to develop.

Nationalism was rampant. In its international economic aspects it took the form of trade restrictions and a variety of national controls on capital and current account transactions. With the demise of the gold standard after 1931, the world economy

---

[35] *Hansard:* House of Commons, Vol. 183, April 28, 1925, p. 58.

became fragmented. Nations tried to insulate themselves from external influences. Thus the world was moving further away from the pre-1914 model of a closely knit, highly integrated international economy.

We cannot hope to describe the events in this period in a comprehensive way because of their complexity and diversity. Instead, we will focus on a few patterns that emerged and on certain features of the experience that proved important in subsequent years.

Managed Flexibility of Exchange Rates

When they cut their ties to gold, many countries were unwilling to let their currencies fluctuate freely in the market. One reason was the still fresh memory of the experience with fluctuating exchange rates in the 1920s. This experience was widely believed to have shown that fluctuating rates were unstable and that they could have harmful effects on the domestic economy of the country concerned. Another, related, reason was a concern about the large sums of liquid short-term capital that might suddenly move from country to country on the basis of political or other rumors. Such hot money movements might cause sharp changes in exchange rates that were not called for by the basic economic situation.

Some countries, therefore, tried to constrain or limit the market fluctuations of exchange rates by operating exchange stabilization funds. Such a fund had to be provided with domestic and foreign assets (gold or foreign currency balances), and it could then buy or sell foreign exchange to counteract sharp changes in exchange rates. If the national currency were weak and its price falling too rapidly, the fund would buy it, paying with its gold or foreign exchange balances. If the national currency rose too rapidly, the fund would enter the market as a seller, accepting payment in foreign exchange.

The objectives of exchange stabilization funds varied from country to country, and, for a given country, they varied from one time to another. Sometimes a fund tried merely to maintain an orderly market, to smooth the daily fluctuations, but not to resist a trend in the exchange rate. Sometimes the fund tried to resist exchange rate changes that it regarded as economically unjustified. The justification for exchange rate changes was always difficult to judge, but if a sudden burst of speculation threatened to drive the exchange rate up or down the fund might "lean against the wind" and try to counteract the effect of such short-term capital flows on its exchange rate. It was argued that since speculative capital movements often reversed themselves in a short time, it was desirable to prevent the swings in the exchange rate caused by such ephemeral factors. After all, as we saw in Chapters 17 and 18, changes in the exchange rate have important effects on resource allocation and income, and these effects should occur in response to basic forces, not the whims of speculators. (This again raises the basic question about the nature of speculation: Is it stabilizing or destabilizing?)

Some countries tried to peg their currencies to another currency, such as the dollar or pound sterling. Then the objective of the exchange stabilization fund would be to maintain the pegged exchange rate within a narrow margin. For example, when Britain went off the gold standard, many countries with close economic ties to Britain pegged their currencies to the pound. The group of countries later came to be called the Sterling Area, and the exchange arrangements among them became somewhat formalized. They kept their reserves in pounds sterling and operated what was essentially a sterling exchange standard. Other countries pegged to the dollar in a similar way. Changes in the dollar-sterling exchange rate thus meant changes in the exchange rates between all Sterling Area and all Dollar Bloc countries. During the 1930s, therefore, many countries developed the practice of holding their foreign exchange reserves in dollars and pounds, depending on which currency area they were in. Dollars and pounds became the two primary reserve, or key, currencies.

Finally, some countries used their exchange stabilization funds as instruments to bring about a deliberate change in their exchange rates. Frequently, the objective was to reduce the value of the currency in order to encourage exports and thus stimulate the domestic economy. Such competitive exchange depreciation, as it came to be called, was seen as a form of economic warfare in the 1930s. With much of the world suffering from unemployment and excess capacity, one country's gains through the income effect of export expansion came at the expense of its trading partners. Competitive exchange depreciation was thus seen as a way to export unemployment and as an aggressive act. Small countries could get away with competitive exchange depreciation more easily than large ones, since they were less likely to face retaliation.

Obviously, the problem was that exchange rates are a matter of mutual, reciprocal concern. They require some form of international cooperation and mutual consent in their determination, but in the 1930s no mechanism or structure existed for multilateral exchange rate agreement. There was a vague groping toward a concept of justifiable exchange rate changes—that is, changes that were warranted on the basis of underlying economic conditions—but it was impossible to state clear, objective criteria for a practical application of this concept. In the Tripartite Monetary Agreement (1936), Britain and the United States accepted the devaluation of the French franc, acknowledged its necessity, and promised not to retaliate. This agreement was a small step toward multilateral agreement on exchange rates. But before many other countries could be induced to join in this agreement, it was overtaken by the outbreak of war.

Exchange Control

Some countries, faced with a choice between maintaining a fixed parity by deflationary pressure and letting their currencies depreciate, were unwilling to accept either alternative. They were particularly reluctant to make this choice when the pressure on the balance of payments came from speculative capital movements: a flight of hot money to other countries. The first alternative was unattractive because the orthodox policy measures of fixed exchange rate analysis, such as raising bank rates, might have little effect on such hot money movements. Fears about the safety of one's capital would not be allayed by a rise in bank rate from 5 to 6 percent. If the exchange rate remained fixed, the real adjustment would have to come through heavy deflationary pressure on the domestic economy, forcing down prices and wages and causing exports to rise, imports to fall. Such pressure would also increase unemployment, which was already high in the 1930s. It seemed incongruous to subject a nation to such hardships merely because of whimsical, capricious speculative flights of capital, or even those caused by rumors of war.

The second alternative (exchange depreciation) was also unattractive to some countries because many of them had recently been through bouts of cumulative depreciation and inflation that had caused great distress and left a heritage of bitter memories. Governments were afraid that if capital flight were allowed to drive down the value of the currency, a cumulative process would again take over. The population was wary and alert to the real income effects of exchange rate changes. When the German mark was under pressure in 1931, for example, German labor unions warned that in the event of devaluation, they would demand a scale of money wages based on the foreign exchange rate. Such a wage policy would largely defeat the purpose of a devaluation.

Several countries in this quandary resorted to exchange control when faced by flights of capital; that is, they left the exchange rate unchanged but imposed various restrictions and controls on monetary transactions between domestic residents and foreigners. Up to now, we have assumed that all holders of money or other financial assets had the right to use this money as they saw fit. They could buy domestic goods and services, they could buy foreign goods and services, or they could transfer funds to other countries through the foreign exchange market at the prevailing exchange rate. We have assumed that every national currency was convertible in this sense, that it could be freely exchanged for other national currencies.[36]

The essence of exchange control is that it restricts this freedom to convert the money of a country into other currencies. Variations in the forms of exchange control are endless, and we will mention only a few examples.[37] When Germany began to experience short-term capital outflows in 1931, it blocked, or froze, the deposits of foreigners in German banks and other assets held in Germany by foreigners. The owners of these money balances and assets were not allowed to withdraw them until the central bank gave them permission to do so. Such a regulation, if it can be enforced, immediately checks the capital flight. It reduces the supply of marks offered in the foreign exchange market, lessens the downward pressure on the mark, and reduces the need for deflationary policies to be initiated in Germany.

This result can readily be seen in our supply and demand diagram of the foreign exchange market in Figure 19-8. Suppose the market is initially in equilibrium at the parity exchange rate $0.40 = DM 1.00, with demand curve D_1 and supply curve S_1. A rumor spreads that the mark is vulnerable, and a short-term capital outflow begins, shown by a shift in the supply curve to S_2. At the parity rate $0.40 = DM 1.00, the supply of marks now exceeds the demand for marks by the amount AB. To remove this excess supply, the German central bank imposes exchange control and forbids the sale of marks for capital transfer. This action

[36]"Convertibility" is a word that has several meanings in international economics. Its original meaning refers to the right to exchange a national currency for gold. Thus Britain restored the gold convertibility of the pound sterling in 1925 when it went back on the gold standard. The pound became inconvertible with respect to gold in 1931, but it could still be freely exchanged for other currencies at the market rate of exchange. One can thus distinguish between *gold* convertibility and *currency* convertibility.

[37]See Howard Ellis, *Exchange Control in Central Europe* (Cambridge, Mass.: Harvard University Press, 1941), for a detailed account.

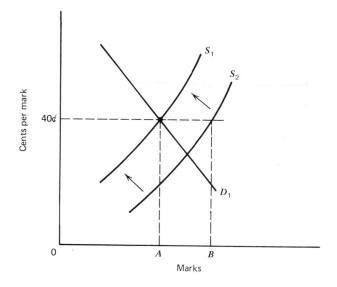

FIGURE 19-8   German exchange control. Restrictions on capital outflow force shift in supply of marks from S_2 to S_1.

suppresses the supply of marks: It prevents the shift of the supply curve to S_2, or one might say that exchange control forces the supply curve to shift back to S_1.

As a temporary expedient, such a policy may be quite effective. But the longer it lasts, the more difficulties it will encounter. Much scope for evasion of the control exists, and to keep controls tight and effective, the exchange control authority will have to screen virtually all transactions in foreign exchange. For example, a bona fide importer may apply for permission to buy $100,000 to pay for imports of timber, but he actually needs to pay only $60,000 for the timber purchased; he intends to put the other $40,000 in a New York bank account. To prevent such evasions, the exchange control authority must check the purchase contract, verify price and quantity, and even check the shipment to be certain that the correct amount of lumber was imported.[38] Similar checks are necessary on the export side. Consequently, to enforce exchange control, exporters must be required to surrender all foreign exchange proceeds from their foreign sales to the exchange control authority. Then the foreign exchange is sold to authorized buyers for approved purposes. This exchange control tends to spread and to require a comprehensive machinery to examine and approve all transactions with the outside world.

When exchange control is used as a more or less permanent system, the authorities are not able to identify a specific source of the excess demand for foreign exchange, as they could in our example of capital flight. All they know, as a rule,

---

[38]Arthur Bloomfield describes many techniques for evasion in his "Speculation and Flight Movements of Capital in Postwar International Finance," *Studies in International Finance,* No. 3 (Princeton, N.J.: Princeton University Press, February 1954).

is that the demand for foreign exchange exceeds the supply of it at the exchange rate they wish to maintain.

Exchange control authorities attempt to deal with the problem of excess demand by simply rationing the available supply of foreign exchange. They allocate it to buyers in accordance with priorities set by government. But first they must get hold of the foreign exchange, which means they must require exporters and other foreign exchange earners to surrender all receipts of foreign currencies to the control authorities. They can then sell it to approved purchasers. Any comprehensive exchange control system must contain a surrender requirement that can be enforced.

Black markets tend to develop in these circumstances, and it is necessary to have severe penalties for violations of the regulations. In Nazi Germany violations were called economic treason, for which the maximum penalty was death.

Exchange control was widely practiced in the 1930s, especially in Central Europe, but also in Latin America and elsewhere. Although initially it was often introduced as a defense against hot money movements, it tended to spread into a comprehensive system of control of all trade and payments. Some nations used exchange control regulations to determine the amounts of different commodities to be imported and exported, and even to determine the geographic pattern of their trade. Exchange control became, in fact, an integral part of the state planning apparatus and was often used as an instrument of economic warfare.

A full-fledged exchange control scheme is, in a sense, at the extreme opposite end of the scale from the closely knit, highly integrated world economy of the pre-1914 gold standard. Under exchange control, a country separates and insulates its economy; it breaks the connections between its prices and those in the outside world. Exchange control is a device that lends itself to the economic nationalism and autarky that were ascendant in the 1930s.

The Devaluation of the Dollar

The depression was extremely severe in the United States. Wholesale prices fell 30 percent from 1929 to 1933; national income dropped 45 percent; unemployment reached 12 million, or 23 percent of the labor force; and exports dropped to 38 percent of the 1929 level in terms of value.

The new administration, which took office in March 1933, was determined to take prompt and vigorous action to improve the economic situation, and it was searching for ideas. One of its primary objectives was to increase the general level of prices, to reflate the economy. Several different methods were used, but one particular method is pertinent here. One of President Roosevelt's advisers, Professor George Warren, argued that an increase in the price of gold (still fixed by the United States at $20.67 per ounce) would automatically and immediately bring about a rise in domestic prices by the same proportion that the gold price was increased. Warren appears to have persuaded President Roosevelt of this thesis,[39] though he did not

---

[39] Seymour Harris, *Exchange Depreciation* (Cambridge, Mass.: Harvard University Press, 1936), Chap. 9, gives a detailed account of this episode and Warren's role in it.

make clear the mechanism through which a gold price rise would be transmitted to the general price level. Our analysis of balance-of-payments adjustment suggests one sequence: The dollar devaluation would stimulate exports, check imports, and tend to cause an inflow of gold, which would in turn cause a rise in the money supply and a rise in prices, either directly or through stimulating investment and other components of aggregate demand. This is a long, slow process, however, and it need not lead to a proportionate increase in prices for many reasons, particularly in 1933, when much idle capacity and unemployment existed.

In any case, soon after he took office, President Roosevelt imposed an embargo on gold exports, thus taking the United States off the gold standard, and in January 1934 the Gold Standard Reserve Act fixed the price of gold at $35.00 per ounce, an increase of 69 percent over the former price of $20.67. (Before this price increase became effective, all privately held gold coins and bullion had been required to be turned in to the U.S. Treasury. U.S. citizens were forbidden to hold gold except for use in jewelry, industry, dentistry, and the like. This prohibition lasted 40 years; it was removed by an act of Congress in 1974.) The Treasury announced that it would buy all gold offered to it at the new price, and it would sell gold bullion to foreign official buyers. The United States was back on a limited gold bullion standard, but with a devalued dollar.

Although the change in gold price did not directly and immediately cause domestic prices to rise by 69 percent (wholesale prices rose 14 percent in 1934, 9 percent in 1935) as predicted by Professor Warren, it did have some significant effects on the international monetary situation. First, it meant a devaluation of the dollar by 41 percent vis-à-vis the currencies of the few countries still on the gold standard: the gold bloc.[40] Thus it made U.S. exports much more attractive to buyers in those countries—that is, it did so to the extent that U.S. prices did not rise by the same proportion as the gold price had increased. Second, it resulted in a huge inflow of gold into the United States as the higher price encouraged miners to expand output and induced hoarders to disgorge their holdings. This golden avalanche continued all through the 1930s and left the United States holding the bulk of the world's known gold stock at the outbreak of war. Third, it tended to cause the dollar to depreciate in terms of the pound sterling and other currencies not on gold. As the U.S. Treasury bought gold, it paid in dollars, and many of these dollars were offered for sale in foreign exchange markets, thus depressing the price of the dollar in terms of other currencies.

This dollar depreciation was particularly important with respect to the pound sterling because of the key currency role it played. As we have seen, Britain's departure from the gold standard led to a sharp fall in the pound. It also released Britain from the necessity to continue its domestic deflationary policy, and as a consequence the British economy had staged a substantial recovery since 1931. Exports were buoyant, employment rose, and production expanded. The depreciation of the dollar was seen as a threat to Britain because it made U.S. goods

---

[40] A rise in the dollar price of gold from $20.67 to $35.00 per ounce (a 69 percent increase) means a fall in the gold value of the dollar from 1/20.67 to 1/35, a decrease of 41 percent.

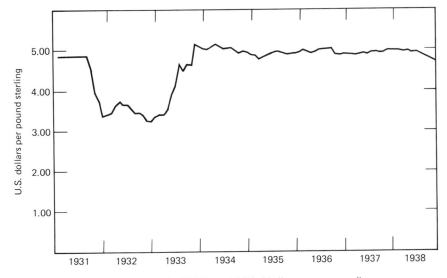

FIGURE 19-9   The British pound, 1931 to 1938 (dollars per pound).

more competitive. In fact, the U.S. devaluation can be interpreted as a competitive depreciation, especially since it was done when the United States had ample reserves and no serious balance-of-payments problem. Recognizing the dangers of competitive exchange depreciation, Britain made some overtures in 1933 to reach a compromise and retain a degree of exchange rate stability, but President Roosevelt was by then determined to go ahead with his gold price scheme to reflate the American economy. As Lionel Robbins remarked, "It was too late. As on an earlier occasion, it had been easier to bamboozle a President than to debamboozle him."[41]

The dollar price of the pound rose in 1933, especially after President Roosevelt embargoed gold exports. It even exceeded the old parity of $4.86 = £1.00, hitting $5.15 (monthly average) in April 1934. Thereafter the rate dropped back and generally stayed near or somewhat above the old parity until 1938, when threats of war in Europe drove it down again. The course of the dollar-pound rate in the 1930s is shown in Figure 19-9. In this period the British Exchange Equalization Account, as it was called, tried to prevent sharp changes in the exchange rate caused, for example, by speculative capital movements, but at the same time it let the rate move in response to basic economic changes. On the whole it succeeded remarkably well. The dollar-pound price fluctuated moderately, and Britain was able to pursue its domestic economic objectives without as much external constraint as had existed in the 1920s.[42] Britain was much better satisfied with its experience with managed flexibility of exchange rates in the 1930s than with the fixed rate gold standard system in the 1920s. In fact, as may be seen in Figure 19-9, after the shocks of the

[41]Lionel Robbins, *The Great Depression* (London: Macmillan, 1934), p. 124.

[42]For an account of this experience, see N. F. Hall, *The Exchange Equalization Account* (London: Macmillan, 1935).

British departure from gold and the dollar devaluation, the pound was remarkably stable in the 1930s. From 1934 to 1939 it fluctuated within a narrow range of 2 to 3 percent around $4.95 and thus remained slightly above the pre-1914 parity that had been sought at such a heavy cost in the early 1920s. Flexible exchange rates turned out to be more stable in practice than fixed rates had been—this despite the political and economic disturbances in the 1930s.

France and the Gold Bloc

Britain's departure from gold and the United States' devaluation of the dollar changed the position of the franc from an undervalued to an overvalued currency in the early 1930s. When the dollar price of gold rose to $35.00 per ounce, the par value of the franc, which was still pegged to gold, soon rose from $0.0392, the level set by M. Poincaré in 1926, to $0.0664. This 69 percent increase in the dollar value of the franc made French goods less competitive and foreign goods more attractive to French buyers, and it thus tended to produce an import surplus in France. The increase had a similar effect in other countries still on the gold standard.

The French government pledged to maintain the gold value of the franc, which meant that it had to exert deflationary pressure on the French economy. In addition, it used import quotas in an effort to hold down imports; that is, the government placed physical limits on the amounts of different goods that could be imported. It chose this method in preference to exchange control.

The government's campaign to stay on gold ran into difficulties because its deflationary measures were unpopular and were opposed by many segments of the population, including labor unions. Furthermore, speculative capital movements began to exacerbate the situation. Fearing that the franc would eventually be devalued, owners of franc assets began to sell them and to convert the franc proceeds into foreign exchange, thus forcing the Bank of France to sell gold to support the franc. As Professor Charles Rist said of a later period, "There is not a single Frenchman who has funds he cannot use who does not reflect whether it might be safer to send them abroad than to keep them home."[43] Throughout the 1930s, capital flight periodically occurred. Since the government shrank from full-fledged exchange control, it had to rely on classical medicine (deflation) and import quotas.

After Belgium devalued in 1935, pressure on the French franc became intolerable, and it was devalued in September 1936 by about 30 percent. It was at this time that the Tripartite Monetary Agreement was signed, in which Britain and the United States accepted the necessity for franc devaluation and agreed not to retaliate against it. The new rate was held for a few months, but capital flight resumed with fresh rumors of further devaluation. These rumors were always denied by the government, but the governments were not long-lived in France in the 1930s, and bear attacks on the franc continued. An exchange stabilization fund was established, but it suffered heavy gold losses when it tried to support the franc. The forward franc was frequently at a discount of 30 to 40 percent (annual basis) as speculators bet on further devaluation.

---

[43]Quoted in Wolfe, *The French Franc Between the Wars, 1919–1939*, p. 172.

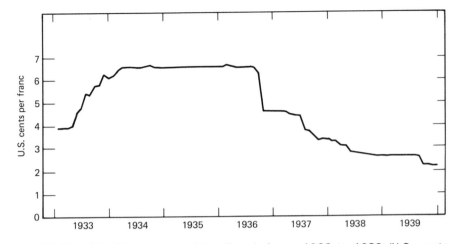

FIGURE 19-10 Monthly average of the French franc, 1933 to 1939 (U.S. cents per franc).

After only nine months of the new gold value, the gold standard was abandoned in June 1937 and the franc was allowed to float, subject only to the interventions of the Exchange Stabilization Fund. Bear attacks continued, and the franc depreciated (Figure 19-10 shows the course of the franc in the 1930s). It seemed like a rerun of the 1920s episode, which did not inspire confidence. The franc fell continuously until April 1938, when a new government under Édouard Daladier made an attempt to peg it to the pound sterling, thus placing France on a sterling exchange standard. At this point the rate was Fr 179 = £1.00, compared to Fr 124 = £1.00 in 1931, before Britain went off gold. (The franc was worth about $0.022 when war was declared in September 1939.)

EPILOGUE

We will pause briefly at this point to reflect on some salient features of the period 1880 to 1940 and perhaps to draw some lessons from it.

In the three decades before 1914, an international monetary system had evolved which linked nations closely together, especially the leading industrial nations. In an expanding world economy, nations were able to achieve external balance while maintaining the fixed exchange rates required by the gold standard. Adjustment was facilitated by a sensitive response of short-term capital movements, by considerable flexibility in prices and wages, and by changes in relative rates of growth. Nations generally accepted adjustments necessary to keep their economies in line with each other.

World War I disrupted this closely knit system, and in the meantime some basic changes occurred in social and political attitudes and institutions and in the world economy which made it difficult, if not impossible, to restore the prewar system.

The interwar period, 1919 to 1940, may be regarded as a period of experimentation, of a search for new ways for nations to manage their economic contacts with each other. A significant element in this experimentation and search was an insistence on the primacy of domestic economic objectives, which was an aspect of the rising nationalism of the time.

Nevertheless, there was a strong drive to restore the gold standard, to reestablish the international economic system that had existed before the war. As we have seen, Britain devoted 12 years (1919 to 1931) to this effort, at great cost to domestic economic welfare. That experience, shared in some degree by several other countries, convinced many people that a system of fixed exchange rates, with domestic economic policy subordinated to the requirements of external balance, was highly undesirable.

Other countries, which cut their currencies free from gold or any other fixed anchor, had equally unsatisfactory experiences. In many cases, as in France, the national currency appeared to become unstable and to depreciate in what seemed to be a cumulative, self-reinforcing fashion. Furthermore, exchange rate changes had effects on the domestic economy, and it seemed that a nation could not pursue its domestic economic objectives and let the external balance take care of itself through exchange rate changes. Whether or not it can remains a controversial matter, not to be settled here, but it is clear that many people were convinced by this experience in the 1920s and 1930s that freely fluctuating exchange rates were unstable and that they could have harmful effects on countries using them.

A third group of countries had to achieve external balance by placing direct controls on transactions with the outside world. These controls took many forms—exchange control, import and export quotas, bilateral trade agreements, and the like—but they all involved substantial governmental planning and decision making on the basis of criteria other than price. They sought to insulate the domestic economy, to separate it or cut it off from direct competitive influences in other countries, or at least to subordinate these influences to decisions made by government on other grounds. This system also encountered many objections: It was cumbersome and inefficient, it placed more demands on governments than they could handle, it tended to make all economic transactions a matter of political negotiation, and it was basically incompatible with a market-oriented economy.

Thus, none of these three main approaches proved very satisfactory, and attempts were made to find a variant, or perhaps a combination, that would work. It also became clear that a cooperative solution was needed. A single nation could not "go it alone," if only because its actions would affect other nations, which might react in various ways. An international monetary system is inescapably a matter of mutual interest; it requires some degree of consent and acceptance on a multilateral basis. We shall examine in Chapter 9 the international agreement that was worked out during and after World War II, an agreement that reflects the experience that has been summarized in this chapter.

For the present, we shall comment briefly on three issues that emerged in the interwar period and created chronic problems for the international monetary system.

The Adequacy of International Reserves

We have discussed the concern that was expressed after World War I about the shortage of gold. Wartime inflation had reduced the real value of gold, and the output of newly mined gold had fallen. Consequently, the ratio of gold to the total money supply (or to money income) was reduced. It was feared that this relative scarcity of gold would put deflationary pressure on the world economy. That was, indeed, the classical process through which the value of money was supposed to be stabilized, as we have seen. Deflation would raise the real value of gold and stimulate gold mining. It was, however, feared that this long-run deflationary adjustment would be too harsh and unpleasant for the postwar world to accept, and ways were sought to avoid it.

Nations were urged to "economize" on gold, and several methods were devised to stretch the world gold stock and thereby to enable the international monetary system to function. These included the withdrawal of gold from private circulation and its concentration in the hands of monetary authorities, the development of a gold bullion standard (in which the gold-standard country was obligated only to sell gold in the form of gold bars of a certain minimum size; later such sales were limited to foreign official institutions), and the development of the gold exchange standard (in which some countries kept their reserves not in gold at all, but in the currency of another country that was on the gold standard). The gold exchange standard necessarily gave certain national currencies, especially the pound sterling and the dollar, a special role. It also increased the potential instability of the system, in that any hint or rumor about the weakness of the reserve currency could lead to a run on its gold stock. Foreign countries holding their reserves in the form of liquid balances in the reserve currency had the right to convert these balances into gold on demand, and they would tend to do so if they suspected that the reserve currency might be devalued against gold.

The decline in prices that occurred in the 1920s did begin to stimulate gold production, and the classical mechanism might have solved the problem of reserve adequacy had it not been complicated by a maldistribution of existing gold. As we have seen, the United States attracted gold in the early 1920s, and France began to do so in 1926. These two countries held 57 percent of the world's monetary gold stock in 1930, and the United States alone held two-thirds of it by 1939. Thus the scarcity of gold was compounded by the absence of any mechanism to redistribute the existing stock.

Short-Term Capital Movements

In the pre-1914 gold standard, short-term capital movements played an important role in the mechanism of balance-of-payments adjustment. Because there was virtually complete confidence in the existing gold parities, short-term capital tended to move into a currency when it dropped below par in the foreign exchange market. The expectation of continued maintenance of the fixed gold parity tended to cause capital movements that supported that parity. Bank rate changes had powerful effects on short-term capital because confidence in gold parities existed.

In the interwar period, short-term capital movements came to be influenced, to a considerable extent, by lack of confidence in the existing gold parities or in existing exchange rate levels (when countries were off gold). Capital flight from a weak currency became a common occurrence. The expectations that a currency would be devalued was enough to cause an outflow of funds, a hot money movement, that would tend to cause the currency to fall in value. In such a climate of expectations, changes in bank rate might have very little effect. If one suspects that the franc may fall 20 percent in the next month or two, an increase in bank rate of 2 or 3 percent will not induce him to keep his funds in franc assets.

Consequently, short-term capital movements became a disturbing element, a constant threat to the stability of an existing exchange rate. Since this was a period of political instability, with frequent changes of governments and recurrent rumors of war, it is no wonder that exchange rates were subject to frequent attacks.

Speculation

Some economists believe that when exchange rates are flexible, speculative capital movements may cause exchange rate changes that are excessive, in some sense, and that these changes may set in motion a sequence leading to further exchange rate movements in the same direction. Thus, they argue that speculation can be a cause of exchange rate instability.

Other economists reject this argument. They say that speculators merely appraise the value of a currency to the best of their ability. If they consider it to be overvalued, they will sell it in the hope of turning a profit when its price falls. If their appraisal is correct, they will make a profit; if it is wrong, they will suffer losses. But, it is argued, speculators cannot alter the basic equilibrium value of the currency. Furthermore, unsuccessful speculators will be forced out of business, and successful (profit-making) speculators will tend through their activities to cause the exchange rate to move toward its equilibrium level (i.e., if the currency is under-valued, speculators will buy it and cause it to rise; if overvalued, they sell and cause it to fall).

The role of speculation is still hotly debated. One of the key issues is whether exchange rate changes caused by speculative activity can themselves bring about changes in the domestic economic situation that make the new exchange rate an equilibrium. That is, can a causal sequence run from speculation to exchange rate change and then to changes in domestic economic conditions that validate those exchange rate exchanges?

Opponents vehemently object to this sequence. The central point of the opponents is that the level of domestic income and prices is largely determined by a country's monetary and fiscal policies. If the authorities do not expand the money supply or give a fiscal stimulus to the economy, then speculative activity cannot cause a change in the equilibrium exchange rate. Prices and income will not rise just because the exchange rate changes.

This argument suggests that the real source of exchange rate instability in the interwar period lies in improper monetary and fiscal policies. Faced with a depreciating franc in the 1920s and 1930s, the French government allowed the money supply and the budget deficit to the treasury to increase. These financial policies then prompted another round of exchange rate changes.

Although most economists probably accept this general view of the matter, some nagging doubts persist. Velocity could rise, thus making it possible for prices to rise with an unchanged money supply. With widespread expectations of depreciation, as in France in 1924 or 1926, the public seeks to exchange its franc balances for foreign exchange, domestic goods, imported goods, or real assets. Their efforts to get out of money and into real assets would increase aggregate demand and tend to raise prices and wages, especially in the short run. In the longer run, if government holds firm, the result may be unemployment and reduced output, not a fall in prices. Government may be just as reluctant to accept these consequences with a flexible exchange rate as it has been reluctant to accept deflationary pressures in a fixed rate system.

The issue remains unsettled in economic analysis, but despite this uncertainty it is clear that many people strongly believe that speculative capital movements were a major cause of exchange rate instability in the 1920s and 1930s. They see the matters we have discussed as interrelated problems of an international monetary system: reserve adequacy, hot money movements, and speculation. These problems continued to cause difficulties after World War II, as we will see in subsequent chapters.

QUESTIONS FOR STUDY AND REVIEW

1. "Under gold standard conditions, as in the pre-1914 period, a sharp increase in British demand for oranges will tend to cause the short-term interest rate in London to rise." Do you agree? Defend your answer.

2. Compare and contrast the French and British experiences with exchange rates and the balance of payments in the 1919 to 1926 period.

3. What are some reasons why the gold standard did not work as well (once restored) in the 1920s as it had worked before 1914?

4. Under a full gold standard (as in pre-1914), what mechanism is supposed to regulate the relationship between the world money supply and the world price level? Explain.

5. What is meant by sterilization of gold flows? How did it figure in U.S. policy in the 1920s?

6. What is the exchange control? Give an example of its use in the 1930s.

7. Why was the interest rate particularly powerful under gold standard conditions?

8. What is the nature of the asymmetry between surplus and deficit countries with respect to the adjustment process in a fixed exchange rate system? How did it arise in the post–World War I period?

SELECTED REFERENCES

Bloomfield, Arthur I. *Monetary Policy Under the International Gold Standard, 1880–1914*. New York: Federal Reserve Bank of New York, 1959.

Bordo, Michael D., and Anna Schwartz, eds. *A Retrospective on the Classical Gold Standard*. Chicago: University of Chicago Press, 1983.

Cassel, Gustav. *Money and Foreign Exchange After 1914*. New York: Macmillan, 1923.

Cooper, Richard N. "The Gold Standard: Historical Facts and Future Prospects," *Brookings Papers on Economic Activity* 1 (1982).

Dulles, Eleanor. *The French Franc, 1914–1928*. New York: Macmillan, 1929.

Nurkse, Ragnar. *International Currency Experience*. Geneva: League of Nations, 1944.

Triffin, Robert. "The Evolution of the International Monetary System." *Princeton Studies in International Finance*, No. 12. Princeton, N.J.: Princeton University Press, 1964.

Yeager, Leland B. *International Monetary Relations: Theory, History and Policy*. New York: Harper & Row, 1976.

CHAPTER

20

THE INTERNATIONAL MONETARY SYSTEM, 1945 TO 1973

Soon after the outbreak of World War II, economic planning for the postwar era began. The hope was that the chaos and turmoil of the interwar period (1919 to 1940) could be avoided. This wartime economic planning was primarily an Anglo-American enterprise, but the emphasis was on global solutions and on international cooperation. In this spirit, delegates from 44 countries convened at Bretton Woods, New Hampshire, in 1944, to negotiate an agreement on the structure and operation of the international monetary system.

The fruits of their labor, the Articles of Agreement of the International Monetary Fund, provided the basis for the international monetary system that existed from 1945 to 1971.[1] In this chapter we will describe the key features of this system,

[1] Actually, two institutions were created at Bretton Woods: the International Monetary Fund and the International Bank for Reconstruction and Development (now called the World Bank), but we will be concerned only with the IMF. For more details, see J. K. Horsefield, ed., *The International Monetary Fund, 1945–1965* (Washington, D.C.: International Monetary Fund, 1969).

analyze its operation, and diagnose its flaws. Although the International Monetary Fund (IMF) still exists, and many of its original functions continue unchanged, in certain essential respects the system that was created at Bretton Woods ended in the 1971–1973 period. An understanding of the nature of that system and the reasons why it ended will help the reader to understand present international monetary arrangements (sometimes called a nonsystem) and the course of recent events. The IMF period also illustrates very well the theory of balance-of-payments adjustment that we discussed in earlier chapters, as well as problems that arise in achieving a satisfactory mechanism of adjustment.

ESSENTIAL ELEMENTS OF THE BRETTON WOODS SYSTEM

The founders of the IMF wanted above all to establish an international monetary order, and thus to avoid the instability and the nationalistic practices that had characterized the interwar period. They sought to provide an orderly method for the regulation of exchange rates, a supplementary supply of international reserves, and a mechanism for the adjustment of balance-of-payments disturbances.

All these matters were highly controversial; they impinged on sensitive areas of national sovereignty and autonomy. The widely different experiences of various nations during the interwar period had given rise to strong differences of opinion about the proper way to deal with these issues. The agreements reached at Bretton Woods can be viewed as a grand compromise, with elements of all the conflicting positions woven into them.[2] Another interpretation is that American power and influence were so great in 1944 that the United States was able to impose its will on most vital issues. In any case, agreement was reached, and most nations outside the Communist bloc became members of the IMF.[3]

We will briefly describe the essential elements of the Bretton Woods system as it existed until 1971.

Exchange Rates

Each member nation agreed to specify a par value for its currency in terms of the U.S. dollar (or its equivalent in gold, i.e., $1/35$ of an ounce). Furthermore, each member agreed to take steps to keep the actual spot exchange rate for its currency within 1 percent of its par value. In practice, this meant that the nation's central

---

[2]We will not describe the fascinating and colorful story of the negotiations and their background. The interested reader should see Richard Gardner, *Sterling Dollar Diplomacy* (New York: McGraw-Hill, 1969), and R. F. Harrod, *The Life of Keynes* (London: Macmillan, 1951).

[3]The USSR declined to ratify the Articles of Agreement. Of the other Communist or ex-Communist countries, Hungary, Romania, Yugoslavia, and China are members. Poland and Czechoslovakia withdrew in the 1950s but have recently rejoined. Switzerland has also declined to join, but may reverse that decision in the near future. Russia and other ex-members of the USSR are now in the process of joining.

bank had to stand ready to intervene in the foreign exchange market, buying the currency when it approached the lower limit and selling it when it approached the upper limit.

As a result of these commitments, the national currencies of member nations were linked together at stable exchange rates, as in the fixed exchange rate system discussed in Chapter 13. (The narrow band of fluctuation permitted, ±1 percent, is analogous to the band that existed in the gold standard between the gold export point and the gold import point.) This stability of exchange rates on a day-to-day basis was greatly desired by countries such as France, which had suffered from the volatile fluctuations of a floating exchange rate during the 1920s and 1930s.

Note that when every currency has its par value stated in terms of the dollar, an exchange rate between any two other currencies is also implied. These implied exchange rates are called *cross rates*. For example, when DM 2.50 = $1.00 and Yen 240 = $1.00, we can readily calculate the cross rate between the DM and the yen: Yen 96 = DM 1.00.

The Articles of Agreement also provided a method for changes to be made in par values. Specifically, if a member found its balance of payments to be in fundamental disequilibrium, it could propose a change in the par value of its currency. On receipt of the proposal, the IMF was required to study the matter and reach a decision to approve or disapprove the change in par value.

Thus did the Bretton Woods compromise combine short-run, day-to-day stability of exchange rates with long-run flexibility. Par values were to be "stable but adjustable," in the popular phrase. The provision for exchange rate flexibility was crucial, especially to the British, who were determined not to be forced to accept internal deflation in order to maintain an inappropriate exchange rate, as in the 1920s. This compromise sought to combine the advantages of both fixed and flexible exchange rates—and thus to satisfy the advocates of each.

Two further points should be made regarding these exchange rate provisions. First, in signing this agreement, nations were for the first time in history submitting their exchange rate changes to international sanction. This represented a significant surrender of national sovereignty to an international organization, a recognition that exchange rates are everybody's business. Even though this provision did not work as it was intended to do, it is remarkable that members accepted this delegation of power, in principle.

The delegation of power was carefully circumscribed, however. The Articles of Agreement stated that the IMF "shall concur in a proposed exchange rate change . . . if it is satisfied that the change is necessary to correct a fundamental disequilibrium" (Art. IV, Sect. 5). Although the key phrase, "fundamental disequilibrium," was nowhere defined, the intent of this provision was to ensure that exchange rate changes could be used to correct chronic and persistent disequilibria in members' balances of payments. A nation would not have to resort to the classical medicine. It was this ability to adjust par values that led Keynes to describe the IMF system as "the exact opposite of the gold standard."[4]

[4]John Maynard Keynes, speech to the House of Lords, reprinted in Seymour Harris, *The New Economics* (New York: Knopf, 1952), p. 374.

Second, because the dollar was the *numeraire* of the system (the standard to which every other currency was pegged), it follows that the United States did not have the opportunity or power to set the exchange rate between the dollar and any other currency. Nor did the United States have a direct responsibility to intervene in the market to stabilize an exchange rate. With respect to exchange rates, it played a passive role. This is known as the *n*th currency problem. With two currencies, there is only one exchange rate; with three currencies, there are two exchange rates; and with *n* currencies, there are $n - 1$ exchange rates. Therefore, in a world that relies solely on national currencies, one nation must relinquish the right to set the exchange rate of its currency. Under the IMF system, the United States accepted the role of the *n*th country.

For its part, the United States agreed to buy and sell gold at the fixed price of $35 per ounce to all foreign official holders, namely, central banks and treasuries.[5] When foreigners accumulated dollars in the course of stabilizing their exchange rates, they had the legal right to use these dollars to buy gold from the U.S. Treasury at the fixed price. The dollar tie to gold was unique; no other country in the world made such a commitment. This U.S. commitment to convert dollars into gold turned out to be a critical element in the Bretton Woods system, as we will see.

Quotas and Drawing Rights

To fulfill its obligation to keep the spot exchange rate for its currency within 1 percent of its par value, a nation must have a stock of international reserves. Such reserves enable it to counter the effect that the day-to-day shifts in the demand and supply of foreign exchange may have on the spot exchange rate—to buy its currency (e.g., with dollars) when it is weak and to sell its currency (for dollars) when it is strong.

Nations held their international reserves in the form of gold and foreign currency balances. Technically, any national currency could be used for this purpose, as long as it was freely exchangeable for other currencies, but in practice nations tended to hold only a few important currencies, especially U.S. dollars and British pounds.

At the end of World War II, most nations had very slender stocks of international reserves. The United States had acquired the bulk of the world's stock of monetary gold; in 1946 it held $26 billion of an estimated world total of $33 billion. Most nations had also drawn down their foreign currency balances to pay for imports.

Consequently, there was much concern about a prospective shortage of international reserves in the postwar period. One objective of the Bretton Woods negotiations was to devise a method to supplement traditional sources of such reserves.

The solution that was adopted involved a system of quotas and drawing rights. Each member nation was assigned a quota, the size of which depended on the economic size of the country. A member nation was required to pay into the IMF

---

[5]Actually, the buying price was $34.9125 and the selling price $35.0875, but this small spread had little economic significance.

one-fourth of its quota in gold or U.S. dollars, the other three-fourths in its own national currency. The IMF thus acquired a fund consisting partly of gold and dollars, partly of a conglomerate of other currencies. It was empowered to lend these funds to member countries to enable them to finance short-term deficits on external account.

Technically, a member nation was allowed to draw a sum of money in a particular national currency and it would, at the same time, pay in the equivalent amount of its own currency. The member nation could use the currency drawn to purchase the excess supply of its own currency being offered in the foreign exchange market. Later, when its balance of payments improved, the member nation would be expected to reverse this transaction, returning the foreign currency drawn and taking back the equivalent amount of its own currency.

Thus these drawing rights are similar to short-term loans, and they must be repaid. Furthermore, a member's right to exercise its drawing rights, beyond the first 25 percent of its quota, is subject to IMF approval. The first 25 percent, called the gold, or reserve, *tranche* (a French word meaning "slice"), is regarded as part of the member's owned reserves, and the IMF cannot deny its use. A member may draw up to four credit tranches, which means that the potential increase in reserves available for a member's use is equal to its quota.

An example will help to illustrate the mechanics of this system. Mexico's original quota was $90 million; it paid $22.5 million in gold or dollars and $67.5 million in Mexican pesos. Mexico had the right to draw up to a maximum of $112.5 million, paying in an equivalent amount in pesos. At that point the IMF would have been holding $180 million in pesos, as follows:

	Initial Quota	Drawings[a]	IMF Holding
Gold or dollars	$22.5 million	−$112.5	−$ 90 million
Mexican pesos	67.5 million	+$112.5	+$180 million
Net	$90 million	0	$ 90 million

[a] 5 tranches @ $22.5 million.

This quota system represented a modest but significant supplement to world monetary reserves. Originally, quotas totaled $8 billion, which then was equal to about 20 percent of world reserves. Subsequently, quotas have been increased several times; by 1990 the total had reached $135 billion, still equal to about 20 percent of total 1990 world reserves. In recent years the IMF has established a number of lending facilities outside of the quota system. Those facilities are described in an appendix to chapter 21 of this book.

Exchange Control

During the interwar period, many nations made use of exchange controls as a means of dealing with their balance-of-payments problems. Holders of money balances in a particular currency, say, German marks, were not free to use the money as they chose. Purchases of foreign exchange required government approval, and governments restricted or prohibited expenditures for some purposes. Such exchange controls were inevitably discriminatory, and they tended to distort the flow of trade. Country A could cut its imports from Country B simply by declining to allow its citizens to buy foreign exchange to pay for such imports.

Consequently, one goal of wartime economic planning was to eliminate the trade-distorting influence of exchange controls. Article VIII of the IMF Charter prohibits the use of exchange controls on current transactions, that is, purchases and sales of goods and services. However, the Bretton Woods negotiators recognized that many nations would not be willing and able to remove all their exchange restrictions immediately after the war ended. They provided (in Article XIV) for the retention of these restrictions during a postwar transitional period. Originally intended to last five years, this transitional period has been allowed to drag on, and many member nations are still operating under Article XIV.

Exchange restrictions are also used to control capital movements. As noted in Chapter 19, short-term capital movements were large and highly volatile during the interwar period. When a fixed exchange rate came under suspicion, or when a rumor about the potential weakness of a currency swept through the financial markets, large flows of hot money could be precipitated, quickly depleting the foreign exchange reserves of central banks and perhaps forcing devaluations that would otherwise be unnecessary.

The IMF Charter allows nations to use exchange controls on capital account transactions to protect themselves from this source of instability. In fact, the Charter places member nations under an obligation to utilize exchange restrictions to control capital movements. They are not supposed to obtain funds from the IMF (under the drawing right scheme) to cover balance-of-payments deficits caused by capital outflows.

In summary, the IMF Charter provided for the (eventual) elimination of exchange controls on current account transactions, and for their permanent retention and use on capital account transactions. This differential treatment of current and capital transactions turned out to be unworkable in practice, however. If all exchange controls were removed on current transactions, trading firms could finance capital movement under the guise of goods transactions. For example, someone who wanted to transfer $1 million from Italy to France could simply pretend to be importing $1 million worth of goods from France, or an importing firm could overstate the invoice price of its actual imports, buying $2 million of foreign exchange when only $1 million was needed. The other $1 million could then be held in France and would represent an illicit capital outflow from Italy.

To prevent these and other devices designed to conceal capital movements, a government would have to operate a full battery of exchange controls, approving every transaction and then verifying its accuracy. Even if bona fide current transactions were routinely approved, the bureaucratic apparatus would be costly and cumbersome, and it would inhibit trade. Consequently, most nations that have accepted Article VIII and dismantled exchange controls on current transactions have also accepted their inability to prevent capital flows. Exchange restrictions on capital movements still exist in these countries—indeed, they are numerous—but it is generally agreed that they are only partially effective and that many loopholes exist through which capital movements can slip.

The Scarce-Currency Clause

A problem that appeared during the interwar period was that surplus countries did not come under as much pressure to adjust their balances of payments as deficit countries did. In a fixed exchange rate system, a deficit country is compelled to take some kind of action to restore equilibrium because otherwise it will exhaust its foreign exchange reserves. A surplus country, on the other hand, does not have an equally imperative compulsion to restore equilibrium. It can accumulate reserves almost indefinitely, especially if it can sterilize the reserve inflow.

We noted this asymmetry in Chapter 19. Britain, a deficit country, applied deflationary pressure on its economy throughout the 1920s, but the surplus countries (France and the United States) declined to share the burden of adjustment. They did not want to let reserve inflows increase their money supplies and push up their price levels. But when surplus countries do not participate in the adjustment process, all of the pressure falls on the deficit country.

The Bretton Woods negotiators, especially the British, were greatly concerned about the prospect that this asymmetry would become a problem in the postwar period. They feared that the United States, with its huge economy undamaged and even strengthened by wartime expansion, would run chronic surpluses in its balance of payments, thus forcing other countries to accept deflationary pressures as they attempted to correct their payments deficits.

To the great surprise and delight of the British, the American negotiators offered a solution to this issue in the form of the scarce-currency clause. This clause (Article VII in the IMF Charter) essentially provides that if the IMF's holding of any national currency should be depleted, that currency could be formally declared scarce, and member nations would be authorized to impose discriminatory restrictions on imports of goods and services from the scarce-currency country. It was expected that surplus countries would be anxious to avoid such discriminatory treatment, and that they would accept some responsibility for removing the balance-of-payments disequilibrium. If they did not, deficit countries could use discriminatory restrictions and be under less pressure to deflate their own economies.[6]

As we will see, these hopes were not realized, and the asymmetry between deficit and surplus countries became a key issue during the 1960s.

[6]In his *Life of Keynes,* R. F. Harrod describes in rather extravagant language his reactions on first seeing the American proposal, sent to him in draft form by Keynes:

> I read on into it, through the scarce currency clause and onwards. I could not believe my eyes or my brain. I read it again and again . . . I was transfixed. This, then, was the big thing. For years we had complained of the United States attitude as a creditor. For months we had struggled in vain to find some formula that would pin them down to a share of responsibility. Now they had come forward and offered a solution of their own, gratuitously. This was certainly a great event. (p. 545).

THE IMF SYSTEM IN OPERATION, 1947 TO 1971

The IMF was in operation under its original charter for about 25 years, from 1947 to 1971. However, there is some debate about how long, if at all, the IMF really functioned as its creators intended. Nevertheless, this so-called Bretton Woods period presents a sharp contrast to the turmoil of the 20 years following World War I. After World War II, the world economy was generally prosperous, no major depression occurred, the monetary system accommodated a rising volume of trade and capital flows with reasonably stable exchange rates, and nationalist excesses such as competitive depreciation were generally avoided. Despite these successes, the Bretton Woods system proved to have a fundamental flaw, one that eventually led to its demise.

In this discussion we will concentrate on the dominant issue during the Bretton Woods period: the role of the dollar and the persistent deficit in the U.S. balance of payments. But first a few words about the postwar dollar shortage.

The Dollar Shortage, 1945 to 1958

At the end of World War II there existed a huge demand for imports. In Europe and Asia, the combatant nations needed materials and equipment to revive and restore their economies; in other parts of the world, a large, pent-up demand existed for imports of goods that had been unavailable during the war years.

The United States, on the other hand, emerged from the war in an extremely strong economic position. Its productive facilities were undamaged and had, in fact, been greatly expanded during the war. It was demobilizing 10 million men, many of them skilled workers, and its industrial capacity was swiftly switching from military to civilian output.

World demand for U.S. goods was enormous, but the world capacity to export was very small. As already mentioned, foreign exchange reserves of most nations were also at low levels. The result was what came to be perceived as an acute dollar shortage. Only the United States had the capacity to produce the desired goods, but the importing nations did not have the dollars to pay for them. Hence, a serious disequilibrium appeared in the world economy: a surplus in the U.S. balance of payments vis-à-vis the rest of the world.

The IMF was unable to cope with this initial crisis of the postwar period. The funds it had acquired through the payment of quotas were a mere drop in the bucket compared to the need. Consequently, the IMF wisely decided not to begin to operate its drawing rights facility until a later date. Exchange rate changes were also believed to be ineffective. Because of very low elasticities, exchange depreciation would neither reduce the demand for imports nor increase the supply of exports in the deficit countries; thus it would not reduce the overall payments deficit. (As economic recovery took place, the validity of this view came into question.)

It was at this point that the United States came forward with the Marshall Plan: a massive program of economic aid to Western Europe. In effect, the United

States made gifts of dollars to enable the recipient countries to finance their import surpluses. For Western Europe alone, these gifts amounted to about $30 billion, an enormous sum in those days. (For future reference we should note that the dollar was not officially declared to be a scarce currency in the sense of Article VII of the IMF Charter. Technically, it was not scarce because the IMF holdings of dollars were intact; the drawing rights facility was not in operation.)

As economic recovery proceeded in Europe and Japan, the trade balance began to swing the other way. This movement was helped along by a series of currency devaluations, some of which may have been excessive. The British pound was depreciated 30 percent against the dollar in 1949 (from £1 = $4.03 to £1 = $2.80), and many other countries quickly matched the British devaluation. Experience varied, but these devaluations did appear to improve the trade balance, though sometimes with a lag of a year or more.

By 1958 the United States had begun to run a significant balance-of-payments deficit. (Actually, on some definitions, the U.S. deficits began as early as 1950, but in the early 1950s the world still perceived the situation as one of dollar shortage.) Foreign holdings of dollars began to rise, and questions were raised about the process through which a different kind of disequilibrium—a dollar surplus—would be corrected.

The Dollar Surplus: A Basic Dilemma

The U.S. balance-of-payments deficits posed a problem and a dilemma for both the United States and the rest of the world: On the one hand, the deficits were welcomed because they increased the world's supply of foreign exchange reserves; on the other hand, they were deplored because they gave the United States a privileged position and tended to undermine confidence in the system.

At first, when the United States began to run small deficits in the 1950s, other countries were pleased to have increases in their reserves and they gladly held the additional dollars they acquired. The U.S. gold stock was very large in relation to its dollar liabilities, and there was full confidence in the United States' ability to convert those dollars into gold.

Beginning in about 1958, however, the modest U.S. deficits became larger and began to be a cause of concern. A few countries, mainly in Europe, found themselves in the unaccustomed position of having to buy more dollars than they wished to hold. As foreign dollar holdings grew, and as it became clear that U.S. efforts to reduce the deficit were not succeeding, the ability of the United States to redeem in gold came into question. Some countries began to ask for gold in exchange for their dollars, and the U.S. gold stock steadily declined.

The gathering crisis and the basis for waning confidence in the dollar are graphically portrayed in Figure 20-1. The U.S. short-term dollar liabilities to all foreigners (official and private) began to exceed the U.S. gold stock in 1960, and U.S. short-term liabilities to official foreigners alone rose above its gold stock in 1965. Actually, the situation was even worse than it appears to be in Figure 20-1, because the United States was using a number of stratagems to make its reserve

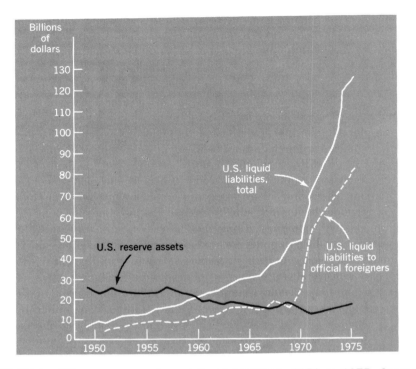

FIGURE 20-1 U.S. reserve assets and liquid liabilities, 1950 to 1975. *Source: U.S. Treasury Bulletin.*

position look better than it really was. For example, it used diplomacy to persuade friendly nations not to convert their dollars into gold despite their legal right to do so; it issued special treasury securities of longer than 12 months' maturity in order to reduce the amount of short-term liabilities; and it placed a variety of restrictions on capital outflows. Since these devices were well known to interested parties, public and private, they did little to instill confidence in the dollar.

In addition, U.S. authorities could take little comfort from the fact that U.S. short-term liabilities to official foreigners did not exceed the U.S. gold stock until 1965. It was clearly understood that if a run on the dollar suddenly began, funds could and would shift rapidly out of private and into official hands.[7]

The fundamental flaw in the IMF system, as Professor Triffin emphasized at an early stage,[8] was that it did not provide any mechanism for orderly growth in world monetary reserves. Such growth was needed as world production and trade expanded, but it could come only in gold or in national currencies. The IMF Charter provided no third alternative.

[7]This distinction is closely related to the distinction between the *liquidity* and *reserve settlements* concepts of balance-of-payments deficits. Controversy raged in the 1960s about the proper concept to use to measure the U.S. deficit.

[8]Robert Triffin, *Gold and the Dollar Crisis* (New Haven, Conn.: Yale University Press, 1960).

U.S. balance-of-payments deficits were supplying the world with needed increases in reserves, but as foreign dollar balances grew in size, the U.S. gold ratio declined, creating a classic crisis of confidence.

Meanwhile, the other potential source of additional reserves, gold mining, was not contributing much. The output of newly mined gold was being held down by the fixed price of $35 per ounce, a price that had remained unchanged since 1934, while prices of other goods and services had risen substantially. Furthermore, most of the newly mined gold was going to the private sector for jewelry, industrial uses, and speculative purposes. Only a small amount found its way into the hands of monetary authorities.

In fact, private demand for gold became so strong in 1960 that it pushed the price in the London gold market above $35 per ounce. At first, this threat was countered by an agreement by a group of central banks to feed gold to that market to hold its price at or just above $35 per ounce. But when this scheme began to cause a decline in monetary gold stocks, central bankers devised a scheme to cut the link between monetary gold stocks and private holdings and to establish a two-price system for gold. Beginning in March 1968, the United States announced that it would buy and sell gold only in transactions with central banks and monetary authorities, and that the price would remain $35 per ounce in this official market. Other central banks agreed that they would neither buy nor sell any gold except in transactions with other monetary authorities. The effect of this arrangement was to freeze the world's monetary gold stock at its existing level.[9] Thereafter, any increase in international reserves had to come from other sources. Under the circumstances, this meant dollars.

The international monetary system now faced a true dilemma: Continued U.S. balance-of-payments deficits would increase dollar balances held by other countries and undermine confidence in the United States' ability to convert those dollars into gold, but elimination of the U.S. deficit would stop the growth in world reserves and tend to hamper world economic growth.

Failure of Adjustment

The nature of the dollar dilemma was clearly understood by 1960, and the persistent U.S. deficit was the focus of intense discussion throughout the 1960s. The obvious question is, Why was this disequilibrium not corrected by the IMF mechanism of adjustment? That correction could have occurred with either stable or flexible exchange rates.

With stable exchange rates, the deficit country is expected to come under deflationary pressures: the classical medicine. Even if the United States had accepted such deflation, the other half of the dilemma would have remained—that is, the

---

[9] It was hoped that when all newly mined gold had to be sold in the private gold market, the price of gold would fall below the official price. South Africa, the world's largest producer, strongly opposed the two-price system because it feared that the price would fall. For a time, South Africa withheld gold, but eventually the price rose far above $35 per ounce, even when South African output was released.

absence of any method for providing needed increases in world reserves. However, the United States was extremely reluctant to exert deflationary pressure on its domestic economy because unemployment was already uncomfortably high. The motto of the Kennedy administration, for example, was to "get this country moving again," to step up the rate of growth. That goal was stressed throughout the 1960s. With a marginal propensity to import then estimated at 5 percent, income would have to fall $80 billion to reduce imports by $4 billion. Such a cost was unthinkable.

Consequently, although the United States sought to stabilize domestic prices and wages, it did not try to force them down. When balance-of-payments deficits and the accompanying gold outflows caused bank reserves to fall, the government did not allow a fall in the money supply to take place. Instead, the Federal Reserve System sterilized or offset the effect of the gold drain on bank reserves. It did so by open-market operations—that is, it bought government bonds in the open market, thus replenishing the reserves of commercial banks. This action can clearly be seen in the reported figures, as shown in Table 20-1. Far from reducing the money supply, the Federal Reserve System took action to expand bank reserves and thus permit an expansion of the money supply. As the gold stock fell $12.4 billion from 1957 to 1968, the Federal Reserve bought treasury securities and expanded credit by $28.5 billion. U.S. policy was clearly aimed at domestic objectives, and the Federal Reserve allowed the money supply to rise as output expanded. In spite of the payments deficit, the money supply rose $57 million between 1957 and 1968: from $136 billion to $193 billion.

Nor did the United States use fiscal policy to apply deflationary pressure. Government expenditures rose steadily from 1958 to 1968, exceeding tax revenues in every year. Even so, unemployment rates remained uncomfortably high during the first half of this period, and in 1964 taxes were sharply reduced in an effort to stimulate the economy. This action was called a declaration of independence from balance-of-payments discipline, since it, like U.S. monetary policy, ran counter to the traditional behavior expected of a deficit nation. Instead of deflating domestic demand, the United States was expanding it. Thus the United States rejected the mechanism of adjustment called for under a fixed exchange rate system.

Despite this rejection, the current account in the U.S. balance of payments improved dramatically from 1958 to 1964. It did so because U.S. prices remained stable in this period, and wages generally increased in proportion to increases in productivity, while prices and wages increased more rapidly in the economies of principal European competitors. Thus a change in relative prices was accomplished by adjustment in the surplus countries. Europeans argued at the time that U.S. deficits were responsible for the inflationary pressures they were experiencing. Under the IMF system, European central banks had to buy the excess dollars by issuing additional supplies of their national currencies. They objected to what they called "imported inflation," although the European central banks could have sterilized these dollar inflows by selling domestic assets, thereby avoiding any inflationary effects.

Even though the U.S. current account improved, the overall balance-of-payments deficit was not removed, or even reduced. The main reason was that the outflow

TABLE 20-1   U.S. Selected Monetary Variables (billions of dollars)

Data	U.S. Securities Held by Federal Reserve	Gold Stock	Member Bank Reserves	Supply of Money
December 1957	24.0	22.8	19.4	135.9
December 1962	30.5	16.0	20.0	147.5
December 1968	52.5	10.4	27.3	193.1

Source: *Federal Reserve Bulletin.*

of capital from the United States to the rest of the world rose greatly from 1958 to 1964.

U.S. firms increased their direct investment in foreign industry, building new plants or buying existing ones in Canada, the United Kingdom, Common Market countries, and many others. Such investments were extremely profitable, and the return flow of interest and profits was an important credit item in the U.S. balance of payments; but when the investments were made, they increased the supply of dollars in the foreign exchange market. The international bond market also revived in the period 1958 to 1963, and a growing volume of foreign bonds was issued in the New York capital market. The efficient operation of the New York market combined with relatively low interest rates and readily available funds to cause a sharp rise in foreign borrowing in the United States.

Foreigners complained that the United States was lending long and borrowing short, thereby profiting at their expense. There was an element of truth in this charge, since the outflow of U.S. funds for direct investment, bond purchases, and bank loans contributed to the excess supply of dollars in the foreign exchange market. When foreign central banks acquired these dollars as a result of their support of exchange rates, they were in effect lending to the United States on a short-term basis.[10]

On the other hand, some economists vigorously argued that the United States was merely performing its role as the world's bank: It was providing a financial intermediation that was needed and wanted by the rest of the world.[11] Europeans preferred short-term assets, and Americans were willing to acquire long-term assets.

[10]When the Chrysler Corporation bought into Simca, the French automobile firm, for $100 million, the Bank of France acquired an additional $100 million which it could hold in a time deposit earning 4 percent interest. The Bank of France was virtually forced to buy the dollars because of its responsibility to stabilize the franc-dollar exchange rate. The net effect of the transaction was that the United States acquired a share of French industry and France acquired a dollar deposit on which it earned a low rate of interest.

[11]E. Despres, C. P. Kindleberger, and Walter S. Salant, "The Dollar and World Liquidity: A Minority View," *The Economist,* February 5, 1966.

The United States imposed a number of exchange controls and restrictions in an attempt to curb capital outflows in the 1960s, but these controls did not reduce the total outflow. They simply changed its form, as the private sector showed great ingenuity in finding loopholes in the regulations and devising ways to slip through them.

Meanwhile, the U.S. deficits continued, and the United States came in for much criticism. General de Gaulle was particularly incensed about what he called the exorbitant privilege enjoyed by the United States, by which he meant its ability to run a persistent deficit in its balance of payments instead of being forced, as other countries were, to correct that deficit one way or another. As his economic adviser, Jacques Rueff, said, the United States had a "deficit without tears." To European critics, it was especially galling that the United States was urging them not to convert their dollars into gold, as was their legal right, because that would threaten the IMF system—that is, it would exhaust the U.S. gold stock and force the United States to break the link between gold and the dollar, a link on which the whole system rested.

This complaint stems from the previously mentioned nth currency problem. Because the dollar was the nth currency, the United States had no obligation to intervene to support any exchange rate. It alone could finance balance-of-payments deficits simply by issuing its own currency. In the bargain struck at Bretton Woods, the United States had accepted a unique obligation of its own: to convert dollar balances into gold at the holder's option. This obligation was supposed to exert a restraining influence on the United States, but it was this discipline that the United States was evading by putting pressure on other nations not to convert their dollars into gold.

In view of the chronic nature of the U.S. deficits, one might have expected exchange rate flexibility to be used to correct the disequilibrium, as provided in the Bretton Woods agreement. The provisions for changing exchange rates had been included precisely to avoid the necessity for nations to undergo the heavy cost of internal deflation.

Almost everyone agreed that exchange rate adjustments were desirable, but there was little agreement about who should take the initiative in making them. One might suppose that the United States, the nation with the largest deficit, would be the logical candidate. But the United States argued that under the terms of the IMF charter, it could not change the exchange rate between the dollar and other currencies. Each other nation had set the official par value for its currency, and each nation was responsible for supporting that rate within a 1 percent band. The dollar was the *numeraire,* the standard to which each other currency was pegged; hence the United States could only play a passive role. Even if the United States devalued the dollar against gold (i.e., increased the dollar price of gold) by, say, 10 percent, that action alone would not change any exchange rate. Other countries would still have to change the official par values of their currencies in terms of the dollar. Furthermore, if they did want to change their par values, then they should have done it. They need not have waited for a change in the dollar price of gold.

This argument led to the conclusion that surplus countries should take the initiative; they should appreciate their currencies against the dollar. For example,

Germany should increase the dollar price of the mark. Only a few countries were in a significant surplus position in any case: Germany, Japan, the Netherlands, Switzerland, and occasionally France, Belgium, and others. These few could remove the disequilibrium in the world payments pattern simply by appreciating their currencies.

The surplus countries vigorously resisted this line of argument, more often with emotion than with economic logic. They said that the United States was the country that was indulging in excessive spending, undertaking too many ambitious programs throughout the world, allowing too rapid a rate of inflation, and generally misbehaving. They, the surplus countries, were acting responsibly by living within their means, controlling inflation, and so on. It was unfair and improper to expect the virtuous countries to take the initiative and bail out the culprit, which also just happened to be the wealthiest and most powerful nation in the world. The United States should put its house in order, start living within its means, and act more responsibly. Any single surplus country also disliked taking action to appreciate its currency, because that immediately made its exports less competitive in all other countries, not just in the deficit country. It was politically difficult to take an action that would tend to reduce output and employment in the export industries.

As a consequence of this impasse, the provisions for exchange rate flexibility in the IMF Charter were not utilized when the system faced its most severe test. A few small currency appreciations did take place (the German mark and the Dutch guilder in 1961, and again in 1969), but they were rare. Most exchange rate adjustments from 1947 to 1971 were depreciations. Indeed, the U.S. dollar itself actually appreciated, on a weighted average basis, during the decade of the 1960s as a result of these currency depreciations by other countries.

This problem of persuading surplus countries to adjust had been anticipated at Bretton Woods. As noted earlier, the British negotiators had expected the United States to be in a strong surplus position, and they wanted somehow to be protected against that hazard. The scarce-currency clause was the result. However, this clause had not been invoked against the United States in the dollar shortage period after World War II, and it was thought politically infeasible to invoke it against Germany and Japan in the 1960s. Furthermore, there was some question about the propriety of taking punitive action against these countries when it was generally agreed that the cause of the disequilibrium was overexpansion of the U.S. economy. It seemed unjust that, as a result of U.S. misbehavior, other countries should be authorized to discriminate against Germany and Japan.

In short, neither mechanism of adjustment—stable or flexible exchange rates—was allowed to operate. Disequilibrium persisted, and eventually an old-fashioned financial panic forced the hand of the monetary authorities.

PERIMETER DEFENSES AND BASIC REFORMS

The failure of adjustment and the persistent disequilibrium in the world payments system received much attention in the 1960s. Responsible authorities reacted to the mounting pressures in two ways: First, they devised a number of schemes to protect and preserve the IMF system and, second, they initiated a series of discussions and negotiations about basic reforms designed to change the structure of the system and remedy its fundamental defects. The preservation schemes (the perimeter defenses thrown up to protect the system) did nothing to improve the adjustment mechanism, whereas the reform discussion proceeded too slowly and was overtaken by events before its modest achievements had much influence.

Defenses

The perimeter defenses took several forms, but their common purpose was to maintain public confidence in the stability of exchange rates between the dollar and other major currencies. In particular, they sought to relieve pressure on the U.S. gold stock and thus to prevent a run on the bank from developing as part of a classic crisis of confidence. These defensive devices included:

1. Swap agreements among central banks, in which open lines of credit were made available on a reciprocal basis. For example, the Federal Reserve Bank of New York and the Bank of Italy agreed to provide each other with short-term funds up to $500 million (or the equivalent in Italian lira), which funds could be drawn on and used to intervene in the foreign exchange market as required to support the existing par values.

2. The issuance of U.S. Treasury bonds to European central banks in exchange for some of their accumulated short-term dollar balances. Some of these securities, known as Roosa bonds, were denominated in foreign currencies, and some were in dollars. In either case, they involved swapping long-term debt (maturity longer than one year) for short-term dollars. It was hoped that this would strengthen the public confidence in the dollar.

3. The two-tier gold market. We have already described the division of the world gold market into official and free-market compartments. One objective was to shield official gold reserves from the influence of the speculative demand for gold.

4. U.S. controls on capital export. The purpose of these controls was to reduce the outflow of capital from the United States in the hope that such reduction would reduce the dollar accumulation of other countries. These controls had little actual effect, however, because the participants in this market showed great ingenuity in finding loopholes in the regulations and devising ways to get around them when capital export was financially attractive.

5. Political pressure to persuade foreign governments to hold dollars and not to present them to the U.S. Treasury in exchange for gold. For example, as a result of negotiations between German and American officials in 1967, the German government promised not to use its dollars to purchase gold from the U.S. Treasury. Friendly governments held dollars, less friendly ones, such as France, asked for gold.

6. Increases in IMF quotas. Several such increases were agreed on. They increased the reserves available to member countries to support the existing exchange rates. The IMF also sponsored a swap agreement among the industrial countries: the General Arrangements to Borrow (GAB).

Reforms

As noted earlier, the fundamental flaw in the IMF system was that nations had to hold their international reserves either in gold or in national currencies, chiefly in dollars. But monetary gold was not increasing, and thus any increases in world reserves had to take the form of dollar balances. These, in turn, tended to erode confidence in the dollar link to gold. Consequently, an important objective of international monetary reform was the creation of a new form of international money that could be used as a monetary reserve in addition to (or instead of) gold and dollars.

After lengthy discussion and debate, the IMF Charter was finally amended in 1968 to authorize the issuance of "Special Drawing Rights," a new money that was supposed to be "as good as gold." The odd name, soon contracted to SDR, was chosen because the new money utilized some features of the original system of quotas and drawing rights in the IMF. When SDRs are created by the IMF, they are allocated among member nations, and each nation is credited with a certain number of SDRs. This is an accounting entry, but it is real money in the sense that a nation can draw against its credit balance in order to settle a payments deficit to another nation. (The SDR was originally defined in terms of gold, and at first SDR 1.00 = \$1.00.) For example, if Italy has a deficit vis-à-vis France, it can cover the deficit by transferring part of its SDR balance to France. Such a transfer leaves the total amount of SDRs unchanged.

After adoption of the SDR amendment, the creation of SDR 9.5 billion was authorized; they were issued in three installments in 1970, 1971, and 1972. It was hoped that this new source of reserves would reduce the rate of increase in dollar reserves and that SDRs might eventually take the place of the dollar as the principal component of official monetary reserves. However, the U.S. payments deficit continued and even increased sharply in 1970 and 1971, thus greatly expanding foreign dollar holdings. The issuance of SDRs did nothing to correct the fundamental disequilibrium in the world monetary system.

Some economists urged that the SDR be made the sole (or principal) form of reserve. They proposed that all nations transfer their existing reserves of dollars, gold, and other currencies to the IMF, receiving in exchange deposit credits in SDR on the books of the IMF. All exchange rates would then be set in terms of the SDR, which would represent an $(n + 1)$th currency. This would remove the asymmetrical status of the dollar and eliminate the privileged position of the United States. A U.S. payments deficit would have to be financed in SDRs, just like that of any other country. If the United States reserves declined, it could propose a change in the dollar-SDR exchange rate, just like any other country.

This idea was much discussed in the 1960s, especially in academic circles, but serious political negotiations to implement it did not take place. Nations were nowhere near a consensus on such a fundamental reform when the crisis struck in 1971. Only then, after the United States had closed the gold window and abrogated the IMF Charter, did serious discussion of basic reform take place in the IMF. The forum was the Committee of Twenty, established under the aegis of the IMF and made up of representatives from the ten largest industrialized countries and ten developing countries. It was at work from 1972 to 1974, and it explored many of the basic issues involved in international monetary reform, but the oil price increase and widespread floating made it clear that no political consensus on these issues could be achieved. The Committee of Twenty filed a report and quietly disbanded in June 1974.[12]

Another reform proposal was simply to let exchange rates fluctuate more or less freely in the marketplace. This too was discussed and advocated most widely in academic circles. Central bankers and treasury officials were almost unanimous in their opposition to such a flexibility; they strongly supported the IMF system of stable par values. When events finally forced many nations to abandon their fixed parities, they did so with great reluctance.

THE FINAL YEARS

Since the reform efforts had failed to produce any substantial results, the IMF system continued to operate in much the same way in its final years. U.S. deficits and waning confidence in the dollar posed a growing threat to this system. As inflationary pressures increased in the United States and tension mounted over the U.S. involvement in Vietnam, a flight from the dollar began in earnest. Holders of dollar assets began to sell them in order to switch into assets denominated in other currencies or into gold. To hold exchange rates steady, central banks had to buy large amounts of dollars.

The U.S. deficit on an official settlements basis rose to $9.9 billion in 1970, but that was only the beginning. Massive outflows occurred in early 1971, and foreign exchange markets were flooded with dollars. Conditions became so hectic that foreign exchange markets were closed for brief periods, and nations imposed exchange controls, allowed currencies to float temporarily, and even set negative rates of interest on foreign-owned deposits—all in a vain effort to stem the tide. The dollar outflow simply swelled further in the summer of 1971. In the first three quarters of that year, the reserve settlements deficit was an incredible $24 billion.

On August 15, 1971, President Nixon bowed to the inevitable and announced to the world that the United States was terminating its commitment to buy and sell gold at $35 per ounce, thus abrogating the IMF agreement. (Foreign central

[12]See Robert Solomon, *The International Monetary System, 1945–1981* (New York: Harper & Row, 1982), Ch. 14, for an authoritative account of the deliberations of the Committee of Twenty.

banks had voluntarily refrained from asking for gold in 1970 and 1971, with some exceptions, so the U.S. gold stock stood at $10 billion on August 15.) The presidential proclamation also called for a depreciation of the dollar of 10 to 15 percent, and stated that the objective was to achieve an improvement of $13 billion in the U.S. balance of trade in goods and services. To encourage (or force) other countries to allow their currencies to appreciate vis-à-vis the dollar, temporary tariff surcharges were imposed on imports.

Despite these drastic steps (the Nixon *shokku,* as the Japanese called it), other countries remained reluctant to allow their currencies to appreciate. They continued to support them at or near the old parities while waiting to see what would happen.

After a four-month period of intense negotiation and discussion, a conference was held in Washington at which the Smithsonian Agreement was hammered out. This agreement, made in December 1971, was essentially an attempt to establish a new set of exchange rates (now called central rates instead of par values) that would restore equilibrium and put the IMF system back on track. The United States bowed to French pressure and agreed to devalue the dollar by $8\frac{1}{2}$ percent (i.e., raise the price of gold to $38 per ounce), but this action was merely a symbolic gesture because the United States did not agree to resume the purchase or sale of gold at that, or any, price. A dollar depreciation against other currencies of about 10 percent was effected in the Smithsonian Agreement, and it was hoped that this depreciation would suffice to correct the U.S. deficit and restore confidence in the dollar.

It did not. Renewed inflationary pressure in the United States stimulated imports, and the dollar continued to be weak. Foreign central banks had to continue their intervention to keep exchange rates within the permitted band (now $\pm 2\frac{1}{4}$ percent) around the new central rates. The dollars they acquired were not convertible into gold or any other standard of value. In fact, the new system placed the world on a dollar standard for all practical purposes.

Within a year the new system was in trouble. In February and March 1973, speculation against the dollar brought a second dollar devaluation (an increase in the nominal price of gold to $42.22 per ounce) and further depreciation of the dollar against the other major currencies. When that depreciation also failed to restore confidence, several nations decided to let their currencies float more or less freely in the foreign exchange market. These floating currencies included the most important ones: the British pound, Canadian dollar, German mark, Japanese yen, French franc, Italian lira, and Swiss franc. Many countries, however, continued to peg their currencies to the dollar or to some other currency.

THE EUROCURRENCY MARKET

A striking innovation in international banking occurred during the IMF period. Commercial banks in several countries began to accept deposits and to extend loans in currencies other than their own national currency. We will briefly describe this activity, which has become known as the Eurocurrency market.

As noted in earlier chapters, creation and control of a nation's money is one of the most sensitive and jealously guarded attributes of national sovereignty. Traditionally, it has been accepted that every nation has an exclusive right to coin and print its own money. When money actually took the form of coin and currency, this exclusive national privilege was generally respected, except by counterfeiters, and even when bank deposits became the principal form of money, the primacy of national control was respected—at least until recently.

In 1960, however, European commercial banks discovered that they could earn handsome profits by accepting deposits in U.S. dollars and by engaging in banking operations in terms of dollars. Since they were dealing almost entirely in bank deposits, or bookkeeping money, it was easy enough to keep accounts in dollars whether the bank was located in London, Paris, or Zurich.

From a modest beginning in 1960, commercial banks proceeded to increase their foreign currency deposits at a rapid rate. Although this market is sometimes referred to as the Eurodollar market, banks in world financial centers now accept deposits and make loans in several other national currencies as well (marks, pounds, francs, and yen are important examples) and commercial banks throughout the world are participating in this market. There is an Asian dollar market centered in Singapore, and many banks collect deposits in branches located in the Bahamas. Thus even the term *Eurocurrency* is not really adequate, although it is much used. Our discussion will primarily concern the Eurodollar portion of the market. U.S. commercial banks are heavily involved through their branches and subsidiaries in foreign financial centers, especially in Europe.

The rise of the Eurodollar market may be interpreted as an evolutionary response of the private banking sector to the need for an international money market. Since no international money exists, commercial banks have proceeded to internationalize some of the national monies, particularly the dollar. These have been made to serve as international monies, and a huge, highly competitive money market has been created. Every important nation is linked into this vast money market, and every nation is influenced by it with respect to credit conditions, interest rates, and so on. Thus it has become a major force pulling toward a more closely integrated world economy. One of the most striking facts about the development of this important institutional form is that it was entirely unplanned. Central bankers watched it grow with some apprehension, but they did not try to suppress it.

How the Eurodollar Market Works

Transactions in the Eurodollar market are extremely simple, in essence. Suppose Firm A, which has a $10 million deposit in a U.S. bank, decides to place that sum in a bank in London (a Eurobank, as we will call any commercial bank in the rest of the world that accepts deposits denominated in dollars and other currencies besides its own national currency). Firm A simply writes a check on its U.S. bank and deposits the check in the Eurobank. The effects of this transaction may be shown in T-accounts, as in Table 20-2. In the U.S. bank, the deposit is simply switched from Firm A to Eurobank 1, leaving its total deposit liabilities unchanged. Firm A now has a time deposit in Eurobank 1, on which it may earn a higher rate of interest (say, 8 percent) than it could earn in a domestic time deposit, and Eurobank 1 now has a $10 million demand deposit in the U.S. bank. Eurodollar deposits are time deposits, with maturities ranging from one day to several years, and they earn interest. (Until recently, banks in the United States were not allowed to pay interest on deposits of less than 30 days' duration, which is one reason Eurodollar deposits have been attractive to firms holding large cash balances.)

Now Eurobank 1 has a $10 million time deposit liability on which it pays 8 percent, and a $10 million asset (demand deposit in a U.S. bank) on which it earns nothing. To hold such a nonearning asset is like holding a hot potato; one wants to get rid of it as quickly as possible. Thus Eurobank 1 will be anxious to convert that deposit into an interest-bearing asset, say, by making a loan or buying an asset. For example, it may place $10 million in a time deposit at $8\frac{1}{2}$ percent interest with an Italian commercial bank (Eurobank 2) that is temporarily in need of funds. (Eurobank 1 may keep a small portion of the demand deposit as a reserve, but in practice reserve ratios are quite small in the Eurodollar market, and we will omit them.) The spreads between interest rates received and paid are very small in the Eurodollar market, as low as $\frac{1}{8}$ or $\frac{1}{4}$ of 1 percent. It is a wholesale market, with large transactions and low margins.

This second transaction can also be shown in T-accounts, as in Table 20-3. In the U.S. bank, the deposit is again simply switched from one holder to another. Eurobank 1 acquires an earning asset, while Eurobank 2 incurs a time deposit liability in return for which it acquires the dollar demand deposit. Note that Eurodollar deposits of $20 million now exist: $10 million payable to Firm A by Eurobank 1 (Table 20-2), and $10 million payable to Eurobank 1 by Eurobank 2 (Table 20-3). This process could be repeated several times, with the amount of Eurodollars increasing each time. The cycle will stop, however, if the dollar demand deposit is used to make a direct payment to a firm in the United States. We can illustrate by taking our example one step further.

TABLE 20-2   The Creation of a Eurodollar Deposit

U.S. Bank			
Assets		**Liabilities**	
		Demand deposit, Firm A	−$10 million
		Demand deposit, Eurobank 1	+$10 million

Eurobank 1			
Assets		**Liabilities**	
Demand deposit in U.S. bank	+$10 million	Time deposit, Firm A	+$10 million

TABLE 20-3   A Eurodollar Redeposit

U.S. Bank

Assets		Liabilities	
		Demand deposit, Eurobank 1	−$10 million
		Demand deposit, Eurobank 2	+$10 million

Eurobank 1

Assets		Liabilities	
Demand deposit in U.S. bank	−$10 million		
Time deposit in Eurobank 2	+$10 million		

Eurobank 2

Assets		Liabilities	
Demand deposit in U.S. bank	+$10 million	Time deposit in Eurobank 1	+$10 million

The Italian Bank, Eurobank 2, now has the demand deposit in the U.S. bank. It too will want to convert this deposit into an earning asset. Let us suppose it lends $10 million to an Italian leather producer (Firm B) at 9 percent interest, and Firm B uses the money to pay for hides it has bought from a U.S. exporter (Firm C). Now the $10 million demand deposit in the U.S. bank is switched from Eurobank 2 to Firm C, an American firm. Firm C may draw checks on this deposit to pay for wages and other expenses, but if these are paid to domestic persons and firms, they will involve monetary circulation within the United States. There is no basis for further rounds of credit creation in the Eurodollar market. However, Eurobank 1 still has a $10 million time deposit liability to Firm A, matched by a time deposit claim on Eurobank 2; and Eurobank 2 still has a $10 million time deposit liability to Eurobank 1, matched by a loan receivable from Firm B. The expansion process in the Eurodollar market stopped because the funds lent to the Italian leather producer were not redeposited in a Eurobank, but were paid to a firm that deposited them in a U.S. bank.

Much discussion has occurred about the extent to which multiple creation of deposits can and does take place in the Eurodollar market. In the absence of any formal reserve requirements, there is no definite limiting value for the multiplier. However, it seems clear that an important factor determining how much multiple expansion of deposits can occur is the extent to which funds lent by Eurobanks are redeposited in the Eurobank system. The larger the ratio of redepositing, the greater the potential for multiple expansion of deposits in the Eurocurrency system.

Although simple in essence, Eurodollar transactions can become intricate in details, with a complex variety of links to trace out. We need not pursue these complications. The main point is that a large external money market now exists, based on dollars. Many governments, persons, and business firms (American, foreign, and multinational) find it to their advantage to place funds (i.e., hold deposits) in Eurobanks, and many governments, persons, and firms borrow in that market.

Why the Eurodollar Market Exists

An obvious question is probably floating through the reader's mind at this point: Why did this money market develop outside the United States? Why aren't banks within the United States doing all this business in dollar loans and deposits?

The first and principal answer is that the Eurodollar market provides a way to circumvent the many regulations and controls that national governments have placed on domestic money markets and bank operations. In the exercise of their sovereign power to operate monetary, fiscal, and other economic policies at the national level, governments have imposed numerous restrictions, regulations, and controls on the use of money and on the operations of commercial banks. The opportunity to escape from this maze of legal restrictions provided much of the stimulus and incentive for the Eurodollar market. We will mention a few examples:

1. Until the mid-1980s U.S. banks were subject to Regulation Q of the Federal Reserve System, which specified the maximum interest rates American banks could pay on time deposits. In the early 1960s the maximum rate was 4 percent. Eurobanks, not subject to Regulation Q, were willing to pay 6 to 8 percent at that time. Consequently, persons and firms with large sums to place in time deposits were induced to hold dollar deposits in the Eurodollar market.

2. During the 1960s the United States imposed a tax on foreign bond issues in New York and placed restrictions on loans to foreigners by U.S. banks. The natural result was that foreigners borrowed money from Eurobanks instead. Furthermore, U.S. firms, facing restrictions on the transfer of funds to finance their subsidiaries in Europe and elsewhere, also turned to Eurobanks for loans. (Note that the U.S. regulations generated both a supply of funds to the Eurodollar market and a demand for loans from it.)

3. Other nations had even more exchange controls and legal restrictions on their citizens than did the United States. Consequently, the opportunity to hold funds in Eurobanks was extremely attractive to firms and individuals in those countries. Eurodollar deposits were subject to no controls, they could be exchanged into any currency, they could be used for payments anywhere in the world, and they were largely beyond the reach of the tax collector.

4. U.S. banks are required to maintain reserves against their deposit liabilities, but Eurobanks are not required to maintain such reserves. Since reserves earn no interest, the requirement to hold them has adversely affected the ability of U.S. banks to compete with their Eurobank rivals. (This factor may be less important now. In 1981 the Federal Reserve System authorized U.S. banks to establish international banking facilities through which they may conduct banking business with foreigners, exempt from domestic regulations such as reserve requirements and interest rate ceilings.)

A second reason for the rapid growth of the Eurodollar market is that it is a highly competitive and efficient market. Eurobanks pay attractive interest rates on time deposits placed with them, and they charge competitive rates of interest on loans they make. As we noted, spreads are small in this market—considerably smaller than in U.S. banks. Eurobanks can operate in this way because they are dealing in large sums, their clerical costs are low because they do not operate a retail banking business, they have no legal reserve requirements to meet, and they are dealing mostly with blue-chip clients whose credit ratings are excellent. If a Eurobank accepts a one-year time deposit of $100 million at 8 percent and simultaneously makes a one-year loan of $100 million to IBM at $8\frac{1}{8}$ percent, its gross profit is $125,000. Operating costs would be low and risk practically nil.

The Effect of the Eurocurrency Market on National Monetary Autonomy

The existence of this huge, highly competitive money market has tended to reduce the ability of any individual nation to operate an independent monetary policy while maintaining a fixed exchange rate. Such a policy usually entails an attempt to raise or lower the domestic interest rate. But, as Geoffrey Bell observed, "short-term funds, like water, find their own level, and there is little that even Canute-minded central bankers can do to arrest the forces of the market."[13] For example, in the 1960s Germany tried to maintain a tight money policy to restrain inflationary pressures. But when interest rates rose in Germany and credit became scarce, German banks had an incentive to seek funds in the Eurodollar market where lower interest rates prevailed. To block that channel, the German central bank placed restrictions on commercial bank access to outside funds, but then German business firms themselves borrowed the funds they needed in the Eurodollar market. The German central bank tried to insulate the German economy by imposing various additional rules and regulations, but these proved to be difficult to enforce. The financial markets have shown great ingenuity in discovering new ways to get around the regulations.

Similarly, if a single country tried to stimulate its economy by pursuing an easy-money policy and reducing interest rates, funds would tend to flow out of that country. If its time deposit rates dropped, firms would shift deposits to the Eu-

[13]Geoffrey Bell, *The Euro-dollar Market and the International Financial System* (London: Macmillan, 1973), p. 70.

robanks. Borrowers would increase their borrowing in the low-interest-rate country and use the proceeds to repay higher cost loans in other places. These actions tend to equalize interest rates in the various financial markets. The United States was in this position in the 1960s. The authorities wanted to keep interest rates low in order to stimulate economic activity and reduce unemployment. Regulation Q was used to limit the rate of interest paid on time deposits. But that led to an outflow of funds to the Eurodollar market, and forced the authorities to introduce a variety of regulations and restrictions designed to curb that outflow. Then, in 1969, the Federal Reserve instituted an extremely tight monetary policy in an effort to stop inflation. Interest rates rose sharply and U.S. banks were put in a double bind—they could not raise their own time deposit rates to attract and hold funds, but short-term interest rates were rising sharply and inducing depositors to switch to other types of assets. In their desperate search for funds, the banks turned to the Eurodollar market. They borrowed $15 billion in 1969, a huge sum at that time. This heavy demand for funds drove up interest rates in the Eurodollar market and, through it, put upward pressure on interest rates in countries in Europe and elsewhere. Their access to Eurodollar funds enabled U.S. banks to escape or at least to moderate the tight-money pressure from the Federal Reserve, but it also transmitted that pressure to the rest of the world.

The advent of floating exchange rates has not greatly changed the role of the Eurocurrency market and the functions it performs. It has continued to grow at a rapid rate since floating began. To a considerable extent, the Eurocurrency market has become a world money market. National money markets are linked into it in many ways. Some scope for an independent monetary policy still exists for countries that maintain a flexible exchange rate, but the monetary authority in one country cannot change its policy without taking account of conditions in this world money market. Through arbitrage, domestic interest rates are kept in line with Eurocurrency interest rates in the same currency.

Interest rates in, say, the U.S. money market are closely linked to interest rates on comparable maturities in the Eurodollar market. For example, at any given time the interest rate on three-month Eurodollar market deposits is about equal to the interest rate on three-month CDs or treasury bills in New York. Similarly, interest rates on Euro-DM deposits are closely linked to interest rates in the German money market. But interest rates on financial assets denominated in Deutsche marks can and do diverge from rates on assets denominated in dollars. As noted in Chapter 13, these differences are related to spot forward exchange rate differentials and to the possibility of exchange rate changes. We will return to this matter in Chapter 21.

The Size of the Eurodollar Market

The volume of Eurodollar deposits has grown tremendously since the beginning of the market in the early 1960s. Net Eurodollar deposits (excluding interbank deposits, which occur when one bank accepts a Eurodollar deposit and then re-deposits the funds in another bank) were only $60 billion in 1966, but grew to

$182 billion in 1973, $1,262 billion in 1983, and $2,703 billion in 1989.[14] This growth occurred despite the phasing out of Regulation Q during the early 1980s. Nondollar Eurocurrency deposits have typically been about one-third of the dollar volume, and this banking sector is no longer entirely European. Singapore, Hong Kong, and Nassau have all become important Eurocurrency banking centers.

Whether the growth of the Eurocurrency markets affects the world's money supply depends on how money is defined. Eurocurrency deposits are time deposits and cannot be used directly as a medium of exchange. When a Eurodollar deposit matures, the holder is paid with dollars in the form of a U.S. bank demand deposit. Those funds can be used directly for payment, while the Eurodollar deposit itself could not be. Eurocurrency deposits would be included in an M2 or M3 definition of money, but not in M1.

Recycling Oil Payments

The Eurocurrency market played a major role in financing the huge current account imbalances that followed the oil shocks of the 1970s. The resulting buildup of international debt produced another difficult problem, however. After the sharp increases in oil prices in 1973 and in 1979, much concern was expressed about the ability of the international monetary system to handle the enormous flows of funds that would be involved. Many experts feared that a crisis or collapse of the system would occur, so massive was the disturbance to which it had to adjust. As it turned out, the system accommodated itself very smoothly to this major shift in direction and amount of international payments. Basically, the mechanism is quite simple. It involves a kind of round-robin, or it could be compared to a game of musical chairs. The Eurocurrency markets played a major role in the mechanism through which payments were made from the oil-importing countries to the oil exporters, especially to members of OPEC. We will explain briefly what the problem was and how it was handled.

The oil price increase meant that oil-importing countries had to pay about $50 billion per year to the OPEC countries. This is an estimate of their current account deficit vis-à-vis OPEC; that is, the $50 billion represents OPEC exports minus their imports of goods and services. It was clear that OPEC nations could not quickly increase their imports to match the sudden huge rise in their exports.

Oil-importing countries had to pay for the oil largely in dollars. Thus in making payments they drew checks on their dollar deposits in U.S. banks. OPEC countries then had to decide what to do with these large receipts of dollars. They chose to place a large part of them in the Eurodollar market—that is, they placed time deposits in Eurobanks. This gave the Eurobanks an immediate increase in their lending capacity, and they were eager to make new loans to match their new deposit liabilities. (Remember, they were paying perhaps 8 percent on those time deposits, and they could not afford to hold nonearning assets.)

---

[14]Data from Morgan Guaranty Trust and the Federal Reserve System.

Many oil-importing countries, having just drawn down their dollar balances and facing the need to pay for next month's oil as well, were eager to borrow dollars from the Eurobanks. When they did borrow, they paid the dollars to OPEC nations, who redeposited them in Eurobanks, thus making possible further loans to oil importers who could then pay for more oil, and so on. This process is what came to be called "recycling the petrodollars." The Eurocurrency market served as a financial intermediary between the oil importers and OPEC. OPEC nations could have made loans directly to oil importers (i.e., sold the oil on credit), but they much preferred to be paid in dollars and then to place deposits in large, prestigious commercial banks such as Barclay's, Chase Manhattan, Bank of America, Lloyd's, and other major participants in the Eurocurrency market. Furthermore, these banks then had to assume the risks of lending to the oil-importing countries. The borrowers were not only industrial countries, but also oil-importing underdeveloped countries throughout the world.

Very large sums were recycled in this way during the 1970s. The process involved a rapid buildup of debt, especially in certain Latin American countries such as Brazil and Argentina. When interest rates rose sharply in the 1980s and exports fell as a result of the worldwide recession, many debtor countries became unable to service their debt—that is, to pay the interest and repay the principal when it became due. The problem was aggravated by the fact that much of the debt was in short-term loans. Even if these loans were renewed (rolled over), the required interest payments rose sharply.

As of 1992 a severe crisis has been averted. Cooperative efforts involving the commercial banks, the International Monetary Fund, and governmental authorities have succeeded in working out refunding agreements that have avoided outright default. We will examine this issue in more detail in Chapter 21.

QUESTIONS FOR STUDY AND REVIEW

1. What is the role of international reserves in the world economy? What have been the main sources of supply of such reserves in recent decades?

2. Summarize the essential elements of the Bretton Woods system. When a disequilibrium appeared in a member nation's balance of payments, through what mechanism was it supposed to be removed?

3. In what sense were speculators offered a one-way bet in the IMF system? Are they now offered the same bet?

4. What exactly was the dilemma of the U.S. balance-of-payments deficit in the 1960s?

5. Explain how the IMF quota system worked. How did drawing rights assist member nations?

6. In the 1960s Europeans complained about the privileged position of the U.S. dollar. What was the basis of these complaints?

7. Write an essay to describe the emergence of the dollar problem in the 1960s, and the causes of the eventual breakdown of the Bretton Woods system.

8. Does the Eurocurrency market have the capacity to create money? If not, why not? If so, how? Explain why there is disagreement on this issue.

9. What is the $n - 1$ problem?

10. State the role of SDRs in the international monetary system: their purpose, mode of creation, and method of distribution and use.

11. In what sense did the United States have a special ability to run balance-of-payments deficits during the Bretton Woods period (1950 to 1971)? Why did it have this ability?

12. What was the meaning and purpose of the scarce-currency clause? Did it achieve its purpose? Why or why not?

13. How were increases in international reserves supposed to be accomplished in the IMF system?

14. The IMF Charter provided for exchange rate changes in the event of a fundamental disequilibrium in the balance of payments. Why didn't such changes occur in the 1960s to help correct the obvious disequilibrium?

15. What was the purpose of the two-tier gold market?

16. What are Eurodollars? Why did the Eurodollar market develop in the 1960s?

SELECTED REFERENCES

Gardner, Richard. *Sterling Dollar Diplomacy.* New York: McGraw-Hill, 1969.

Gilbert, Milton. *Quest for World Monetary Order.* New York: John Wiley, 1980.

Harrod, Roy F. *The Life of Keynes.* London: Macmillan, 1951.

Little, Jane. *Euro-Dollars: The Money-Market Gypsies.* New York: Harper & Row, 1975.

McKinnon, Ronald I. "The Eurocurrency Market. *Essays in International Finance,* No. 125. Princeton, N.J.: Princeton University Press, December 1977.

Meier, Gerald M. *Problems of a World Monetary Order.* New York: Oxford University Press, 1982.

Rolfe, Sidney E., and James Burtle. *The Great Wheel: The World Monetary System.* New York: Macmillan, 1973.

Scammell, W. M. *The International Economy Since 1945.* New York: St. Martin's Press, 1980.

Solomon, Robert. *The International Monetary System 1945–1981: An Insider's View.* New York: Harper & Row, 1982.

Southard, Frank. "The Evolution of the International Monetary Fund." *Essays in International Finance,* No. 135. Princeton, N.J.: Princeton University Press, December 1979.

Triffin, Robert. *Gold and the Dollar Crisis.* New Haven, Conn.: Yale University Press, 1960.

RECENT EVENTS IN INTERNATIONAL MONETARY RELATIONS: 1973 TO THE PRESENT

As was noted in the previous chapter, many major industrialized countries shifted to a regime of flexible or floating exchange rates in early 1973. This change occurred not because the academic arguments for floating exchange rates had been accepted, but because the previous system of fixed parities had collapsed twice within a period of two years (August 1971 and January/February 1973) and it was not clear what set of parities would succeed. Except for the subsequent decision of several European Community countries to maintain fixed parities among themselves and to float as a bloc relative to the rest of the world, the countries shifting to flexible exchange rates in 1973 have retained that approach.

Flexible exchange rates are not universal, however; most nations still maintain some form of fixed exchange rates, and only 27 nations were floating independently as of early 1991 (Table 21-1).

Most developing countries have chosen to retain fixed exchange rates and have expressed the wish that the industrialized countries would return to that approach. Developing countries often fear that a floating exchange rate will mean excessive exchange rate volatility (although that has also been a problem for industrialized countries) and prefer the Bretton Woods system as it existed until 1971.[1] A few developing countries, however, such as Nigeria, Argentina, and Bolivia, have experimented with flexible exchange rates with some success.

TABLE 21-1   Exchange Rate Regimes of IMF Member Countries as of March 31, 1991

Exchange Regime	Number of Countries
Pegged to the dollar	27
Pegged to the French franc	14
Pegged to another currency	5
Pegged to the SDR	6
Pegged to another currency composite	34
Subtotal, pegged	86
Limited flexibility relative to the U.S. dollar	4
Members of the European Monetary System	10
Peg, adjusted frequently on the basis of payments indicators	5
Managed floating or wide band allowed around a peg	22
Independent floating rate	27
Subtotal, other than pegged	68
Total	154

Source: 1991 International Monetary Fund, *Annual Report,* p. 102.

[1] For analysis of the problems facing developing countries as a result of the decision of many industrialized nations to adopt flexible exchange rates, see Carlos Diaz-Alejandro, "Less Developed Countries and the Post–1971 Financial System," *Princeton Essays in International Finance,* No. 108, April 1975. Also see Stanley Black, "Exchange Policies for Less Developed Countries in a World of Floating Exchange Rates," *Princeton Essays in International Finance,* No. 119, December 1976.

A VERY BRIEF HISTORY OF THE U.S. FLOAT

The March 1973 adoption of flexible exchange rates by the major industrialized countries was widely expected to be temporary. Fixed exchange rates were still viewed as the normal and preferred system, and it was thought that when the floating rates settled in a narrow range they could be re-fixed. The IMF had already begun discussions about how to reform the system through the Committee of Twenty (C-20). It was expected that those discussions would simply proceed under the new temporary arrangements.

The oil embargo of late 1973 and the 1974 increase in the price of oil from $3 to $8 per barrel changed everything. The OPEC countries suddenly had a huge current account surplus (over $70 billion in 1975, declining to the $40 billion range in following years), and there was no way to predict how or where this money would be invested. In light of the payments instability that could result from shifts in OPEC investment patterns, as well as other uncertainties resulting from higher oil prices, it did not appear feasible to return to a set of fixed parities. As a result, flexible exchange rates were accepted as the normal system for industrialized countries, despite widespread opposition among central bankers and finance ministry officials. This change was formalized in amendments to the IMF Articles of Agreement that were adopted in Kingston, Jamaica, in 1976.[2]

The U.S. dollar, which had depreciated in 1973, recovered in the following three years, and the system had settled into a relatively stable pattern by 1975–1976. In 1977, however, a new U.S. secretary of the treasury publicly stated that he thought the dollar was too strong and that it should float down. This unfortunate statement, combined with considerable uncertainty about the new leadership of the Federal Reserve Board, led to a depreciation of the dollar, which came under speculative attack by the summer and fall of 1978. A number of U.S. allies organized a rescue package for the dollar in late 1978, but worsening U.S. inflation continued to create doubts about its future. In late 1979, however, the newly appointed chairman of the Federal Reserve Board, Paul Volcker, presided over a sharp tightening of U.S. monetary policy.

In early 1981, in part because of increasing market confidence that Chairman Volcker's policies would succeed in breaking the U.S. inflation, a large volume of capital began flowing into the United States and the dollar began a long appreciation. By the time it peaked in early 1985, the dollar had appreciated by over 60 percent in nominal effective terms and by approximately 40 percent in real terms. A 40 percent real appreciation of the dollar meant a disastrous decline in the cost and price competitiveness of U.S. firms operating in international markets. Exports declined and imports grew enormously, resulting in huge trade and current account deficits.

---

[2]For a more detailed coverage of the international financial history of this era, see B. Diane Pauls, "U.S. Exchange Rate Policy: Bretton Woods to Present," *Federal Reserve Bulletin,* November 1990, pp. 891–908. See also Robert Solomon, *The International Monetary System, 1945–1976: An Insider's View* (New York: Harper & Row, 1977), Chs. 14–18. For an evaluation of the first decade of flexible exchange rates, see J. Shafer and B. Loopesko, "Floating Exchange Rates after Ten Years," *Brookings Papers on Economic Activity,* No. 1, 1983, pp. 1–86.

This appreciation can be seen as resulting primarily from an extremely unusual set of macroeconomic policies in the United States. The Kemp-Roth tax cut of 1981 combined with a large increase in military expenditures to produce large federal budget deficits. The resulting increase in the U.S. Treasury borrowing coincided with a tight monetary policy, resulting in very high interest rates. These high rates, combined with the widespread conviction that U.S. inflation was being controlled, caused capital inflows that bid the dollar up to levels at which U.S. products were uncompetitive in world markets. Fiscal and monetary policies were being directed in opposite directions, and the result was an exchange rate that severely damaged large parts of the U.S. tradable goods sector. The industrial and agricultural Midwest, which is particularly dependent on export markets, was injured severely by this situation and suffered through a slow recovery from the early 1980s recession. One benefit of the overvalued dollar, however, was that it did force U.S. tradable goods prices down and helped to end the inflation that had plagued the U.S. economy in the late 1970s and early 1980s. For U.S. producers of tradable goods and for their employees, however, this benefit of an overvalued dollar was difficult to appreciate.

In early 1985 the dollar, then widely viewed as overvalued, finally peaked and started to depreciate. This was in part the result of an earlier easing of U.S. monetary policy, which had helped generate a recovery from the 1982 recession. This decline was encouraged by U.S. official intervention in the exchange market, which had been lacking during the period of appreciation. During the first Reagan administration, the Department of the Treasury was committed to a clean float, and exchange market intervention was not used to slow the rise of the dollar. The replacement of Donald Regan by James Baker as secretary of the treasury, however, led to a change of policy and the float became considerably less clean. In late 1985 the new secretary of the treasury met with the finance ministers of the major industrialized countries at the Plaza Hotel in New York, where it was agreed that the dollar was still too high and that coordinated intervention should be used to produce a further depreciation.

The other industrialized countries accepted this view in part because enormous U.S. trade deficits had led to a rapid increase in protectionist sentiment in the United States. It was feared that if the dollar did not fall to levels at which the U.S. trade account could recover, the Congress would pass protectionist legislation with a sufficient majority to override a presidential veto, thus threatening a breakdown of the carefully constructed postwar trading system.

The dollar continued to decline in 1986 and early 1987, leading to another meeting of the finance ministers at the Louvre in Paris, at which it was decided that existing exchange rates were approximately correct and that no further depreciation of the dollar was needed. The goal of intervention, and perhaps of loose coordination of monetary policies, was then to be to stabilize exchange rates at close to existing levels. Despite this intention, the dollar appreciated by over 10 percent in 1988–1989, which was seen as a threat to the further recovery of the U.S. trade balance. In 1989–1990, however, this appreciation was reversed, and by the end of 1990 the dollar had fallen slightly below its 1988 lows. Despite declining U.S. interest rates, the dollar rose slightly during the first part of 1991, perhaps owing to the effect of the rapid conclusion of the Gulf War on market confidence.

Although the dollar began to depreciate in early 1985, the U.S. trade account continued to deteriorate until 1987 and began a slow recovery only in 1988. Economists have usually found that the trade account responds to the exchange rate with a lag of a year or slightly more (the so-called J-curve), but this lag was far longer than expected. The reasons for the length of the lag remain unclear, but the continuing strong recovery of the U.S. economy in 1986–1988 meant growing imports that added to the trade deficit. Perhaps it was more significant that the long period of an overvalued dollar had reduced many industries within the U.S. tradable goods sector to shadows of their former selves. These industries could not respond quickly to the opportunities created by the lower dollar of the late 1980s; thus the recovery of the U.S. trade balance was delayed until they could rebuild productive capacity.

Despite the 1987–1989 recovery, the U.S. trade and current accounts remained in deficit by about $100 billion at the end of the decade. This current account deficit ultimately reflects the gap between U.S. investment needs and extremely low savings rates. As was noted in Chapter 14, the current account surplus is simply the excess of domestic savings over investment, and vice versa. Because of both low private savings rates and enormous federal deficits (public dis-saving), the overall savings rate for the U.S. economy has been only about 15 percent, which is far lower than in competing countries.[3] Even with a modest 17 to 18 percent of GNP being invested in the private sector (and that is gross investment, net investment being far lower), a current account deficit of 2 to 3 percent of GNP has been needed to provide the necessary resources because of the low savings rates.

CONTINUING QUESTIONS ABOUT FLEXIBLE EXCHANGE RATES

As suggested in Chapter 18, flexible exchange rates have not performed as their supporters predicted. The period of almost two decades of floating has produced a number of disappointments, the most important being unexpectedly large volatility in both nominal and real exchange rates. Supporters of this system had widely predicted that nominal rates would move only to approximately offset differing rates of inflation, leaving real exchange rates largely unchanged. This expectation was not realized, and changes in real rates were both large and very disruptive.

Even during the 1970s real exchange rates were far from constant, but the dollar became far more volatile in the 1980s. Between 1973 and 1979 the average real exchange rate change for 16 currencies of industrialized countries was 6.8 percent, but the larger shock was the real appreciation of the dollar by over 40 percent in

---

[3]The behavior of savings rates in the United States and in other industrialized countries is discussed in Harold Rose, *The Question of Savings* (Washington, D.C.: British-North America Committee, National Planning Association, 1991).

1981–1985, followed by an equally large real depreciation in 1985–1988.[4] (See Figures 21-1 to 21-3.)

Real exchange rate movements of these magnitudes are quite disruptive, and there has been a growing desire among central bankers and finance ministry officials to avoid them. A real depreciation raises the prices of tradable goods relative to those of nontradables, thus redistributing income within the economy. The tradables sector gains, at the cost of losses of real income to the nontradables sector. A real appreciation has the opposite effect, as the tradables sector loses real income. The 1981–1985 behavior of the dollar devastated the tradables sector of the U.S. economy, and some of the affected industries have only recently recovered.

This redistribution of incomes can sometimes have sizable regional impacts across an economy. The U.S. Midwest, for example, has a particularly heavy concentration of export industries in both agriculture and manufacturing, so the appreciation of the dollar in the early 1980s was very damaging to that region. As noted in Chapter 17, most of western Canada is oriented toward the production of exports (oil, metals, grain, forest products), whereas Ontario produces more nontradables such as services. Therefore a real depreciation of the Canadian dollar shifts real incomes from Ontario toward the west.

If these movements of real exchange rates were long-run or permanent responses to terms-of-trade movements or changes in competitiveness, they might be accepted as necessary, but it can readily be seen in the graphs presented here that this has not been the case. Large changes in real exchange rates have often been caused

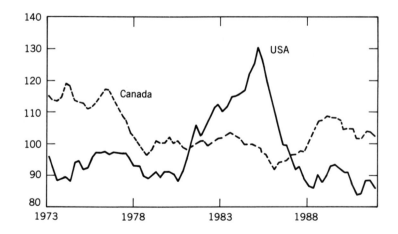

FIGURE 21-1. United States and Canada—Real effective exchange rate. *Source:* Morgan Guaranty Trust.

[4]Pieter Korteweg, "Exchange-Rate Policy, Monetary Policy, and Real Exchange Rate Variability," *Princeton Essays in International Finance,* No. 140, December 1980.

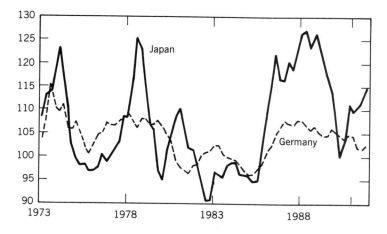

FIGURE 21-2. Germany and Japan—Real effective exchange rate. *Source:* Morgan Guaranty Trust.

by temporary factors and have later been reversed, the rise and fall of the dollar during the 1980s being the most striking example of that pattern.

The widespread desire to avoid or at least limit such real appreciations and depreciations has increasingly constrained national monetary policies, which cancels one of the strongest original arguments for floating exchange rates. The Meade

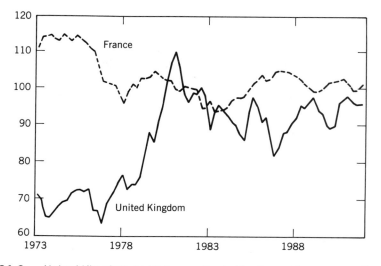

FIGURE 21-3. United Kingdom and France—Real effective exchange rate. *Source:* Morgan Guaranty Trust.

conflict cases, which were discussed in Chapter 16 for a regime of fixed exchange rates, are reappearing in a new form. The desire to limit the depreciation of a currency strongly implies the need for a tighter domestic monetary policy, which may conflict with a domestic goal of macroeconomic expansion. Similarly, a real appreciation could be stopped with an expansionary monetary policy, which could conflict with a desire to control inflation.

If a currency is depreciating when a recession appears to be starting, the central bank faces a clear conflict: The desire to stabilize the exchange rate implies tighter money, whereas the desire to expand the domestic economy implies the opposite. An appreciation during a period in which inflation is a threat creates the same type of conflict.

Under fixed exchange rates, monetary policy had to be managed to avoid unacceptable payments disequilibria, which often meant conflicts with domestic macroeconomic goals. Under flexible exchange rates, monetary policy has to be managed to avoid unacceptable exchange rate volatility, which can also create frequent conflicts with domestic macroeconomic goals. It is not clear that domestic monetary policies are much more independent in a regime of flexible exchange rates than they were under the parities of Bretton Woods.

SOURCES OF REAL RATE VOLATILITY

The reasons for the unexpected volatility of both nominal and real exchange rates are far from clear, but a number of possible explanations have been proposed. It is clear from commercial bank traders that the exchange markets are dominated by capital flows, most of which are short term and speculative in nature. Current account transactions are reportedly responsible for less than 10 percent of all foreign exchange trading in New York. This means that the asset market or portfolio balance approach to exchange markets is more relevant than the more traditional elasticities or absorption approaches. The monetarist model of the balance of payments, which can be viewed as a special case within the asset market approach, produces an important argument for volatility in the form of Dornbusch overshooting, as discussed in Chapter 18. Currency substitution, as discussed in Chapter 15, implies large shifts in relative demands for currencies whenever changes occur in inflationary expectations and in expected real rates of return on money balances. Such changes in desired currency balances could easily produce large exchange rate changes. The stock-adjustment or portfolio balance model of capital flows (Chapter 15), which is also part of the asset market approach to the balance of payments, suggests that when expected yields change, there will be large but temporary flows of capital, which would also imply exchange rate volatility.

Whatever the reasons for large exchange rate movements, the governments of the major industrialized countries have decided that they should be avoided. This decision implies coordinated exchange market intervention and considerably less independence for national monetary policies than was foreseen by academic supporters of flexible exchange rates.

PROTECTIONISM AND FLEXIBLE EXCHANGE RATES

Returning briefly to the subject of protectionism and mercantilism, the adoption of flexible exchange rates has not had the effect of reducing political pressures for restrictions on imports. These pressures have instead worsened. Individual industries are still successful in gaining congressional approval for quotas and other protectionist policies, although recent presidents have vetoed most of the resulting proposals. The fact that protection for one industry produces exchange rate impacts that harm other tradable goods industries is not widely understood, and this argument is seldom raised in political debates over import restrictions. The hope that the existence of flexible exchange rates would discourage or eliminate protectionist campaigns has not been realized.

ALTERNATIVES TO FLEXIBLE EXCHANGE RATES

It is easier to conclude that the existing system of managed floats has performed imperfectly than it is to design an attractive replacement. Widespread unhappiness with the experience of the last two decades has led to a variety of proposals for reform, but none of them has gained sufficient support to threaten current arrangements. It may be worthwhile, however, to review briefly some of the proposals.

Since the exchange rate volatility of recent years has been widely blamed on enormous speculative capital flows, it is occasionally suggested that such transactions be prohibited, taxed, or otherwise discouraged. Exchange market controls could be used to make such capital flows illegal, or an exchange market tax could be used to discourage them.[5] A closely related alternative would be the maintenance of a dual exchange rate, with all capital transactions segregated into a market that operated on the basis of a clean float.[6] Capital flows would then have to balance, meaning that net capital flows would equal zero. A fixed or at least a more stable exchange rate would be maintained for current account transactions. The goal of all such proposals is to protect current transactions, and therefore real economic activity, from shocks resulting from large shifts in the capital account.

All these proposals have at least two major disadvantages. First, international capital flows move a scarce productive resource from less to more productive locations. Prohibiting or discouraging such flows must result in a less efficient allocation of the world's capital stock, thereby making the world economy less productive. Second, exchange controls or taxes on capital account transactions are easily evaded, and the imposition of such systems therefore invites widespread cheating.

---

[5]Such proposals can be found in J. Karekin and N. Wallace, "International Monetary Reform: The Feasible Alternative," *Federal Reserve Bank of Minneapolis Quarterly Review,* Summer 1978, pp. 2–7, and in J. Tobin, "A Proposal for International Monetary Reform" in *Essays in Economics: Theory and Policy* (Cambridge, Mass.: MIT Press, 1982), pp. 488–494.

[6]For a discussion of systems of dual and multiple exchange rate systems, see Susan Collins, "Multiple Exchange Rates, Capital Controls, and Commercial Policy," in R. Dornbusch and L. Holmes, eds., *The Open Economy: Tools for Policy Makers in Developing Countries* (New York: Oxford University Press, 1988), pp. 128–164.

False invoicing or transfer pricing is one of the more obvious ways of moving capital despite such rules. This involves the use of false or misleading prices on international trade transactions in order to move capital. If, for example, an investor in India wants to purchase assets in the United States despite legal prohibitions on such transactions, he could simply understate export prices on invoices. If this investor is exporting garments to the United States which have a value of $250,000 and the investor has a cooperative importer in New York, the invoice may show exports of only $150,000, which is the amount actually remitted back to India. The cooperative importer then invests the other $100,000 in the United States on behalf of the exporter. There is no way of knowing how common such underinvoicing is, but many believe it is a widespread means of evading both exchange controls and ad valorem tariffs. In addition, multinational firms can use it to shift profits from high-tax to low-tax jurisdictions.

Exchange controls have generally been found to become less effective the longer they are in operation because people find more ways to evade them.[7] Dual exchange rates have the same problems because false invoicing can be used to shift capital account transactions into the current account market. When Belgium maintained such a dual rate system, with a higher value for the Belgian franc for current account than for capital transactions, it was widely rumored that Belgium's trade statistics for one year showed imports of eggs from the Netherlands, which exceeded the number of eggs laid by all Dutch hens that year. The story may be apocryphal, but its underlying point is valid; exchange controls or dual exchange rates encourage graft and cheating, and therefore ought to be avoided.

A crawling peg that follows purchasing power parity is sometimes proposed as an alternative to either fully fixed or flexible rates. Under this approach a fixed exchange rate is maintained, but frequent parity changes are made to offset the difference between local and foreign rates of inflation. If, for example, Brazilian prices are rising by 40 percent per year, while inflation in the rest of the world averages 4 percent, the Brazilian government can devalue the currency by 3 percent per month, for an annual total of 36 percent, which equals the difference between local and foreign rates of inflation.

This approach has been used with some success in developing countries with high rates of inflation, but it has the disadvantage of not allowing for other sources of balance-of-payments disequilibria. If differing rates of inflation were the only source of payments problems, this reform proposal would be attractive, but that is obviously not the case. Changing terms of trade, shifts in rates of return to capital, and a variety of other factors affect the balance of payments, and a purchasing power parity crawl does not provide a route to payments adjustment when they occur.

Finally, there is the option of returning to rigidly fixed exchange rates. A few years ago there was considerable public discussion of reviving the gold standard,

---

[7]See the *IMF Survey*, November 24, 1980, p. 372, and V. Argy, "Exchange Rate Management in Theory and Practice," *Princeton Studies in International Finance*, No. 50, October 1982, pp. 77–78.

but that proposal is no longer under active consideration, in part because of fears that unstable gold production in South Africa or Russia could result in unstable monetary policies in the countries that were tied to gold. Ronald McKinnon's proposal for close coordination of monetary policies among the major industrialized countries has received more serious consideration. He would have these countries set target exchange rates based on current purchasing power parities, and then use coordinated shifts in monetary policy to keep market rates close to those parities.[8]

This proposal has disadvantages that are similar to those of the Bretton Woods system. It would leave national central banks with little or no independence in managing domestic aggregate demand, particularly in the Meade conflict cases discussed in Chapter 17. What would the Federal Reserve System do, for example, if the dollar fell significantly below its target parity just as the U.S. economy entered a recession? The coordination rules would call for a tightening of U.S. monetary policy when the domestic economy called for the opposite. It is not clear that such a system of monetary policy coordination could survive a series of such policy conflicts, particularly if they occurred shortly before national elections. It is sometimes suggested facetiously that the major industrialized countries should first coordinate the timing of their elections, perhaps setting them at the same time every four years. Close monetary policy coordination and stable exchange rates could be maintained for three years, with each country being allowed to do whatever it wanted during the year before elections.

The current system of managed floating exchange rates will likely be maintained for the time being, but if exchange rates return to the volatile behavior of the early and mid-1980s, fixed exchange rates could be considered more seriously. Loose and informal coordination of monetary policies and of exchange market intervention will probably continue as a way to reduce exchange rate volatility, with countries being allowed to act more independently if faced with clear conflict situations.

The broad lesson of recent experience is that open economies cannot escape some degree of vulnerability to macroeconomic shocks that originate abroad, and that policy independence will always be partially constrained by balance-of-payments or exchange rate considerations. The only way to avoid these costs of interdependence is to maintain an autarkic economy. The economic performance of countries, such as Albania, that have tried to remain in autarchy suggests the enormous costs of such economic isolation. Trade and other international transactions produce huge efficiency gains and other advantages. Vulnerability to foreign economic shocks and constraints on macroeconomic policies are unavoidable costs of these benefits. Some degree of exchange rate flexibility and modest reforms of the international monetary system can be used to limit these problems, but it does not appear that they can be eliminated.

---

[8]R. I. McKinnon, "Monetary and Exchange Rate Policies for International Financial Stability: A Proposal," *Journal of Economic Perspectives,* Winter 1988, pp. 83–104. See the following comments on the McKinnon article by R. Dornbusch and J. Williamson in the same issue of that journal for doubts about this proposal.

THE EUROPEAN MONETARY SYSTEM

Shortly after the breakdown of the IMF par value system, several European countries began to operate a joint float, a scheme in which they linked their currencies together by limiting the range of exchange rate fluctuation between any two currencies in the group. The result was that the currencies of participating countries moved together vis-à-vis the dollar, rising or falling as a group. The moving band, its width fixed by the permitted range of fluctuation between member currencies, traced a snakelike path as it floated against the dollar; financial journalists promptly dubbed it the European snake.

The active participants in this scheme have varied as countries joined and then withdrew. The joint float led to the creation, in 1979, of a European Monetary System, which was seen as a step in the direction of monetary union. Members agreed to maintain the exchange value of their currencies within $2\frac{1}{4}$ percent of each other (except for Italy, which was allowed a 6 percent range). At present there are nine full members (Belgium, Denmark, France, Ireland, Italy, Germany, Luxembourg, the Netherlands, and the United Kingdom).

The European Monetary System has introduced a new currency, the European Currency Unit (ECU), which is a composite currency (or basket) made up of fixed amounts of the currencies of the participating countries. The hope is that the ECU may eventually become an actual circulating currency and serve as a medium of exchange and a store of value for the European Community. It is, in fact, beginning to be used in a modest way. Some banks accept deposits in ECU, a few bond issues have been denominated in ECU, and tourists can buy ECU traveler's checks. (An ECU traveler's check can be cashed in any of the member currencies, but there is not yet an actual ECU currency, despite its name.)

It now appears that the European Monetary System may indeed evolve into a full monetary union. Monetary policy coordination appears to be far closer than it previously was, and there is increasing discussion in Europe of rigidly fixing internal exchange rates and then of replacing the national currencies with the ECU.[9] Either rigidly fixed rates or a single currency would, of course, eliminate any independence for national monetary policies. A single monetary policy would have to be determined by Community authorities, and it is not yet clear what institutional arrangements will be made to accomplish this step. An EMS board, made up of officials from each of the national central banks, with weighted voting on the basis of the size of national economies, is a likely possibility, but arrangements are not yet settled.

How would this system function if, for example, a recession prevailed in Italy and Spain, leading them to favor an expansionary monetary policy, while Germany

---

[9]For discussions of the current prospects for the European Monetary System, see Horst Unger, "Europe: The Quest for Monetary Integration," *Finance and Development,* December 1990, pp. 14–18. Also see Alberto Giovannini, "The Transition to European Monetary Union," *Princeton Essays in International Finance,* No. 178, November 1990. For an earlier analysis of the prospects for European monetary integration, see J. C. Ingram, "The Case for European Monetary Integration," *Princeton Essays in International Finance,* No. 98, April 1973. For the most recent views on this subject, see Peter B. Kenen, *EMU after Maastricht* (Washington, D.C.: Group of Thirty, 1992).

and the other northern European countries remained more prosperous and favored a tight monetary policy? The policy needed by Italy and Spain would conflict with that desired by other members. Thus, monetary policy would probably be unavailable to deal with Spanish or Italian business cycles. If all members of the bloc experienced the same timing of macroeconomic cycles, an integrated monetary system would present few problems. However, under the more realistic assumption that the phasing of cycles will differ among countries, such integration leaves individual countries unable to use monetary policy to resist recessions.

The question of whether a country or group of countries is the proper size to be an optimum currency area was raised by Robert Mundell in the early 1960s.[10] He argued that a currency bloc should be no larger than the area over which labor was mobile, so that regional recessions could be dealt with through labor moving to where jobs were more plentiful. If France was a currency area, for example, a localized recession in Paris could be handled in part by having people move to other parts of the country. A currency area consisting of the whole continent of Europe, however, faces difficulties because it is hard for workers to move across national boundaries, for example, from Italy to Germany, if there is a recession in the south. Distance and language barriers make such mobility more difficult; Therefore the EMS may be larger than optimum in terms of Mundell's argument.

This problem exists in any geographically large monetary union, including the United States. During the mid-1980s, for example, most of the United States was relatively prosperous, but oil-producing regions such as Texas and Oklahoma were in a serious recession. The fact that the Dallas Federal Reserve Bank is part of a monetary union of 12 districts meant that it was impossible to design a monetary policy that would encourage recovery in Texas without accelerating inflation elsewhere in the country. Since it is difficult or impossible for labor to move quickly from Texas to other parts of the country, the United States may be larger than an optimum currency area in terms of Mundell's argument.

If the European Monetary System does evolve toward a full monetary union, individual member countries are likely to face circumstances similar to those faced by the Dallas Federal Reserve District during the mid-1980s. There are sizable advantages to a European monetary union, including reduced transactions costs for trade and other transactions, more convenient management of EEC institutions and taxes, and the ending of a history of inflation in southern Europe. This approach requires, however, that individual member countries give up all monetary independence, which means the loss of a major domestic macroeconomic tool and a significant part of what has normally been viewed as national sovereignty.

---

[10] R. Mundell, "The Theory of Optimum Currency Areas," *American Economic Review,* September 1961, pp. 657–665. For the argument that an optimum currency area should be considerably larger in order to encourage stability in the price system, see R. I. McKinnon, "Optimum Currency Areas," *American Economic Review,* September 1963, pp. 717–725.

CHANGES IN THE ROLE OF THE SDR

The 1976 amendments to the Articles of Agreement of the IMF included changes in the definition of the SDR and in the interest rate charged for its use. Originally, the SDR was defined as the gold content of one U.S. dollar, but that definition became unacceptable to other countries when the link to gold was cut. The SDR is now equal to a basket of the five currencies that are most important in world trade. At present the value of an SDR equals the following amounts of each of the five currencies:

U.S. dollar	0.5720
Deutsche mark	0.4530
French franc	0.8000
Japanese yen	31.8000
Pound sterling	0.0812

Source: IMF Survey, September 1991, p.8.

The interest rate that is applied to countries using their SDR allocations is a weighted average of short-term yields in the five countries whose currencies make up the SDR. New allocations of SDRs occurred in 1979, 1980, and 1981, but there have been none since then. When U.S. inflation was very serious in the late 1970s and early 1980s, there was some thought that the SDR would replace the dollar as the dominant reserve asset, but the return to relative price stability in the United States has restored the dollar to its previous position as a widely acceptable reserve asset, and the SDR has not become as important in the international financial system as was expected a few years ago. An appendix to this chapter provides further information on the various activities and functions of the International Monetary Fund.

LATIN AMERICAN DEBTS AND U.S. BANKS

The Latin American debt crisis, which was a dominant topic of discussion in international economics a few years ago, has faded somewhat from public and professional consciousness, but the problem remains serious and deserves brief coverage here.[11]

Latin American countries have frequently had problems meeting debt repayment schedules; U.S. banks have a long history of absorbing loan losses in that part of the world. The 1980s experience, however, was far worse than anything experienced earlier. A number of Latin American countries borrowed heavily from banks in the

---

[11]There is an enormous literature on the subject of the LDC debt crisis, but one useful gathering of papers on the subject is J. Sachs, ed., *Developing Country Debt and Economic Performance: The International Financial System* (Chicago: University of Chicago Press, published for the National Bureau of Economic Research, 1989). See also B. Eichengreen, "Historical Research on International Lending," *Journal of Economic Perspectives,* Spring 1991, pp. 149–170.

United States and elsewhere in the late 1970s and early 1980s, with the total of such debts exceeding $300 billion by 1982 when the lending slowed. The largest debtors were Brazil and Mexico, but others such as Argentina, Peru, and Venezuela borrowed far more than was prudent. At the end of 1989, Brazil was indebted in the amount of $115 billion, Mexico $97 billion, and Argentina $60 billion, with considerably more than half of all these debts being owed to private banks.

Most of the debtor countries were able to meet interest payments and avoid serious problems in the 1970s, but in the early 1980s they became unable to meet debt-servicing schedules, and the problem became a crisis in 1982. A variety of plans (Baker, Brady, etc.) have been proposed to solve or at least ease the problem, but success has been limited, and many countries are still not current on interest payments. Mexico, Venezuela, and Chile are all doing quite well, but Brazil (the largest single debtor), Argentina, Peru, and Ecuador are all badly in arrears. The 1990 increase in the price of oil made it easier for Mexico and Venezuela to meet payment schedules but worsened the situation for Brazil and other debtors that import large amounts of oil.

These debts have been a serious problem for the United States because they have threatened the financial stability or perhaps even the solvency of some large U.S. banks. Many of these institutions made loans in Latin America whose total amounts approached or equaled their net worth. Hence, if all these loans went into default, the net worth of the banks would be destroyed, and they might become candidates for closure by the Federal Deposit Insurance Company. Debt rescheduling, writeoffs, and other arrangements have eased this problem for some banks, but it remains a threat for others. A number of Japanese banks have also absorbed large losses on loans to Latin American countries.

This indebtedness also requires that Latin American governments adopt adjustment policies that are politically unpopular at best. As shown in Chapters 16 and 17, the policies necessary to produce a major improvement in a country's trade account are often painful. Many Latin American countries had to live with such policies throughout the 1980s, resulting in a decade of little or no growth, and of deteriorating economic and social conditions.

Causes of the Debt Crisis

The causes of the debt crisis of the 1980s begin with the OPEC price shocks of the 1970s. A number of oil importers such as Brazil and Chile found that their trade accounts deteriorated badly when oil prices rose, and they decided to borrow to finance these costs rather than undertake painful payments adjustment policies. The surplus oil-producing countries of the Middle East had large current account surpluses to invest and placed much of this money in U.S. and British banks. The banks needed borrowers for these funds just when nonoil LDCs wanted to borrow, with the result that imprudent loans were made.

Oil producers such as Mexico and Venezuela decided to accelerate their development plans on the basis of prospective increases in oil revenues and were viewed as excellent credit risks by the banks. They spent even more than their extra oil income and borrowed the difference. Later, when oil prices fell in the mid-1980s, they were unable to meet repayment schedules.

The prices of most raw materials were quite firm through the mid-1970s, which made it possible for countries such as Brazil to survive higher oil prices, but primary product prices started to decline in the late 1970s, making the situation of countries such as Brazil far worse. IMF data indicate that the terms of trade of primary product producers declined by about 40 percent between 1975–1979 and 1987.[12]

Increased interest costs on floating rate loans were another major problem for debtor countries. The post-1965 inflation had made banks very wary about making loans at fixed interest rates for long periods of time, so credits to developing countries typically had adjustable or floating interest rates. Because most loans were tied to Eurodollar deposit rates (LIBOR, the London Interbank Offer Rate, which is the interest rate on interbank dollar deposits in London), the cost of servicing them rose or fell with monetary conditions in the United States and Europe. The tightening of monetary policy by the U.S. Federal Reserve System at the beginning of the 1980s was very expensive for countries such as Brazil. LIBOR, which had been as low as 6 percent in 1976, reached 18 percent in 1981–1982. Every percentage point rise in interest rates cost Brazil an additional $700 million and Latin America as a whole, an extra $2,500 million per year.[13]

The fiscal, monetary, and exchange rate policies that were maintained in Latin American countries during the 1970s and 1980s were another major contributor to the crisis. Most of these countries have a long history of large government budget deficits, which are financed by the central bank, that is, monetized. The resulting inflation quickly causes current account deficits, and foreign loans are sought as a way to avoid painful payments adjustment. Devaluations are delayed even though the currency is obviously overvalued, which worsens the current account deficit and increases the need for external borrowing. IMF austerity programs are badly needed in such countries, but they are very unpopular and so governments resist them. Borrowing from New York banks was frequently seen as a way of avoiding going to the IMF, where difficult conditionality requirements would be imposed.

The flight of private capital from Latin America to what were viewed as safer investment climates was another reason for the debt crisis. One study concluded that $61 billion left Argentina, Mexico, Peru, Uruguay, and Venezuela during the 1974–1982 period. This is 40 percent of the total foreign borrowing by these countries during that eight-year period.[14]

Finally, there is the question of why supposedly sophisticated and knowledgeable bankers in New York (and London and Tokyo) lent such vast sums of money to

---

[12]R. Dornbusch, in J. Sachs, ed., *Developing Country Debt and Economic Performance,* pp. 354–355.

[13]Ibid, pp. 336 and 353.

[14]J. Cuddington, "Capital Flight: Estimates, Issues, and Explanations," *Princeton Studies in International Finance,* No. 58, December 1986, pp. 6–7. See also D. Lessard and J. Williamson, *Capital Flight and Third World Debt* (Washington, D.C.: Institute for International Economics, 1987).

countries with a poor history of debt repayment and weak economies. Many of the same banks made large loans to these countries in the 1920s and absorbed massive losses on those loans in the 1930s. Institutional memories appear to be surprisingly short.

Lending to foreign governments has always been particularly risky because the lender cannot foreclose on real assets if the loan goes into default. The early history of banking is full of failures caused by kings failing to pay foreign bankers who had no way to force repayment. Unfortunately, it seems that each generation of bankers has to relearn these lessons.[15]

Possible Solutions

Unfortunately, there are no easy solutions for the problem of Latin American debts. Many U.S. and foreign banks have written off large amounts of these loans, and further writeoffs are likely. A few countries, such as Chile and Mexico, have managed their economies well in recent years and now have a good chance of reducing their indebtedness to reasonable levels. Others, such as Peru, seem to have made little progress. IMF-designed austerity programs (devaluations combined with tight fiscal and monetary policies), though helpful, are painful and politically unpopular.

Debt/equity swaps are a recent innovation that has made a modest contribution to the progress of some countries. In such a swap, a bank sells its financial claim on a Latin American government for dollars at a sizable discount (often 30 to 50 percent) to a private firm. This firm then sells the debt back to the Latin American government for local currency, which it uses to cover the costs of a direct investment.

A Japanese car company, for example, might buy $40 million in Mexican debt from Sumitomo Bank for $24 million. The car company then sells the debt to the government of Mexico for Mexican pesos worth $40 million (or perhaps less) at the current exchange rate. The pesos are then used to pay the local costs of building a car parts factory in Mexico, which is used to supply Japanese-owned factories in the United States. The Japanese bank gets partial repayment in hard currency, Mexico is able to repay its loan in pesos, and the car company gets a parts factory in Mexico at a discount. A number of these swaps have been done, but they cannot be sufficient to deal with debts of the volume of those in Latin America. Another policy option that would provide some help is discussed in Exhibit 21-1.

The likely outcome is a long, painful period in which Latin America lives with more macroeconomic austerity than it would prefer, U.S. and other foreign banks absorb more writeoffs in the weakest countries, and the banks develop a stronger institutional memory. It should not be necessary for every generation of bankers to relearn the lesson that lending to foreign governments, particularly in developing countries, is extremely risky.

---

[15]For a discussion of the tendency of bankers to underestimate the riskiness of foreign lending, see J. Guttentag and R. Herring, "Disaster Myopia in International Lending," *Princeton Essays in International Finance,* No. 164, September 1986.

How to Help Latin Debtor Nations

The enormous Latin American loan writeoffs by Citibank, Chase Manhattan and other New York banks, combined with earlier moratoriums on interest payments by Brazil and Ecuador, make it abundantly clear that attempts by the International Monetary Fund and the Administration to deal with the debt crisis have failed. The Baker Plan, which has been comatose for months, is now dead. It should be obvious to even the most optimistic officials that new policies are needed.

Latin American debtor countries must increase their export revenues sharply if interest payments are to be made and if there is to be any hope of reducing outstanding loan balances. Although austerity and devaluations have improved trade performance in many countries, the human costs have been far too large for this approach to be sustained. Something else is needed to help these countries sharply increase export revenues. While useful and even necessary, austerity and exchange rate adjustments are not sufficient.

My suggestion is that we shift our import markets toward debtor countries. In theory, the United States does not have bilateral trade policies but instead maintains a uniform multinational trade policy that treats all exporting countries equally. Actual trade policies are, however, very different. A variety of quota arrangements are used to allocate market shares among exporters; these quotas should now be shifted toward those countries that need additional export revenues to make debt payments, and away from countries that lack debt problems or have sizable trade surpluses.

The arrangements for textiles and garments are probably the largest available target for such reallocation. Under this system, which has operated since the early 1970's, United States imports of textiles and gar-ments are limited by annual volume, and the right to export individual items to this market is divided among exporting countries on the basis of historic market shares. Since American prices for these products are considerably higher than those prevailing in world markets, exporters who receive quota allocations earn large windfall profits. There's almost universal agreement among economists that this quota system is absurd, but it is far too well entrenched and too popular to be abandoned.

If Washington is going to allocate shares of what amount to windfall profits among textile exporters, why not shift them to countries that need additional export revenues to make debt payments?

Taiwan, with a 1986 trade surplus of $15 billion and foreign exchange reserves of about $50 billion, enjoys a large quota allocation and, consequently, reaps sizable windfall profits in our textile market. Brazil is also an efficient exporter of textiles and garments, so part of Taiwan's quota might be shifted to Brazil in order to improve debt repayment prospects. Such reallocations of textile quotas should be carried out over a number of years to allow both those countries losing quotas and those gaining them to adjust to the new market situation.

Changes in textile and garment quotas alone would not be sufficient to make a major impact on Latin American debt, but similar quotas in other product areas could be reallocated. Brazil and Mexico, for example, could receive larger steel quotas at the expense of countries in Europe and Asia. Coffee and sugar imports are also controlled by quotas that might be shifted toward debtor countries.

There are two problems with this policy change. First, it implies acceptance of quotas as a way of regulating trade, which contradicts the overwhelming view among economists that quotas are the worst form of trade policy. But since we already insist on maintaining quotas for products such as textiles and steel, we should at least allocate them on the basis of need for export revenues to repay debts.

The second problem is that this policy would send a message to developing countries that the only way to maintain favored access to the United States market is to be heavily in debt. American bankers would therefore have to be told to avoid becoming overextended in a new group of developing countries. After their unhappy experiences so far, the bankers' motto should be "once burned, twice warned."

EXHIBIT 21-1.   *Source:* From *The New York Times*, Robert M. Dunn, Jr., ©The New York Times, Op. Ed. page, June 26, 1987. Reprinted by permission.

PROSPECTIVE ISSUES DURING THE REMAINDER OF THE 1990S

The disintegration of the Soviet bloc and of the USSR itself has created international financial problems as well as opportunities. One question is how the new countries are to be integrated into the world financial system.[16] For reasons that are not entirely clear, the Bush administration resisted full IMF and World Bank membership for what remains of the USSR until early 1992. The IMF would appear to be the obvious source of technical advice and loans during the restructuring of the Soviet economy. One strategy for the United States would have been to insist on a full membership in the Fund and on the acceptance of a standard stabilization program by Moscow before more large-scale aid from the industrialized countries were made available.

It has been fairly standard practice for developing countries in financial trouble to be told to arrange a drawing from the IMF with the associated conditionality requirements before further help is forthcoming from the industrialized countries. This approach would appear to be relevant to Moscow. Despite the lack of full Russian membership in the World Bank and the Fund, planning for the restructuring of the Russian financial system and economy already involves a major role for both institutions. The financial requirements for reconstructing the economies of Russia, the new countries emerging from what was the USSR, and other Eastern European countries will be enormous, which leads to the issue of a shortage of world savings.

It was noted in Chapters 12 and 14 that one group of countries can invest more than they save only if they can run current account deficits, which requires that the rest of the world run a current account surplus and save more than it invests. The 1990s appears to be a decade in which a large number of countries should be in the first situation, but in which there is a decided lack of countries in the second

---

[16]For a discussion of possible domestic and international monetary arrangements for Russia and the rest of what was the USSR, see O. Havrylyshyn and J. Williamson, *From Soviet Disunion to Eastern Economic Community?* (Washington, D.C.: Institute for International Economics, 1991).

situation. There does not appear to be a sufficient volume of excess savings in the industrialized countries to provide for the needs of both Eastern Europe and the developing world.

During the 1980s the United States ran large current account deficits and invested more than it saved, which produced a sufficient shortage of savings in world financial markets to result in high real interest rates and great difficulty for many LDCs in attracting enough capital to maintain normal growth rates. At least during that decade, however, Germany ran large surpluses and Eastern Europe was not a huge net borrower. Germany will now need all the savings it can produce in its western sector to finance the reconstruction of its new eastern sector, making it unlikely that Germany as a whole will run current account surpluses during the remainder of the decade. It is far more likely that Germany will run current account deficits, which it will finance by selling some of its previously accumulated net creditor position. Germany's situation eliminates one major lender from world financial markets. In addition, Poland, Hungary, and the other countries of Eastern Europe will be borrowing massive sums, as will Russia and the other countries emerging from the USSR.

This situation raises the question of whether any funds and resources will be available for Latin America, Africa, and the poorer parts of Asia. A period of very tight world capital markets appears to be likely. This situation would be eased, of course, if the United States would cease saving less than it invests and running a current account deficit. The world financial system will function far better during the remainder of this decade if the United States returns to its role during the 1950s and 1960s of saving more than it invests, running a current account surplus, and lending to the rest of the world.

Another continuing issue will be the desire of the major industrialized countries both to avoid exchange rate volatility and to maintain the ability to manage national monetary policies that are targeted at domestic macroeconomic stability. As has been argued earlier in this book, there is an inherent conflict between the goals of exchange rate stability (or balance-of-payments equilibrium) and truly independent monetary policies. The industrialized countries very much want to avoid the exchange rate volatility of the 1980s, which implies coordinated monetary policies. If their business cycle patterns differ, such coordination will be difficult, particularly as national elections approach. The conflict between internal and external balance still exists, and it is likely to be seen again whenever a major industrialized country such as the United States faces a recession when its currency is depreciating, or wants to restrain inflationary pressures when its currency is appreciating.

Finally, there is the broader issue of whether the U.S. economy will remain as closely tied to that of the rest of the world as it became during the 45 years after World War II. American voters accepted the need for foreign aid expenditures, trade liberalization, the maintenance of armed forces abroad, support for the World Bank, the IMF, and other international agencies, and a variety of other expensive international programs because of the cold war. As long as the USSR was perceived as a major threat to the United States, American taxpayers were willing to spend large sums of money and undertake other difficult policies to contain Moscow.

Now that the threat is gone, some American commentators are suggesting a return to the relative isolationism of the period before World War II. This is still a small minority view, but it may become harder to convince American voters of the need to spend money on foreign aid, undertake painful trade liberalization policies, and generally remain actively involved in the world economy now that Moscow is no longer a serious threat.

Many developing countries probably miss the cold war, because it allowed them to attract attention and foreign aid from both sides of the conflict. It is not clear just how interested the United States will remain in the problems of the Third World now that the former USSR is no longer competing for its allegiance. An interesting paradox in this situation is that ten years ago the USSR would have been overjoyed if the United States had withdrawn from involvement with the rest of the world. Now Russia and its neighbors need U.S. help and therefore would prefer that the United States resist any temptation to return to isolationism. One can only hope that American taxpayers and voters will realize that this country has responsibilities and interests in the rest of the world that go beyond the cold war and that a return to isolationism would therefore be very unwise.

QUESTIONS FOR STUDY AND REVIEW

1. The United States has allowed the dollar to float since 1973, yet the United States has reported large balance-of-payments deficits on a reserve settlements basis. What is the explanation for this apparent paradox?

2. "If nations have different rates of inflation, then exchange rates between their currencies cannot remain fixed." Do you agree? Explain.

3. What are the principal objections to (or arguments against) a system of floating exchange rates? How do these stand up in the light of experience with floating rates since 1973?

4. Exchange rate fluctuations since 1973 appear to be larger than warranted by the underlying economic circumstances in the nations involved. What reasons have been offered to explain this experience?

5. From 1965 to 1981, the price level in Switzerland rose from 100 to 150, while the U.S. price level tripled (rising from 100 to 300). If the exchange rate in 1965 was SW Fr 4 = $1.00, approximately what would you expect it to be in 1981? Explain why.

6. Academic supporters of flexible exchange rates began the 1970s with some strong expectations as to how that system would operate. Which of those expectations have and have not been realized?

7. "Flexible exchange rates, like democracy, is not the best system; it is merely the least bad." Explain.

8. How can central banks be caught in a new version of the Meade conflict cases under floating exchange rates?

9. On what grounds might one conclude that the current membership of the European Monetary System is too large to be an optimum currency area?

10. "Latin America lived very well in the 1970s, but the region paid for its sins in the 1980s." Explain. Who else paid for those sins?

SELECTED REFERENCES

Branson, W. "Exchange Rate Policy after a Decade of Floating." In J. Bilson and R. Marston, eds. *Exchange Rate Theory and Practice*. Chicago: University of Chicago Press, 1984.

Collins, S. "Multiple Exchange Rates, Capital Controls, and Commercial Policy." In R. Dornbusch, *The Open Economy: Tools for Policy Makers in Developing Countries*. New York: Oxford University Press, 1988.

Cuddington, J. "Capital Flight: Estimates, Issues, and Estimates." *Princeton Study in International Finance,* No. 58, December 1986.

Giovannine, A. "The Transition to European Monetary Union." *Princeton Essays in International Finance,* No. 178, November 1990.

IMF *Annual Report*. Washington, D.C.: International Monetary Fund, 1990.

McKinnon, R. "Monetary and Exchange Rate Policy for International Financial Stability: A Proposal." *Journal of Economic Perspectives,* Winter 1988.

Pauls, B. Diane. "U.S. Exchange Rate Policy: Bretton Woods to Present." *Federal Reserve Bulletin,* November 1990, pp. 891–908.

Sachs, J., ed. *Developing Country Debt and Economic Performance: The International Financial System*. Chicago: University of Chicago Press, 1989.

Shafer, J., and B. Loopesko. "Floating Exchange Rates after Ten Years." *Brookings Papers in Economic Activity,* No. 1, 1983, pp. 1–86.

Williamson, J. *The Exchange Rate System*. Washington, D.C.: Institute for International Economics, 1983.

World Bank, *World Debt Tables*. Washington, D.C.: World Bank, 1989.

IMF SURVEY

Supplement on the I.M.F.
A Publication of the International Monetary Fund
September 1991[1]

IMF FACILITIES AND POLICIES ARE ADAPTED IN RESPONSE TO MIDDLE EAST CRISIS

During 1990/91, IMF membership increased by four countries—the Republic of Bulgaria, the Czech and Slovak Federal Republic, the Mongolian People's Republic, and Namibia—to 155. At the same time, the IMF adapted its facilities and policies to help its members cope with the effects of the Middle East crisis, and committed a total of SDR 5.6 billion to support macroeconomic and structural policies in member countries. In addition, the IMF continued to implement the strengthened cooperative strategy for resolving members' arrears problems. In June 1990, two members—Guyana and Honduras—cleared their overdue obligations.

At the 1990 Annual Meetings, Governors requested the Executive Board to explore ways in which the IMF could assist members most severely affected by events in the Middle East. In response, the IMF modified a number of facilities and policies, as follows:

• the amount of financing available to members under arrangements was modified or rephased, as appropriate, to take into account the effects of developments in the Middle East on member countries;

• the lower annual, three-year, and cumulative borrowing limits under the enlarged access policy were suspended until December 31, 1991;

• total financing available under the enhanced structural adjustment facility (ESAF) may be increased at the time of the midterm reviews of such arrangements;

• a fourth year of ESAF support will be permitted for countries that complete their current ESAF arrangements before November 1992;

• an oil import element was introduced into the compensatory financing facility until the end of 1991 to compensate for sharp, unexpected increases in oil and natural gas import costs;

• the coverage of compensatory financing under the compensatory and contingency financing facility (CCFF) was expanded to include losses resulting from shortfalls in receipts from pipelines, canals, shipping, transportation, construction, and insurance;

• an external contingency mechanism may be attached to stand-by and extended arrangements at the time of a review, provided it is done at least six months before the expiration of the underlying arrangement.

IMF PROVIDES FINANCIAL ASSISTANCE TO OVERCOME BALANCE OF PAYMENTS DIFFICULTIES

Tranche Policies

First credit tranche. Member demonstrates reasonable efforts to overcome balance of payments difficulties in program. Performance criteria and purchase installments not used. Repurchases are made in 3 ¼ –5 years.

Upper credit tranches. Member must have a substantial and viable program to overcome its balance of payments difficulties. Resources normally provided in the form of standby arrangements that include performance criteria and purchases in installments. Repurchases are made in 3 ¼–5 years.

Extended Fund Facility

Medium-term program aims at overcoming structural balance of payments maladjustments. A program generally lasts for three years, although it may be lengthened to four years, where this would facilitate sustained policy implementation and achievement of balance of payments viability over the medium term. Program states policies and measures for first 12-month period in detail. Resources are provided in the form of extended arrangements that include performance criteria and drawings in installments; repurchases are made in 4 ½–10 years.

Enlarged Access Policy

Augments resources available under stand-by and extended arrangements. Applicable policies on conditionality, phasing, and performance criteria are the same as under the credit tranches and the extended Fund facility. Repurchases are made in 3 ½–7 years, and charges are based on the Fund's borrowing costs.

Structural Adjustment Facility (SAF)

Resources are provided on concessional terms to low-income developing member countries facing protracted balance of payments problems, in support of medium-term macroeconomic and structural adjustment programs. Member develops, and updates, with assistance of the Fund and the World Bank, a medium-term policy framework for a three-year period, which is set out in a policy framework paper (PFP). Detailed annual programs are formulated prior to disbursement of annual loans, and include quarterly benchmarks to assess performance. Repayments are made in 5 ½–10 years.

Enhanced Structural Adjustment Facility

Objectives, eligibility, and basic program features of this facility parallel those of the SAF; differences relate to provisions for access, monitoring, and funding. A PFP and a detailed annual program are prepared each year. Arrangements include quarterly benchmarks, semiannual performance criteria, and, in most cases, a midyear review. Adjustment measures are expected to be particularly strong, aiming to foster growth and to achieve a substantial strengthening of the balance of payments position. Loans are disbursed semiannually, and repayments are made in 5 ½–10 years.

Compensatory and Contingency Financing Facility

The compensatory element provides resources to a member for an export shortfall or an excess in cereal import costs that is due to factors largely beyond the member's control. The contingency element helps members with IMF-supported adjustment programs to maintain the momentum of adjustment efforts in the face of a broad range of unanticipated, adverse external shocks. Repurchases are made in 3 ¼–5 years.

Buffer Stock Financing Facility

Resources help finance a member's contribution to an approved international buffer stock. Repurchases are made in 3 ¼–5 years.

Financial Support

The IMF approved 20 new arrangements during 1990/91, including 13 stand-by arrangements; 2 extended arrangements; and 2 arrangements under the structural adjustment facility (SAF) and 3 arrangements under the ESAF. In addition, 11 countries made drawings under the CCFF totaling SDR 2.1 billion. Commitments to 5 Eastern European countries accounted for almost two thirds of the IMF's total commitments during 1990/91.

Ninth Quota Review

In June 1990, the Board of Governors authorized an increase of 50 percent in IMF quotas, to approximately SDR 135.2 billion. (Following the adoption of this resolution and the subsequent membership of four additional countries, total quotas will increase to about SDR 136.7 billion.) The increase will not come into effect before the Third Amendment of the IMF's Articles of Agreement, which will provide for the suspension of voting and related rights of members that do not fulfill their obligations.

IMF BOARD OF GOVERNORS EXERCISES MANY POWERS THROUGH EXECUTIVE BOARD

The organizational structure of the IMF is set out in its Articles of Agreement, which provide for a Board of Governors, an Executive Board, a Managing Director, a staff of international civil servants, and, potentially, a Council.

The highest authority of the IMF is the Board of Governors, which consists of a Governor and an Alternate appointed by each of the IMF's member countries (155 countries as of September 1, 1991). The Governors are usually ministers of finance or central bank governors, but sometimes hold other positions of ministerial or comparable rank.

The Articles, as amended in 1978, provide that the Board of Governors may establish a Council as a permanent body of the IMF at the ministerial or comparable level to supervise the management and adaptation of the international monetary system and to consider any proposals to amend the Articles of Agreement. The Board of Governors has not established a Council, but has continued to rely on the Interim Committee, which was established at the 1974 Annual Meetings.

The Interim Committee, a temporary advisory body, has a composition and scope of concern comparable with those contemplated for the Council but does not have decision-making authority under the IMF's Articles. A second advisory body, the Joint Ministerial Committee on the Transfer of Real Resources to Developing Countries (the Development Committee), was also established in 1974 by the Boards of Governors of the IMF and the World Bank to consider development issues.

The Board of Governors meets once a year at the Annual Meetings to review the work of the IMF, but may meet or vote by mail at other times. It has delegated many of its powers to the Executive Board, which conducts the IMF's day-to-day business. The Executive Board is in continuous session at IMF headquarters in Washington. The Executive Board, which was originally (in 1946) composed of 12 Executive Directors, has increased in size with the growth of the IMF's membership, and today consists of 22 Executive Directors. At present, 6 Executive Directors are appointed by individual countries: France, Germany, Japan, Saudi Arabia, the United Kingdom, and the United States. The other 16 Executive Directors are elected by groups of the remaining members.

The Executive Board deals with a wide variety of policy, operational, and administrative

matters, which include surveillance of members' exchange rate policies, provision of IMF financial assistance to member countries, consultations with members, and comprehensive studies on important issues.

The Executive Board also selects the Managing Director of the IMF, who serves as its Chairman. The Managing Director, under the direction of the Executive Board, conducts the ordinary business of the IMF.

MEMBERS' QUOTAS GUIDE
THEIR ACCESS TO IMF RESOURCES

Each member of the IMF has a quota, expressed in SDRs, that is equal to its subscription in the IMF. The quota, which reflects the relative size of the member's economy, is the most fundamental element in its financial and organizational relations with the IMF. It determines a member's voting power in the IMF, which is based on 1 vote for each SDR 100,000 of its quota plus the 250 basic votes to which each member is entitled. Each member's quota also determines its access to the financial resources of the IMF, and its share in allocations of SDRs by the IMF. A member is generally required to pay 25 percent of any increase in its quota in SDRs or in currencies of other members selected by the IMF, with their concurrence; it pays the remainder in its own currency.

Initial Quotas

The initial quotas of the original members of the IMF were related to, but not strictly determined by, the Bretton Woods formula, which included such basic variables as average import and export flows, gold holdings and dollar balances, and national income. This formula served as the basis for determining initial quotas of new members until the early 1960s.

In April 1963, a number of other quota formulas were introduced, which, taken together, were used to determine initial quotas of new members and increases in quotas. These formulas employ economic data relating to GDP, current account transactions, the variability of current receipts, and official reserves.

Quotas of New Members

When a country applies for IMF membership, the IMF staff makes a quota calculation for the new member and compares it with the quota calculations and other relevant data of existing members of comparable economic size and characteristics. The staff then prepares a paper for the consideration of a committee of the Executive Board. After the country has agreed to the proposed terms and conditions for membership—including the amount of the initial quota proposed by the committee and the proportion of the applicant's subscription to be paid in reserve assets—the full Executive Board considers the committee's recommendations and, upon its approval, forwards a proposed membership resolution to the IMF's Board of Governors. After the membership resolution is approved by the Board of Governors and appropriate legal and procedural steps are effected, the country signs the Articles of Agreement and becomes a member.

As of September 1, 1991, 155 countries were members of the IMF, and total quotas amounted to SDR 91.1 billion. The newest member, the Mongolian People's Republic, joined the IMF in February 1991. It became the fourth member to join the IMF during the past 12 months; the others were Republic of Bulgaria, the Czech and Slovak Federal Republic, and Namibia. Applications for membership have been received from Albania, Switzerland, and the U.S.S.R.; these applications are being processed.

CURRENT AND PROPOSED IMG QUOTAS
(million SDRs)

Member	Current	Proposed	Member	Current	Proposed	Member	Current	Proposed
Afghanistan	86.7	120.4	Greece	399.9	587.6	Paraguay	48.4	72.1
Algeria	623.1	914.4	Grenada	6.0	8.5	Peru	330.9	466.1
Angola	145.0	207.3	Guatemala	108.0	153.8	Philippines	440.4	633.4
Antigua and Barbuda	5.0	8.5	Guinea	57.9	78.7	Poland	680.0	988.5
			Guinea-Bissau	7.5	10.5	Portugal	376.6	557.6
Argentina	1,113.0	1,537.1	Guyana	49.2	67.2	Qatar	114.9	190.5
Australia	1,619.2	2,333.2	Haiti	44.1	60.7	Romania	523.4	754.1
Austria	775.6	1,188.3	Honduras	67.8	95.0	Rwanda	43.8	59.5
Bahamas, The	66.4	94.9	Hungary	530.7	754.8	St. Kitts & Nevis	4.5	6.5
Bahrain	48.9	82.8	Iceland	59.6	85.3	St. Lucia	7.5	11.0
Bangladesh	287.5	392.5	India	2,207.7	3,055.5	St. Vincent & Grenadines	4.0	6.0
Barbados	34.1	48.9	Indonesia	1,009.7	1,497.6			
Belgium	2,080.4	3,102.3	Iran	660.0	1,078.5	Sao Tome & Principe	4.0	5.5
Belize	9.5	13.5	Iraq	504.0	864.8			
Benin	31.3	45.3	Ireland	343.4	525.0	Saudi Arabia	3,202.4	5,130.6
Bhutan	2.5	4.5	Israel	446.6	666.2	Senegal	85.1	118.9
Bolivia	90.7	126.2	Italy	2,909.1	4,590.7	Seychelles	3.0	6.0
Botswana	22.1	36.6	Jamaica	145.5	200.9	Sierra Leone	57.9	77.2
Brazil	1,461.3	2,170.8	Japan	4,223.3	8,241.5	Singapore	92.4	357.6
Bulgaria[1]	310.0	464.9	Jordan	73.9	121.7	Solomon Islands	5.0	7.5
Burkina Faso	31.6	44.2	Kenya	142.0	199.4	Somalia	44.2	60.9
Burundi	42.7	57.2	Kiribati, Republic of	2.5	4.0	South Africa	915.7	1,365.4
Cambodia	25.0	25.0				Spain	1,286.0	1,935.4
Cameroon	92.7	135.1	Korea	462.8	799.6	Sri Lanka	223.1	303.6
Canada	2,941.0	4,320.3	Kuwait	635.3	995.2	Sudan	169.7	233.1
Cape Verde	4.5	7.0	Lao People's Dem. Rep.	29.3	39.1	Suriname	49.3	67.6
Central African Rep.	30.4	41.2				Swaziland	24.7	36.5
			Lebanon	78.7	146.0	Sweden	1,064.3	1,614.0
Chad	30.6	41.3	Lesotho	15.1	23.9	Syrian Arab Republic	139.1	209.9
Chile	440.5	621.7	Liberia	71.3	96.2			
China	2,390.9	3,385.2	Libya	515.7	817.6	Tanzania	107.0	146.9
Colombia	394.2	561.3	Luxembourg	77.0	135.5	Thailand	386.6	573.9
Comoros	4.5	6.5	Madagascar	66.4	90.4	Togo	38.4	54.3
Congo, People's Rep. of	37.3	57.9	Malawi	37.2	50.9	Tonga	3.25	5.0
			Malaysia	550.6	832.7	Trinidad and Tobago	170.1	246.8
Costa Rica	84.1	119.0	Maldives	2.0	5.5			
Côte d'Ivoire	165.5	238.2	Mali	50.8	68.9	Tunisia	138.2	206.0
Cyprus	69.7	100.0	Malta	45.1	67.5	Turkey	429.1	642.0
Czechoslovakia[1]	590.0	847.0	Mauritania	33.9	47.5	Uganda	99.6	133.9
Denmark	711.0	1,069.9	Mauritius	53.6	73.3	United Arab Emirates	202.6	392.1
Djibouti	8.0	11.5	Mexico	1,165.5	1,753.3			
Dominica	4.0	6.0	Mongolia[1]	25.0	37.1	United Kingdom	6,194.0	7,414.6
Dominican Republic	112.1	158.8	Morocco	306.6	427.7	United States	17,918.3	26,526.8
			Mozambique	61.0	84.0	Uruguay	163.8	225.3
Ecuador	150.7	219.2	Myanmar	137.0	184.9	Vanuatu	9.0	12.5
Egypt	463.4	678.4	Namibia[1]	70.0	99.6	Venezuela	1,371.5	1,951.3
El Salvador	89.0	125.6	Nepal	37.3	52.0	Viet Nam	176.8	241.6
Equatorial Guinea	18.4	24.3	Netherlands	2,264.8	3,444.2	Western Samoa	6.0	8.5
Ethiopia	70.6	98.3	New Zealand	461.6	650.1	Yemen, Republic of	120.5	176.5
Fiji	36.5	51.1	Nicaragua	68.2	96.1			
Finland	574.9	861.8	Niger	33.7	48.3	Yugoslavia	613.0	918.3
France	4,482.8	7,414.6	Nigeria	849.5	1,281.6	Zaïre	291.0	394.8
Gabon	73.1	110.3	Norway	699.0	1,104.6	Zambia	270.3	363.5
Gambia, The	17.1	22.9	Oman	63.1	119.4	Zimbabwe	191.0	261.3
Germany	5,403.7	8,241.5	Pakistan	546.3	758.2			
Ghana	204.5	274.0	Panama	102.2	149.6			
			Papua New Guinea	65.9	95.3			

[1] Became a member after May 30, 1990.

Data: IMF

Ninth General Review of Quotas

In accordance with the IMF's Articles of Agreement, the Board of Governors is required, at intervals of not more than five years, to conduct a general review of quotas and to propose any adjustments that it considers appropriate. These adjustments take into account the growth of the world economy and changes in the economic positions of members.

At the end of May 1990, the Executive Board submitted a resolution to the Board of Governors proposing an increase of 50 percent in IMF quotas, to approximately SDR 135.2 billion. (Following the adoption of this resolution and the subsequent membership in the IMF of four additional countries, total quotas will increase to about SDR 136.7 billion.) At the same time, the Executive Board submitted a separate draft resolution proposing a Third Amendment of the IMF's Articles of Agreement, which provides for the suspension of voting and related rights of members that do not fulfill their obligations under the Articles.

Members have until December 31, 1991, to consent to the proposed increases; this period may be extended by the Executive Board. However, no increase in quotas can become effective before the date of the IMF's determination that, during the period ending December 30, 1991, members having not less than 85 percent of total quotas on May 30, 1990 have consented to the increases proposed for them and, thereafter, that members having not less than 70 percent of total quotas on May 30, 1990 have so consented. Members with overdue financial obligations to the General Resources Account may not consent to their proposed increases until they become current.

In accordance with the understanding reached by the Interim Committee in May 1990, no increases in quotas under the Ninth Review shall become effective before the effective date of the Third Amendment of the Articles. The Interim Committee urged members to make every effort to ensure that the resolutions to increase quotas and to amend the Articles were effective before the end of 1991. If it appeared that they might not be effective by this date, the Committee would consider what steps might need to be taken.

The quota increases proposed for members were reached in the following manner: 60 percent of the overall increase was distributed in proportion to current individual quotas, and the balance of 40 percent was distributed in the form of selective adjustments to bring members' shares more into line with their relative positions in the world economy. In addition, Japan's proposed quota was increased further to equal that of Germany. The proposed quota increases for Canada, France, Germany, Italy, the United Kingdom, and the United States were also adjusted in such a manner that the proposed increases in quotas of all other members were not affected. Special adjustments were also made in the proposed quotas of Antigua and Barbuda, Bhutan, Maldives, and Seychelles, and for other members with current quotas of less than SDR 10 million.

In accordance with the Articles of Agreement, the Board of Governors must conduct the Tenth General Review of Quotas not later than March 31, 1993. However, the Interim Committee noted at its May 1990 meeting that "the review could be conducted earlier if there is a clear need to do so."

SURVEILLANCE OF MEMBERS' EXCHANGE RATE POLICIES

The IMF is mandated to "exercise firm surveillance over the exchange rate policies of its members" to help assure orderly exchange arrangements and promote a stable exchange rate system. It carries out this responsibility with the active participation of its member countries.

The IMF's appraisal of exchange rate policies is made within the framework of a comprehensive analysis of the general economic situation and the policy strategy of the member. In its latest review of surveillance, the Executive Board recognized that the scope of appraisal had broadened to include structural and other issues relevant to understanding broad macroeconomic developments and the context in which macroeconomic policies are formulated and implemented.

The IMF fulfills its surveillance responsibilities in two principal ways. First, the Board regularly examines each member's economic policies and performance and their interaction with economic developments in other countries. These examinations are based on staff reports, prepared on the basis of consultation discussions with the authorities of member countries.

Second, the Board holds regular (usually twice a year) discussions on the world economic outlook, which allow for review of members' policies from a multilateral perspective and for systematic monitoring and analysis of the global economic situation. The Board also holds, somewhat more frequently, discussions on exchange market developments in the major industrial countries. In addition, the Managing Director participates in meetings of finance ministers and central bank governors of the seven major industrial countries (Group of 7), to which he brings a global perspective that helps in analyzing international policy interactions.

The IMF contributes to international policy coordination through its work on key economic indicators and alternative medium-term economic scenarios. The IMF staff prepares medium-term projections for a range of indicators used to monitor and review the policies and performance of the large industrial countries. These indicators—which the IMF has been refining since 1986—include real growth of GNP or GDP, growth of real domestic demand, gross private investment, GDP deflators, general government financial balances, external current account balances, and primary commodity prices. The IMF staff also prepares, for the Board's consideration, medium-term scenarios that illustrate the effects of alternative policy paths and identify potential conflicts that may need to be addressed.

In its most recent biennial review of surveillance, the Executive Board reaffirmed the role of surveillance in promoting orderly underlying economic and financial conditions and a stable exchange rate system. Recognizing the broadened scope of surveillance, the Board has encouraged more selective coverage, so that consultations focus on core issues with substantial implications for price stability, economic growth, and the balance of payments from both national and international perspectives. The Board also reaffirmed that the world economic outlook would continue to play a crucial role in providing a multilateral framework for surveillance, and as a basis for integrating the analysis of individual countries into a larger multilateral context.

EVOLUTION OF IMF-CREATED INSTRUMENT IS LINKED TO ROLE AS PRINCIPAL RESERVE ASSET

The SDR is an international reserve asset created by the IMF and allocated to its members to supplement existing reserve assets. The IMF has allocated a total of SDR 21.4 billion in six allocations since the SDR was created in 1970. As of April 30, 1991, holdings of SDRs by member countries amounted to 3.6 percent of their total non-gold reserves.

All member countries of the IMF are participants in the SDR Department. They are eligible to receive allocations of SDRs and may use SDRs in transactions and operations among themselves, with prescribed holders (of which there are now 16), and with the IMF itself.

The SDR is also the unit of account of the IMF. The value of the unit is determined daily on the basis of a basket of five currencies: the U.S. dollar, the deutsche mark, the French franc, the Japanese yen, and the pound sterling. The SDR valuation basket was revised on January 1, 1991. The five currencies used in the basket remained the same, but their weights were revised to reflect changes in their relative importance in international trade and finance. The revised basket will be in effect until December 31, 1995.

The SDR interest rate, which is determined weekly, is a weighted average of the yields on specified short-term domestic obligations in the money markets of the five countries whose currencies make up the SDR's valuation basket. The financial instruments included in the SDR interest rate basket were reviewed in 1990 and, with effect from January 1, 1991, the interest rate on the two-month private bill used for the Japanese yen component was replaced by the rate on three-month certificates of deposit, and the interest rate on three-month interbank deposits used for the French franc component was replaced by the rate on three-month French treasury bills. The instruments for the U.S. dollar (market yield for three-month U.S. treasury bills), the pound sterling (market yield for three-month U.K. treasury bills), and deutsche mark (three-month interbank deposit rate in Germany) remained unchanged. The changes in the instruments reflect changed circumstances in financial markets resulting from innovation and deregulation.

SDR VALUATION ON AUGUST 26, 1991

Currency	1 Currency Amount	2 Exchange Rate on August 26	3 U.S. Dollar Equivalent
Deutsche mark	0.4530	1.74780	0.259183
French franc	0.8000	5.93500	0.134794
Japanese yen	31.8000	136.96000	0.232185
Pound sterling	0.0812	1.67980	0.136400
U.S. dollar	0.5720	1.00000	0.572000
			1.334562

SDR 1 = U.S.$ 1.33456
US$ 1 = SDR 0.749310

Column 1: The currency components of the SDR basket.

Column 2: Exchange rates in terms of currency units per U.S. dollar except for the pound sterling, which is expressed in U.S dollars per pound.

Column 3: The U.S. dollar equivalents of the currency amounts in Column 1 at the exchange rates in Column 2—that is, Column 1 divided by Column 2 except in the case of the pound sterling, for which column 1 is multiplied by column 2.

Note: The value of one US dollar in terms of the SDR is calculated as the reciprocal of the total of column 3, i.e., 1 ÷ 1.334562.

Data: IMF Treasurer's Department

SDR Allocations

The IMF has the authority to create unconditional liquidity by allocating SDRs to participants in the SDR Department. The IMF cannot allocate SDRs to itself or to prescribed holders. Decisions on allocations of SDRs are made for basic periods that run consecutively. The amount allocated to a participant is in proportion to its quota at the time of allocation.

In deciding on the timing and amount of SDR allocations, the IMF must determine that there is a long-term global need to supplement existing reserve assets. The most recent allocation was made on January 1, 1981. A total of SDR 4.1 billion was allocated to the 141 countries that were members of the IMF at that time.

Use of SDRs

Members with a balance of payments need may use SDRs to acquire foreign exchange in a transaction *with designation,* that is, one in which another member, designated by the IMF, provides a freely usable currency in exchange for SDRs. The IMF may designate members to provide currencies in exchange for SDRs on the basis of the strength of their balance of payments and reserve positions. A member's obligation to provide currency does not extend beyond the point at which its SDR holdings amount to three times its net cumulative allocation. However, the IMF and a participant may agree on a higher limit.

IMF members may use SDRs in a variety of voluntary transfers. These include transactions *by agreement*—that is, spot exchanges of SDRs for other monetary assets—and *in operations* among themselves and with prescribed holders:

- to obtain any currency in transactions by agreement with other members, provided that the transaction is made at the official exchange rate against the SDR as determined by the IMF;
- in swap arrangements, in which a member may transfer SDRs to another member in ex-

SDR INTEREST RATE CALCULATION FOR THE WEEK BEGINNING AUGUST 26, 1991

Currency	1 Currency Amount	2 Interest Rate	3 Exchange Rate Against the SDR	4 Product
Deutsche mark	0.4530	9.3075	0.43122500	1.8182
French franc	0.8000	9.7600	0.12667000	0.9890
Japanese yen	31.8000	7.2600	0.00546228	1.2611
Pound sterling	0.0812	10.3708	1.26368000	1.0642
U.S. dollar	0.5720	5.5500	0.74614800	2.3687
				7.5012

SDR interest rate 7.50

Column 1: The currency components of the SDR basket.

Column 2: Short-term interest rates on specific domestic obligations, as of Friday, August 23.

Column 3: Exchange rate as of August 23, expressed in terms of SDRs per currency unit.

Column 4: Product of columns 1 through 3.

Data: IMF Treasurer's Department

change for an equivalent amount of currency or another monetary asset, except gold, with an agreement to reverse the exchange at a specified future date and at an exchange rate agreed to by the participants;

• in forward operations, in which members can buy or sell SDRs for delivery at a future date against currency or another monetary asset, except gold, at an exchange rate agreed to by the members;

• to make loans of SDRs, at interest rates and maturities agreed to by the parties (repayments of loans and payments of interest may be made with SDRs);

• to settle financial obligations;

• as security for the performance of financial obligations, in either of two ways: (1) members can pledge SDRs, which can be earmarked for the duration of the pledge by being recorded in a special register kept by the IMF, or (2) members can agree that SDRs will be transferred as security for the performance of an obligation and that the SDRs will be returned to the transferor when its obligation under the agreement has been fulfilled; and

• in donations (grants).

In addition, SDRs may be used under special arrangements in operations under the Supplementary Financing Facility Subsidy Account, the Trust Fund, the structural adjustment facility, and the enhanced structural adjustment facility. Special arrangements are needed for these operations because the IMF's Special Disbursement Account and accounts administered by the IMF may not hold SDRs directly.

No transactions with designation have taken place since September 1987. All exchanges of SDRs for currency since then have been through transactions by agreement, which declined to SDR 5.3 billion in FY 1991 from SDR 6.8 billion in FY 1990. Transactions by agreement in recent years have been facilitated by revolving buying and selling (two-way) arrangements for voluntary SDR transactions,

which currently allow the IMF to arrange potential exchanges of SDR 2.0 billion for U.S. dollars, deutsche mark, Japanese yen, French francs, and pounds sterling. While maintaining the SDR holdings of participating members within the desired ranges, these arrangements have facilitated the smooth functioning of the SDR system by accommodating excess demand or supply of SDRs without recourse to the designation process.

Prescribed Holders of SDRs
The IMF has the authority to extend the range of official holders of SDRs beyond its member countries and the IMF's General Resources Account. It has designated, as of July 31, 1991, the following 16 organizations as prescribed holders: the African Development Bank and the African Development Fund, the Andean Reserve Fund, the Arab Monetary Fund, the Asian Development Bank, the Bank for International Settlements, the Bank of Central African States, the Central Bank of Western African States, the East African Development Bank, the Eastern Caribbean Central Bank, the International Bank for Reconstruction and Development (World Bank) and the International Development Association, the International Fund for Agricultural Development, the Islamic Development Bank, the Nordic Investment Bank, and the Swiss National Bank.

Valuation of the SDR
The value of the SDR in U.S. dollar terms is calculated daily by the IMF as the sum of the values in U.S. dollars, based on exchange rates quoted at noon in the London market, of specified amounts of the five currencies in the valuation basket. These amounts are derived from the agreed percentage weights of these currencies, using average exchange rates for the three months that ended on December 31, 1990. The agreed weights are 40 percent for the U.S. dollar, 21 percent for the deutsche mark, 17 percent for the Japanese yen, and 11 percent each for the French franc and the pound sterling. The

weights broadly reflect the relative importance of the currencies in international trade and payments, based on the value of the exports of goods and services of the member countries issuing these currencies and the balance of these currencies held as reserves by members of the IMF during 1985–89. An illustrative calculation of the value of the SDR in terms of the U.S. dollar is shown in the accompanying table.

SDR Interest Rate

The interest rate on the SDR is determined weekly on the basis of the yields on Friday of the specified short-term domestic obligations included in the SDR interest rate basket. For the week beginning August 26, 1991, the rate of interest on the SDR was 7.50 percent. The accompanying table illustrates how this rate is calculated.

A member whose holdings of SDRs exceed its net cumulative allocation earns interest on those excess holdings, and a member whose holdings are less than its net cumulative allocation pays charges at the same rate on its net use of SDRs. Interest is credited, and charges debited, quarterly.

On April 30 of each year, an assessment is levied on each participant, in proportion to its net cumulative allocation, to cover the expenses of conducting the business of the SDR Department. The rate for the financial year ended April 30, 1991 was 0.0172629 percent of net cumulative allocations.

Unit of Account

The SDR is used as a unit of account or as a basis for the unit of account by a number of international and regional organizations. The SDR has also been used to denominate private financial instruments; however, the market for private SDR deposits is still limited. The use of the SDR as a unit of account is explained, in part, by the fact that the value of the SDR (in terms of any one currency) tends to be more stable than that of any single currency in the basket, since movements in the exchange rate of any one of the component currencies will tend to be partly or fully offset by movements in the exchange rates of the other currencies.

Currency Peg

As of June 30, 1991, the currencies of six member countries were pegged to the SDR. The value of the member's currency under such an arrangement is fixed in terms of the SDR and then calculated in terms of other currencies by reference to the SDR value of those currencies as published by the IMF.

ARTICLE IV CONSULTATIONS PROVIDE FRAMEWORK FOR SURVEILLANCE OF IMF MEMBERS' POLICIES

IMF staff meets regularly with government officials of each member country to gather current economic and financial information and to review economic policies and developments. In principle, these consultations are annual, and take place in accordance with a decision adopted in 1977. The IMF analyzes economic developments and policies in member countries; examines members' fiscal, exchange rate, and monetary policies and performance, and balance of payments situation; and assesses the impact of policies—including exchange and trade restrictions—on members' external accounts.

In addition, consultations help draw attention to the international implications of policies and developments in the economies of individual countries. They also help the IMF to deal promptly with members' requests for the use of IMF financial resources and with proposed

Article VIII: Countries Undertake
To Refrain from Exchange Restrictions

One of the main purposes of the IMF is to facilitate the expansion and balanced growth of international trade. In this context, the IMF seeks to contribute to the promotion and maintenance of high levels of employment and real income and to assist in establishing a multilateral system of payments with respect to current transactions between IMF members. One way that the IMF endeavors to achieve these objectives is by helping to eliminate restrictive practices in the exchange and payments areas—one of the basic purposes of the IMF as set out in Article I and a specific objective of Article VIII of the IMF's Articles of Agreement.

Members accepting the obligations of Article VIII, Sections 2(a), 3, and 4 undertake to refrain from imposing restrictions on the making of payments and transfers for current international transactions and from engaging in discriminatory currency arrangements or multiple currency practices without the approval of the IMF.

Since December 1990, two members have notified the IMF that they have accepted the obligations of Article VIII, Sections 2(a), 3, and 4 of the Articles of Agreement—Cyprus (January 9, 1991) and Tonga (March 21, 1991). Tonga is the seventieth member to accept these obligations.

changes in policies or practices that are subject to IMF approval. Article IV consultations enable the staff and the Executive Board to draw on, and learn from, the broad experience of the membership over an extended period of time.

SDR RATES

Week Beginning	Rate of SDR Interest and Charges (percent)
September 2	7.45
September 9	7.33

The rate of SDR interest and charges is calculated weekly, by reference to a combined market interest rate, which is the weighted average of interest rates on specified short-term domestic obligations in the money markets of the five countries whose currencies constitute the SDR valuation basket (U.S. dollar, deutsche mark, Japanese yen, French franc, and pound sterling). The interest rates used are those that prevail each Friday. For the latest weekly rates call (202) 623-7171.

Data: IMF Treasurer's Department

In practice, the scope of Article IV consultations depends on the characteristics of the member country and on the prevailing external economic environment. In recent years, increasing attention has been devoted to determining whether a country's balance of payments position can be sustained over the medium term and to finding ways that structural policies can enhance economic performance.

Article IV consultations are held annually with most member countries, although a few countries have longer consultation cycles of up to two years. That is, within the framework of annual consultations, some member countries schedule consultations under a "bicyclic" procedure, which was introduced in 1987 to help reduce the frequency of Board discussions while ensuring the quality of surveillance. Although a staff report is issued to the Executive Board for each annual consultation, in these cases, the interim consultation—held every second year—is completed without a Board discussion unless a discussion is requested by a Board member or the Managing Director.

CONDITIONALITY: FINANCIAL SUPPORT FOR MEMBER COUNTRIES COMPLEMENTS ECONOMIC POLICY CHANGES

In providing financial support to any member country, the IMF must be assured that the member is pursuing policies that will ameliorate or eliminate its external payments problem. Use of the IMF's general resources must be in accordance with the provisions of the IMF's Articles and the policies adopted under them. This requirement, known as conditionality, seeks to strike an appropriate balance between financing and policy changes.

As part of conditionality, the use of the IMF's resources in the credit tranches is linked to the member's progress in implementing policies geared to restoring balance of payments viability and sustainable economic growth. A viable payments position is one that a country can finance on terms compatible with its development prospects and its debt-servicing capacity, without resorting to restrictions on trade and current payment. IMF-supported programs are designed to restore domestic and external balance in the economy.

Flexible Approach

Conditionality is not a rigid set of operational rules. The Executive Board undertakes periodic reviews of conditionality, and, on many occasions, it has adjusted the policies and practices relating to the use of the IMF's general resources. In its most recent discussion of issues related to conditionality and program design, in July 1991, the Executive Board affirmed that the current guidelines on conditionality, which the Board adopted in 1979, remain broadly appropriate. These guidelines provide for the phasing of purchases and include the injunction that objective indicators for monitoring performance—performance criteria—be limited to those variables necessary to ensure the achievement of the objectives of the programs. The guidelines also:

• emphasize the need to encourage members to adopt corrective measures at an early stage of their balance of payments difficulties;
• stress the necessity of paying due regard to members' domestic social and political objectives, as well as their economic priorities and circumstances, including the causes of their balance of payments problems;

• provide for a flexible approach on the number and content of performance criteria, which may vary because of members' diverse problems and institutional arrangements; and
• stress that IMF arrangements are not contractual agreements with the member, but are instead decisions of the IMF that set out the conditions for financial assistance from the IMF.

Basis for Conditionality

Conditionality is an essential element of the IMF's role in helping member countries to alleviate their balance of payments problems. It is also designed to ensure that members who use IMF credit will be able to meet the repayment schedule, thereby maintaining the revolving nature of IMF resources.

If the balance of payments problem is temporary and self-reversing, adequate financing on a temporary basis is all that is needed. However, it is neither desirable nor feasible to finance balance of payments deficits over a protracted period without reducing or eliminating the underlying causes. At the same time, applying corrective measures without the necessary financing would render the process of adjustment more difficult. The IMF's provision of financing to support a member's policy adjustments and its catalytic role in attracting financing from other sources allow the adjustment period to be extended, thereby making the process less severe than it would otherwise be.

Conditionality in Practice

The IMF takes a pragmatic approach in helping members formulate economic reform programs. Given the diversity of IMF members' situations, it would be inappropriate to apply any one model of adjustment to all members. Each IMF-supported program is designed by the member country concerned in close collaboration with the IMF staff. The process involves a comprehensive review of the member's economy, including the causes and nature of its balance of payments problems and an analysis of the policies needed to achieve a sustainable balance between the demand for, and the availability of, resources.

IMF-supported programs emphasize certain key aggregate economic variables, including domestic credit, public sector deficits, international reserves, and external debt. They also emphasize key elements of the pricing system—including the exchange rate, interest rates, and, in some cases, the prices of commodities—that significantly affect the country's public finances and foreign trade, and the supply response of the economy.

During a stand-by or extended arrangement in support of a member's program of reform, its performance is monitored through performance criteria, which are selected according to the economic and institutional structure of the country, the availability of data, and the desirability of focusing on broad macroeconomic variables, among other considerations. The IMF approach also embraces all aspects of economic policies that affect the supply of, and demand for, resources.

The impact of IMF-supported programs on other economic variables—such as income distribution, employment, and social services—depends in large part on decisions affecting the detailed execution of policy measures, which are the responsibility of the government. These decisions include how credit should be allocated, where public expenditures should be restrained, and which tax and subsidy measures should be applied. While questions of income distribution do not form part of IMF conditionality, the IMF attaches considerable importance to improving program design to protect the poor from the possible short-run adverse effects of policy adjustments. The IMF will, upon request, explore with the authorities the distributional consequences of alternative approaches to economic policy reforms.

Growth-Oriented Adjustment

To succeed, a program must elicit an adequate response from the supply side of the economy. Interest rates and exchange rates are particularly important, since they influence saving and investment decisions and, therefore, a member country's growth prospects. In emphasizing certain aspects of members' economic objectives—such as strengthening the current account of their balance of payments and promoting economic growth—policy adjustments supported by the IMF focus on such supply-related actions as export-promotion policies and measures to increase the efficiency of government spending. These measures help to eliminate a country's imbalances while enhancing its growth prospects. However, while the IMF now places more emphasis on measures to expand the supply of resources and broaden the productive base, it still supports demand-side measures, which remain essential to the creation of a stable economic environment conducive to sustainable growth.

In light of the greater emphasis on the structural aspects of IMF-supported programs, close collaboration between the IMF and the World Bank is important. Coordination between the IMF and the World Bank is particularly important in developing programs that support members' requests for resources available under the IMF's structural adjustment and enhanced structural adjustment facilities.

IMF PROVIDES RESOURCES TO MEMBERS UNDER VARIOUS FACILITIES

The IMF's financial resources are made available to its members through a variety of facilities and policies, which differ mainly in the type of balance of payments needs they address and in the degree of conditionality attached to them.

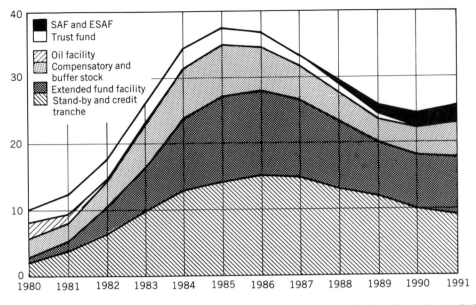

FIGURE 21A-1 Total Fund Credit Outstanding to Members (including Trust Fund, SAF, and ESAF), Financial Years Ended April 30, 1980–91

The IMF derives its finances from

• resources in the General Resources Account, which may be used to provide balance of payments financing to all members and are obtained from members' subscriptions and the IMF's borrowing;

• resources in the Special Disbursement Account, which are used for concessional balance of payments assistance to low-income developing members through the structural adjustment facility (SAF) and the enhanced structural adjustment facility (ESAF), and are derived from the reflow of Trust Fund resources (originally derived from the proceeds of the sale of a part of the IMF's gold holdings during 1976–80); and

• resources in the ESAF Trust, which are used by the IMF, as trustee, for concessional balance of payments assistance to low-income developing members and are derived from members' loans and donations.

The rules governing access to the IMF's general resources apply uniformly to all members. Access to these resources, which is determined primarily by the member's balance of payments need and the strength of its adjustment policies, is set within well-defined limits in relation to the members' quota. However, under the IMF's Articles of Agreement, it may allow members access to its general resources in excess of these limits in exceptional circumstances.

General resources are used to finance standby and extended arrangements, as well as special facilities that are open to all members, including the compensatory and contingency financing facility and the buffer stock financing facility. Members may also make use of general resources under temporary policies and facilities that are financed with borrowed resources. For example, in 1981, as a follow-up to its supplementary financing facility, the IMF established a policy of "enlarged access" to its resources. This policy helps members whose balance of payments needs are large relative to their quotas by augmenting its own resources with resources available through borrowing arrangements.

The IMF makes available other resources, in addition to its general resources, to provide low-income developing countries with relatively long-term balance of payments assistance at concessional rates of charge. Concessional assistance in amounts related to members' quotas is provided through loans under the SAF and the ESAF.

Reserve Tranche

A member has a reserve tranche position in the IMF to the extent that its quota exceeds the IMF's holdings of its currency in the General Resources Account, excluding holdings arising out of purchases under all policies on the use of the IMF's general resources. A member may purchase up to the full amount of its reserve tranche at any time, subject only to the requirement of balance of payments need. A reserve tranche purchase does not constitute a use of IMF credit and is not subject to charges or to an expectation or obligation to repurchase.

Credit Tranches

The credit tranche policy is the IMF's basic policy on the use of its general resources. Credit is made available in four tranches, each equivalent to 25 percent of a country's quota. Members may request stand-by arrangements in excess of this limit in the context of the enlarged access policy.

A first credit tranche purchase raises the IMF's holdings of the purchasing member's currency in the credit tranches to no more than 25 percent of quota. Generally, a member may request use of the IMF's resources in the first credit tranche when confronted with relatively minor balance of payments difficulties; the financial assistance is made available if the member demonstrates that it is making reasonable efforts to overcome its difficulties. A member may also request use of the first credit tranche as part of a stand-by arrangement.

Subsequent purchases are made in what are collectively known as the "upper credit tranches." A member may use the IMF's resources in the upper credit tranches if it adopts policies that provide appropriate grounds for expecting that the member's payments difficulties will be resolved within a reasonable period. Such use is almost always made under stand-by or extended arrangements.

Stand-by Arrangements

A stand-by or extended arrangement assures the member that it will be able to make purchases from the IMF, up to a specified amount, during a given period, as long as it has observed the performance criteria and other terms specified in the arrangement. The length of stand-by arrangements has typically been between 12 and 18 months in recent years, but it may extend up to 3 years. Repurchases of credit tranche drawings financed with ordinary resources are made $3\frac{1}{4}$–5 years after each purchase.

Purchases of the amounts available under a stand-by arrangement in the upper credit tranches or under an extended arrangement are "phased"; that is, they are made available in installments at specified intervals during the period of the arrangement. The member's right to draw is subject to observance of performance criteria and other specified conditions. These criteria typically cover credit policy, government or public sector borrowing requirements, and policies on trade and payments restrictions. Performance criteria also frequently cover the contracting or net use of short-, medium-, and long-term foreign debt, and changes in external reserves.

Performance criteria allow the member and the IMF to assess the member's progress in carrying out policies during the stand-by or extended arrangement, and they signal the need for possible corrective policies. When performance criteria have not been observed, further purchases are permitted only after the IMF and the member reach understandings—following consultations and Executive Board action—for the resumption of purchases.

Extended Fund Facility

Under the extended Fund facility (EFF), which was established in 1974, the IMF may provide assistance to members to meet their balance of payments needs for longer periods and in amounts larger in relation to quotas than under the credit tranche policies.

A member that requests an extended arrangement is expected to present a program outlining the objectives and policies for the whole period of the extended arrangement, as well as a detailed statement of the policies and measures that it will follow in each 12-month period. In May 1988, the Executive Board agreed that, in cases where a country has a strong adjustment program, more IMF resources could be made available by increasing actual access within the current limits; and in exceptional circumstances, access might extend beyond existing quota limits. Also, disbursements and performance criteria can now be phased semiannually, provided that appropriate monitoring of macroeconomic developments is ensured. In addition, the period of an existing extended arrangement over which purchases are phased—normally three years—may be lengthened, where appropriate and at the request of the member, to four years.

Purchases under extended arrangements are made from ordinary resources until the outstanding use of ordinary resources in the upper credit tranches and under the facility equals 140 percent of the member's quota. Members may also request extended arrangements in excess of this limit in the context of the enlarged access policy. Repurchases of drawings of ordinary resources are made 4½ to 10 years after each purchase.

Enlarged Access Policy

The enlarged access policy enables the IMF to provide additional financing, from borrowed resources, to members whose payments imbalances are large in relation to their quotas. The enlarged access policy is used when the member needs more financing from the IMF than is available to it in the four credit tranches or under the extended Fund facility, and when its problems require a relatively long period of adjustment and a longer repurchase period.

POTENTIAL CUMULATIVE DISBURSEMENTS UNDER ARRANGEMENTS AND FACILITIES (PERCENT OF MEMBER QUOTAS)

Under stand-by and extended arrangements[1,2]	
Annual	90–110
Three-year	270–330
Cumulative	400–440
Special facilities	
Compensatory and contingency financing facility (CCFF)	
Export shortfall[3]	40
Excess cereal import costs[3]	17
Contingency financing[4]	40
Optional tranche[3,5]	25
Combined[6]	122
Buffer stock financing facility	45
Under SAF and ESAF arrangements	
Structural adjustment facility	
First year	20
Second year	30
Third year	20
Cumulative	70
Enhanced structural adjustment facility[1]	
Cumulative	250

[1] Under exceptional circumstances, the amounts disbursed may exceed the limits shown.

[2] The application of the lower access limits was temporarily suspended as of November 1990 until December 31, 1991.

[3] Until end 1991, access for export shortfalls, cereal import excesses, and the optional tranche may alternatively be used to compensate an excess in oil import costs.

[4] A sub-limit of 35 percent of quota applies on account of deviations in interest rates.

[5] May be applied to supplement the amounts for export shortfalls, excess in cereal imports costs, or contingency financing.

[6] When a member has a satisfactory balance of payments position—except for the effect of an export shortfall or an excess in cereal costs—a limit of 83 percent of quota applies to either the export shortfall or the excess cereal costs; a joint limit of 105 percent of quota applies.

The enlarged access policy is financed by resources borrowed for this purpose, in conjunction with ordinary resources. The "mix" of ordinary and borrowed resources is determined in accordance with the IMF's mixing policy. All repurchases of drawings financed with borrowed resources under the enlarged access policy, irrespective of the facility under which they are made, fall due 3½ to 7 years after each purchase.

The current access limits on stand-by and extended arrangements, individually or combined, are 90 or 110 percent of quota annually; 270 or 330 percent of quota over three years; and 400 or 440 percent of quota on a cumulative basis, net of repurchases. In November 1990, following a sharp increase in many members' external financing needs as a result of events in the Middle East, the lower of these limits were suspended through the end of December 1991. The limits, which may be exceeded in exceptional circumstances, exclude drawings under the compensatory and contingency financing and buffer stock financing facilities. For a member that has access to IMF resources under a stand-by or an extended arrangement involving enlarged access, the amounts available for enlarged access are apportioned between ordinary quota-based resources and borrowed resources.

The policy on enlarged access and access limits under this policy are reviewed annually by the Executive Board. In the latest review, in June 1990, the Board decided to leave the limits unchanged. In light of the expected full utilization of available credit lines, the Executive Board, in September 1990, decided to substitute ordinary resources for borrowed resources where needed to meet commitments, once borrowed resources have been drawn down fully. Such substitution will apply only until the quota increases under the Ninth General Review become effective or the end of 1991, whichever is earlier. The amount of IMF financial assistance provided in individual cases is determined by guidelines that the IMF reviews periodically.

FINANCING HELPS MEMBERS ADJUST TO UNEXPECTED EXTERNAL DISRUPTIONS

Financing under the compensatory and contingency financing facility (CCFF) compensates countries for shortfalls in export receipts, excesses in the cost of cereal imports, and excesses in oil import costs, to protect members pursuing IMF-supported economic programs from the effects of unexpected external disruptions.

Compensatory Financing

Compensatory financing was first introduced in 1963 to help members experiencing—for reasons largely beyond their control—balance of payments problems resulting from temporary declines in export earnings below their medium-term trend, particularly as a result of fluctuations in commodity prices. Initially, compensatory financing only covered merchandise exports, but the range of exports covered has expanded over the years. In 1979, the facility was broadened to include shortfalls in receipts from two categories of services: tourism and "workers' remittances" (earnings of citizens working overseas that are repatriated to the home country). In 1981, a new window was added to the facility to allow compensation for countries faced with an excessive rise in the cost of imports of cereal products.

In December 1990, as part of the IMF's policy adaptations in light of events in the Middle East, the Executive Board further widened the range of services eligible for compensatory financing to cover most services, including earnings from pipelines, canal transit fees, shipping, transportation, construction, and insurance. At the same time, the Board allowed quicker access to compensatory credit—by permitting the member to use estimated, rather than actual, data for the entire shortfall year to calculate the earnings shortfall (compared with a maximum of six months' estimated data previously).

The CCFF's new oil element, which was also introduced in December 1990, compensates members for sharp rises in the cost of their imports of crude petroleum, petroleum products, and natural gas. The oil element will remain in force until the end of the 1991 calendar year.

Export Shortfalls

To receive compensatory financing, a member must have a balance of payments need. The export shortfall or the cereal and oil import excesses must be temporary and attributable to circumstances largely beyond the member's control. For members whose balance of payments problems go beyond the effects of an export shortfall, the use of the compensatory financing element requires that the member cooperate with the IMF in finding appropriate solutions to its balance of payments difficulties. For purchases on account of an oil import excess, the member must satisfy the IMF that it is pursuing appropriate energy policies.

The calculated shortfall is the amount by which a country's export earnings in the shortfall year are below the value of their medium-term trend. This trend is defined as the geometric average of export earnings during the five years centered on the shortfall year. Projected export earnings for the two years after the shortfall may not be more than 20 percent above the level of actual export earnings in the two years before the shortfall.

An excess in cereal import costs is calculated as the difference in the cost of such imports in a given 12-month period from their arithmetic average cost for the 5 years centered on that year. An excess in cereal or oil import costs is compensated only in combination with an export shortfall. Where there is an export excess, this excess is deducted from the excess in cereal or oil import costs to determine the amount of compensation.

Contingency Financing

A contingency mechanism may be attached to an IMF arrangement at the request of the member concerned. Under this mechanism, financing is provided to cover part of the net effect of unfavorable deviations in highly volatile and easily identifiable variables affecting the current account (which are beyond the member's control) on the member's balance of payments. The variables covered could include, for example, main export or import prices or international interest rates. Deviations in the variables covered by a contingency mechanism are measured in relation to baseline projections, which are established at the start of an arrangement or at the time of a review of an arrangement that has at least six months remaining. The contingency mechanism is triggered once net deviations in the key variables exceed a threshold level and it is clear that these deviations have not been offset by movements in other variables affecting the current account that are not covered by the mechanism.

Favorable deviations—such as an unexpected increase in export prices—may trigger the symmetry provision. This could result in an increase in the reserve target under the IMF-supported program, a reduction in the amount available under the IMF arrangement, or an early repurchase of previous contingency purchases.

Access Limits

The current overall access limit under the CCFF is set at 122 percent of a member's quota. Sublimits provide maximum access equivalent to 40 percent of quota under the contingency element; 40 percent of quota that may be used either for the export element or the oil element; 17 percent of quota that may be used either for the cereal element or the oil element; plus an "optional" 25 percent of quota, which may be used to supplement any of the four elements of the CCFF.

Drawings under the CCFF are additional to those under regular credit tranche policies. This means that a member's use of IMF resources under these special facilities may increase the IMF's holdings of the member's currency beyond the limits set for credit tranche policies.

Buffer Stock Financing Facility

Another special facility, the buffer stock financing facility (BSFF), was established in 1969 to help finance IMF members' contributions to approved international commodity buffer stock schemes, provided that members demonstrated balance of payments need. Drawings may be made for buffer stock financing up to the equivalent of 45 percent of quota. The member is expected to show its willingness to cooperate with the IMF to find, where required, appropriate solutions to its balance of payments difficulties. In April 1990, the IMF decided that the BSFF may be used to finance eligible members' contributions to the 1987 International Rubber Agreement. No drawings have been made under this facility for the past six years, and no credits under this facility are outstanding.

CONCESSIONAL FACILITIES
ASSIST POORER COUNTRIES

The IMF's Executive Board established the structural adjustment facility (SAF) in March 1986 to provide balance of payments assistance on concessional terms to low-income developing countries. The facility is funded by the resources of the Special Disbursement Account, which are derived from reflows from the IMF's Trust Fund. Established in 1976 to provide balance of payments assistance on concessional terms to eligible members, the Trust Fund made its final disbursements on March 31, 1981. Total resources available for disbursements are projected at SDR 2.7 billion. In December 1987, the Executive Board established the enhanced structural adjustment facility (ESAF), which is financed from SAF resources and grant contributions.

The SAF provides loans to support the medium-term macroeconomic and structural adjustment programs of low-income developing member countries with protracted balance of payments problems. The objectives are to help these countries establish the conditions for sustained growth, to strengthen their balance of payments position, and to facilitate orderly relations with creditors and a reduction in trade and payments restrictions. Of the 61 countries currently eligible for SAF resources, China and India—the 2 largest—have indicated that they do not intend to borrow from the facility, thereby making more resources available to other eligible countries.

The amount potentially available to each eligible member under a SAF arrangement is equal to 70 percent of the member's quota. Loan disbursements are made in three annual installments equivalent to 20 percent of quota in the first year, 30 percent in the second year, and 20 percent in the third year. SAF loans carry an annual interest rate of 0.5 percent, with repayments to be made semiannually, beginning 5 ½ years and ending 10 years after each disbursement.

An eligible member seeking to use SAF resources develops, with the assistance of the staffs of the IMF and the World Bank, a policy framework for a three-year adjustment program, which is set out in a policy framework paper (PFP). The PFP describes the authorities' macroeconomic and structural policy objectives and priorities and the measures that they intend to adopt during the three years. It assesses the member's external financing needs and possible sources of finance. The PFP is also intended as a means of catalyzing and coordinating financial and technical assistance in support of the adjustment program. The PFP is reviewed by the Executive Board of the IMF and by the Executive Directors of the World Bank in the Committee of the Whole, and is updated annually on a three-year rolling basis.

The first annual loan disbursement under the SAF is made available after the Executive Board approves the three-year SAF arrangement and the first annual arrangement thereunder. In requesting these arrangements, the member is expected to present a program, consistent with the PFP, that describes the specific objectives and policies it will pursue during the three-year program period and the first annual program. The second and third loan disbursements are made available after the IMF approves annual arrangements for those years.

Performance during a program year is monitored with reference to benchmarks that reflect the program's key elements. Financial benchmarks, which are specified on a quarterly basis, usually cover monetary, fiscal, and external debt variables. Structural benchmarks are also usually specified for key structural policies. Although disbursements are not directly related to the observance of benchmarks, deviations would indicate the need for policy adjustments under the subsequent annual program.

The objectives, eligibility, and basic procedural features of the ESAF—including the role of the PFP—parallel those of the SAF. Differences between the SAF and the ESAF relate largely to the monitoring and the strength of the programs and to the access to, and the funding of, the facilities. The adjustment measures adopted under programs supported by the ESAF are expected to be particularly ambitious, with a view to fostering growth and achieving a substantial strengthening of the balance of payments position during the three-year period. The 61 countries eligible for the SAF are also eligible for the ESAF.

When the ESAF was established, China indicated that it did not intend to use ESAF resources in the present circumstances, and India indicated that, unless its balance of payments position deteriorated fundamentally, it did not expect to borrow from the facility. Eligible members may request arrangements under either the SAF or the ESAF.

In 1990, in conjunction with developments in the Middle East, the Executive Board supported the possibility of rephasing and augmenting resources under ESAF arrangements to help members cope with external shocks. The Board agreed that the total amount of an ESAF arrangement could, unlike in the past, be augmented on the occasion of a midyear review.

The Board also decided to permit a fourth year of ESAF support for eligible members, provided such support is approved before November 30, 1992, which is the deadline for commitments of resources under new ESAF arrangements, and so long as resources are available. The Board stressed that a fourth-year ESAF arrangement—which should not be seen as an entitlement—would be appropriate to assist members whose past policy performance had been satisfactory and who had adopted strong measures in response to external developments.

ESAF arrangements are funded by ESAF Trust resources, which are derived from special loans and donations—and together are targeted to reach SDR 6 billion—and by amounts remaining undisbursed under SAF arrangements. Access under ESAF arrangements differs according to members' balance of payments needs and the strength of their adjustment efforts. An eligible member country may borrow a maximum of 250 percent of its quota under a three-year arrangement, although this limit may be exceeded under exceptional circumstances up to a maximum of 350 percent of quota. ESAF access is expected to average about 150 percent of quota.

As with the SAF, ESAF loans are repaid in 10 semiannual installments, beginning 5 ½ years and ending 10 years after the date of disbursement. The interest rate on ESAF loans is currently 0.5 percent a year but will be reviewed periodically by the Executive Board. Monitoring under ESAF arrangements is conducted on the basis of quarterly financial benchmarks and structural benchmarks, as under the SAF. In addition, performance criteria are established on a semiannual basis for financial aggregates and key structural policies. Policies and performance are reviewed at midyear. ESAF loans are disbursed semiannually, initially upon approval of an annual arrangement and subsequently based on the observance of performance criteria and after completion of the midyear review.

GUIDELINES FOR IMF SUPPORT

The Interim Committee, at its meeting in April 1989, recognized the central role the IMF should play in debt-reduction operations through its policy guidance and financial support. It proposed that the IMF provide support, in appropriate cases, for debt and debt-service reduction in connection with appropriate flows of new money from the private sector. The Executive Board has developed broad guidelines—to be kept under review and expected to evolve in the light of experience—for IMF support of such operations.

The IMF's role in the debt strategy is part of its ongoing efforts to adapt its policies to assist member countries in coping with their debt problems. The ultimate objective of the debt strategy is to ensure satisfactory growth with balance of payments viability and to restore spontaneous access to financial markets for the debtor countries. The basic conditions for the success of this strategy continue to be

- growth-oriented adjustment and structural reform in debtor countries;
- a favorable global economic environment; and
- adequate financial support from official (bilateral and multilateral) and private sources.

The Guidelines

The IMF will provide financial support for debt and debt-service reduction under the new guidelines, provided that it is satisfied that

- the member is pursuing an economic adjustment program with strong elements of structural reform, in the context of a stand-by or extended arrangement;
- voluntary, market-based debt and debt-service reduction will help the country regain access to financial markets and achieve external payments viability with economic growth; and
- financial support for debt and debt-service reduction represents an efficient use of scarce resources.

In assessing the quality of a member's adjustment and structural reform program, the Executive Board will give emphasis to policies designed to improve the climate for saving and investment, help reverse capital flight, and attract private capital inflows.

Amount of Support

The guidelines provide that the proportion of IMF resources committed under a stand-by or extended arrangement that could be set aside to finance operations involving a reduction in the stock of debt would generally be about 25 percent, although the exact proportion would be determined on a case-by-case basis. Drawings on set-aside amounts are normally to be phased—in line with the member's performance under the adjustment program—but in some cases, more money could be made available in the initial purchase, in accordance with the specific financing needs of the member's debt-reduction plan.

Initial purchases under the set-aside can be made available from the outset of an arrangement if the Executive Board is satisfied that the debt-reduction plan is market related and consistent with the program objectives. Otherwise, purchase rights would accumulate, and purchases would be made available upon completion of the Board's review of the debt-reduction plan.

The IMF is prepared, in certain cases, to provide additional access to its resources, provided that such support would be decisive in promoting cost-effective debt and debt-service reduction and in catalyzing other financial resources. Such additional access—up to 40 percent of the member's quota—can be used as collateral for debt instruments paying below-market interest rates in connection with debt- or debt-service-reduction operations. Actual access is determined on a case-by-case basis in view of the magnitude of the member's balance of payments need, the strength of its adjustment program, and its efforts to contribute its own resources to support debt and debt-service reduction.

The timing of actual disbursements to the member is based on specific operations. The member would be expected to make early repurchases of amounts drawn under a commitment of additional access to the extent that the amounts were not used within an appropriate period for the purposes described in the member's request.

Financing Assurances
The objectives of the IMF's policy on financing assurances are to ensure that

• adjustment programs are fully financed;
• financing is consistent with a return of the country to a viable balance of payments position and with its ability to repay the IMF;
• the burden of financing is shared equitably; and
• orderly relations between the member country and its creditors are maintained or reestablished.

In 1989, the IMF modified its policy on financing assurances in view of changes in the financial environment and the possibility that debtors and creditors might, in some cases, need time to agree on appropriate financing packages. The IMF may—on a case-by-case basis—approve an arrangement before the conclusion of a financing package between the member and its commercial bank creditors if prompt IMF support is essential for program implementation, negotiations with banks have begun, and a financing package consistent with external viability is expected to be concluded within a reasonable period.

INCOME REFLECTS CHARGES ON FACILITIES AND REMUNERATION PAID TO CREDITOR MEMBERS

The IMF seeks to achieve a positive net income each financial year to add to its reserves, after covering its expenses and paying remuneration to its creditors, while retaining a concessional element in the rate charged to members.

Reviews of the IMF's income position take into consideration developments that affect the cost and use of its resources, including the financial consequences of overdue obligations, which are shared between debtor and creditor member countries. Periodic charges due from a member in arrears to the IMF by six months or more are treated as deferred rather than current income. Under the burden-sharing mechanism, an amount equal to charges deferred during a quarter is generated in a symmetrical fashion by an upward adjustment of the rate of charge and a downward adjustment of the rate of remuneration for that quarter, subject to certain limitations.

In addition, revenues generated through burden sharing are allocated to the IMF's Special Contingent Accounts (SCAs). The first account (SCA-1) was established in 1987 in recognition of the need for additional precautionary balances in view of the protracted overdue obligations of some members. The second account (SCA-2) was established in June 1990 as part of the strengthened cooperative strategy on overdue obligations.

The resources for the SCA-2 are generated by an increase of 0.35 percent in the rate of charge and a reduction in the rate of remuneration to yield three times the amount generated by the increased rate of charge, subject to the floor on the rate of remuneration set in the Articles. These resources are intended to protect the IMF in view of the risks associated with credit extended by the General Resources Account in the context of IMF-monitored rights accumulation programs and to provide additional liquidity to contribute to the financing of encashments. The extended burden-sharing mechanism for the SCA-2 is designed to generate SDR 1 billion over a period of about five years.

For financial year 1990/91, the target amount of net income, which was added to the IMF's reserves, and the amount placed in the SCA were each set at SDR 69.8 million. In addition, a total of SDR 142.3 million was placed in the SCA-2. Unpaid charges due from members with protracted arrears and contributions to the SCA-1 resulted in an average adjustment to the basic rate of charge of 98 basis points, and in an average adjustment to the rate of remuneration of 94 basis points.

Adjustments under extended burden sharing for the SCA-2 further increased the basic rate of charge by an average of 29 basis points and further reduced the rate of remuneration by an average of 67 basis points, to 81.7 percent of the average SDR interest rate. For the financial year, the adjusted rate of charge on the use of the IMF's ordinary resources averaged 8.92 percent, and the adjusted rate of remuneration averaged 7.18 percent.

Since financial year 1989/90, the basic rate of charge on the use of ordinary resources has been set as a proportion of the weekly SDR interest rate. The Executive Board set the proportion at 91.3 percent at the beginning of 1990/91 and, upon review at midyear, reduced the proportion to 87.8 percent for the remainder of the year. On June 7, 1991, this proportion was further reduced retroactively for the year as a whole to 87.0 percent, resulting in an average rate of charge of 7.65 percent before adjustments under the burden-sharing mechanisms.

The Board also decided to continue in 1991/92 the proportional relationship between the basic rate of charge and the SDR interest rate. The proportion, which will be reviewed at midyear, was set at 96.6 percent, so as to achieve a target amount of net income of 5 percent of reserves.

Net income for financial year 1990/91 amounted to SDR 69.8 million after the retroactive reduction of the rate of charge, and was added to the IMF's reserves, which rose to SDR 1.5 billion on April 30, 1991. Total precautionary balances, which include amounts in the SCAs, reached SDR 1.9 billion at the end of 1990/91.

IMF ADDRESSES PROBLEM
OF OVERDUE FINANCIAL OBLIGATIONS

Overdue financial obligations to the IMF remained a serious problem in 1990/91. The total amount of overdue obligations rose from SDR 3.3 billion at the end of 1989/90 to SDR 3.4 billion at the end of 1990/91, of which almost all was due from members in arrears to the IMF by six months or more. Nevertheless, the absolute increase and the rate of growth of overdue obligations over the financial year were the lowest since 1983. And the number of ineligible members was reduced from 10 to 8, as Guyana and Honduras settled their arrears to the IMF in June 1990.

The reduction and elimination of overdue financial obligations to the IMF are essential to maintain the cooperative nature of the institution and to preserve its monetary character. During the past year, the IMF continued to implement the strengthened cooperative strategy for resolving members' arrears problems. This strategy has three main elements: (1) the prevention of new arrears; (2) intensified collaboration among the members concerned, the IMF, and other multilateral and official bilateral financial institutions to resolve existing protracted arrears; and (3) remedial action to be taken if a country with protracted arrears fails to cooperate with the IMF.

As a complement to preventive measures, the deterrent element of the cooperative strategy was strengthened in 1990. The Executive Board further defined the procedures and timetable for the application of remedial measures, which had been endorsed in 1989, and two new instruments were added—communications with IMF Governors and heads of selected international financial institutions and a declaration of noncooperation. In addition, the timing of procedures for dealing with members with overdue obligations were tightened. A maximum time limit has been set between the date of emergence of arrears to the IMF and a declaration of in-

eligibility, and the timing of a declaration of noncooperation and the initiation of procedures for compulsory withdrawal has been made explicit. The deterrent element also includes the possible use of the suspension of voting and related rights, once the Third Amendment of the Articles of Agreement, which would make such a suspension possible, becomes effective.

Progress continues to be made under the cooperative strategy. In addition to the countries that cleared their arrears to the IMF (Guyana and Honduras), a number of countries have continued to pursue policies aimed at restoring growth and external viability as they cooperate with the IMF in addressing the problems of their arrears. For countries that have not been cooperating with the IMF, remedial measures have been applied with flexibility.

Rights Approach

In May 1990, the Interim Committee endorsed the concept of a "rights" approach, under which a member with protected arrears could earn rights—based on sustained performance during the period of a "rights accumulation program" monitored by the IMF—toward future financing once its arrears to the IMF have been cleared. Such programs would generally span a period of about three years. Upon the successful completion of a rights accumulation program, clearance of the member's arrears, and approval by the IMF of a successor arrangement, the member would be able to cash in its accumulated rights as the first disbursement under the successor arrangement.

Future financing could be made available from the IMF's general resources, or, for countries eligible to use the structural adjustment facility (SAF), from the general resources, the SAF, the enhanced structural adjustment facility (ESAF), or some combination as determined by the Executive Board. The Interim

Committee endorsed the proposal that the IMF pledge up to 3 million ounces of gold, if needed, as additional security for use of ESAF resources in connection with the financing of accumulated rights.

In the context of the collaborative approach, in April 1991 the Executive Board decided to suspend the application of special charges in the General Resources Account for members in protracted arrears to the IMF if the IMF endorses an IMF-monitored or a rights accumulation program for that member, or if the IMF determines that (1) the member is actively cooperating with the IMF toward clearance of its arrears, and (2) the member has undertaken not to increase its overdue obligations to the IMF above a specified ceiling. For those members (specified in the decision) that had already undertaken to make payments to the IMF equivalent to their obligations falling due, special charges were to be suspended effective May 1, 1991, or when the level of their arrears was reduced to or below a specified level, whichever was later, provided the member continued to make payments equivalent to maturing obligations.

Eligibility for the rights approach is limited to those of the 11 members with protracted arrears at the end of 1989 that adopt an economic program that can be endorsed by the Executive Board as a rights accumulation program by the time of the spring 1992 Interim Committee meeting.

CENTRAL BANKS AND OTHER OFFICIAL ENTITIES HELP AUGMENT IMF RESOURCES

Although the financial management of the IMF is based on the principle that quota subscriptions are, and should remain, the basic source of financing, borrowing has provided an important temporary supplement to the IMF's ordinary resources.

To date, the IMF has borrowed only from official sources, including the treasuries and central banks of member countries and one nonmember country (Switzerland), and the Bank for International Settlements.

Borrowings from official sources have been used to supplement the IMF's ordinary resources and to finance members' purchases under the present enlarged access policy. In addition, the IMF has the authority, which so far it has not used, to borrow from private sources. On August 30, 1991, all credit lines available to the IMF to finance the policy on enlarged access had been fully drawn, except that SDR 0.4 billion was temporarily invested in the Borrowed Resources Suspense Account pending its use to finance purchases of borrowed resources.

There are no undrawn borrowing agreements at this time, although the IMF may borrow up to SDR 17.0 billion from the Group of 10 industrial countries under the General Arrangements to Borrow (GAB) and a further SDR 1.5 billion under a borrowing arrangement with the Saudi Arabian Monetary Agency (SAMA) in association with the GAB, when supplementary resources are needed to prevent a breakdown of the international monetary system. The GAB, in its original form in 1962, was a four-year revolving borrowing agreement that provided that its 10 industrial country members—later joined by Switzerland under an associated agreement—would lend resources to the IMF, if necessary, "to forestall or cope with an impairment of the international monetary system." These arrangements have been extended and revised several times. The present GAB and the associated arrangement with SAMA are effective through December 1993.

GLOSSARY

Absolute advantage. The argument, associated with Adam Smith, that trade is based on absolute differences in costs. Each country will export those products for which its costs, in terms of labor and other inputs, are lower than costs in other countries.

Absorption condition. A Keynesian analysis of the conditions necessary for the success of a devaluation, namely, that output must grow relative to the domestic use of goods and services, and that domestic savings must grow faster than investment. Associated with Sidney Alexander.

Ad valorem tariff. A tariff that is measured as a percentage of the value of the traded product.

Appreciation. An increase in the exchange market value of a currency that occurs in a floating exchange rate regime.

Arbitrage. Purchase of a good or an asset in a low-price market and its riskless sale in a higher price market. If arbitrage is possible, prices should be forced together, differing by no more than transport or transactions costs.

Articles of Agreement of the IMF. The founding document of the International Monetary Fund that defines the Fund's functions. Agreed to at the Bretton Woods Conference in 1944 and amended since then.

Asset market model of the balance of payments. A group of models of the balance of payments or the exchange rate which views foreign exchange as a financial asset rather than as a claim on real goods. Capital transactions, rather than current account transactions, dominate these models. Foreign exchange is bought or sold in order to facilitate financial transactions rather than merchandise trade, and the models are based on supply and demand functions for financial assets.

Balance of payments. A set of accounts that represents all transactions between residents of one country and residents of the rest of the world during a period of time, normally a year.

Base money. The total volume of member bank reserve accounts and currency created by a central bank. The stock of base money, sometimes known as high-powered money, is central in determining the money supply of a country.

Basic balance. A balance-of-payments surplus or deficit measured as the sum of the current account and the long-term capital account. Excludes short-term capital and flows of foreign exchange reserves.

BB **line.** Combinations of interest rates and levels of domestic output which will produce equilibrium in the balance of payments.

Bilateral exchange rate. The price of the local currency in terms of a single foreign currency.

Border trade. Trade that occurs when the exact same good is traded in both directions across a border. It takes place when two countries have a long border and transportation costs across the border are less than within each country for a heavy or bulky good.

Brain drain. The movement of scientists, engineers, and other highly educated people from developing to industrialized countries, which imposes a loss of public investment in education on the developing country.

Cable transfer. A means of transferring foreign exchange from one economic agent to another. An electronic message instructs a bank to transfer funds from the account of one party to that of another.

Call. An option contract that allows the owner to purchase a specified quantity of a financial asset, such as foreign exchange, at a fixed price during a specified period. The owner is not required to exercise the option. The price at which the option can be exercised is known as the strike price.

Capital account balance. A country's total receipts from the sale of financial assets to foreign residents minus its total expenditures on purchases of financial assets from foreign residents. These assets include both debt and equity instruments.

Cartel. A collusive arrangement among sellers of a product in different countries, which is intended to raise the price of that product in order to extract monopoly rents.

C.I.F. Cost, insurance, and freight. This measurement of the value of imports includes the cost of the goods itself, insurance, and freight.

Clean floating exchange rate. A rate that obtains when an exchange rate is determined solely by market forces. The central banks not only fail to maintain a parity, but also refrain from buying or selling foreign exchange to influence the rate.

Clearing House International Payments System (CHIPS). The electronic system among banks in New York and other major foreign financial centers, which is used to transfer foreign exchange, that is, to complete foreign exchange market transactions.

Commercial policy. Government policies that are intended to change international trade flows, particularly to restrict imports.

Common market. A group of countries that maintain free trade in goods among the membership, share a common external tariff schedule, and allow mobility of labor and capital among the members.

Community indifference curve. A line that shows all the combinations of two goods which provide the community with the same level of welfare, that is, to which the community would be indifferent. A set of these curves can be used to show increases in community welfare as more goods are made available.

Comparative advantage. The argument, developed by David Ricardo in the early nineteenth century, that mutually beneficial balanced trade is possible even if one country has an absolute advantage in both goods. All that is required is that there be a difference in the relative costs of the two goods in the two countries and that each country export the product for which it has relatively or comparatively lower costs.

Conditionality. The policy under which the International Monetary Fund makes large loans (drawings) to member countries only if they pursue exchange rate and other policies that can be expected to improve the borrowing country's balance-of-payments performance and make the repayment of the loan possible.

Consumer surplus. The difference between what a consumer would be willing to pay for a product and its market price.

Countervailing duty. A tariff imposed by an importing country which is intended to increase the price of the goods to a legally defined fair level. Often used in export subsidy cases.

Covered return. The rate of return on an investment in a country after allowance for the cost of a forward contract to move the funds back to the country of the investor.

Credit. A transaction that results in a payment into a country. Exports, receipts of dividend and interest payments, and purchases of local assets by foreigners are all credits in a country's balance-of-payments accounts.

Crowding out. The argument that government budget deficits do not increase GNP because the deficits crowd out or discourage other private transactions, perhaps through higher interest rates resulting from government borrowing.

Currency board. An institution which fulfills the role of a bank, but which is not allowed to own domestic financial assets. Its only financial assets are foreign exchange reserves, meaning that its ability to create base money, and thereby increase the domestic money supply, is strictly regulated by the balance of payments.

Currency substitution. The argument that national currencies are often viewed as substitutes and that firms switch from holding one currency to another in response to changes in expected yields and risks.

Current account balance. A country's total receipts from exports goods and services minus its local expenditures on imports of goods and services. Also includes unilateral transfers such as gifts and foreign aid.

Customs union.   A group of countries that maintain free trade in goods among the membership and a common external tariff schedule.

Deadweight loss.   The loss from a tariff or other restrictive policy that is a gain to nobody. A pure efficiency loss.

Debit.   A transaction that results in a payment out of a country. Imports and purchases of foreign securities are debits in a country's balance-of-payments accounts.

Debt/equity swap.   An exchange that occurs when a bank sells financial claims on a foreign government to another firm at a discount, and that firm allows the debtor country to pay the debt in local currency, which it uses to finance a direct investment in the debtor country. Frequently used in Latin America to ease the burdens of excessive debt.

Depreciation.   A currency's decline in exchange market value in a flexible exchange rate system.

Devaluation.   A condition that arises when a government or central bank changes a fixed exchange rate or parity for its currency in a direction that reduces the value of the local currency compared to foreign currencies.

Dumping.   Selling a product in an export market for less than it sold for in the home market or for less than the importing country views as a fair value, which is usually based on estimates of average cost.

Economic union.   An agreement among a group of countries to maintain free trade among themselves, a common external tariff, mobility of capital and labor among the members, and some degree of unification in their budgetary and monetary systems.

Economies of scale.   Conditions characterized by the decline of long-run average costs as an enterprise becomes larger. Economies of scale frequently exist when fixed costs are particularly important in an industry.

Effective tariff.   A measurement of the amount of protection provided to an industry by a tariff schedule which allows for tariffs on inputs that the industry buys from others, as well as for the tariff on the output of the industry. The effective tariff can be negative, which means that the government policy is discriminating against local firms and in favor of imports, if tariff levels on inputs are sufficiently higher than the tariff on the final good.

Embargo.   A complete prohibition of trade with a country. U.S. trade with Libya and Cuba, for example, is under an embargo.

Escape clause.   A provision of U.S. law which allows temporary protection for U.S. industries that are under particular pressure from imports.

Eurodollar market.   Banking markets in Europe, and elsewhere outside the United States, in which time deposits are accepted and loans are made in U.S. dollars. Similar arrangements exist for such offshore banking in other currencies.

European Currency Unit (ECU).   A currency unit that is made up of the currencies of the countries in the European Monetary System. It is only a unit of account at present, but is scheduled to become the circulating currency of these countries later in this decade.

European Monetary System (EMS).   The phased unification of the monetary systems of the members of the European Community. Fixed exchange rates and coordinated monetary policies now exist, and this system is scheduled to result in a single European currency, the ECU, by the end of the century.

Exchange market intervention.   Purchases or sales of foreign exchange by a central bank which are intended to maintain a fixed exchange rate or to affect the behavior of a floating rate.

Exchange Rate Mechanism (ERM).   The arrangement through which the members of the European Monetary System maintain the exchange rates among their currencies within a narrow band.

Export-led growth.   Policies in developing countries that are designed to encourage economic growth which is based on rapid growth of exports sales. Widely used in East Asian countries.

Factor-price equalization.   The argument that international trade that is based on differences in relative factor endowments, as predicted by the Heckscher-Ohlin theorem, will tend to reduce or eliminate international differences in factor prices. Free trade between Australia and Japan, for example, would reduce land prices in Japan and increase them in Australia until land prices in the two countries became equal or at least similar. Associated with Paul Samuelson and Wolfgang Stolper.

Factor intensity reversal. A situation in which it is impossible to rank clearly or identify the relative factor intensities of two products, because one is more labor intensive at one set of relative factor prices, but the other becomes more labor intensive at another set of relative factor prices. Factor intensity reversal can occur when it is far easier to substitute one factor for the other in one industry than it is in the other industry.

F.A.S. Free along side. This measurement of the value of exports includes the price of the goods shipped to the side of the ship, but without loading costs.

Floating exchange rate. An exchange rate for which a government or central bank does not maintain a parity or fixed rate, but instead allows to be determined by market forces.

F.O.B. Free on board. This measurement of the value of exports includes the price of the goods loaded on the ship, but without the cost of international shipping and insurance.

Foreign exchange reserves. Foreign financial assets held by a government or central bank which are available to support the country's balance of payments or exchange rate. Includes holdings of gold, the country's reserve position in the International Monetary Fund, and claims on foreign governments and central banks.

Foreign trade multiplier. The Keynesian multiplier adjusted to allow for the existence of foreign trade. The marginal propensity to import makes this multiplier lower than that which would prevail for the economy without trade.

Forward exchange market. A market in which it is possible to purchase foreign exchange for delivery and payment at a future date. The quantity and exchange rate are determined at the outset, but payment is made at a fixed future date, frequently in 30, 60, or 90 days.

Free-trade area. A group of countries that maintain free trade among the membership, but where each country maintains its own tariff schedule for trade with nonmembers.

Futures market for foreign exchange. A market that is similar to the forward market except that all contracts mature on the same day of the month, a secondary market for the contracts exists, and the amounts of money in the contracts are smaller. Futures contracts are traded in commodity markets rather than through commercial banks.

General Agreement on Tariffs and Trade (GATT). An institution, located in Geneva, which carries on international negotiations for trade liberalization, settles disputes among countries over existing trade agreements, and attempts to maintain international rules with regard to trade policies.

Generalized System of Preferences. A preferential trading arrangement in which industrialized countries allow tariff-free imports from developing countries while maintaining tariffs on the same products from other industrialized countries.

Gold standard. A monetary system in which governments or central banks maintain a fixed price of gold in terms of their currencies by offering to purchase or sell gold at fixed local currency prices. Exchange rates are then determined by relative national prices of gold.

Heckscher-Ohlin theorem. The argument, developed by two Swedish economists in the 1920s, that international trade patterns are determined by the fact that countries have different relative factor endowments and that different products require different relative factor inputs. Each country will export those products that require a great deal of its relatively abundant factor of production.

Hedging. Undertaking a financial transaction that cancels or offsets the risk existing from a previous financial position.

Immiserizing growth. Economic growth that is so strongly biased toward the production of exports, and where the world demand for these exports is so price inelastic, that the world price falls sufficiently to leave the country worse off than it was before the growth occurred.

Import substitution strategy. A development policy in which economic growth is to be encouraged by repressing imports and by encouraging the domestic production of substitutes for those imports.

Industrial strategy. The argument that the growth of industries within an economy should not be left to market forces but should instead be guided by government policies. The government should choose industries that have strong prospects and encourage their growth, perhaps by maintaining barriers to imports.

Infant industry protection. The argument that an industry's costs will be high when it is beginning, and it will therefore need protection from imports to survive. If provided with a period of protection, the industry's costs will decline and it will be able to prosper without protection.

Intellectual property. Property developed through research and other creative efforts which is supposedly protected by law. Examples include patents, copyrights, and trademarks.

Interest rate parity. The forward discount on a currency, measured as an annual rate, should equal the local interest rate minus the foreign interest rate.

Intraindustry trade. Trade that occurs when a country both exports and imports the output of the same industry. Italy exporting Fiat automobiles to Germany and importing VWs from Germany would be an example of intraindustry trade.

IS **line.** Combinations of interest rates and levels of domestic output which will equate savings and intended investment, thus producing equilibrium in the market for goods.

Isoquant. A curve representing all the combinations of two factors of production which will produce a fixed quantity of a product. A set of isoquants can be used to represent a production function for two inputs.

J-curve effect. The possibility that after a devaluation or depreciation, a country's balance of trade will deteriorate modestly for a brief period of time before improving by far more than enough to offset that loss.

Law of one price. The argument that international differences in prices for the same commodity should be arbitraged away by trade. If the exchange rate is 5 pesos per dollar, a product that costs $1 in the United States should cost 5 pesos in the other country. This law is frequently violated in oligopolistic markets.

Law of the second best. The argument, associated with Richard Lipsey and Kelvin Lancaster, that when an economic distortion exists which cannot be removed, government intervention may be necessary to minimize the losses resulting from that distortion. Many arguments for protection are examples of this law.

Leontief paradox. The 1953 research finding by Wassily Leontief that U.S. exports were more labor intensive than U.S. imports, which contradicts the predictions of the Heckscher-Ohlin theorem.

LM **line.** Combinations of interest rates and domestic output which, given a money supply, will clear the domestic market for money.

London Interbank Offer Rate (LIBOR). The market-determined interest rate on short-term interbank deposits in the Eurodollar market in London, frequently used as the basis for floating interest rates on international loans. A country might borrow at LIBOR plus 1 percent, for example.

Long position. Owning an asset or a contract to take delivery of an asset at a fixed price with no hedge or offsetting position. A long position is profitable if the price of the asset rises, and vice versa.

Managed or dirty floating exchange rate. A policy in which a government or central bank does not maintain a parity and instead allows the exchange rate to change to some degree with market forces. The government or central bank buys or sells foreign exchange, however, when it is displeased with the behavior of the market. Such intervention is intended to produce exchange market behavior which the government prefers.

Marginal propensity to import. The percentage of extra or marginal income which residents of a country can be expected to spend on imports.

Marginal rate of substitution. The rate at which an individual or a group of people would be willing to exchange one good for another and be no better or worse off. Equals the ratio of the marginal utilities of the two goods, which equals the slope of an indifference curve.

Marginal rate of transformation. The rate at which an economy can transform one good into another by moving productive resources from one industry to another. Equals the ratio of the marginal costs of the two goods, which equals the slope of the production-possibility curve.

Marshall-Lerner condition. The elasticity of demand and supply conditions that are necessary for a devaluation to improve a country's balance of trade.

Mercantilism. The view that a government should actively discourage imports and encourage exports, as well as regulate other aspects of the economy.

Monetarist model of the balance of payments. A view of the balance of payments, or the exchange rate, which emphasizes excess demands for, or supplies of, money as causes of exchange market disequilibria. An asset market approach to the balance of payments in which domestic and foreign assets are viewed as perfect substitutes.

Most-favored-nation status (MFN). When a country promises to offer the country having most-favored-nation status the lowest tariff which it offers to any third country.

Multi-Fibre Arrangement (MFA). A system of bilateral quotas in the markets for textiles and garments in which each exporting country is allowed to send a specified quantity of various textile or garment products to an importing country per year.

New International Economic Order. A list of requests by the underdeveloped countries for improvements in their trading and development prospects, to be largely financed by the industrialized countries. The agenda was actively discussed during the 1970s, but interest in it declined in the 1980s. The most important element in the agenda was a system of price support programs for primary products which are exported by developing countries. This system would have been similar to the U.S. farm support program, but world-wide in scope. Fears of enormous costs and resource allocation inefficiences led the industrialized countries to resist this and other parts of the NIEO program.

Nominal effective exchange rate. A weighted exchange rate for a currency relative to the currencies of a number of foreign countries. Trade shares are frequently used as the weights.

Nontariff barrier. Any government policy other than a tariff which is designed to discourage imports in favor of domestic products. Quotas and government procurement rules are among the most important nontariff trade barriers.

Offer curve. A curve that illustrates the volume of exports and imports that a country will choose to undertake at various terms of trade. Also known as a reciprocal demand curve.

Official reserve transactions balance. A measurement of a country's balance-of-payments surplus or deficit which includes all items in the current and capital accounts. It excludes only movements of foreign exchange reserves. Also known as the official settlements balance of payments and occasionally as the overall balance.

Open economy macroeconomics. Macroeconomic models that explicitly include foreign trade and international capital flow sectors.

Opportunity cost. The cost of one good in terms of other goods which could have been produced with the same factors of production.

Optimum currency area. The area within which a single currency or rigidly fixed exchange rates should exist.

Optimum tariff. A tariff that is designed to maximize a large country's benefits from trade by improving its terms of trade. Optimum only for the country imposing the tariff, not for the world.

Organization for Economic Cooperation and Development (OECD). An organization consisting of the governments of the industrialized market economies, headquartered in Paris. It provides a forum for a wide range of discussions and negotiations among these countries, and publishes both statistics and economic research studies on these countries and on international trade and financial flows.

Overshooting. A condition that occurs when the price of an asset, such as foreign exchange, is moving in one direction but temporarily moves beyond its permanent equilibrium, before coming back to its long-run value. Associated with Rudiger Dornbusch's analysis of the response of a floating exchange rate to a shift in monetary policy.

Par value. A fixed exchange rate, denominated in terms of a foreign currency or gold.

Petrodollars. Funds resulting from OPEC current account surpluses which are placed in Eurodollar or other offshore bank deposits.

Policy assignment model. A model of balance-of-payments adjustment under fixed exchange rates in which it is possible to reach both the desired level of domestic output and payments equilibrium through the use of fiscal and monetary policies. Associated with J. Marcus Fleming and Robert Mundell.

Portfolio balance model. A view of the capital account or of the overall balance of payments which emphasizes the demand for and supply of financial assets. Concludes that capital flows in response to recent changes in expected yields rather than in response to differing levels of expected yields. That part of the asset market approach to the balance of payments in which domestic and foreign assets are viewed as imperfect substitutes.

Predatory dumping. Temporary dumping designed to drive competing firms out of business in order to create a monopoly and raise prices.

Preference similarity hypothesis. The argument that trade in consumer goods is often based on the fact that a product that is popular in the country in which it is produced can most easily be exported to countries with similar consumer tastes. Associated with Stefan Linder and sometimes known as Linder trade.

Producer surplus. The difference between the price at which a product can be sold and the minimum price which a seller would be willing to accept for it.

Production function. A graphical or mathematical representation of all the combinations of inputs which will produce various quantities of a product. Can be represented with an isoquant map if only two inputs exist.

Purchasing power parity. The argument that the exchange for two currencies should reflect relative price levels in the two countries. If yen prices in Japan are on average 200 times as high as dollar prices in the United States, the exchange rate should be 200 yen = $1. Associated with Gustav Cassel.

Put. An option contract that allows its owner to sell a specified amount of a financial asset, such as foreign exchange, at a fixed price during a specified period of time. The owner of the option is not required to exercise the option. The price at which the asset can be sold is known as the strike price.

Quota. A government policy that limits the physical volume of a product which may be imported per period of time.

Quota rents. The extra profits that accrue to those who get the right to bring products into a country under a quota. Equal to the difference between the domestic price of the product in the importing country and the world price times the quantity imported.

Real effective exchange rate. The nominal effective exchange rate adjusted for differing rates of inflation to create an index of cost and price competitiveness in world markets. If a country's nominal effective exchange rate depreciated by 5 percent in a year in which its rate of inflation exceeded the average rate of inflation in the rest of the world by 5 percentage points, its real effective exchange rate would be unchanged.

Real interest rate. The nominal interest rate minus the expected rate of inflation. Current saving and investment decisions should be based on the real interest rate over the maturity of the asset.

Real money supply. A nation's money supply divided by the price level in that country. The real money supply, which represents the purchasing power of the nation's money supply, is critical in determining the demand for goods and services, as well as for financial assets, in a monetarist model.

Relative factor endowments. The relative amounts of different factors of production which two countries have. India has a relative abundance of labor, while the United States has a greater relative abundance of capital.

Relative factor intensities. The relative amounts of different factors of production that are used in the production of two goods. Textiles and garments are relatively labor intensive, whereas oil refining is relatively capital intensive.

Revaluation. An increase in the value of a currency in terms of foreign exchange by changing an otherwise fixed exchange rate.

Rybcyznski theorem. The argument, associated with Thomas Rybcyznski, that if the supply of one factor of production increases, when both relative factor and goods prices are unchanged, the output of the product using that factor intensively will increase and the output of the product using the other factor of production intensively must decline.

Section 301. A provision of U.S. trade law which allows retaliation against the exports of countries maintaining what the United States views as unfair trade practices such as allowing the theft of U.S. intellectual property by local firms.

Short position. Having a contract to sell an asset in the future at a fixed price with no hedge or offsetting position. A short position is profitable if the asset declines in price, and vice versa.

Singer-Prebisch hypothesis. The argument developed by Hans Singer and Raul Prebisch that developing countries face a secular decline in their terms of trade owing to a trend toward lower prices for primary commodities relative to prices of manufactured goods.

Smoot-Hawley Tariff. A very high level of tariffs adopted by the United States in 1930 which caused a dramatic decline in the volume of world trade. It is widely believed to have worsened the great depression.

Special Drawing Rights (SDRs). A foreign exchange reserve asset created by the International Monetary Fund. The value of the SDR is based on a weighted average of the U.S. dollar, the DM, the yen, sterling, and the French franc.

Specie flow mechanism. A balance-of-payments adjustment mechanism in which the domestic money supply is rigidly tied to the balance of payments, falling in the case of deficits and rising when surpluses occur. Associated with David Hume.

Specific factors models. Short-run models of international trade which are based on the assumption that factors of production are not mobile among industries. Free trade harms all factors of production employed in the import competing industry, and benefits all factors in the export industry, in a specific factors model.

Specific tariff. A tariff that is measured as a fixed amount of money per physical unit imported—$500 per car or $10 per ton, for example.

Spot market. The market for an asset, such as foreign exchange, in which delivery is in only one or two days.

Sterilization. A domestic monetary policy action that is designed to cancel or offset the monetary effect of a balance-of-payments disequilibrium. When a payments surplus increases the domestic money supply, an open-market sale of domestic assets by the central bank will cancel this effect and will constitute sterilization.

Stolper-Samuelson theorem. The argument that in a world of Heckscher-Ohlin trade, free trade will reduce the income of the scarce factor of production and increase the income of the abundant factor of production in each country. Under rather demanding assumptions, wage rates will be equalized across countries, as will returns to capital.

Strategic trade policy. The argument that trade policy, including protection, should be used to encourage the growth of domestic industries which the government feels to have strong prospects in world markets. This usually involves trying to choose industries in which rapid technical advances are likely and where growing world markets exist.

Swap. A transaction in which one security or stream of income is exchanged for another, frequently with a contract to reverse the transaction at a date in the future. In foreign exchange, a swap means the purchase of a currency in the spot market and its simultaneous sale in the forward market.

Tariff. A tax on imports or exports imposed by a government.

Tariff of Abominations. A very high schedule of tariffs imposed by the United States in 1828.

Terms of trade. The ratio of a country's export prices to its import prices. High terms of trade imply large welfare benefits from trade, and vice versa.

Trade adjustment assistance. The practice of providing financial aid for industries injured by growing imports or for their employees. When tariffs are reduced, trade adjustment assistance is sometimes promised for import-competing industries.

Trade balance. A country's total export receipts minus its total import expenditures during a period of time, usually a year.

Trade creation. An efficiency gain that results from the operation of a free-trade area because more efficient firms from a member country displace less efficient local producers in the domestic market.

Trade diversion. An efficiency loss that results from the operations of a free-trade area because less efficient firms from a member country displace more efficient producers from a nonmember country. It occurs because of the discriminatory nature of the tariff regime. The member country faces no tariff in the import market, whereas the nonmember still faces a tariff.

Trade-related investment measures (TRIMs). Government policies in which foreign direct investments in a country are allowed only if the investing firm promises to meet certain trade performance goals. Frequently, the firm must promise to export a specific percentage of its output or strictly limit its purchase of imported parts or other inputs.

Transfer pricing. The practice of using false or misleading prices on trade documents in order to evade ad valorem tariffs or exchange controls, or to shift profits within a multinational firm from a high tax rate jurisdiction to a low tax rate jurisdiction. Also known as false invoicing.

U.S. Trade Representative. An official of the executive branch of the U.S. government who is responsible for carrying on negotiations with foreign governments on foreign trade issues. Previously known as the Special Trade Representative.

Vernon product cycle. The observation that a country such as the United States will frequently export a product that it has invented only for as long as it can maintain a technical monopoly. When the technology becomes available abroad, perhaps because a patent has expired, production grows rapidly in foreign countries where costs are lower, and the inventing country experiences a decline in its production of the product because of a rapid growth of imports. Associated with Raymond Vernon.

Voluntary Export Restraint (VER). A way of maintaining a quota by evading the GATT prohibition on such quantitative limits. The exporting country agrees to maintain limits on its sales, frequently in order to avoid a more damaging protectionist policy by the importing country. Sometimes known as an Orderly Marketing Agreement (OMA).

Walras Law. The idea that excess demands must net out to zero across an economy in a general equilibrium framework, because if there is an excess demand in one market, there must be an offsetting excess supply in another market. Associated with Leon Walras.

INDEX